AF715022

Labour Law in Turkey

Labour Law in Turkey

Third Edition

Toker Dereli
Yeşim Pınar Soykut Sarıca
Aslı Taşbaşı

This book was originally published as a monograph in the International Encyclopaedia of Laws/Labour Law and Industrial Relations.

Founding Editor: Roger Blanpain
General Editor: Frank Hendrickx
Volume Editor: Frank Hendrickx

Wolters Kluwer

Published by:
Kluwer Law International B.V.
PO Box 316
2400 AH Alphen aan den Rijn
The Netherlands
E-mail: lrs-sales@wolterskluwer.com
Website: www.wolterskluwer.com/en/solutions/kluwerlawinternational

Sold and distributed by:
Wolters Kluwer Legal & Regulatory U.S.
920 Links Avenue
Landisville, PA 17538
United States of America
E-mail: customer.service@wolterskluwer.com

ISBN 978-94-035-3406-0

e-Book: ISBN 978-94-035-3766-5
web-PDF: ISBN 978-94-035-3776-4

This title is available on www.kluwerlawonline.com

The Authors

Dr Toker Dereli (1936) received his BA from the Faculty of Economics, Istanbul University, having majored in economics, industrial relations and labour law. He joined the Department of Labour Economics and Industrial Relations of the same faculty as a research assistant in 1961. Dr Dereli completed his graduate studies at the Cornell ILR School (MS, 1964) and Istanbul University (PhD, 1965). He became an associate professor in 1969 and a full professor in 1975 at the Faculty of Economics, Istanbul University.

Professor Dereli worked as a visiting professor at Temple University (1971–1973 and 1982–1984) and at McMaster University (1991–1992), where he taught courses on collective bargaining, labour relations, human resource management and organizational behaviour for a total period of five years. In the autumn semester of the 1981–1982 academic year, he taught a comparative labour course at the Faculty of Law, Catholic University of Leuven. He also taught various subjects at Boğaziçi University (1976–1996) and several other Turkish universities as well as in his own institution, Istanbul University, since the mid-1960s. His publications include nine books and many articles in his areas of interest.

Professor Dereli has worked as a mediator-arbitrator in many labour disputes. He was the President of the Turkish Industrial Relations Association until 2012 and has been actively involved as a consultant in the various labour law reform projects of his country, including the preparation of the original draft for the new Labour Act of Turkey. From 1989 to 2008, he acted as the spokesperson for the Turkish government on the ILO's Conference Committee.

Professor Dereli was the Dean of the Faculty of Economics, İstanbul University, for four years (1999–2003), from where he retired in May 2003. He also served for one term on the Board of Directors of Türkiye İş Bankası (2002–2005) and after his retirement from İstanbul University, he taught at Işık University in Şile, İstanbul until the year 2019.

The Authors

Dr Yeşim Pınar Soykut Sarıca is an Associate Professor at Işık University, Management Department. Her research areas are labour relations and social politics. She conducted funded scientific research projects in fields like employee and industrial relations in Turkey and microcredits for women. She has also worked as a short-term consultant with FSWW (the Foundation for the Support of Women's Work). She has several articles in national and international journals and is the author of books and book chapters in the field.

Dr Aslı Taşbaşı is an Associate Professor of Economics and the Head of Economics Department at Işık University, İstanbul. Her research focuses on economic sustainability, particularly on its extensions of labour market. Awarded with a TUBITAK (the Scientific and Technological Research Council of Turkey) scholarship, she conducted research at the Department of Economics, Lund University, Sweden, during her PhD studies. Dr Taşbaşı also received a UNESCO grant for her research on economic policy. Her articles have been published in many international academic journals. She is also the author of several book chapters and the editor of two books in the field.

Table of Contents

List of Abbreviations

AFL-CIO	American Federation of Labour and Congress of Industrial Organizations
AID	Agency for International Development
AKP	Justice and Development Party
ANAP	Motherland Party
BAĞ-KUR	Tradesman and Craftsmen and Other Self Employed Social Insurance Institution
BASK	Confederation of Independent Public Servants Unions
CGT	General Confederation of Labour in France (French: Confédération Générale du Travail)
DİSK	Confederation of Progressive Labour Unions of Turkey
DSP	Democratic Leftist Party
DTP	Democratic Party of Turkey
DYP	True Path Party
ECS	Economic and Social Council
ETUC	European Trade Union Confederation
EU	European Union
GDP	Gross Domestic Product
GNP	Gross National Product
Hak-İŞ	Confederation of Righteous Labour Unions of Turkey
ICFTU	International Confederation of Free Trade Unions
İİBK	Public Employment Services Organization
ILO	International Labour Organization
IMF	International Monetary Fund
İŞKUR	Employment Organization of Turkey
ITS	International Trade Secretariats
JHSU	Joint Health and Safety Units
MÇP	Nationalist Workingmen's Party (*Milliyetçi Çalışanlar Partisi*)
MHP	National Action Party
OECD	Organisation for Economic Co-operation and Development

List of Abbreviations

OHSB	Occupational Health and Safety Boards
PDLEO	Provincial Directorates of Labour and Employment Organization
PPP	Purchasing Power Parity
CHP (RPP)	Republican People's Party
SHP	Social Democratic People's Party
SEEs	State Economic Enterprises
TİP	Turkish Labour Party
TİSK	Employers' Confederation of Turkey
TKİ	Coal Enterprises of Turkey
TUIK	Statistics Institute of Turkey
TÜRK-İŞ	Confederation of Labour Unions of Turkey
SPO (DPT)	State Planning Organization
WFTU	World Federation of Trade Unions
YHK	Supreme Arbitration Board

Acknowledgements

With heartfelt gratitude to the late Professor Roger Blanpain, a superb colleague and the memory of Professor John P. Windmuller, both giants of comparativism in labour relations.

Acknowledgements

General Introduction[1]

Chapter 1. The General Background

§1. Geography

1. Turkey is 779,452 square km (300,948 square miles) in size, which is about three times the size of the United Kingdom or one-twelfth that of the United States. About 97% of that area is a peninsula extending between the Black Sea and the Mediterranean. There is also a small area in Eastern Thrace, which constitutes the most southeasterly part of Europe. The landscape of the country is dominated by mountains, not only in the east but on the Black Sea and Mediterranean coasts as well. Surrounding the mountainous areas are smaller but agriculturally rich sub-regions. There is a huge plateau in Central and Eastern Anatolia, which is suitable for growing wheat and related products. The terrain to the east and south of the Aegean region also favours agriculture – mostly figs, raisins, tobacco and cotton – and the Black Sea has a fertile coastal strip as well, good for raising hazelnuts, tobacco, tea and citrus fruits. The Turkish climate varies almost as much as its topography, thus influencing the country's agricultural potential to a considerable extent. Turkey is well endowed with most of the basic minerals, with the exception of crude oil, which meets only about one-fifth of the country's domestic consumption. However, neither the mineral nor the crude oil reserves have yet been fully surveyed. Turkey's major supplies for the world market are chromite and boron minerals as well as industrial products in varying quantities, i.e., household appliances, textiles, electronic equipment and autos, due to the expansion of the country's industrial production in recent years. Geography provides Turkey with significant tourism potential, thereby creating additional income, which in turn helps reduce foreign-trade imbalances in the economy. Turkey's location at the crossroads of East and West has, through the past ages, endowed it with a rich cultural heritage as well as historical monuments of the Greek–Byzantine times and the Ottoman–Turkish era.

1. In this monograph, for reasons of space economy, only the pronoun 'he', without prejudice to the pronoun 'she', is used to denote the third person. The terms 'employee' and 'worker' are used synonymously and interchangeably. For labour law concepts, the terminology of the International Labour Organization has been adopted for purposes of uniformity.

I. Social and Cultural Values

2. A few studies in the management literature have approached the themes, such as the Turkish business mentality, the work ethic and traditions from a historical perspective. Here the main themes concentrate first on the research about the reasons why industrial and economic development lagged behind the levels achieved by the Western countries that had realized their march on economic development and modernity long before the Muslim nations of the east. Inquiry into the historical trends from medieval times to the twentieth century could be a starting point for our purposes. While during medieval times, the Turkish-Ottoman society seemed to make important headway as opposed to Medieval Europe, Turks were unable to catch up with the developments which Europe could attain through such transformations as the renaissance, 'enlightenment' revolution, the French revolution and the industrial revolution.

3. Deliberations on the cultural values of a nation necessarily calls for some inquiry into the role of religion in shaping these cultural values over time. This brings us to the theme of Islam's effects on Turkish culture, at least from a speculative, broad-based perspective. It has been a known theme that although the medieval Moslem world had shown considerable progress by establishing contacts with the Greek philosophers of antique times (through translations of their works into their native languages), with the closing of the Moslem minds to such intellectual deliberations during the reign of Nizamülmülk's Selçuk empire (which ultimately led to the suppression of free and rational thinking of Moslem philosophers by İmam Gazali). This was a phenomenon which necessarily lengthened Islam's middle ages that must be regarded as one of the major reasons causing the ending of the Moslem world's development, intellectually, scientifically and economically. Thus, Islam's 'middle ages' seem to have outlasted the middle ages of western societies.[2]

4. By refusing the importance of 'rationality, science and philosophy', İmam Gazali accentuated the superiority of religious revelation and interpretation of the word of the Koran over rationality and science as though the two were mutually exclusive and could never be reconciled. Although there were remarkable analysts like İbni Rüşt (Avereos) and others who opposed Gazali and valued instead rational thinking and philosophy, the transition to the streamlining of Gazali's approach marked the beginning of the closing of the Moslem mind, a kind of intellectual suicide which ultimately created the modern Islamist crisis, epitomized by great divisions in and among major Moslem sects.[3]

5. The Ottoman elites of the seventeenth century became aware of the superior position of Europe, yet they attributed their decline behind the west to the progress

2. For a comprehensive new study on the subject, *see* Merdan Yanardağ, İçtihat Kapısı, İslam Dünyasının Süren Ortaçağı, Kırmızıkedi, 2022, 366 pp.
3. Robert R. Reilly, *The Closing of the Muslim World* (National Review Online 2010), as cited in Merdan Yanardağ, İçtihat Kapısı as cited by Yanardağ, *ibid.*

of the west in military technology rather than their own attenuation in scientific rationality and research. This is still epitomized by various discourses in some Turkish Moslem circles (e.g., the popular belief that every human discovery has bas been foreseen and foretold in the Koran, that the progress of Europe was also preceded by the weakening of Christian values, that every advantage brought about by western science and technology is preordained to benefit the Moslem world anyhow).

6. Despite the fact that the Ottoman-Turkish culture was unable to catch up with the renaissance and industrial revolution, coupled with the failure to launch reforms in Islamic thinking and practice, Turkey was the first country in the Moslem world which demonstrated a serious endeavour to break away from the medieval values of Islam. What its founder Kemal Atatürk aimed to accomplish following his military victories against western powers was to offset the losses caused by having missed the renaissance of the west and the industrial revolution. His reforms imposed from above which were in fact an extension of the young Turks movement of the nineteenth century, generated quick results, albeit with some unanticipated dysfunctions several decades later, which reflect traces of the so-called political Islam. Although religion has been used in the past as an ideological apparatus by the state to accomplish social and political consensus, political Islam seems to have entailed during the last few decades in Turkey a serious ideological polarization. All these developments of the recent past notwithstanding, Islam still constitutes in Turkey a broad base for the cultural values of Turkish society.[4] This point may be exemplified by the following verses from the Koran and the prophet's dictums, among many others: 'There is nothing for man in the world other than what he deserves for his labour'; 'Can those who know versus those who don't know be equal?'; 'Go and find science even though it may exist as far away as in China'; 'Pay the workingman his wages before the sweat on his forehead has dried.'

7. The craftsmen guilds were the main occupational-commercial organizations of medieval times; a comparison of their main characteristics in Western and Turkish societies could serve as a starting point. Guild system was based on rules, one of which was the respect for contracts (agreements) made between real and legal persons; this legal principle was referred to as the 'rule of good-faith negotiations and loyalty to one's contract' or promise to contract. For successful transactions in society, the principle 'culpa in contrahendo' liability is that in a contractual relationship, the party who is at fault during the negotiation stage and has therefore caused harm to the other party must compensate for the damage of the injured party. So, strict observance of 'obligation liability or tort liability' was held to be the essence of a healthy commercial transaction,[5] which is a rule that should prevail in any healthy commercial relationship. It was strictly observed in the guild system of medieval times, but being rather short-lived, ended by the end of the seventeenth century in the Ottoman-Turkish society, although remnants of it could survive in various countries that made up the empire.

---

4. M. Yanardağ, *ibid.*
5. K. Oğuzman, *Law of Obligations (Contracts)* 121 (Kluwer Law International 1996), translated by T. Dereli.

8. In this environment, guilds were voluntary associations of persons pursuing the same trade, art or profession, united under a distinct organization of their own, regulating the affairs of the trade by their own laws and rules, their main objectives being to protect and promote the interests of their members. They were especially careful in protecting the quality and ethical standards of the trade or craft; in order to qualify as skilled craftsmen, high competence standards were to be observed in entering the trade or craft, so in this respect, guilds were somewhat monopolistic organizations. A few scholarly studies using the Weberian approach to the rise of capitalistic development have pinpointed the weakening trends of ethical values inherent in the guild system; these area also trends that caused the Ottoman-Turkish society to fall behind the tenets of the enlightenment revolution, renaissance and then industrial revolution in the medieval Muslim world. The deep-rooted faith in 'loyalty to contract' waned through time and now seems to be no longer a virtue (cultural value) in the underdeveloped societies of the middle east. In fact, the craftsmen's guilds were the only form of strong institutional arrangement in the Ottoman Empire until the first half of the nineteenth century. Manufactured goods of the western countries weakened the guilds considerably. And they finally disappeared after the 1860s with the proclamation of new legislation, the *Mecelle,* which combined the liberal economic principles of western capitalist countries and the tenets of Islam, thus undermining their monopolistic character by encouraging freedom of enterprise. But the truth, as accentuated by many writers, is that the value of loyalty to one's contractual promise is no longer widely believed and practised in commercial transactions.[6] In the early industrialized countries, craft unions were the first workers' organizations as there was some degree of continuity between guilds and labour unions. But in Turkey, simply because there was no longer any viable craft existence at the inception of the labour union movement (the 1940s and after), craft unions would never gain any strength, although the law, especially from the beginning, had by no means prohibited their appearance.

9. Westernization efforts of Kemal Atatürk were interpreted by some prominent historians as a step towards Turkey's catching up with a 'belated Turkish renaissance'; whether or not this view could be considered a viable idea remains to be tested in the course of time.

10. It should be noted that, except for a few micro-level behavioural studies, no comprehensive attitudinal research (e.g., F-scale type of questionnaire by Adorno et al.) has been done on the values of the Turkish working class and managerial groups in recent decades, particularly. The following few paragraphs dwell therefore on the somewhat outdated data of the pre-1960 decades.

11. The main focus of social organization in Turkish society is predominantly the 'nuclear family' in urban centres and 'extended family', generally in rural areas, of which the father or the eldest male is the unchallenged head. The average rural Turk is still a good Moslem and tends to be puritanical. In the village, status is

6. S. Ülgener, *İktisadi İnhitat Tarihimizin Ahlak ve Zihniyet Meseleleri* (İstanbul Üniversitesi İktisat Fakültesi, 1957).

attached to the elderly, the religious head (*imam*), the government official, the soldier and the owner of good livestock and land. In the earlier stages of Republican westernization, because of some resentment of state-imposed changes, a certain degree of suspicion was attached to the government official and the secular school teacher, a phenomenon which has disappeared over time. Although during the early republican period, the industrialization elite encouraged the state sector of the economy, stimulation of the private enterprise system by legislation gave rise to the emergence of a Turkish bourgeoisie which in turn facilitated further changes towards industrialization. The stimulation of the economy through the private sector after the 1950s has gradually given rise to a bourgeoisie which in turn facilitated further changes towards industrialization, accompanied by a private sector managerial class. And if the army, whose role has been traditionally important in the westernization of the country, was treated in the same category as the public servants and intellectuals, one could speak of a unique salaried middle class in Turkish society, a coalition of bureaucrats, army officers and intellectuals,[7] notwithstanding that the armed forces of Turkey have been losing much of its prominence during the recent decades.

12. It was this kind of 'salaried' middle class unique to Turkey that helped Atatürk accomplish many of his reforms (economic-industrials well as rational-scientific). Using the model proposed by Kerr et al. in their well-known study in the early 1960s, Industrialism and Industrial Man, of the five types of industrializing elites 'dynastic', 'middle class', 'revolutionary intellectuals', 'colonial administrators' and 'nationalist leaders', Kerr et al. had referred to Turkey's development model as being one under the guidance of a mixture of 'revolutionary intellectuals' and 'nationalist leaders.' This model is destined to change towards industrialization forms under other elite types.[8] Atatürk's genius as a social planner was to see economic development within a comprehensive behavioural matrix. He destroyed the political and temporal power of the organized religion; he established secular schools, he simplified the alphabet and he degraded the traditional form of dress by ordering the wearing of Western attire. Through such institutional changes, he undermined rural isolation and encouraged modernization. 'Owing perhaps too long military tradition and the necessity for discipline as the price of holding an empire and establishing a republic, the Turks have been accustomed to authoritarian ways.'[9]

13. The application of state-led investments during the 1930s encouraged economic development and began to give rise to a new industrial working class. Though wealth and income level provided some influence in urban areas, occupational prestige was not necessarily related to these factors only. Upon the peasant's transition to urban areas, his standards used to change; he was now more likely to

---

7. Z.F. Fındıkoğlu, *The Social Stratification Related with the Turkish Social Changes* 20 (1–4) (İstanbul Üniversitesi İktisat Fakültesi Mecmuası 2011).
8. C. Kerr et al., *Industrialism and Industrial Man* 88–89 (Harvard U. Press 1960).
9. *Caldwell, Lynton K.* (1957) *Turkish Administration and the Politics of Expediency Toward the Comparative Study of Public Administration* 117-144, at 129 (in William J. Siffin ed., Department of Government).

look up to professional men. The high degree of skill and education became more appreciated. As for the working class, white-collar jobs were more valued as opposed to manual labour, but depending on special time periods, manual labourers gained higher status as unionism and the right to collective bargaining, if recognized, helped to increase their income levels. In spite of resentment and a certain degree of suspicion against government authorities, the Turk identified himself through many centuries with his state and armed forces. Turkish people generally looked upon their government as a friendly leader to be trusted above private persons.

14. An important characteristic of the Turkish society that has been frequently cited in the past was the lack of class consciousness. Nonetheless, extreme class distinctions were readily observable by the way authority relationships were observed. For a long time in the past early Republican period the worker's high respect towards and dependence on his immediate superior within the highly centralized organizations, his loyalty to duty and observance of status symbols provided clear clues for class distinctions. 'In interpersonal behaviour the contrast between those in authority and their subordinates is very striking.'[10]

15. There has always existed a considerable degree of upward mobility in Turkish Society. Traditionally, however, the Turks were oriented toward the military and bureaucratic occupations, leaving commercial pursuits to minority groups. It was only after the 1950s following Turkey's adopting multi-party democracy that the Turks began becoming significant in the field of commerce and industry. It was often stated that the Turk was individualistic' in terms of voluntary cooperation, a characteristic that accounts for the relative failure of cooperative organizations and up until the second half of the twentieth century, of the corporate type of enterprise and for that reason, the state should pioneer economic development. Most probably, this policy had been supported 'by elements of the bureaucracy whose positions might be adversely affected by the growth of substantial private enterprise.'[11]

16. A national cultural value important in labour-management relations seems to be related to attitudes towards 'conflict', which is likely to be clearer in some other authoritarian cultures. It rests on the belief that conflict is bad and undesirable per se, necessarily leading to aggressive and harmful interpersonal behaviour. This implies what Friedland has called a 'consensus-oriented' culture.[12] Conflict is looked upon as misunderstanding rather than disagreement and undesirable confrontation due to conflict of interests. Parties believe that their future relations will deteriorate considerably once they engage in advocating their views aggressively on a face-to-face basis. Expressing one's own ideas and trying to put forward new conditions that are natural components of the democratic process were not regarded as

10. Norman B. Bradburn, *Interpersonal Relations Within Formal Organizations in Turkey*, XIX(1) The Journal of Social Issues 66 (January 1963).
11. Caldwell, *supra*, p. 125.
12. George Friedland's reference in the course on social problem of industrialization., Cornell University, 1962.

acceptable social behaviour. It does not mean that in a consensus-oriented environment aggressive behaviour does not erupt. On the contrary, it may take extreme forms once the parties have had to be involved in the open, face-to-face expression of conflict.[13]

17. Owing partly to the 'consensus-oriented' nature of the Turkish culture, the actors of the industrial relations system have, over the course of time, welcomed the presence of a third party to act as the conciliator, arbitrator or overseer to forestall the eruption of serious conflict within the system. Even in sectors where there is no legal ban on the right to strike, the government (council of ministers, or now the President) must always be present to end the conflict through the 'suspension of the strike' which legally culminates in compulsory arbitration. This is a restriction for which Turkey has been taken to the agenda of the International Labour Organization's (ILO) supervisory organs almost every year.

18. In Turkey until the 1960s, the philosophies of management and industrial relations were threefold and antipathetic to the presence and activities of labour unions. The younger and technically trained managers in both the public and private sectors used to look at unions as obstacles to the expansion of the industry. The organizational behaviour model used during those times was of the 'custodial' type (paternalistic, i.e., 'be good to your employees' policy where personnel policies depended on welfare programs at best with employee dependence based on economic resources, fair wages and fringe benefits, especially in the state sector. However, a small segment of these managers recognized that a production-centred attitude was not to be sufficient and that some sort of employee representation was inevitable. The older paternalists who were found in the upper ranks of state enterprises and some of the older and larger private plants looked on unions as rivals for the allegiance of workers and resisted workers' organizations. For the third group comprising the commercial profit-makers who had entered sectors such as textiles, food-processing and other light industries since 1950, labour unions were also looked at hostile institutions as obstacles to higher profits and effective exploitation. In Turkey 'the supportive and participative model of Newstrom would gradually enter the scene in the 1960s only in the minority of enterprises. Presently of course each model is in the process of constant change and has been evolving over the course of time.[14]

19. As opposed to private sector employers, state economic enterprises (SEEs) had always provided substantial programs of fringe benefits for workers, subsidizing free supplements to wages such as housing, medical care, meals, training and

13. A study made on Turkish businessmen has afforded a picture of the father as stern, forbidding, remote, domineering and autocratic. Few of the men interviewed had ever argued with their fathers, and those who had did so at the price of an open break with him. Norman M. Bradburn, *An Achievement, and Father Dominance in Turkey*, 67(2) Journal of Abnormal and Social Psychology 464–465 (November 1963).
14. For the autocratic, custodial, supportive, collegial and system models, *see* J.W. Newstrom, *Organizational Behaviour* Ch. 2 (McGraw Hill/Irwin 2011).

education, work clothes, heating allowance and the like.[15] A benevolent paternalism yet accompanied by authoritarian practices dominated their personnel policies which were later imitated by the educated managers of the private sector. Describing the state sector as more progressive than private sector employers may seem rather ironic, but this observation was true due to certain factors unique to the Turkish culture. It was not before the 1960s that this difference began to vanish. Especially at the inception of state investment programs, most management positions were assigned to engineers educated by the state for this purpose plus military personnel retired or resigned from the army.[16] These men brought with them the disciplinary practices of the army as well as the paternalistic philosophy of their profession. Paternalism, however, was by no means confined to the state sector; it was also found in domestic private firms, particularly in centres where industry and family-owned plants had existed for some time. Both types of organizations were generally authoritarian, but state enterprises were characterized more by a subtle paternalism with their higher wages, fringe benefits and better working conditions in the hope that the modern Turkish state was paving the way for the creation of a healthier and more productive workforce. Most private firms, especially the majority where ownership and management had been separated even before the 1950s, followed a 'naive paternalism', a 'be good' policy; while some, 'now an outmoded' approach, 'be strong-' policy of autocratic management with unfavourable attitudes towards labour unions.

20. In state enterprises, the underlying view of management's relation to labour was one of broad-gauge leadership on management's side, loyal acceptance and deference to this leadership on labour's side.[17] These enterprises identified themselves with the young regime. Related to this phenomenon was the high degree of centralization in their administration. This caused managers to seek formal authority from above before taking any action or simply pushing decisions upward in the organization for resolution. This in turn resulted in delays and inefficiency.[18] Age of the enterprise seemed to separate attitudes more decisively. 'The older organizations retained a traditional set of attitudes dating from the earlier days of the Republic; they had financial and political security, a broader and less urgently production-minded point of view'.[19] They were likely to be more independent of the higher authorities in their personnel policies.

21. In both types of organizations, striking distinctions were found between white-collar and manual workers. Protective labour legislation covered only blue-collar workers until the year 1971 after which year white-collar workers were subjected to the same act as manual workers. The popular feeling was that formal

15. Rosen M. Sumner, *Turkey*, in *Labour in Developing Economies*, 251–296, at 264 (Walter Galenson ed., Univ. of California Press 1962).
16. R.W. Kerwin, Türkiye'de İşletme İdarecildrinin Bugünkü Durumu' Sosyal Siyaset Konferansları, Vols 9–11, p. 56.
17. Rosen, *supra*, p. 132.
18. R.V. Prestus, *Weberian v. Welfare bureaucracy in Traditional Society*, 6(1) Administrative Science Quarterly 13 (June 1961).
19. Rosen, *supra*, p. 131.

education was a means for promotion into a privileged managerial class. For this reason, educated people did not welcome the idea of starting their careers at the foreman level. Unlike the US legislation, foremen were and are still regarded, as 'employees' in Turkey and usually were organized in the same union as the workers. Foremen were considered to be merely workers somewhat upgraded by the employer. Their number was often seen as exceeding the needs of the plant. For status reasons, some of the engineers were assigned minor white-collar supervisory positions, which normally would have called for foremen by the rank-and-file employees. Since prestige and status considerations were great in Turkey, the injured pride of these engineers prevented them from being good foremen.'[20]

22. The problem of high labour turnover was faced by management not only as it related to the uncommitted peasant-type blue-collar workforce but also to white-collar employment except for the civil service personnel in public employment.[21]

23. The cultural variables alluded to above were the observed tendencies in Turkey during the 1950s and 1960s mostly. Of course, there is no question about the fact that there have been important changes since then as a result of global tendencies and large-scale international cultural contacts among nations. With the widespread expansion of management training programs, the organizational behaviour model of most large corporations must have reached the level of 'the supportive and participative' models, if not 'collegial, using the phraseology of Newstrom. Authoritarian tendencies embedded in Turkish culture must have tended to thin out if not withered away completely, now replaced by more open, equal and democratic relations facilitated by the expansion of multiparty and pluralistic democracy in Turkey. Suffice it to say, therefore, that there is a need for more research on the cultural variables of Turkey affecting labour-management relations.

§2. Population and Demographic Trends

24. The Turks appeared in world history in the sixth century AD. Their original homeland lay in and around the Altai mountains in Central Asia. The direction of their migration due to climatic, political and economic reasons was from east to west. The Turkish nation took shape in Anatolia (Asia Minor) during the centuries of Selçuk and Ottoman power. Because of large-scale migrations, intermarriages, wars and dislocations, the Turkish nation today exhibits a wide variety of ethnic groups. Within the meaning of nationhood, however, members of all ethnic groups are regarded as being 'Turkish' and 'citizens of the Republic of Turkey'. The language, Turkish, comprised of mainly modern Turkish vocabulary, predominantly rooted in the Oghuz dialect but also enriched by Arabic and Persian words through a long acculturation process during the past centuries, belongs basically to a subgroup of the Ural-Altai languages family. The Turks' conversion to Islam in the

20. Kerwin, *supra*, p. 57.
21. Bradburn, *Interpersonal Relations Within Formal Organizations in Turkey*, *supra*, pp. 64–65.

tenth century paved the way for Turkish expansion in the Muslim world as well as in Europe until at least the eighteenth century.

Turkey's population more than quadrupled between 1927 and 1993. Due to the high birth rate, the population reached 45 million in 1980 and 60 million in 1993. Projections for the year 2000 estimated the country's population at 66,834,000. According to the General Census of 31 December 2010, however, Turkey's population reached 73,722,988. By the year 2013, it stood at 76,667 864. In 2020 it reached 83,614362 and in 2021 84,680273 people 50.2 of which were male. Nearly two-thirds of the population (76.3%) live in urban locations. The ratio of male population is 50.2% while the female ratio is 49.8%. Due to family planning measures, the rate of population increase began to drop in the 1990–1995 period. And owing to increasing urbanization trends coupled with rising incomes and family planning, it fell to an average annual rate of 1.8% in the 2000s. The population is estimated to stabilize somewhere between 95 and 98 million by the middle of the twenty-first century.

Due to the high fertility and population increase rates of the past decades, Turkey's population reflects a young-age structure. While the proportion of individuals between the ages of 20 and 54 was 44% in 1990, it had risen to 52% by the year 2010. Certainly, this presents opportunities as well as challenges to public authorities, including the provision of gainful employment for the youth entering the labour market every year. There are indications, though, which signal a slight aging trend, but this is negligible at present. As it gains momentum in the years ahead, new problems are likely to affect the social security system of the country.

§3. National Income

25. Turkey enjoyed high growth rates between 2002 and 2017. According to data from the Turkish Statistical Institute (TURKSTAT), Turkey's gross domestic product (GDP) for the year 2004 was USD 390,387 million and per capita income for the same year was USD 5,862, even USD 9,844 million when adjusted by PPP (purchasing power parity). GDP for 2009 further increased to USD 616,703 million, while per capita income reached USD 8,560 (USD 12,339, PPP). By April 2011, the economy had already grown 8.8%; while the overall rate was 11% as can be seen in Table 1, an impressive performance indeed. But it was believed that much of that growth was fuelled by increasing imports and consumption rather than a genuine boost in the supply of goods and services.

Table 1 Turkey's Main Economic Indicators (2010–2020)

Year	*GDP (in Bil. US$ PPP)*	*GDP per capita (in US$ PPP)*	*GDP (in Bil. US$ nominal)*	*GDP per capita (in US$ nominal)*	*GDP growth (real)*	*Inflation rate (in Percent)*	*Unemployment (in Percent)*	*Government debt (in % of GDP)*
2010	1,281.0	17,376.4	776.6	10,533.5	8.4%	8.6%	11.1%	39.7%
2011	1,454.1	19,459.8	838.5	11,221.4	11.2%	6.5%	9.1%	36.2%
2012	1,550.7	20,504.4	880.1	11,637.9	4.8%	8.9%	8.4%	32.4%
2013	1,703.7	22,221.4	957.5	12,489.0	8.5%	7.5%	9.0%	31.2%
2014	1,860.5	23,945.5	938.5	12,079.3	4.9%	8.9%	9.9%	28.5%
2015	2,022.9	25,691.1	864.1	10,973.6	6.1%	7.7%	10.3%	27.4%
2016	2,116.2	26,513.6	869.3	10,891.2	3.3%	7.8%	10.9%	28.0%
2017	2,282.3	28,242.5	858.9	10,628.9	7.5%	11.1%	10.9%	28.0%
2018	2,406.5	29,345.6	779.7	9,508.0	3.0%	16.3%	10.9%	30.2%
2019	2,471.3	29,719.2	760.5	9,145.8	0.9%	15.2%	13.7%	32.7%
2020	2,545.9	30,448.7	719.9	8,610.0	1.8%	12.3%	13.1%	39.8%

Source: TURKSTAT web site, www.tuik.gov.tr, 2022.

26. However, while productivity growth has slowed in the last decade, efforts to support growth with credit booms and demand stimulus have increased domestic and external vulnerabilities. Especially the second half of 2018 witnessed macroeconomic instability that can be described by high private sector debt, permanent current account deficits financed by short-term portfolio flows, high inflation and high unemployment. The country experienced an exchange rate crisis in 2019 that resulted in poor growth performance. While the economy was just recovering in early 2020, the COVID-19 crisis hit, yet Turkey was still among the few countries to achieve positive growth (1.8%) in 2020, thanks to the government's credit pressure.

27. With the effect of the relaxation of the COVID-19-related measures in 2021, Turkey became the country with the highest economic growth performance (11%) among the G20 countries. On the other hand, although the interest rate cuts since September had a positive impact on demand, they increased macroeconomic instability and combined with the effects of the Ukraine-Russia war, this situation had negative repercussions for 2022. While the lira depreciated to record lows, inflation soared to record highs. External and fiscal buffers worsened as the Central Bank resorted to foreign exchange reserves to support the lira and the Government introduced tax rate cuts and fuel subsidies to dampen the impact of inflation.

28. Apart from all these, the high energy and carbon intensity of the Turkish economy makes it vulnerable to global energy supply and price fluctuations which poses a challenge for Turkey's exporters in the context of global and regional decarbonization policies. For a more inclusive and sustainable recovery, structural problems such as low female labour force participation, widespread informality (COVID-19-induced contraction hit informal workers the most) and other challenges related to the labour market must be addressed. Forecasts for the future mainly consider high inflation and limited consumption expenditures due to declining consumer confidence, discouragement of foreign investments due to uncertainty about geopolitical factors and financial conditions and the negative impact of the war in Ukraine on foreign demand and commodity prices. In particular, it is thought that rising energy and food price inflation will hurt the poor the most and will endanger getting out of poverty after the pandemic.

29. Studies conducted by the Statistics Institute of Turkey (TUIK) and formerly by the State Planning Organization (SPO (DPT)), reveal a pessimistic picture, reflecting the rather distorted nature of income distribution in Turkey, as shown in Table 2.

Table 2 Income Distribution in Turkey by Years

%of households	*1968*	*1973*	*1987*	*1994*	*2002*	*2013*	*2016*	*2019*	*2020*
Poorest 20%	3.0	3.5	5.24	4.9	5.3	6.1	6.2	6.2	5.9
2nd 20%	7.0	8.0	9.61	8.6	9.8	10.7	10.6	10.9	10.6
3rd 20%	0	12.5	14.06	12.6	14.0	15.2	15.0	15.2	14.9
4th 20%	20.0	19.5	21.15	19.0	20.8	21.4	21.1	21.4	21.1
Richest 20%	60.0	56.5	49.94	54.9	50.1	46.6	47.2	46.3	47.5
Ratio of richest 20% to poorest 20%	20	16.1	9.5	11.3	9.5	7.7	7.6	7.5	8.1
Gini coefficient	0.56	0.51	0.43	0.49	0.44	0.40	0.40	0.39	0.41

Source: Data derived by the authors from SPO and TUIK, 2022.

30. A quick comparison of the respective rates in different years shows that there has not been a significant change in income distribution among the percentiles in question. One should note, however, the slight effect of the differences in methods used in these surveys. The absence of significant ameliorations in income distribution is attributable to problems exacerbated by economic shocks, unemployment and neo-liberal economic policies which have generally ignored social development since the 1980s. The fall in the Gini coefficient implies that there was a certain amelioration in income differentials in 2013, as compared to the year 2002. In urban areas, it fell from 0.44 to 0.39 and in rural areas from 0.42 to 0.37. The Gini coefficients for the selected years between 2002 and 2013 were as follows: 0.42 in 2003, 0.40 in 2004, 0.38 in 2005, 0.43 in 2007,0.41 in 2010 and 0.40 in 2012, indicating that there have been slight ameliorations in income distribution in Turkey. 50.4% of the richest 20% lived in urbanized and 47.7% in rural areas by the year 2021. The Gini coefficient, which was 0.49 in 1994, fell to 0.41 in 2020, reflecting a slight improvement.

§4. Labour Force and Employment

31. Despite the increase in the 15+ age group of the population and the gradual increase in the civilian labour force, a continued diminishing trend was observed in the labour force participation rate. It fell to 63% in 1983 from 67% in 1978; from 56.7% in 1990 to 53.2% in 1994; from 49% in 2000 to about 47% in 2004; during the first decade of the 2000s, it varied between 47 and 50%. However, it was calculated as 50.8%, with a slight increase in 2013. By the year 2022, the participation rate stands at 52.5%. The participation and unemployment rates are both sensitive to monthly fluctuations in economic activity and are therefore adjusted seasonally.[22]

32. Basic data given by 2013 were as follows: labour force 28,271 (in thousands); employment 25,524,000; the unemployed 2,747,000; labour force participation rate 50.8%; employment rate 45.9%; unemployment rate 9.7%. The male participation rate is 71.5% while the ratio for women is only 30.8. The declining rate of female participation is a point of concern, especially in the face of Turkey's efforts for accession to the European Union. The ongoing migration of the rural population to urban areas accounts for most part for the drops in the labour force participation rate. While in agriculture women are counted in the labour force as unpaid family workers, their withdrawal from work life as well as the difficulties they encounter in finding adequate employment in urban centres, together with the increasing rate of schooling for children, contribute also to the decline in the overall labour force participation rate. Thus, in spite of the increasing overall population as well as of the working-age population, labour force participation rates show declining trends over the years. (It should be noted, however, that changes are sometimes caused by the different methods adopted by TUIK.) Suffice it to say that the process of shifting away from agriculture to services and industry continued in the 1990s and 2000s. In 2013 the share of agricultural employment was 23.6%, of industry 26.4% and of the services sector 50%.

33. Having suffered from several major shocks (i.e., the Gulf wars of 1991 and 2004 adversely affecting the Turkish economy, the financial crises of 1994, 1999,

22. These percentages as well as the following statistics draw basically on the database of the Statistics Institute of Turkey (TUIK).

2001 and 2010, as well as the earthquakes of 1999), Turkey had to deal with a high level of unemployment during the past decades. The employment rate, which is an important indicator of labour market performance, decreased from 44.8 to 42.3% in the fourth quarter of 2003 compared with the results of the same quarter of 2002. In recent years the unemployment rate has fluctuated roughly between 10 and 13% according to the quarterly household labour force surveys of the TUIK. By February 2005, it stood at 11.7%. In April 2010, the rate was 12%; in March 2011, it fell to 10.8% and eased down to 9.2% in June 2011; but the fact that the non-agricultural unemployment rate during the same period was 13.4%, while 'the young unemployment rate' (of those in the 15–24 age group) was as high as 19.3%, was a matter of concern indeed. On the other hand, while the rate of underemployment – meaning employment in substandard jobs, unproductive or part-time employment where jobholders are in fact in search of full-time productive work for which they are qualified – was 7% in the year 2000; it dropped to around 5% by the end of 2003 which is still a high rate. Combined with the prevailing unemployment rate, therefore, a ratio of about 16–20% (unemployment + underemployment) level presents the authorities with serious challenges to cope with, especially in light of Turkey's efforts to accede to the European Union. If so-called discouraged workers – meaning those who, due to repeated failures in finding adequate jobs, have given up the search for work – are also considered, the level of actual unemployment would be still higher. As for the educated youth unemployment where the ratio was 29.8 in 2002, it declined to 25.4% in 2003; but the rate of underemployment for the educated young during the same period rose to 7.6% from 6.8%, a phenomenon showing that the educated young are employed on substandard jobs where their skills are underutilized. Among the OECD countries, by the data of 8 October 2021 Turkey ranked as the top country with the longest weekly working time.

34. As for the distribution of employment by occupational status, the ratio of wage and salary earners in non-agricultural employment in March 2013 was 64%, the self-employed 23.9% and unpaid family workers 12.1%. Over the years the ratio of wage and salary earners has tended to rise owing to the expansion of the industry and services sectors. The ratio of self-employed to non-agricultural employment seems to have dropped slightly since the 1990s, while during the same period the ratio of unpaid family workers has somewhat increased. The last two groups are certainly encompassed within the bulk of agricultural employment.

35. The relatively satisfactory levels of economic growth achieved in the Turkish economy despite the absence of corresponding increases in employment, a tendency called 'jobless growth', is, among other factors, also attributed to the temptation of employers to attain higher volumes of production with the same size of workforce. The stagnating low level of wages (or falling real wages) plus engaging the same number of employees in overtime work despite legal restrictions, seem to have contributed to the ongoing growth rates. Although the increase in production continued in 2003 and growth reached an impressive level of 9.9% in 2004, 8.8% in 2011 and yet 4% in 2013; real wages declined, signifying a deterioration in income distribution. The causes and problems of 'jobless growth' were the themes of much debate on employment in the 2000s.

36. The dominance of an informal labour market is also a considerable problem in Turkey, as emphasized by the European Commission in the progress reports on the projected EU accession of Turkey. Research studies estimate the scale of the informal market (unrecorded economy) was about 52–53% of Turkish GNDP in 2003. As for employment, the share of the informal sector in non-agricultural employment was reported to run as high as 40% during the 1990s. In March 2011 it still stood at a rate of 41.3% (82.6 in agriculture and 27.7 in the non-agricultural sector). The high rate of informal employment entails substandard working conditions, unfair competition *vis-à-vis* employers active in the formal sector, shifting sizeable portions of employment away from social security and labour legislation coverage.[23] The Ministry of Labour and Social Security (namely İş-Kur) as well as several public and private agencies (e.g., the SPO, labour and employers' unions) have been engaged recently in a number of research projects to ease unemployment and ameliorate labour market functioning in Turkey.

37. The European Union emphasizes that Turkey should accelerate its efforts to develop a national employment policy in line with the European Employment Strategy. It must strive for higher employment rates and reduce the levels of youth and female unemployment. The extent of informal employment also remains a concern. A national integrated strategy for promoting social inclusion should also be created.

38. In recent years a sizable population whose precise number is not known but is estimated to be not below 5 million foreigners, most of whom are roughly from Middle Eastern countries, notably Syria, have moved to Turkey illegally, either as refugees or immigrants, a problem that has caused considerable political and economic controversy. This is also one of the various factors which seem to make the informal unemployment problem even worse.

§5. The Political System

39. The disintegration of the Ottoman Empire following its defeat in the First World War was marked by the occupation of Anatolia by the Entente powers of the West. The war for Independence initiated in 1919 under the leadership of Mustafa Kemal Atatürk led to the foundation of the Turkish Republic in 1923. The Ottoman Empire was a theocratic state based on Islam, governing many diverse ethnic and religious groups in harmony for centuries. The Turkish Republic is, as emphasized in its Constitution, a secular democratic state of law. From the proclamation of the Republic in 1923 to the end of the second World War, the new regime used rather authoritarian methods to rapidly meet the urgent needs of building a modern nation-state. Since 1946 Turkey has been governed by multiparty democracy based on free elections. In order to do away with the drawbacks of 'majority representation' which usually led to the domination of a single party, the 1961 Constitution emphasized a

23. For more on the labour market and employment situation in Turkey, *see* T. Dereli, P. Donders & K. Senger, *Description of the Formal and Informal Labour Market in Turkey*, working paper prepared in conjunction with the MATRA Project in 2004.

pluralistic democratic society and brought electoral procedures based on 'proportional representation'. Presently the election system is based on proportional representation buttressed by the requirement of receiving at least 10% of the general vote for any political party to be represented in the Parliament. Notwithstanding these initiatives, the result had often been the formation of weak coalition governments saddled with instabilities and political uncertainties in the recent past. While the 1960s and 1970s were characterized by the gradual consolidation of pluralism and freedoms, the economy was still a mixed one, involving state and private enterprises together and following essentially import-substitution policies. It was during the 1980s and 1990s that neo-liberal policies gained momentum, with a strong emphasis on the outward opening of the economy. The early 2000s, on the other hand, seem to be marked rather by initiatives aiming to expand human rights, at least, in legal rhetoric, though perhaps not paralleled by actual practice.

40. The general elections in the spring of 1999 resulted in a coalition government of three parties (the Republican People's Party (RPP) from left of centre, Motherland Party (Anavatan Partisi-ANAP) from right of centre and National Action Party (MHP) from the nationalist right). In the general elections held on 3 November 2002, only two of the 32 contesting parties were able to win the minimum 10% of the total poll which a party needs in order to qualify for representation in Parliament. (Under the existing system, it is impossible to achieve a genuine representation which is distorted by the 10% barrier, as votes cast for parties which fall below it are wasted to the benefit of those which cross the barrier. For the upcoming 2023 elections, the new election law has reduced the 10% barrier to 7% as a favour to the National Action Party which has formed an alliance with the ruling Justice and Development Party (AKP).)

41. In 2002, namely right of centre AKP and left of centre RPP could enter the Parliament. AKP came to power with 34% of the popular vote, winning 363 seats of the Parliament out of 550. The results of the following 2007 elections were similar, in that the AKP which won 46.5% of the general vote came to power as the single dominant party to form the government. In the 2011 elections, AKP won its third and most resounding electoral victory whereby 50% of the voters cast their votes for it, resulting in AKP's winning 326 seats of the Parliament. Although AKP's ideology was described as 'democratic conservatism', in Turkey after 2010 there seemed to be signs of a disguised march towards authoritarianism, as implied by restrictions on freedom of speech, alleged derogations from 'due process of law' and the prevalence of 'partisan' appointments.

42. The last two decades in particular have witnessed in Turkey the attenuation of the principle of the 'separation of the legislative, executive and judicial powers', with the increasing politicization of the judiciary over which the executive has been wielding higher degrees of influence. The Kurdish insurgency (an ethnic separationist movement) growing in south-eastern Turkey since the 1980s is a serious threat aimed at destabilizing the political system and slowing down economic development. To solve the Kurdish insurgency, the AKP, under the leadership of Prime Minister (now the President) Recep Tayyip Erdoğan, initiated a move called 'the

Kurdish Opening Up Initiative', aiming to expand the scope of human rights for the Kurdish minority, a critical strategy whose ultimate target and contents were not disclosed to the public properly. For the settlement of the Kurdish question, the agreement called 'the opening up of the Kurdish problem' turned out to be a failure for a number of reasons, leaving behind only sorrow and frustrations on the part of those who had instigated it, the Kurds, liberal intellectuals and the government (Tayyip Erdoğan) etc.

43. Local elections of 30 March 2014 resulted in AKP's victory with 43% of the votes of the participating electorate while (CHP RPP) the major opposition party followed it with 39%, CHP votes concentrated mainly in coastal areas as usual. Local elections of 2019 were seriously controversial wherein, after much debate and court actions, the RPP won astounding victories over the AKP in major coastal cities. Although Turkey's democracy has been traditionally based on a parliamentary constitutional system, wherein the Parliament elects the President from within and then the President, having a rather coordinating role, used to appoint the Prime Minister as the chief of the executive branch to be followed by the Prime Minister's forming the Council of Ministers (cabinet), the 2010 constitutional change foresaw the election of the nation's President through direct votes of the people. The presidential election materialized on 10 August 2014, with quite a low rate of electorate participation and yet accompanied by a very vocal election campaign pressed forward by Tayyip Erdoğan aggressively which, despite all the allegedly corrupt practices ascribed to the AKP government, eventually led to his election as the 12th President of the Republic, with 51.8% of the votes of the participating electorate. His close rival, the candidate nominated jointly by the CHP and MHP, followed him with 38.9%. Looking at his rhetoric and deeds, Erdoğan's ultimate aim seemed to be to change Turkey's democracy to a purely presidential system of government, but given the composition of the present Parliament, this was a target hard to realize as it required the restructuring of the Constitution accordingly.

44. Pursuing policies embedded in religious sectarianism is apt to lead to the division of the social system into extreme poles. The Gülen ideology, which was originally an integral part of the AKP policies, was later involved in a major conflict with AKP interests, whereby the Gülen community was dubbed by the AKP as the (so-called) 'parallel structure' defying the authority of the Turkish state.

45. The close-knit alliance between the Gülen movement and Erdoğan's AKP was known since the 1980s as well as the fact that the real target of the Gülen community was motivated by an Islamist ideology to convert Turkey's socio-political fabric into a state based on Islamist canon law principles since the 1980s. With the support of the AKP Gülen was able to infiltrate the state apparatus, the armed forces and the educational system of Turkey. But this cooperation between Gülen and AKP was disrupted by a conflict of interests which erupted on 15 July 2016 as a coup instigated by the pro-Gülen elements in the army. The uprising by the forces sympathizing with Gülen ideology was suppressed by the reactions of the army's core elements faithful to Atatürk's principles as well as by Erdoğan's sympathizers, as a result of which the attempted coup could not succeed. However the 'so-called 15th of July 2016' uprising as well as the struggle to eradicate it led to many harmful consequences for Turkish democracy, resulting in the drastic change in Turkey's constitutional structure after 2017, weakening the Turkish armed forces by the dismissal of the country's valuable military resources by successive 'decrees' with the force of law (KHKs) in the following decade. With more than so-called KHKs enacted after the introduction of the new regime (Erdoğan's new presidential system) in 2017 many important changes in Turkey's social and economic fabric were imposed from above (e.g., the closing of military schools and war colleges, expulsion of a sizable number of public employees for whom lawsuits for reinstatement are still lingering on unsolved. The result has been the attenuation of the power of the judiciary, the police and the army, accompanied by a complex web of problems which are likely to lead to unanticipated dysfunctions for the future political system, the unity of the nation and, for that matter, naturally, the industrial relations system of the country.

46. AKP's appeal seemed to centre around its religious-conservative appeal to the masses. It is estimated that, with this appeal alone, it sustains a sizeable crystallized ratio of votes (about 20%). The remaining ratio of support for it was accounted for by its populist policies, material concessions to its committed supporters as well as investments in mass construction projects, transportation systems and public works undertaken by loans which increase the public debt of the nation. A remarkable feature of the 2014 presidential election campaign was the dominant discourse of the candidates which focused mainly on religious and conservative topics, the use of heated arguments and attacks by the candidates against the cultural and ethnic identities of their opponents, rather than concrete economic and social policy issues. Thus, in Erdoğan's mission statements, 'value premises' predominated heavily over 'fact premises'. Labour and social policy issues had no place on the agenda of the local and presidential election campaigns. Insofar as the main themes of this monograph are concerned, this represents a pessimistic future for the labour relations system and the social policy agenda of the country.

47. The new government's programme was announced and debated in the Parliament on 4 September 2014. Among the priorities of the programme of the Turkish 62nd government was the finalization of the Kurdish 'opening up' initiative, it was the struggle against the so-called parallel structure and further democratization of the political system – i.e., removal of the barriers to freedom of speech, but no specific measures were envisaged to realize these goals. The new government also seemed willing to revive relations with the European Union. But suffice it to say that the EU–Turkey negotiation process is not likely to gain momentum unless Turkey implemented the long-awaited reforms in its industrial relations system (namely the required ameliorations in Act No. 6356 on Unions and the Collective Labour Agreement), which, among other items, was a precondition for opening up of negotiations on the chapter with the EU on social policy and employment.

48. Finally, as predicted in the earlier updates of this monograph, with a national referendum held on 16 April 2017, the constitutional structure of Turkey was changed drastically from the 'parliamentary democracy' format to a strictly authoritarian 'one man-rule', in an attempt to supposedly provide efficiency and speed in governmental actions, a quasi-presidential system unique to Turkey. Various phases of this major change were subject to criticisms of the opposition (i.e., the application of a referendum of vital importance under 'emergency law' circumstances, the narrow margin of 'yes' votes 51% as opposed to 49% 'no' votes, allegedly fraudulent practices in the counting of the ballots, Erdoğan's running for president without resigning first from his seat as the prime minister). Under the new Constitution the number of deputies members of the Grand national assembly, was raised to 600 from 500. The eligibility age for voting was lowered to 18 from 25 years of age. The term of office for the national assembly members was increased to five years from four. The deputies' power to monitor and check the executive (president and ministers) was removed by repealing the deputies' power to question the members of the executive. Thus the principle of the separation of three powers (checks and balances, in a general sense) was weakened. 'The council of ministers' as a concept, was disbanded, with the monopolization of all the executive power to be vested now in the President. The legislature's law-making power was attenuated by enlarging the power of the President to issue executive orders with the force of law. The deep-seated concept of law-maker grand national assembly in Turkey was replaced by executive orders and presidential decrees. The so-called ministers ow who are merely civil servants appointed by the president would not carry any accountability towards the grand national assembly. They are just public functionaries to be appointed and ousted by the President, if and when deemed necessary. The president while in office may keep his party allegiance which would necessarily turn the system into a party-state.

49. Among other outcomes of the transition to the so-called presidential governmental system has been the attenuation of Turkey's legal and judicial system, weakening of the role of the legislature in making the budget, attenuating the relatively high independence enjoyed by judges and prosecutors and decline in the popular belief in 'due process of law'. Under the new system of 2017, judges and prosecutors are to be controlled by the President who would staff the Council of Judges and Prosecutors.

50. Coupled with the rising levels of high inflation and unemployment, discontent with the authoritarian policies of Erdoğan has been giving important signals pointing to a possible failure in the upcoming general elections of 2023. The AKP-MHP alliance aiming to forestall such a failure has already made changes in the Election Law with a view to consolidating its position., among which is the reduction of the election barrier to 7% from the present 10%. This and the 7% barrier, as well as forming alliances with other parties, are perceived by the AKP as avenues paving the way for another victory. However major opposition parties committed also to forming another broad-based alliance with a view to returning the system to the earlier form of 'parliamentary democracy', one that is even stronger and healthier than the one which existed before 2017 are determined to eradicate the power of the AKP-MHP alliance.

51. Most sympathizers with the opposition share the fear that the AKP's ultimate goal is to realize a transition of Turkey from a modern secular state of law based on Atatürk's principles to a 'hybrid regime' built basically on a combination of '*shariat*' ('Islamic canon law principles' and the pretext of certain material signs of modern technology).

§6. The Legal and Judicial System

52. The Turkish system of private and public law is based essentially on legislative enactment. Upon the foundation of the Republic, the basis of Turkish private law was the Swiss law and consequently the legal system was laid on the Roman German tradition. Labour legislation, however, is rather eclectic in character, mirroring the social and economic conditions of the country and the nation.

53. The Turkish judicial system comprises an intertwined network of ordinary courts of first-level as well as national-level High Courts. The former, which include also labour courts, deal with civil and criminal disputes which mainly fall into the domain of private law, while the latter deal, in general, with both public and private-law-related disputes and include the Constitutional Court, the Council of State (the High Court of Public Administration) and the Court of Cassation. Ordinary courts are staffed by the Ministry of Justice which appoints judges and public prosecutors. There is no jury system in Turkey. If appeals are made, the review of judicial decisions of the civil and criminal courts, including labour law cases, is undertaken first by regional intermediate courts of appeal and then by the Court of Cassation. The 2nd, 7th and 9th divisions of the Court of Cassation deal with individual and collective labour disputes; the 10th division with social security disputes and the 21st division is in charge of adjudicating occupational health and safety disputes.

54. Courts of first instance justice are established in every township; they are in charge of settling legal disputes specified by their special legislation, like the criminal court of justice, under the chairmanship of a single judge and two member judges, but usually one judge except for commercial courts. First-instance labour courts of justice deal with the settlement of disputes between employees and employers or employer's representatives emanating based on employment contracts or employment legislation. Where they do not exist due to the low number of labour disputes, first-instance courts of justice perform their functions. The now-outdated Labour Courts Act of 1950 had to be amended with the establishment of intermediate regional courts of appeal with a view to upgrade efficiency and speed by the new Labour Courts Act. The appeal system has also been upgraded by the new Labour Courts Act. In the first stage, the process includes 'mediation as a precondition for filing a lawsuit with the labour court. However, there is now also mediation foreseen in the settlement of disputes of a general nature. Before treating mediation for labour disputes, summarizing mediation in a general sense may be a good starting point.

§7. Mediation in Legal Disputes (General)

55. In an attempt to alleviate the work load of the general court system and to speed up the adjudication of legal disputes in Turkey, the legislature enacted the Mediation Law Act No. 6325 on 7 June 2012. The objective of the Act No. 6325 was to set forth the procedures to apply to the settlement of legal disputes through the mediation process first in disputes of private law on matters where the parties can freely dispose of transactions which apply to foreigners also. Disputes which involve claims emanating from in-family violence are not subject to mediation. Where mediation foreseen in the Labour Courts Act is silent the pertinent clauses of Act No. 6325 shall be applicable. Article 2 of Act No. 6325 provides basic definitions for the mediator as well as the pertinent administrative provisions, like the Directorate of Mediation to be formed within the General Directorate of Legal Matters in the Ministry of Justice, the relevant institutions of the government, local administrations and their associated enterprises. The term 'board' refers to the board of mediation and 'registry' means the roster of mediators. Following this general framework, mediation as an alternative dispute settlement mechanism, the legislature passed the new Labour Courts Act No. 7036, on 12 October 2017 which foresaw the implementation of mediation as a precondition before going to the labour court in labour disputes (a topic to be discussed below at greater length.) It should be noted that the mediation has been regulated as an essentially voluntary procedure in Acts No. 6325 and No. 7036 both. The parties have equal rights in their application to the mediation process.

§8. Higher Courts of Appeal

56. The Constitutional Court vets and supervises the constitutionality of laws through cases brought before it. The Conflict of Laws Court is competent to clarify and eliminate conflicts and confusions caused by the contradictory provisions which may be found in different laws. The absence of intermediate courts of appeal between the ordinary courts and High Courts has resulted in the overburdening of the latter with too many cases appealed for review and reversal, thus leading to overly delayed and at times even conflicting awards. With a view to alleviating the work load of the High Courts of Appeal and inculcating more efficient results from the judicial system, work under way to establish intermediate-level Courts of Appeal (*istinaf mahkemeleri*), a goal which was on the agenda of the Ministry of Justice and envisaged also by the new Act of Civil Procedure This goal has already been accomplished . While the Court of Cassation reviews and, if deemed necessary, reverses the lower courts' decisions, the intermediate courts will have the power to gather evidential facts directly and decide rapidly on the merits of the cases.

57. Notwithstanding such initiatives, the once widespread belief in the independence of the judiciary seems to be waning in Turkey, since as a result of recent amendments, the courts seem to have been packed with a considerable number of new judges allegedly loyal to the executive branch. It should be acknowledged, however, that the independence and neutrality of labour courts, as well as the Court of Cassation and Constitutional Court, for that matter, as perceived by the public, have not yet been affected adversely.

58. The main sources of law are legislative acts as well as bylaws, decrees and regulations that complement legislation. Thus, where a pertinent provision in legislation exists, it must be applied when appropriate. Article 1 of the Civil Code states, clearly, however, that if there is no applicable provision in legislation, custom should prevail and in the case where there is no applicable custom either, the void should be filled by a rule set forth by the judge himself who then must act as how he himself would legislate on the issue if he were the law-maker. Moreover, the judge, in all his applications, must make use of 'jurisprudence' (case law) and the teachings found in legal doctrine.

59. The predominant role played by legislation notwithstanding, the judiciary has made important contributions to the development of a viable labour law system in Turkey. The legislative acts alluded to in the ensuing chapters helped create an industrial jurisprudence system and rules to govern labour–management relations. Collective bargaining determined not only the earnings of workers but also the administration of discipline and workplace rules, as well as the settlement of grievances. The accumulation of court-articulated rules and the decisions of arbitration boards have made Turkish industrial relations both rich and complicated within a relatively short time.

Chapter 2. Categories and Definitions of Social Law

60. Social legislation in Turkey consists mainly of labour law on the one hand and social security law on the other.

§1. Labour Law

61. Labour law is concerned 'with labour or work', either intellectual (white collar) or manual (blue collar) in character, carried out in a position of subordination (dependence), that is, when a person works under the command, authority and control of an employer. Turkish labour law requires the presence of other elements for the definition of 'employee', but subordination is the first and foremost element from which the other ingredients (i.e., 'working in a job' and 'for wages') are derived. If there is no element of subordination, as in the case of self-employment, labour law does not apply. Labour law can be defined as the aggregate of legal rules governing the relationships between employers and employees who exercise their labour or work in a subordinate position. In Turkey, labour law is concerned with the relationship between employers and employees in both the private and public sectors. However, the legal position and rights of public servants in the public sector are governed by administrative law rather than by labour law. SEEs engaged in the production and marketing of goods, energy and services (e.g., textiles, cement, steel, sugar, tobacco, electricity and the like) and public corporations like the State Railways or Turkish Airlines have been given the legal form of a quasi-private corporation although they are financially and administratively controlled by the state. Many such SEEs and some public corporations have been slated for privatization since the mid-1980s.

62. Persons with 'employee' status working in such public organizations which are subject to the general and annexed budgets as well as those working in municipalities, government-operated schools and universities fall within the scope of labour law, while public servants in the same institutions are subject to the Public Servants Act. As in many other countries, labour law is divided into two main parts: individual labour law and collective labour law.

§2. Individual Labour Law

63. Individual labour law is concerned mainly with the relationship between the employer and the employee on an individual basis. Its main topics include the following:

- definitions of employees, apprentices and trainee students, employers and employers' representatives, the physical premises such as the establishment and the enterprise, the scope of labour – law in terms of activities, etc.;
- the individual employment contract (or labour contract) (categories, the legal capacity to conclude, form and content of the contract);

- the rights and duties of the employer and the employee in the course of the employment relationship;
- working time and organization of work;
- the ending of the individual employment contract (termination and breaking), severance pay, problems of job security, covenants of non-competition;
- inventions by employees;
- settlement of individual labour disputes and labour courts.

§3. Collective Labour Law

64. Since the passage of the Trade Unions Act of 1947, and particularly the enactment of collective bargaining legislation with the right to strike in 1963, collective labour relations have become extremely important in Turkish labour law. They include such subjects as:

- union freedoms;
- the organization, structure and functions of labour unions and employers' unions;
- collective bargaining (competence and authorization, certification, structure and territory of bargaining, legal nature of collective agreements);
- settlement of collective labour disputes (mediation and arbitration);
- strikes and lock-outs;
- exceptions of the right to strike and recourse to compulsory arbitration;
- workers' participation in management.

§4. Social Security Law

65. The Social Security Organization was established in 1965 by Act No. 506 of 1964 which governed various branches of social security as the successor to the earlier Workers' Insurance Organization. Act No. 506, as amended by Act No. 4958 of 6 August 2003, covered all branches with the exception of family allowances. It excluded agricultural workers, the self-employed and public servants for which there were different schemes of social security. Act No. 506 was amended many times in the past and more recently in 2003, as a result of which the system has become quite complicated and confusing over the years. Attempts to reform the system with a view to creating uniformity in norms and bringing the administration of various branches under a single umbrella gained momentum in the early 2000s. Further, in an effort to extend the scope of health services so as to cover all segments of the population, work on the creation of a general health system was in progress. All of the branches of social security specified in the ILO Convention 102, except family allowances, exist in Turkey. As a general rule, the principle of equal treatment exists. Contributions to entitlements from social security schemes are the same for men and women. However, there is preferential treatment of women with regard to retirement age and age limits for children as standard beneficiaries or survivors.[24]

66. Contributory social insurance systems of the state were the following: the Public Servants Retirement Fund Act No. 5434 of 1949; the Social Insurance Act No. 506 of 1964, covering workers (employees); the Self-Employed Insurance Act No. 4956 of 2003, covering tradesmen, small artisans and other self-employed persons; the Social Insurance Act of the Self-Employed in Agriculture Act No. 2926 of 1983; the Agricultural Workers' Social Insurance Act No. 2925 of 1983, covering agricultural workers working on a temporary basis in the private sector; and the Unemployment Insurance Act No. 4447 of 1999.

67. The financial crisis plaguing the social security system was exacerbated in the 1990s. In order to restore the actuarial integrity of the system, the rules on retirement were overhauled in 1999, but implementation of the new law was delayed until 2002. Under the previous system, women could choose to retire at age 38, provided they had twenty years of continuous employment. For men, the thresholds were 43 years of age and twenty-five years of employment. Under the new system, for a new entrant, the minimum age of retirement was made 58 for women and 60 for men, with varying transitional periods for those already working and covered. A new Act No. 5502 amended Article 30 of Act No. 3146 and Social Insurance Organization, Bağ -Kur and Public Servants Retirement Fund were merged under one name, the Social Security Institution, thereby transferring the relevant functions to the merged Institution and abrogating various related provisions (Official Gazette, 20 May 2006, No. 26175).

68. In an effort to reduce the state's role in social security, a new private pension scheme for workers and the self-employed was enacted in 2001. The new private pension scheme based on voluntary contributions to which employers can also contribute on behalf of their employees is to be managed by private companies and supervised by the Treasury.

69. Following reform efforts to overhaul the social security system, the Act on Social Insurance and General Health Insurance, No. 5510, was passed on 31 May 2006 (Official Gazette 16 June 2006, No. 26200). Article 2 of Act No. 5510 defines the scope of social security in the following manner:[25] the beneficiaries of social insurance and general health insurance, employers, health service providers and in terms of the implementation of this Act, real persons as well as all types of public and private law corporate bodies and other institutions and organizations of a non-corporate nature. Article 4 of Act No. 5510 indicates which other categories shall

24. For more on social security law, *see* N. Süral, *Worker's Social Security Schemes with Special Reference to Recent Amendments*, working paper for the MATRA Project, 2004.
25. This section on Social Security law is based on M. Demircioğlu, *Labour Law in Turkey* 115–123 (translated by T. Dereli, İstanbul Chamber of Commerce Publications, No. 2010-43, 2010).

be treated as insured persons in terms of the implementation of this Act. These categories are the following: village and district heads; and in the case of the self-employed and independent workers, persons subject to income tax due to earnings derived from independent occupations; persons exempt from income tax but listed in small trades and artisans registers; shareholders of corporations on the management board of commandite companies and all partners of other companies and participations; persons engaged in agricultural activities; and certain categories employed in public administration units. Atypical types of work are subjected to contribution deductions on the basis of *pro rata temporis*. In an attempt to integrate atypical employment categories, some amendments have already been made to the Social Insurance Act, but further work may be needed to consider some of the outstanding cases.[26]

70. Act No. 5510 treats social security branches within two groups: (1) short-term social insurance branches and (2) long-term social insurance branches. Short-term branches include (a) work accidents, (b) occupational disease, (c) illness and (d) maternity.

I. Short-Term Insurance Branches

A. *Work Accidents*

71. Article 13 defines a work accident as an incident which disables the insured person physically or mentally, either immediately or afterwards. The relevant elements are as follows: (1) The incident has occurred while the 'insured' was at the workplace; (2) If the 'insured' was working independently on his own behalf, the incident occurred as a result of the work carried out by himself but in conjunction with the work performed at the establishment of an employer; (3) If the insured working for an employer was sent on an errand to a place outside the establishment, the incident has occurred while he was not engaged in doing his main duty; (4) In accordance with labour legislation, during the breastfeeding periods allowed for the nursing 'insured' mother she is working for an employer and (5) During the transportation of the 'insured' to and from the workplace by a vehicle provided by the employer.

72. The work accident must be communicated to the competent security forces immediately and to the Social Security Institution within three working days at the latest. The Social Security Institution may conduct investigations to determine if the incident reported qualifies as a work accident. If the investigations conclude that the communications are incorrect, all payments made by the Institution shall be recovered from the persons who have made the false declarations.

26. For a more comprehensive work in English, *see* Kübra D. Yenisey, *Social Security Law in Turkey*, *International Encyclopaedia of Laws* (R. Blanpain, gen. ed., Kluwer 2013).

B. Occupational Disease

73. Article 14 defines an occupational disease as a case of temporary or permanent disease, bodily or mental disability suffered by the 'insured' due to the nature of his work or as a result of performing the relevant operations. It must be authenticated by examining (1) the report of a health board and the related documentation duly prepared by health service providers authorized by the Social Security Institution and (2) the audit reports and other required documents investigating the working conditions at the workplace as well as the associated medical findings drawn up by the Health Board of the Social Security Institution, if deemed necessary.

C. Illness

74. Article 15 defines illness as a state of sickness falling outside the scope of occupational disease and work accident and causing disability for the 'insured'.

D. Maternity

75. In view of Article 15, maternity refers to cases of illness or disability due to pregnancy and motherhood of the insured woman and the insured wife of insured man, starting from the commencement of pregnancy up to the first eight weeks and in the case of multiple pregnancies up to the first ten weeks of giving birth to the child of the woman who was earning income from her work.

76. Benefits provided for work accidents, occupational disease, illness and maternity are as follows. Benefits to be provided by the Work Accidents and Occupational Health Insurance are (1) providing the 'insured' with a daily temporary disability payment for the duration of temporary disability; (2) assigning the 'insured' a permanent disability income; (3) compensating the entitled survivors of the 'insured' deceased as a result of a work accident or occupational disease with income; (4) granting a marriage payment to girls who have been assigned such income and (5) providing the 'insured' deceased as a result of a work accident or occupational disease with a funeral payment.

77. The 'insured' is paid a daily temporary disability benefit for the duration of his/ her illness or maternity. As for maternity insurance, the 'insured' is also paid a nursing allowance for each living child at a current rate fixed by the management board of the Social Security Institution and approved by the minister.

II. Long-Term Insurance Branches

A. Disability

78. Article 25 of Act No. 5510 addresses disability. Upon the request of the 'insured' or the employer, disability is to be authenticated according to reports based on the examination of medical documents duly prepared by the health boards of health service providers authorized by the Social Security Institution. The 'insured' is considered disabled if it is found by the Health Board of the Institution that he/she has lost a certain portion of his/her earning power in the occupation. For a worker employed by the employer or self-employed or independent worker and for an employee working in public institutions as well as the person who is identified as having lost his capacity to work, the 'insured' is considered disabled if he/she has lost at least 60% of his/her earning power due to a work accident or occupational disease.

79. In order to benefit from a monthly disability salary, the 'insured' must (1) be considered disabled; (2) must have been insured for a minimum of ten years, having paid contributions for a total of 1,800 days; (3) must have sent a written request to the Institution upon leaving his/her job due to disability.

B. *Old Age and Retirement*

80. Old age insurance benefits are the following (Article 28): (1) provision of old-age salary; or (2) making a lump-sum payment. In addition to the condition of having paid the relevant amounts of social security contributions, presently 58 is the age of retirement for women and 60 for men, which (beginning on 1 January 2036) will increase progressively over the years and reach 65 for both men and women by January 2048 (Article 28, as amended on 17 April 2008). To be entitled to retirement, a female worker under 4/a status must have paid insurance contributions for 3,600 days, insured for fifteen years and completed the age of retirement (58 for women and 60 for men). The last one (the age condition) has become a serious political question recently for a large portion of the working population. A male worker under 4/a status will have access to retirement by having paid insurance contributions for 4,500 days, insured for twenty-five years and completed the age of 60.

81. Following the serious mining accident in Soma plant in May 2014, among other changes the retirement age which was 55 for all workers employed in the mining sector has been reduced to 50, Article 41 of Act No. 6552. Unworked days shall be considered as having been actually worked in terms of the computation of social insurance contributions.

82. A recent significant issue in Turkey's social security system is the so-called people stuck with the age requirement for retirement question. With a view to warrant the financial sustainability of the social security system, the age requirements cited above were computed quite carefully despite strong reactions from groups that wished to retire earlier. However recently groups of people referred to as 'people stuck with the age requirement' have been voicing their demands for the revision of their retirement to conditions which were effective prior to the date before the act had gone into effect, i.e., September 1999. In solving this issue, the government's first option seems to be requiring the presence of the insured person having paid a certain number of contribution days, or bringing 'new (lower) retirement age limits' for men and women.

C. Death

83. Benefits to be granted to the survivors of the deceased 'insured' are the following: (1) survivors' salary; (2) lump-sum survivors' benefit; (3) marriage benefit to girls who receive survivors' salary; (4) funeral payment.

84. Social insurance contribution rates are as follows: (Article 81) the contribution rate for disability, old age and death insurance is 20% of the earnings of the 'insured' which serve as a basis for contributions. 9% of the contribution is the share of the 'insured', while 11% must be paid by the employer.

85. As for long-term insurance branches, contribution rates are to be fixed by the Social Security Institution; they vary between 1% and 6.5% based on the degree of danger posed by the occupation for health and work accident incidents.

86. Unemployment insurance is governed by Act No. 4447 which covers those insured employees working under employment contracts according to Act No. 5510. Coverage is mandatory, starting from the date on which the persons involved begin working. The following payments are made and services provided to the 'insured' who are unemployed: (1) unemployment payment, (2) insurance contributions disbursed in conjunction with Act No. 5510, (3) finding employment, (4) occupational training with a view to developing skills, (5) occupational counselling and training, labour force adjustment and community work services, labour market research and planning. Expenses incurred for these functions shall be met by the Unemployment Insurance Fund.

87. Contributions are as follows: of the monthly gross earnings serving as a basis for contributions computed in accordance with Act No. 5510, 1% to be paid by the 'insured', 2% by the employer; and 1% by the state. The amount of unemployment pay is 40% of the daily average (gross) earnings of the 'insured', computed over his/her four months' earnings which serve as the basis for contribution payments.

88. The number of days for which unemployment benefits shall be granted to the 'insured' is computed in the following manner. Provided that the 'insured' has worked without interruption by paying insurance contributions for the last 120 days before the termination of his/her employment contract within the last three years, the unemployed employee (1) who has worked as insured and paid contributions for 600 days, for a duration of 180 days; (2) who has worked as insured and paid contributions for 900 days, for a duration of 240 days and (3) who has worked as insured and paid contributions for 1,080 days, for a duration of 300 days.

89. In order for the employee to be entitled to unemployment pay, the conditions are: (1) the employment contract must have been terminated by the employer according to the relevant notice terms, or (2) the employment contract must have been terminated by the employee for just cause, or (3) the employment contract must have been terminated by the employer for just cause due to reasons other than the employee's immoral or malicious conduct, or (4) the fixed-term contract must have ended up on the expiration of its fixed term, or (5) the employee must have been laid off due to the transfer or closing of the establishment or due to the change of work or the nature of the establishment.

90. Although 'domestic services' are, according to Article 4 of Act No. 4857, outside the scope of the Labour Act, in view of a novel provision they shall be subject to social insurance coverage if they are engaged by the same household for a minimum of ten days in a month. However, those whose employment falls below ten days a month may be voluntarily insured based on their own will (Article 40 of Act No. 6552), the new so-called bag law of 2014. However, domestic caretakers (i.e., babysitters and home maids) employed by the same person on a continuous basis are to be covered by social insurance.

91. As for social security coverage, in 2019, the number of the actively insured is 22.000.964; the number of the passively insured (insured dependents) is 12.977.719; and the dependence ratio (active/passive ratio) was 1.8 according to data provided by the Turkish Ministry of Family, Labour and Social Services.

§5. Legal Nature

92. Since the present monograph deals mainly with labour law and industrial relations in Turkey, social security law is not studied to any extent except when certain labour law practices are intertwined with rules governing the social insurance scheme. Labour law and social security law both have an 'imperative' character in Turkey. However, a distinction is made between those provisions of labour law which are 'absolutely imperative' (absolutely binding) and those which are 'relatively imperative'. The 'relatively imperative' provisions can be improved upon by individual employment contracts or by collective agreements, but only in favour of employees (e.g., provisions on minimum wage, working time, wages, remuneration for overtime work, etc.). Although the same concept applies to social security law, collective agreements have rarely provided anything above the minimum retirement pensions, let alone in the field of disability and sickness benefits. The 'absolutely imperative' provisions are those which must never be altered, even in favour of employees (e.g., the ceiling levied upon the maximum amount of severance pay). Due to the pro-labour and protective character of labour law, the number of such 'absolutely imperative' clauses is quite limited in Turkish labour law. Contraventions of 'absolutely imperative' clauses may be declared null if nullity is invoked by the protected party. The period within which nullity can be invoked differs in relation to the subject matter, as alluded to in the ensuing chapters. Moreover, employment contracts and collective agreements must not contravene public order and general morals. There are penal sanctions to be applied in the case of violations of imperative provisions of both individual and collective labour law, but such sanctions are rarely used.

Chapter 3. Historical Background of Labour Law and Industrial Relations in Turkey

93. The history of labour law and industrial relations in Turkey can be studied within six periods.

§1. THE PRE-REPUBLICAN PERIOD

94. In the Ottoman period, the earliest known labour legislation dates from the year 1865. This and most of the subsequent protective measures were aimed at regulating the working conditions of coal miners in Ere li and the surrounding coal mining zones. As for occupational organizations, the craftsmen's guilds were the only form of institutional arrangement in the Ottoman Empire until the first half of the nineteenth century, but self-evidently the guilds were quite different from the trade unions of nineteenth-century Europe and America, both in terms of structure and functions. Manufactured goods from Europe weakened the guilds to a considerable extent and they finally disappeared in the 1860s with the proclamation of a new civil code, the *Mecelle*, which combined the liberal economic principles of Western countries and the tenets of Islam deeply embedded in Turkish society. The major instrument of labour regulation in the *Mecelle* – for which work, begun in 1865, was completed in 1876 – was the individual lease contract that viewed the employment relationship as a special form of hiring of labour. Following the declaration of the short-lived First Constitution of 1876, a series of protests, demonstrations and work stoppages by labour groups occurred in the major towns of the Empire but were suppressed with police intervention. Upon the proclamation of the Second Constitution in 1908 – which recognized the freedom of association – there was an outbreak of strikes in Istanbul, mainly against the foreign-operated establishments. Some of these took the form of general strikes and spread to Izmir, Aydin and several other towns. The reaction of the government was to suppress these work stoppages. Union organization and strikes were prohibited in public services and utilities and previously organized unions in such services most of which were under foreign operation – the trams, public utilities and services – were abolished by the enactment of the Work Stoppages Act of 1909. This Act stood out as the first legal document inhibiting employee organizations in Turkey, for though its scope was limited, there was virtually no significant industrial workforce outside such sectors during this era. The Work Stoppages Act permitted unionism outside the public services, however, and established conciliation mechanisms for the settlement of labour disputes. It remained in force until the year 1938.

95. Because of the suppression of almost all union activity, left-wing political organizations were formed between 1909 and 1920 to manage the labour protest. During the Independence War against the Entente powers (1919–1922), a few protest movements by sporadic labour groups developed, but unionism did not emerge in the formal sense. On 12 September 1921, Acts Nos. 151 and 114 were passed, again with a view to protect coal miners by regulating their working conditions in the Zonguldak and Ereğli regions.

§2. The Republican Period (The Era of Liberalism, 1923 to Early 1930s)

96. When peace returned the one-party regime of the new Republic established in 1923 did not encourage the development of associations and particularly of labour unions in spite of the liberal provisions of the 1924 Constitution and the 1926 Civil Code, the latter adapted from the Swiss legal system. In fact, the Restoration of Peace Act, passed in 1925 with a view to facilitating the launching of Atatürk's reform programs, discouraged the establishment of class-based organizations. The new regime realized the significance of engaging in sustained efforts toward economic development. However, in tackling this task it was confronted with a depressing legacy from the past. At this stage, Turkey was saddled with inherited debts and the destructive effects of several decades of war. In February 1923, delegates representing farmers, traders, industrialists and workers assembled in Izmir for the new regime's first Economic Congress. Although the need for a mixed economic system was stressed at that Congress, together with the active role which the government should play in the country's development, the period until the early 1930s was marked by a liberal economic policy. In 1924 a draft labour bill was prepared, but could not be enacted into law due to the reactions of forces that insisted on the adoption of a more comprehensive and protective labour code.

97. Because private capital and entrepreneurial skills were in short supply and due to the worldwide effects of the Great Depression, the regime had to adopt etatist principles of economic development during the 1930s. The early 1930s witnessed several efforts to devise a draft bill on labour law, but the actual materialization of such efforts had to wait till the year 1936.

§3. The Etatist Era (The Period of Intervention)

98. The major practical expression of the etatist philosophy was Turkey's first five-year industrialization plan, drawn up in 1933 and put into operation between 1934 and 1938. The plan provided for the establishment of a series of industrial plants designed to reduce Turkey's need for imported consumer and intermediate goods as well as to create employment. It was during this period that Turkey's well-known SEEs like Sümerbank and Etibank were founded.

99. The Work Stoppages Act of 1909 remained in effect until 1938, and as a result, unions could still be established, at least theoretically, in sectors which did not fall within the category of public services. An amendment to the Penal Code passed in 1933 dealt specifically with the prohibition of work stoppages and their punishment. In 1936 the legislature passed the Labour Code (No. 3008), the major piece of protective labour legislation, which remained in force until 1967. Its enactment coincided with the implementation of the first five-year plan. It also followed Turkey's entry into the ILO in 1932. The Keynesian policies of the 1930s as well as the traditionally paternalistic attitude of the Turkish state towards labour–management relations also accounted for the introduction of this Act at a time when there was still no substantial industrial workforce or labour conflict in Turkey.

100. The main instrument of this code was the individual employment contract, and its coverage was limited to manual employees (blue-collar workers) only. As in the past, relations with white-collar employees were to be regulated by the provisions of the Obligations Act which was an adjunct to the Civil Code of 1926. Also, only those establishments with an average of ten or more workers over the year were covered. (In 1952 coverage was extended to establishments with four to nine workers in cities with 50,000 or more inhabitants.) The Labour Act of 1936 tightened the already-existing restrictions on strikes and lock-outs by bringing legal penalties and establishing a full-fledged compulsory arbitration mechanism for the settlement of interest disputes. It also created a mechanism for the election of employees' representatives in workplaces who would encourage communication between workers and employers and act as the first step in handling collective interest disputes on behalf of workers within the compulsory arbitration system. The banning of strikes and labour unions under the 1936 Act may be attributed to the Republican Party's (RPP) populist philosophy that Turkey was not a class-divided society and that labour's interests were well protected by a paternalistic state.

101. In 1938, the Turkish Parliament, prompted by the threats posed by political developments in Europe, passed a new Associations Act and prohibited the formation of organizations based on class, race or religion, thus reiterating the prohibition on forming unions as well.

§4. Labour Unionism Without Collective Bargaining and the Right to Strike (1946–1963)

102. After World War II Turkey adopted multi-party democracy and there followed an era of liberalism as far as the right of association was concerned. In 1946, the Ministry of Labour was established, which proceeded to open a series of official public employment agencies as well as exercise general supervision over labour problems. The Social Insurance Organization, with a scheme to cover industrial accidents and maternity benefits, was created in the same year. The Associations Act of 1938 was amended, and in 1947 legislation specifically addressing the formation of unions was passed.

103. The Unions Act of 1947 adopted several democratic principles. Union freedoms and voluntary unionism were emphasized. No person could be forced to join or refrain from joining a union or withdraw (resign) or refrain from withdrawing from a union. Prior permission from administrative authorities was not required to set up a union. However, the Act of 1947 carried several restrictive measures as well. For example, labour and employers' unions were to be 'national' organizations in the sense that they should view national interests above their own economic and organizational goals. Like the Labour Act of 1936, the Trade Unions Act too was limited in scope to manual employees, thus excluding white-collar employees from the right to unionize, the only exception to this restriction is a special act concerning journalists which was passed in 1952. Also, those who worked for small businesses, such as a grocery store or a small tradesman, could not unionize even though they might be defined as wage-earners.

104. Parts of the 1947 Act violated certain trade union freedoms, such as the provisions which, in some cases, put unions under government control. The activities and finances of a union could be controlled at any time by the administrative authority of a given locality. Also, unions should not join international organizations without the consent of the government, nor could they engage in political activities. The annual amount of membership dues was limited to TL 120 per member (about USD 15 at the 1950s rate of exchange), and by subjecting unions to the provisions of the Associations Act, the legislature restricted their freedom to increase the rate of dues, to own property and to improve their financial strength in general. But, most important of all, the Act of 1947 re-emphasized the bans on strikes and lock-outs. However, Turkey ratified the ILO Convention on the Right to Organize and to Bargain Collectively (No. 98, 1949) in 1951, but the Freedom of Association and Protection of the Right to Organize Convention (No. 87, 1948) was not ratified until 1993, probably due to its extensive coverage which seemed to extend into the orbit of the right of public servants to organize and the right to strike.

105. Of special significance in the early 1950s was the formation of Türk-İş, the Confederation of Turkish Labour Unions, as a national centre in 1952. There were also important legal developments. In 1950 labour courts were established by Act No. 5521 (which is still in force) in order to deal with rights disputes. By means of special legislation in 1950, labour unions were empowered to play some part in the conciliation and compulsory arbitration mechanisms and to conclude agreements with employers. The Obligations Act of 1926 carried some vaguely stated provisions which entitled employee groups to enter into the so-called general agreements, but the bans on strike action made it virtually impossible for unions to bargain collectively with employers. Nevertheless, labour unions became very active in initiating collective labour disputes under the compulsory arbitration scheme in the years following the 1950 amendment.

§5. The Liberal Industrial Relations Era: The Post-1963 Period (Free Collective Bargaining with the Right to Strike)

106. The Political Reformation of 27 May 1960, prompted and implemented by the collaboration of intellectuals, the armed forces and bureaucrats – a coalition of forces which has traditionally been the innovating element in Turkish society enabled Turkish unionism and industrial relations to gain new momentum. Among its other progressive clauses, the new Constitution of 1961 established in Articles 46 and 47 trade union freedoms, the right of employees to bargain collectively with employers and the right to strike. However, the rights which the new Constitution conceded were to be governed by special legislation, and it was in July 1963 that the required enactments – the Trade Unions Act No. 274 and the Collective Agreements, Strikes and Lock-outs Act No. 275 which covered both white-collar and blue-collar workers – were passed by the Turkish Parliament. Among the major factors facilitating the introduction of the new industrial relations system, one could cite the impact of external forces, such as ILO Conventions and Recommendations, as well as softening government attitudes towards organized labour, the emerging belief that collective bargaining with the right to strike was an indispensable component of pluralistic democracy, and the threats triggered by the gradual growth of left-wing ideologies in Turkish society. The adoption of a decentralized decision-making system in industrial relations was viewed as an urgent matter despite the resistance of certain anti-union forces. But the most salient feature of these developments was the fact that these new rights, for which workers in the West had striven for almost a century, were granted rather abruptly from above. Despite the sporadic demands of Türk-İş for the right to strike during the late 1950s, the new legislation could not be viewed as an outcome of continued pressures by workers from below.[27]

107. Following the 1960 political changes various Turkish unions, and particularly Türk-İş, received the government's permission to affiliate with international labour organizations. It was not long before these international bodies began to play a significant role, especially in the area of drafting new legislation and the education of union officials. Assistance was extended by bodies like the Organisation for Economic Co-operation and Development (OECD), the International Confederation of Free Trade Unions (ICFTU), the International Trade Secretariats (ITS) and the ILO. The grants and technical assistance programmes of US agencies like the Agency for International Development (AID), and later the technical aid programmes of the Asian and African Free Labour Institute (AAFLI) of the American Federation of Labour and Congress of Industrial Organizations (AFL-CIO) which began in 1974, became one of the major forces shaping the character of the new industrial relations system in Turkey.

108. Among other legislative developments in the industrial relations field during the post-1963 era should be mentioned the creation of a limited 'workers' participation' scheme in the management of certain SEEs. This was first established by Act No. 440 in 1964 and then put into effect by a special bylaw in 1966. A workers' representative was entitled to participate in the management boards of the SEEs and certain public corporations 'which employed a considerable number of workers'. He was to be elected to the management board of the enterprise by the management committee of the union concerned. The government was empowered by Act No. 440 to identify which state enterprises and corporations would qualify as employing a 'considerable number of workers'.

27. For a legal and sociological study of these developments in Turkey, *see* T. Dereli, *The Development of Turkish Trade Unionism: A Study of Socio-political and Legislative Dimensions* (Sermet Publishing (1968; the revised version of a MS thesis submitted to the School of Industrial and Labour Relations, Cornell University, June 1964).

109. Act No. 624 concerning the formation of unions by public servants was passed in 1965, as had been foreseen in Article 46 of the 1961 Constitution; but because they were denied the right to bargain collectively and to strike, these unions remained rather insignificant. They were intended to operate as consultative, 'meet and discuss' type of organizations through participation in joint committees established by the Public Servants Act. Though public servants, and particularly public school teachers, set up many unions during the late 1960s, they did not have any role in the determination of their members' working conditions. However, teachers' unions became actively involved in left-wing politics and therefore were susceptible to occasional harassment by the government.

110. There was no significant change in the Collective Agreements, Strikes and Lock-Outs Act during this period. However, by passing Act No. 1317 in 1970, the legislature amended certain articles of the Trade Unions Act (No. 274). While some of these changes were of minor importance, a few others (i.e., the imposition of numerical requirements for unions to be active nationwide) proved to be quite controversial and triggered mass protests and worker uprisings which, along with other political developments, ultimately led, on 12 March 1971, to the military intervention which temporarily suspended democratic freedoms in Turkey. Later, upon an objection filed by the Turkish Labour Party (TİP), the Constitutional Court repealed some of these provisions of Act No. 1317 amendments, ruling them unconstitutional.

111. This era witnessed the creation of new organizations which played significant roles in Turkish industrial relations in the following years. In 1962 the Employers' Confederation of Turkey (TİSK), and in 1967 the left-wing Confederation of Progressive Labour Unions of Turkey (DİSK), which had ties to the TİP set up in 1961, were established.

112. A new Social Insurance Act (No. 506) was passed in 1964 with a view to improving the already-existing workers' insurance scheme established in 1946. More important than this, however, a new Labour Code dealing with the individual employment relationship and overhauling various features of the 1936 Labour Code was adopted in 1967 but actually came into force in 1971 as the new Labour Act (No. 1475) which remained in force until 2003. The most significant aspect of Act No. 1475 was its expanded scope in contrast to the 1936 Code. In dealing with the individual employment relationship it covered, as did the Trade Unions Act of 1963, white-collar as well as blue-collar workers, and its scope was extended to all establishments, even those employing only one worker. However, there were certain types of work and workers: the great bulk of agricultural workers, workers employed by small artisans and the like, who were still excluded from its coverage. By abolishing the local minimum wage commissions, the Labour Act of 1971 also provided for centrally determined minimum wages to be revised at least once every two years. Parallel to this new Labour Code, amendments to the legislation on white-collar press workers and maritime workers were made by two separate acts (Nos. 212 and 854, respectively). The transitional government formed during the 12 March 1971 military intervention effected certain changes in the 1961 Constitution, one of which was the abolition of the public servants' right to organize. Following this constitutional amendment, the Parliament repealed the Public Servants' Unions Act of 1965 (No. 624), thus depriving them of the right to organize at a time when these unions were struggling for the right to strike.

113. Perhaps the most controversial development of the 1970s was Act No. 1927, passed in 1975, amending and supplementing certain sections of the Labour Act No. 1475. Its significance lay in its new clauses pertaining to 'severance pay' for workers and dismissals. Due to the absence of employment security and unemployment insurance, severance pay had always played an important role in providing workers with some degree of income and job security in the event of dismissals. The amendment increased the compensation from fifteen days' pay to thirty days' pay for the employee each year of service. While under the previous system it was payable to a worker who had been employed in an establishment for at least three years, Act No. 1927 lowered the required minimum period to one year and also expanded the scope of the 'contract termination' categories which entitled the worker to severance pay. Since the levels set by the Labour Act were automatically exceeded by collectively bargained arrangements, the impact of the new severance pay legislation on employers was allegedly profound, touching off heated debates in labour–management circles.

114. In the 1970s it was often argued that a consequence of rising labour costs would be the likelihood of employers' being tempted to use labour saving rather than labour-intensive techniques in an economy which was riddled with a high rate of unemployment. Such an effect would run counter to the employment-creating objectives set out in the five-year economic plans as well as to the unions' avowed goals of providing employment security for their members. It was natural that in those years, due to restrictions on currency transfers, employers' response to rising wages by massive lay-offs could not be immediate. But the tendency for the volume of employment to contract as a result of increased wage bills made itself felt. Also due to the many wage supplements and fringe benefits which did not have any link to the time worked, the variable character of labour costs weakened, tending to take on the characteristics of fixed costs over a period of time. It was argued that even in the economy of Turkey based on import-substitution policies then, Turkish industries would lose their comparative advantage in international markets insofar as labour costs were concerned, and this could have adverse effects on the economy's international balance of payments. A frequently heard criticism directed against unions was that collective bargaining and union power were the main causes of the inflationary pressures in the economy.

115. During the 1970s employers' complaints centred on the allegation that soaring labour costs tempted them to lay-off increasing numbers of workers or even to close their factories permanently, thus creating combined adverse effects both on employment levels and economic growth of the country. Another argument addressed the impact of the unions' policy of obtaining flat rate, across-the-board wage settlements rather than percentage or merit-based wage increases. In some plants, flat-rate increases caused unrest in the higher labour grades by narrowing wage differentials among 'skilled' and 'semi-skilled, unskilled' categories. This created difficulties for managers in their recruitment of skilled technicians, foremen and the like. Some unions had begun towards the late 1970s to realize the unanticipated adverse effects of flat-rate increases not only for management but also for their own security, particularly in plants where skilled workers constituted a significant portion of the workforce. In order to, at least, maintain the already narrowed wage differentials, they endeavoured to incorporate percentage increases into their demands.

116. In the Turkish mixed economy, the state always played an important role, not only as the third 'actor' of the industrial relations system but also as an employer through its profit-motivated enterprises. During the 1960s and 1970s the public sector paid higher wages and fringe benefits than those paid by the private sector. This was probably due to the state's deep-rooted paternalistic approach and the ongoing effects of neo-Keynesian policies, as well as to its traditional tendency to be the leading force in labour questions. However, a closer study showed that the state sector was characterized by higher wages, on average, for semi-skilled and unskilled employees, while in the private sector skilled employees received better remuneration than their counterparts in the public sector. The differences between the two sectors obstructed attempts to establish a rational wage structure in Turkey. Moreover, public sector managers chose to conduct their bargaining negotiations separately at enterprise level, independent from private sector employers' unions and this prevented harmonization of collective bargaining agreements both in time and in content. Private sector employers' unions aspired from the very beginning to conduct their negotiations jointly with the public sector, or at least to coordinate their bargains with those of the latter, but attempts in this direction were never successful, mainly because of the reluctance of the public sector to form a united front with private sector employers.

117. The proposals embodied in the third five-year plan to set up an Industrial Relations Unit to coordinate collective bargaining in the public sector and to establish a Wages and Incomes Council for the whole economy did not materialize either. One reason for the failure of initiatives to form such neo-corporatist central organs was, of course, the presence of several factors which had caused collective bargaining to operate mainly at local levels. But failures in this area were due mostly to the organizational problems of employers, both in the public and private sectors, rather than to the structure of labour unions. However, the government in power in 1978 ventured to restrict wage hikes to cost of living indices by adopting a new document termed the 'social contract'. After long negotiations with Türk-İş, the then Prime Minister Ecevit was able to persuade the Confederation, whose affiliates were better organized in the public sector than DİSK, to abide by the rules of the 'social contract'. The government was willing to implement the 'social contract' as a guideline for collective bargains in both sectors and formulated it in broad terms by pledging to strengthen workers' participation in management and to launch various labour law reforms including job security for workers. The main thrust of the 'social contract', however, was to maintain the purchasing power of workers in 1978 and afterwards at the level obtained in 1976, the year in which workers had acquired the highest increase in their real wages. With the shifting of political power to the right-wing Justice Party in 1979, the 'social contract' was abandoned, only to leave its mark as a short-lived experiment in the history of Turkish industrial relations.

118. As the 1970s came to a close, however, reactions were brewing against the Turkish unions' philosophy which so far had been aimed solely at furthering the narrow class interests of their members. The inflated number of unions at various levels (about 900 in 1980), often dubbed as 'union inflation', had become a major source of concern for the government as well as for employers and the well-entrenched unions themselves. Turkish social legislation had indeed manifested a vertical growth, leaving various social groups – agricultural workers, public servants, employees working for small tradesmen and the like – outside its scope. Therefore, the problem involved the creation of a more equitable income distribution within the social strata as well. The 'social contract' was, in fact, an attempt to strike a balance between free collective bargaining and the need to impart a sense of self-restraint into unions' behaviour for the sake of maintaining price stability and spreading welfare to other groups in society which so far had been excluded from the coverage of social legislation.

119. In the late 1970s, Turkish labour relations were adversely affected by increasing inflation and growing political instability. In 1977 and 1979, there was an unprecedented level of strike activity, and in the first nine months of 1980, 1,303,253 workdays were lost due to strikes. Together with the effects of various internal problems within the unions, and heightened militancy on the part, mainly, of the DİSK leadership, these circumstances had placed the Turkish labour movement in a very vulnerable position by September 1980. A horrifying surge of political violence from the extremist partisans of both left and right compelled the army leaders to intervene. On 12 September 1980, General Kenan Evren, the Chief of General Staff, installed himself and his five-man National Security Council as a temporary government. Among certain other political changes, the new regime suspended the activities of several labour unions and levied a ban on strikes and lock-outs. It also issued Act No. 2316 (dated 11 October 1980) concerning the appointment of trustees (curators) for trade unions whose activities were suspended, and Act No. 2364 on the Reactivation of Expired Collective Agreements in Cases of Social Necessity which would remain in force until legislative amendments to Acts Nos. 274 and 275 could be made and put into force.

§6. The Post-1980 Era up to the Present

120. The '12 September 1980' intervention was followed by a transitional period during which the Supreme Arbitration Board (YHK) reactivated many collective agreements lopsidedly, as they expired, after revising wages and fringe benefits. In May 1983, coupled with the revival of multiparty democracy, a new era of industrial relations began in Turkey. Its instruments were Act No. 2821 on Unions and Act No. 2822 on Collective Agreements, Strikes and Lock-Outs.

121. Together with Act No. 1475 dealing with the individual employment relationship, these two Acts, as amended in 1986, 1988, 1995 and 1997 with a view to expanding the scope of trade union freedoms, established the legal environment of industrial relations in Turkey. With few exceptions, this legislation covered all manual and white-collar workers in both the public and private sectors; however, public servants and certain public functionaries, including the newly created 'contract employee' category in the SEEs, were denied the right to unionize and bargain collectively. The 1983 legislation set out to eliminate the abuses and malfunctioning aspects of the previous system, but these 'positive motives' were accompanied by 'negative motives' with respect to a few dimensions of union freedoms. Thus new laws further restricted strikes, expanded the scope of compulsory arbitration, imposed certain limitations on union membership, and instituted heavier penalties for violators. Some of the new restrictions had their basis in Articles 51 to 54 of the 1982 Constitution. Ironically, efforts to correct abusive practices of the past, for example, by creating a neat and centralized structure, speeding up the bargaining process, eliminating fraud by unions, and strengthening union democracy, at the same time engendered new malfunctions, among them intertwined rules, entangled procedures, and complicated time intervals to be observed if unions were not to incur penalties or lose bargaining rights, as alluded to in the succeeding chapters.

122. The attempt to tidy up the trade union picture through legislation after 1980 focused on creating a neat, centralized structure and on reducing the number of unions. To this end, 'national-industrial unionism' having been declared the sole organizational principle, the number of industries according to which unions might be organized was cut from 32 to 28. The stipulation that at least five unions active in different industries must come together to found a 'confederation' likewise served to create a less factionalized organizational environment. By 1990, the 750 unions in existence a decade earlier had been brought down to 69 unions, and of these only 41 seemed to meet the 10% industry representation requirement to gain bargaining status. That requirement was probably the most instrumental factor in reducing the number of unions. Türk-İş and its affiliates had already had the elimination of the federations and the creation of a centralized structure as goals since the early 1960s, so they were content with these results. The Ministry of Labour and Social Security and most employers, too, preferred fewer and bigger unions because this eased the process of ascertaining which unions had bargaining status and because it was hoped that the end of union inflation would reduce the sharp political divisions within the labour movement that had characterized the pre-1980 era. By July 1996 there were 92 unions in Turkey, and of these only 48 met the minimum 10% requirement which was the precondition for acquiring bargaining rights.

123. Although the union structure was centralized at the industry level, the focus of bargaining was reduced to local levels. At the same time, the requirement that a union, in order to be entitled to bargain on behalf of a plant (establishment) or enterprise (company), should represent at least 10% of the workers in the industry and more than half of the workers in the plant or company tended to curb on the freedom to bargain without the impediment of smaller, newly established unions, a circumstance that has become a major issue in union and ILO circles. There has been a tendency, however, for multi-employer or 'group' bargaining to become more common over the course of time. Particularly in the public sector, entire branches are occasionally covered by concurrent company (enterprise) agreements, thus in effect creating an industry-wide agreement.

124. The 1982 Constitution placed major restrictions on the political activities of the unions. Unions were forbidden to pursue political objectives, engage in political activities, establish relations with political parties, or use the name or symbols of political parties. Despite legal harassment, however, Turkish unions frequently engaged in various forms of political activity, justifying their political involvement by arguing that they were simply furthering the economic and social status of their members as permitted by the law. Article 52 of the Constitution prohibiting unions' political activities was repealed in 1995, meaning that new legislation was pending to govern unions' involvement in politics in a more liberal fashion. This void was recently filled by Act No. 4277 of 28 June 1997.

125. Elaborate prescriptions for mediation and detailed regulations relating to strikes and lock-outs are other features of the post-1980 system of industrial relations. To be considered legal, strikes and lock-outs must have been called by the competent parties and conducted in conformity with the rules; their purpose must be solely work-related. General strikes, sympathy strikes, politically motivated strikes and lock-outs, work slowdowns, sit-ins and similar forms of concerted action were all illegal. Compared to the 1963 legislation, Act No. 2822 expanded the scope of strike restrictions. For those establishments and activities where strikes and lock-outs were prohibited, Act No. 2822 prescribed a compulsory arbitration mechanism to follow the mediation process. About one-fifth of the unionized workforce is engaged in those areas subject to compulsory arbitration, a ratio criticized for being high in a country committed to free collective bargaining and the right to strike.

126. Strikes and lock-outs were not permitted during a state of war or full or partial mobilization, and they could be prohibited in the event of major disasters adversely affecting daily life and temporarily restricted in the case of martial law or 'extraordinary emergency law' circumstances. What is more, a lawful strike or lock-out deemed likely to endanger public health or national security may be suspended for sixty days by government order and taken to compulsory arbitration at the end of that period if the parties to the dispute have failed to reach an agreement. This last provision has been denounced repeatedly since 1984 both by Türk-İş and the ILO. Türk-İş has also been highly critical of the composition of the YHK, arguing that because the workers are underrepresented, arbitration awards are generally slanted against worker interests. In the event, the government has been reluctant to make use of these powers and did so only on about ten occasions between 1984 and 1992.

127. After a hiatus caused by 12 September 1980 military intervention, the unions quickly restructured themselves, and although disillusioned by the restrictive character of the 1983 legislation, they became indispensable elements of Turkey's post-1983 democracy. By the end of 1990, despite the reduction of unions through forced mergers, total union membership had reached its pre-1980 level of just over 2 million. At that time, union density, in terms of the total labour force, remained at around 10%, but in terms of the potentially unionizable workforce of 3,573,426 wage earners, according to the Ministry of Labour statistics, it reached approximately 58%. The drop in the size of the potentially unionizable workforce from about 4 million in the pre-1980 period to 3.5 million was due, among other things, to legal restrictions on union membership, the creation of the contract employee status that disallowed union membership, and the increase in the number of public servants who were not permitted to join unions. However, a high union density ranging between 99 and 75% was achieved in certain industries (i.e., general services; food and allied branches; communications; energy; textiles; banking and insurance; mining; metalworking; petroleum, chemicals and rubber; and railways).

128. The government's promotion of strict stabilization policies based on wage restraint prompted Türk-İş and its affiliates to oppose the ANAP, the right-wing conservative party in power since the 1983 elections which strictly adhered to neo-liberal economic policies. It did so largely because of the pressures generated from within by the Social Democratic faction of the Confederation. Moreover, since rank-and-file members of even some of the more moderate Türk-İş affiliates were former DİSK members, the unions felt compelled to take a tougher stance in wage negotiations and demonstrated an increasing propensity to strike. At the same time, due to legislation that encouraged employers to organize more effectively, the post-1983 era witnessed growth in the power of employers' unions, particularly in the metalworking, petroleum, chemicals and rubber and food and textile industries.

129. The complex network of intertwined rules and regulations notwithstanding, collective bargaining gained momentum and began to operate with fair efficiency. On average, about 2,000 such agreements were concluded annually through the 1980s and early 1990s covering nearly one million workers. Yet the record of Turkish industrial relations between 1980 and 1990 was far from encouraging. Government policies of stabilization, involving wage restraint particularly, in the public sector, produced a drop in workers' purchasing power. The contrast between economic and political 'liberalism' and the limitations imposed on free collective bargaining appeared as an intolerable contradiction to the unions and the friends of labour, which they tended to blame on the decision makers as well as on external organizations, such as the International Monetary Fund and the World Bank. Labour unions reacted to the tough bargaining approach of employers with increased strike activity at a level exceeding that of the strike-prone the late 1970s.

130. In addition to inflation, which ran at an annual average rate of 60%, inter-union rivalry, and stronger organization and stiffer bargaining approaches by employers, both public and private, the increase in strike activity could be attributed to the intervention of political party leaders in some major strikes with the aim of expanding their political base, the failure of mediators to produce acceptable solutions, and the high wage demands brought to the bargaining table by the unions.

Frequently, the unions, in order to compensate for the losses incurred in their purchasing power since the year 1978, insisted on wage hikes of from 400 to 700%. Employers, who faced stiff national and international competition, usually responded to the resulting high-cost agreements with mass lay-offs, hiring replacements at the prevailing minimum wage, or contracting work out to third parties.

131. The increase in reported lay-off cases during the organizing drives of unions was also noteworthy. Despite legal provisions protecting union freedoms, employers used pressure to keep workers outside the union or to force them to resign from the union even after the latter's certification as the bargaining agent, thereby diminishing the union's bargaining and strike power. In spite of the apparent gains achieved in collective agreements, therefore, unemployment, declining union memberships and reduced average wages became the order of the day.

132. Union attempts to maintain bargaining status have been hampered by employer endeavours to expand the scope of the 'non-covered' workers category in collective bargaining. Union membership was also adversely affected by the rising number of white-collar and part-time employees, particularly in the services sector. In 1991, heightened demands by public servants to organize their own unions led to controversy. Although several such organizations were formed, the decisions of the judiciary wavered, then ebbed and flowed, with public authorities sometimes taking immediate action to close them down. The ILO demanded that Turkey permit at least those public servants not directly engaged in the administration of the state (such as public school teachers and postal and communications functionaries) to organize unions in accordance with Article 6 of ILO Convention No. 98 of 1949 on Right to Organize and Collective Bargaining which Turkey ratified in 1951, but the issue remained unresolved.

133. As none of the political parties won sufficient votes in the general elections of 20 October 1991, a coalition was formed by the centre-right True Path Party (DYP) and the left-of-centre Social Democratic People's Party (SHP). While in opposition, both parties had made various promises, including constitutional changes. For this reason, the new government was welcomed by organized labour as a development that would pave the way for better times for the workers. In fact, there were signs of softening management attitudes to major collective agreements during the first half of 1992. Days lost due to strikes showed a steady decline in 1992, 1993 and 1994. The Minister of Labour, who was an SHP deputy, prepared various labour law reform bills, but a draft law on the creation of an iron-clad job security system, with reinstatement rights for unjustified dismissals, ran into serious opposition from employers. In the spring of 1992, proposed amendments designed to liberalize trade union and collective bargaining rights further and new draft bills on unemployment insurance and public servants' unions, also proceeded slowly and kindled considerable controversy. In 1992, the Parliament ratified six ILO Conventions, among them ILO Convention No. 87 of 1948 on Freedom of Association and Protection of the Right to Organize, Convention No. 135 of 1971 on Workers' Representatives and Convention No. 151 of 1978 on Labour Relations in the Public Service, but the proposed ratification of Convention No. 158 of 1982 on Termination of Employment was vetoed by the President. Plans by the Ministry of Labour for the establishment of a tripartite, top-level Labour Council, led to the hope that quasi-conservative mechanisms could be devised to generate sustained peace and viable solutions within the system.

134. The early 1990s were characterized by political instability and weak coalition governments in Turkey. During the second DYP-SHP coalition (5 July 1993 to October 1993), the economy was hit by a severe economic crisis in 1994 which led to heightened unemployment and an unprecedented level of inflation (120%). However, employers in modern industries, coming to agreements with labour unions, softened the impact of the crisis by exercising various flexible labour practices, thereby deviating from the rigid rules of labour legislation – i.e., temporary lay-offs, granting workers unpaid and paid leaves of absence, job sharing and partial close-downs. On 26 July 1995, amendments made to Article 53 of the Constitution recognized the freedom of public servants to organize unions, with limited negotiation rights but not the right to conclude binding collective agreements and in 1994 ILO Convention No. 158 on the Termination of Employment was ratified by the Parliament, two significant developments which required the enactment of enabling legislation for implementation.

135. The year 1995 was marked, however, by an upsurge of increased strike activity (4,838,241 workdays lost), particularly in the public sector (4,249,920 days lost) which had important political repercussions as well. Neither the short-lived DYP-CHP, nor the ANAP-DYP coalitions (30 October 1995 to 6 March 1996 and 6 March 1996 to 28 June 1996, respectively) could deliver any of their promises to labour. However, the Economic and Social Council (ESC), a tripartite body including also the representatives of various interest groups, was formed by a Prime Minister's declaration, with a view to promoting dialogue in an advisory capacity. Although the ESC was a positive step to further social dialogue, it did not prove to be an effective mechanism due to its large size and inability to convene at frequent intervals (on the other hand, the Tripartite Consultation Board established in conjunction with the Labour Act of 2003, No. 4857, in line with ILO Convention 144, turned out to be much more active in promoting dialogue on legislative reforms of the 2000s). The formation of the religious-right Refah Partisi (Welfare Party) and DYP coalition on 28 June 1996 and then the ANAP-DSP (Democratic Leftist Party) and DTP (Democratic Party of Turkey) coalition government on 12 July 1997, together with unchecked inflationary pressures and unstable political conditions, rendered the future of public policy toward unions and industrial relations uncertain. All the legal and political obstacles notwithstanding, Turkish labour unionism still stood as a viable ingredient of democracy. According to the official statistics of the Ministry of Labour in July 1996, it represented, with a total membership of 2,708,784 organized in 92 unions, 66.86% of a potentially unionizable workforce in Turkey.

136. The late 1990s and early 2000s were marked by the devastating effects of a major earthquake as well as three serious financial crises (1999, 2001 and 2008). These shocks created unprecedented levels of unemployment and drops in real wages which were more serious in the private than the public sector. General elections held in April 1999 brought a coalition government by the RPP, the ANAP and the MHP which, in the general elections of 3 November 2003, was ousted by the victory of right-wing AKP. The years 2004 and 2005 witnessed ongoing efforts by the AKP to start negotiations for Turkey's accession to the European Union. Although the major policy-makers and the greater part of public opinion were obsessed with the initiation of accession talks scheduled to begin on 3 October 2005, full EU membership still seemed to remain a far-off goal for Turkey.

137. Among the major labour law developments of the last two decades, the enactment of the new Labour Act No. 4857 of 10 June 2003 stands as the major landmark of the recent past. Combining flexibility measures and job security, the Labour Act was based on a draft bill prepared by a nine-member committee of academicians, as was its predecessor Act No. 4773 of 2002 on job security, in compliance with the relevant ILO Conventions and EU Directives. Introduction of unemployment insurance scheme into the social security system in 1999 plus the revision of retirement ages for men and women in the same year, the passage of Public Servants' Unions Act No. 4688 in 2001 and the adoption of Act No. 4904 in 2003 on the Employment Organization of Turkey (İş-Kur) were some of the major legislative developments. Further, the passage of a new Associations Act No. 5253 and the Penal Code No. 5237 in 2004 carrying new sanctions to circumvent anti-union behaviour as well as protections against sexual harassment and the freedom to work at the workplace paved the way for making relevant changes in labour legislation. In an attempt to amend basic legislation on collective labour relations in order to bring it into conformity with ILO standards and EU norms, as well as to do away with malfunctions or abuses of the past, a committee of academicians was formed in 2005 by the initiative of the Ministry of Labour and Social Security. As the social partners prodded the government for further changes, this draft bill was followed by several subsequent texts in the ensuing years, but due to a lack of consensus between the social partners, they all failed even before coming to the agenda of the Parliament. Further attempts at legal reform included draft bills, prepared by the Ministry of Justice by mid-2005 on a new Obligations Act (law of contracts) as well as a new Commercial Code (corporate law) both of which have been enacted recently, bringing various new clauses relating to employment relations as well.

138. Due to economic, technological and institutional setbacks adversely affecting unions elsewhere in the globalizing world, the union movement and collective bargaining together with strike activity had lost much of its clout at the onset of the twenty-first century. According to the official statistics of the Ministry of Labour and Social Security by July 2011, there were 3,232,000 members (likely to be an overstated figure), organized in 94 labour unions (of which only 51 met the 10% industry representation condition to qualify for collective bargaining), reflecting a union density of 59.9% of the potentially unionizable workforce (which was a total of 5,398,296 workers, excluding public servants). A union density as high as 60% was likely to be a far-fetched figure. Because of allegedly inflated membership figures and the difficulty of monitoring memberships due to workers' flitting from union to union, a more realistic ratio was estimated to stand at around 30%. As of 2009, approximately 560,000 were covered by collective agreements.[28]

139. On the other hand, Ministry of Labour and Social Security statistics give union density as 8.88% by July 2013 where 1,032,166 workers were union members out of a base figure of 11,628,806 workers (agriculture included). This is certainly a more realistic indicator. Union density was 23.35% in banking, 22.46% in communication, 20.19%, in energy, 18.63% in general services, 18.31% in mining, 15.21% in metal and 13.31% in food. Because the OECD data considers mainly collective bargaining coverage in its calculations, it gives union density in Turkey for the year 2013 as 4.5%, meaning only about half of the union members have access to collective labour agreements.

140. Labour unions tend to put the blame for the meagre state of union density in Turkey on restrictive industrial relations legislation as well as unfriendly governmental policies. While these arguments may carry some weight, adverse effects engrained in structural characteristics of the labour force and economy cannot be overlooked. The unemployment problem Turkey has been wrestling with is certainly at the root of many industrial relations questions. The size of the informal economy which has featured prominently in recent debates stands out as another significant negative factor, for though there is no legal impediment to unionization in informal employment, union penetration is virtually impossible. In fact, one reason why union density is overstated in official statistics is the exclusion of informal wage earners in the calculations. The penetration of unions in small to medium enterprises which comprise the larger portion of the Turkish economy is also extremely low. Union activities are usually frowned upon by small- and/to medium-sized enterprise (SME) employers and employees are reluctant to join unions for fear of losing their jobs.

141. A new package of amendments to the 1982 Constitution of Turkey by Act No. 5982 (published in the Official Gazette on 13 May 2010 and approved by a national referendum held on 12 September 2010) lifted some of the constitutional constraints on freedom of association. It has (a) repealed the ban on the worker's simultaneous membership to more than one union in the same branch of activity (industry), (b) removed the restriction on the co-existence of more than one collective agreement in the establishment, thus paving the way for a possible multi-layered collective bargaining structure, (c) abolished the labour union's liability for damages inflicted by the strikers' intentional or faulty conduct and (d) lifted the prohibition on general, political or sympathy strikes and lock-outs as well as work slow-downs. Paradoxically, however, the amendments did not remove some of the constitutional restrictions which were subject to ILO criticisms for many years in the past, like recourse to compulsory arbitration in strikes and lock-outs that may be suspended by the government for reasons of public health or national security. But, as an important positive development, the constitutional amendment had given public servants' unions the right to conclude binding collective agreements with the

28. Statistics of the Ministry of Labour and Social Security, Ankara, 2009.

administration (albeit, with no right to strike). If the parties fail to come to an agreement at the negotiation stage, the decision of the 'public servants' arbitration board' shall become binding as a collective agreement. Further, among its provisions, the amendment emphasized the role and function of the ESC now as a constitutional institution. While these issues were significant for freedom of association in Turkey, there still seemed to be a need, to make the pertinent changes in legislation in order to bring the law into conformity with these new provisions, as well as to improve the Turkish industrial relations system in response to national conditions and to the requests of the ILO and the European Union.

142. Following the Constitutional changes of 12 September 2010, the years 2011 to 2014 represent a degree of stagnation in labour union activism. While union density continued to fall, in the realm of legislation affecting labour relations major developments were the passage of the new Obligations Act No. 6098 of 11 January 2011 which came into effect on 1 July 2012, the new Act on Civil Procedures, No. 6100 of 12 January 2011 which came into effect on 1 October 2011, the Public Servants' Union Act, No. 4688, as amended in 2001 and 2004 and lately in 2012 by Act No. 6289, the Act on Unions and the Collective Labour Agreement of 2012, No. 6356 (on which the AKP-dominated legislature, despite sustained efforts of social dialogue, stalled on delivering most of the long-awaited reforms), and as perhaps a positive step in response to the staggering rate of industrial accidents, the adoption of a comprehensive piece of legislation, the Occupational Health and Safety Act of 2012, No. 6331 were all noteworthy developments.

143. Several national and international circles called on the President to veto Act No. 6356 on grounds of its unconstitutionality and alleged violation of the principles of freedom of association, but President Gül ratified the Act. There was, however, a pending lawsuit filed with the Constitutional Court by the major opposition party RPP (CHP)for the nullification of about thirty articles of Act No. 6356. On 22 October 2014, the Constitutional Court ruled a few articles of Act No. 6356 as null. Below are the relevant articles struck out by the Constitutional Court, the original articles of Act No. 6356 are cited first with the author's evaluation and analysis, then followed by references to the Constitutional Court's overruling decision which declared them as null and void.

144. The 10th Meeting of the Labour Council (an *ad hoc* body annexed to the Ministry of Labour and Social Security with a view to promoting dialogue on legislative proposals) was convened in September 2013 with its agenda focused mainly on three issues, the 'severance pay fund', 'subcontracting' and the 'legalization of temporary work agencies', but despite a great deal of rhetoric, no viable compromises could be achieved among the stakeholders.

145. Of more recent origin, a comprehensive piece of legislation termed the 'bag law' (*torba kanunu*) No. 6552, was passed on 10 September 2014 amending about 149 articles in 24 different Acts and executive orders. It includes provisions for workers and their dependants aggrieved as a result of the May 2014 Soma mining accident as well as for all workers employed underground, on the rights of workers employed by subcontractors, work permits of foreigners, on public servants, on unions and collective bargaining as well as for workers in general, the social security system and amnesty for or the restructuring of individual and public debts (concerning taxes, social security contributions) and occupational health and safety, etc. As there were other industrial accidents causing loss of lives in the mines after the Soma incident, a new *torba kanunu* (bag law) was enacted in 2015.[29]

146. With the exception of a major change in the political system of Turkey – i.e., the transition from a well-established parliamentary democracy to a 'presidential' system in the year 2017-, there has been almost no significant development since the year 2015, particularly in the industrial relations area. Adversely affected by rising inflation, high unemployment and attenuation of democracy accompanied by an unprecedented concentration of power in the executive branch, the industrial relations scene of Turkey was not exposed to any noteworthy development. The stagnation in union and collective bargaining activity seemed to continue. In an attempt to alleviate the workload of labour courts, the legislature passed the new controversial Labour Courts Act which foresaw instituting the 'mediation' process as a precondition before recourse to court action for litigation in labour disputes. Also, after much debate and controversy, legislation on 'temporary work agencies' was finally passed on 6 May 2016, Act No. 6715.

147. With the exception of the 'social contract', which in 1978 Prime Minister Bülent Ecevit had co-signed with Türk-İş, there has never been an institutionalized form of wage and incomes policies in Turkey. Faced with serious economic difficulties Ecevit had put in place this agreement with Türk-İş, covering the public sector only whereby labour agreed to self-restrain unions' wage increase demands in return for concessions to workers (e. job security legislation, workers' participation in the management boards of SEEs). Despite great expectations, though, the social contract turned out to be a short-lived experiment. The present system has a constitutionally guaranteed, high-level ESC. Although there is a strong need for the potential contributions of ESC, it has not been called on by Erdoğan during his terms, either as prime minister or president. Therefore, due to the absence of a worthwhile 'neo corporatist existence, our present monograph does not include any section on Incomes Policies', nor any paragraph on 'works councils' or 'elected workers' representatives'. However, in the text below, there will be several references to these topics for their applications in Turkey, however limited.

148. The following paragraphs of this monograph deal with major labour law and industrial relations developments which have taken place after the 2015 edition. Like in the past updates, in this 2022 edition too the author's choice has been to sketch first the historical background of certain notions in Turkish industrial relations and then introduce the latest developments. The objective is to shed light on the reasons which account for the present stage of labour law and practice

29. T. Dereli, '6356 Sayılı Sendikalar ve Toplu İş Sözleşmesi Kanunu: Süreçler, Sorunlar ve Öneriler', *Çimento İşveren*, Vol. 28, No. 1, Ocak 2014, pp. 17–19.

(e.g., in the structure of unions, the level and territory of collective bargaining, right to strike, public servants' labour relations, etc.)

Chapter 4. Sources of Turkish Labour Law

149. Turkish labour law practices derive mainly from two broad sources; namely the 'official' and 'private' sources of labour law.

§1. Official Sources of Labour Law

150. These can be studied within two separate and yet interrelated categories: 'national' and 'international sources' of labour law in Turkey.

I. National Sources

A. *Legislation*

151. Legislative action is naturally the most important source. As in other legal jurisdictions, the Turkish Constitution of 1982 stands as the most prominent source and one which takes precedence over other areas of legislation. Article 2 of the Constitution states that the Turkish Republic is a state based on democracy, secularism, rule of law and social justice. Related to this general principle are those provisions of the Turkish Constitution in Articles 48–55 and 60–62 which lay down a general framework for labour law in Turkey. Under the heading of 'basic social and economic rights and obligations', the state has been assigned the duty of ensuring that everyone receives an equitable share of the national income, that economic and social inequalities be eliminated and that the economically weak and underprivileged are accorded special protection.

152. Among the provisions envisaged in Articles 48 to 55 of the Constitution concerning labour law are the individual's right to work and to enter into contracts in any chosen area (Article 48); the right of every individual not to be employed in work which does not suit his age, physical condition or sex (Article 50), the obligation of the state to protect working people by taking adequate social, economic and financial measures (Article 49); the right to paid vacations (Article 50); the right of employees and employers to form and join unions (Article 51); the right of employees and public servants to organize and to conclude collective agreements (Article 53); the right of employees to strike and employers' resort to lock-out (Article 54); the state's responsibility to take measures for the provision of a just wage in order to provide workers with a decent living (Article 55); and the right of every individual to benefit from social security measures (Article 60).

153. As mentioned above, the major labour legislation in Turkey consists, at present, of the following statutes: the Labour Act (No. 4857, dated 10 June 2003); the Maritime Labour Act (No. 854, dated 20 April 1967); the Act concerning Labour–Management Relations in the Press (No. 5953, dated 13 June 1952, as amended by Act No. 212, dated 4 January 1961); the Unions and the Collective Labour Agreement Act, No. 6356, dated 18 October 2012; Obligations Act, No.

6098, dated 11 January 2011; and the Occupational Health and Safety Act No. 6331, dated 20 June 2012. Of recent origin, the so-called bag legislation (*torba kanunu*) No. 6552, dated 10 September 2014 has, among a number of other pieces of legislation on the restructuring of taxation and financial debts, brought amendments to the Labour Act, the Act on Unions and the Collective Labour Agreement and the Social Insurance Act as well as to a few executive orders with the force of law.

154. On 28 November 2014, the text of a new Act on the Istanbul Arbitration Centre was published in the Official Gazette. In view of this new legislation, the said Centre having corporate status and subject to private law will deal with resolving disputes by using arbitration and other alternative dispute settlement mechanisms related to national and international-level commercial conflicts. The Centre will be composed of a general congress, administrative and auditing boards, national and international arbitration councils and a general secretariat. The general congress will include 25 members from various organizations as well as representatives from labour and employers' confederations with the largest membership.

155. To the extent they are related to our subject matter, these changes with the exception of the new Istanbul Arbitration Centre, have been incorporated into the text of the present monograph.

156. In addition to the above-stated legislation, one should cite also the Public Servants' Unions Act No. 4688, dated 25 June 2001, as amended by Act No. 5198, dated 24 June 2004 and recently in 2012; the Social Insurance and General Health Insurance Act No. 5510, dated 16 June 2006, the Social Security Institution Act No. 5502, dated 20 May 2006; and the Labour Courts Act No. 5521, dated 30 January 1950.

157. There are also several acts of a more general nature, with provisions that seem to extend into the labour–management relations area. The Associations Act of 2005, the Civil and Obligations Code, the Act on Civil Procedures, the National Holiday and General Vacations Act, the Weekend Holiday Act, the Act on Noon Rest Periods and the Act on Jobs and Services open specifically to Turkish citizens as well as the Act on the Employment Organization of Turkey could be cited in this category.[30]

B. Executive Sources

158. Bylaws (*tüzük*) issued by the government are also significant sources of Turkish labour law. They are subject to scrutiny by the Council of State (the High Court of Administration) which is the supreme judicial body in matters of public administration. Such bylaws are designed to indicate the ways and means whereby legislative acts are to be implemented. Suits can be brought before the Council of State if they carry clauses contrary to prevailing acts. The Council of State can

30. For a comprehensive list of labour legislation in Turkey, *see* the List of Statutes given above.

repeal bylaws by final judicial awards. Since Turkish labour law relies heavily on legislative enactment, the need to issue detailed bylaws has arisen quite frequently.

159. In addition to the above-stated category of executive regulations, the government also issues decrees (decisions of the Council of Ministers) dealing with the application of labour legislation. The legal basis of these decrees is found in the respective acts. They are usually issued in conjunction with the recommendation of the Ministry of Labour, and here the review of the Council of State is not required. For example, the Social Insurance Act has provided that its extension to workplaces where only one worker is employed as well as to the spouse and children of the insured person is to be implemented through decrees of the Council of Ministers. This provision has helped to expand the scope of the Social Insurance Act.

160. The third type of executive source is the 'regulation' (*yönetmelik*) which can be issued by a public or military organization in order to govern the implementation of legislation or bylaws as regards their respective fields of jurisdiction. Regulations are published in the Official Gazette as other sources and may be repealed by the Council of State if they violate prevailing acts and bylaws. Turkish labour law has been enriched by the promulgation of various regulations by the ministries including the Ministry of Labour and Social Security and such agencies as the Social Insurance Organization and Public Employment Organization of Turkey. In fact, the Labour Act as well as other legislation on employment relations has foreseen the issuance of regulations. In its relevant articles, the new Labour Act foresaw issuing regulations, a method which is more practical compared to adopting bylaws, as borne out by the publication of many regulations by the Ministry of Labour and Social Security in a relatively short period of time.

C. *Judicial Sources*

161. The judgments passed by the courts constitute another important source of labour law in Turkey. Court decisions help to clarify the conflicting provisions of labour legislation as well as to interpret existing legislation so as to meet newly emerging needs. Among the main judicial sources in the field of labour law are the verdicts of the Constitutional Court, the Conflict of Laws Court, the Court of Cassation (the highest Court of Appeals in private law) and the Council of State (the highest judicial organ dealing with and among public agencies) (*Danıştay*). Disputes in private law are to be settled by a system of first-level courts and, at the level of appeal, by intermediate-level courts of appeal and then by the Court of Cassation.

162. Court trials are conducted within the framework of 'judicial competence' requirements set forth in the Act on Civil Procedures, at civil courts of peace and lower courts which act as courts of first instance. The review of first-instance courts' verdicts is made by the Court of Cassation through a legal procedure termed 'the request for reversal'. The verdicts whose reversal cannot be requested have been shown in the Act on Civil Procedures. Verdicts not requested to be reversed within the set time limits as well as verdicts whose reversal may not be requested by definition become final without recourse to the Court of Cassation.

163. A verdict whose reversal has been requested is reviewed by the competent division of the Court of Cassation. With the intent of having it corrected, a request may be made, for reasons indicated in the Act on Civil Procedures, against the verdict of the Court of Cassation which has upheld or turned down the verdict of the first instance court. If no request for reversal of the verdict is made or if such request is made but turned down, the lower court verdict upheld by the Court of Cassation becomes final and effective. On the other hand, in the event of a verdict turned down by the Court of Cassation, the first instance court has the right to resist. If it does not resist and contest, it must finalize the trial along the lines embodied in the verdict of the Court of Cassation which has abrogated the first-instance court's verdict.

164. If the first-instance court resists the ruling of the Court of Cassation which has abrogated its verdict, the dispute is referred to the General Council of the Court of Cassation, convened with the participation of all divisions, for review. The verdict of the first instance court becomes final and definitive if the General Council gives its approval. If the General Council does not consider the resistance by the lower court appropriate and thus abrogates its verdict, the latter must abide by the ruling of the Court of Cassation.

165. If, in interpreting and executing legal provisions or filling in the voids in legislation, disagreements arise between the various divisions of the Court of Cassation or the decisions of the General Council, the Court of Cassation, again with the full participation of all division heads, renders a 'unification of jurisprudence award' with the intent of eliminating conflicting opinions on jurisprudence and formulating a universally acceptable principle on the subject. Like legislation, unification of jurisprudence awards (hereafter referred to as 'unification awards') is published in the Official Gazette. While rulings by the divisions of the Court of Cassation and the General Council are not binding on the judges in other lawsuits on similar disputes, unification awards bind both the courts and the Court of Cassation in similar events.[31] Therefore such awards carry a great deal of weight.

166. However, in settling the disputes they are confronted with, judges are also expected to take the rulings of the 9th division and of the General Council of the Court of Cassation into consideration. In this sense, judge-made decisions seem to constitute a labour law source of secondary importance. A frequently heard criticism directed against the High Court is that its rulings have not been consistent in similar cases. This criticism notwithstanding, court rulings and especially unification awards have played an increasing role in shaping the general character of labour law in Turkey, particularly during the last forty years or so.

31. The Act on the Court of Cassation, 4 Feb. 1983, No. 2797, Art. 45/V.

II. International Sources

167. Being a member of various international and supranational organizations, Turkey has undertaken a number of international obligations. In the field of labour law, Turkey was influenced by the conventions and recommendations of the ILO. Although Turkey joined the ILO as a member in 1932, its actual participation dates from the establishment of the Ministry of Labour in 1945. Article 90/V of the 1982 Constitution of Turkey (like the previous 1961 Constitution) provides that 'ratification of agreements with international organizations rests upon the legislative action of the Turkish Grand National Assembly, and international agreements ratified and put into effect following the approval of the President do have the force of law; no appeal may be made to the Constitutional Court on the grounds of their alleged unconstitutionality'. The wording of Article 90/V of the Constitution has caused the question of the position of such ratified international agreements in the hierarchy of the sources of labour law to become a matter of controversy. Likewise, decisions of international courts (e.g., the European Court of Justice) are held to be binding as ratified international conventions.

168. In an effort to bring the same clarity to this issue and help pave the way for the adaptation of national norms to those of the European Union, an amendment made in May 2004 added a third sentence to Article 90 of the Constitution. It reads: 'In disputes arising from the conflict between ratified international agreements on fundamental rights and freedoms and national legislation on corresponding topics, the provisions of international agreements shall prevail'. Though the new subsection is clear enough, there is no doubt that actual implementation will be saddled with problems of controversies and conflicting interpretations.[32]

169. The first significant controversy resulted from Erdoğan's denunciation of the İstanbul Convention on 'Fighting Violence Against Women' Convention' singlehandedly with a presidential decision overnight; this was in contradiction to the wording and spirit of the Constitution's Article 90. This action is now likely to be on the agenda of 'women's rights groups' as well as the opposition parties. This convention which was ratified with the support and acclaim of the AKP initially aimed to stop violence against women which had become a serious matter of great concern. Its denunciation by Erdoğan so abruptly on 20 March 2021, it was feared, might pave the way for further presidential actions against other international agreements, even the ratified conventions of the ILO for that matter. The principle foreseen for the ratification of international conventions requiring the approval of the Grand National Assembly beforehand was thus bypassed by a one-sided decision of the President. It was likely motivated by the male-dominated values of the Turkish culture prevalent within the family. Currently the opposition parties as well as the concerned women's groups are determined to fight through available appeal mechanisms the '18 July 2022 decision of the High Court of Administration' (*Danıştay*)

32. On possible problem areas, *see* M. Gülmez, 'Sendikal Haklara İlişkin Sözleşmelerin İç Hukuka Üstünlüğü ve Yasalalarımızdaki Aykırılıklar', *Çalışma ve Toplum*, 2005, pp. 11–56.

which has turned down with a 'three-to -two' vote the request of the RPP for the reversal of the said presidential decision.

170. The following are some of the major ILO Conventions which Turkey has ratified: Unemployment Convention, No. 2; Forced Labour Convention, No. 29; Fee-Charging Employment Agencies Convention, No. 34; Underground Work (Women) Convention, No. 45; Minimum Age (Industry) Convention (revised) No. 59; Labour Inspection Convention, No. 81; Freedom of Association and Protection of the Right to organize Convention, No. 87; Employment Service Convention, No. 88; Public Contracts (Labour Clauses) Convention, No. 94; Protection of Wages Convention, No. 95; Right to Organize and Collective Bargaining Convention, No. 98; Minimum Wage Fixing Machinery (Agriculture) Convention, No. 99; Equal Remuneration Convention, No. 100; Social Security (Minimum Standards) Convention, No. 102; Abolition of Forced Labour Convention, No. 105; Discrimination (Employment and Occupation) Convention, No. 111; Employment Policy Convention, No. 122; Minimum Age (Underground Work) Convention, No. 123; Maximum Weight Convention, No. 127; Workers' Representatives Convention, No. 135; Tripartite Consultation (International Labour Standards) Convention, No. 144; Labour Relations (Public Service) Convention, No. 151, Termination of Employment (Job Security) Convention, No. 158.

171. By the year 2014, Turkey had ratified 58 ILO Conventions. The most recent convention adopted on 21 November 2014 was No. 167 concerning Safety and Health in Construction. With the exception of Conventions Nos. 87 and 151 ratified in 1993 and Convention No. 158 in 1994, the government used to pursue the policy of bringing national legislation into conformity with the ILO standards first and only then ratifying the convention concerned. With Conventions Nos. 87, 151 and 158, Turkey seemed to deviate from this rather cautious policy of ratification.

172. With the progress made in 2005 in respect of Turkey's projected membership to the European Union, the three sources of secondary EC Law have taken on a great deal of importance in the scanning and upgrading process of Turkish labour legislation, namely (a) the regulations, (b) the directives and (c) the decisions taken by the Council and the Commission. In addition, the rulings of the European Court of Justice are binding on national judges.

173. Of secondary importance has been the impact of the European Economic Community Agreement; the European Social Security Agreement concerning Old Age, Disability and Death, and the European Social Security Agreement in Fields Other Than Old Age, Disability and Death; Customs Union Agreement; and the European Social Charter. Parallel to the growth of the number of Turkish workers employed in Europe and elsewhere since the early 1960s, various bilateral agreements as regards placement, employment conditions and social security rights have been signed between Turkey and Germany, France, Austria, Belgium, Sweden, Denmark, Switzerland, Britain, the Netherlands, Australia and Libya.

§2. PRIVATE SOURCES OF LABOUR LAW

I. Collective Labour Agreements

174. Since the passage of the Collective Agreements, Strikes and Lock-Outs Act (No. 275) in 1963, the system of collective bargaining has become an important element in shaping the character of labour relations in Turkey. Prior to 1963, 'the rules of work' (in conjunction with the provisions of the Labour Act) which were imposed unilaterally by the employer determined the nature of working conditions at the workplace. At present, however, collective labour agreements concluded between labour unions and employers' unions or employers at establishments, enterprises or multiemployer levels take precedence over other sources of labour law except for the absolutely mandatory clauses of legislation. The normative provisions of collective labour agreements which regulate working conditions are regarded as objective legal rules binding on both the employees and the employer.

II. The Individual Employment Contract

175. The employment contract serves as a source in the individual employment relationship between the employer and the employee. It does not create objective rules per se. It only establishes a subjective legal relationship between the employee and employer who, by their mutual consent, determine their rights and obligations. The norms thus created in accordance with the principle of 'freedom of contract' are binding on the parties. Several restrictions have, however, been placed on the 'freedom of contract' in Turkish labour law and they will be dealt with in the pertinent paragraphs below.[33]

III. The Rules of Work

176. Article 29 of the now-repealed Labour Act of 1936 (No. 3008) required employers to draw up written 'rules of work', describing the working conditions, discipline procedures, workers' health and safety measures, etc. 'Rules of work' which should not contravene legal provisions were to be enforced in the establishment following the approval of the Regional Directorate of Labour or the Ministry of Labour. The Collective Agreements, Strikes and Lock-outs Act of 1963 (No. 275) repealed the legal compulsion to establish such 'rules of work'. Since collective bargaining marked the beginning of an era of 'joint decision making', the abolition of this lopsided practice was quite natural.

177. However, the practice of 'rules of work' has not been altogether prohibited. The parties are free to devise 'rules of work' in the establishments if they wish to do so. Despite the freedom to bargain collectively, establishments not covered by any collective agreement still exist. A document called 'rules of work' governing

33. On these, *see also* N. Çelik, *İş Hukuku Dersleri* 117–121 (Beta 2013).

labour–management relations over and above the minimum standards set by legislation still seems to be an important source at such workplaces.

178. Also, one may encounter 'rules of work' at enterprises where labour relations used to be regulated by elaborate collective labour agreements but where unions, due to various de-unionizing forces, have lost their bargaining status. Also, in establishments where collective agreements are in force, the practice of 'rules of work' is still carried out. In this last case resort to 'rules of work' usually takes three different forms.[34]

179. Parts of a collective labour agreement are sometimes referred to as 'rules of work' or in some cases, parties to the collective labour agreement choose to treat a certain segment of the agreement separately under the heading of 'rules of work', dealing with topics like work discipline, workers' health and safety, etc., in a detailed fashion. In this category 'rules of work' constitutes only a certain part of the collective labour agreement. Some collective labour agreements indicate that the employer is entitled to draw up 'rules of work' in those areas not covered by the agreement on the condition that these rules must not be contrary to the provisions set forth in the agreement. This means that 'rules of work' in this category fall outside the scope of, but are, in fact, a supplement to the collective labour agreement.

180. Due to the fact that the Labour Unions Act No. 2821 and now Act No. 6356 (as well as Act No. 274 of 1963) have defined the 'employer's representative' too narrowly, thus broadening the definition of 'employee' so as to cover managers, department heads, foremen and the like, a conflicting situation prevails for management in Turkey. Since such personnel is, by definition, allowed to join labour unions because they are treated as employees, employers have improvised means of excluding them from the coverage of collective labour agreements and have thus given rise to the concept of 'covered' v. 'non-covered' employees. While such managerial personnel, normally considered 'employer's representatives' according to the Labour Act, No. 1475 and now Act No. 4857, can still retain their membership status in unions (Article 2, Act No. 2821), they are left outside the scope of collective agreements and their status and working conditions are sometimes regulated in separate 'rules of work'. They are usually granted better remuneration and employment conditions than the 'covered' employees. Which categories and how many of such potentially unionizable employees are thrust outside the collective labour agreement generally depends on the bargaining power of the parties and on the mutual concessions they make in negotiations.[35]

181. The legal nature of the rules of work is a disputed matter in Turkish labour law. According to one view, the 'rules of work' is contractual in the sense that the employer makes the content of the proposed contract known through the terms set out in the 'rules of work', and the employment contract is concluded when the

34. M. Ekonomi, *İş Hukuku* 25–27 (1980).

35. *See* Part II, Ch. 5, §4 below for more on the concepts of 'covered' versus 'non-covered' employees and the status of the individual employment contract vis-à-vis the collective agreement.

employee accepts these terms. Another view holds that by issuing 'rules of work', the employer becomes entitled to unilaterally impose objective and obligatory legal norms which the employee must abide by at the establishment. This latter view has lost validity during the post-1963 era since Acts Nos. 275 and now 2822 have abolished the legal requirement of establishing 'rules of work'. Accordingly, it is the collective agreement which should take precedence in determining the nature of employment conditions at the establishment. The generally accepted view at present, therefore, is that the 'rules of work' are a supplement to the employment contracts or the collective agreement; they are subjective legal norms established and agreed upon by the parties themselves.[36] As the rules of work are supplements to the collective agreement or the employment contract one would surmise that in the hierarchy they should be positioned above the relatively binding provisions of legislation. Although in most cases they aim to lay down the playing field for working conditions in a detailed fashion, their place should not be relegated to a level below the relatively imperative provisions of labour legislation.

IV. Custom

182. The role of custom in Turkish law in general and in Turkish labour law, in particular, has been a diminishing one due to the increasing role of legislation, the impact of which has not declined despite the enhanced role of collective bargaining since the early 1960s. However, custom has not disappeared entirely from the Turkish labour scene. The Obligations Act of 1926 makes references to custom in relation to employment contracts in Articles 326, 329, 331 and 337. Also, the Labour Act (No. 1475) referred to custom in Articles 40, 64 and 65. Thus, custom still plays a certain role in Turkish labour law. The labour courts decide whether or not a certain practice qualifies as 'custom'. In order to be considered 'custom', a work rule should meet two criteria: the first is the objective criterion, that is, it must have been entrenched as a continued and regular practice, while the second is the subjective criterion, which means that there must be a common belief as to the necessity of obeying the rule. Collective agreements have paved the way for creating certain customs. The normative provisions of an expired collective agreement which, by law, are to remain in force until the conclusion of the new agreement occasionally take on the force of custom even when similar provisions are not explicitly worded in the new agreement. The transportation of workers to and from the workplace has thus become a general practice in many establishments. According to a decision of the Court of Cassation, repealed government regulations may also be treated as custom if they have become entrenched practices.[37]

183. Thus, a related concept is the 'entrenched workplace practice'. Nevertheless, certain workplace practices implemented one-sidedly by the employer do not

36. The Court of Cassation has also upheld this view. Court of Cassation, 9th Div., 13 Jun. 1966, 4633/5262; 22 Feb. 1971, 384/236. (In the verdicts of the Court of Cassation cited in this monograph, the first number after the date signifies the main file while the second the decision number.)
37. Court of Cassation, 9th Div., 25 May 1973, 42409/18766.

qualify as a source of labour law per se. However, coupled with certain other elements, they may have become an embedded part of the employment contract. Bonuses granted by the employer or fringe benefits are a case in point. In the opinion of the Court of Cassation, a bonus awarded by the employer for more than three years becomes an entrenched workplace practice.[38] Each case should be assessed in light of surrounding circumstances by looking into whether or not an objective criterion or condition is required. An entrenched practice, if held to exist, may be altered only upon the mutual consent of the parties in view of Article 22 of the Labour Act.[39]

184. The violation of rights based on custom did not entitle the aggrieved party to initiate a rights dispute to culminate in a strike or lock-out action under the previous system. Under the present system which has prohibited strikes and lock-outs for rights disputes, however, it is held that, if the collective agreement has made reference to custom, the union or the employer may resort to court or to voluntary arbitration if the custom which has become part of the collective agreement is violated.

§3. The Hierarchy of the Sources of Labour Law

185. The general principle underlying the hierarchy of the sources of Turkish labour law is aimed at the improvement of workers' employment conditions. The study of the hierarchy of official national and international sources as opposed to that of unofficial sources is a convenient working framework.

186. The hierarchy within the official national sources is as follows: ratified international agreements, Constitution of the Turkish Republic, labour laws, bylaws, decrees and regulations which have been issued in accordance with the laws.

187. International agreements put into operation in accordance with appropriate procedures have the same legal effect as national laws. As Article 90/V of the Turkish Constitution stipulates, all international agreements ratified by Turkey through legislative enactment take precedence over other sources of law, since no appeal may be made against them before the Constitutional Court on the grounds of their alleged unconstitutionality. As mentioned above, the wording of Article 90 has been further strengthened by the 2004 amendment.

188. With regard to the position of official sources (laws) *vis-à-vis* collective agreements, the latter are held to take precedence over the former only insofar as the collectively bargained provisions are more favourable for the workers. If there is a conflict between a legislative clause and the collective labour agreement, that which is more favourable for the employee shall prevail. Legal provisions which are supplementary in character automatically become effective in cases where there are

38. Court of Cassation, General Council Decision, 5 Feb. 2003, 2003/9-11/54.
39. Court of Cassation, 9th Div., 27 Sep. 2004, 5272/2002.

no relevant provisions in the collective agreement. When supplementary legal provisions contradict the collective labour agreement the provisions of the latter prevail. However, some principles of labour law, particularly those pertaining to public order and general good morals, are construed as being absolutely binding on the parties. On the other hand, those rules of labour law which are relatively binding may be superseded by individual employment contracts or collectively bargained provisions which are more favourable for the employees covered by collective agreements. It should also be noted that the number of absolutely binding provisions is quite limited in Turkish labour law.

189. The hierarchy of the sources of labour law can be depicted in the following manner:

- ratified international agreements (namely the ILO Conventions and the EU Law); (in particular, their clauses on fundamental rights and freedoms); and decisions of the European Court of Human Rights;
- the Constitution;
- legislation which is absolutely binding; (decrees with the force of law, Presidential decisions, executive orders, which, with the new Presidential system of the Constitution of 2017, seem to have taken precedence over legislative acts);
- unification of jurisprudence awards of the Court of Cassation, intermediate courts of appeal and other High Courts of Appeal;
- collective labour agreements;
- individual employment contracts;
- relatively binding provisions of legislation;
- supplementary legal provisions;
- custom, and entrenched workplace practices.

Chapter 5. The Ministry of Labour and Social Security: Organization and Functions

190. Presently governed by Act No. 3146 of 18 January 1985, the Ministry of Labour and Social Security was established by a special Act (No. 4841) in 1946. It succeeded the Bureau of Labour and Department of Labour, both of which were attached to the Ministry of Economy. According to Article 1 of Act No. 4841, the Ministry of Labour is charged with 'regulating labour conditions, increasing the workers' standard of living, harmonizing relations between employees and employers for the benefit of the country, improving the productivity of the workforce and taking measures to provide for full employment and social security'. These functions are consistent with the principles set out in the Turkish Constitution of 1982 in Articles Nos. 48, 49 and 50, as will be indicated below. The Ministries of Labour and Social Security were merged in 1983 under the name of the Ministry of Labour and Social Security (hereafter occasionally referred to as the Ministry of Labour for reasons of convenience and accustomed usage of the term). Presently governed by Act No. 3146 of 18 January 1985 on the Organization and Functions of the Ministry of Labour and Social Security, the objectives of the Ministry of Labour and Social Security are to regulate and supervise labour and employer (management) relations and to protect the rights and promote the interests of workers employed abroad (Article 1). Functions and duties of the Ministry have been defined in Article 2 which states that the Ministry, in addition to its duties cited in this Article, performs other functions and services assigned to it by other relevant legislation. These duties and functions cover a wide array of activities not only in the area of individual labour law but also in collective labour relations which have increased considerably since the passage of Acts No. 2821–2822 and now Act No. 6356. The Ministry is composed of certain central organs which are complemented by regional organizations and units in foreign countries.

§1. Central Organs

191. The 'associated' and 'annexed' organizations of the Ministry of Labour and Social Security are shown by Article 30 of Act No. 3146 which has been amended by Act on the Social Security Institution, No. 5502. The Ministry of Labour is headed by the Minister himself and his Deputy Minister. In the central organization of the Ministry, there are various General Directorates with well-articulated functions conferred by Act No. 3146 (i.e., the General Directorate of Labour, General Directorate of the Social Security Organization, the General Directorate of Labour Affairs Abroad, and General Directorate of Workers' Health). Although the Employment Organization of Turkey (*İş-Kur*) established by Act No. 4904 has been defined as an independent entity with financial and administrative autonomy, the same Act links it in general terms to the Ministry of Labour. The structure of the Ministry is composed of the central organization, organization in foreign countries and the related boards of the Ministry itself. With an amendment made in Article 12 of the Act on the Employment Organization of Turkey by an executive order (Official Gazette 2 November 2011, No. 28103), the local organization of the Ministry which included the regional directorates of labour has been linked to the Employment Organization of Turkey and named the Provincial Directorates of Labour and Employment Organization (PDLEO), coined in the relevant legislation (e.g., Act No. 6356) as 'the competent authority'.

192. The 'associated organizations' are the Training and Research Centre of the Ministry and the Savings and Mutual Aid Fund of the Ereğli Coal Basin Workers. The Ministry's 'annexed' organizations' are the Social Security Institution, the Employment Organization of Turkey (*İş-Kur*) and the Labour Inspectorate.

193. The Ministry of Labour may set up PDLEOs wherever it deems them to be necessary and insofar as budgetary constraints permit to do so. Each PDLEO is in charge of fulfilling the tasks assigned to it in a certain province or several provinces. The tasks of the PDLEO include those functions prescribed by other pieces of labour legislation (such as acting as the first step in the resolution of authorization disputes for collective bargaining or the mediation process in accordance with Act Nos. 2821–2822 and now by Act No. 6356), as well as the functions directly imputed to the Ministry by Act No. 3146. PDLEOs are not autonomous units; they are mere adjuncts of the Ministry, subject to its instructions and supervision.

194. As an annexed organization, the Social Security Institution established by Act No. 4947 in 2003 is in charge of coordinating the work of social security institutions and the Employment Organization of Turkey. The Social Insurance Institution established on 6 August 2003 is in charge of the application of social security legislation to insured employees. Linked to the Social Security Institution, it has financial autonomy.

195. The Ministry of Labour and Social Security may appoint labour attachés to work in Turkish Consulates and labour advisors to work in embassies, permanent representatives and Turkish missions abroad. Such advisors and attachés are under the direction and supervision of the Ministry's General Directorate of Turkish Workers Employed Abroad. They must endeavour to protect the rights and interests of Turkish workers and to help them in the solution of various problems which they may face in their employment relations abroad. They must establish relations with trade unions and employers' organizations as well as follow the developments in the fields of labour law, social security and social policy in the foreign country where they are stationed, and send periodic reports concerning such developments to the Ministry of Labour in Ankara.

196. In addition to the above-mentioned organizations and functionaries, the Ministry of Labour may call upon the advisory services of the Labour Council which is an *ad hoc* annexed body composed of representatives from the ministries concerned as well as from employees' and employers' organizations. It may convene on dates specified by the Ministry of Labour and Social Security and act as a consultative and study committee on labour matters brought before it, such as giving opinion on draft bills concerning proposed labour legislation or on other labour problems.

§2. The Supervision and Inspection of Working Conditions (Labour Inspectorate)

197. Because the inspection of working conditions concerns public order and the nation's health, the state has the obligation and the right to carry out supervision and inspection in establishments to see to it that labour legislation is properly enforced (Article 91, the Labour Act). The ILO Convention No. 81 which was ratified by Turkey by Act No. 5690, ensures the fulfilment of the inspection function by a central organ. This function has been assigned to the Ministry of Labour and several other official bodies. The actual inspection of workplaces is performed by labour inspectors who are officials attached to the regional directorates of labour. Labour inspectors supervise and inspect not only the workplaces subject to the general Labour Act No. 4857, Articles 91–93, but also those undertakings covered by the Maritime Labour Act, Article 49 and the Press Labour Act, Article 24.

198. The Ministry of Labour may also employ experts – engineers, medical doctors and chemists acting in the capacity of labour inspectors in order to supervise the implementation of bylaws and regulations. These experts as well as the inspectors employed by other public bodies must report on the results of their inspections and the measures taken to the Ministry of Labour. A bylaw governing the details of labour inspection was issued in 1979 (Official Gazette, 28 August 1979, No. 16378). Employees and employers as well as other persons concerned are under the obligation to provide labour inspectors with all the information they request and to cooperate with labour inspectors whenever they are summoned to report on pertinent facts and evidence (Article 92(2) of the Labour Act). During their inspections, labour inspectors must not obstruct to the extent possible the normal operation of the establishment; they must not disclose private and confidential information as well as commercial and trade secrets about the employer and establishment unless otherwise necessitated by the nature of the investigation. The records kept by labour inspectors are valid until the contrary is proven. Concerning the claims of workers, the interested parties may have recourse to the labour court within thirty days. Application to the labour court shall not preclude the collection of the worker's claims.

§3. The Public Employment Organization of Turkey (İş-Kur)

199. In Turkey, 'employment services' was organized as a state monopoly until 2003. Despite the variety of functions conferred on the previous Public Employment Services Organization (İİBK), it should be noted that most of İİBK activities had centred on providing jobs for the unemployed within the country and on regulating the flow of Turkish workers to foreign countries. By special regulations, the public sector was required to recruit workers through the İİBK, and employers in both the private and public sectors were under the obligation to hire a certain number of disabled persons and ex-convicts through the İİBK under Article 25(5) and (10) the previous Labour Act No. 1475.

200. With the outward opening of the Turkish economy in the early 1980s and coupled with the growing demand for more efficient utilization of human resources and flexible work arrangements, the need to overhaul employment services was also felt in Turkey. As temporary and part-time work and subcontracted labour were practised in Turkey on a larger scale in recent years, the need to liberalize employment services and to permit the operation of fee-charging private placement agencies made itself felt more strongly. Some private consulting firms had already circumvented the existing legal restrictions, particularly in so far as the search for and placement of executives and skilled employees were concerned. The İİBK, whose accomplishments had centred mainly on the public sector, seemed ill-equipped to tackle the problems of today's markets, particularly in respect of the privatization trends which would eventually lead to the contraction of employment in the public sector. Efforts were undertaken by the İİBK itself to improve the structure and overhaul the functions of the organization as well as to permit the operation of private employment agencies under its supervision and licensing. Thus, a shared management model of the labour market was believed to function better than one monopolized solely by the state. With a view to introducing the necessary changes, new legislation on improving the structure and functions of the organization under the new name İş-Kur and amending the pertinent articles of the Labour Act as well as issuing a new bylaw on the licensing and inspection requirements of the private employment agencies had become an urgent matter. Yet due to procedural difficulties, enactment of the İş-Kur Act was delayed until 2003.

201. Article 90 of the Labour Act of 10 June 2003, No. 4857, provides the following: 'The task of acting as an intermediary in providing employees with jobs suitable to their qualifications and in finding employees for different kinds of work needed by employers shall be performed by the Employment Organization of Turkey (İş-Kur) and by private employment agencies which shall be permitted to function in this capacity'. The Employment Organization of Turkey is governed by its special law, Act No. 4904, dated 25 June 2003. Articles No. 17–20 of Act No. 4904 deal with the establishment, licensing and operation of private employment agencies under the supervision of İş-Kur.

202. In addition to its employment services, İş-Kur is also in charge of administrating the unemployment insurance scheme and as such is linked to the Social Security Organization of the Ministry of Labour and Social Security.

Part I. The Individual Employment Relationship

Chapter 1. Definitions, Concepts and Scope of Turkish Labour Law

§1. 'Employees' (Workers)

203. Labour law is concerned basically with the rights of employees[40] and employers in their employment relations. The relationship between the employee and employer is generally dealt with by individual labour law while organized relations between collective entities (labour unions *vis-à-vis* employers or employers' organizations) are governed by collective labour law. In Turkey, the individual employment relationship – which is the subject of Part I of this monograph – is regulated by four main Acts, namely the Labour Act No. 4857, the Maritime Labour Act No. 854, the Act on Labour –Management Relations in the Press No. 212 (hereafter referred to as the Press Labour Act) and the Obligations Act No. 6098.

I. The Concept of 'Employee' according to the Labour Act

204. In view of all these legislative acts, an employee is a real person who works under an employment contract. The Labour Act No. 4857 has defined 'the employee' in Article 2 by emphasizing merely the elements of 'a real person working under an employment contract', thus leaving out the elements of 'working in a job' and 'for wages' which existed in the previous Labour Act No. 1475. These two additional elements are now included in the definition of the employment contract in Article 8(1) of Act No. 4857. The Collective Agreement, Strike and Lock-out Act of 1983, No. 2822 (which was one of two major instruments of collective labour law, the other being the Unions Act of 1983, No. 2821) also viewed the employee along the same lines, but Act No. 2821 and now the Unions and the Collective Labour Agreement Act No. 6356 have departed from this general definition by somewhat broadening the categories (that is, by including also those working under a publishing contract, transportation contract, agency contract, ordinary partnership

40. For purposes of uniformity in terminology, the term 'employee' rather than 'worker' has been used in this monograph, though the two terms are certainly synonymous.

or commission contract in the definition of the 'employee'). However, the category of employees that have access to collective bargaining and strike rights is only those working under an employment contract.

205. On the other hand, the Social Insurance Act No. 506 makes reference to 'insured persons' (insurance holders), a concept which also includes some unpaid employees and district guards who are under 'public servant' status as well as those whose work is based on an 'employment contract' in general.

206. It should be noted that, unlike the Labour Act of 1936 which covered only blue-collar employees (that is, manual or manual and intellectual in which case the manual aspect should be predominant), the Labour Act No. 4857 covers both manual and white-collar employees, as did its predecessor the Labour Act No. 1475. Nor does the work have to be performed in the private sector in order for the person to gain 'employee' status. Employees in the public sector are also covered by the Labour Act as well as by the legislation on collective labour law, provided that their employment relationship is based on an employment contract.[41] As will be alluded to below in detail, those working in the public sector are divided into two main categories, namely (1) public sector employees and (2) public servants and other public functionaries (e.g., public sector 'contract employees'). While the latter are excluded from the definition of 'employee', the former (public sector employees) whether they work for SEEs or for any other divisions of the government are 'employees'. Public servants and public sector contract employees are governed by special legislation of administrative law as well as by the Public Servants Unions Act' which does not recognize public servants' the right to strike. It should be noted here that the public servant–employee distinction is a controversial issue in Turkish practice.[42]

II. Persons Considered 'Employees' by the Trade Unions Act

207. As indicated above, the Unions Act of 1983, No. 2821 and now Act No. 6356, like the previous 1963 Unions Act of 1963, have adopted a broader concept of 'employee'. While in the Unions Act the major criterion is still the employment contract, Article 2(4) provides that a person performing work for wages as independent professional activity in accordance with transportation, job, agency, publishing, commission or ordinary partnership contract (other than employment contract)

41. Following this line of reasoning, the Court of Cassation ruled long ago that although the work they performed was of a public sector character, the sanitary employees in a municipality should be considered as 'employees', as their relationship to the municipal authority was predicated on an employment contract; therefore, they could join the labour union and enjoy the right to bargain collectively and to strike. Court of Cassation, 9th Div., 12 Sep. 1967, 7547/7805; Court of Cassation, General Council Decision, 3 Apr. 1968, 132/228.
42. For more detailed information on the employee–public servant distinction and public servants' right to organize, *see* below Part II, Ch. 10.

shall be regarded as 'employees' but only in terms of the second and sixth sections of Act No. 6356, meaning they shall not have recourse to provisions on collective bargaining.

208. Due to the denial of the right to bargain collectively and strike to these categories, no viable union movement has been developed by them so far.

209. Those deemed to be 'public servants', however, are to be distinguished from other public sector employees whose work is based on an employment contract rather than on civil service legislation and who are therefore clearly defined as 'employees'. But since during the past decades various public sector employees who were placed in civil service positions have somewhat arbitrarily been vying for 'employee' status, claiming that they display the same features as those who are employed under an employment contract, the employee–public servant distinction became a very controversial and complicated issue in the public sector.

210. As the economic and social status of public servants who were denied the right to unionize and bargain collectively deteriorated considerably over the years – in relative as well as in absolute terms *vis-à-vis* the employees in general – the demands of public servant categories to be defined as 'employees' gained momentum and eventually led to the emergence of 'public servants' unions' in the 1990s. Responding to these demands, the legislature passed the Act on Public Servants' Unions. Yet, because the right to conclude binding collective agreements and to strike was not recognized by that legislation, unrest and controversy still remained on the agenda. With a view to launching a reform programme in the public sector personnel regime, several draft bills were debated in the recent past, but no concrete results have yet been achieved in practice.

III. Apprentices and Trainees

211. Because apprenticeship is based on the apprenticeship contract, the relationship of the apprentice to the employer is not considered to be an employment relationship. The subject of the apprenticeship contract is the acquisition of a certain trade or skill by the apprentice. The apprentice may be performing certain work while learning the trade, but work as such is not an essential element of the contract. Therefore, with the exception of the Act's provisions on occupational health and safety, apprentices do not qualify as employees within the scope of the Labour Act No. 4857. Also, the Court of Cassation holds that the time spent under the apprenticeship status shall not be reckoned as part of the worker's entitlement to seniority rights.[43] (Nevertheless, Article 5 of the now-repealed Act No. 1475 stated that the Labour Act would not cover apprentices under the age of 18, thus implying indirectly that apprentices over the age of 18 were to be accorded the protection of the Labour Act. Certainly, this provision did not grant 'employee' status to apprentices; it merely entitled them to benefit from the protective coverage of the Labour

43. Court of Cassation, 9th Div., 26 Apr. 2007, 3873/13120.

Act. In practice there were frequent cases of alleged abusive practices by employers employing children under the pretext of an apprentice contract, thus avoiding the requirements of labour legislation, including the obligation to pay at least the legal minimum wage. Confronted with such allegations, the Court of Cassation passed several judgments aimed at preventing the employment of young persons under apprenticeship status).[44]

212. The apprenticeship contract is regulated, in a somewhat loose manner, in relation to the provisions of employment contract by the relevant Articles of the Obligations Act of 1926. In conjunction with the work on this matter, Act No. 2089 on Apprentices, Journeymen and Master Workmen was passed in 1977 which was later replaced by Act No. 3308 of 1986 on Apprenticeship and Vocational Training. Act No. 3308, like its predecessor, covered certain establishments where the Obligations Act would not apply.

213. Major categories not covered by Act No. 3308 were establishments registered by chambers of agriculture, engineering, the bar and medical-pharmaceutical associations and certain public institutions. The name of Act No. 3308 was changed to Vocational Training Act by the amendment made by Act No. 4702 in the year 2001.

214. The coverage of the Vocational Training Act has changed considerably after the amendment of 2001 by Act No. 4702 and the passage of the new Labour Act No. 4857 in 2003. Article 2 of the Vocational Training Act provides that 'the Act shall cover the occupations, organizations and the establishments of the public and private sectors as well as vocational and technical training and education institutions to be designated by the Vocational Training Board'. By enabling the Vocational Training Board to determine the scope, some flexibility has been introduced, but if the Board restricts the coverage, the mandate of the Obligations Act may tend to be broader, an ambiguous point which may be viewed as a shortcoming for the promotion of an effective vocational training system. On the other hand, Article 4 of the new Act No. 4857 dealing with exceptions provides that without prejudice to the provisions on occupational health and safety, the Labour Act shall not apply to apprentices. Thus, unlike the approach adopted by Act No. 1475 which covered apprentices above the age of 18, Act No. 4857 has purged out all apprentices outside the scope of labour legislation except for its protective provisions on occupational safety and health. Further, according to Article 13 of the Vocational Training Act, 'provisions of the Obligations Act relating to apprenticeship contracts shall not be applicable in establishments and occupations where the Vocational Training Act is implemented'.

215. In view of Article 3 of the Vocational Training Act, an apprentice is a person whose motive is to improve his knowledge, skill and work experience required

44. Court of Cassation, 9th Div., 28 Mar. 1973, 36098/6625; 14 Sep. 1977, 9778/13293; 10th Div., 20 Feb. 1975, 321/982. For an analysis of these rulings, *see* A.M. Demircioğlu, İHU, 1978/I, İş K. 5 (No. 2); C. Tuncay, İHU, 1975, SSK. 3 (No. 2).

by a particular vocation by working within a vocational field. Article 13(2) provides that the apprenticeship contract must be concluded in written form between the employer and the legal guardian or representative of the apprentice, or the apprentice himself if he has reached the legal age. The Act also provides that with a view to preparing them for a vocation, those who have completed their primary education may have access to training in workplaces as apprentice candidates before they gain the status of an apprentice (Article 9). In the meaning of the Vocational Training Act, apprentices bear 'student status', therefore they are not to be considered in the thresholds foreseen for employees (Article 11). For the same reason, the Unions Act and the Collective Labour Agreement Act (Nos. 2821, 2822 and 6356 respectively) should not apply to apprentices. Article 10(1) has levied age limits on apprenticeship. The requirement is to have completed the age of 14 and to be below the age of 19. However, those above the age of 18 may be admitted to apprenticeship training programs geared to their age and educational levels if they have not undergone apprenticeship training before. The duration of apprenticeship is to be determined by the Ministry between a minimum of two and a maximum of four years. The employer must pay the apprentice a wage consistent with his age, which must not be less than 30% of the prevailing minimum wage (Article 25(1)). The wage shall be exempt from all taxes. The apprentice shall be granted paid annual vacation for the duration of one month (Article 26).

216. The Act also regulates the status and conditions relating to journeymen and master workmen. However, if these categories work in subordination to an employer, they shall be treated as employees subject to the Labour Act and Social Insurance Act as well as to the legislation on collective labour law.

217. Trainee students admitted to an establishment on an internship basis are not considered employees either. The sole purpose of the trainee's presence in the establishment is acquisition of practical experience in an area in which the trainee already has a certain degree of theoretical knowledge. In a legal sense, he does not create any value for the employer who is therefore under no obligation to pay him wages. Although in practice trainees are paid a nominal amount by the employer, payment made voluntarily as such is not denoted as wage in the legal sense. For similar reasons, trainee students are not subject to any of the aforementioned labour legislation, with the exception of legislation and regulations on occupational health and safety (Article 77 of the Labour Act).

IV. Persons Undergoing Rehabilitation

218. Article 4(1h) of Act No. 4857 provides that it shall not cover persons undergoing physical or mental rehabilitation. The purpose of rehabilitation is the restoration or improvement of the working capacity of a physically and/or mentally handicapped person. Since their work is not wage-oriented, persons subject to rehabilitation cannot be considered 'employees'. The Social Insurance Act No. 506 has defined rehabilitation as medical treatment and/or occupational training provided for partially or totally disabled persons in order to enable them to carry on working in their own occupations or in a different occupation. In a legal sense, there is no employment contract between the person undergoing rehabilitation and the employer. Needless to say, a disabled person may be working for an employer in accordance with an employment contract. In this case, he must be viewed as an employee who may or may not have passed through a rehabilitation period but who has the capacity to work at a job accommodated to his physical and mental capabilities. As a matter of fact, Article 30 of the Labour Act has made it mandatory for employers to hire certain categories and numbers of disabled persons.

§2. 'Employer'

I. In General

219. Article 2(1) of the Labour Act defines an 'employer' as any real person or corporate body or a non-corporate institution or organization employing other person(s) as employee(s). Public entities as well as private persons or corporate bodies shall also be considered as 'employers'. Likewise, ministries and certain public agencies bear 'employer' status even though they may not have corporate status. (A good example is the Ministry of National Defence which operates many workplaces such as repair shops, armed forces clothing centres and bakeries. In this sense, the Ministry is the employer of thousands of workers employed in its establishments.)

220. An employer is a person who has the right to require the fulfilment of the obligation to perform a certain type and amount of work and also to issue commands in the administration of the establishment. However, these two categories of rights may emanate from different persons. While the former belongs to the owner of the establishment, the latter may be wielded by the person who actually manages the establishment. The person who actually manages can be a real person empowered to engage in legal procedures. In cases where the owner is deprived of carrying out legal procedures or where it is a corporate body, the 'right to expect work to be performed' and the 'right to issue commands' may be combined in the same person. In such instances, both entities are to be regarded as 'employers'. In a 'corporate form of company', the corporate body is the employer because it employs employees. However, real persons making up the management board (board of directors) of the corporation are to be considered as employers as well, since in such an enterprise the right to manage has been vested in that board. On the other hand, Article 62 of the Collective Agreements, Strikes and Lock-outs Act No. 2822, entitled 'employers', stated that the 'provisions of this Act as to the rights and obligations of the employer also apply to persons performing the duties of an employer or an employer's representative, even if their remuneration is determined by law'. A similar clause is found in Article 39(7) of the new Act No. 6356. Here the phrase 'those participating in collective negotiations as representatives of the employer are to be treated as employer's representative and that 'they may not benefit from the collective labour agreement' is important in making the said distinction.

221. It should be noted, however, that employers' representatives in the real sense in the meaning of Act No. 6356 are those authorized to manage at the highest level of the organization (i.e., the enterprise). This definition excludes the employer's representative in view of the Labour Act No. 4857 used in the broad sense of the term who is authorized to wield the right to manage in the name of the employer within circumscribed limits.

222. It is also generally held that the real persons constituting the board of directors of a corporate body are regarded as 'employers', along with the legal personality of the corporate body itself. Members of the board of directors (or management board) possess the right to formulate policies and issue commands which the employees are required to abide by. This applies both to private and to public sector enterprise management boards. As a legal entity, the corporate body has the right to request the employee to fulfil his obligation to work, but it is the management board (and its members as real persons) that exercises the right to manage employees with the authority delegated to it by the corporate body. Management board members are defined as employers and as such are to be distinguished from employer's representatives who also possess delegated authority to manage within specified limits.

II. According to the Unions and the Collective Labour Agreement Act

223. The Unions Act No. 2821 defined the employer in broad terms. In the view of Article 2(3), any person or corporate body and non-corporate public bodies employing persons who were entitled to form employees' unions and to join such unions were to be deemed as 'employers' for the purposes of this Act. As also is the case under Act No. 6356, not only persons employing employees under the employment contract but also persons who employ those working under a publishing contract, job contract, agency contract and transportation contract and ordinary partnership contract are also entitled to form and join employers' unions. Furthermore, any person in the position of the employer's representative authorized to manage the whole enterprise is treated as an employer for the purposes of this Act (Article 2(2) of Act No. 6356). The definitions inferred from Act No. 6356 are therefore similar to those found in previous collective labour law concepts.

224. The Collective Agreements, Strikes and Lock-outs Act No. 2822 also defined those persons employing employees under an employment contract as 'employers'. However, according to the amendment to Act No. 2822 in 1986 by Act No. 3299, the institutions and establishments in the public sector are to be treated as integrated entities even though they may belong to different organizations with different corporate statuses provided they are in the same industry. As such they shall conclude enterprise-level collective agreements whereby the entity by definition shall be deemed as the employer. Furthermore, as indicated above, Article 62(2) provides that any person holding a position as the employer's representative in an establishment and acting as the employer party to a collective agreement or during collective negotiations, even if only as a representative, would be treated as an employer for the purposes of this act. The same meaning is inherent now in Article

39(7) of Act No. 6356, as indicated above. However, this person was not regarded as an employer's representative under the Unions Act.

§3. 'Employer's Representative'

I. According to the Labour Act

225. According to Article 2(4 and 6) of the Labour Act No. 4857, the term 'employer's representative' means any person acting on behalf of the employer and charged with the direction of the work in the establishment or the enterprise. The employer is directly liable to the employees for the conduct and responsibilities of his representative acting in this capacity. This definition contains two basic elements. The first element is 'acting on behalf of the employer'. This requires that some 'representative authority' be delegated. The second element implies functioning in the direction of work, the establishment or the enterprise within the framework of the said 'representative authority' delegated to him. In fact, employer representatives are employees working for the employer under an employment contract. The fact that they have been granted some representative authority in the direction of work and the establishment does not alter their 'employee' status. As Article 2(5) states, the status of an employer's representative does not abrogate the rights and obligations which that person has as an employee. The Labour Division of the Court of Cassation has confirmed the view that 'foremen', while bearing the legal status of 'employer's representatives', also possess 'employee' status as they work for an employer under an employment contract.[45]

226. According to Article 2(4), the employer must be answerable for the conduct of his representative and bound by the obligations contracted by the latter as his representative in relation to other employees. This means that the employer shall assume total responsibility for the conduct of his representative. But the employer's representative's liability is limited to the extent of his administrative authority within the boundaries of the representative function delegated to him. As Article 2(5) states, any obligations and responsibilities for which the employer is liable under this Act shall also be assumed by his representative. But the latter's responsibility should not be construed as meaning financial liability nor would it cover every area in the management of the establishment. Suffice it to say that the employer's representative carries criminal liability. A foreman or technical supervisor shall not of course be held responsible for the inadequate payment of, say, minimum wages or severance pay to the employees under his supervision.

II. According to the Unions and the Collective Labour Agreement Act

227. In contrast to the rather broad definition of the employer's representative in the Labour Act, the Unions Acts (No. 2821 and 6356) have defined the 'employer's

45. Court of Cassation, 9th Div., 14 Oct. 1968, 8835/12837.

representative' in a rather narrow manner. According to Article 2(1 e) of Act No. 6356. 'any person authorized to manage an entire enterprise in the name of the person or corporation or non-corporate public bodies considered to be an employer' shall be treated as an 'employer's representative for the purposes of this Act'. And 'employer's representatives' shall be considered to be the 'employer' in the implementation of this Act. The main criterion here is the authority to manage the entire enterprise and not just the authority to manage a certain establishment or branch office or to supervise certain types of work as in the case of a foreman. The person who is generally referred to as the 'general manager' or 'general director' or 'the CEO' is thus considered to be the employer's representative as he has the authority to manage an entire enterprise. An enterprise comprises several establishments and workplaces whose managers are not regarded as employer's representatives under the Unions Act No. 6356, but who under the broader definition of the Labour Act No. 4857 are viewed, along with all the other middle and lower managerial categories, as employer's representatives.

228. The conflict between the definitions given by the two Acts with regard to the 'employer's representative' has given rise to various problems in Turkish trade unions and collective bargaining practices. Persons regarded as employer's representatives according to the Trade Unions Act are treated as 'employers' under this Act and are thus entitled to join employers' unions, while other managerial categories who are considered to be 'employer's representatives' in view of the Labour Act can join trade unions along with the rank-and-file members. There is even the possibility of foremen and other first and middle-line supervisors being appointed as shop stewards by the union and more often than not this is what has actually happened in practice.

229. In line with this reasoning, the Court of Cassation has upheld the opinion that the managers of banks' branch offices should be deemed as 'employees' since they are not in a position to manage the entire enterprise – which is the bank's corporate personality as a whole – and can therefore join trade unions if they choose to do so.[46] Because conflicts of interest are apt to arise from the unionization of such managerial personnel, the parties to collective bargaining have devised the concept of 'covered v. non-covered employees', i.e., certain categories of employees with varying degrees of managerial authority who are legally and potentially unionizable are excluded, by mutual agreement of the parties, from the coverage of collective agreements.

230. For the purposes of job security, Act No. 4857 seems to have somewhat broadened the concept of employer's representative. Article 18(5)V of Act No. 4857 provides that 'this Article and Articles 19 and 21 and the last subsection of Article 25 shall not be applicable to the employer's representative and his assistants (meaning, for example, vice-presidents of a corporation) authorized to manage the entire

46. Court of Cassation, 9th Div., 18 Apr. 1968, 512/5105. The High Court has issued similar verdicts on the same topic.

enterprise as well as the entire establishment provided that the manager of the establishment is also authorized to recruit and to terminate employees. This means that the said categories may not have access to the job security provisions of the Labour Act.

231. It is held that the definition adopted by the Unions Act is also applicable for collective bargaining purposes. At present, in view of Act No. 6356, the employer's representative who is authorized to manage the entire enterprise shall not be considered in the computation of thresholds for collective bargaining authorization as well as in the strike ballot.

§4. The Principal Employer and the Subcontractor

232. The relations between the employer, the subcontractor and the subcontractor's employees were always a controversial and much-debated matter under the previous Labour Act No. 1475, particularly as the subject pertained to the collective bargaining process. With a view to bringing some clarity to this matter, Act No. 4857 brought in new provisions in Article 2(6,7) that read as follows:

> The relations between the principal (main) employer and the subcontractor who undertakes to carry out work in auxiliary tasks related to the production of goods and services or in a certain section of the main activity due to operational requirements and for reasons of technological expertise in the establishment of the principal employer and who engages the employees recruited for this purpose only (exclusively) in the establishment of the principal employer is called 'the principal employer–subcontractor relationship'. The principal employer shall be jointly liable with the subcontractor for the obligations ensuing from the Labour Act and from employment contracts of the subcontractor's employees or from the collective agreement to which the subcontractor has been a signatory.

233. The rights of the principal employer's employees shall not be restricted by means of their engagement in work by the subcontractor and no principal employer–subcontractor relationship may be established between the employer and his ex-employee. Otherwise, and in general, based on the premise that the principal employer-subcontractor relationship was a simulated act, the employees of the subcontractor shall be treated as employees of the principal employer. The main activity shall not be divided and assigned to the subcontractor, except for operational and work-related requirements or except in jobs requiring expertise for technological reasons.

234. With a view to circumventing abuse, Article 2 of the Labour Act seems to have embodied certain restraints imposed on the use of subcontractor labour.[47] First, the principal employer–subcontractor relationship shall be applicable only when the

47. For an analysis of present legislation on the establishment of employer – subcontractor relationship,

subcontractor undertakes work in the 'auxiliary tasks' or 'in a section of the main activity' by assigning his employees only (exclusively) to the establishment in question. In other words, the relationship between the employer and a contractor who undertakes to complete, say, some construction activity on the work site of the employer is not to be construed as meaning subcontractor work within the meaning of Article 2 with the associated consequences envisaged for this relationship. Certainly, the contractor in this example may establish with someone a principal employer–subcontractor relationship in his sphere of construction work where he will be acting as the main employer himself.

235. Second, establishing such a relationship shall necessitate the presence of operational requirements and (and/or, according to some interpretations) technological expertise which cannot be met by the establishment itself. The word 'and' here may be construed as meaning 'or' as well. Obviously interpreting and justifying the presence of these two elements together, as advocated by those who wish to restrict the misuse of subcontracted work to the extent possible, will probably lead to various difficulties in practice. In fact, some circles have insisted to interpret the expressions of operational requirements and technological expertise as two conditions which must coexist. However, the Court of Cassation has not supported this approach. In the opinion of the High Court, however, the main thrust here is on technological expertise.[48] In order to eliminate misunderstandings on this issue, an amendment in the wording of the article is recommendable. Tasks auxiliary to the main activity shall mean, as in the past, cleaning, cafeteria services, loading and unloading activities and the like.[49] Such work may be temporary or permanent.[50] Needless to say, the subcontractor does not bear the status of the employer's representative in this relationship. His relation to the principal employer is based on a job contract or a similar commercial contract rather than an employment contract.

236. The element of 'joint liability' aims to protect the rights of the subcontractor's employees emanating from labour legislation, employment contracts and the collective agreement. Joint liability means that, in seeking redress for his claims, the

---

see S. Süzek İş Hukuku, İstanbul, Beta, 2008, pp. 141–165; K. Arıcı, Yeni İş Kanunu ve ve Alt İşveren İlişkisinin Sınırlandırılması Sorunu, İstanbul, 2006, Toker Dereli'ye Armağan, İ.Ü.İktisat Fakültesi Mecmuası, 55.cilt, No. 1, pp. 485–510. E. Ünsal, '4857 Sayılı Yasaya Göre Asıl İşveren-Alt İşveren İlişkisinin Kurulması', İş Hukuku ve Sosyal Güvenlik Hukuku Dergisi, Legal, No. 6, 2005, pp. 536–544; A. Güzel, 'İş Yasasına Göre Altİşveren Kavramı ve Asıl İşverenAltİşveren İlişkisinin Sınırları', Çalışma ve Toplum, No. 1, 2004, pp. 31–65.

48. Court of Cassation, 9th Div., 13 Oct. 2008, 32916/26551; 21 Jan. 2010, 12349/582.
49. In a case the High Court ruled that where the cleaning, loading and unloading activities were contracted out as a result of a tender and the plaintiff (contractor) was found to fall outside the scope of the lawsuit, with the alleged simulated act deemed unfounded, the employee (plaintiff) should not have access to the collective agreement to which the principal employer was the signatory party (Court of Cassation, 9th Div., 24 Jan. 2005, 30506/1232). The High Court also concluded that where the subcontractor's employees were doing the same tasks as those of the principal employer's employees and where the subcontractor' employees were terminated upon their joining the labour union and the employer hired new replacements on the same day, the employer (defendant) was the real (principal) employer. (Court of Cassation, 9th Div., 31 Jan. 2005, 31850/2487).
50. N. Çelik, *İş Hukuku Dersleri*, Beta, İstanbul, 2013, p. 48.

aggrieved employee of the subcontractor can have recourse either to the subcontractor (his own employer) or to the principal employer. The judge shall decide whether or not the principal employer can have recourse to the subcontractor for compensation as well as what the amount of compensation should be.

237. The liability of the principal employer shall be limited by the subcontractor's obligations pertaining to auxiliary tasks or a section of the main activity, rather than other contract work like construction or repairs to be executed in the establishment by a third party. This was already the judgment of the judiciary under the previous system.[51]

238. A crucial point here concerns those cases where employees have worked under different subcontractors without interruption in the same establishment. The High Court has concluded that the last subcontractor is liable not only for the period during which the employee had worked under him but also for the period during which the employee was employed by the previous subcontractor. The previous employer's liability is limited by the wage rate which prevailed at the time of his handing the employee over to the last subcontractor, who has the right to have recourse to the previous employer.[52]

239. Further, for the establishment of the principal employer-subcontractor relationship within the meaning of Article 2, the subcontractor's employees must have been assigned only to the designated work undertaken by the subcontractor in the establishment, a requirement which was also stipulated under Act No. 1475. This means that joint liability shall not be applicable for the subcontractor's employees who are rotated among different types of work and to different establishments of the employer.[53] The transfer of the establishment or the activity therein wholly to the subcontractor or to another employer shall bring an end to the principal employer–subcontractor relationship.[54] For the protection of the wages of subcontractor's employees, Act No. 4857 has foreseen additional safeguards in Article 36.

240. Other limitations placed on the principal employer–subcontractor relationship are as follows. With an amendment to Article 3 of the Labour Act No. 4857 by Act No. 5763 of 26 May 2008, the subcontractor must register his domain of activity as a separate establishment with the regional directorate of labour; to do this, he must provide a written agreement concluded with the principal employer and attach this agreement to the relevant documents to be delivered to the regional directorate. A regulation has been issued on the contents of that agreement (Official Gazette, 27 September 2008, No. 27010). Parallel requirements of pertinent notifications have been foreseen in Act No. 5510 on Social Insurance and General Health Insurance.

51. Court of Cassation, 21st Div., 4 Jul. 1995, 2660/3844; Court of Cassation, General Council Decision, 7 Feb. 1996, 9-902/44.
52. Court of Cassation 9th Div., 26 Apr. 2004, 9899/9416.
53. Court of Cassation, 9th Div., 25 Jun. 1992, 6240/7357; 19 Nov. 2001, 18581/17882; 25 Jan. 2010, 32292/1149. For a somewhat contrary view, *see* M. Kutal, 'Toplu İşHukuku Açısından Alt İşveren ve Sorunları', *Kiplas*, 1990, Eğ itim Semineri Bildirisi, p. 222.
54. Court of Cassation, 10th Div., 11 May 2001, 19/3691.

Due to the problems which plagued mainly collective labour relations in the past, Act No. 4857 provides that 'the rights of the principal employer's employees must not be restricted by way of their engagement in work by the subcontractor' (Article 2(7)). Although this principle aims to prevent certain abusive practices of the past – e.g., the temptation to put the principal employer's employees under the control of the subcontractor or to forfeit such employees' right to collective bargaining by including subcontractor's employees in the thresholds for collective bargaining, thereby reducing the unions' bargaining status, it is at the same time likely to create certain problems in practice. Some would argue that, in view of Article 2/VII, the employee terminated by the employer for a valid reason might be unable to be employed by the subcontractor, a practice which may hamper the freedom of contract. Obviously, it will be difficult to regard all such practices as simulated acts and here too achieving viable solutions will depend on the sound interpretations of the judiciary.

241. The provision that 'no principal employer-subcontractor relationship may be established between the employer and his ex-employee may be viewed as a contravention of the principle of 'freedom of contract'. While the underlying motive is still the prevention of some abusive practices of the past, an employer's agreement with an ex-employee to conclude in good faith a subcontracting relationship may be entirely normal and sometimes necessary for reasons of expertise or operational requirements. The article might stress merely the presence of malicious and abusive motives in order to revoke the validity of the subcontractor relationship in alleged simulation cases and leave the rest to the interpretation of the judge.

242. Lastly, 'the main activity (of the establishment) must not be divided and assigned to subcontractors, except for operational and work-related requirements or in jobs requiring expertise for technological reasons'. This means that the principal employer's employees must not be employed at the same time in a section of the main activity which, due to operational requirements and for reasons of technological expertise, has been assigned to a subcontractor and his employees. Where the main activity has been divided and assigned to subcontractors, the principal employer's employees must not be employed in such divided activities.[55] Again, the underlying motive is to ward off abuses of the past whereby the majority union in the establishment was denied authorization for collective bargaining simply by the employer's assigning part of the main activity to the subcontractor. One could encounter cases where, for instance, half of the employees in the same assembly line were those recruited by the subcontractor, as a result of which the union that represented the majority of the employees in the establishment would lose its bargaining status. To find a solution, the Court of Cassation, relying on the 'joint liability' concept, ruled in its earlier verdicts that the 'subcontractor's employees' should also be included in the threshold for collective bargaining. Certainly, this was a misinterpretation artificially expanding and exaggerating the scope of 'joint liability'. However, the Court changed its stance later by ruling that the principal employer

55. Court of Cassation, 9th Div., 26 Jun. 2006, 15117/18653; 5 Oct. 2009, 35910/25679.

would be jointly liable with the subcontractor only to the extent of the latter's obligations towards his employees stemming from the collective agreement to which he was a signatory. Apparently, the present clause in Article 2 of Act No. 4857 was motivated by the obfuscations which had beset workplace-industrial relations in the past. Yet, some view also the phrase 'except for operational and work-related requirements or in jobs requiring expertise for technological reasons' as vague and difficult to verify, thereby paving the way for still other abuses in the future.

243. It is understood from subsection 2 of Article 2 that the sanction applied in the case of abuses shall be to regard the employees of the subcontractor as employees of the principal employer from the very beginning. In the original draft bill, the said sanction was included in the last sentence of Article 2. The phrase which provides that 'the main activity shall not be divided' as the last sentence in the final legislated text, has certainly been a misplacement. Paradoxically, however, paragraphs (8) and (9) annexed to Article 2 by Act No. 5538 which entered into force on 12 July 2006 seem to have brought about more favourable conditions for public entities in their use of subcontracted work. In view of paragraph (8):

> in public institutions and organizations established by law or by the power given by law as well as in partnership corporations in whose capital such public entities own a minimum 50% of shares, the employees of the contractor, in the context of Act No. 4734 on public tender contracts or according to the provisions of other relevant legislation, shall not be appointed to the positions in these public entities nor shall they benefit in any way from the rights.

244. In other words, the sanction foreseen in Article 2(7) that 'otherwise … the employees of the subcontractor shall be treated as the employees of the principal employer from the very beginning' shall not be applicable to such employees. Consequently, the restrictions envisaged for private-sector employers will not be binding on public-sector employers. Thus the constraints in Article 2(6) and (7) concerning the applicability of subcontracting have been relaxed considerably for the public sector. And 'requests by employees working in partnership corporations to be assigned to positions in the same public entities shall also be subject to the same restrictions foreseen in paragraph (7), Article 26.

245. It should be noted that the favourable treatment accorded to the public sector is a clear violation of the principle of equality enshrined in Article 10 of the Constitution.[56] In fact, if challenged, the Constitutional Court may revoke paragraphs (7) and (9).[57]

56. Süzek, *supra*, pp. 164–165. For another critical analysis, *see* S. Şen, 'Alt İşverenlik Ucubesi', *Türk-İş Dergisi*, Mayıs-Haziran 2011, No. 394, pp. 39–52.
57. The Court of Cassation ruled, however, that joint liability would not apply in this case if simulation was involved in this relationship (Court of Cassation, 9th Div., 2 Jul. 2012, 22196/25136).

246. The new so-called bag law, Act No. 6552, dated 10 September 2014, has brought amendments to various articles with a view to expand the scope of subcontracting in the public sector. Some of the changes seem to protect job rights of subcontractor's workers (e.g., wages, severance pay) while some others, by way of references to 'public tenders' legislation, are likely to facilitate the use of subcontracting in the public sector further. Special protective measures will be mentioned in the relevant paragraphs. Those of a more general nature are as follows in summary form: as a replacement to Article 36(5) of the Labour Act, Article 3 of Act No. 6552 provides: 'When work is subcontracted to the sub-employer, the main employer is under the obligation to check the payment of wages to subcontractor's workers upon the request of these workers or on a monthly basis, and if there are any unpaid wages, by deducting the outstanding sums from the subcontractor's entitlements, to deposit the unpaid amounts to workers' bank accounts'.

247. Concerning the employment of subcontracted labour in the public sector, Article 10 of Act No. 6552 provides the following: (1) the types of public institutions and organizations where subcontract labour can be employed in auxiliary services shall be designated by the Council of Ministers by considering the constraints set forth in Article 2 of the Labour Act as well as the criteria established by the judiciary, pursuant to taking the opinion of the Ministry of Labour and Social Security, Under-secretary of the Treasury and the Head of the State Personnel Department, as well as the proposal of the Ministry of Finance, labour and employer confederations and public servants' confederation. Depending on their relevant legislation and other special clauses in related laws, municipalities may also purchase such services; (2) public tender may be initiated by public administrations in a section of the main work as well as in tasks required by the nature of the work or necessitated for technological expertise.

248. Owing to demands of labour unions and the RPP (the major opposition party) the government decided to place subcontracted works of the public sector into permanent official positions in the public organizations and institutions. In fact, the number of subcontracted employees had increased at a staggering rate reaching a number as high as 750,000 by the year 2022, of which about 350,000 were working for the municipalities and the rest in hospitals and institutions of higher learning. Although the process had to be completed within the year 2022, only about one-fifth of this figure seems to have been placed into more secure positions in the public sector, where the duration of the employment contract will be elevated to three years from one, with the status of employment being 4/C or perhaps 4/E as a new category in view of the Public Servants Act No. 657. From the debate that goes on, it is understood that those employed in the main tasks of the establishment, rather than those working in auxiliary activities, shall be given precedence. The contemplated process has not been completed yet, pending the determination of the political will after the upcoming elections of 2023. While it is hoped that these workers will enjoy more stable employment in their new positions after the process is fully completed, the protections afforded to them by Article 2 of Act No. 4857 (strict definitions, the joint liability clause, etc.) will apply only to subcontracted workers in the private sector.

249. In view of decree No. 375 promulgating the subcontractors' workers 'placement in the permanent positions of the public sector, the said workers' employment period shall not be extended beyond their retirement dates in accordance with the social security legislation.

250. Concerning subcontracting and the process of privatization, the related legislation provides: 'In order to participate in a public tender which will involve employment of workers under a subcontractor in administrations slated for privatization, obtaining the permission of the Directorate of Privatization Administration' and in the case 'SEEs, the permission of the Undersecretary of Treasury, is necessary'. Subcontracted workers shall not be engaged in tasks other than those for which they have been employed. Violators shall be subject to administrative fines.

251. In the event of collective bargaining, Article 13 provides:

> On condition that the subcontractor firm grants authorization, collective bargaining may be conducted by one of the public employers' unions to which public administrations within the scope of the central administration is affiliated; in such a case, the cost increase which may arise shall be met by the relevant organization concerned.

252. Article 14 foresees that public tender for works of a continuous nature shall be held for a period of not less than three years.

253. According to Article 12, within 120 days of the publication of Act No. 6552, subcontracted workers in local (municipal and provincial) administrations may be transferred to other tasks or establishments among the units or associated institutions of the same local administration. From the debate which continues on the issue of subcontracting in the public sector, it is understood that with a provision in a possible forthcoming new 'bag law', it will be foreseen that 'where simulation (falsification or abuse) is detected by the court in a subcontracting relationship, subcontracted workers shall be treated as the employees of the main employer (the relevant public unit) from the beginning and placed in its permanent positions'.

254. The new Labour Courts Act provides in its Article 13(15) that where a mediation process has been initiated with a request for reinstatement of the terminated employee in situations where the main employer-subcontractor relationship exists, in order for the agreement to materialize both employers must participate in the mediation meeting, with their congruent declarations of mind, due to the unique nature of this trial.[58]

58. Ü. Narmanlıoğlu, 'İşe İade Davalarında Arabuluculuk'. Sicil Dergisi, no. 38, 2017, p. 2148.

§5. The Scope of the Labour Act as regards the Premises Covered

I. Establishment

255. The concepts, 'establishment' and 'enterprise' (*Betrieb–Unternehmen* in German), are significant in terms of the application of labour legislation. While in general the establishment has a narrower connotation implying the premises where goods or services are produced in a technical sense, 'enterprise' is a broader concept in the application of the Unions Act and the Collective Labour Agreement Act No. 6356.

A. The Establishment

256. Article 2(1) of the Labour Act defines the establishment as 'the unit (entity) wherein the employees and material and immaterial elements are organized with a view to ensuring the production of goods and services by the employer'. Also, all premises used by reason of the nature and execution of the work and organized under the same management, including all facilities annexed to the establishment such as rest and recreational rooms, day nurseries, dining rooms, dormitories, bathrooms, rooms for medical examination and nursing, places for physical and vocational training and courtyards as well as the vehicles are deemed to be part of the establishment. The establishment is an integrated organizational entity within the meaning of the annexed and adjunct facilities and vehicles (Article 2(2,3)).

257. Involved in the Act's definition is the combination of material elements (buildings, labour, machinery and equipment) as well as immaterial elements (patents, experience, inventions and relations with customers) with a view to producing goods and services. Second, these elements must be kept continuously together by the employer who wishes to attain certain goal(s). As such, the establishment contributes technically and indirectly to the economic goals of the enterprise.

B. Boundaries of the Establishment

258. From the definitions given by the Labour Act, it follows that all premises used by reason of the nature and execution of the work and organized under the same management and oriented towards the same technical goal must be considered in drawing the boundaries of the establishment. If there is no relationship between these premises and the nature of the main activity, then the presumption must be made that more than one establishment exists. An employer may certainly have more than one establishment. Also, the same employer can carry on the same type of work in two or more separate establishments independent of each other. Certainly, the requirement of pursuing the same technical goal is not easy to clarify in every case. In the event of a restaurant and a pharmacy owned by the same employer, the two entities shall be considered separate establishments. But the distinction is not so clear when the same employer operates a factory producing pharmacies and has also a marketing office for selling his products. Here one should scrutinize first to see whether or not the marketing office constitutes an important part of the organization. Having been registered by the regional directorate of labour would not be a sufficient condition in order to qualify as an establishment.[59]

259. Among the factors to be considered, the following could be cited: the performance of the activities which fall into the domain of the subject matter in which the establishment is involved, independent arrangement of the payrolls and documentation of entry and exit of the employees by that entity and the like.[60]

260. There is no requirement for the premises to be located in the same physical area or even to be close to each other, but the physical distance should not be too great to preclude them from being under the same management. Otherwise, the work sites would be considered independent establishments even though they may be directed towards the same technical goal. Here, the co-existence of the conditions, i.e., 'unity in terms of management and in terms of technical goal' must be emphasized. In cases where different employers are active in the same building, each shall be considered to have his independent establishment. Likewise, a subcontractor carrying out work on the premises of another employer is deemed to be operating an independent establishment with his own employees.

261. In contrast to Act No. 1475, the new Labour Act No. 4857 seems to have somewhat broadened the boundaries of the 'establishment' with a view to considering contemporary developments and also bringing more clarity to the concept. In the past, the decisions of the judiciary as to the nature of the establishment and its annexed facilities were not consistent; for example, a printing press and the administrative centre of the newspaper printed therein, both belonging to the same employer, were considered as a single establishment as the two entities complemented each other; several establishments of a mining company located in different towns and the management of that company were designated as a single establishment while in a similar case the two entities were regarded as separate establishments. The central office and sales branches of the same employer, ticket sales offices and fuelling and cargo sites of airline companies were treated as separate and independent establishments. The broader and more comprehensive definition set forth by Act No. 4857 is likely to dissipate conflicting judgments. However, the broader scope may make it more difficult for labour unions to acquire collective bargaining status at the establishment level since the minimum 50% plus 1 threshold will be harder to attain.

59. Court of Cassation, 9th Div., 7 Jun. 1985, 6069/6260; 8 May 1997, 8063/8456.
60. Çelik, *supra*, pp. 55–60.

C. The Transfer of the Establishment or One of Its Sections

262. Unlike Act No. 1475, the new Labour Act No. 4857 regulates the transfer of the establishment as well as its likely consequences for the existing employment contracts of the employees involved. Article 6 provides: 'When, due to a legal transaction, the establishment or one of its sections is transferred to another person, employment contracts existing on the date of the transfer in the establishment or in the section transferred shall pass on to the transferee'. Computation of all the entitlements based on the employee's length of service, the transferee must act, in regard to the transactions concerning the employee, according to the date on which the employee had started work under the transferor (Article 6(2)).[61] In a transfer executed in accordance with the above provisions, the transferor and transferee shall be jointly liable for the obligations which had materialized before the transfer and which should be defrayed on the date of the transfer. The liability of the transferor is limited, however, to the two-year period following the date of the transfer (Article 6(3)). Provisions on joint liability shall not be applicable in cases where the corporate status ceases to exist as a result of a merger, participation or where the corporate type is changed (Article 6(4)). The transferor or transferee is not authorized to terminate the employment contract solely because of the transfer of the establishment or a section thereof, nor shall the transfer entitle the employee to terminate the contract for just cause.

263. Where the employment contract of the employee has been terminated after the transfer of the establishment, the lawsuit for reinstatement must be filed by the transferor, meaning the mediation process as a precondition for court action must be initiated with the transferee employer. In this case, different alternatives may be at stake, depending on the dates on which the transfer has taken place. The flexible nature of mediation should allow different solutions based on the agreement between the plaintiff and defendant where the mediator should act as a facilitator.

264. The transferor's or the transferee's right of terminating the employment contract for reasons necessitated by economic, technological or organizational changes as well as the employer's and the employee's right to terminate the contract for just cause is reserved (Article 6(5)). The provisions mentioned above shall not be applicable in the event of the transfer of the establishment as a result of liquidation of the employer's assets due to his insolvency (Article 6(4)).

265. The provisions of Article 6 are generally consistent with the past rulings of the judiciary on this matter.[62] Joint liability is construed to mean the employee's right to direct his claims to either the transferor or the transferee. However, the

61. Court of Cassation, 9th Div., 7 Mar. 2005, 18134/7308; 16 Sep. 2008, 27199/23898.

62. Court of Cassation, General Council Decision, 25 Nov. 1987, 9-382/874; Court of Cassation, 9th Div., 19 Jan. 1988, 11294/144; 9 May 1994, 2379/7056; 3 Apr. 1997, 746/6660; 9 Jun. 1999, 9604/10073; 3 Nov. 1999, 13788/16676; 23 Dec. 2003, 9002/22524. In the opinion of the High Court, where the existence of unpaid wages to which a terminated employee was entitled is proven, the employer who has taken over the establishment with all its assets and debts is also to be held liable. Court of Cassation, 9th Div., 12 Oct. 2004, 13687/22962.

transferor may not be held liable jointly with the transferee for the obligations which materialize after the date of the transfer.[63] Regarding severance pay, the Court of Cassation was of the opinion that in the face of the absolutely mandatory nature of the maximum amount of severance pay and the penalty foreseen in Article 98 of the Labour Act No. 1475, joint liability would not be applicable in the case of the transfer of the employment contract. Article 7 of the draft bill for the new Labour Act had envisaged the concept of 'the transfer of the employment contract to another employer', but this proposal was not incorporated into Act No. 4857. In the presence of this void, problems which may arise in practice due to the actual transfer of an employment contract will have to be evaluated in light of existing legal norms. However, with the enactment of the present legislation, and coupled with the abolition of the said penalty, the incompatibility of the transfer of the employment contract and Article 14 is no longer an issue. Therefore, contingent on the employee's consent and the agreement between the transferor and the transferee to that effect, the transfer of the employment contract is possible at present.[64]

266. As stated in the meaning of Article 6, provisions on the transfer of the establishment should be applicable not only in the event of an absolute and permanent transfer such as through a sale contract but also in the case of a temporary and fixed-term transfer such as through a lease contract.

267. The new Commercial Code of Turkey also includes provision for the transfer of employment relations in the event of divisions, mergers and changes in the nature of corporations. Article 178 provides that:

> the full or partial division of the company, unless the worker refuses, the employment contracts of workers shall pass over to the transferee with all the rights and obligations accrued until the date of the transfer. If the worker does not comply, the employment contract expires upon its legal termination. The transferee and the worker are obliged to abide by the contract until the date of its termination. The transferor employer and the transferee are jointly liable for the workers' accrued claims. Unless otherwise decided or understood from the facts of the situation, the employer must not transfer the rights stemming from the employment contract to third persons. The workers may request that their accrued claims be guaranteed in some way and the shareholders of the company who were responsible for the debts of the corporation before the company's division shall continue to be held jointly liable for the obligations based on the employment contracts until their termination.

268. Provided that the required conditions are met, the provisions of the Commercial Code seem to be more favourable for workers than those of Article 6 of the Labour Act.

---

63. Court of Cassation, 9th Div., 25 Sep. 2003, 2336/15352.
64. Çelik, *supra*, p. 66. Court of Cassation, 9th Div., 16 Jun. 2008, 41042/15622. Çelik 27th edn, 2014, pp. 164–167.

D. Opening, Declaring and Closing the Establishment

269. The setting up and opening of the establishment are subject to the permission of the municipal authority and other interested agencies. This matter is not regulated by the Labour Act. However, Article 3 of the Labour Act No. 4857 foresees the declaration of the establishment to the regional directorate of labour. As Article 3 provides the employer who sets up or takes over an establishment covered by this Act, who completely or partly changes the nature of his business, or who permanently closes down an establishment due to the completion of work or for any other reason must, within one month, inform the regional directorate of labour of the name and address of the establishment, the number of employees working, the field of activity of the establishment, as well as the beginning and ending date of the work, name or title of employer and of employer's representatives, if there are any (Article 3(1)).

270. The employer who does not comply with this requirement is subject to a fine (Article 98). The subcontractor must also make notification for his own establishment set up to produce goods or services in his capacity as subcontractor (Article 3(2)). The documents submitted for the registered establishment of the subcontractor may be controlled by labour inspectors with a view to detecting alleged cases of simulation. If a simulated act is detected as a result of the said examination, the report shall be communicated to the employers. The employers may file an objection to this report within 30 working days from the date of notification. The trial filed upon objection to these transactions shall be finalized within four months by the court through simple hearing procedures. In the event of appeal to court's decisions, the Court of Cassation shall award its definitive verdict within six months. Objections against these reports by public authorities must be made to competent labour courts and actions against such court decisions shall be concluded by recourse to other relevant channels (Article 3(2) as amended by Act No. 6552).

271. However, registration of commercial corporations shall be executed by using the documents sent by the official registrars of commerce; these documents shall be forwarded by the official registrars to the relevant regional directorates of the Ministry of Labour and Social Security within one month (Article 3(3)). In temporary work envisaged in Article 10, there is no requirement to declare the establishment.

272. The employer may freely close down his establishment, temporarily or permanently at any time he wishes. Only 'in the event of closing the entire establishment which entails a definite and permanent stoppage of activities, the employer must notify, at least 30 days prior to the intended closure, solely the regional directorate of Labour and the Employment Organization of Turkey' (Article 29(6)).

273. As a rule, the employer does not have to show a reason for the closure. Exceptions to the rule are found in the sphere of collective bargaining activity. The Court of Cassation upholds the view that upon the finalization of the process of authorization for collective bargaining,[65] the employer may close the establishment only for economic reasons[66] or, upon the communication of the mediator's report to the parties, for justifiable reasons necessitating the closure.[67] On the other hand, the decision of the employer to close down the establishment without just cause after the labour union had announced its decision to strike would be denoted as an unlawful lock-out.[68]

274. The existence of certain conditions relating to occupational safety and health may require suspension of activities or the closure of the establishment upon the decision of the safety committee. In this case, the employer has the right to appeal to the labour court within six working days.

II. The Concept of the Enterprise

275. Turkish law makes a distinction between the concepts of the 'establishment' and the 'enterprise'. As mentioned above, the concept of 'enterprise' is also significant for the definition of 'employer's representative' according to union legislation. The enterprise is broader than the establishment in the sense that it may comprise various establishments as well as just a single one. While an establishment is generally conceived of as pursuing a technical goal, the enterprise is profit-oriented. For example, a bank is regarded as an enterprise while its branches are treated as establishments aimed at helping the enterprise achieve its economic goals. However, the economic motive is not necessarily embedded in the concept of enterprise. A non-profit service organization like a public hospital may not have the profit motive as its main goal. An establishment (*işyeri*) is roughly the equivalent of the German term *Betrieb* or the American concept 'plant', whereas the enterprise (*işletme*) would mean *Unternehmen* or 'company'. Enterprise takes on a specific connotation according to the Unions and the Collective Labour Agreement Act No. 6356, where establishments in the same industry branch belonging to the same employer constitute an integrated entity to be covered by a single collective agreement at this level.

§6. The Scope of the Labour Act No. 4857 as Regards Activities

276. In view of Article 1(2) of the Labour Act No. 4857, 'with the exception of those cited in Article 4, this Act shall apply to all the establishments and to their employers, employer's representatives and their employees, irrespective of the subject matter of their activities'. Also, 'establishments, employers, employer's representatives and employees shall be subject to this Act irrespective of the date of notification to be made to the regional directorate of labour under Article 3'.

65. *See* Part II, Ch. 5, §4 below.
66. Court of Cassation, 9th Div., 15 Jan. 1979, 1199/670; 1 Mar. 1991, 2643/3142.
67. Court of Cassation, 9th Div., 15 Jun. 1990, 6798/7405.
68. Court of Cassation, 9th Div., 8 Jul. 1977, 8399/10606.

277. Article 4 provides that the following activities and employment relationships shall not be subject to Act No. 4857:

(a) Sea and air transport activities. Due to the unique characteristics of maritime work, employees engaged in transport activities at sea or on lakes and rivers have been protected by special legislation (Maritime Labour Act, No. 854). However, loading and unloading activities at ports and landing stages are subject to Act No. 4857 (Article 4(2, a, f)) as well as work by sea producers whose activities are not covered by the Maritime Labour Act and not deemed to be agricultural work. Also excluded from the coverage are air transport employees whose employment conditions bear special features. But, unlike sea transport there is yet no special protective legislation relating to air personnel. Notwithstanding this exception, the only categories excluded from the coverage are persons directly involved in flying (e.g., pilots, stewardesses). Ground activities are subject to the provisions of Act No. 4857. As ruled by the Court of Cassation, labour disputes relating to flying employees must be settled by normal courts of law of first instance rather than labour courts.[69]

(b) In establishments and enterprises employing fewer than 50 employees where agricultural and forestry work is carried out (Article 4, b). Article 111(1) of the Labour Act provides that the Ministry of Labour and Social Security shall determine in a regulation whether or not an activity is to be deemed industrial, commercial, agricultural or forestry work. This provision is significant in terms of the applicability of certain articles to employees working in the said branches (e.g., in view of Article 73 of the Labour Act, 'children and young workers who have not completed the age of 18 must not be employed in night work in activities deemed to be industrial'). And another regulation shall indicate the working conditions, employment contracts, wages and organization of work of agricultural and forestry employees (Article 111(3)). The Ministry makes the said determination according to a list published in the Official Gazette dated 28 February 2004.

By November 2005, however, there was a void created by the Constitutional Court's decision overruling the authority of the Ministry to make this determination, thereby bringing uncertainties to various obligations of employers, e.g., safety boards and safety engineers. In view of Article 4(2 c, d and e), the following agriculture-related activities have been included in the coverage of Act No. 4857: (1) agricultural crafts and activities in workshops and factories manufacturing implements, machinery and spare parts for use in agricultural operations, (2) construction work in agricultural establishments and (3) work performed in parks and gardens open to the public or subsidiary to any establishment.

The need for passing separate legislation to protect agricultural employees because of the unique character of agricultural work was frequently voiced in the past. Incorporation of this category into the coverage of Act No. 4857 is

69. Court of Cassation, 9th Div., 8 Apr. 1997, 1996/22816; 1997/7054. But in the presence of a collective agreement in air transportation, the dispute between the union member and the employer must be resolved by the labour court (Court of Cassation, 9th Div., 6 Oct. 2008, 2008/25218).

therefore a controversial matter eliciting criticisms from various quarters.[70] Protection of their working conditions by special regulations is not a viable solution either. Issues such as paid vacations, notice pay and severance pay of agricultural employees cannot be dealt with under the Labour Act since the categories excluded from coverage (i.e., those in undertakings which employ fewer than 50 employees) are subject to the pertinent articles of the Obligations Act. Nevertheless, in view of Article 113 of Act No. 4857, Articles 32, 35, 37 and 38 (wages, protected portion of the wage, wage account slip and fine deductions from wages) shall be applicable to employees working in agricultural establishments.

(c) Any construction work related to agriculture which falls within the scope of family economy.
(d) In works and handicrafts performed without outside help and carried out in the home by members of the family or close relatives up to the third degree (third degree included).
(e) Domestic services. Services performed by servants, maids, etc., within homes are excluded from the scope of Act No. 4857. The work relationship of such persons is governed by the Obligations Act. However, according to Act No. 2552 of 2014, domestic care workers employed by the same person for more than ten days in a month are under the scope of the Labour Act and social security legislation.
(f) Apprentices, without prejudice to the provisions of the Labour Act on occupational health and safety. The repealed Labour Act No. 1475 had foreseen this exception only for apprentices below the age of 18. Act No. 4857 has broadened the exception so as to cover all apprentices, with the stipulation that they must be protected by the provisions on occupational health and safety as foreseen in the European Union labour norms.
(g) Sportsmen. In general, employment relations of professional sportsmen are subject to the Obligations Act No. 3813 on the Foundation and Functions of the Football Federation of Turkey regulates employment contracts of professional football players. However, professional coaches employed by the sports club are covered by the Labour Act.
(h) Persons undergoing rehabilitation.
(i) Establishments employing three persons (employees) and falling within the definition given in Article 2 of the Tradesmen and Small Handicrafts Act No. 507. This exception which existed also in the previous legislation was retained in the present Labour Act No. 4857. Since, except for the categories cited above, the Act applies to all establishments including even those employing only one person, manual or white-collar, this exception concerning persons engaged by small businesses like blacksmiths, tailors, shoemakers, barbers and similar businessmen employing three or fewer employees can hardly be justified on any ground. In view of Article 113 of the Labour Act, however, Articles No. 32, 35, 37 and 38 shall apply to such employees as well.

70. Çelik, *supra,* pp. 72–73; M. Kutal, 'İş Güvencesi Yasası, No. 4773', *Çalışma Hayatımızda Yeni Dönem Semineri*, 2002, p. 22.

278. The exceptions cited in Article 4 of Act No. 4857 are prone to general criticism apart from the critical views expressed above. As the ILO and EU favour the expansion of protective social law so as to cover all working people, including the self-employed as well as the underprivileged segments of the labour market, it will prove to be even more difficult to justify bringing exceptions to the cited categories who are working under an employment contract.

§7. The Scope of the Maritime Labour Act

279. With the exception of loading and unloading works at ports, sea transport activities are governed by the Maritime Labour Act, subject to certain conditions. Article 1 provides that Act No. 854 applies to seamen working under an employment contract – as well as to their employers – in ships of a hundred or more gross tons bearing the Turkish flag at sea, on lakes and rivers. The same Act shall be applicable if ships belonging to the same employer amount to a hundred gross tons or more, or if five or more seamen are employed by the same employer. The Council of Ministers may decide, however, to apply the Maritime Labour Act to ships, seamen and their employers even when they do not normally fall within its scope due to the absence of the above-stated preconditions (Article 1(4)). Provisions of Act No. 854 as to working conditions and employment of seamen are distinct from those of Act No. 4857, reflecting the different nature of work at sea.

§8. The Scope of the Press Labour Act

280. Although employees engaged in press and media activities have not been excluded from the coverage of Act No. 4857, relations between journalists (white-collar press workers) and their employers are regulated by a different Act, carrying special clauses, Press Labour Act No. 5953 of 1952, as amended by Act 212 in 1961.

281. Those working for wages in non-manual jobs which fall within the scope of the Press Labour Act are considered to be 'journalists' (Article 1(2)). Employment contracts and conditions of manual press workers, on the other hand, are governed by the Labour Act No. 4857. Both categories are entitled to join unions established in their respective branches of activity. Demarcations are not always clear, however, leading at times to overlapping jurisdictions.

282. Perhaps owing to the vulnerability of the political power *vis-à-vis* the press, journalists seem to have been overprotected over the years as compared to the status of other groups covered by labour legislation in such matters as redundancy payments, paid vacations, etc. Perceptions of under-rewarding by members of groups covered by the Labour Act, may lead to alleged violations of the principle of equal treatment set out in the new Labour Act No. 4857.

Chapter 2. The Individual Employment Contract

§1. The Notion

283. The Labour Act No. 4857 defines the employment contract as 'an agreement whereby one party (the employee) undertakes to perform work in subordination to the other party (the employer) who in turn undertakes to pay him wages' (Article 8(1)). The concept is also used in the definition of the employee: 'the employee is a real person working under an employment contract' (Article 2(1)). But neither the Maritime Labour Act nor the Press Labour Act provides a definition of the employment contract; the only definitions given relate to the concept of the 'seaman' and the 'journalist' in the respective Acts. The definition given by the Obligations Act, the first legal source dealing with employment relationship in the Republican era, provides that 'the employment contract is that type of agreement under which the employee performs a definite or indefinite service in return for which the employer pays him a certain wage'. Missing in this definition is the element of 'subordination', a concept which is now correctly included in the definition given by the new Labour Act. In fact, the Constitutional Court had emphasized back in 1967 that an employment contract should comprise three ingredients: (a) performance of work, service or task, (b) payment of a certain wage and (c) subordination. Indeed, a person working under an employment contract is subordinated to his employer, that is, he performs an agreed-upon service under the control and supervision of the employer.[71]

284. The 'subordination' element is important in distinguishing the employment contract from other contract types such as the job contract (*locatio conductio operis/ istisna akdi*) or the agency (*vekalet*) contract. In the former, one party is under the obligation to accomplish a certain task, work or product, without the subordination element being present. The party, called the contractor, undertakes the manufacture of a thing, in consideration of a price to be paid by the other party, called the principal. In the latter case, a person (agent) undertakes the obligation to do something, a legal transaction or a material act for another person (client). In neither case, the element of subordination (of the contractor or the agent to the principal or the client, respectively) is present, nor is the payment of wages required for the contract to materialize.

285. The individual employment relationship is regulated by four different acts in Turkey, namely the Labour Act, the Obligations Act (law of contracts), the Maritime Labour Act and the Press Labour Act. Those covered by the Labour Act are subject to its provisions on the employment contract, while employment contracts of seamen and journalists are governed by their respective legislation. Those who fall outside the scope of all that legislation work under the provisions of the Obligations Act governing the employment contract. In addition, as regards matter not regulated by the provisions of the said legislation, provisions of the Obligations Act

71. Court of Cassation, 26–27 Sep. 1967, 19631/366, 1967/29.

shall apply as they are of a more general nature. The Obligations Act of 1926, No. 818, has been replaced by new legislation, Act No. 6098, on 11 January 2011 that came into effect on 1 July 2012. Public servants whose relations with the state and other public bodies do not depend on an employment contract are subject to the Public Servants Act No. 657.[72]

286. The employment contract establishes a personal relationship between the employer and the employee. As such, work to be performed by the employee is as a general rule a personal attribute that cannot be transferred, unlike the case in a lease, loan or sales contract. The employment contract also imposes obligations on both parties. In those cases where there are no rules in the Labour Act, provisions of the Obligations Act shall be applicable, provided they are not contradictory to the essential principles of the employment relationship. Also, an employment contract, fixed term or open-ended, has a certain continuity in the sense that the parties' mutual obligations tend to prevail in a continuous manner, whether for a short or long period. In view of Article 2(2) of Act No. 4857, 'the special relationship established between the employee and the employer in conjunction with the employment contract is the 'employment relationship'. Although the Act uses the two terms almost synonymously, it should be noted that the concept of 'employment relationship' is somewhat broader than that of the 'employment contract', since various entitlements to be earned by the employee (i.e., severance pay, paid annual vacation) are computed on the basis of the date on which the employee has actually begun work rather than the date of the formal conclusion of his contract.

287. A crucial point here is 'the transfer of the employment contract to another employer'. This concept differs from the temporary employment contract where posting (loaning) the employee to another employer (user undertaking) which does not change the employee's employer (as explained in paragraphs 214–216 below). Although the transfer of the employment contract was foreseen in the original draft of Act No. 4857, it was not incorporated in the Labour Act during the Parliamentary process. This void has now been filled by Article 429 of the new Obligations Act No. 6098. While Article 205 of Act No. 6098 regulates the transfer of the contract in general terms, Article 429 governs the transfer of the employment contract. Since as a general rule, provisions of the Obligations Act shall apply in cases where the Labour Act is silent, the parties are free now to agree to transfer the existing employment contract. In view of Article 429, the employment contract may be transferred to another employer only upon the written consent of the employee. Following the transaction entailing the transfer, the transferee shall become the employer party to the transferred contract with all the rights and obligations involved. The date on which the said employee started work under the transferor employer shall be treated as the beginning point in the computation of his entitlement to rights based on length of service (seniority). With the transfer, the content of the contract shall not be subject to change. It is held that the worker's written consent must be obtained at the time of the transfer which will involve a permanent transfer of the rights and obligations. For the transfer to materialize, however, it is

72. Constitutional Court, 26–27 Sep. 1967, 1963/336, 1967/29.

espoused that a written transaction is needed involving a triangular declaration of mind between the transferor, the transferee and the employee. But the worker may approve the transfer between the previous and the new employer afterwards. Article 429 does not carry any notion of 'joint liability', but by way of analogy to Article 6 of the Labour Act on the transfer of the establishment or a section thereof, as well as Article 14 on severance pay, holding the presence of joint reliability has been proposed for this relationship as well.[73]

288. As in other countries, the emergence of atypical employment relationships in recent decades has necessitated the revision of various labour law concepts in Turkey, including the adoption of new employment contract categories which were not foreseen in the previous legislation. With a view to bringing flexibility to this issue, the Labour Act No. 4857 provides that 'the parties are free to draw up the employment contract in a manner commensurate to their needs, without prejudice to the limitations brought by legislation; employment contracts may be concluded for a definite (fixed-term) or indefinite (open-ended) period. In terms of the manner of working, these contracts may be concluded on a full-time or part-time basis, or with a trial clause (probation term) or in any other form' (Article 9(1,2)).[74]

289. Article 8(1) states that the employment contract is not subject to any form unless the contrary has been stipulated by the Act. However, a written form is required for employment contracts with a definite (fixed) period of one year or more. Such written contracts are exempt from the stamp tax and all kinds of fees (Article 8(2)).

290. In cases where no written contract has been made, the employer is under the obligation to provide the employee with a written document, within two months at the latest, informing him of the general and special conditions of work, the daily or weekly working time, the basic wage and any wage supplement, time intervals for remuneration, the duration of the contract if it is a fixed term contract and conditions concerning the termination of the contract. This requirement shall not apply, however, in the case of fixed-term contracts whose duration does not exceed one month. If the employment contract has expired before the lapse of two months, this information must be communicated to the employee in written form on the expiration date at the latest (Article 8(3)).

§2. The Types of Individual Employment Contract

I. Employment Contracts for Continual and Temporary Work

291. A distinction is drawn between 'continual' and 'temporary' employment contracts. Employment that, owing to its nature, lasts only up to thirty days is

73. Nuri Çelik, *İş Hukuku Dersleri*, İstanbul, Beta, 2014, 27th edn, pp. 164–167.
74. In this monograph, the concepts 'employment contract for an indefinite period' and 'open-ended contract' are used synonymously. The same holds for the concepts 'employment contract for a definite period' and 'fixed-term contract'.

temporary, and employment which requires a longer period is continual. This distinction is based on an objective criterion, that is, the nature of the work itself, rather than on any subjective will or decision of the parties. The 'length of employment' criterion is not how long it has actually taken to complete a given work, but rather how long time would be required to complete it under normal conditions.[75] An employer may try to complete certain work within twenty-five days by operating his plant twenty-four hours a day on a three-shift basis, but if the nature of the said work requires a period of, say, two or three months, the employment contracts of his employees must be considered 'continual'. Employees on repair work, which is transitory by its nature, on the other hand, shall be deemed to have continual employment if they are permanent employees of an establishment engaged for repair work. The distinction between continual and temporary employment is significant for the applicability of certain provisions of the Labour Act. According to Article 10(2) of Act No. 4857, Articles 8, 12–15, 17, 23–31, 34, 53–59, 75, 80 and transitional Article 6 shall not apply to temporary work. If employment is temporary, provisions of the Obligations Act shall apply to matters addressed in the cited articles.

II. Employment Contracts for a Definite and Indefinite Period

292. An employment contract is deemed to have been made for an indefinite period where the employment relationship is not based on a fixed period. An employment contract for a definite period is one that is concluded between the employer and the employee in written form, for work of a specified term or which is based on objective conditions like the completion of a certain work or the occurrence of a certain event (Article 11(1)).

293. In the text of the framework agreement of 18 March 1999 which was subsequently given legislative effect through Council Directive 1999/70/EC, there is no requirement for the establishment of objective reasons for the first use of fixed-term employment contracts.

294. The prevention of abuse is regulated only with regard to successive fixed-term employment contracts. However, the present text of Article 11/I, by using the phrase 'for work of a specified term', gives the impression that the first use of a fixed-term contract also requires an essential reason such that the work in question must be of a certain duration. By restricting the freedom of the parties to fix an expiration date, this interpretation is likely to restrict the first conclusion of fixed-term contracts. For the moment, this is a controversial point. While most EU jurisdictions do not require the presence of essential reasons for the first conclusion of fixed-term contracts, the Turkish Labour Act has gone further than the directive in protecting the fixed-term employee and requires an objective justification for the first conclusion of a fixed-term contract. However, this is an option not generally taken in the EU Member States, nor in the original draft of the Turkish Labour Act

75. Court of Cassation, 9th Div., 13 Oct. 1969, 7308/9759.

which simply mentioned for fixed-term contracts the phrase 'whose duration is fixed by the parties in terms of time and date' rather than 'for work of a specified term' (Article 12, original draft).

295. The reasons cited by the government for Article 11 in the final text also attest to the fact that the underlying rationale does not imply any requirement for the objective justification for the first conclusion of a fixed-term contract. The prevention of abuse has been regulated only with regard to successive (chain) contracts, as indicated below. In academic circles, however, some argue for the prevention of abuse even in fixed-term contracts concluded only once.[76] While this confusion may be settled by the rulings of courts, the author believes that it is advisable to carefully reconsider the definition of fixed-term contracts to the extent that an objective reason need not be demonstrated for the first use of a fixed-term contract when the parties freely determine its duration and/or expiration date.

296. 'An employment contract for a definite period must not be concluded more than once except when there is an essential reason which necessitates making repeated (chain) contracts. Otherwise, the employment contract is deemed to have been made for an indefinite period from the very beginning' (Article 11(2)). The same principle is held to apply according to the Obligations Act, Article 430(2): 'Chain contracts based on essential reasons shall maintain their status as contracts made for a definite period' (Labour Act Article 11(3)). In fact, many past and recent decisions of the Court of Cassation of Turkey have confirmed this principle.[77]

297. The stipulation foreseen in Article 11(1) that all contracts made for a definite period must be concluded in written form is clearly ill-conceived and contradictory to the provision of Article 8(1) which provides that the written form is required only for definite term contracts whose duration is at least one year or more.

298. The only solution to deal with the contradiction in Article 11(1), then, could be to treat the 'written form' notion of Article 11 as a broad principle covering the requirement of written form as well as the duty to provide the employee with a written document in cases where no written contract has been drawn up. Apparently, the original draft bill prepared by the committee of academicians was not saddled with this contradiction. Besides, the wording of the draft bill was more consistent with the EU Directive. Without referring to written form, it defined a fixed-term contract as one whose duration was determined in terms of a certain time and date or which could be inferred from objective factors such as the type, nature and purpose of the

76. For such views, *see, e.g.*, Çelik, *supra*, pp. 90–95; G. Alpagut, 'Belirli Süreli İşSözleşmesi', *Mercek*, Ocak 2004, pp. 73–91.

77. Renewal of fixed-term contracts with teachers on a yearly basis is based on the notion of essential reasons; this does not turn the contract into an open-ended one. Because of the automatic expiration of the term in fixed-term contracts, the employee is not entitled to notice and severance pay (Court of Cassation, 9th Div., 26 Apr. 2000, 2291/6305). But depending on a clause in the employment contract, the non-renewal of a contract with no just reason enables the employee to receive severance pay (5 Apr. 1994, 5717/5181). The renewal of the contract with the faculty at a university converts the contract into an open-ended one (4 Jun. 2007, 7323/17668; 13 Apr. 2009, 2153/10426).

work undertaken by the employee. Past verdicts of the Court of Cassation had also attached the same interpretation to the meaning of fixed-term contracts. Also, the notion in Article 11/II stating that a fixed-term contract once repeated should automatically turn into an open-ended contract has also been emphasized by the High Court in its various decisions in the past.

299. Parallel to the relevant provisions of Article 5 on the principle of 'equal treatment', Article 12 deals with the limitations on the distinction between fixed-term and open-ended contracts. 'An employee working under an employment contract with a definite term must not be subjected to differential treatment in relation to a comparable employee working under an employment contract with an indefinite period' (Article 12(1)).

300. Divisible amounts for a given time period relating to wages and other monetary benefits to be given to an employee working under a fixed-term contract shall be paid in proportion to the length of time during which the employee has worked. In cases where seniority (length of service) in the same establishment or the same enterprise is treated as the criterion in order to take advantage of an employment benefit, the seniority criterion foreseen for a comparable employee working under an open-ended contract shall apply to an employee with a fixed-term contract, unless there is a reason justifying the application of a different seniority criterion for an employee working under a fixed-term contract (Article 12(2)).

301. The comparable employee is the one who is employed under an open-ended contract in the same or similar job in the establishment. If there is not such an employee in the establishment, then an employee with an open-ended contract performing the same or similar job in a comparable establishment falling into the same branch of activity shall be considered as the comparable employee (Article 12(3)).

302. These new principles foreseen in Article 12 are consistent with the provisions of the framework agreement of the social partners put into effect by the EU Council Directive No. 99/70.

303. Since they were not contained in the previous legislation, the interpretation of the 'comparable employee' is likely to cause practical problems in the event of labour disputes which therefore will have to be solved by expert opinions and judicial decisions. In past practice, the same principles were applied in the computation of the employee's severance pay as well as his entitlement to paid annual vacation. Under the new system, the same principles shall be applicable to other employment conditions as well.

III. Part-Time and Full-Time Contracts

304. Under the now-repealed Act No. 1475, there was no regulation concerning part-time employment although it was widely practised in the recent past. The void was filled by the rulings of the judiciary. The new Labour Act No. 4857 brought provisions on this matter consistent with the pertinent EU norms.

305. Act No. 4857 provides that 'the employment contract shall be considered a "part-time contract" if the normal weekly working time of the employee has been fixed considerably shorter in relation to a comparable employee working full-time' (Article 13(1)). The basic criterion is, then, a comparison to be made in proportion to the normal weekly working time. Part-time work may be executed in various ways, i.e., working part-time on all days of the week, working only a few days of the week full-time and in the remaining days shorter hours or not working at all. Domestic services, cleaning and preparatory work, work by company physicians, lawyers and engineers and work by women or students employed at supermarkets are typical examples of part-time work in Turkey.

306. The phrase 'working time to have been fixed considerably shorter than the normal weekly time' used in the definition is likely to cause confusion in practice. The example given in the meaning to Act No. 4857 is work which is less than at least two-thirds of the normal full-time weekly working time. It seems safe to say at this point that practical applications as they are interpreted and settled by the parties as well as by the judiciary will pave the way for clearer constructions of part-time work in practice.

307. As a limitation placed on part-time work, Article 13(2) stipulates that an employee working under a part-time employment contract must not be subjected to differential treatment in comparison to a comparable full-time employee solely because his contract is part-time unless there is a justifiable cause for differential treatment. The divisible benefits to be appropriated to a part-time employee in relation to wages and other monetary benefits must be paid in proportion to the length of his working time proportionate to a comparable employee working full-time' (Article 13(2)). A comparable employee is one who is employed full-time in the same or a similar job in the establishment. If there is no such an employee in the establishment, an employee with a full-time contract performing the same or similar job in an appropriate establishment which falls into the same branch of activity shall be considered as the comparable employee (Article 13(3)).[78]

308. These provisions of Article 13 are in conformity with the framework agreement put into effect by Council Directive No. 97/81.

309. What all this means is that a part-time employee must have access to all the fringe benefits (e.g., bonuses, premiums, child allowances, heating allowances, holiday pay) granted to full-time employees but only in terms of divisible amounts in proportion to the length of his work unless there is an agreement to the contrary. As explained in the Act's statement of reasons on which the said article is based, a part-time employee who works fifteen hours a week will be entitled to only one-third of the full-time employee working forty-five hours a week. Similarly, an

78. Court of Cassation., 9th Div., 8 Dec. 2009, 44744/33940.

employee working only two days a week shall not have access to paid weekly rest days; workers engaged in work only during afternoons will not take advantage of the transportation service assigned to employees beginning the workday in the morning. On the other hand, if the employees are paid a transportation allowance, a part-time employee working every day shall receive that allowance in full while the part-time employee who is employed only on certain days will be paid the said allowance prorated in accordance with the length of his working time.

310. Self-evidently part-time employment contracts may be concluded for an indefinite or definite term or for continual work or temporary work. In the computation of the employee's length of service (i.e., for severance pay, notice term or notice pay), the total period between the beginning and end dates of his contract shall be considered, rather than the total actual time he has worked. Also, as there is no provision to the contrary, an almost commonly held view is that a part-time employee is entitled to annual vacation in full.[79]

311. Again, in line with Council Directive No. 97/81, 'if there are vacant positions suited to the qualifications of employees working in the establishment, employees' requests to move into full-time from part-time jobs or vice versa must be taken into consideration; vacancies must be announced without delay (Article 13(4)).

312. Remuneration for part-time employees may be freely determined by the parties, provided the wage to be paid for a given period of time must not be less than the amount of the legal minimum wage corresponding to the same time period. In such types of work, the total amount of hours worked by the employee in a month should be computed first and then the level of legal minimum wage corresponding to this amount must be determined.[80] Part-time employees have access to all the entitlements of collective labour law and benefit from the provisions of the collective agreement in force, with the exception of those benefits granted exclusively to full-time employees.

IV. Work on Call Contracts

313. The concept 'work on call' or 'call work' is a special form of part-time employment contract regulated in Article 14 of Act No. 4857. An 'employment relationship which foresees the performance of work by the employee upon the emergence of a need for his services, as agreed on by the parties in the written employment contract, qualifies as a part-time employment contract based upon work on call' (Article 14(1)). Work on call, not unknown in past Turkish practices and referred to as a special form of part-time employment contract in the various

79. *See* Çelik, *supra*, p. 106. Termination of part-time employment contracts is subject to the same rules foreseen for full-time contracts.
80. Court of Cassation, 9th Div., 16 Dec. 2003, 4877/17229.

decisions of the High Court[81] is now regulated as one of the flexible working arrangements by the new Labour Act which has bolstered it by certain protective measures.

314. Article 14(2) provides that 'in the event the employee's working time has not been determined by the parties in terms of time slices such as a week, month or year, the weekly working time of the employee shall be considered to have been fixed as twenty hours. The employee shall be entitled to wages irrespective of whether or not he is engaged in work during the time announced for work on call.' Implicit in this article is the notion of working time and wage flexibility, construed to mean as the possibility of the parties' agreeing to a period longer or shorter than twenty hours. However, there is a strong likelihood that the twenty hours will be regarded as an absolutely binding minimum, construed to mean that the parties may not agree on shorter hours in individual or collective agreements.

315. Also, 'unless the contrary has been decided, the employer who has the right to request the employee to fulfil his obligation to work must make the said call at least four days in advance. The employee is obliged to perform the work upon the call communicated to him within the said time limit (i.e., notice at least four days in advance). If the daily working time has not been decided in the contract, the employer must engage the employee in work for a minimum of four consecutive hours at each call' (Article 14(3,4)). As these provisions indicate, legislation has recognized considerable freedom to the parties of the 'work on call' contract while bringing at the same time certain protective measures to apply in the absence of any agreement to the contrary. Notwithstanding such regulations, however, labour was quite critical of work on call during the legislative debates on grounds of its alleged infringement on secure and stable employment.

V. Employment Contract with a Trial Clause

316. A continual employment contract with a trial (probation) clause enables the parties to establish their rights and duties over a short period before their relationship becomes definitive. Article 15 of Act No. 4857 allows the employer and the employee to agree on a trial period, both in contracts for a definite and indefinite period during which time either party may terminate the contract without observing the notice term. Not all employment contracts are to be conceived of as containing a trial clause; in other words, in order for the contract to qualify as one with a trial clause, the parties must have agreed on a trial clause. Nor may such a contract be conceived of as comprising two separate contracts, one for the duration of the probation period and the other for a definite or indefinite period. There is one contract only and it is not binding on the parties during the trial period. This category of employment contract should be distinguished, however, from a contract whose aim is solely 'trial' where the contract automatically expires upon the completion of its duration.

---

81. Court of Cassation, 9th Div., 29 Jun. 1998, 9346/10981; 17 Apr. 2001, 1039/6436.

317. In contracts which carry a trial clause, the trial period must not exceed two months, which may be extended to not more than four months by collective agreement (Article 15(1)). The length of the trial period may be different for different employee categories. Some collective agreements envisage a three-month trial period for skilled employees and a one- or two-month period for the unskilled. The beginning of the trial period is the date on which the employee has actually started work rather than the date on which the contract has been concluded. The trial period is not discontinued in the event of the employee's illness or the suspension of the execution of the contract during a strike or lock-out. If either party believes that inserting a trial clause into the contract has not served its purpose due to illness or a work stoppage, he is free to terminate the contract and then agree on a new trial clause by concluding a new contract after the incident is over.

318. During the trial period, either party is free to terminate the contract without having to give advance notice or pay compensation. The employee's entitlement to wages and other benefits for the days he has worked is protected. Compensation may be claimed, however, if termination within the trial period is held to be abusive. If neither party has terminated the employment contract by the end of the trial period, the contract becomes binding on the parties as a regular contract the termination of which will then depend on general principles regarding the ending of employment contracts with a definite or indefinite period. The trial period is to be included in the employee's total length of service in the establishment in computing his entitlements related to length of service (i.e., notice pay, severance paid, paid annual vacation).

319. The employee's entitlement to wages during the trial period should be construed to cover all wage-related payments in a broad sense, including wages for weekly rest days, pay for national and public holidays and, when the required conditions are present, bonuses, premiums and other fringe benefits. Whether or not the employee shall benefit from a collective agreement which is in force at the establishment during his trial period depends on the provisions of the collective labour agreement as well as the respective provisions of the Unions and the Collective Agreement Act, No. 6356.

320. In the Maritime Labour Act, trial period foreseen for contracts with an indefinite period must not exceed one month (Article 10). According to the Press Labour Act, it must not exceed three months for the journalist in the first job of his career (Article 10). The Obligations Act provides that a trial period not to exceed two months may be foreseen in the employment contract during which the parties are free to terminate the contract without having to respect the notice term (Article 433(1)).

321. Subjecting a rehired employee to a trial clause is held to violate the principle of good faith,[82] except where the rehired employee is to be employed in a position which is entirely different from his previous job, or if considerable changes

82. K. Oğ uzman, *Hizmet Akdinin Feshi*, İstanbul, 1955, p. 16.

have been made in work methods (e.g., introduction of automation, computer technologies).[83] Nor is a trial clause permitted when the employer is under a legal obligation to rehire certain of his previous employees.

VI. Employment Contracts Based on a Gang (Team) Contract

322. The contract concluded between an employer and a gang (or team) of employees represented by one of the employees acting as the gang leader is called a gang contract (Article 16(1)).

323. The gang contract must be made in writing irrespective of the duration of employment contracts emanating from it. The gang contract must indicate the name and identity of each employee separately (Article 16(2)). It does not become effective on the date on which it is signed by the employer and the ganger. Once each employee named in the gang contract begins work, an employment contract is deemed to have been concluded between the employer and the employee with the conditions specified in the gang contract. Thus, various individual employment contracts emanate from a single gang contract. The ganger is considered to have fulfilled his obligation once each employee has begun work (Article 16(3)). However, in the event that a named employee does not start work following the signing of the gang contract, the ganger is to be held liable according to Article 128(1) of the Obligations Act.

324. The employer or his representative must pay each employee's wages directly to him as that employee named in the gang contract begins work. For the gang leader's acting as an intermediary or for any other reason, no deductions may be made on his behalf from the wages of employees who form the gang (Article 16(4)).

VII. Temporary Employment Contracts

325. Temporary employment relationship, based on a triangular employment relationship involving the temporary transfer of employees to other establishments within the structure of a holding company or the same group of companies was a known practice in Turkey, generally with the purpose of meeting the needs of employers of related companies for skilled labour or for joint projects. In some cases, with a view to head off lay-offs, employers who faced financial difficulties assigned some of their employees to employers of related companies. Act No. 4857 has now brought some clarity to this complicated issue by regulating it with a view to dispel the prevailing controversy, albeit from a somewhat narrow point of view. From the wording of Article 7, it is inferred that temporary work agencies assigning their employees to third parties on a professional basis for which the original draft bill had brought detailed regulations are not permitted to function.

83. T. Esener, *İş Hukuku*, 1978, p. 137.

326. 'A temporary employment relationship is established when, in order to have work performed similar to what the employee was doing, the employer transfers the employee, upon obtaining his written consent at the time of transfer, to another establishment within the structure of the same holding company or the same group of companies or to another employer. While after such transfer the employment contract between the employer and the employee continues to be in effect; the employee is obliged to perform work for the employer with whom the temporary employment relationship has been established (transferee). While the employer who is the party to the temporary employment relationship has the right to give commands to the employee, he is under the obligation to provide him with the necessary training against health and safety risks. Temporary employment relationship which must be concluded in written form may be established for a period not to exceed six months, and it may be renewed twice if required (Article 7(1,2)). And the employee's consent must be obtained in each renewal.

327. In this triangular relationship, while the employment contract between the transferor and the employee subsists, the employee is obliged to perform the work – which he has undertaken in view of this contract – for the transferee employer who has the right to give him commands. The transferee's right to give commands to the employee is limited, however, to his right to manage the establishment. Also, it is held that the employer (transferor) who is the party to the employment contract maintains his right to give commands to the employee on such matters as access to paid annual vacation.[84]

328. The transferor's obligation to pay the employee's wages shall continue. The employer with whom temporary employment relationship has been established (transferee) shall be jointly liable with the employer (transferor) for the employee's unpaid wages for the period during which the employee was engaged in his establishment as well as for the duty to protect the employee and the payment of social security contributions (Article 7(3)). If the temporary employee continues working under the transferee employer despite the expiration of the said renewals, it is held that an employment contract is formed between the two.[85]

329. Act No. 4958 of August 2003 on Social Insurance Organization, by referring to the social insurance rights of temporary employees mentioned in Article 7 of the Labour Act No. 4857, provides that the transferee (user employer) has the duty to communicate the identities of temporary employees to the Social Insurance Organization, and holds the transferor and transferee employers jointly liable for social insurance transactions concerning such employees (Article 37).

330. For the payment of damages which the employee has inflicted due to his own fault in relation to the establishment and his employment, the employee shall be liable to the employer (transferee) with whom temporary employment relationship has been established (Article 7(4)).

84. E. Akyiğit, *Ödünç İş İlişkisi*, Ankara, 1995, p. 138.
85. Court of Cassation, 9th Div., 16 Jun. 2008, 41042/15622.

331. Though the Labour Act is silent, it should be recalled that the employee has a duty of loyalty to both employers, implying for instance such obligations as refraining to disclose trade secrets of the transferee as well as of the transferor. As regards the employer's obligation to treat the employee equally, it is also held that both the transferor and the transferee are obligated to observe and respect the principle of equal treatment towards the employee.[86] However, as the obligation to pay the employee's wages and wage-related supplements rests on the transferor, his duty of equal treatment shall be limited solely to such payments. The transferee, on the other hand, must not make any discrimination as regards his rights to give commands and manage, i.e., organization of work, doing night work and assignment of tasks between his employees and the temporary employee who has similar qualifications.

332. In establishments where collective dismissals have taken place, no temporary employment relationship may be established in jobs affected by the collective dismissal within the six-month period following the collective dismissal (Article 7(7)). Unless the contrary is understood from the employee's temporary employment contract, the provisions of Act No. 4857 relating to other rights and obligations of the employee also apply to his relationship with the employer with whom temporary employment relationship was established (Article 7(5)).

333. The closing of the establishment or a section thereof belonging to the transferee employer where the temporary employee has been working shall not entail the termination of the employment contract. However, the occurrence of a similar reason at the establishment of the transferor employer may result in the termination of the temporary employment relationship.[87]

334. If the employer who has taken over the employee temporarily is the party to a collective labour dispute which has reached the strike and lock-out stage, the employee must not be engaged in work during the execution of the strike and lock-out. Provisions of Act No. 6356 on Unions and the Collective Labour Agreement are, however, reserved. The transferor employer must engage such employees in work at his own establishment (Article 7(6)). This means that the temporary employee must not work at the transferee's establishment affected by a strike or lock-out, without prejudice to a situation where the employee is designated among those who must not participate in a lawful strike or lock-out.[88] In this case, he shall perform his obligation to work at the establishment of the transferor. The Act is silent, however, on the employee's participation in a strike or lock-out which has affected the transferor's establishment. As the employee is attached to the transferor with his employment contract, one could safely argue that he could be entitled to exercise his constitutional and legal rights to participate in a lawful industrial action affecting his main workplace.

86. Çelik, *supra*, p. 115.
87. Ö. Ekmekçi, '4857 Sayılı İş Kanununda Geçici (Ödünç) İş İlişkisinin Kurulması, Hükümleri ve Sona Ermesi', *LEGAL*, No. 2, 2004, p. 374.
88. *See* paras 338 below.

335. As for the temporary employees union and collective bargaining rights, he may only become a founder of or join a union organized in the branch of activity which covers the establishment of the transferor employer, again by way of the nature of his employment contract. And for the same reasons, he may avail himself exclusively of the collective agreement covering the transferor's establishment if the conditions foreseen by Act No. 6356 are present. Nevertheless, provisions of the collective agreement covering the transferee's establishment and relating to working time, rest breaks and employer's management rights shall apply to the temporary employee as well.

336. The original draft bill prepared by the tripartite academic committee had envisaged the operation of temporary work agencies, based on the same notion of the triangular relationship but on a professional basis. It envisaged certain protective rules, yet left still further details to a regulation to be issued in conjunction with provisions on labour market management. Due to intensive labour opposition, the article was deleted from the text during the parliamentary process. Act No. 4857 permitted in Article 90 only the operation of private employment agencies as an intermediary to provide employment services for job seekers and employers. At present, private employment agencies are licensed and supervised by the Employment Organization of Turkey and they must not charge employees any fees, except for high-level managers and certain occupational categories determined by a regulation.

337. However, the triangular temporary work relationship is practised on a professional basis by certain agencies, albeit informally and with no legal basis. In so doing, these agencies rely, for the most part, on the principal employer–subcontractor relationship which, by way of its quite different nature, leads to controversy. In order to legalize temporary work agencies in Turkey, the draft bill for the Act of 26 June 2009 on Amendments to the Labour Act, Social Insurance and General Health Insurance Act annexed Article 7A to the Labour Act No. 4857 by which it set out to regulate the conditions of temporary work on a professional basis in accordance with the guidelines of EU Directive No. 2008/104/EC. But, due to active lobbying by labour unions, the President vetoed Article 7A for several reasons, among them basically for the void existing in the observance of the principle of equal treatment. Following this initiative of 26 June 2009, the draft bill for the Act of 25 February 2011, No. 6111 (which covered a broad range of provisions in many different areas), revived Article 7A with more elaborate provisions, but this proposal too was struck out during the final legislative enactment. Labour unions claim that temporary workers are doomed to employment mainly in lower-paying, substandard jobs with no employment protection. In addition to the difficulties in organizing them, unions believe that this category of work clearly violates the principle of just wage embodied in Article 55 of the Constitution. These views notwithstanding, the submission of the issue to the agenda of the Parliament in the near future is quite likely. In this effort, matters like the optimum number of temporary workers to be employed, their right to organize and bargain collectively, the designation of the industry branch wherein they can organize, their job security as well as the principle of 'equal treatment' should be given due consideration.

VIII. Legislation on Temporary Work Agencies

338. Because of the strong reactions against the proposed introduction of temporary work agencies in Turkey, posting of workers by an employer to other employers on a commercial basis was not allowed until the enactment of Act on Amendments to the Labour Act and the Act on the Employment Organization of Turkey, No. 6715, 6 May 2016. Article 7 of Act No. 4857 was amended with a view to permit the establishment and operation of temp if carried out by a licensed private employment agency in a limited number of sectors under the strict supervision of İş-Kur. It must be noted that the salient characteristic of the new Act on temps is the extremely rigid and overly detailed legal rules and regulations. This is due partly to the motive to ward off possible attacks and admonitions by labour unions and partly to the tendency of the legislature to prevent abusive practices. Faced with opposition mainly from labour unions who feared that their organizing efforts would be greatly impaired by the fragmentation of the workforce as such and felt that at least a minimum level of recognition could pave the way for at least initiating the operation of temps on a legal basis. In the face of global developments and adoption of the related EU directive, this was perceived now as a necessary step to take. So this was a 'pass the law now and see what happens' approach. Regardless of the legislature's motives, though, the Act's likely effects are difficult to forecast. But experience so far implies that it will have only a minimal effect on the creation of a flexible labour market. Despite the existence of a legal environment now how big illegal temp activity exists in Turkey is not known.

339. Article 7 of Act No. 4857 provides the following definitions: 'In the temporary employment relationship, the private employment agency is the employer. The temporary employment relationship through the private employment agency shall be established by concluding a written employment contract between the temporary worker and the private employment agency as well as a written contract for the provision of temporary worker between the private employment agency and the user employer. In the contract for the provision of temporary worker, the beginning and end dates of the contract, the nature of the work to be performed, the service fee of the private employment agency and the special obligations of the user employer and the private employment agency (if there is any) shall be indicated. No clauses shall be allowed preventing the temporary worker from having access to the services of the Employment Organization of Turkey or of another private employment agency or, upon the completion of the worker's obligation to work, preventing him from working at the user employer's establishment or of another employer. In the employment contract with the temporary worker, the minimum time period within which the temporary worker may terminate the contract for just cause if he is not called back to work must be designated. This time period may not exceed three months.

340. Temporary employment relationship through a private employment agency licensed by the Employment Organization of Turkey (İŞKUR) may be established in the following sectors:

> In cases indicated in par. 5 of Article 13 (part-time work) and Article 74 of Act . 4857 (women on maternity leave) and in other cases where the employment contract has been suspended; (b) in seasonal agricultural works; (c) in domestic works; (d) in works not considered as part of the establishment's daily activities and in intermittent works; (e) in activities of an urgent nature for purposes of occupational health and safety or upon the emergence of 'force majeure' factors which affect production considerably; (f) in the event of an unforeseeable increase in the average capacity of the establishment to produce goods and services necessitating the establishment of temporary employment relationships; (g) with the exception of seasonal works, in cases of periodic increases in the workload.

341. The contract for the provision of temporary worker may be made for the duration of the cases cited in subparagraph (a) of the second paragraph, and without regard to any limit, for a total period of eight months duration in cases cited in subparagraphs (b) and (c); and for a maximum duration of four months with the exception of subparagraph (g). The contract may be renewed only twice, not to exceed a total period of eight months with the exception of subparagraph (g). Upon the expiration of the designated time period. The user employer shall not employ temporary workers for the same activities within the following six-month period.

342. No temporary employment relationship under the second paragraph of Article 7 as indicated above may be permitted for a period of eight months where a collective dismissal has occurred according to Article 29 of the Labour Act 4857, and it shall not be permissible in public organizations nor in underground mining activities. And according to Article 65 of Act No. 6356 on Labour Unions and Collective Labour Agreements, the user employer must not employ temporary workers during the execution of a strike and lock-out.

343. Act No. 6715 has brought other stipulations as to the establishment of TWAs, conditions for their licensing and supervision, revocation of their licenses and penalties for certain offenses as well as obligations for checking if the employees' wages have been paid properly. In the event the temporary employment relationship continues despite the expiration of the time indicated in the employment contract, an open-ended employment contract shall be deemed to have been established between the user employer and the worker starting from the date of the expiration of the contract. In this case, the private employment agency shall be responsible for the worker's wages accrued and for the oblige to protect the worker as well as for the payment of the worker's social security contributions, limited by the duration of his employment contract.

344. The act has also brought short amendments to the Labour Act as regards to 'work on call and telework'.

§3. CONDITIONS FOR CONCLUDING A VALID EMPLOYMENT CONTRACT

345. As a general rule, an employment contract is concluded upon the mutual agreement of the employer and the employee who must have the necessary legal capacity and whose consent must be expressed in accordance with the relevant provisions of the Labour Act; and where the Labour Act is silent, by reference to the pertinent articles of the Civil Code and Obligations Act.

I. The Legal Capacity to Conclude an Employment Contract

346. The parties to an employment contract must have legal discretion (that is, the ability in a legal sense to distinguish right from wrong). Those under interdiction (because of drunkenness, misuse of family property, etc.) may conclude employment contracts only with the consent of their guardians.

347. In view of the new Civil Code, married persons are free to enter into employment contracts; neither the husband nor the wife has to obtain the permission of the other party in his (her) choice to work in an occupation or job; however, in the choice of an occupation or job, the integrity and interests of the marriage relationship shall be considered (Article 192).

348. As a rule, a person who has not reached the age of majority (that is, the full of age 18) can be a party to an employment contract provided that he (she) has the necessary discretion and has obtained the explicit consent of his parent or guardian. If the minor is living away from his parents with their permission, he (she) may enter into an employment contract without having to receive their consent. In addition to such general rules, the Labour Act has brought the following restrictions.

349. Employment of children who have not reached the age of 15 is prohibited. However, children who have reached the full age of 14. as well as their primary education, may be employed in light works that will not hinder their physical, mental and moral development, and for those who continue their education, in jobs that will not prevent their school attendance (Article 71(1)). On the other hand, employment of boys under the age of 18 and women irrespective of their age in underground or underwater work like in mines, cable-laying and the construction of sewers and tunnels is prohibited (Article 72). Furthermore, 'children and young employees under the age of 18 must not be employed on industrial work during night hours' (Article 73/I).

350. Young employees and children who have not completed the age of 16, as well as persons who have not received any training in their field of activity, shall not be employed in arduous and dangerous work. In fact, a regulation has been issued, showing the categories of works deemed to be arduous and dangerous (Official Gazette, 16 June 2004, 25622). Employment in arduous or dangerous works is permitted only on condition of the provision of a medical certificate (Article 86). In the event of children between 14 and 18 years of age their fitness for the job to be performed must be certified by a medical report before they are admitted to employment, with due consideration of the nature and conditions of the job in question.

351. Act No. 2007 of 1932 (as amended in 1954) which restricted the employment of foreign nationals in certain occupations has now been repealed by Act No. 4817 on the Work Permits of Foreigners. Under the present Act No. 4817, unless otherwise foreseen in the bilateral or multilateral agreements to which Turkey has been signatory, foreign nationals must obtain a work permit before beginning work in Turkey, for short-term or for an indefinite period, whether for self-employment or under an employment contract (Article 4(1)). Act No. 4817 has brought detailed procedures concerning the work permits to be issued to foreigners.

352. Also, a regulation has been issued on the implementation of Act No. 4817.[89] Act No. 4817 has also amended the various provisions of legislation in this area. More recently, Act No. 6552 of 10 September 2014 (the so-called bag law) has expanded some of the rights granted to foreign workers. For example, those who fall into the scope of Act No. 6458 on Foreigners and International Protection may be granted work permit without limit. Those who have been granted long-term work permit may have access to all the rights of persons who possess long-term resident permits. A work permit without limit may be cancelled upon the request of the foreigner concerned or the employer as well as for reasons indicated in the relevant legislation. The entry into and exit from Turkey of foreign workers with work permits shall be communicated to the Ministry of Labour and Social Security by the Ministry of Internal Affairs. Turkey's prospective accession to the European Union may require still further amendments to the existing legislation.

353. A novel provision in Act No. 6552 provides that 'workers who have been sent to Turkey by a country with which Turkey has not signed a social security agreement for employment for a period of more than three months shall be taken under the coverage Turkey's social security system'.

II. Restrictions Placed on the Freedom of Contract

354. Related to the notion of freedom of contract in employment, as foreseen in Article 48 of the Constitution, persons (employers or employees) are, as a rule, free to enter or not to enter into contractual relationships for employment or on any matter whatsoever. However, this freedom – which may be limited only for reasons of public interest – has been restricted by law for certain cases. Restrictions which usually entail also the compulsion (requirement) to conclude employment contracts with certain employees apply to the conclusion, content and form of the employment contract.

355. In the event of collective dismissals and the closing of the entire establishment which involves, a definite and permanent stoppage of activities, the employer

89. Official Gazette, 29 Aug. 2003, as amended on 24 Apr. 2004.

must make a notification, at least thirty days prior to the lay-off or the closure, to the Public Employment Organization of Turkey and post the relevant announcement at the establishment. If the employer wishes to employ employees for the same kinds of jobs within six months of the lay-off date, he must call back the laid-off employees whose occupational skills are suitable (Article 29(6)).

356. In view of Article 30 of the Labour Act as amended by Act No. 5763, dated 26 May 2008, in establishments employing 50 or more employees, employers shall employ disabled persons at a ratio of 3% in the private sector, and disabled persons at a ratio of 4% and ex-convicts at a ratio of 2% in the public sector in jobs consistent with such persons' occupational skills and physical and mental capacities.

357. For an employer who has more than one establishment within the boundaries of a certain province, the number to be employed shall be computed according to the total number of his employees, taking account of employees both with open-ended and fixed-term contracts. Taking their working time into consideration, part-time employees shall be converted into full-time numbers. In the computations of the ratios, fractions up to one-half shall be omitted; those above half shall be elevated to one (Article 30(2,3)). Priority in hiring these categories must be given to those who have become disabled during their previous employment in the establishment, Article 30(2).

358. Employers shall recruit these employees through the Public Employment Organization of Turkey (Article 30(3)). The qualifications of the employees who shall be employed in the context of this clause, the types of jobs in which they may be engaged, the special conditions to apply as well as their occupational orientation and how they shall be recruited professionally are indicated in a regulation of the Ministry of Labour and Social Security. Employment of ex-convicts shall be carried out without prejudice to the special provisions of laws concerning services related to public security.

359. No disabled person shall be employed in any underground or underwater work. And employees engaged in underground or underwater works shall not be taken into consideration in determining the threshold mentioned above. Also, in considering the minimum '50 workers' threshold', apprentices, trainees, those undergoing vocational training, subcontractor's employees, temporary workers and private security guards are not to be taken into account (Article 30(4)).

360. Act No. 4857 has not envisaged any legal sanction for violators of the obligation to employ disabled persons and ex-convicts; however, the payment of an administrative fine has been included in Article 101. The monies thus collected are to be appropriated, by a mixed committee under the coordination of the Employment Organization of Turkey, for the vocational training and rehabilitation of the disabled and ex-convicts as well as to aid in the setting up of self-employment projects for such people.

361. If employees who leave their employment to carry out military or statutory duties apply to their employer within two months of the completion of such duties, the employer shall rehire them, by giving priority over other applicants, when there is a vacancy equal or similar to their previous jobs and under the prevailing conditions. If there is no vacancy, the employer shall rehire them for the first job which will become vacant. If the employer does not fulfil his obligation to conclude the employment contract with such a person despite the presence of required conditions, he shall pay the ex-employee applying for reemployment compensation equal to three-months' wages (Article 31(4)).

362. The employer must give priority to applicants who have left his establishment due to disability but who have later recovered should they wish to resume their previous jobs, either immediately if vacant positions are available, or if not, when vacancies occur in their previous jobs or in other corresponding jobs, subject to the prevailing employment conditions. If the employer fails to respect this obligation despite the presence of the said requirements, he must pay the applying ex-employee compensation equal to his six months' wages (Article 30(5)).

363. As explained below in more detail, the employer must reinstate the chairman and members of the administrative board of labour organizations who have lost their positions for specified reasons, within one month of their application for reemployment, provided they have made such an application within one month of the termination of their duties as professional labour union officials. The reinstatement shall be to their previous jobs or to similar jobs, under the prevailing conditions (Article 23(1,2) Act No. 6356).[90] However, since according to the formulation of the new Act No. 6356, the employment contract of the worker who leaves his job upon being elected as a labour union administrator is to be considered as 'suspended' (and not terminated), this category should perhaps be cited as a case of 'reactivation of the 'suspended contract' rather than considered among the cases of 'compulsion of the employer to enter into employment contract with certain persons'.

364. Under certain conditions to be explained below, the employer must employ according to the Occupational Health and Safety Act No. 6331 workplace physician(s) and engineers or technical staff in charge of industrial safety.

365. The law has also brought certain remedies with a view to prevent the abusive exercise of the right to conclude employment contracts. If the employee quits work before the expiration of a fixed-term contract or without respecting the notice term of an open-ended contract and accepts employment under another employer, the new employer shall also be liable to the previous employer jointly with the employee if he has led the employee to act in this manner, or if he was aware of the employee's behaviour, or if he keeps the employee in his service even after becoming aware of the employee's action (Article 23 of the Labour Act).

---

90. Assurance of workers' organization management, Court of Cassation, General Council Decision, 2020/4547.

366. Furthermore, the law has prohibited any discrimination by the employer between union members and non-members in his recruitment policies, thereby prohibiting abuses in the conclusion of employment contracts in regard to freedom of association (Article 25, Act No. 6356).

A. *The Form of the Employment Contract: The Right to Determine the Form Freely, and Its Limits*

367. As a rule, the employment contract is not subject to a special form unless the contrary has been stipulated by legislation (Labour Act Article 9, Obligations Act Article 394(1)). However, 'written form is required for employment contracts with a fixed term of one year or more' (Article 8(2)). Such written contracts are exempt from the stamp tax and all kinds of fees. According to the rulings of the Court of Cassation, written form is a condition of proof rather than a condition of validity.[91] On the other hand, a gang (team) contract must always be made in written form irrespective of its duration. In this category, written form is a condition of validity.[92]

368. In cases where no written contract has been made, the employer is under the obligation to provide the employee with a written document within two months at the latest, showing the general and special conditions of work, the daily or weekly working time, the basic wage and any wage supplements, the time intervals for remuneration, the duration if it is a fixed-term contract and conditions concerning termination of the contract. However, this rule shall not apply in the case of fixed-term contracts whose duration does not exceed one month. If the employment contract expires before the lapse of two months, the above-mentioned information must be communicated to the employee in written form on the expiration date at the latest (Article 8/III).

369. The wording of Article 8 is consistent with the EU Directive No. 91/533. Unlike the now-repealed Labour Act No. 1475 which had envisaged the provision of such a written document only upon the request of the employee, it must now be delivered to the employee irrespective of any request whatsoever.

370. There is no specific requirement to form employment contracts subject to the Obligations Act (Article 314). However, all employment contracts subject to the Maritime Labour Act (Article 5) and the Press Labour Act (Article 4) must be concluded in writing in order to be valid.

B. *Limitations on the Right to Determine the Content of the Employment Contract Freely*

371. As a rule, in view of the Obligations Act, the subject matter of the employment contract must not involve work that is impossible to fulfil; and it must

91. Court of Cassation, General Council Decision, 19 Mar. 1986, 1984/9-555, 1986/251.
92. Court of Cassation, General Council Decision, 9 Feb. 2000, 2000/13-77, 2000/63.

not be contrary to mandatory legal norms, to public order, general good morals and individual rights.

372. Certain categories of employees who, upon their application, shall be reengaged in work by the employer (i.e., the laid off employees who are to be called back if the employer wishes to recruit employees within six months following the lay-off, employees whose disability (Article 30) or statutory duties and military service (Article 31) have ended, as well as union officials who have lost administrative positions in unions, must be remunerated under the prevailing employment conditions rather than at rates that were effective when they had left the establishment). The motive here is apparently to protect the employee's wage income and other working conditions. Similarly, except for the benefits granted to employees by the collective agreement, the employer must not make discrimination in terms of working conditions between union members and non-members (Article 25(2), Act No. 6356).

373. Further limitations have been envisaged by Act No. 6356 respecting collective agreements: 'unless otherwise stated in the collective agreement, individual employment contracts must not be contrary to the collective agreement; provisions contrary to the collective agreement are to be supplanted by the terms of the collective agreement' (Article 36(1)). And, 'unless the collective agreement provides for the contrary, non-striking employees must not have access to the benefits brought by a collective agreement signed following a strike' (Article 39(8)), meaning that their employment contracts are to remain below the collectively bargained rates. Nonetheless, collective agreements generally grant this permission to employees who have not participated in the strike action.

III. Nullity of the Employment Contract

374. An employment contract shall be considered null and void if it is fraught with deficiencies concerning competence of the parties, the form when required, if it contravenes public order and general good morals, or if it entails work which is not legally permissible or possible. Nullity and avoidance take effect retroactively and may be invoked by any person or dealt with directly by the judge. Also, nullity may affect only a certain part of the contract if the said defects are related solely to that part, Obligations Act (Article 27(2)).

375. Taking the protective nature of labour law, however, the Court of Cassation has ruled that in the employment of a person despite legal restrictions – e.g., in work where women or employment of children below a certain age is prohibited – the employment contract must not be considered null and void retroactively.[93]

93. Unification award of the Court of Cassation, 18 Jun. 1958, 20/9.

376. The employment contract is to be considered valid even in cases where it was concluded under a gross mistake, fraud, threat or a simulated act, but avoidance and nullity may be invoked here by the protected party retroactively from the beginning. However, due to the protective nature of labour law, it is affirmed that nullification should be effective as of the date of the request by the protected party.[94]

94. Çelik, *supra*, p. 136.

Chapter 3. Duties of the Parties in the Course of the Employment Relationship

§1. Duties of the Employee

I. Duty to Work

377. The main duty of the employee is the performance of work. Apart from special provisions agreed upon in the employment contracts and the collective agreement, major rules concerning the conditions and scope of the employee's duty to work in Turkish law are as follows.

378. Because the employee's personality, capabilities, skills and experience were considered in the conclusion of his employment contract, he is obliged to render the work himself unless the contrary was agreed or is implicit in the nature of the work (Obligations Act, Article 395). The work for which the employee was hired may neither be transferred by him to someone else nor may it be inherited by his heirs after his death. This provision envisaged by the Obligations Act is not mandatory. The parties may agree to the contrary in the employment contract or collective agreement, or it may be inferred from the facts of the situation. As a rule, the employee's duty to work continues even after the establishment is taken over by a different employer.

379. The employee must abide by the mandatory rules of labour legislation, individual employment contract and the collective agreement. He must fulfil his obligation to work. If he refuses, after being warned, to perform his duties, the employer may terminate his employment contract for just cause (i.e., without having to respect the term of notice or to pay any indemnities) (Article 25, Labour Act No. 4857). As a rule, the employee is obliged to perform the duties envisaged in his employment contract. The employer must not force him to render duties not agreed upon in the contract, nor may he ask him to do things contrary to law.

380. If the employees' duties have not been clarified in the employment contract, then he must carry out the orders given to him by the employer in equity and along the goals of the establishment. The employee performs his duties at the time and place – which is generally the establishment – agreed in the contract. Unless the employee gives his consent, he must not be transferred to another establishment owned and/or operated by the employer. He is not obliged to work if his place of employment is moved to a distant location. Such unilateral changes will be considered as breach of contract. Apart from these general principles, essential alterations in the employee's workplace and working conditions have been subjected to special procedures set out in Article 22 of the Labour Act No. 4857. Unless there is an agreement to the contrary, the employee is not allowed to work for himself or for another employer during working hours. If there is an agreement to the contrary, however, the new employer would acquire the right to command work from him. The exception to this rule is the conclusion of an employment contract made with specific reference to the personality of the employer per se.

381. Unless there is an agreement to the contrary or inferred from the facts of the situation, the employer shall not transfer his right to command work from the employee to another person (Obligations Act, Article 429). In fact, temporary work which has been regulated in Article 7 of Act No. 4857 is, somehow ironically, based on this notion. Under special conditions set out in Article 7 and upon receiving the consent of the employee, the employer may assign him to another employer within the structure of the same holding company or group of companies for a certain period.[95] According to a ruling of the Court of Cassation, the employer may transfer his right to command work from the employee to another employer either temporarily or on a continuous basis.[96] As mentioned above, whether this could be done on a professional basis is a dubious matter under the present Turkish law. As temporary work agencies which were envisaged in the draft bill were deleted from the text of Act No. 4857, temporary work through professional agencies is not to be deemed permissible according to majority opinion under the present legislation. If such agencies continue leasing out employees on a commercial basis, they will have to predicate their *raison d'être* on the general spirit of Article 429 of the Obligations Act until at least new regulations are enacted to this effect. Yet this practice as well as predicating the triangular relationship as such on employer–subcontractor relationship is likely to entail legal problems. As indicated above, even draft laws in this area have not materialized so far, let alone enacted legislation.

382. The employee must perform the work with care and diligence. As stated in Article 25/II (i) of the Labour Act, if the employee either wilfully or through gross negligence imperils safety or damages machinery, equipment or other articles or materials in his care, whether these are the employer's property or not, and the damage cannot be offset by his thirty day's pay, the employer may break the employment contract for just cause. There is no objective criterion concerning the degree of care and diligence, so it has to be determined in accordance with the nature of the employment contract and the extent of the employee's knowledge, skills and vocational competence as required by the job in question (Obligations Act, Article 396(1)). However, in the opinion of the Court of Cassation, if in his recruitment the employee's competence or skill was not given due consideration for the job for which he was to be employed, termination of his contract without notice and severance pay as well as claims of compensation for the damage caused by him were not justified.[97]

383. Under the Obligations Act, the employee is liable to his employer for the damage he inflicts if he is guilty of misconduct during the execution of the employment contract (Obligations Act, Article 400(1)). Also, if an employee working under a continual employment contract with a fixed or indefinite term leaves his job before the expiration date or by not giving due notice and takes a job with a new employer,

95. Çelik, *supra*, p. 137.
96. Court of Cassation, 7 May 2001/7889. In this ruling, however, the High Court referred mainly to temporary work under the concept 'leasing out – loaning – of the employee'.
97. Court of Cassation, 9th Div., 11 Nov. 1986, 87194/10063; 6 Oct. 1992, 3068/10904; 31 Mar. 2008, 29966/7020.

the new employer must pay compensation at a rate to be fixed by the court – without prejudice to the employee's own liability – for the loss caused to his former employer by his breach of contract if (a) the new employer has caused the employee to act in this manner or (b) if he has engaged the employee in work even though he was aware of the employee's behaviour or (c) if he has retained the employee in his service even after becoming aware of the employee's behaviour (Labour Act, Article 23).

384. Furthermore, as provided by Article 25/II (h, i) of the Labour Act, the employer may break the employee's contract without observing the notice term and paying any compensation if the latter refuses, after being warned, to perform his duties and inflicts damage due to negligence and lack of sufficient diligence.

II. The Obligation to Abide by the Instructions and Orders of the Employer

385. The employee is obliged to abide by the instructions and orders given by his employer. The employer's instructions and orders emanate from his right to manage the establishment. The Employer's right to issue orders and instructions is limited, however, by the mandatory provisions of the law, the collective agreement, the needs of the establishment and the requirement that the work be performed in accordance with prevailing custom. The employee is not under any obligation to obey orders and instructions which exceed these limits. Here three issues which give rise to problems in practice deserve special attention – namely, the search of employees during access to and departure from the establishment, the 'no smoking' regulations and restriction of alcohol on the premises.

386. The Constitution and the Civil Code of Turkey both protect the privacy of individuals, but it is generally accepted that the employee should tolerate the search and control procedures introduced by the employer with the object of safeguarding industrial safety and health and preventing theft, provided that the employee's consent on this issue is obtained by way of the employment contract or the collective agreement. Even in cases where there is no clarity in the employment contract or collective agreement, custom or the principle of honesty may necessitate such search and controls.[98] However, search as such must not be implemented in an arbitrary or humiliating manner. Besides, there must be objective reasons stemming from the nature of the establishment or the operations. Although the search and controls must be carried out in a non-discriminatory fashion, they may be limited, by applying objective criteria, only to certain categories if large numbers of employees are involved. The new Obligations Act has set forth a new duty for the employee, i.e., the duty to deliver back the tools and equipment back to the employer and to settle the accounts with him upon the completion of work (Article 397).

387. A 'no-smoking' rule unilaterally imposed by the employer is enforceable only if established by law (i.e., Act No. 4207), the collective agreement or the

98. Çelik, *supra*, p. 142.

employment contract. In operations where there is a danger of fire, the employer may impose the 'no-smoking' restriction based on the occupational health and safety provisions of the Labour Act, Article 77. The employer may terminate the employment contract of the employee who smokes outside the area assigned exclusively to smoking and who thus endangers occupational safety in the establishment.[99] The employer may also establish the 'no-smoking' rule in operations where smoking on the job is bound to reduce output.[100] Besides, the employer may impose smoking bans by relying on the provisions of Act No. 4207 on the prevention of harm from smoking and consumption of tobacco products.

388. As a rule, it is unlawful for an employee to enter an establishment while drunk or under the effect of narcotics or to consume alcohol or to take narcotics on the premises. The employer may determine, however, the circumstances and times for the consumption of alcoholic beverages in parts of the establishment treated as subordinate facilities. This general restriction does not apply to employees assigned to quality control in establishments where alcoholic beverages are manufactured or who have to consume alcohol in establishments which hold a license to serve liquor or to those employees allowed to consume alcoholic beverages with customers owing to the requirements of the job, Article 84.

III. The Duty of Loyalty

389. This duty has two phases, namely (a) the duty to act and (b) the duty to abstain from acting, with a view to protect the interests of the employer and the establishment. The employee must render his services in a way commensurate with the interests, reputation and prestige of the employer; he must take the necessary precautions to protect the employer from possible harm and must inform him of events such as theft, work irregularities and machine failures which may hinder the efficient functioning of the establishment. Further, the employee must leave his work in an adequate and orderly manner. As regards the duty to abstain from acting, the employee must not engage in any behaviour which may be detrimental to his employer. Such behaviour is implied, perhaps in an indirect manner, in Article 25/II (b, d and e) of the Labour Act concerning immoral, or malicious conduct which enables the employer to break the employment contract without having to observe the term of notice and paying any compensation. Of special importance in this respect is behaviour cited in subsection (e), like committing dishonest acts against the employer such as breach of trust, theft or disclosure of the employer's trade secrets. Since Article 25/II refers to 'other similar behaviour' in violation of the honesty and fair dealing principle, behaviour such as accepting bribes,[101] failing to hand over to the employer money which belongs to the establishment,[102] fraudulently

99. Court of Cassation, 9th Div., 2 Nov. 2004, 1934/24692.
100. M.E. Ekonomi, *İş Hukuku*, İstanbul, 1984, pp. 125–126.
101. Court of Cassation, 9th Div., 1 Dec. 1994, 16908/17076; 16 Oct. 1995, 10862/3191; 28 Apr. 1998, 2415/7814.
102. Court of Cassation, 9th Div., 15 May 1996, 37186/10548; 28 Oct. 2010, 14806/1477.

altering receipts and forgery in documents,[103] sleeping[104] or reading a newspaper on the job, spending the bank's deposits for his personal gain and risking the assets of the bank through irregular procedures,[105] working at another establishment while calling in sick,[106] engaging in competition against the employer by doing business with customers of the bank where he is employed[107] have all been held to conduct contrary to the duty of loyalty. In such cases, the employer may terminate the worker's open-ended employment contract immediately or the fixed-term contract without having to await the expiration of the contract term. In addition, he may also sue the employee for legal damages (Article 26(2)).

IV. Covenant of Non-competition

390. As a rule, the employee is not allowed to compete against his employer during the life of his employment contract. The employee's competition with the employer within the duration of his employment contract is treated as a violation of the duty of loyalty whereby the employer may break the contract for breach of trust according to Article 25/II(e).[108] Once the contract ends, however, the employee regains his freedom of enterprise. But the employee may, by subscribing to a covenant of non-competition, waive his right to compete with the employer even after the expiration of his contract which has enabled him to be acquainted with the employer's customers or to learn his trade secrets. Thus, the employee undertakes not to engage in a competing business or to enter into an employment relationship with a competitor of his employer after the termination of his present employment contract. The covenant of non-competition is regulated by the Obligations Act, Article 444. Contravention of a non-competition clause may be further sanctioned by a penal compensation clause inserted into the employment contract (Obligations Act, Article 179 (according to which the employee is to be held liable even though the employer may have suffered no damages)). The Court of Cassation has passed judgments whereby it has found the amount of penal compensation excessive, ruling that it should be lowered to a reasonable amount. But the employee must also pay any extra losses he has inflicted on the employer if the damage caused exceeds the agreed-upon compensation (Obligations Act, Article 446(2)).

391. In order to conclude a valid employment contract with a non-competition clause, it must be made in writing, with the type of business activity, place and

103. Court of Cassation, 9th Div., 27 Nov. 1972, 14317/31230.
104. Court of Cassation, 9th Div., 26 Feb. 1968, 13713/2260; 27 Apr. 1992, 17320/4704; 2 Nov. 1998, 13707/15475. Nevertheless, the Court of Cassation has ruled that the first instance of sleeping is a reason for termination for a valid reason rather than for just cause (Court of Cassation, 9th Div., 9 Feb. 2009, 11037/1879).
105. Court of Cassation, 9th Div., 15 Feb. 1988, 12134/1179; 26 Sep. 1996, 16627/17899.
106. Court of Cassation, 9th Div., 29 Apr. 1991, 14468/7693; 29 Apr. 1991, 14468/7693; 13 May 1991, 5888/6405; Court of Cassation, General Council Decision, 29 May 1991, 9223/315.
107. Court of Cassation, 9th Div., 26 May 1997, 4847/9797.
108. The Court of Cassation has ruled that the employee's involvement outside working hours in business activity on his own behalf but without obtaining his employer's permission is a breach of trust. Court of Cassation, General Council Decision, 18 Oct. 1995, 6-670/813.

duration clearly specified (Obligation Act, Article 444). Besides, the stipulated non-competition clause must not threaten the economic future of the employee in an unjust manner (Article 45(1)).[109] According to a new clause, the duration of the non-competition clause must not exceed two years. The worker must possess action competence and the clause must be limited to a certain place, type of work and time (Article 445(1)). The Act has clarified the cases which invalidate the clause on non-competition (Article 447). No lawsuit based on the non-competition clause may be instituted against the employee where the employment contract is terminated by the employer for no just cause or by the employee for just cause.

392. Also, the non-competition clause becomes invalid when it is understood that the employer no longer has any real interest in the employee's acceptance of non-competition (Article 447(1)). And naturally, the covenant expires upon the termination of the employment contract by the employer for no just cause or by the employee for just cause (Article 447(2)).

§2. Duties of the Employer

I. The Duty to Pay the Employee Wages

393. Among the duties of the employer, the obligation to pay employees wages for the work they perform is probably the most important one. Because of its special significance, the duty to pay wages will be dealt with separately under the special heading 'Remuneration' in Chapter 5.

II. The Duty to Protect the Employee

394. As part of the employer's duty to protect the employee, the Labour Act of Turkey of 2003, No. 4857 provided various articles on occupational health and safety which were generally in compliance with EU norms. And following this legislation, a considerable number of government regulations on occupational health and safety were published and came into force.[110] As in the course of time, some of these regulations were replaced by new ones and a few others were abrogated by court decisions, there appeared a serious void in this area. In an effort to do away with the emerging deficiencies and to fill in the voids, the legislature, overhauling most of the existing measures, adopted an entirely new and comprehensive text titled the Occupational Health and Safety Act, No. 6331 which, with the protraction of some of its articles to future dates, took effect on 30 June 2012.

109. Court of Cassation, 9th Div., 6 Jul. 1999, 8262/12073. In this specific case, the covenant involved the employee's acceptance of not working in any bank, which the Court interpreted as an unjustified commitment that would endanger the economic future of the employee unconditionally and therefore should be declared invalid. Similarly, a non-competition clause to apply to the whole country must be deemed invalid, but a non-competition clause may cover a certain province or region (9th Div., 24 Dec. 2009, 26954/36971).

110. For the measures foreseen by Act No. 4857, *see* the 2011 edition of this monograph.

395. Act No. 6331 has regulated the employer's and, where relevant, the employees' obligations on health and safety in more concrete and detailed terms than the repealed provisions of Act No. 4857. In view of Article 2(1) of Act No. 6331, its provisions shall apply to a wide array of activities and establishments, covering not only employees but also, except for a few groups, all working people, establishments, occupations of both the public and private sectors, their employers and employer's representatives, apprentices and trainees, irrespective of their occupations. For reasons of convenience, the terms 'employees' and 'workers' shall be used in this text to denote the broader concept of 'working people'. Exceptions cited by the Act are the following: Turkish armed forces (excluding military factories, care centres, military tailoring shops and the like which are within the scope of the Act); general security forces and activities associated with the under-secretariat of the National Intelligence Organization; activities of units in charge of urgent intervention in the case of national disasters; domestic services; those people producing goods and services on their own behalf without employing workers; rehabilitation activities of law enforcement agencies, including construction of training and security services (Article 2(2)).[111]

396. The employer's duty to protect his employee is based, for the most part, on the provisions of Act No. 6331 which, along with the related bylaws and regulations in this field,[112] are of a mandatory nature. The Act's provisions have also set forth parallel obligations and duties on the employee. As a general rule, 'employers must take all the necessary measures and maintain all the needed means and tools in their establishments in order to ensure occupational safety and health of their employees'. Likewise, the Obligations Act has imposed the same duty on the employer as well (Article 417(1) of the Obligations Act). Also, 'the employees are under the obligation to respect and abide by the measures taken in the field of occupational health and safety'. The employee's duty to observe safety and health measures is significant in articulating the employer's liability in lawsuits filed against the employer in order to cover damages caused by industrial accidents or occupational diseases.[113] The employer may terminate the employee's employment contract for just cause if the latter has failed to respect and obey safety and health measures.[114]

397. Article 4(1) of Act No. 6331 has set forth the general rules concerning the employer's duties in this area: the employer is under the obligation to ensure all the measures for the health and safety of all the working people in his establishment, i.e., taking all the measures including the elimination of occupational risks, provision of training, launching and providing the necessary means and tools; readapting the health and safety measures to changing circumstances, improving the existing situation; monitoring the application of health and safety measures at the workplace

111. For more information, *see* N. Salper Süzek, *İş Hukuku*, 10th edn, 2014, pp. 863–935.
112. N. Çelik, *İş Hukuku Dersleri*, 23rd edn, 2010, pp. 165–177. Consistent with the provisions of Act No. 4857, a considerable number of regulations were published to govern this issue.
113. Court of Cassation, 9th Div., 25 Jun. 1990, 4838/7758.
114. Court of Cassation, 9th Div., 29 Sep. 2000, 20215/2369.

and eliminating the deficiencies, making risk assessments and analyses; ensuring the suitability of his employees to their work assignments from the standpoint of health and safety considerations; and taking measures to keep the unauthorized personnel away from areas which pose a special danger to life.

398. To ensure compliance with and supervision of occupational safety and health measures at the establishment, the employer must provide the employees with information on occupational risks as well as their legal rights and obligations and the necessary training on occupational health and safety.[115]

399. In view of Article 78 of Act No. 4857, the Ministry of Labour and Social Security, after taking the opinion of the Ministry of Health, would issue bylaws and regulations with a view to ensure the adoption of occupational safety and health measures, the prevention of work accidents and occupational diseases as well as the arrangement of working conditions for persons who must be protected because of their age, sex and special circumstances. Based on this clause, the Regulation on Occupational Health and Safety (Official Gazette, 9 December 2003, No. 25811) was published first as the basic document, followed later by the publication of the Regulation on Occupational Health and Safety in Temporary and Fixed-Term Jobs (Official Gazette, 15 May 2004, No. 25463). The Regulation of 9 December 2003 was declared invalid by the Council of State since such basic texts should be governed by bylaws rather than regulations.[116] During the ensuing years, the Ministry of Labour and Social Security issued a sizable number of regulations adapted from the relevant EU directives on the technical aspects of occupational health and safety.[117] Now under the new Act No. 6331, most of these regulations are no longer valid.

400. Act No. 6331 has now delineated the duties of employees in respecting health and safety matters. Workers must obey the employer's instructions on health and safety and refrain from jeopardizing the health and safety of their co-workers who may be adversely affected by their actions (Article 19(1)).

401. Workers must use the machinery, equipment, dangerous materials and other means of production in a manner consistent with the training and instructions given by the employer. They must not alter these devices arbitrarily (Article 19(2 a)); they must use the protective equipment and supplies correctly (Article 19(2 b)); they must inform the employer or the workers' representative immediately when they

115. The High Court holds that safety training should include not only providing employees with the necessary information but it should also make them fully aware in a proactive manner of the importance and implementation of safety measures. In the special case under consideration the employer was found at fault for not having taken sufficient care in this sense. Court of Cassation General Council Decision, 16 Jun. 2004, 21-365, 2004/369.

116. Council of State decision, 10th Div., 24 May 2004, 2004/1942.

117. For more details on the subject of occupational health and safety, *see* in particular Sarper Süzek, *İş Hukuku*, p. 513; S. Süzek, 'İşçilerin İşSağlığı ve Güvenliği Konusunda Hakları ve Yükümlülükleri', *Legal İş Hukuku Dergisi*, 2005, No. 6, pp. 610–622.

notice defects in the protective devices or an imminent danger posed by the machinery, equipment, installations and buildings (Article 19(2)c) and cooperate with the employer and workers' representative for the elimination of defects and legal contraventions detected by inspection authorities (Article 19(2)c); as well as for the provision of health and safety in their own sphere of activity (Article 19(2)d).

402. As mentioned above, the employee's duty to observe and respect health and safety measures is significant also for the employer's or the employee's liability in lawsuits filed for covering damages caused by industrial accidents or occupational diseases.[118] In case of the employee's failure to respect these measures, the employer may break the worker's employment contract for just cause.[119]

403. The employer must provide workers with proper training on health and safety. This training must be given before the worker begins work as well as in the case of the change of the workplace or the work itself; change of the equipment used and, in the event of application of new technology, training must be renewed in response to emerging risks and, if necessary, repeated at regular intervals (Article 17(1)). The employer must inform the Social Security Institution of any industrial accident within three days following the accident (Article 14(2)).

404. Act No. 6331 has foreseen the publication of implementation regulations. Transitional Article 2 states that the provisions of regulations issued in conjunction with Articles 78–81 and 88 of Act No. 4857 which are not contrary to Act No. 6331 shall be applicable until the publication of new regulations. Suffice it to say that, although not on all pertinent topics yet, several such regulations have already been published, as mentioned in the ensuing paragraphs.

405. With a view to promoting general policies and strategies as well as developing recommendations and proposals on occupational health and safety, a top-level National Occupational Health and Safety Council shall be set up in view of Article 21 of Act No. 6331.

406. Another important measure is the establishment of occupational health and safety boards (OHSB) in establishments where a minimum of fifty employees are employed and continuous work is performed for more than six months (Article 22);[120] the employer has a duty to employ safety experts as well as the liability of safety experts in relation to occupational accidents and diseases.[121] Employers are under the obligation to enforce the decisions of the OHSB taken in accordance with the pertinent legislation According to Article 6 of the Regulation on OHSBs, the

118. Court of Cassation, 9th Div., 13 Nov. 1984, 8256/9776; 25 Jun. 1990, 4838/7758.
119. Court of Cassation, 9th Div., 29 Sep. 2000, 20215/2369.
120. For criteria used in computing the '50 worker threshold', *see* Murat Demircioğlu and Hasan Ali Kaplan, '6331 Sayılı İş Sağlığı ve Güvenliği Yasası Çerçevesinde İşyerinde İş Sağlığı ve Güvenliği Örgütlenmesi', *Sicil İş Hukuku Dergisi*, 2013, No. 30, pp. 9–10.
121. Ş. Eşra Başkan, 'İş Güvenliği Uzmanı Çalıştırma Yükümlülüğü ve İş Güvenliği Uzmanlarının İş Kazası ve Meslek Hastalıklarından Doğan Sorumluluğu', *Çimento İşveren Dergisi*, Vol. 28, No. 4, July 2014, pp. 20–319.

board shall be composed of the following persons: the employer or the employer's representative; work safety expert; workplace physician; person in charge of human resources, personnel management, social affairs or financial matters in charge of employee-related procedures; the civil defence expert, if there is one; the foreman or supervisor; workers' representative (if more than one, the chief representative).

407. According to a new provision, apprentices and trainees shall not be considered within the number of workers at an establishment from the standpoint of Act No. 6331 on Occupational Health and Safety. Health personnel other than the establishment physician shall be employed only in establishments within the 'very dangerous' category with 10 or more workers (Article 16 of Act No. 6552).

408. Act No. 6331 also carries provisions on the establishment of OHSBs in cases where the main employer–subcontractor relationship lasting more than six months exists. Where separate boards have been established, the main employer shall be in charge of ensuring cooperation and coordination between the OHSBs in the execution of the boards' decisions. If one OHSB has been formed by the employer, the subcontractor shall appoint an authorized representative to help provide the necessary coordination between the two (Article 22(2 a and b)). In a similar manner, the main employer who is not obliged to form a board in his establishment shall appoint an authorized representative to ensure cooperation and coordination with the board formed by the subcontractor (Article 22(2c)). If the total number of employees of the main employer and the subcontractor does not require the formation of boards, a board jointly established by the main employer and the subcontractor shall be set up where the coordination shall be fulfilled by the main employer (Article 22(2c)). Where more than one employer operates in the same work area leading to the formation of a multitude of boards, the employers shall supply information to one another on respective board decisions which may have effects on their operations (Article 22(3)). A regulation dated 15 January 2013, No. 28532, has been published to clarify and regulate the working methods of OHSBs.

409. As Act No. 6331 provides, 'any employee faced with a serious and imminent danger may make an application to the OHSB or to the employer if there is no board, and request the verification of the case along with the decision for the implementation of necessary measures. The OHSB must hold an urgent meeting. The board or, where relevant, the employer, must decide on the case immediately and prepare a written report. The decision shall be communicated in written form to the employee or workers' representative (Article 13(1)). If the board or the employer reaches a decision consistent with the employee's request, the employee may abstain from working until necessary measures are taken. Wages and other associated benefits accrued for the time the employee has refrained from working shall be protected. In cases where serious and imminent danger cannot be avoided, the employees, without having to respect the procedure indicated in subsection (1), may leave the dangerous zone and take shelter at a secure place. The employees' rights shall not be restricted for their participation in such conduct (Article 13(3)).

410. The employee working under an employment contract may terminate his contract according to the relevant provisions of law if the necessary measures were not taken in spite of his request. Public employees or public servants subject to a collective agreement are deemed as having actually worked during the unworked period in relation to this article. According to some views in the teaching, the employee must obtain the board's decision not only to exercise his right to abstain from working but also for terminating his contract for just cause by relying on Article 24(2)f of the Labour Act, No. 4857.[122]

411. If an imminent danger to the life of employees, buildings or adjunct facilities, working methods or equipment is found to exist, operations shall be suspended and stopped until the elimination of the said danger, taking account of the risks involved as well as the area and working people that may be affected. Operations shall also be stopped if risk assessment has not been made in establishments in the 'highly dangerous' category like mines, metal-working and construction sites as well as in plants processing dangerous chemicals (Article 25(1)). Following examinations based on the determination of an inspector authorized to make health and safety inspections, a committee of three inspectors may decide to stop operations within two days of verifying the danger. If the facts require an urgent intervention, the inspector making the determination shall stop operations to be effective until the decision of the committee (Article 25(5)).

412. The decision to suspend operations shall be communicated to the local public authority and the Provincial Directorate of Labour and Employment within one day. The decision shall be implemented by the local public authority within twenty-four hours. However, the decision for urgent intervention shall be implemented by the local public authority on the same day (Article 25(3)).

413. The employer may appeal the decision to stop and suspend operations to the competent labour court within six working days of the enforcement of the resolution to suspend operations. The employer's objection shall not affect the enforcement of the decision to suspend operations. The court shall handle the appeal of the employer with a final ruling within six working days. Upon the employer's written notice to the Ministry that defects requiring suspension have been eliminated, the employer's request shall be concluded following inspections at the establishment within seven days at the latest (Article 25(5)). Procedures concerning suspension have been clarified in a regulation.[123] Article 25(6) provides that the employer must pay the wages of employees who, due to the suspension of operations, have not worked, or he must give them other work commensurate with their occupations (Article 25(6)).

414. With a view to preventing occupational health and safety risks and ensuring necessary protections against these risks, the employer is under the obligation to assign workplace physicians and other health personnel as well as safety experts

122. Çelik, *supra*, p. 182.
123. Official Gazette, 15 Mar. 2013, No. 28603.

from amongst his employees. In the absence of qualified personnel in his workforce, the employer may meet this requirement, wholly or partially, by having access to the services of 'joint health and safety units' (JHSU)). Thus, irrespective of the nature of activity, the employer must employ occupational health and safety professionals. The employer must meet all the needs of these professionals as well as the institutions from which he receives such service (Article 6b). However, considering the risk level involved and the number of employees working in his establishment, he may undertake to perform this function himself provided that he has the required qualifications and certificates.

415. A Regulation on Workplace Physicians has been published, describing their training, powers and responsibilities as well as their certification and working times. Another Regulation has been published on safety experts, their powers and responsibilities, their training, classification and working times according to the risk categories involved, based on the relevant articles of the Act.[124]

416. The JHSU is defined as an entity having the necessary equipment and personnel that can supply health and safety services to establishments associated with public institutions and organizations, organized industrial zones and companies operating under the Commercial Code of Turkey. According to the Regulation on Occupational Health and Safety, the JHSU must employ at least one full-time workplace physician, one safety expert and other health staff (Article 12(1)). In either case, that is (1) where the occupational health and safety staff are employed from amongst the employees of the establishment and (2) where services are provided by the JHSU, a contract has to be co-signed by the employer and the respective health and safety experts (Article 14(1)).

417. Article 20, Act No. 6331 has set forth the functions and the relevant procedures for the election or appointment of 'workers' representatives' whose number shall vary between one and six depending on the number of employees at the establishment. Where they exist, union shop-stewards may also perform the functions foreseen for workers' representatives.

418. An important duty of the employer is to ensure the collaboration and coordination between his occupational health and safety personnel or service providers in charge of carrying out health and safety work at his establishment as well as the implementation of the measures proposed by them, in written form and in compliance with the relevant legislation. Article 9 of the Regulation puts the expert in charge of informing the employer, in written form the measures to be taken in relation to occupational health and safety. Act No. 6331 also foresees keeping an approved register to be co-signed by the workplace physician and safety expert, showing the health and safety recommendations to be undertaken in the establishment. The matters contained and co-signed in the register shall be deemed to have been communicated to the employer who has to submit it to authorized inspectors upon request.

124. For further details, *see* the article by Demircioğlu and Kaplan, *supra*, pp. 14–19.

419. Act No. 6331 offers three alternatives to the employer in the provision of health and safety services: as the first option, the employer may employ such professionals as employees in his workforce. The second alternative for the employer is to buy out these services from OHSUs; and third, the employer may perform such services himself if he has the necessary qualifications. Given the constraints envisaged by Article 2 of the Labour Act and the possible problems which may arise, it seems unrealistic to propose the performance of health and safety services through subcontractors.

420. In an attempt to bolster health and safety measures further, Act No. 6331 foresees government support for small undertakings. With the exception of public organizations and institutions, establishments with fewer than ten workers in the 'very dangerous' and 'dangerous' categories shall be entitled to have access to government support. The expenses shall be met by the Social Security Organization through funds to be transferred from the contributions paid for short-term social insurance branches.

421. The duty to apply occupational health and safety professionals applies not only to establishments subject to the Labour Act but also to employers and employees covered by the Maritime Labour Act, Press Labour Act and the Obligations Act. Because of this vast coverage and the sheer numbers involved, the applicability of health and safety requirements under the new Act raises questions, especially with respect to the availability of qualified personnel and the need to provide supervisory inspection mechanisms as well as to align and coordinate the activities of various public agencies involved. Furthermore, the collection of administrative fines which are relatively quite high will not be easy. Also, the employer's duty to make risk analyses and assessments will bring additional hardships to small and medium-sized enterprises. It is for these reasons that the duty to employ health and safety experts has been postponed for certain establishments in different groups (i.e., in establishments with fewer than 50 workers in 'dangerous' and 'very dangerous' risk categories, the Act will go into effect on 1 January 2014; in 'mildly dangerous' category, on 1 July 2016; and for other establishments, six months after the passage of the Act on 30 June 2012).

422. The employer may be held legally liable for material and moral damages in the event of the employee's death, injury or occupational disease. Though legislation has cited many of the protective measures which should be taken by the employer, judicial opinion holds that the employer's duty to protect his employee should be construed to mean also covering efforts to prevent other risks which may arise in the normal operation of the working life. However, there must be a reasonable causal relationship between the outcome (damage caused) and the care that should have been taken.[125] If the employee is covered by the social insurance system, a considerable portion of such damages is met by the Social Insurance Organization. However, the Social Insurance Organization is entitled to have recourse to

125. Court of Cassation, 9th Div., 8 Jul. 1985, 6725/7403; 8 Apr. 1992, 2500/3929; 21st Div., 10 Jun. 1999, 3763/4119; General Council Decision, 5 Feb. 2003, 21–23, 2003/56.

the employer, to third persons and to their employers to recover payments for damages. The employer may also be held liable for damages above and beyond the benefits provided by the Social Insurance Organization (Obligations Act, Article 53).[126] However, there are differing views on the legal basis of the employer's liability.[127]

423. The employee involved in a work injury may claim compensation for the loss in his capacity to work (Obligations Act, Article 112 and 417(3)). In cases where there is a causal relationship between the unlawful actions, the bodily damage (including mental or moral anguish) and the loss inflicted,[128] the employee or his survivors and others deprived of his support or entitled on his behalf may also claim compensation for immaterial damages (Obligations Act, Article 56). But the employee who was at fault in full in the work accident may not demand compensation for immaterial damages.[129] Also, persons whose livelihood was regularly provided by the deceased employee can also file suit for the damages they suffer from the death of the employee due to the employer's failure to take adequate safety and health measures (Obligations Act, Article 56).[130] Legal actions filed for work injuries are subject to statutory limitations of ten years.

424. In addition to legal liability, the employer is also subject to criminal liability in case of his failure to take adequate safety and health measures. The employer or his representative shall be liable to pay a certain fine for each health and safety measure not taken. A fine of the same amount shall be applicable for each ensuing month to the extent that the said measures have been not taken. The obligation to take protective measures covers also other cases of the duty to act in honesty and good faith. In this connection, the employer must take the necessary measures to protect the employee against intrusions into the employee's personality and dignity as well as sexual harassment by other employees and third persons.

425. Considering the sheer number of industrial accidents, Turkey tops the list of countries in Europe and ranks as the third country worldwide. According to the statistics of the Social Security Institution, the number of work accidents was 69,227 in the year 2011 alone where 2,700 persons lost their lives. The number of occupational diseases was 697 in the same year. In Turkey, the mines and shipbuilding yards have proved to be high accident-prone zones traditionally. Despite the presence of Act No. 6331, the recent mining accident of 13 May 2014 in Soma is noteworthy in terms of lost lives (301 miners according to the official figure given) and the strong nationwide reactions it has elicited. As a result, in order to demand the payment of damages, a considerable number of lawsuits have been

126. Court of Cassation, 9th Div., 15 Mar. 1988, 614/2979; 21st Div., 14 Oct. 1997, 5076/6413, in addition to many earlier decisions of the High Court. For the employer's liability, however, it is held that the employer's fault or failure in taking safety measures must be proven. Court of Cassation, General Council Decision, 3 Feb. 2010, 21-36/67.
127. Çelik, *supra*, pp. 187–189.
128. Court of Cassation, Unification Award, 22 Jun. 1966, 7/7; Court of Cassation, 9th Div., 16 Mar. 1989, 12884/2409.
129. Court of Cassation, 21st Div., 27 Apr. 1995, 2143/1921.
130. Court of Cassation, 9th Div., 27 Jun. 1994, 5375/10126.

instituted by the affected survivors and persons against the Soma Holding, the corporate company which has been operating Soma mines, based on a lease contract with the parent corporation, Coal Enterprises of Turkey (TKİ) The incident was proof to the basic argument that the implementation of legislation is as significant as its passage and content, however elaborate it may be.

426. The major coal mining accident following Soma occurred at Amasra in the State Coal Enterprises of Turkey on 14 October 2022, taking the lives of 42 miners. Like Soma, the Amasra accident and the resulting plight of miners also elicited strong reactions from the opposition parties, media and local people. Among the possible causes were cited factors like insufficient safety measures, the contraction of the employment volume through the years leading to higher levels of work load, insufficient auditing by management, poor ventilation and the general inertia of the law enforcement units in penalizing those that were responsible.

III. The Duty of Equal Treatment

427. The constitutional basis of the duty of equal treatment is found in Article 10 of the Constitution of Turkey. In view of Article 10 of the Constitution, 'every person is equal before law irrespective of differences in language, colour, sex, political thought, religion, sect and other similar features'. According to the subsection annexed to this Article in 2004, 'men and women have equal rights; the State must take measures to provide for this equality'. Still another subsection added to the same Article by the 2010 Constitutional amendment by Act No. 5982 provides the following: 'The measures taken in this regard cannot be construed as meaning contrary to the principle of equality, and special measures taken for children, the elderly, the disabled, the survivors of war casualties and veterans shall not be construed as contravening the principle of equality.'

428. Article 5 of the new Labour Act No. 4857 has incorporated this constitutional principle into labour law by providing that 'no discrimination based on language, race, sex, political opinion, philosophical belief, religion and sect or similar reasons is permissible in the employment relationship'. Article 5 further delineates the principle of equal treatment by adding that 'unless there are essential reasons for differential treatment, the employer must not make any discrimination between a full-time and a part-time employee or an employee working under a contract made for a definite period and one working under a contract made for an indefinite period' (Article 5(2)). Also, 'except for biological reasons or reasons related to the nature of the job, the employer must not make any discrimination, either directly or indirectly, against an employee in the conclusion, conditions, execution and termination of his/her employment contract due to the employee's sex or maternity' (Article 5(3)).

429. As the exceptions cited in the above subsections of Article 5 imply, the concept of 'equal treatment' should not be taken literally. The employer must not discriminate among his employees who occupy the same or similar positions in his establishment. The crucial point is the compromise to be made between the 'freedom of contract' and the duty of 'equal treatment' among employees. Once this duty is construed to mean as treating employees in comparable positions who perform similar tasks equally, attention should then be focused on drawing up the limits and exceptions to this general rule.

430. Compared to the now-repealed Labour Act No. 1475, Act No. 4857 has thus brought more elaborate rules on the duty of equal treatment which is essentially consistent with EU directives. Article 5 also addresses the issue of equality in remuneration by providing that 'different remuneration for similar jobs or for work of equal value is not permissible'. And 'application of special protective legal measures due to the employee's sex shall not justify paying him/her a lower wage' (Article 5(4,5)).

431. Legislation has also foreseen the sanctions to apply in the event of violations. 'If the employer violates the above provisions in the execution or the termination of the employment relationship, the employee may demand compensation up to his four months' wages plus other claims of which he was deprived, without prejudice to the provisions of Article 25 of the Unions and the Collective Labour Agreement Act. Without prejudice to the provisions of Article 20 of the Labour Act (concerning invalid terminations where the burden of proof is on the employer), the burden of proof in regard to the alleged violation by the employer of the above-stated rules on equal treatment rests on the employee. However, if the employee shows a strong likelihood (presumption) of such a violation, the burden of proof that the alleged violation has not materialized shall rest on the employer' (Article 5(6,7)).

432. Also Article 122(a) of the new Penal Code No. 2537 provides that any employer who, during the recruitment process, makes discrimination among the candidates based on language, racial background, political opinion, religion or sect or similar reasons, without prejudice to the employer's right to select the suitable candidates, shall be sentenced to a prison term from six months up to one year.

433. As indicated above, the duty of equal treatment is not construed to have an absolute meaning to apply literally in every case. It is generally held, for example, that differential treatment is possible in terms of wages to be paid due to differences among employees as to their skill, training, seniority, merit or dexterity. If employees are granted flat-rate (across the board) wage increases, however, the Court of Cassation holds that the principle of equal treatment should apply in a strict manner.[131]

434. The duty of equal treatment does not apply to the termination of employment contracts. Except for cases where the contract is terminated without a valid reason or where termination is abusive, the employer may terminate the contract of

131. Court of Cassation, 9th Div., 11 Sep. 1967, 3479/7519; 13 Feb. 1986, 12199/1604; 3 Apr. 2000, 1034/4713; 7 Dec. 2006, 12851/32166; 18 Sep. 2007, 28938/26952; 29 May 2009, 32183/7045.

whomever he wishes by giving adequate notice according to Article 17. The same holds true in the event of termination for just cause in accordance with Article 25. It is affirmed, for example, that the employer may terminate a certain employee for his absenteeism even though there might be other employees who have also been absent from work.[132] One should argue, however, that in terminating the employee in such a discriminatory fashion, there ought to be an objective criterion, like the past disciplinary record of the employees.

435. There are certain cases where the duty of equal treatment is construed as having an absolute meaning. Provision by the employer of fringe benefits such as bonuses, premiums, family allowances, etc., for certain employee categories that meet certain criteria is a case in point. Under such circumstances, the employer must not discriminate against any employee who meets the same criterion. The employer is free, however, to extend the fringe benefits to all of his employees or to a certain group or groups of employees, provided that he applies objective criteria in grouping his employees. The employer's duty of equal treatment applies to cases where such benefits are granted only at his own initiative. In cases where providing such benefits has been articulated by the individual employment contract or the collective agreement, the appropriate basis of benefits is then such legal sources rather than the principle of equal treatment.

436. Likewise, instructions and orders given by the employer based on his right to manage must be consistent with the principle of equal treatment for employees in similar positions; that is, the employer must not discriminate among his employees in similar categories in such matters as the implementation of the 'no-smoking rule', in gate search and controls, in the distribution of work including overtime work, in holiday or night work. But here too the collective agreement may have modified the employer's duty of equal treatment.

437. As a rule during a strike, the employer is free to engage or not to engage in work the non-striking employees (Article 64(1), Act No. 6356). However, the Act is not clear as to whether or not the employer may make discrimination in his employment policy among employees who refuse to participate in the strike. Based on the premise that the employer's freedom of action pertains to all the non-striking employees, the generally accepted opinion based on the principles of 'honesty' and 'equal treatment' is that he should not demonstrate any preference in engaging in work employees from among the non-strikers.[133] If he intends to employ such employees, he must give work to all of them without any discrimination whatsoever.

438. Deviation from the principle of equal treatment is possible only when the law permits it. A major limitation is found in the general principles of 'good faith,

132. Çelik, *supra*, p. 197. However, this is a disputed matter in legal teaching. For example, Tuncay's opinion on this matter is in the opposite direction. *See* C. Tuncay, *İş Hukukunda Eşit Davranma İlkesi,* İstanbul, 1982, p. 209.
133. Çelik, *supra*, p. 199.

honesty and fair dealing' embodied in Article 2 of the Civil Code. Constraints have also been laid down in Article 5 of the Labour Act mentioned above. No provisions contrary to these principles may be included in any collective labour agreement or individual employment contract. Furthermore, Article 25 of the Unions and the Collective Labour Agreement Act, No. 6356, emphasizes that it shall be unlawful for any employer to discriminate between employees who are members of a labour union and those who are not, or those who are members of another labour union, with respect to recruitment, the arrangement and distribution of work, promotion, wages, bonuses, fringe benefits, social assistance and application of discipline rules or provisions regarding other questions including the termination of employment. However, collective agreement provisions on wages, bonuses and other benefits are to be reserved (Article 25(2)) (meaning that only members – as well as non-members who pay solidarity dues to the signatory union – may benefit from such collectively negotiated monetary items). Regarding termination of the worker's employment contract for union-related reasons, however, there seemed to be some degree of uncertainty with respect to applying the principle of 'equal treatment', as will be emphasized below with respect to Article 25(5). Fortunately, however, this uncertainty has been eliminated by the recent ruling of the Constitutional Court

IV. The Duty to Provide the Employee with a Certificate of Employment on the Expiration or Termination of the Employment Contract

439. The employer must furnish the employee who leaves his employment for any reason whatsoever with a certificate stating the nature and duration of his employment. The employee who suffers a loss or the new employer who has recruited him may claim damages from the previous employer for the latter's failure to furnish the certificate on due time or for the incorrect information contained in the certificate (Article 28/I, II).

V. Employer's Other Duties

440. The employer must provide the employee with adequate paid weekly rest days (Article 46), annual vacation with pay (Article 53) and rest breaks during working hours (Article 68). Furthermore, the employer must pay the employee who has invented something new during his employment a fair amount if the invention has some economic value (Obligations Act, Article 427). The Decree on the Protection of Patent Rights[134] mentions a regulation to be issued by the Ministry of Labour and Social Security which would provide for the equitable pay rates and the arbitration procedure to apply in the event of disputes concerning inventions by workers. This regulation has not been issued yet.

134. Decree No. 551, Official Gazette, 27 Jun. 1995, 22326.

Chapter 4. Organization of Work and Working Time

§1. Normal Working Time

441. The Working Time Regulation issued by the Ministry of Labour and Social Security[135] in conjunction with Article 63 of Act No. 4857 defines working time as time spent by the employee in work. The Labour Act considers certain time slices not worked by the employee as part of the statutory hours of work (Article 66) and provides that rest breaks shall not be considered as part of the working time (Article 68).

442. The maximum working time which was previously forty-eight hours a week was reduced to forty-five hours by Act No. 2869 in 1983. The working time arrangements in the Labour Act No. 1475 were, however, quite rigid and the need for flexibilization was often voiced by employers' circles and academicians throughout the 1990s.[136] In response to such demands, the new Labour Act did bring various flexible working arrangements on working time as well as on types of work, taking account of the relevant EU directives.[137]

443. Article 63/I provides that 'in general terms, weekly working time is forty-five hours maximum. Unless the contrary has been decided, working time shall be divided equally by the number of week days worked at the establishment.' So, as in the previous system, working time may be divided by the number of weekdays on an equal basis, depending on whether full or only partial work is carried out on Saturdays, as foreseen in Article 4/II of the Regulation. If work is done six days of the week, daily working time is 7.5 hours; if work is only 5 hours on Saturdays, daily working time shall be (48–5 = 40:5 =) 8 hours.

444. According to a new clause added to Article 63(1) by Act No. 6255 of 2014, the working time of workers employed at underground mines shall be thirty-six hours weekly, to be not more than six hours daily (Article 7, Act No. 6225).

445. Provided that the parties have so agreed, however, working time may be distributed over the days of the week in different forms on condition that the daily working time must not exceed eleven hours in any case. But, within a period of two months, the average weekly working time of the employee must not exceed the weekly normal working time (forty-five hours). Insofar as the weekly working time does not exceed forty-five hours, there shall be no need to put into use the 'balancing' act even if daily working times may have varied.[138] This balancing period (two months) may be increased up to four months by collective agreement (Article

135. Official Gazette, 6 Apr. 2004, No. 25425.
136. For details on the previous system, *see* the 1997 edition of this monograph.
137. For detailed information in the English language, *see* the article by N. Süral, 'Reorganization of Working Time and Modalities of Employment Under the New Turkish Labour Act', *Middle Eastern Studies*, Vol. 41, No. 3, May 2005, pp. 407–420.
138. Court of Cassation, General Council Decision, 14 Jun. 2006, 9-734/382; Court of Cassation, 9th Div., 8 Nov. 2006, 7802/29417; 21 Oct. 2008, 25716/28014.

63(2)). Flexibilization as such is consistent with EU Directive 93/104. So if the employer and employee agree, the working time may be distributed to the workdays differently; no longer is there a rigid requirement to divide forty-five-hour weekly working time by the workdays equally. Second, the possibility is brought to raise the weekly working time even above forty-five hours in some weeks, provided that within a two-month period the average weekly working-time of the employee must be equalled to forty-five hours. In other words, the practice of the so-called compressed work week is applicable.

446. The balancing (equalizing) period may be increased up to four months by collective agreement. Employees' consent may be obtained through individual employment contracts, or when this is not practical, through the acceptance by the employees of the pertinent provisions inserted into the rules of work or personnel regulations drawn up by the employer, or through collectively negotiated arrangements. As for the employees concerned, balancing act may be implemented on the basis of the whole establishment, or a section thereof or on the basis of the individual employee.

447. The balancing period is the time span between two to four months beginning from the first day of the application of the compressed work week. In any case, the employer is held to have the initiative either through implicit or explicit individual agreement or through joint decision-making by way of collective agreement. Because working time is a non-monetary issue, an adjustment made in respect to the balancing period shall be binding not only on the members of the signatory union but on all employees working in the establishment, in view of Article 25 of Act No. 6356. The collective labour agreement, if there is one, shall take precedence in any case, as it does have an automatic and binding effect on individual employment contracts. The rules on flexible working arrangements are therefore relatively binding which may be altered only in favour of employees. A collective agreement clause may envisage the distribution of weekly working time to the workdays – not to exceed eleven hours daily – equally or on a differential basis. The ceiling on the length of the balancing period is, of course, mandatory and cannot be altered. In the balancing period, the employee shall not be entitled to overtime pay even when his weekly working time exceeds forty-five hours in some weeks due to the application of the 'compressed' workweek (Article 41(1)).

448. Further, 'depending on the nature of the activity, the beginning and ending times of work may be arranged differently for employees' (Article 67). Thus, flexitime arrangements which were already implemented in some enterprises have also been introduced formally into labour legislation.

449. Thus if the employer calls on compressed workweek upon agreeing with the worker or if agreed in the collective labour agreement he engages the worker in work for more than forty-five hours weekly, he must put into practice what is called 'balancing' within two months, or four months if the collective labour agreement carries a clause to that effect. The two concepts are not on a par; they are separate entities, the latter applicable if agreed to in the collective labour agreement. Of course, a balancing period up to four months rather than two is more beneficial to the employer. The 'two or four months balancing period refers to the time span beginning with the first day on which the implementation has begun and extends into the following two or four months, depending on the agreed time span.

450. To practise the compressed work week, there is no requirement to get an official permission as in the case of 'short time work, for instance. Nor is there any mention that balancing has to be made on a yearly basis. If the application of compressed workweek has started on, say, 15 June, the balancing act must be completed by 15 October (i.e., within four months according to the collective labour agreement). Whether or not the employer may restart a new round of compressed workweek applications before the initial balancing act is completed is not clear. If he does, it is likely to complicate the process even further.

451. Balancing shall be implemented by letting the worker work shorter hours or doing no work during the times which fall outside the application of compressed workweek(s) so as the normal working time shall not exceed the average weekly working time (forty-five hours). How the worker's working shorter hours or doing no work will be distributed throughout the balancing act is not clear; they may coincide with any time slice within the balancing period. As an example, suppose there is an establishment operating five days of the week; if the worker has been engaged in work fifty-five hours weekly for three weeks, he will work thirty-five hours weekly within the following three weeks, in which case his average weekly working time will not have exceeded forty-five hours normal weekly working time. The fact that no upper ceiling has been foreseen for the worker's weekly working time was criticized in the teaching on grounds of the worker's health and safety considerations. Suppose again that the worker, in a six work day establishment with eleven hours of work maximum daily, may be asked to work up to sixty-six hours weekly. The draft bill for the Act had mentioned that in compressed work week applications there should be a reasonable additional ceiling on the daily working time.

452. If the employee has worked more than forty-five hours weekly during the application of the compressed workweek and yet terminated for any reason without the implementation of the so-called balancing act, he shall be entitled to overtime pay for each hour above the forty-five-hours. Because balancing act is complicated and requires expertise, and due to the effects of recession rather than good times, compressed workweek and balancing act seem to be the least utilized form of flexibility measures envisaged by Act No. 4857. On the contrary, short-time work (or shortened workweek) was widely used by many enterprises hit by recession.

453. In moving vehicles engaged in jobs and establishments on highways, railways as well as lakes and rivers which are not subject to the Maritime Labour Act, the working time may not be divisible by the workdays as provided by Article 63 explained above. Therefore, in jobs and establishments where, due to their nature, the application of daily and weekly working times is not possible as foreseen in Article 63, procedures to provide for the implementation of working time in a manner not to exceed the legal daily working time and by allowing a balancing period of up to six months have been indicated in a regulation[139] issued by the Ministry of Labour and Social Security, in conjunction with Article 76 of the Labour Act.

454. The Labour Act treats the following unworked periods as part of the daily working time (Article 66/I):

(a) the time required for employees working in mines, stone quarries or any other underground or underwater work to descend into the pit or vestibules or to the actual workplace and to return from there to the surface;
(b) travelling time if the employee is sent by the employer to a place outside the establishment;
(c) the time during which the employee has no work to perform pending the arrival of new work but remains at the employer's disposal;
(d) the time during which the employee who ought to be performing work within the scope of his duties in the establishment is sent on an errand for his employer or is employed by him in his household or office, instead of performing his own duties;
(e) the time allowed to a female employee who is a nursing mother to enable to feed her child;
(f) the time necessary for the normal and regular transportation of groups of employees engaged in the construction, maintenance, repair and alteration of railways, roads and bridges to and from a workplace at a distance from their place of residence;
(g) However, 'time for transportation to and from the establishment which is not a requirement of the activity but is provided by the employer solely as a form of amenity shall not be reckoned as part of the statutory working time' (Article 66(2)).

455. As regards the last category (g), it has been clearly stated that transportation not required by the nature of the work performed but provided by the employer solely as a form of fringe benefit is not to be reckoned as part of the statutory hours of work. In practice, however, it has often been difficult to distinguish transportation time due to the requirements of the work per se from those cases where transportation is provided merely as a form of amenity. To clarify the issue, the Court of Cassation has ruled on several occasions that, in established settings where the nature of work is stable and permanent, time spent for transportation to and from the workplace should not be treated as part of the normal working time even though the place of work might be far from any centre of habitation.[140] In this case, the provision of transportation qualifies only as an extra service of the employer for social reasons. So, adhering to the exact wording of the article, the Court holds that the period which must be reckoned as part of the normal working time is only the time spent on the transportation of employees to worksites involved in activities such as

139. Official Gazette, 6 Apr. 2004, 25425.
140. Court of Cassation, General Council Decision, 21 Oct. 1970, 9-501, 600/318/443; Court of Cassation, 9th Div., 18 Feb. 1976, 34811; 14 Sep. 1976, 11249/17901; 27 Nov. 1984, 10531/10466.

the construction, maintenance, repair and alteration of railways, roads and, bridges where, upon the completion of certain work, operations are normally moved on to other sites.

456. In normal working time, it should be noted that, in conjunction with Article 63(5) a regulation prepared jointly by the Ministry of Labour and Social Security and the Ministry of Health has been issued, indicating the types of work where the daily working time must be seven and a half hours maximum or less for health reasons.

§2. Night Work

457. For the purposes of the Labour Act, 'night' means the part of the day beginning not later than 8 pm, ending not earlier than 6 am and lasting not longer than eleven hours in any case (Article 69(1)).

458. According to the nature and requirements of certain activities or regional characteristics of the country, regulations may be issued with a view to moving back the beginning of night work to an earlier hour or, in determining the methods to implement the provisions of the first subsection of this article, to rearrange summer and winter hours or to fix the beginning and ending of daily working time, or to apply payment of extra wages to certain night work, or to prohibit night work altogether in establishments where there is no economic necessity for night work (Article 692).[141]

459. As different rules apply to night work, ascertaining whether or not the nature of certain operations qualifies them as night or day work is significant since some operations may fall into both day and night hours. In view of the regulation adopted in accordance with Article 76(2) of the Labour Act, the legal provisions applicable shall be determined according to which more than half of the working time falls into day or night hours. If, for example, 5 hours of a 7.5-hour working day coincide with night hours, the provisions on night work shall apply. Where the two slices are of equal length, principles concerning night work should also be implemented.[142]

460. Due its implications for employee health, the Labour Act has provided certain safeguards, thereby limiting the implementation of night work. 'Night work must not exceed seven and half-hours' in any case (Article 69(3)). Therefore, no overtime can be worked at night hours (Article 41(6)).

461. Further, 'suitability of the employees for night work must be certified with a health report to be obtained before they begin work. Persons who are employed on night work shall be subjected by the employer to a periodic health examination

141. Regulation on operations carried out in successive or rotating shifts, 7 Apr. 2004, 25426.
142. Çelik, *supra*, p. 364.

at least once every two years. The costs of health examinations shall be borne by the employer' (Article 69(4)). 'The employer shall assign, to the extent possible, the employee who produces documentary evidence showing that his health has been impaired as a result of night work to a suitable job in the day shifts' (Article 69(5)).

462. As regards shift work, 'the employer is under the obligation to submit to the relevant regional directorate of labour the list of employees who shall be employed on night shifts as well as a copy of the health reports issued before they had started working in the establishment and then given periodically' (Article 69(6)). Also, 'in establishments where operations are carried on day and night by alternating shifts, the changing of shifts shall be so arranged that employees are engaged on night work for not more than one week and are then engaged on day work the following week. Alternation of work on night and day shifts may also be carried out on a two-week basis. The employee whose shift will be changed shall not be reengaged on the other shift unless allowed a minimum rest break of eleven hours' (Article 69(7,8)). Besides, employees engaged in shift work are entitled, on a rotating basis, to a weekly paid rest day of not less than twenty-four hours (Regulation on operations carried out in successive or rotating shifts, No. 25426, Article 11). Also, employees doing shift work must be granted breaks in conjunction with Article 68 of Act No. 4857.

463. Restrictions on night work have been foreseen for young employees and women. Article 73 provides that children and young employees under the age of 18 must not be employed on industrial work during night hours. The principles and methods for employing women who have completed the age of 18 on night shifts are indicated in a regulation issued by the Ministry of Labour and Social Security upon receiving the opinion of the Ministry of Health (Article 73(2)). These restrictions do not apply to workplaces like hospitals, pharmacies, restaurants, hotels and theatres which fall outside the scope of Article 73.

§3. Compensatory Work

464. The rigid rules of Act No. 1475 did not permit the employers to call on compensatory work in order to offset the lost time caused by economic recession or force majeure or the like. The flexibility brought by Act No. 4857 makes this possible now. Article 64 provides that 'in cases where time worked has been considerably lower than the normal working time or where operations are stopped entirely due to *force majeure* or on the days before or after national and public holidays or where the employee has been granted time off upon his request, the employer may call upon compensatory work within two months in order to compensate for the time lost due to unworked periods'. Compensatory work may be done before or after the emergence of the conditions which necessitate such work.

465. Compensatory work shall not exceed three hours daily, and in any case it must not exceed the maximum daily working time (eleven hours) (Article 64(2)). However, compensatory work may not be carried out on holidays (Article 64(3)).

Notwithstanding this last restriction, it should be noted that, for employees who work five days of the week, thereby using the sixth day (Saturday) as free time, compensatory work may be executed on Saturdays provided the daily working time on such a Saturday should not exceed eleven hours.[143] Implementation of compensatory work shall not be permissible on statutory or contractual holidays.

466. Time lost due to cases of force majeure cited in Articles 24(3) and 25(3) shall be subject to compensatory work, as Article 64(1) suggests, but here other events of an extraordinary nature may also qualify as force majeure. The wage the employee is entitled to receive in return to compensatory work performed is generally his normal wage.[144] In accordance with the Regulation on Working Time, the employer must specify according to which reason(s) indicated in Article 64 compensatory work is required as well as the date of beginning to perform this type of work.[145]

§4. Short-Time Work

467. In an attempt to head off dismissals in unexpected crisis situations under the rigid rules of Act No. 1475, some employers usually allowed their employees to take unpaid leaves or put them on a shortened workweek rather than calling on massive lay-offs. To create a legal framework for such incidents, Act No. 4857 envisaged new rules in Article 65 under the title 'short-time work and its pay'. Article 65, which was later abrogated by Act No. 5763, was transferred with almost the same wording (except for some details on short-time work benefits), to the annex Article 2 of Act No. 5763 by way of making references to Act No. 4447 on Unemployment Insurance. It provides that 'the employer who employs workers under employment contracts subject to the Unemployment Insurance Act No. 4447 may call on short-time work, for a duration not to exceed three months, by temporarily reducing the weekly working time considerably or in the event of suspension of operations wholly or partially'. The Regulation issued in conjunction with this Article provides that 'short-time work means the reduction of the weekly working time at the establishment or a section thereof at a ratio of one-third or where operations are suspended wholly or partially for a minimum duration of four weeks. The employees shall be paid short-time work benefits corresponding to the time not worked' (annex Article 2). To call on short-time work, the employer must fulfil certain procedures:

> The employer who temporarily shortens the weekly working time or who temporarily suspends work wholly or partially in his establishment due to a general economic crisis or *force majeure* must communicate this matter, along

143. M. Ekonomi, 'Telafi Çalışması', *İş Hukuku ve Sosyal Güvenlik Hukuku Dergisi*, Ekim-, KasımAralık 2004, No. 4, p. 1257.
144. For details on wages, *see ibid*., pp. 1258–1260.
145. For short-time work, *see* E. Akyiğit, Kısa Çalışma, TÜHİS, August/November 2004.

with the reasons, immediately to the Employment Organization of Turkey (İş-Kur) and to the union signatory to the collective agreement if there is one. The acceptability of the request shall be decided by İş-Kur and ultimately by the Ministry of Labour and Social Security.

468. The methods and procedures were indicated in the regulations of the Ministry of Labour and Social Security, published in the Official Gazette, 31 March 2004, 6 April 2004 and 13 January 2009.

469. These Regulations on short-time work and its pay[146] brought some clarity to certain issues. For example, the criterion for 'time considerably shorter than' should be understood as reduction of the working time at a ratio of at least one-third of normal working time. The notion 'general economic crisis' would refer to economic recession of a national or international scope as well as a sectoral crisis which affects the national economy to a considerable extent.[147] Force majeure refers to such unanticipated and external events as earthquakes, fire, floods, epidemic or war which are not attributable to the employer's mismanagement and which partially or completely disrupts the performance of the establishment.[148] The Ministry has to make a determination as to whether or not the case in question qualifies as an economic crisis or force majeure. Recourse to judicial process is possible against the determination of the Ministry.

470. The Unemployment Insurance Act Annex Article 2(4) has laid down other details concerning short-time work: The amount of daily benefit for the worker is 60% of his daily gross earnings computed as the daily average of his last 12 months' earnings. But its amount shall not exceed 150% of the monthly minimum wage fixed for workers above the age of 16 designated according to Article 39 of the Labour Act. The transfer of contributions for social insurance branches and transactions concerning health services for workers who benefit from short-time work payments shall be executed in accordance with the relevant procedures foreseen by Act No. 5510. Payments as short-time work benefits shall be deducted from the computed duration of entitlement to unemployment insurance benefits. The Council of ministers has the power to extend short-time work benefits up to six months and the said deductions from unemployment insurance benefits.

471. Among the flexibility measures, short-time work proved to be a widely used practice indeed, especially in times of economic crisis, as evidenced by the number of regulations issued. (By annex articles to Act No. 4447, the maximum period of three months was elevated to six months and the rate of benefit would be paid with a 50% increase, limited only temporarily to the years 2008, 2009 and 2010.) Short-time work shall not exceed the period during which force majeure was

146. Ö. Ekmekçi, *Kısa Çalışma ve Kısa Çalışma Ödeneğinin Uygulamasına İlişkin Sorunlar*, Sicil, Haziran 2009, pp. 49–59.
147. Çelik, *supra*, p. 367.
148. *Ibid.*, pp. 367–368.

effective and in any case three months. In order to have the right to insurance benefits for short-time work, the employee must meet the conditions required for entitlement to unemployment benefits, except for the case of his termination, both in terms of his length of employment and the number of days for which unemployment insurance contributions should have been paid. The daily amount of benefit for short-time work is the same as the unemployment benefit. In the event of force majeure, payment of unemployment benefits shall commence after the lapse of the one-week period envisaged in subsection (3) of Article 24 and Article 40 (i.e., payment of half-wages up to one week). The employer may close the establishment within the duration or at the end of the short-time work practice.

472. Afterwards, with an amendment to the Unemployment Insurance Act No. 4447, Act No. 6111 of 12 February 2011 (*torba kanun*), enlarged the scope of short-time work, providing that short-time work may be implemented also in cases of sectoral and regional crisis situations; and the rate of daily benefit was increased to 60% of the daily gross earnings of the worker, computed as the daily average of the worker's last 12 months' earnings. Further, the government was empowered to extend the duration of short-time work benefits up to six months as well as to decide whether or not they will be deducted from the unemployment benefit (Act No. 6111 also brought various subsidies to social insurance contributions and amnesty for social insurance debts).

473. As these amendments were not perceived to be sufficient, a new Regulation was issued on 30 April 2011 and published in the Official Gazette on 30 April 2011, No. 27920, replacing the Regulation of 13 January 2009.

474. The new Regulation has defined the meaning of the general, sectoral and regional economic crises. The scope of short-time work was further clarified by providing that the concept would refer to the temporary reduction of the working time practised in the establishment or in a section thereof, at a ratio of at least one-third of the working time and entailing the stoppage of work, either entirely or partially, for a minimum of four weeks. The employer contemplating implementing short-time work for the above reasons has to communicate his request to the Employment Organization as well as to the labour union signatory to the collective agreement, if there is one, indicating also the information concerning workers who will do short-time work and attaching the required documents to the application. The employer's application as well as the extent of the alleged national, sectoral or regional crisis shall be evaluated and then decided upon by the management board of the Employment Organization. Thus, according to the new Regulation, the feasibility of the application shall be determined directly by the authority of İş-Kur rather than by the inspectors of the Ministry of Labour, which was the case under the previous Regulation. To have access to benefits, the worker's application is not required. The duration of the benefit is equal to the length of short-time work actually carried out, provided that it shall not exceed three months, to be computed monthly on the basis of the length of short-time work actually done. The amount of the benefit is the same as in the aforementioned Act No. 6111.

475. With respect to different modalities of working time, reference should also be made to categories of work where the daily working time must be fixed at seven and half hours maximum or less for health reasons. A Regulation on that matter prepared jointly by the Ministry of Labour and Social Security and the Ministry of Health was published in the Official Gazette on 6 April 2004, No. 25425. Articles 4 and 5 of the Regulation cite the types of work where the daily working time must be seven and half hours maximum and those where it should be less than this amount. Employees working on such jobs may not be engaged in work on other jobs upon the expiry of the time limits imposed, and no overtime work is permissible in the types of work mentioned in the Regulation, Article 7.

§5. Overtime Work and Work at Extra Hours

476. Overtime work may be performed for purposes such as the country's interest, the nature of the operation or the need to increase output. Overtime work is work which, under conditions specified in Act No. 4857, exceeds forty-five hours a week. In cases where the balancing act is applied in accordance with Article 63, work which exceeds a total of forty-five hours a week shall not be deemed overtime work provided the average working time of the employee does not exceed the normal weekly working time, Article 41 of the Labour Act No. 4857.

477. It follows from this definition that the criterion for overtime work is work that exceeds the forty-five-hour weekly working time rather than work which lasts longer than the daily working time – which was the case under the Labour Act No. 1475. Any work which is in excess of the daily working time will be deemed overtime if the total weekly working time is more than forty-five hours, as also substantiated by the High Court which has ruled that overtime cannot be computed on the basis of the monthly working time.[149]

478. Act No. 4857 also brought a new concept, namely 'work at extra hours'. As Article 41(3) provides, 'in cases where the weekly working time has been set by contract at less than 45 hours, work that exceeds the average weekly working time … and which may last only up to 45 hours weekly is deemed to be work at extra hours'. A regulation on the working methods of overtime work has been published in conjunction with the last subsection of Article 41 (Official Gazette 6 April 2004, No. 25425, hereafter referred to as the Overtime Regulation).

I. Types of Overtime Work

479. Turkish labour law refers to three kinds of overtime work:

(1) normal overtime work, performed for reasons such as the national interest, the nature of operations or the need to increase output;

149. Court of Cassation, 9th Div., 24 May 2004, 1404/12423.

(2) compulsory overtime work: 'All or some of the employees may be required to work overtime either in the case of a breakdown, whether actual or threatened, or in the case of urgent work to be performed on machinery, tools or equipment or in the case of force majeure, provided that overtime work shall not exceed the time necessary for the normal operating of the establishment. In these cases employees must be allowed an adequate time for rest' (Article 42(1));

(3) overtime work in emergency situations: 'During periods of mobilization, the Council of Ministers may, if it deems it necessary and limited only to that period, extend the daily hours of work up to the maximum of which the employees working in establishments serving the needs of national defence are capable, according to the nature of operations and urgency of the needs in question' (Article 43(1)). Also, under the National Protection Act (No. 3780), the government was empowered to extend the hours of work; although this Act has been repealed, some of the subsequent government decrees which extended the hours of work remain in force, as envisaged in Act No. 79 which repealed the National Protection Act in 1960. Further, under the Emergency Administration Act of 1983, No. 2335, working time may be increased in areas where emergency administration has been declared (Article 8) and governmental decrees may be promulgated in case of heavy economic crises (Article 10(1)).

II. Conditions Concerning Overtime Work

480. In normal overtime work the employee's consent must be obtained (Article 41(7)). This consent may be obtained at the time when the employee is hired, or later. According to the Regulation on overtime work,[150] the employer may obtain the employee's approval in written form at the beginning of each year and keep it in the employee's personnel file (Article 9(2)).

481. The requirement to obtain the permission of the regional directorate of labour which existed under Act No. 1475 is no longer required. The employee's consent must also be obtained in the case of work at extra hours (Regulation, Article 9(1)). In the opinion of the Court of Cassation, the employee is under the obligation to do overtime work once the condition of 'approval' has materialized and the employer's instructions concerning overtime work communicated to the employee. If the employee refuses to do overtime, the employer may break the employment contract according to Article 25(2h) unless there is a collective agreement provision to the contrary.[151]

---

150. Regulation on Overtime and Work at Extra Hours, Official Gazette, 15 Apr. 2004, No. 25434.

151. Court of Cassation, 9th Div., 5 Jun. 1980, 6852/6755. 22 Oct. 2010, 2551/4290. On the other hand, in the opinion of the Court of Cassation, the termination of the employee whose prior approval had not been obtained and yet had done overtime work in the past, with his wages paid regularly, shall be considered justified if he refuses to do overtime (9th Div. 8 Oct. 2007, 11936/29817).

482. All or some of the employees may be asked to do compulsory overtime work in order to enable the normal operating of the establishment in which case provisions of Article 41(1,2,3) shall apply (Regulation Article 9(1)). For overtime in emergency situations, a decision of the Council of Ministers to that effect is needed (Article 43). The employee's consent to compulsory overtime work also under emergency situations is not required (Regulation Article 9(1)).

483. Article 41(8) states that total overtime work shall not be more than 270 hours in a year. Act No. 4857 does not refer to any daily or weekly ceiling with respect to the maximum length of overtime (other than the yearly figure of 270 hours). The three-hour weekly maximum foreseen in the draft bill was struck out during the legislative process. Recalling that even in the application of 'compressed work week' the employee's maximum working time must not exceed eleven hours daily (Article 63(2)). This eleven-hour daily maximum shall also comprise the overtime hours that can be worked in a work day, provided the total overtime work in a year must not exceed 270 hours. Unlike Act No. 1475, Article 99/B (2), Act No. 4857 has not envisaged any penal sanctions for overtime work done in excess of this maximum. The Court of Cassation has usually compelled the employer in many of its rulings to defray legal overtime wages also for work performed in excess of the 270-hour yearly maximum.[152] In many cases, though, it has found pay requests for excessive overtime hours as unrealistic and inconsistent with the nature of human capacity, therefore turning them down.[153]

484. Workers employed in mines may not be engaged in overtime work, except for reasons cited in Article 42 (compulsory overtime) and Article 43 (extraordinary overtime). Miners doing overtime work in categories cited as 'compulsory' and 'extraordinary overtime' shall be remunerated for each hour exceeding the weekly thirty-six hours by increasing the normal hourly wage at a rate not to be less than 100% (Article 41 as amended by Article 4 of Act No. 6552).

485. As regards compulsory overtime work, its duration may not exceed the limits necessary to ensure the normal operation of the establishment. Any overtime work executed in accordance with Act No. 79 mentioned above must not be longer than three hours daily.

III. Overtime Wages

486. Wages for each hour of overtime must be remunerated at one and half times the normal hourly rate (Article 41(2)). In overtime for miners in the compulsory' and 'extraordinary overtime' categories, wage must not to be less than the double of the normal hourly wage. In work at extra hours, each extra hour must be remunerated at one and a quarter times the normal hourly rate (Article 41(3)). In operations

152. Of the many decisions, *see*, *e.g.*, Court of Cassation, 9th Div., 20 Nov. 2007, 26362/34664; 29 Dec. 2009, 19722/38425.
153. Çelik, *supra*, p. 375.

where wages are paid on a daily, weekly or monthly basis the hourly wage is calculated first and then any overtime work is remunerated in accordance with the foreseen increment. When piece rates are involved, the overtime rate is to be fixed on the basis of the wages earned for each extra hour worked. Where difficulties are encountered in computing the hourly amount of wages earned for each extra hour worked, the total number of pieces produced within the remuneration period – say, a week or a month – is to be divided by the total number of normal and overtime working hours worked. Thus, the hourly wage earnings corresponding to the average hourly amount produced becomes the basis on which the rate with a 50 or 25% increment is to be computed.

487. The Court of Cassation holds that in the event of a dispute the employee who claims overtime pay must prove that the corresponding overtime was requested by the employer.[154] However, the employer's instructions on that matter may not be explicit. The employee's claim for overtime pay may be justifiable even in cases where the employer has not given written instructions to that effect if his request concerns work which could be performed only through overtime work.[155] Further, if the employer who has actually seen and known of overtime work done and yet has remained silent, it is not appropriate to treat that work as having been performed without the employer's instruction.[156] The Court has also approved the parties' agreeing in the employment contract to consider overtime payments as part of the normal wage.[157] But, the Court accepts this only up to the legal limits; any extra work beyond these limits cannot be considered part of the contract and therefore must be compensated according to the requirements concerning overtime rates.[158]

488. 'If the employee who has worked overtime or at extra hours so wishes, instead of receiving overtime pay, he may use as free time one hour and thirty minutes for each hour worked overtime and one hour and fifteen minutes for each extra hour worked' (Article 41/IV). The employee shall use the free time to which he is entitled within six months, within his working time and with no deduction from his wages (Article 41/V). The employer must go along with the employee's wish, since using free time has been linked to his will. The Regulation provides that the employee must inform the employer in written form of his right to free time which he shall then use in conformity with the requirements of the work and establishment, starting from the date indicated by the employer (Regulation on overtime

---

154. Court of Cassation 9th Div., 21 Apr. 1972, 26738/12364; 15 Oct. 1974, 25820/22200; General Council Decision, 29 Dec. 1973, 91/1229; 9th Div., 17 Sep. 1979, 9524/11091; 5 May 1981, 1183/6549; 19 Feb. 2002, 17563/2912.
155. Court of Cassation, General Council Decision, 3 Mar. 1982, 9-1702/932; 15 Jan. 2002, 14044/204; 25 Sep. 2003, 2312/15347; 9th Div., 25 Sep. 2003, 2312/15347; 1 Apr. 2008, 32439//7134; General Council December 29 Apr. 2009, 9-87/147.
156. Court of Cassation, 9th Div., 17 Sep. 1979, 9524/11091.
157. Court of Cassation, 9th Div., 25 Mar. 1965, 2729/2832; 4 May 1965, 1622/3810; 30 Apr. 1973, 24456/14208; 4 Feb. 1991, 9547/1004; 14 Sep. 1999, 11364/13215.
158. Court of Cassation, 9th Div., 15 May 1997, 5352/9310; 23 May 2000, 3151/7421.

work, Article 6/II). The employee who has not been enabled to use his free time within six months should have the right to claim its corresponding wages.[159]

IV. Activities Where Overtime Work Is Prohibited

489. According to the Regulation on overtime work cited above, overtime work is prohibited in operations were the hours of work must be fixed at 7.5 hours or less, in night work, in the mines, in sewage, cable laying and tunnel construction and similar underground or underwater work (Article 7). Persons below the age of 18 as well those whose state of health has been reported by a physician as being unsuitable for such work – even though the contrary has been decided by the employment contract or the collective agreement – are not permitted to work overtime. Further, persons engaged in part-time work and female employees under confinement as well as nursing mothers shall not do overtime work (Article 8).

V. Overtime Work in Other Labour Legislation

490. The Maritime Labour Act of 1967, No. 854, does not specify the reasons which may necessitate overtime work but provides that work performed above the hours of work prescribed in Article 26 is overtime (eight hours daily and forty-eight hours weekly, to be divided equally by the number of work days). Certain activities which must be performed due the nature of maritime work (i.e., emergency work, fire, evacuation, rescue work, collision at sea and time for health formalities, customs work) shall not qualify as overtime work (Article 28(3)). There are no limits on the length of overtime for seamen, and obtaining employee's consent is not required. The remuneration which must be paid for each hour of overtime must not be less than 25% above the normal hourly rate (Article 28(2)). The employer or his representative must keep a record of the overtime worked in a separate register certified by the notary public. He must pay the seaman his overtime pay in full on the day, at the place and for the period decided in the employment contract for normal wage payments (Article 28(4,5)).

491. For white-collar press employees who are covered by the Press Labour Act, working time that exceeds eight hours daily, either during the day or at night, is considered to be overtime work. Overtime work for such employees must not be longer than three hours daily. Overtime work for less than half an hour is reckoned as 'half-an-hour' and overtime for more than half an hour is rounded to 'one hour'. Overtime pay is one and a half times the wage for each extra hour worked. For overtime work after 12 pm; however, the employee is entitled to an additional wage, meaning 2.5 wages altogether for each additional hour worked, Act No. 6523 as amended by Act No. 212 of 1961, annex Article 1.

159. P. Soyer, 'Çalışma Süresinde Esneklik Sağlayan Düzenlemeler', *Yeni İşYasası Sempozyumu*, İstanbul, 2003, p. 193.

§6. Preparatory, Complementary and Cleaning Operations

492. These are activities which must be carried out before and after normal working hours to ensure the operation of the establishment. The provisions on the organization of work which shall not apply to employees engaged in preparatory, complementary and cleaning operations generally carried out before and after normal working hours, or to what extent, under which conditions and with what modifications they must apply to such employees have been indicated in a regulation[160] prepared by the Ministry of Labour and Social Security in accordance with Article 70. This Regulation is applicable in cases where such work is executed by the core employees of the establishment in addition to their main tasks. If such work is performed by employees recruited especially for this purpose; however, the general principles of Act No. 4857 shall apply (Article 2(1,2)).

493. The additional time which the regular employees can spend on such extra work must not exceed two hours daily (Article 5). Daily working time may not exceed eleven hours in any case. Total overtime for such extra work must not exceed 270 hours in a year. If it does not cause technical problems, the employees concerned must be given a break of not less than half an hour between their regular work and preparatory, cleaning and complementing operations (Article 10). Employees doing such work must be compensated at one and a half times their hourly rate for each extra hour spent on such work (Article 15).

§7. Breaks

494. 'Employees must be allowed a rest break approximately in the middle of the working day fixed with due regard to the customs of the area and to the requirements of the work' (Article 68/I). The purpose of the break is to enable the employee to rest and to satisfy his ordinary needs such as to eat and drink. The duration of breaks has been linked to the length of daily working hours in the following manner:

(a) 15 minutes, when the work lasts for not more than four hours;
(b) half an hour, when the work lasts for more than four hours but less than seven and a half;
(c) one hour, when the work lasts for seven and a half hours or more.

> 'These are minimum durations and the full period must be allowed at each break. The break periods may, however, be split up by employment contract where the climate, season, local custom or nature of the work so requires' (Article 68(2,3)).

160. Official Gazette, 28 Apr. 2004, 25446.

495. 'Breaks may be taken at the same time or at varying times by the employees at the establishment' (Article 68(4)). 'The breaks are not reckoned as part of working time'; therefore the employer is not obliged to pay any wages for these periods (Article 68(5)).

496. The employee may use the break period freely as he wishes. He may spend it outside the establishment. The Court of Cassation has ruled that, if during the break the employee has remained at the employer's disposal pending the assignment of work, the break period should be considered as part of the working time even though he has not actually worked.[161] But if the employee proves that he has been forced to work during the break, the break period is to be considered overtime. There may also be collectively bargained tea or smoking breaks of short duration. The Court of Cassation has held that if the total daily working time has not lasted longer than 7.5 hours, such collectively negotiated short periods during which the employee is engaged in work should not be reckoned as overtime work.[162] Also, according to the Court, the denial to give breaks to the employee does not entail the payment of overtime wages to him,[163] and the employee's spending the break period at the workplace (for example, firemen) is not construed to mean that he has been denied to use the rest break.[164] In the opinion of the Court, the employee who eats his lunch at his work taking care of possible breakdowns and attending machinery is not entitled to overtime pay but the compensation foreseen in the collective agreement should be paid to him.[165] In work areas where there are collectively negotiated 'no smoking' provisions, this restriction should not apply to employees who, by the nature of their work, may smoke without any limitations.[166]

161. Court of Cassation, 9th Div., 25 May 1971, 970/13112 (If in the establishment the working time is longer than 10 hours daily, the break must be 1.5 hours. Court of Cassation, 9th Div., 8 May 2007, 275/06/1455530; April 2009, 34510/12278; 16 Jun. 2011, 18211/18264; 30 Apr. 2012,7031/15007.
162. Court of Cassation, 9th Div., 29 Jan. 1974, 1015/1575. 17 Oct. 1991, 13727/18182.
163. Court of Cassation, 9th Div., 6 Jun. 1986, 4931/5981.
164. Court of Cassation, General Council Decision, 14 Oct. 1992, 9-385/577.
165. Court of Cassation, 9th Div., 26 Oct. 1987, 9437/9596; 29 Sep. 1997, 14003/16572.
166. Court of Cassation, 9th Div., 20 Oct. 1975, 24847/47252.

Chapter 5. Remuneration

§1. The Notion

497. Remuneration (compensation) is one of the main duties of the employer. It is the counterpart of the employee's duty to work. Though based on the freedom of contract, remuneration is also regulated by protective provisions because of its predominantly socio-economic character. Partly because of its social nature, the employer is obliged, in a number of cases, to pay his employees' wages even when no work may have been performed. Wages are protected not only in connection to the employment contract but also in respect to the employee's relations with third parties. As defined by the Labour Act, 'wage is, in general terms, the amount of money paid in cash by the employer or by a third party to a person for the work performed by him' (Article 32). The burden of proof that the wage has been paid, rests on the employer.[167]

498. In addition to the concept of wage in this general sense, however, account must also be taken – in the calculation of wages corresponding to notice pay (Article 17(6,7)) and of wages which form the basis of severance pay (Article 14(11), Act No. 1475) as well as compensation for abusive terminations, for example – of other pecuniary contractual and statutory benefits measurable in terms of money to be paid to employees. This phase of the broader wage concept having been confined to specific cases, then, what is meant by 'wage' is therefore the basic (hourly or piece, percentage and the like) rate which constitutes the base for all wage increases and wage related payments.

499. The employee's actual wage is sometimes understated in the payroll or wage receipt. Such records signed by the employee without any reservation does not indicate that the signed document reflects the employee's actual wage. In such cases the actual wage level of the employee must be determined by taking account the nature of work, length of the employee's service, his work experience as well as wages paid to comparable employees, thus considering all evidential facts together.[168] The same rule shall apply in cases where the wage has not been addressed in the employment contract.

500. The Obligations Act sheds light on the notion of 'wage level' by providing that 'the employer must pay the amount of wage agreed in the individual

---

167. Court of Cassation, 9th Div., 13 Apr. 1990, 1590/4963; 22 Jun. 1993, 15087/10838; 14 Sep. 2000, 7291/11615; 1 Jun. 2006, 36947/5997.
168. Court of Cassation, General Council Decision, 25 Dec. 1987, 523/1106; 9th Div., 14 Mar. 1988, 873/2968; 24 Nov. 1998, 13630/16619; 20 Feb. 2002, 17168/3006, 10 Nov. 2003, 5553/19021, 9 Jun. 2004, 1342/14381. In later decisions the Court of Cassation ruled that the comparable wages should be should be investigated through inquiries from labour and employers' unions: 20 Oct. 2008, 29446/27965; 30 Apr. 2009, 41392/12134; 3 May 2010, 25178/12039, 29 Feb. 2012, 45076/6466.

employment contract or the collective labour agreement, or if there is no clause in the collective labour agreement, a comparable wage to be not lower than the minimum wage (Article 401).

501. Thus, from the legal standpoint, three sources seem to be significant in determining the wage level, namely (a) the collective agreement, (b) the individual employment contract and lastly (c) custom. This means that the employment contract becomes significant if there is no collective labour agreement or if the wage level decided in the employment contract is higher than that which has been collectively bargained; and finally custom will prevail if neither of the first two sources exists.

502. Article 5 of the Labour Act provides that differential remuneration for similar jobs or for work of equal value shall not be permissible. Application of special protective provisions due to the employee's sex shall not justify paying her (him) a lower wage. In the event of violation, the employee may request compensatory damages up to her (his) four months' wages plus other claims of which she (he) was deprived.

§2. Forms of Remuneration

503. Wages may be paid on a time basis (per hour, per day, per week, etc.) or on the basis of performance (e.g., piece rate) or according to results or percentage made by way of tips (Articles 49, 51). The Social Insurance Act makes references to premiums, bonuses, commissions and to profit-sharing (Article 77, Social Insurance Act). Similar references are found in the Obligations Act. In practice payments according to time, pieces, results and percentages are cited as 'wages', while premiums, bonuses, commissions and profit-sharing are usually mentioned as wage supplements.

I. Time Wages

504. Time wages are quite common in Turkish practice. In this category, changes in performance, both in terms of quantity and quality, do not affect the wage level directly; however, the employee may be held liable for having abused the duty of diligence if his performance falls below an acceptable minimum (Obligations Act, Article 396). This liability is rather indirect, though, since it is tied not to the employee's failure to obtain some predetermined result, but to his failure to perform work with diligence and care.

II. Piece-Rate Wages

505. Piece-rate wages are applicable in cases where results of the work performed are measurable in terms of divisible amounts such as pieces, metres or tons produced. Piece-rates are encountered mostly in the textile industry in Turkey. Although piece-rates have certain advantages (e.g., encouraging the employee to produce and earn more), they may entail several drawbacks as well (e.g., tempting the employee to overwork and causing harm to his health, or affecting quality adversely). There is also the likelihood that, due to the slowing-down of the work processes or the employee's being assigned fewer or smaller tasks than customary, the employee's income may fall below the level he would attain if he had worked on a time basis. In this case, the employer is required to make up the gap by figuring out the difference; otherwise the employee is entitled to break the contract for just cause (Article 24(2 f)). In some cases, with a view to do away with such drawbacks, mixed remuneration systems combining time wages and piece rates are put into effect; for example the employee may be put essentially on a piece-rate system, but a minimum hourly wage is also guaranteed; or, coupled with the hourly wage, the employee is paid a specified premium if he produces above a certain number of pieces. Also, the employee must be paid at least the collectively bargained or legal minimum wage if the income he earns falls below these levels. Piece-rate work must be carried out in conjunction with the prevailing working-time arrangements. If the employee engaged on a piece-rate system works overtime, he must be paid overtime wages accordingly.

506. 'Wages by results' to be obtained (*götürü ücret*) could be considered a special version of the piece-rate system. It is generally used in operations that are not continuous by their nature and where unit determination is difficult. Usually a lump-sum payment is fixed as the wage for the result(s) to be obtained and the applicable rules are similar to those in piece-rate systems.

III. Percentage Wages and Tips

507. Employees working in establishments such as hotels, cafes, restaurants, casinos, music and dance halls, clubs, fast-food stands and bars serving alcoholic beverages are usually paid time wages; but occasionally they may be remunerated on a percentage basis; and in some cases combinations of time and percentage wages may be used. Where a percentage wage system is used, the employer must pay all the employees in the establishment such sums of money, without deduction, as are obtained by the employer's adding to the customer's bill a percentage service charge and any amounts of money voluntarily left by costumers with the employer or collected under the employer's direction (Article 51(1)). The employer or his representative is under the obligation to produce documentary evidence that, upon receiving these sums of money, he has apportioned the exact amounts to his employees without deduction (Article 51(2)). The obligation to distribute the monies thus collected is to all the employees of the establishment and not merely to employees involved with direct services to the employees. It is held, however, that the employer is not responsible to apportion the tips left with the employee voluntarily.[169]

508. In line with Article 51(3) a regulation has been prepared and published by the Ministry of Labour and Social Security indicating the principles and rates applicable in the apportionment of the sums collected by means of additions among the employees according to the nature of jobs performed (Official Gazette, 26 February 2004, No. 25387).

IV. Premiums

509. While the above-mentioned categories are treated as 'wages', premiums, bonuses, commission wages and shares calculated on the basis of realized profits are generally considered to be wage supplements in Turkish practice. Premiums which are generally designed to reward extra work (e.g., overtime pay), heavier or hazardous working conditions, increased effort or superior performance may be granted by the employer unilaterally or may have been set out in the employment contract or the collective agreement. However, a continued practice of premium payments unilaterally by the employer can, in the course of time, become entrenched as an employment condition which may give the employee the right to request it periodically.

V. Bonuses

510. Bonuses which are a special form of remuneration paid on certain occasions such as the ending of the working year or in fixed or variable intervals, with a view to motivating employees or to encourage sound labour–management relations, constitute a part of wages if provided for, implicitly or explicitly, in the employment contract or the collective agreement.[170] Even when practised by the employer unilaterally, the bonus qualifies as a wage supplement rather than a donation or gift and is therefore subject to the regulations on wages. The criterion for the bonus is the prevailing wage rate at the time of the bonus payment. Also, if granted by the employer unilaterally but at repeated intervals, it may become part of the entrenched working conditions.[171] Unless decided in the employment contract or the collective agreement or held to be part of the entrenched working conditions due to repeated applications, the employer is free to give or not to give bonuses, or to award such payments to certain categories of employee; but he must not discriminate between the employees within a certain category. Likewise, without prejudice

169. Çelik, *supra*, pp. 155–156. In case of controversy, however, the Court has judged that in the absence of clear witness testimony, the amount of a reasonable tip must be decided via inquiries through professional organizations (Court of Cassation, 9th Div., 27 May 2008, 1648/12819).
170. Court of Cassation, 9th Div., 12 May 1982, 3883/4794.
171. Court of Cassation, 9th Div., 7 Aug. 1969, 1938/640.

to the rights of union members and non-members who pay solidarity dues to the signatory union, no distinction should be made in the payment of bonuses between members of the labour union and those who are not (Article 25(2), Act No. 6356).[172] The employee whose employment contract is terminated at an establishment where bonuses are paid is entitled to bonus remuneration on a prorated basis.[173]

511. Because increasing the number of bonus payments by successive collective agreements had become a widespread practice in the 1970s, Act No. 2448 of 1981 put a ceiling on bonuses, according to which employees who are to be paid bonuses under Act No. 6772 are to be awarded, in addition to the extra payments they receive, a maximum of two bonuses, while those outside the scope of Act No. 6772 may be granted by collective agreements a maximum of four – and those working exclusively in underground operations, five – bonuses a year. However, the Court of Cassation has held that employees with extraordinary performance may be granted a 'motivating bonus' beyond these legal limits.[174]

512. Commission wage refers to the sum of money generally paid to an employee as a percentage of the work he has performed for the employer. Used in certain commercial operations, commission wage resembles the piece-rate system since here too the employee is remunerated according to his performance.

513. In some enterprises such as banks and similar financial institutions, a certain percentage of realized profits is distributed to employees, a practice referred to as profit-sharing. To be distinguished from distributing profits to shareholders, profit-sharing is deemed to be a wage supplement for which the employee, unlike the shareholder, cannot hold the employer responsible for the mismanagement of the enterprise.

514. Both the commission wage and profit-sharing are wage supplements, but neither of them seems to have much significance in Turkish practice.

§3. The Place and Method of Remuneration

515. As a rule, the wage must be paid in Turkish lira at the establishment or it must be deposited into a specially opened bank account. If the wage has been decided in terms of a foreign currency, it shall be paid in Turkish lira according to the currency rate on the date of payment (Article 32(2)). However, if remuneration through a bank account is the preferred method, a wage slip has to be delivered to the employee in each payment. Wage payment must not be made in bonds, coupons

172. Court of Cassation, 9th Div., 25 Mar. 2013/13993 2014/10049.
173. Court of Cassation, 9th Div., 7 Mar. 1972, 26708/6932; 5 Dec. 1994, 13251/17231; 18 Feb. 2010, 17167/3984.
174. Court of Cassation, 9th Div., 12 Jun. 1990, 8137/8212. Notwithstanding this, however, the Court has ruled that no bonus payment may be requested for an unworked period; Court of Cassation, 9th Div., 24 Nov. 2005, 9819/37165.

or papers claimed to represent the national currency or by any other means whatsoever (Article 32(3)). Although the Act is not clear, it is affirmed that wage payments by bank cheques, postal cheques or mail remittances which can be cashed easily are also valid, provided the employee has given his consent[175] to this method of payment.

516. No wage payments may be made to employees in bars and similar entertainment areas where alcoholic beverages are served as well as in retail stores, with the exception of employees working in such establishments (Article 32(6)). The Maritime Labour Act provides that the wages of seamen must be paid at the place indicated in the employment contract (Article 29(2), the Maritime Labour Act).

§4. The Time of Remuneration

517. The Labour Act provides that wages may be paid on a monthly basis at the latest. But the intervals of remuneration may be reduced down to one week by employment contract or by collective agreement (Article 32(4)). Also, upon the termination of the employment contract, the employee's wage claims as well as all the benefits based on the employment contract and law must be paid to him in full (Article 32(5)).

518. The employee may terminate the employment contract before its expiration date or, in the case of an open-ended contract, by not having to respect the term of notice if the employer fails to make out a wages account or to pay wages in conformity with the Labour Act or the terms of the collective agreement or the employment contract (Article 24/II-e).

519. If the employee is remunerated on a monthly basis he may request advance payment from the employer since, too often as a wage-earner, he rarely can manage himself until the end of the month. According to the Obligations Act Article 406, the employer may make payments to him in proportion to his service by way of advances, but for this the following conditions must be fulfilled: (a) the employee must be in need, (b) the amount he requests must have been already earned, (c) the requested advance payment must not pose a difficulty or cause harm to the employer. In practice, half of the employee's monthly wage is paid to him on the 15th or 20th day of the month. After reimbursement of the advance, the remainder is paid to him at the end of the month if the advance payment was made on the 15th day of the month. If the advance was made on the 20th day of the month, then the remainder is paid on the 5th day of the following month.

§5. Wage Slip

520. In wage payments which the employer makes at the establishment or through a bank, he must deliver to the employee a signed slip showing the wage

175. N. Çelik, *supra*, pp. 160–161.

account and bearing the special mark of the establishment. The account slip must include all payments, supplements and deductions, payments for alimony and garnished deductions. These transactions are exempt from all stamp taxes and fees (Article 37).

521. The prescribed statutory time limit for wage claims is five years (Article 32). The right of the employee to claim his wage (that is, each accrued remuneration) ceases to be operative after the lapse of five years from the date on which his wage became due (Obligations Act, Article 149(1)). This means that the statutory limitation does not have to go into effect upon the termination of the employment contract. It is to be calculated for each wage claim which has become due irrespective of the duration of the employment contract.

522. In the event of default, the legal rate of interest shall apply to wage claims. The same rate shall apply to wage claims for holiday pay, overtime pay, paid annual vacation and bonuses. In suits for fulfilment in the case of rights disputes based on a collective agreement, the party held liable to fulfil must pay, as of the date of his default, the highest interest rate charged by banks to credits used in business transactions (Act No. 6356, Article 53(2)). On the other hand, the highest interest rate applicable to bank deposits shall be charged to realized severance pay claims.

§6. Protection of Wages

523. Not more than one-fourth of the wages may be garnished, seized, transferred or assigned to a third party. However, any maintenance allowances awarded by a court to members of the employee's family whom he is required to support shall not be included in this sum. Rights of persons entitled to alimony shall be protected (Article 35).

524. Also, the part of the employee's wages required to support himself and his family may not, without the consent of the employee, be deducted and swapped for any debt (Obligations Act, Article 144(3)).

525. In the event of the employer's going bankrupt, wage claims of employees including severance pay and notice pay for the one-year period preceding the implementation of bankruptcy proceedings must be granted priority following the claims of public organizations and other guaranteed (pledged or mortgaged) claims. In other words, ordinary creditors' claims shall be met only after public and guaranteed debts and wage-earners' claims have been fully reimbursed (Act of Bankruptcy, Articles 206, 207). Similar priorities shall also apply in the case of seizure (attachment, foreclosure) of the employer's property (Act of Bankruptcy, Article 289(3)). Also, if the employer fails to repay his debts due to insolvency, the employee may request some guarantee for a reasonable period, and if the employer fails to fulfil his obligations within the specified period, the employee may terminate his employment contract (Obligations Act, Article 436).

526. In line with the EU Directive 36/80, Article 33 of the Labour Act had foreseen another protective device to guarantee the payment of a certain portion of employees' wages. The provisions of Article 33 were later transplanted into the Unemployment Insurance Act No. 4447 as annex Article 1. In the case of the employer's inability to pay as evidenced by the declaration of a concord by him or the issuance of a certificate attesting to his insolvency, bankruptcy or postponement of bankruptcy, a separate Wages Guarantee Fund shall be established within the Unemployment Insurance Fund with a view to meet the employees' wage claims for the last three months accruing from the employment relationship, In such cases, the worker shall be remunerated on the basis of his basic wage, provided that he has worked at the same establishment within the one-year period prior to the employer's being declared as 'unable to pay'. The Wages Guarantee Fund shall comprise 1% of the annual amount of unemployment insurance contributions paid by employers.

527. A regulation has been adopted in conjunction with the Wage Guarantee Fund and published in the Official Gazette on 18 October 2004, No. 25617. It is held that the part of the employees' wage claims which cannot be met by the wages Guarantee Fund are still to be protected by the above-stated general provisions.[176]

528. Protection of wages is also an issue addressed in relation to the wage claims of contractors' employees engaged in public contract works. Parallel to ILO Convention No. 94 of 1949 concerning public contracts, Article 36 provides that public agencies administered by the general and annexed budgets, local governments, SEEs and banks and organizations established under special laws must ensure, before making any progress payment to a contractor carrying out construction work (i.e., construction of buildings, bridges, railways and roads) as well as repair work, that all the employees hired for such work have been paid their wages adequately by the contractor or a subcontractor, and if there are any employees who have not yet been paid, as determined by the payrolls to be produced by the contractor or subcontractor on demand, must deduct the appropriate amounts from the progress payment to the contractor and pay the employees' wages that are due. Before any progress payment is made to a contractor a notice by the public agency concerned must be prominently displayed in written form in places where the employees gather together. The agency concerned is not liable, however, for any wage claims exceeding the amount of three months' earnings to which the employee is entitled.

529. Any transaction involving a transfer, takeover, sequestration, foreclosing or enforced sale on the guarantees and entitlements accorded by the said contractors to the employers (agencies) concerned may be implemented only on the sum obtained after apportioning the wage claims of the employees who have been employed in such ventures. Any foreclosure and enforced sale imposed on the equipment, materials, raw, semi-finished and finished products and other assets in the establishment of an employer for his debts to a third party is applicable only on the sum obtained

176. Ö. Eyrenci, 'İşin Düzenlenmesi İle İlgili Yeni Düzenlemeler', *Yeni İş Yasası Semineri*, İstanbul, 2003, p. 157.

after apportioning the wage claims of the employees for the three-months' period preceding the date on which the decision for forced sale was taken (Article 36(3,4)).

530. All other employers responsible within the meaning of Article 2/VI of the Labour Act are also authorized to use the powers given to public legal bodies and other organizations referred to in this article (Article 36(5)).

531. Even before the incorporation of the above provision into the Labour Act No. 4857, a Council of Ministers Order in 1988 and subsequent to it, the General Specifications on public works, provided that the contractor's employees must not be remunerated at levels below wages and working conditions for comparable jobs prevalent in the same industry as fixed by law and collective agreements. The reference made to collectively bargained wage levels has in the recent past led to controversy in judicial rulings as well as in the complaints brought by Türk-İş before the ILO's supervisory machinery.

§7. Deduction of Fines from Wages

532. No employer may impose a fine on an employee's wages for reasons other than those indicated in the collective agreement and the employment contract. The employee must be notified immediately, together with the reason, of any fines deducted from his wage (Article 38(1)).

533. Deductions made in this way must not exceed the employee's two days' wages in any one month, or in the case of piece work or amount of work to be performed, the wages earned by the employee in two days (Article 38(2)). These deductions shall be credited within one month to the account of the Ministry of Labour and Social Security in a bank established in Turkey and must be designated by the Ministry for use in the training of and social services for employees. Every employer shall keep a separate account in his establishment showing such deductions. A committee presided over by the Minister of Labour and Social Security and including employees' representatives shall decide where and to what amounts the fines thus collected are to be used. Rules for the establishment and working methods of this committee shall be indicated in a regulation (Article 38(3)). The employer who violates Article 38 shall be held liable to pay a fine foreseen in Article 102/b.

534. Article 62 provides that 'no deductions of any kind may be made from an employee's wages on grounds that the daily or weekly working hours applicable to any type of work have been reduced by law, or by reason of the fulfilment by the employer of any legal obligation or because of any mandatory obligation imposed on the employer by the provisions of this Act'. Naturally the restriction addressed in Article 62 does not cover the reduction of working time by collective agreement or employment contract. In other words, the employee who has accepted employment on the basis of a forty-two-hour working week, for instance, cannot request remuneration for a forty-five-hour working week which is the maximum foreseen in Article 63. Self-evidently the employer may conclude employment contracts or collective agreements involving working hours of either more or less than forty-two hours per week, at prevailing or increased wage rates. What Article 62 means is that the employer is not allowed to lower employees' wages if he reduces working time unilaterally – without the employees' consent, or if such reduction in working time is necessitated by a legal obligation. It does not pertain to lowering wages as a result of changed working conditions mutually agreed to by the parties of the employment contract or the collective agreement,[177] although the Court of Cassation has predicated some of its rulings on this article even in cases where wages were reduced by the agreement of the parties.[178]

§8. Non-payment of the Wage on the Day Due

535. 'The employee whose wage has not been paid within twenty days of the date on which it was due, except for *force majeure*, may refrain from fulfilling his obligation to work.' Even when refraining from work by employees based on their personal decisions takes on the character of a concerted action, it shall not be treated as a strike. The highest interest rate applicable to bank deposits shall be levied on wage-related debts of the employer who has defaulted to pay wages on the day they were due.[179]

536. Employment contracts of employees shall not be terminated solely because they have refrained from working due to the employer's default; no replacements shall be hired, nor may their work be performed by others' Article 34(1, 2).

537. This new clause in the Labour Act seems to fill an important void in Turkish practice. It aims to head off allegedly unlawful industrial action in the form of employees' collective refusal to work to protest the non-payment of wages which in the past had resulted in allegations of illegal strikes which in turn used to lead to mass lay-offs. Despite resistance by employers who asserted that strike action was again made possible for rights disputes – apparently not recognized by the Constitution of 1982 – labour unions hailed it as a significant gain. Furthermore, the employee retains the right to break his employment contract for the non-payment of his wage according to Article 24/II-e. Besides, the worker has the right to receive severance pay. Payment of wages only partially does not affect the worker's right to terminate and demand severance pay.

177. Çelik, *supra*, pp. 166–168.
178. Court of Cassation, General Council Decision, 21 May 1986, 1985/9–110, 1986/546; Court of Cassation, 9th Div., 1 Apr. 1991, 13699/6898; 29 Jan. 1996, 26217/893; 2 Jul. 1997, 10825/13495. Wage may be reduced by agreement of the parties, 28 Dec. 2004, 4975/29754.
179. According to a ruling of the Court of Cassation, however, the employee's claim for the reimbursement of the twenty days' unpaid wages should be overruled since he had refrained from working on his own volition. Court of Cassation, 9th Div., 10 Feb. 2005, 13259/3782. However, the High Court's position on this matter seems to have changed in favour of the worker (*see* Court of Cassation, 9th Div., 16 Nov. 2009, 10493/31940.

538. Under the title of 'violation of the freedom to work', the new Penal Code No. 2537 has brought penal sanctions to apply against the offenders who violate the duty to pay wages. Persons who exploit needy people by paying them no wages or who refuse to pay adequate wages or who subject them to working or accommodation conditions incompatible with human dignity shall be indicted to a prison term from six months up to three years or to a major fine, Article 117(2). Further, persons who, by using force or exerting threats, compel employees and their employers to lower or raise wages or push them into accepting new agreements shall be sentenced to the same penalty, Article 117(4).

§9. THE MINIMUM WAGE

539. Article 39 of the Labour Act deals with the principles of minimum wage fixing: 'with the object of regulating the economic and social conditions of all employees working under employment contract, and irrespective of the coverage of the Labour Act, the minimum limits of wages shall be determined every two years at the latest by the Ministry of Labour and Social Security through the Minimum Wage Fixing Board' (Article 39(1)). Thus, provisions on minimum wages apply to all employees working under employment contracts covered by the Labour Act, Maritime Labour Act, Press Labour Act as well as the Obligations Act in general. Apparently, the rationale underlying the broad coverage of Article 39 is the general motive of providing social justice in conformity with Articles 49 to 55 of the Constitution which impute to the state the tasks of providing social justice and a just wage for the working people.

540. The Minimum Wage Regulation as foreseen by Article 39 and published in the Official Gazette 1 August 2004, No. 25540 defines the minimum wage as the 'daily wage sufficient to meet the minimum needs of the employee relating to food, housing, clothing, health, transportation and education at current prices'. It is inferred from this definition that only the needs of the employee himself are taken into consideration.

541. However, as some writers argue, minimum wage should be construed as meaning a level sufficient to meet the needs of not only the single employee but also those of his (her) potential dependants.[180] As a matter of fact, in minimum wages certain increments were made in some years in the past to account for the employee's family as well. The phrase 'regulating economic and social conditions of employees' as envisaged in Article 39 also attests to this broader concept of the minimum wage. Notwithstanding these views, minimum wage practice of recent years has comprised only the single employee. Further the fact that minimum wage is subject to income tax brings heavy criticisms from labour unions and pro-labour circles.

---

180. Çelik, *supra*, pp. 170–175; M. Kutal, Asgari Ücret, İstanbul, 1969, p. 325; T. Centel, *İşHukukundaÜcret*, İstanbul, 1988, p. 186; M. Demircioğ lu and T.Centel, *İş Hukuku*, İstanbul, 2003, p. 118.

542. Furthermore, the minimum wage level also affects the salary of public servants who, being subject to public law, are outside the scope of labour legislation. According to Article 146 of Act No. 1897, which amended the Public Servants Act No. 657, the minimum monthly salary to be paid to public servants must not be less than the monthly amount of the current minimum wage.

543. A minimum wage may be fixed on a local, regional or national basis, for a branch of activity or for all branches nationwide. No discrimination based on sex or age is permissible (Regulation, Articles 2 and 3). However, a minimum wage is fixed for those above and below the full age of 16 separately. The minimum wage-fixing board shall, in determining the minimum wage and, according to the coverage mentioned in Article 2, take into consideration the social and economic conditions and cost of living indices for wage-earners, and if these do not exist, general cost of living indices, current wage levels and the nature of the branch(es) of activity (Regulation, Article 5).

544. No remuneration below the minimum wage level is to be allowed. Any agreement below that level (by employment contract or collective agreement) is void. In such a case, the employee's pay must automatically be elevated to the legal minimum wage level. However, an employee working only part-time for an employer is not entitled to receive the full minimum wage. He shall receive only the fraction of the minimum wage corresponding to the length of time of his daily work. Likewise, the employee who has concluded employment contracts with different employers shall not be paid the minimum wage separately by each employer. In this case, the employee's remuneration must not be less than the prorated amount of the minimum wage adjusted to the length of time worked under each employment contract.

545. As a rule, minimum wage is fixed on a daily basis, and adjustments are made accordingly for monthly, weekly and hourly wages as well as for performance – based and piece-rate systems (Article 4). As indicated above, the wage of the employee working part-time in more than one establishment is to be prorated according to the total number of working hours and days worked.[181]

546. The employee who works full-time according to normal working time may not be remunerated below the minimum wage level. If the contrary is found to be the case, the severance and notice pay of the employee must be computed according to the legal minimum wage.[182] Self-evidently the employee also has the right to break the contract for just cause and file legal action to claim damages (Article 24).

181. Court of Cassation, 9th Div., 5 May 1975, 7229/29109; 9 Oct. 1978, 11787/14975; General Council Decision, 15 Dec. 1978, 1977/10-519, 1978/1142; 16 May 1994, 7505/7380; 3 Jul. 1996, 9759/15333.

182. Court of Cassation, 9th Div., 18 Dec. 1997, 18159/21849; Court of Cassation General Council Decision, 12 Mar. 2003, 21143/159.

547. Minimum wage-fixing relates only to the basic wage; in other words, wage supplements and fringe benefits are not considered in fixing the minimum wage.[183]

548. No deductions may be made from the minimum wage as a result of granting employees fringe benefits (Regulation, Article 10-III).

549. Minimum wages are fixed by a central board. The Minimum Wage Fixing Board, presided over by one of its members to be designated by the Ministry of Labour and Social Security, shall be composed of the General Director of Occupational Health and Safety or his deputy, the chairman of the Economic Statistics Department of the State Institute of Statistics or his deputy, representative of the Under-Secretariat of Treasury, the head of the relevant department of the SPO or his representative, five employee representatives from different branches of activity elected by the highest-ranking labour organization representing the majority of employees and five employer representatives elected by the employer organization representing the majority of employers. The Board meets with at least then members present and takes its decisions by majority vote. In the event of a tie, the chairman has a casting vote (Article 39/II).

550. Before the legislation of 1971 (Act No. 1475), minimum wages used to be fixed by local commissions. By establishing a central board, Act No. 1475 gave birth to a centrally-fixed minimum wage system and thus eliminated the complications which had arisen from differentiated minimum wage levels under the old system.

551. Due to serious industrial accidents in May 2014 at Soma coal mines, Act No. 6552, envisaging the improvement of coal miners' working conditions and in response to mass protests, set forth in Article 9 the following rule by adding an annex article to the Mining Act No. 3213, dated 4 June 1985, which says: 'In establishments in group 4 cited in Article 2 of this Act where lignite and coke are extracted, the wage to be paid to underground workers shall not be less than twice the amount of the minimum wage determined in accordance with Article 39 of the Labour Act, No. 4857.'

552. Decisions of the Board are mandatory and final, meaning that the Ministry of Labour is not authorised to alter them. But, like every administrative action, decisions of the Board are subject to the judicial review of the Council of State. If the Council of State repeals the decision of the Board, the minimum wages already paid in accordance with the Board's decision do not constitute a vested right for employees.[184] The Board's decision comes into force at the beginning of the month following the date of its publication in the Official Gazette. Certainly, the employee whose wage has been paid below the minimum wage level has the right to access to legal

183. Metin Kutal, 'Asgari Ücret Kavramı', *İHD* Vol. 1, No. 5, p. 427.
184. Court of Cassation, 9th Div., 6 Feb. 1968, 1822/1418 and 1799/1417.

action to recover his/her claims; besides he/she can terminate the employment contract for just cause in accordance with Article 24/II; likewise the employer may be sentenced to the fine set out in Article 102(a) of the Labour Act.

553. Once the minimum wage is fixed every two years and, in recent years, more often, all wages below the new minimum prevailing at the establishment, either by collective agreement or employment contracts, must be elevated to the increased level. Correct calculation of the erosion in real wages due to high inflationary pressures has become a serious issue of concern for workers as well as for the general working population and retirees (pensioners). And this has made 'minimum wage fixing' in more frequent time intervals an urgent matter. It is estimated that on the average about 50% the working population in Turkey live on the minimum wage level; in other words half of the wage and salary earners receive the minimum wage on average.

554. The term 'minimum wage' is also used to denote the floor of collectively bargained wages. In the past a controversial point was the temptation of unions to win wage increases over and beyond the new legal minimum wage The Court of Cassation had ruled, however, that the negotiated wage increase should apply to actual wages rather than being treated as an additional increment based on the difference between the new and the previous minimum wage levels.[185]

555. Likewise, in the event of the minimum wage increase succeeding in time the implementation of a collectively negotiated wage increase, the union may not request the adding the collectively negotiated increase onto the minimum wage level if the actual wage is already above the new minimum wage.[186] However, as a general tendency of wage behaviour, a new minimum wage level indirectly boosts up all wages, especially collective bargaining wages throughout the economy.

§10. Pay for Time Not Worked Within Working Hours

556. The general rule is to pay for time worked, but there are certain categories when pay for time did not work such as national holidays, weekly rest day and paid annual leave, all of which are explained in the pertinent paragraphs below.

557. However, the law also entitles the employee, under certain circumstances, to receive remuneration even though he may not actually have worked within normal working hours. These circumstances can be studied under three headings: (1) If the employer, without wishing to terminate the employment contract, refuses to

185. Court of Cassation, General Council Decision, 16 Dec. 1972, 9-1313/1400; For a contrary view asserting the imposition of the minimum wage difference on collectively bargained wages, *see* S. Reisoğ lu, 'Toplu İş Sözleşmeleri Açısından Asgari Ücret', *TÜHİS*, Kasım 1988, 9; and the Court of Cassation decision in the same direction cited by Reisoğ lu, 9th Div., 13 Sep. 1988, 5863/7997.
186. Court of Cassation, 9th Div., 30 May 1975, 13044/33203.

accept the labour of the employee (*mora creditoris*), (2) when it becomes impossible for the employee to render his service and (3) force majeure.

I. *Mora Creditoris*

558. An employer's default to accept the employee's labour has been envisaged in the Obligations Act which provides, in Article 408 that 'if the employer defaults to accept his labour, the employee is entitled to request the payment of his wage even though he may not have performed the work agreed upon in the employment contract, provided that the amount the employee has saved by not performing the work or the amount he has gained by doing, or failed to gain by not doing some other work, must be deducted from his wage'. Parallel to the Obligations Act, the Labour Act sets forth a general rule in Article 66(1) (c): 'the time during which the employee has no work to perform pending the arrival of further work, but remains at the employer's disposal, shall be reckoned as part of the statutory hours of work'. However, the provision envisaged in the Obligations Act is also significant, especially in practice, as it indicates what should be done in the event of *mora creditoris*. For the presence of *mora creditoris*, however, the employer's refusal to accept the employee's labour should not have stemmed from a just cause.[187] In the past when job security was absent in Turkish labour law, court rulings had established a link between unjustified dismissals and *mora creditoris*.

II. Sickness, Pregnancy, Military Duty

559. There are provisions in legislation which require remuneration in certain cases when it becomes impossible for the employee to perform work, such as sickness, pregnancy and military duty. Collective agreements may also regulate some of these matters as well as ensuring the payment of wages in the event of the birth of a child, death of the spouse or of relatives, civic duties such as serving as a witness in court, and other justified leaves of absence.

560. Only that category of salaried employees who are paid their wages on a monthly basis are entitled to remuneration during sickness (Article 49(4)). The difference between their wages and the temporary disability benefits paid by the Social Insurance Organization must be met by the employer. Such employees also receive their wages in full when they are on leave for any reason (Article 48(2)). If they have worked on national and public holidays, they shall be paid an additional one day's wage for each such holiday on which they have worked. In other categories of wage payments, the employer is not obliged to pay wages for sickness or any leave of absence unless the contrary has been decided in the employment contract or the collective labour agreement.

187. K. Tunçomağ, *İş Hukuku-I*, İstanbul, 1979, p. 251.

561. During pregnancy the female employee is not entitled to remuneration, as her contract is deemed to have been suspended during the periods foreseen in Articles 25/I and 74, since as a general rule no wages are to be paid for the period during which the employee fails to report to work due to the suspension of the employment contract (Article 25/I, last sentence). Such an employee is to be paid temporary disability benefits by the Social Insurance Organization for the days she is absent from work due to pregnancy and confinement.

562. A female journalist, on the other hand, is to be granted maternity leave with pay equal to half her wages starting from the seventh month of her pregnancy until the end of the second month following the birth of her child; any benefits granted by other organizations shall not cause a reduction in the above-mentioned wage (Press Labour Act, Article 16).

563. The Labour Act does not provide any protection for the wages of employees who leave their employment to do military duty. The only protection is the suspension of the employment contract, with no wages involved, for a period of from two to three months if the employee has been called up, after the completion of his regular compulsory military service, to take part in manoeuvres, or if he has left his employment to perform statutory labour service. Journalists, on the other hand, who are on similar short-term military duty or drafted for partial or general mobilization are entitled to receive their wages (Press Labour Act, Article 16(1,2)). Moreover, the journalist drafted for the first time to do his regular military service must be paid half his last wages throughout the duration of his service (Article 16(3)).

III. Force Majeure

564. An employee must be paid half his wage, for each day up to one week if he cannot work or is not given work because of force majeure, as provided in Articles 24/III and 25/III of the Labour Act, which also enable both the employee and the employer respectively to terminate the employment contract without having to respect any term of notice.[188]

188. *See also* Arts 24/III and 25/III of the Labour Act.

Chapter 6. Weekly Rest Day, Paid Vacations and Annual Leave with Pay

§1. Weekly Rest Day

565. The 1982 Constitution of Turkey has guaranteed, in Article 50(3 and 4), the right of every working person to paid vacations, a weekly rest day and paid annual leave. The Labour Act as well as other legislation has brought various provisions addressing these issues. According to the Weekly Rest Act No. 379 (Official Gazette 21 January 1924, No. 54), all establishments in places with a population of 10, 000 or more must allow employees a weekly rest day, Article 1, and employees should not be forced to work more than six days a week (Article 2). Violation of these rules entails a fine (Article 10). Only agriculture, hunting, fishing, forestry and related activities have been excluded from the weekly rest day requirement (Article 3).

566. Normally employees take their weekly rest on Sundays; however in certain establishments and activities which must carry on their operations continuously – such as hospitals, pharmacies, public baths, public utilities, transportation services, hotels and restaurants, bakeries, vegetable and fruit sellers, some construction and farm products-processing operations, etc. – Sunday may not serve as the weekly rest day for all employees, but those who do not benefit from the Sunday rest must be allowed another rest day with pay each week (Articles 4, 5).

567. Similarly employees like guards and janitors who are employed on security, maintenance and similar services even on Sundays as well as employees in establishments excluded from the weekly rest day in accordance with Articles 1, 4, 5 and 6 of Act No. 79 must be allowed another rest day with adequate remuneration each week.

568. Article 46(1) of the Labour Act provides that 'the employees covered by this Act must be allowed to take a rest for a minimum of 24 hours (weekly rest day) without interruption within a seven-day period, provided they have worked on the days preceding the weekly rest day as indicated in Article 63' (concerning working time).

569. It follows from this that a part-time employee working half days on all the workdays of the week shall be entitled to a weekly rest day with pay, while a part-time employee working three workdays of the week shall not receive pay for the weekly rest day. As a rule, however, 'for the non-worked weekly rest day, the employer shall pay the employee's daily wage, without any work obligation in return' (Article 46(2)).

570. The employee who works on Sunday in establishments excluded from Sunday rest – as alluded to above – and takes his weekly rest on some other day of the week shall receive only one day's pay for his work on Sunday.[189]

571. Employees engaged in work on their weekly rest day (Sunday or another day of the week) are paid their weekly rest day wages plus one and a half times that wage, since work exceeding forty-five hours is held to be overtime.[190] Thus, altogether, the employee is paid two and a half days' wages for having worked on his weekly rest day. In some of the major collective agreements, unions have been able to increase overtime pay for work on weekly rest days even further. In the event of shift work, however, the employee who starts his shift at, say, 24.00 pm on Saturday and works until 8.00 am on Sunday is not treated as having worked overtime, since this is the natural result of shift work and the employee is to be allowed another day off of the week as his rest day.[191]

572. The law provides that, in order for the employee to benefit from a paid weekly rest day, certain non-working periods shall be reckoned as part of the requirement to have worked a certain length of time as set out in Article 63. These are (a) time periods deemed to be part of the working time although no work has been done (Article 66), and any periods of holidays with or without pay, either statutory or contractual; (b) up to three days of leave of absence in the event of the employee's marriage and up to three days leave in the event of the death of the employee's mother, father, spouse, brother or sister and child; (c) any leave granted by the employer and any sick or convalescent leave based on a medical report, subject to a maximum of one week (Article 46(3)).

573. If the employer, without being obliged to do so by force majeure or economic reasons, suspends work on one or more days of the week, those days on which no work has been done shall be reckoned as days worked in order to have access to paid weekly rest day (Article 46(4)). If work is suspended in an establishment for more than one week on account of force majeure, the half-wages payable to employees up to one week for days not worked due to force majeure in accordance with Article 24/III and Article 25/III shall be paid also for the weekly rest day (Article 46/V). 'In establishments where a percentage wage system is in effect, the wage for the weekly rest day shall be paid to the employee by the employer' (Article 46(6)). In that case, the weekly rest day pay shall be computed by dividing the total wage income for that week accumulated on a percentage basis by the number of days worked'.

---

189. Court of Cassation, 9th Div., 18 Jun. 1974, 20266/12804; 3 Nov. 1988, 9281/11508; 1 Feb. 1990, 9833/899; 30 Oct. 2001, 14351/16856; 23 Feb. 2010, 14745/4500.
190. Court of Cassation, 9th Div., 27 Sep. 1984, 7043/8302; 23 May 1996, 37960/11745; 9 Apr. 2012, 2011/44976; Court of Cassation, 22nd Div., 22 Jan. 2013, 10831/372.
191. Court of Cassation, 9th Div., 17 Feb. 1975, 74/27048; 13 Feb. 1986, 11819/1609.

574. The Obligations Act also provides that the employer must allow the employee a full weekly rest day on Sundays and, if working conditions do not permit it, on another day of the week (Article 421(1)).

§2. National and Public Holidays

575. Employees in establishments covered by the Labour Act must be paid a full day's wages for the national and public holidays on which they have not worked; if they work instead of observing the holiday, they must be paid an additional full day's wage for each day (Article 47(1)). In this case, wage claims are to be based on wages realized in their respective terms rather than the last current wage.[192] In view of a significant ruling of the Court of Cassation ensuring the reimbursement to the plaintiff worker several claims, 'if engaged in work even for one hour on a public or national holiday the worker shall be entitled to a full day's wages' (construed as meaning in fact to two days' wages altogether within the context of Article 47 of the Labour Act) (Court of Cassation, 9th Division, 15760/2020, 4806).

576. Employees who work intermittently as the need for their service arises shall not be paid holiday wages for holidays which coincide with the intervals when no work is performed.[193] 'In establishments where a percentage wage system is in effect, the wage for the national and public holiday shall be paid to the employee by the employer' (Article 47(2)).

577. According to Act No. 2429 on National and Public Holidays (as amended on 20 April 1983): the National Holiday is the 29 October, the anniversary of the date on which the Republican regime was founded in 1923; it starts in the afternoon of the 28 and continues on the 29 October. Public holidays are the following: 23 April, National Sovereignty Day; 19 May, the Youth and Sports Day; 15 July, Democracy and National Unity Day; 30 August, Victory Day; 1 January, the New Year Day; the Ramadan Holiday, three and a half days and the Sacrifice Day, four and a half days (dates rotating according to Arabic calendar).

578. If the weekly rest day coincides with the national holiday or a public holiday, the employee is entitled to only one-day's wages.[194] This is the widely shared interpretation and also the opinion of the Court of Cassation. Likewise, in establishments where employees do not work on Saturdays, the employee must be paid only one-day's wages if Saturday coincides with the National Holiday or a public holiday.[195]

192. Court of Cassation, 9th Div., 18 Feb. 2002, 101/2797.
193. Court of Cassation, 9th Div., 23 Sep. 1996, 15976/17646.
194. Court of Cassation, 9th Div., 18 Feb. 1970, 10027/11680.
195. Court of Cassation, 9th Div., 20 Jun. 1974, 30174/12817.

579. Likewise, if the last day of the public holiday coincides with Friday and the employee has been engaged in work on the following Saturday, he cannot claim holiday pay.[196]

580. All establishments, public and private, must suspend their operations on the National Holiday (29 October). On other public holidays, only official establishments have to close down. Collective agreements or employment contracts may carry provisions as to whether or not operations would continue on the National Day and public holidays in establishments, private or public, which are covered by the Labour Act. Where there is no clause in the collective agreement or the employment contract, the employee's consent is required for work on such days (Article 44(1)).

581. Regarding the suspension of operations on the National Day, the question arises as to the establishments where, due to the nature of work, operations must be carried out continuously. Since the continuity of operations is a necessity in such establishments, it could be inferred from the wording of Article 44 as well as Article 47, that, they shall be permitted to operate on 29 October as well.[197]

582. Article 47(1,2) provides that 'employees in establishments covered by the Labour Act shall be paid a full day's wages for the National and public holidays on which they have not worked; if they work instead of observing the holiday, they shall be paid an additional full day's wages for each day worked. Where a percentage wage system is in effect, the wage for the National and public holidays shall be paid to the employee by the employer'.

583. According to Article 50, 'the following payments shall not be considered for the purpose of calculating payments in respect of National Day or for public holidays or weekly rest days: Overtime pay and incentive premiums, wages paid to permanent employees of the establishment when they are employed outside normal working hours in preparatory, complementary or cleaning operations; and fringe benefits'. Thus, Article 50 implies that only the basic wages are to be taken into account in computing holiday pay, as also upheld by the Court of Cassation.[198]

§3. Calculation of Holiday Pay According to the Type of Remuneration System

I. In General

584. Article 49(1) provides that holiday pay of an employee is the daily amount he receives in proportion to the total sum of the days he has worked. Article 49 foresees the methods of calculating holiday pay in relation to the different remuneration

196. Court of Cassation, 9th Div., 23 Oct. 2003, 17723/17653; 23 Oct. 2005, 17723/17653.
197. Çelik, *supra*, p. 387.
198. Court of Cassation, 9th Div., 1 Apr. 1985, 810/3317; 3 Nov. 1998, 15053/16953.

systems, namely according to hourly, daily and weekly wage as well as for salaried employees remunerated on a monthly basis mentioned below.[199]

585. In an hourly wage system, the holiday pay of an employee is 7.5 times his hourly rate (Article 49(3)). If the employee's wage has been determined on a daily basis, it serves as the basis for holiday pay. Where the employee receives his daily wages on a monthly basis, however, the wages for days on which he has not worked shall naturally be deducted from his monthly pay, thereby implementing subsection I of Article 49 according to which, for the holiday, the employee shall receive the daily amount in proportion to the total sum of the days he has worked. The same rule shall also be applicable in the case of weekly wages. On the other hand, 'holiday pay of an employee working at a piece or job rate or on a percentage basis shall be computed by dividing his total earnings within a pay period by the number of days he has worked during that period' (Article 49(2)).

II. Holiday Pay for Salaried Employees

586. Some employees, and especially white-collar employees who are paid on a monthly basis, are referred to as 'salaried employees'. Article 49(4) provides that 'Articles 46, 47 and 48(1) shall not be applicable to salaried employees who are remunerated monthly in full despite the days they are absent from work due to illness, leave of absence or for any reason whatsoever'. This means that such employees will draw full pay for the month even though they may have been absent from work on some days. If deductions are made from their monthly pay for any reason for the days on which they are absent from work, then such employees shall not be treated as 'salaried', meaning that they will be paid even for no work on weekly rest days and holidays. If salaried employees work on national and public holidays, they must be paid double for each such holiday on which they have worked. It follows from the foregoing statements that even in the case of salaried employees there may arise a need to determine the daily wage, which is to be computed by dividing the monthly salary by 30. This is also required for purposes of computing the salaried employee's severance pay.[200]

587. Article 49(2) has clarified the link between the salaried employees pay and the temporary disability benefits to be met by the Social Insurance Organization, a statement that was missing in the Labour Act of 1971, No. 1475. This subsection provides that 'the disability compensation paid by the Social Insurance Organization due to sickness shall be deducted from the wage paid to the salaried employee remunerated on a monthly basis'. Article 49(2) has thus eliminated the ambiguities which existed on this matter under Act No. 1475.

199. *See* below 'Annual Leave with Pay'.
200. Court of Cassation, 9th Div., 4 Feb. 1971, 14850/1384; 12 Jan. 1976, 33477/1670; 30 Oct. 2001, 14351/16851; 31 Mar. 2003, 1377/5437.

§4. Annual Leave with Pay

588. 'Annual leave with pay' (or paid annual vacation) is based, like the weekly rest day and holidays, on the rights of rest granted to every working person by Article 50 of the Constitution of Turkey. A regulation on annual leave with pay was published to that effect in the Official Gazette of 3 March 2004, No. 25391. Buttressed by provisions of an imperative character, paid annual leave reflects the social character of Turkish labour law. The Labour Act, No. 4857, as its predecessor Act No. 1475, sets out the principle that the employee shall not waive his right to annual leave with pay (Article 53(2)), and if an employee is found to have accepted gainful employment during his paid vacation period, he may be asked to reimburse the leave remuneration already paid to him (Article 58). The change of employer or transfer of the establishment shall not affect the rights of employees to annual leave with pay.

I. Conditions

589. Employees, in establishments covered by the Labour Act, who have completed at least one year of service since their recruitment, including the trial period, must be granted annual leave with pay (Article 53(1)). Seasonal employment and partial work with interruptions shall not be counted,[201] nor is a prorated leave permissible for employment which has lasted less than a year.[202] The employee shall use his annual leave with pay computed for each year of service within the following year of employment (Article 54(4)). The length of the 'one-year service' which must elapse for the employee's entitlement to his upcoming annual leave with pay shall commence from the day on which his entitlement to his previous annual leave became effective, to be computed towards the following year (Article 54(3)).

590. In the computation of the length of service of an employee in order to qualify for annual leave with pay, the total period during which the employee was employed in one or more establishments belonging to the same employer shall be taken into consideration. Furthermore, any length of time spent by the employee in an establishment covered by the Labour Act plus any length of time previously spent by the same employee in an establishment belonging to the same employer but not covered by this Act shall also be considered (Article 54(1)).

591. The same rule is applicable in the event of the transfer of the establishment or one of its sections in conjunction with Article 6 of the Labour Act. It could be inferred from all this that under these circumstances the employee's employment in various establishments need not be continuous to qualify for annual leave. A controversial issue has been the entitlement to paid annual leave of an employee who has worked under the same employer with interruptions. The decisions of the Court

201. Court of Cassation, 9th Div., 25 Mar. 1996, 31346/6089.
202. Court of Cassation, 9th Div., 3 Oct. 1980, 10970/10666; 21 Nov. 1989, 10143/10077; 24 Jan. 1991, 9621/518; 21 Sep. 1999, 11435/14354.

of Cassation have tended to hold that if previous entitlements have not been cleared either by letting the said reemployed employee actually use his annual leave with pay in respective past periods or by clearing his entitlements upon previous termination(s) of his employment contract, these unused or uncleaned periods shall be added to outstanding paid annual leave calculations. If already used or cleared (paid) upon the termination(s) of his employment contract, no such additions may be made.

592. If the employee has been served a notice of termination, the notice term must not be included in the computation of the one year period required in order to qualify for annual leave with pay.[203]

593. For the employee whose termination was declared invalid by the court and as a result reengaged in work (Article 21(1)), the unworked period between the termination date and the date of reengagement in work should be taken into consideration for his entitlement to annual leave with pay irrespective of the limitations on wages and other claims.[204]

594. The provisions on annual leave with pay are not applicable to employees working in seasonal or other occupations which, owing to their nature, last less than one year (Article 53(3)). Because this rule denies annual leave to seasonal employees employed in various establishments on a regular basis, it has often been criticized in the teaching.

595. Employees on part-time contracts and on-call contracts, however, are entitled to have access to annual leave like full-time employees. They must be allowed to use their paid annual leave for each year of employment within the following year, and no discrimination between them and full-time employees is permissible in view of Article 13 of the Regulation on Annual Leave with Pay.

II. Unworked Periods Considered as Part of the One-Year Requirement to Qualify for Paid Annual Leave

596. In determining the rights to annual leave with pay, the periods cited below shall be deemed as having been worked (Article 55):

(a) days on which the employee fails to report to work owing to an accident or illness (however, time which exceeds the period foreseen in subsection I (b)

203. Court of Cassation, 9th Div., 6 Jul. 2004, 8053/17234. In a decision of the Court of Cassation, the prior periods of employment which were already disposed of by way of making notice and severance pay to the employee should not be considered in his later entitlements to annual pay (Court of Cassation, 9th Div., 30 Jan. 2007, 12556/1252). Later in 2009, the Court changed its stance by ruling that the said periods could be combined (9th Div., 5 Nov. 2009, 11592/30499).
204. S. Süzek, *İş Hukuku*, p. 60.

of Article 25 shall not be treated as worked. This period is related to the employer's right to terminate the employee's contract for health reasons);

(b) days on which the female employee is not permitted to work before and after her confinement, in accordance with Article 74;

(c) days on which the employee is unable to report to work through having been called up for military exercises or for the fulfilment of a statutory obligation, other than military service (up to a maximum of ninety days in a year);

(d) fifteen days of any period during which the employee has not worked because of the temporary but uninterrupted suspension of operations for longer than one week owing to force majeure, on condition that he has subsequently resumed work;

(e) time periods reckoned as having been worked, envisaged in Article 66; (f)weekly rest days and national and public holidays;

(f) half-days of leave granted in addition to Sundays to employees working in radiological clinics, in accordance with the regulation issued under Act No. 3153;

(g) days on which the employee is unable to report for work because of having to attend meetings of mediation and arbitration boards, acting as an employees' representatives on such boards, serving as an employees' or union representative on boards, committees or meetings organized under the relevant legislation or attending conventions, conferences or committee meetings of international organizations dealing with labour matters;

(h) up to three days' leave on the occasion of the employee's marriage and up to three days' leave on the occasion of his parent's, spouse's, sibling's or child's death;

(i) other leave granted by the employer;

(j) annual leave with pay conferred on the employee in pursuance of the application of this Act.

The time spent by the employee on strike is not considered as part of the one-year requirement.[205] Likewise, term of notice in the termination of the employment contract is not reckoned as part of the one-year requirement for access to the right to annual leave with pay even when the contrary has been decided in the collective agreement.[206]

If within the one-year period the employee's work is interrupted for reasons other than those enumerated in Article 55 above, the expiry date of the one year of employment which must have elapsed for the employee's entitlement to paid annual leave shall be shifted to the following year of service by adding additional time to compensate for the outstanding gaps caused by interruptions (Article 54(2)).

205. Court of Cassation, 9th Div., 6 Jul. 2004, 8053/17234.

206. Court of Cassation, 9th Div., 25 Jan. 2000, 17281/325; 25 Jan. 2001, 16671/1258.

III. Length of Annual Leave with Pay

597. As for the duration of paid annual leave, Article 53(4) of Act No. 4857 provides the following:

(a) 14 days if the employee's length of service is between one and five years (five included);
(b) 20 days if it is more than 5 and less than 15 years;
(c) 26 days if it is 15 years and more (15 included).

598. Concerning workers employed underground, the length of paid annual leave shall be granted by adding four days to each category of seniority, as amended as a supplement to Article 53 of the Labour Act) by Act No. 6552 (Article 5).

599. For employees below the age of 18 and above the age of 50, the length of annual leave with pay must not be less than twenty days (Article 53(5)).

600. National holidays, weekly rest days and public holidays which coincide with the duration of annual leave may not be included in the annual leave period (Article 56(5)), meaning that they shall be added to the leave period. However, in the event of a five -day work week, unworked Saturdays shall not be added to the annual leave period'. 'The length of annual leave may be extended by employment contracts or collective agreements' (Article 53(6)).

IV. Implementing Annual Leave with Pay

601. The employee must not be engaged in work (albeit for wages) during his annual leave entitlement; likewise, unless dictated by business necessity and personal reasons, annual leave entitlement may not be used on a protracted and accumulated basis although the employee's right to past entitlements must be protected in any case. In principle, the employee's constitutionally guaranteed right to rest must be given priority, although many employees would rather prefer to relinquish that right and instead receive wages by working during the leave period, thereby doubling their income. The Court of Cassation has ruled that under the constitutional and legal principles safeguarding the right to annual leave, written request by the employee during the course of his employment relationship waiving his rights and future claims to annual leave with pay cannot be deemed valid, which is also construed to mean that he must be paid his accrued entitlements upon his retirement.

602. In the event of the employee's illness during his annual leave period, it may be affirmed that the addition of the days on which illness as officially authenticated by a medical report would be a fair solution as there is no clear provision on that matter. Article 56(4) which provides that 'other kinds of leave, with or without pay, granted by the employer or taken by the employee as convalescent or sick leave must not be deducted from annual leave' seems to substantiate this solution. Further, the indivisibility of annual leave by the employer (Article 56(1)) as well as the ban on the employee's working during his annual leave (Article 58), attests to the basic motive underlying annual leave with pay which is to ensure a full rest period for the employee.

603. 'If the employee so requests, the employer must grant him up to four days' leave without pay in order to make good his round-trip travel time, on condition that the employee provides documentary evidence that he is spending his annual leave at a place other than that where the establishment is located' (Article 56(6)). If, despite such an arrangement, the employee spends his annual leave at the place where the establishment is located, the employer may break the contract for just cause, as this behaviour shall be deemed to be a breach of trust in contravention of the duty of loyalty.

604. 'Annual leave with pay may not be divided by the employer. This leave must be granted without interruptions and in conformity with the number of days indicated in Article 53. However, leave periods foreseen in Article 53 may be divided, by mutual consent, into three parts at the maximum, provided that one of the parts shall not be less than ten days' (Article 56(1,2,3)).

605. According to the Regulation on Paid Annual Leave, the employee must inform the employer one month in advance in writing of his request to use the annual leave to which he is entitled. The employer shall transmit this request to the vacation committee or, where there is no established committee, to persons who act in this capacity (Article 7(1,2)). The vacation committee or the employer does not have to comply with the employee's request. However, in the preparation of the vacation roster, employees' requests must be given due consideration to the extent possible, and in evaluating the requests for leave which coincide with the same dates, priority must be given to those who have longer seniority in the establishment and in relation to the dates on which employees had taken their leaves in the past year. In the opinion of the Court of Cassation, the authority to determine the timing of annual leave belongs to the employer in the final analysis, meaning that the employee cannot decide on the timing as he wishes.[207] Also, the employee cannot break the contract for just cause on grounds of the denial by the employer of his request to use his leave on a certain date.[208]

606. 'The employer must keep a roster showing the paid annual leave taken by the employees working in his establishment' (Article 56(6)). The employer should be held liable for the employee's annual leave pay where the latter's having used annual leave cannot be proven by the employer.[209] In the event that signed receipts are produced by the employer attesting to the fact that the employee has used paid

207. Court of Cassation, 8th Div., 30 Nov. 1998, 15055/16955; 20 Mar. 2000, 298/2934.
208. Court of Cassation, 9th Div., 24 Dec. 1997, 18437/22430; 20 Jun. 2006, 15954/17843.
209. Court of Cassation, 9th Div., 20 Oct. 1992, 3597/11536; 12 May 1997, 3746/8791; 11 May 1999, 4981/8748; 23 Mar. 2000, 536/3250; 30 Apr. 2009, 41415/12145.

annual leave, the court should not hold the employer liable for the reimbursement of past leave pays merely by relying on the testimony of witnesses.[210]

607. According to the Regulation on Annual Leave with Pay, the employer may also grant a 'general' (or collective leave) on condition that it must cover all employees in the establishment during the period between the beginning of April and the end of October. In this case the vacation committee shall arrange and announce the leave roster in such a manner as to enable employees to start taking their leave on the same date and yet to show the expiration of the leave period for each employee depending on the employees' entitlements to paid annual leave, taking into account their requests for round-trip travel time (Article 10(2)). The period of 'general leave' can be scheduled by the employer or his representative in such a manner as to also cover those employees who are not yet entitled to annual leave with pay. However, the date on which these employees shall be allowed to take their paid annual leave will be subject to general principles if this practice is discontinued in the years that follow (Article 10(3)).

608. Concerning annual leave in the event of employment under subcontractors:

> For workers who continue working at the same establishment although their 'subcontractor employer' has changed, the length of paid annual leave shall be computed by considering the total time they have worked at the same establishment. The principal (main) employer is under the obligation to check to see if workers employed by the subcontractor have used their annual vacation periods to which they were entitled as well as to make sure that they have used their vacations in the relevant years. The subcontractor shall deliver one copy of the vacation rosters to the main employer, as amended by Article 6 of Act No. 6552, as a supplement to Article 56 of the labour Act.

V. Remuneration During Annual Leave

609. If the employee is paid according to time, the rules relating to holiday pay are also applicable to remuneration during annual leave. In this case, the major step is the determination of the daily wage.

610. For employees who are not paid daily, monthly or weekly but who are remunerated according to an indefinite period of time or amount of money, such as a piece-rate, commission, profit-sharing or percentage, the annual leave pay must be computed on their overage daily earnings by dividing the total wages earned during the previous year by the number of days actually worked during that year. For

210. Court of Cassation, 9th Div., 26 Jun. 1996, 3645/14404. The roster must also include the actual dates of the employee's taking the leave and his returning to work (Court of Cassation, 9th Div. 7 Feb. 2005, 13529/3151).

employees working on a percentage basis, wages for annual leave must be paid by the employer apart from the amount of money derived from current percentage earnings (Article 57(3,5)).

611. As in pay for national or public holidays and weekly rest days, only the basic wage shall be considered in annual leave pay; that is, in line with Article 50, overtime and incentive premiums, the wages paid to permanent employees when they are employed outside normal working hours in preparatory, complementary and cleaning operations and fringe benefits shall not be included in determining the leave pay (Article 57(2)).

612. The employer must pay the employee who will use his paid annual leave the remuneration corresponding to his leave period either as a lump-sum or as an advance payment prior to the beginning of his leave. Wages for weekly rest days, national and public holidays which coincide with annual leave shall be paid to the employee in addition to his annual leave pay (Article 57(1,6)).

613. Any annual leave pay that is due to not yet drawn by an employee must be paid to him or other persons entitled on his behalf. This rule applies also when the employee's contract is terminated. The wage level for such accumulated past leave pays is the employee's last wage prevailing on the date of the termination of the contract rather than wage levels in the relevant years. The periods of leave to be considered, however, are to be those belonging to the respective years than the one which was effective in the last year.[211] The employee who has not requested to take his annual leave during his employment must not be denied the payment of his annual leave pay.[212] However, he may not claim entitlement to past leave pays if the employer produces documentary evidence (signed payrolls, for example) that he has used annual leave in the past.[213]

614. Where the employment contract was terminated by the employer, the terms of notice indicated in Article 17 and the leave of absence to be allowed according to Article 27 must not overlap with the annual leave periods (Article 59(3)). It should be noted that the employee's right to paid annual leave with pay is valid even in the case where his employment contract was terminated by the employer for just cause in line with Article 25/II. In view of Article 53(2) of Act No. 6356, where leave periods or pay levels have been fixed by collective agreement, the highest interest rate charged for business loans shall be imposed on the defaulting employer for the arrears in question.[214]

615. Article 59(2) provides that statutory limitations on wage claims for paid annual leave (which in principle is five years for wages according to the Obligations Act) shall begin as of the date of the termination of the employment contract

---

211. Court of Cassation, 9th Div., 30 Jan. 2002, 16766/170.
212. Court of Cassation, 9th Div., 14 Nov. 1995, 13622/34214.
213. Court of Cassation, 9th Div., 26 Oct. 1996, 17254/24326.
214. Court of Cassation, 9th Div., 12 Nov. 1997, 14619/18911.

(rather than upon the maturation of each claim in the respective years). Apparently, this new provision has removed the uncertainties which existed on this matter under the previous system.

VI. Annual Leave According to Other Legislation: The Maritime and Press Labour Acts

616. Seamen employed by the same employer or on board the same vessel under one or more employment contracts for at least six months during any one calendar year are entitled to annual paid leave. The length of annual leave for seamen employed for a period of between six months and one year must be, for each year, not less than fifteen days, or in the case of seamen who have completed at least one year's service, not less than one month. One month's annual leave may be divided into two parts by mutual consent of the parties, on condition that all of this leave is taken within the same calendar year to which it applies. The seaman may request from the employer or employer's representative travelling time without pay of up to seven days. He must not be forced to take his paid annual leave in a foreign port or at a place other than that where he had concluded his employment contract (Article 40).

617. Journalists employed by daily newspapers for a minimum of one year, either on a continued basis or with interruptions, must be granted four weeks' annual paid leave. Journalists employed by periodicals other than daily papers must be granted two weeks' paid leave for every six months of service (Press Labour Act, Article 21).

VII. Compatibility of Rest Days and Paid Annual Leave with European Union Norms

618. The new Labour Act of Turkey is predominantly in line with the requirements of the Working Time Directive 93/104/EC. However, according to the Matra Project under which articles of Act No. 4857 were scanned with a view to assess the Act's compatibility with Directive 93/104/EC, the one-year qualifying period for entitlement to paid annual leave as well as the foreseen lengths of annual leave seem to be in contravention of the Working Time Directive. Article 7 of the Working Time Directive lays down the right to four-week's annual leave for all employees which, in appropriate cases, may be given on a *pro rata temporis* basis. This shortcoming is particularly relevant in respect of employees under relatively short fixed-term contracts. Therefore, the Labour Act has to be revised to incorporate fully the requirements of Article 7 of the Directive.

Chapter 7. The Suspension of the Execution of the Individual Employment Contract

§1. The Notion

619. The suspension of the employment contract means that the agreement between the parties remains in existence, but that the obligations which the parties have to fulfil towards each other are temporarily suspended, in which case the employee does not fulfil his duty to work and consequently the employer would not, in principle, be obliged to pay him wages. As in the case of the employee being allowed by his employer to take a graduate course of study, for example the parties may also agree between themselves to suspend the execution of the contract for a certain period. In various forms of paid leaves and rest periods during which the employee does not work, the contract is not deemed to have been suspended since the employee's certain obligations – except for the duty to work – as well as the employer's obligation to pay him wages are still operative.

§2. Conditions Which Require the Suspension of the Execution of the Individual Employment Contract

I. Military Service or Statutory Labour Service

620. If an employee is called up – outside the period of his compulsory military service – to take part in military manoeuvres, or if he leaves his employment to perform statutory labour service, his employment contract is suspended for at least two months on condition that the employee must have been employed for a minimum of one year. Employees who have been employed for more than one year must be allowed two additional days for each additional year of service, provided that the total period of absence may not exceed ninety days. If the employee's absence exceeds the stipulated suspension periods (i.e., from sixty days up to a maximum of ninety days), 'the contract is deemed to have been terminated by the employer' (Article 31(1,2,3) of the Labour Act). Unless otherwise stated in special legislation or in the collective agreement, the employee is not entitled to his wages during that period which must elapse before the contract may be deemed to have been terminated. If notice to terminate the contract is given by the employer or the employee during the period of suspension, the term of notice takes effect after the expiration of the suspension period. However, this provision is not applicable in cases where the contract is for a definite period which expires during the suspension period (Article 31(4)).

621. In the event that the employer terminates the employment contract of an employee who is taking his annual leave, the term of notice shall not become operative until the end of the leave period.

622. Further, priority in filling vacancies must be given to employees who have left their employment to carry out military or other statutory duties and who make application within two months of the completion of such duties (Article 31(5)).

II. Strikes and Lock-Outs

623. Article 67(1)of the Unions and the Collective Labour Agreement No. 6356 states explicitly that where an employee is affected by a lawful strike or lock-out, his rights and obligations under the employment contract are suspended until the end of the strike or lock-out. The legal consequence of this principle is that the employer is not permitted to engage another employee in a permanent or temporary capacity or to employ any other person in substitution for an employee whose rights and obligations under the employment contract have been thus suspended (Article 68(1)). Also, an employee whose rights and obligations accruing from the contract are suspended as a consequence of a lawful strike or lock-out is not permitted to accept other employment; if he does, the employer may terminate his employment contract without having to observe the term of notice and to pay compensation (Article 68(3)). Also the employment contract of an employee who leaves his employment to act as a union administrator on a professional basis is to be suspended.

III. Illness, Pregnancy or Confinement

624. In cases of illness or accident which are not attributable to the employee's fault and which are due to reasons outside those set forth in subsection (a) of Article 25/I – i.e., employee contracting a disease or suffering an injury on his own fault – and in cases of pregnancy or confinement, the employer may terminate the employment contract if recovery from the said incidents lasts for more than six weeks beyond the notice terms set out in Article 17.

625. In cases of pregnancy or confinement, the period mentioned shall begin at the expiration of the time stipulated in Article 74 – eight weeks before and eight weeks after giving birth. (In addition, if the female employee so wishes, she shall be granted an unpaid leave up to six months.) No wages are to be paid for the period during which the employee fails to report to work due to the suspension of his (her) employment contract (Article 25/I-b). During her pregnancy and confinement, the female employee is entitled to maternity benefits to be met by the Social Insurance Organization. Only those categories of 'salaried' employees who are paid on a monthly basis are entitled to remuneration during sickness.

Chapter 8. The Ending of the Individual Employment Contract: Expiration, Termination

§1. The Ending of the Employment Contract by Means Other Than Termination

I. Mutual Consent of the Parties

626. A valid employment contract may be brought to end by the parties' mutual consent (referred to as *ikale* in Turkish legal terminology). If the employer and the employee so agree, they may cancel the employment contract made for a definite period before its expiration date. The same holds true for employment contracts made for an indefinite period (open-ended contracts); the parties may agree, by mutual consent, to end such an employment contract without having to give advance notice. The agreement may occasionally be implicit, as is encountered in practice where the employee expresses his wish to quit and the employer indicates his consent in a written note. Likewise, an employee's contract in the public sector is implicitly ended when the employer changes his status to that of a public servant upon receiving his consent. In such cases the parties may agree to end the contract either immediately or subsequent to the lapse of a certain time period; in the absence of either, the contract is deemed to have ended on the day of the parties' mutual agreement.[215] Following the adoption of job security legislation in 2003, there seems to be an increase in terminations by way of *ikale*, allegedly with the covert employer's intention to thwart litigation by workers for reinstatement/ compensation. Based on the concept of 'abusive termination', the Court of Cassation has ruled such terminations invalid in several cases, but the controversy on this issue continues.[216]

627. The employment contract is deemed to be valid even if it has been concluded under mistake, improper pressure, threat or fraud; but the party claiming the presence of such factors may dissolve the contract by notifying the other party within the time periods and conditions set forth in the Obligations Act (Articles 28, 30, 36–39).

628. This means that the employment contract has come into existence as a valid one but the wronged party may invoke its invalidation in which case the contract is deemed to have remained in force until the date of its cancellation. Also, upon a suit filed by either party, any conditions in a contract found to be contrary to imperative law, public order or good morals may be revoked by the court.

---

215. N. Çelik, *İşHukuku Dersleri*, İstanbul, 2013, p. 205. The parties' agreement relating to the employee's working for a period commensurate with the notice term and involving the payment of severance pay is valid (Court of Cassation., 9th Div., 13 Mar. 2007, 37425/6511); 25 Jun. 2011, 1650/ 15398.

216. N. Geref, 'Iş Sözleşmesinin ikale Sözleşmesi ila Sona Ermesi', *Calisme uc Toplum* No. 31, 2011/, pp. 43–58.

II. Death

629. The employment contract ends if the employee dies, Obligations Act, Article 440, without any obligation to give notice for termination. This is natural since, in principle, the employment contract establishes a personal relationship, and the employee's obligation to work cannot be transferred to his heirs. However, in respect of severance pay which normally is paid in certain cases of contract termination, heirs of the deceased employee shall have access to the severance pay to which he was entitled. However, the death of the employer does not cause the employment contract to cease automatically unless it has been concluded *intuitu personae* (Obligations Act, Article 441(1)). As a rule, rights and obligations of the employer based on the contract pass on to the heirs of the deceased employer who may terminate the employment contract only according to the general provisions of law. If the contract has been made *intuitu personae* of the employer, however, his death brings the contract to an end even though it may have been concluded for a definite period. If, in this case, the employee suffers any losses, he may request a fair compensation from the employer's heirs (Article 441(2)).

III. Expiration of the Definite Time Period (in Fixed-term Contracts)

630. Fixed-term contracts end with the expiration of the specified period or on the specific date indicated.[217] Unless otherwise agreed to by the parties, there is no need to give advance notice (Obligations Act, Article 430(1)). Also, the duration of a fixed-term contract may have been linked to the materialization of a certain event(s) or the completion of certain work. Duration of the fixed-term contract can also be inferred from the purpose of the activit(y)(ies) (i.e., seasonal agricultural work, campaign work).[218] The employment contract is deemed to have been extended if, despite the expiration of its duration, the employee continues working with no opposition from the employer. The new contract is held to be of the same duration as the previous one, but it may not be longer than one year, Obligations Act (Article 430). The same rule shall apply in the event of fixed-term contracts based on essential reasons, as foreseen in Article 11 of Act No. 4857.[219]

631. As inferred from the wording of Article 430 of the Obligations Act, the ending of a fixed-term contract may have been predicated on the serving of a notice despite the presence of a clearly stated expiration time. If notice is not served, the contract shall be deemed to have been extended for the same length of time as the duration of the employment contract, rather than one year. If neither party gives notice, the contract turns into an open-ended contract (Article 430(4)). Clearly this type of arrangement is valid only in fixed-term employment contracts based on an essential reason; nor should it be confused with a mutually agreed clause inserted

217. For the controversy over the first use of a fixed-term contract.
218. Article 11 of Act No. 4857.
219. Çelik, *supra*, pp. 203–204.

into the contract foreseeing that the fixed-term employment contract may always be terminated by giving notice before its expiration.[220]

632. The duration of an employment contract for a definite period may not exceed ten years, nor can it be made for the lifetime of either party. After ten years the employee may cancel such a contract at any time by giving six-month advance notice with no obligation to pay compensation (Article 430(3)). If the employer terminates a fixed-term contract before its expiration date without just cause, the employee may request his wages for the remaining period, but not notice pay. If a contract with a fixed duration of more than one year is terminated by the employer without just cause or by the employee for just cause, the employee is entitled to receive severance pay.

633. Even before the enactment of the new Labour Act No. 4857 in 2003, the Court of Cassation, with a view to protecting the employee and forestalling the abuse of the freedom of contract, treated the renewal of a fixed-term contract as a contract made for an indefinite term.[221] Act No. 4857 addresses this issue more clearly now and provides in Article 11(2) that 'an employment contract for a definite period must not be concluded more than once, except when there is an essential reason which may necessitate the conclusion of repeated (chain) contracts. Otherwise, the recurring contracts are deemed to have been made for an indefinite period from the very beginning.' As can be inferred from the wording of Article 11, it should be held that a fixed-term contract shall be converted into an open-ended one upon its first renewal. However, 'chain contracts based on essential reasons shall maintain their status as contracts made for a definite (fixed-term) period' (Article 11(3)). This last point is also consistent with the views expressed in various rulings of the Court of Cassation, that is, recurrent fixed-term contracts shall be treated as separate contracts, provided there are socially justifiable reasons which entail the conclusion of repeated contracts for a definite term. Renewal of one-year employment contracts of private school teachers subject to Act No. 625 is one such case in point. The teacher is not entitled to notice pay or severance pay upon the expiration of his contract.[222] However, if, based on a clause inserted into the contract, the employer notifies the employee of the non-renewal of his contract with no just cause involved, the employee is entitled to severance pay.[223]

§2. At-Will Termination of the Individual Employment Contract

I. Notification of Termination; The Notion

634. In conjunction with the concept of freedom of contract, the parties to an employment contract (the employer and the employee) are both free to terminate it

220. Court of Cassation, 9th Div., 25 Mar. 1996, 1995-31346/1996-6089.
221. Court of Cassation, 9th Div., 7 May 1998, 5745/8434; 21 Sep. 1999, 9537/14061.
222. Court of Cassation, General Council Decision, 1 Jul. 1992, 9-335/448; 9th Div., 27 Dec. 1994, 14771/18626; 26 Apr. 2000, 2291/6305.
223. Court of Cassation, 9th Div., 5 Apr. 1994, 5717/5181.

by notifying the other party unilaterally. While this notion is in essence valid, Labour Act No. 4857 has, by bringing a certain degree of job security, restricted the freedom of some employers to unilaterally terminate the employment contract with no reason.

635. Declaration of will to terminate the contract is called 'notice of termination'.

636. 'Contracts made for an indefinite period may be terminated by either party by respecting a certain term of notice in advance (Obligations Act, Article 431, Labour Act, Article 17). On the other hand, contracts with a definite or indefinite period may be terminated for just cause with no obligation to respect an advance notice term (Obligations Act, Article 435, Labour Act, Articles 24, 25). In both categories, that is, in the former case where a term of advance notice must be respected and in the latter where no notice term has to be observed, a clear and precise notification to end the contract must be made to the other party. (In daily usage of Turkish legal terminology, however, it has been customary to refer to the former category as termination with notice, and to the latter as prompt (immediate) termination without notice.) Although notice to terminate the contract must be expressed in clear and precise terms, the Court of Cassation holds that the termination may also be inferred from the behaviour of the terminating party in the natural course of events.[224] In any case termination entails a new legal formation.[225]

637. Notice of termination is the unilateral expression of the notifying party that he no longer considers himself bound by the employment contract. In principle, notice engenders its legal consequences when it reaches the other party. It is not possible to withdraw the intent to terminate the contract once the notice has reached the other party. However, according to the general principles of the Act of Obligations (Article 10), the notifying party may withdraw it before notice has reached the other party or before the other party has become informed of it. Article 109 of the Labour Act provides that the notification must be served to the person concerned in written form, in clear terms, and upon obtaining his signature.[226] The refusal to sign must be documented on the spot in written form, as a report drawn up to that effect forthwith. It is a commonly held view that the form set out in Article 109 is a condition of proof rather than a condition of validity, as substantiated by most of the rulings of the Court of Cassation. Therefore an oral notice is also valid, but in the event of a dispute, a written notice serves as a condition of proof. In a few cases, however, the High Court has required the existence of written form as a condition of validity.[227]

---

224. Court of Cassation 9th Div., 20 Oct. 1997, 13230/17815; 17 Dec. 1997, 17655/21738.
225. Çelik, *supra*, pp. 205–208.
226. However, notices within the scope of Act No. 7201 shall be served in accordance with the provisions of the said Act.
227. Court of Cassation, 9th Div., 5 Jun. 1964, 3330/3682; 8 Mar. 1966, 948/1968; 3 Oct. 2000, 9309/12891.

638. Notice of termination may be given any time within or outside working hours, in the establishment or at any place. However, if notice is served at an inconvenient time or place, its refusal is held to make termination invalid.[228]

639. On the other hand, the behaviour per se may signify a clear indication of the wish to terminate (e.g., the employee just quitting his job without any notice). In this case, the contract is deemed to have been terminated, but termination is regarded as being 'irregular' or 'unfair'.[229]

II. Types of Notice of Termination

A. *Termination by Means of Respecting a Term of Notice*

640. Termination by way of observing a notice period applies only to open-ended contracts. An exception to this general rule has been foreseen only for fixed-term contracts made for life-time or for those whose duration exceeds ten years. The Obligations Act provides that the employee may terminate such a contract upon the lapse of the ten-year period (Article 430(3)). The length of time between the notification of the decision to terminate the employment contract and the date on which the contract shall end constitutes the term of notice. The obligation to respect the terms of notice has been imposed on both parties. The aim is to mitigate the effects of the unilateral decision of the employee or employer to terminate the contract by giving the employee a chance to look for a new job while he still has an income and by providing the employer with adequate time to recruit a replacement.

641. Terms of notice which were regulated by Article 13 of the now-repealed Act No. 1475 are reiterated, without any change as regards the length of each term category, in Article 17 of the new Labour Act No. 4857, ranging between two and eight weeks depending on the length of service of the employee. Provisions found in Articles 18–21 are, however, new as they relate to new rules on job security. Terms of notice envisaged in Article 17 shall apply to all regular terminations except for terminations for just cause, while provisions in Articles 18–21 apply only to those who are covered by the new job security regulations.[230] The last subsection of Article 17 deals with payment of compensation for abusive terminations, construed to mean it shall be applicable only to those who are outside the coverage of job security.

---

228. Çelik, *supra*, pp. 207–209.
229. For examples, *see* Court of Cassation, 9th Div., 21 Dec. 2005, 16325/40325; 6 Jul. 2009, 1426/19511.
230. For details on the new job security system, *see also* the article in English by N. Süral, *Employment Termination and Job Security under New Turkish Labour Act*, 41(2) Middle Eastern Studies 249–268 (March 2005).

1. Terms of Notice

642. Article 17(1) provides that 'before terminating an employment contract made for an indefinite period, a notice to the other party must be served by the terminating party'.

The contract shall then terminate:

(a) in the case of an employee whose employment has lasted less than six months, at the end of the second week following the serving of notice to the other party;
(b) in the case of an employee whose employment has lasted for six months or more but for less than one-and-a-half years, at the end of the fourth week following the serving of notice to the other party;
(c) in the case of an employee whose employment has lasted for one-and-a-half years or more but for less than three years, at the end of the sixth week following the serving of notice to the other party;
(d) in the case of an employee whose employment has lasted for more three years, at the end of the eighth week following the serving of notice to the other party.

643. These are minimum periods and may be increased by contract between the parties (Article 17/(2)). The beginning of the term of notice takes effect from the day on which notice reaches the other party. The day on which notice is given is not counted.

644. The parties to an employment contract have occasionally agreed on differential lengths for terms of notice; for instance, notice term to be respected by the employer is foreseen, usually in collective agreements, to be longer than that which must be respected by the employee. However, the validity of such agreements is a matter of controversy. It is generally held that the increase in terms of notice should be of equal length for either party.[231] The new Obligations Act provides in Article 432(5) that if different notice terms for the parties have been decided, the longer one shall apply to both parties. The minimum periods set out in Article 17 may, however, be evaded by agreement of the parties who may decide to terminate the contract before the expiration of the notice term.[232]

645. In the opinion of the High Court, a penal clause inserted into the employment contract which requires the employee to pay the employer a certain sum in the event of his terminating the contract before a designated maximum duration on his own will whereas the employer was held liable to pay only the amount corresponding to the notice period if he would terminate the contract for no just cause should not bind the employee.[233] In this case the employee should pay only the sum foreseen for the employer. The amount exceeding this level should be considered

231. Çelik, *supra*, pp. 213–214.
232. Court of Cassation, 9th Div., 21 Feb. 1994, 2473/2638.
233. Court of Cassation, 9th Div., 17 Nov. 1992, 8777/12603; 26 Jun. 1997, 10135/13040; 30 May 2002, 1228/9321. *See also*, M. Demircioğ lu, *İş Hukukunda Cezai Şart, Prof Dr. Ali Güzel'e Armağan*, Cilt 1, İstanbul 2010, pp. 159–172.

invalid.[234] The judge must intervene in the event of excessively long notice terms in the collective labour agreement.[235] Furthermore, the judge, by taking account of the time periods worked and unworked proportionately, has been empowered to make a reasonable reduction in the amount set forth as a penal condition, in accordance with Article 161 of the Obligations Act.[236]

2. Rights and Duties During the Term of Notice (Permission to Seek New Employment Within the Term of Notice)

646. During the term of notice, the employment contract subsists with all the explicit and implicit obligations and rights involved. The employer must continue to provide work for the employee at the same wage rate and under the same working conditions and the employee must continue working. Also, legal provisions regulating relations between the parties are in full force throughout the term of notice. Special provisions must also be respected (e.g., where the contract is terminated by the employer, term of notice envisaged in Article 17 and the leave of absence to be granted under Article 19 to enable the employee to seek new employment must be included in the one-year period required in order to qualify for paid annual leave).

647. From the standpoint of the employee the provisions of a collective agreement are considered to be in full effect until the end of the term of notice. Also, the employee benefits from a collective agreement signed at any time during the term of notice, or signed after its expiration but made retroactive so as to take effect when the employee's contract (including the term of notice) was still in force.[237]

648. The party who has given notice to terminate the employment contract cannot withdraw his decision unilaterally during the term of notice. However, within this period the said decision may be abrogated with the consent of the party to whom notice has been served. In this case, the contract remains in effect as it is. Certainly, upon the expiration of the term of notice, the parties may agree to conclude a new contract which is deemed to have been made with the same conditions as the previous one unless the contrary is indicated. The parties may also agree to establish an uninterrupted connection between the two contracts. Such a contract

234. Court of Cassation 9th Div., 26 Mar. 1997, 22867/6102; 21 Jun. 2004, 22636/534; 22 Jun. 2004, 226/534.
235. Court of Cassation., 9th Div., 12 Mar. 2009, 41150/6661.
236. Court of Cassation, General Council Decision, 15 Oct. 1997, 9-846/822; 9th Div., 14 Feb. 2005, 14528/4135. However, a penal clause requiring the employee not to terminate such a contract if a relatively long and costly training has been provided as a condition for his employment should be binding on the employee (Court of Cassation, 9th Div., 29 Mar. 2000, 507/4100; 10 Mar. 2004, 14720/4609.) In another ruling, the maximum amount has been held to be the total of notice pay and the compensation for abusive termination (Court of Cassation, 9th Div., 14 Jul. 2008, 2449/20203).
237. Court of Cassation, 9th Div., 30 Apr. 1992, 16845/4784.

entails certain advantages for the employee (e.g., longer length of service and notice pay in the event of a new termination, more severance pay, etc.).

649. During the term of notice the employer must grant the employee a permission to seek new employment within working hours without any deductions from his wage. The time devoted to this purpose should not be less than two hours daily, and if the employee so requests such hours may be added together and taken at one time. But if the employee wishes to use these hours at one time, he must do so on the days immediately preceding the day on which his employment shall cease and must inform the employer in advance' (Article 27(1)). If the employer does not grant the employee permission for seeking new employment or allows less time than that stipulated in this article, he must pay the employee the wages corresponding to the time to which he was entitled (Article 27(2)). If the employer makes the employee work during the time to be allowed for seeking new employment, he must compensate him at twice the amount of wages he is entitled to in addition to his wage entitlement for no work corresponding to the time which should be allowed for seeking new employment (Article 27(3)).

650. In the opinion of the Court of Cassation, the employer does not have to grant this permission for the weekly rest days, holidays and general vacation days which the employee uses, and the employee is not entitled to wages for seeking employment on such days.[238]

651. Permission to be absent from work to seek new employment is to be granted to the employee regardless of which party is terminating the contract. But the employee who terminates the contract because of or after having found employment elsewhere is not permitted to avail himself of this provision; if he finds other employment during the term of notice, he must inform the employer promptly and stop using the remaining time to seek new employment.

652. Also, the employee's request is not a necessary condition for his entitlement to leave of absence for the purpose of seeking a new job. His request is significant only to the extent of the time and form of taking the leave. If the employee wishes to take these hours together, he must so inform the employer, for reasons of good faith, on the day on which notice is given or on the following day.

653. In principle the employer has the right to decide at what times of the day the leave of absence is to be taken, but attention must be paid to giving the employee an effective chance to look for a job. If the employer is the party who has given notice of termination, he must indeed have taken all the possible precautions to continue operations without interruption. Also the employee may request that leave period be convenient so as to enable him to seek a job effectively. If the employer refuses the employee's request with respect to the timing of the leave even though that request does not seem to interfere with operations, the employee may

238. Court of Cassation, 9th Div. 23 Dec. 2008, 427/34976; General Council decision, 27 Jan. 2010, 9-593/20.

break the contract for just cause in line with Article 24/II-e. If the employee exercises his right to leave of absence without informing the employer and/or decides on the times of such leave unilaterally, the employer may terminate the contract for just cause – due to absenteeism as foreseen in Article 25/II (g) and (e), breach of trust. The employer is also entitled to break the contract of an employee who pretends to be looking for a job even though he has already found employment elsewhere (Article 25/II-e). If the term of notice has for any reason elapsed without the leave for the purpose of seeking new employment being granted to or used by the employee, the employer must compensate the employee for the wages corresponding to leave periods to which he was entitled. In the case the employer has terminated the contract without observing the term of notice, he must pay the employee compensation corresponding to his wages for the term of notice. In this case, the employee is not entitled to leave pay since such pay is already included in the notice pay. The same holds true when the employer terminates the contracts by paying the employee in advance the wages for the term of notice (notice pay).

3. Termination of the Employment Contract by the Advance Payment of Wages Corresponding to the Term of Notice; Notice Pay

654. Like the previous Labour Act, Article 17(5) of Act No. 4857 provides that 'the employer may terminate the employment contract by paying the employee his wages corresponding to the term of notice'. Implementing termination by advance notice pay was widely practised by employers during the past decades.

655. It was later incorporated into Act No. 1475 as a provision deemed to be favourable both to the employer and employee. It is very likely that the employee to whom notice of termination has been given may manifest low morale and reduced performance, consequences detrimental to the employer. On the other hand, the employee who gets his wages in advance (notice pay) can spend all his time to seek a new job more effectively. In the calculation of wages corresponding to the term of notice, it is the last gross wage of the employee, plus any contractual and statutory benefits measurable in monetary terms granted to him that will be considered.

656. Certainly termination by advance notice pay is not to be construed to mean the same thing as prompt termination for just cause where the contract is deemed to have ended with all the related consequences on the day notice is given.[239] However, in many of its verdicts, the Court of Cassation has ruled in the contrary direction.[240]

657. Disregarding the notice term in the calculation of the employee's length of service entails the denial to the employee of various entitlements like bonuses,

239. *See*, Labour Act, Art. 17(5) of Act No. 4857.
240. Court of Cassation, 9th Div., 15 Apr. 1998, 4994/6703; 28 Jun. 1999, 10450/11622; 25 Jan. 2000, 17281/325; 11 Apr. 2000, 2616/5001; 25 Jan. 2001, 16671/1258.

severance pay, paid annual leave as well as the collectively negotiated wage increases which coincide with the term of notice. In the past, however, the Court of Cassation ruled that although terms of notice were related to public order and thus were of a mandatory character, the employee's vested rights corresponding to his term of notice should also be safeguarded in the event of termination by the advance compensation of his notice pay.[241] More recent verdicts of the Court of Cassation have been wavering, however, being slanted against or for this interpretation. If it is concluded, for instance, that the employer's decision was motivated by an abusive intention to deprive the employee of the benefits to accrue from an upcoming collective agreement, the employee should have access to all his vested rights coinciding with his term of notice.[242] Contrary to some of its earlier verdicts, the Court has also held that collectively bargained provisions entitling the employee to benefits accruing within the notice term after advance payment had been made should be held valid.[243]

658. To conclude, one should state that, controversial verdicts of the Court of Cassation notwithstanding, when the employee is terminated through the advance payment of his wages, his term of notice must be considered in the calculation of his severance pay and paid annual leave as well as any legal and collectively bargained wage increments and bonuses which have accrued within the term of notice even though he may not have actually spent that time in the establishment. The basis for advance notice pay is the employee's last basic wage plus whatever wage supplements, monetary or measurable in monetary terms, that he has been receiving.

4. Irregular Termination (Non-observance of the Duty to Give Notice) and Compensation (Notice Pay)

659. The party (employer or employee) who terminates the employment contract by violating the conditions related to respecting the term of notice must pay compensation to the other party corresponding to the wages for the term of notice (Article 17(4)). Because notice pay here is construed to mean compensation for payment of damages in the legal sense, claims for such payments cease to be valid after the lapse of ten years (statutory limitations). Notice pay shall be computed over the employee's gross wage; this is applicable even where the plaintiff is the employer.[244] The plaintiff has the burden of proof to verify that the term of notice was not respected or that a shorter notice was given; he does not need proof of the damage because the notice pay is designated by law as a fixed amount. If, in the event of an irregular termination, the employee has soon found a job or the

241. Court of Cassation, General Council Decision, 29 May 1963, 4-39/59; also 9th Div., 30 Mar. 1992, 16854/4784.
242. Court of Cassation, 9th Div., 8 Apr. 1991, 4473/7311; 2 Jan. 1999, 12252/16507; also General Council Decisions, 3 Feb. 1999, 9-35/54 and 5 May 1999, 9-258/276.
243. Court of Cassation, 9th Div., 3 Mar. 1997, 20450/3710; 13 Mar. 2001, 19901/3852; 1 Mar. 2003, 13738/3488; 11 Apr. 2003, 21541/5474; 11 Mar. 2004, 4474/4788; 11 Mar. 2004, 4475/4789.
244. Court of Cassation, 9th Div., 30 Nov. 1998, 14272/16876; 1 Nov. 1999, 16223/16478.

employer a replacement, notice pay may be requested in full.[245] Termination with a term of notice which is shorter than that stipulated by the law also qualifies as an irregular termination.[246]

660. It should be noted also that, in view of Article 17(6), the employer's non-observance of the rule of giving notice or his terminating the contract by paying in advance the wages corresponding to the term of notice shall not preclude the application of Articles 18–21 on job security (to those employees subject to job security, certainly).

661. As in advance notice pay explained above, in the computation of notice pay, all the monetary benefits plus other benefits which can be measured in monetary terms emanating from the employment contract, the collective labour agreement (payments like bonuses and premiums), or law shall be taken into consideration, in addition to the basic wage defined in Article 32(1) of the Act (Article 17(6)). The same rule applies to the computation of the employee's severance pay. Subvention interest for unpaid notice pay shall be charged as of the date on which the defendant was in default of payment.[247] If, however, the claim is based on a collective labour agreement, the highest interest rate charged to business transactions shall apply, as foreseen in Act No. 6356.[248]

662. The question of whether or not the parties may agree to increase notice pay for irregular terminations is a controversial matter. While the Court of Cassation holds that terms of notice may be increased as foreseen in Article 17, notice pay as payment of damages for irregular termination must not be altered by contracts, as it is related to public order.[249] This view was criticized in the teaching, especially in relation to another ruling of the High Court which held that because the term of notice is a relatively binding provision, advance notice pay may be increased in favour of the employee.[250] If claimed by the employer, however, notice pay must be computed on the basis of the legal notice term.[251]

663. With the introduction of new rules on job security into Turkish labour law, agreements restricting the right of employers to terminate the employment contract seem to have lost their significance in Turkish practice.[252] Especially in the presence of Article 21(5) which provides that the rules on the consequences of termination 'must not be altered by any agreement whatsoever and any agreement

245. Çelik, *supra*, pp. 214–215.
246. Court of Cassation, 9th Div., 25 Dec. 1996, 17132/24194; 15 Oct. 1997, 13629/17701; 12 Mar. 2009, 41150/6661.
247. Court of Cassation, General Council Decision, 12 Jun. 1991, 9-287/349.
248. Court of Cassation, 9th Div., 11 Mar. 1997, 3866/4816.
249. Court of Cassation, 9th Div., 12 Jan. 1980, 15645/63.
250. Court of Cassation, 9th Div., 4 Mar. 1998, 564/3399.
251. Court of Cassation, 9th Div., 29 Sep. 1998, 11002/13716.
252. On the restriction of the employer's right to terminate by the collective labour agreements, *see* para. 746 below.

provisions to the contrary shall be considered null and void', negotiated compensations for unjustified terminations including punitive damages which exceed the legally established limits have been prohibited. It is held that the same limits shall apply to the categories which fall outside the scope of job security provisions.[253] Since the exclusions relate to small workplaces where unions can hardly organize, restrictions to be brought by collective labour agreements as such do not seem to be a realistic possibility in any case.

5. Abusive Termination and Its Consequences

664. Under the present system provisions on job security are applicable only to persons employed in establishments with 30 and more employees and who also meet a minimum seniority of six months (Article 18(1)).[254] In other words, in terminating employees who do not meet these criteria, the employer does not have to depend on a valid reason, meaning that the employer and employee are free to terminate an open-ended contract by observing the notice requirements laid down in Article 17. The only restriction here relates to the payment of compensation by the employer if his act has been motivated by the abusive exercise of the right to terminate. Article 17(6) provides that 'in cases where the employment contract of employee who falls outside the scope of Articles 18–21 by definition of Article 18(1) has been ended by the abusive exercise of the right to terminate, the employee must be paid compensation amounting to three times the wages for the term of notice. If the requirement to give notice has not been observed either, the employee must be paid also the compensation for notice pay' (Article 17(6)).

665. In abusive termination, ending the contract is seemingly lawful and regular, but the employer is deemed to have acted with a covert and abusive intention in dismissing the employee. Article 13/c of the now-repealed Labour Act No. 1475, in dealing with abusive termination, also included the phrase 'dismissal due to the membership of the employee to a labour union or to his filing a grievance or in any other case where there is manifest abuse of the right to terminate the employment contract', but Article 17 of Act No. 4857 does not address the 'union membership' element since this dimension is now protected under Article 18 of the new Labour Act as well as under Article 25 of Act No. 6356 on Labour Unions and the Collective Labour Agreement.

666. The burden of proof in abusive dismissal is on the employee.[255] The Court of Cassation has upheld the view that the termination due to the employee's filing

253. Çelik, *supra*, pp. 308–312.
254. Also (according to Art. 18/VI), Arts 18–19, 21 and 25/III shall not be applicable to the employer's representative and his assistants authorized to manage the entire enterprise as well as the employer's representative managing the entire establishment if he is also authorized to hire and terminate employees.
255. Court of Cassation, 9th Div., 7 Apr. 1997, 621/6829; 27 Jan. 1999, 19528/1646; General Council Decision, 9 Jun. 1999, 9-47/490; 21 Jun. 2000, 97/27/8950.

a grievance against the employer with the official authorities constitutes abusive dismissal irrespective of whether the grievance itself is justified or not; the mere fact that a relationship can be proven to exist between the dismissal and the employee's filing the grievance is sufficient to hold that the termination was the result of the abusive exercise of a right.[256] If in the event of abusive termination the rule to give notice has not been observed either, the employee must receive notice pay as well, in addition to the compensation for abusive termination which is three times the wages for the term of notice (Article 17(6)).

667. For employees who are not covered by Articles 18–22 on job security of the Labour Act, the prevailing protective remedy is the payment of the above compensation in the event of abusive dismissals. It is hoped that, as in the past, the judiciary will keep shedding light with its interpretations on various allegedly abusive dismissals.[257] On abusive termination, Article 160(2) of the Maritime Labour Act carries provisions similar to Article 13/c of Act No. 1475. The Press Labour Act does not address this issue, but, since, in line with the reasoning of the Court of Cassation, the Labour Act should prevail in cases where other legislation is silent, provisions of the Labour Act on abusive terminations are applicable to employees covered by the Press Labour Act as well.

668. In addition to compensation for abusive dismissals, the Unions and the Collective Labour Agreement Act No. 6356 has foreseen even a stronger remedy for the employee's discriminatory treatment by the employer due to his membership to a union or participation in union activities in which case compensation shall not be less than the employee's total annual wages (Article 25(1,2,3)). However, at the time of this writing, the interpretation of Article 25 was a disputed and controversial matter under Act No. 6356. 'In the event of union-related dismissals, the employee may file legal action in accordance with Articles 18, 20 and 21 of the Labour Act No. 4857' (construed as meaning 'only workers who can have access to job security protection of the Labour Act No. 4857). If it is determined that the employment contract was terminated for a union-related reason, the employee shall be entitled to receive the 'union compensation'. In case of non-reinstatement, the compensation envisaged in Article 21(1) of Act No. 4857 (i.e., job security compensation up from four to eight months' wages) shall not be payable' (Article 25(5)). According to the dominant view in the teaching, given the clear and yet confusing

256. Court of Cassation, 9th Div., 17 Feb. 1965, 410/D-4/66; 4 Oct. 2006, 4253/25767, 11 Jun. 2006, 32353/18337.

257. For example, the Court of Cassation has held that where the employer has recruited new replacements for a number of terminated employees, allegations of abusive dismissal should be deemed justified (Court of Cassation, 9th Div., 11 Sep. 1991, 9229/9809). The refusal to engage employees in work by the employer who has decided to discontinue operations due to his inability to pay excessive wage demands emanating from a new collective labour agreement should not be treated as abusive dismissal (Court of Cassation, 9th Div., 6 Dec. 1993, 15719/17895). Likewise, the High Court has not held terminations due to economic crises, as verified by the Prime Minister's circulars, to be abusive (Court of Cassation, 9th Div., 13 Mar. 1996, 4900/5688; 18 Jan. 2000, 17262/124). Termination of a married female employee upon her becoming pregnant as confirmed by a medical report is, however, an abusive dismissal (Court of Cassation, 9th Div., 27 Mar. 1997, 2900/6115; 288 May 1997, 6254/10175).

wording of Article 25, union compensation shall be payable only to workers who are within the scope of job security provisions, i.e., who are employed in establishments with a minimum of 30 or more workers. Since employees below the scope of the 30-worker threshold can have access only to the lower compensation for abusive dismissal, Article 25(5) is perceived as a clear violation of the principle of equal treatment and freedom of association for a sizable portion of the workforce. Nevertheless, the last sentence of Article 25(5) has led to confusion and controversy by providing that 'the reluctance of the employee to file suit according to the above-mentioned provisions of Act No. 4857 shall not preclude him from requesting the said 'union compensation'.

669. It should be noted that the compensation foreseen as a remedy for union-related issues – to be not less than the employee's total annual wages – shall apply not only in the aggrieved person's dismissal, but also in the case of other discriminatory practices mentioned in Article 25, as upheld by the various past rulings of the Court of Cassation. Uncertainty has arisen only for scope of the category 'union-related terminations', which, of course is more important than other discriminatory practices during the employment relationship. Fortunately, however, this confusion has been eliminated by the 22 October 2014 decision of the Constitutional Court which has enabled all workers to receive union compensation for union-related dismissals.[258]

670. On the other hand, the compensation envisaged for employer's discriminatory practices in violation of the principle of 'equal treatment' (to be up to the employee's four months' wages (Article 5)) is a different category; as such it must not be confused with abusive dismissal compensation. The same should hold true in the distinction between compensation for discriminatory practices and compensation for the employee's union-related activities.

B. *The Scope of Job Security in Relation to Provisions on Change in Working Conditions and Collective Dismissals*

671. Article 22 deals with change in working conditions and termination of employment the subject matter of which concerns those who fall into the scope of job security. But, as there is no similar provision in the Act for those who are outside the scope of job security, it is affirmed that, as implicit in its first and last subsections, certain dimensions of Article 22 shall apply to all employees. In the first place the last subsection of Article 22 which provides that 'by mutual agreement the parties may always change working conditions and that changes in working conditions may not be made retroactive' is applicable to all employees. Second, the statement that 'changes that are not made in conformity with the procedure of serving a written notice to the employee and not accepted by the employee within six working days shall not bind the employee' is again applicable to all employees. If in this case the employee does not accept the offer for change, the employer will either

258. *See* below for more on this controversial topic.

abandon his offer or will very likely terminate the contract by paying the employee notice pay and severance pay to which he is entitled. The employee's claim to compensation for abusive dismissal will depend on the presence of special circumstances. If the employer does not terminate the contract and yet refuses to accept the labour of the employee, the legal consequence shall be deemed to be an unfair dismissal. On the other hand, the employees covered by job security provisions are entitled to have recourse to judicial process in accordance with the provisions of Articles 17 and 21 (Article 22 (last subsection)).

672. Similarly, except for the provision foreseen in the last subsection of Article 29 for employees who are under the scope of job security regulations, Article 29 on collective dismissals shall apply to all employees. The subsection of Article 29 provides that 'the employer must not make use of the provisions on collective dismissals with the covert aim to evade and prevent the application of Articles 18–21 on job security; otherwise the employee may file suit according to these articles'. This means that all employers irrespective of the scope of job security regulations will have to abide by the rules concerning collective dismissals which will be explained below.

C. *Termination of the Employment Contracts of Employees Who Are Covered by the Job Security Provisions of the Labour Act*

673. Protection of an employee's job was a long-debated issue in Turkey dating back to the late 1970s. Due to socio-economic developments of the last two decades and especially the heightened demands by labour unions, Turkey ratified in 1994 ILO Convention 158 on the Termination of Employment with the Initiative of the Employer by Act No. 3999. The problem in the ensuing years was to soften employers' reactions and to reach a compromised solution in determining the limits to be placed on the concept of freedom of contract. Finally, a draft bill prepared by a nine-member tripartite committee of academicians was passed by the Parliament as Act No. 4773 on Job Security in the year 2002. Provisions of this Act concerning termination of employment were transposed with some modifications into Act No. 4857 which came into force on June 2003.

674. During the legislative process, employers demanded the revision of the legislation on severance pay. According to them since an unemployment insurance scheme had been put into practice in 1999, there was no longer a need to maintain the 'inflated' amounts of severance pay in addition to the new job protections brought by the Labour Act. To meet employers' requests, the committee of academicians prepared also a draft aiming to establish a severance pay fund, making severance pay payable basically only upon the employee's retirement out of a fund to be established, but in the face of reactions from both labour unions and employer organizations (and for different reasons), the new proposal could not reach the stage of legislative enactment. At the moment, therefore, Article 14 of the now-repealed Labour Act No. 1475 was left in force. There is, however, an increasing demand emanating from employer circles for the revision of severance payment regulations.

675. In principle, the provisions on job security are limited to a certain segment of the coverage of the Labour Act. However, Article 116 of the Labour Act provides that Articles 18–21 on job security and Article 29 on collective dismissals of the Labour Act shall apply by analogy to those covered by the Press Labour Act as well. With a view to expand the scope of employment protection to all categories as envisaged in ILO Convention 158, job protection for employees subject to the Maritime Labour Act and the Obligations Act in general was suggested in the draft bill of the academic committee, but it has not been implemented yet.

676. Article 18(1) of Act No. 4857 provides that the employer who terminates an employee working under an open-ended (indefinite) employment contract and who has completed a minimum seniority of six months in an establishment with 30 or more employees must depend on a valid reason for such termination connected with the capacity or conduct of the employee or based on the operational requirements of the establishment or service. Thus, Article 18, in laying down the components of the concept of job security also delineates the limits of its scope. But in access to job security coverage for workers employed underground, the 'six months seniority' condition shall not be required, as amended by Article 2 of Act No. 6552.

677. The requirement to depend on a valid reason in terminating the employment contract is, therefore, applicable only to establishments with 30 or more employees. Notwithstanding this threshold, since this criterion is held to be relatively binding, the parties' agreeing in the collective agreement to apply job security in establishments with fewer employees should be binding.[259] It should be noted, however, that as establishments engaged in agricultural and forestry work employing more than 50 employees have been taken under the coverage of the Labour Act, the scope of job security in agriculture and forestry is limited by the criterion of 'establishment with 50 or more employees'.

678. Although a disputed matter the numerical limitation placed on the scope of job security (30 or more generally, and more than 50 employees in agriculture) is in line with ILO Convention 158 which permits the placement of limitations on the scope of job security in terms of the size of undertakings if national conditions so require.

679. In the first job security Act No. 4773 the scope was limited to establishments with 10 or more employees. The present '30 criterion' is now open to criticism for it denies job security to a great majority of wage-earners, employed not only in small but also medium-sized establishments. It is also in conflict with 'the principle of reasonable measurement' criterion enshrined in Article 13 of the Constitution. Upon complaints of labour unions, this increased threshold is also criticized by the ILO Committee of Experts in its observations on Convention 158 for the year 2005.

---

259. Court of Cassation 9th Div. 26 May 2005, 12317/19404; 22 Oct. 2010, 4905/4260.

680. 'In the event the employer has more than one establishment in the same branch of activity, the number of employees shall be computed on the basis of the total number of employees in these establishment' (Article 18(6)). However, employees employed in transitory work (lasting only up to thirty days by its nature), trainees in the establishment and students undergoing vocational training, apprentices, employees of the subcontractor insofar as the obligations of the subcontractor are concerned and temporary employees posted to the employer are to be excluded in determining the 30-employee threshold. If the units of a group are represented by different corporate (legal) personalities, the thresholds are to be considered separately for each. The threshold includes full-time and part-time employees as well as employees working under fixed-term and open-ended contracts since the Labour Act has not brought exceptions to any of these categories The same holds true for seasonal employees.[260] Temporary employees posted by the employer to another employer in accordance with Article 7 shall also benefit from job security provisions in their continuing relationship with their main employer. The same protection shall apply to the subcontractor's employees in their employment relationship with the subcontractor (i.e., their own employer).[261]

681. As for the employee's length of service which must be observed for his entitlement to job security provisions, 'the six-month' minimum seniority of the employee shall be computed on the basis of the sum of his employment periods in one or different establishments of the same employer (Article 18(4)). As the Act does not refer to continuity of employment, interrupted employment periods must be combined in computing the minimum six-month employment of the employee. And in cases where the employee has not completed the minimum six-month service, the employer does not have to show a valid reason in terminating the employment contract.

682. Another category excluded from the coverage of job security provisions (Articles 18, 19, 21 and the last subsection of Article 25) is the employer's representative and his assistants authorized to manage the entire enterprise as well as the employer's representative managing the entire establishment but who is also authorized to recruit and to terminate employees (Article 18(5)). This means that in an incorporated company, for instance, the president and vice-presidents of the corporation itself as well as the general managers of establishments (for example, branches of a bank) have also been excluded from job security coverage if they are also empowered to hire and terminate employees.[262]

---

260. Court of Cassation, 9th Div., 22 Feb. 2006, 320/3898.

261. If, however, a simulated act is proven to exist between the main employer and the subcontracted workers, the latter shall be included in the threshold for the main employer's establishment. Court of Cassation, 9th Div., 18 Dec. 2009, 247/37746.

262. For definitions of the 'enterprise' and 'establishment' and 'employer's representative' in this context, *see* paras 145–150 above. For a critical evaluation of this broadened concept of 'employer's representative' in relation to job security, *see* E. AkyiAit, 'İşveren Vekilinin İşGüvencesi', *Kamu-İş*, Vol. 4, No. 4, 2004, pp. 63–78. The status of the employer's representative in this regard can be inferred from the organization chart, employment contract and provisions of the personnel rules of work. Court of Cassation, 9th Div., 1 Feb. 2010, 13573/1817.

683. The requirement that the employer must depend on a valid reason when he terminates the employment contract applies to contracts of indefinite duration (open-ended), as provided in Article 18. Since fixed-term contracts automatically expire upon the lapse of the specified term, they are to be excluded from employment protection, as also permitted by Article 2/a of ILO Convention 158. But employees under fixed-termed contracts must be accorded sufficient protection against abusive dismissals as envisaged in Article 2/3 of the Convention. Obviously, the Labour Act of Turkey No. 4857 has foreseen the abusive conclusion of fixed-term contracts with the covert aim of denying job protection to the employee. Article 11 provides that a fixed-term contract must not be concluded more than once except when there is an essential reason which may necessitate repeated (chain) contracts; otherwise the contract shall be deemed to have been made for an indefinite period from the very beginning. It is clear that, in this case, the employee will have access to provisions on job security.

D. *Valid Reasons for Termination*

1. The Notion

684. The employer who terminates the open-ended contract of an employee must depend on a valid reason for such termination connected with the capacity or conduct of the employee or based on the operational requirements of the establishment or service (Article 18(1)). In order to shed light on practice, the text on the reasons for the article provided various examples and explanations for valid reasons. Valid reasons for termination are those which, although not as serious as the cases mentioned in Article 25 (termination for just cause, summary dismissal), affect adversely the normal functioning of the workplace or the obligation of the employee to perform his duties adequately.[263] Reasons connected with the capacity of the employee may be his productivity or performance being lower than those working in comparable jobs,[264] decrease in his concentration on the job, incapacity to learn and improve himself, frequent illnesses which adversely affect his ability to perform his duties adequately, inability to adapt, especially if he has reached retirement age. Reasons connected with the employee's conduct may be the following: to do harm to the employer or to threaten to give repeated harm, to cause unrest in the workplace by borrowing money from co-workers or provoking them against the employer, to perform his work poorly or inadequately despite warnings, to engage in frequent and long telephone conversations, frequent tardiness or walk-arounds, to cause frequent and unnecessary disputes with co-workers, to establish relations

263. *See, e.g.*, the ruling of the Court of Cassation, 9th Div., 2 Feb. 2005, 92049/2901.

264. On the question of low productivity and insufficient performance, *see* the ruling of the Court of Cassation, 9th Div., 24 Jun. 2004, 3740/15625. In the opinion of the High Court, the alleged low performance must be scrutinized by expert opinion at the establishment to see if the job is compatible with accepted job standards and if so, the employee's performance must be compared with that of other employees doing comparable jobs. Further, whether low productivity is of a temporary or permanent nature must be determined. Further, objective standards must be used to measure performance (18 Mar. 2008, 27584/5327; 9 Mar. 2009, 6142/20570).

with other people which may hinder the work flow and the working environment. Valid reasons which are based on the operational requirements of the establishment or service may emanate from inside or outside the establishment. The following examples are those valid reasons which may emanate from outside the organization: reduced sales, decreased demand and plummeting orders, energy shortages, economic crisis, a general stagnation in the market, loss of foreign markets, disruption of work due to raw material shortages and the like. Adoption of new work methods, downsizing, application of new technologies, abolition of certain sections or jobs (restructuring) are valid reasons emanating from inside the organization.

685. It is generally accepted that the employer should call on termination only as a last resort. Before terminating, he must have stopped overtime work, shorten working time with the employee's consent, institute flexible work patterns, transfer employees to other sections, retrain them for other jobs and the like. The Court of Cassation has already issued rulings along these dimensions.[265] Terminations following the increases in production and overtime work have been declared null and void.[266]

686. In a similar fashion, the Court of Cassation ruled terminations based on the alleged reason of economic crisis invalid because the actual case was a reduction in profits rather than a real loss and about 80 employees were hired prior to the said terminations; therefore the measure of 'last resort' had not been respected.[267] On the other hand, reductions in the workforce of public economic enterprises by encouraging early retirements were deemed valid since the need for privatization had made such reductions necessary.[268]

687. A crucial point is the distinction to be made between the concept of 'valid reasons' stemming from the capacity or conduct of the employee and those 'just cause' cases envisaged in Article 25/II for summary dismissals. Apparently such distinctions may at times be quite precarious and difficult to make. A reasonable method could be to evaluate each case in the light of the examples given in the reasons for the relevant articles and then to use meticulous legal judgment to determine whether the case necessitates application of Articles 18–21 or Article 25/II whose consequences for the employee may be quite different.[269] The principle of 'last resort' must be observed in terminations due to the capacity or conduct of the

265. Court of Cassation, 9th Div., 27 Oct. 2003, 18257/17985; 11 Dec. 2003, 20222/20604; 15 Apr. 2004, 6141/7644.
266. Court of Cassation, 9th Div., 8 Jul. 2003, 12442/13123; 29 Dec. 2003, 23204/22988.
267. Court of Cassation, 9th Div., 27 Oct. 2003, 18257/17985; 10 Nov. 2003, 18296/18920; 11 Jul. 2005, 21402/2448.
268. Court of Cassation, 9th Div., 23 Oct. 2003, 18090/17878; 29 Jan. 2004, 23159/1418. For an analysis of court decisions involving requests for reinstatement, *see* Ömer Ekmekçi, 'Yargıtay'ın İşe İade Davalarına İlişkin Kararlarının Değ erlendirilmesi', *İşHukuku ve Sosyal Güvenlik Hukuku Dergisi*, Legal, No. 1, 2004, pp. 165–182.
269. For High Court rulings addressing the fine distinction between termination for just cause and termination for a valid reason, *see* Court of Cassation, 9th Div., 24 Jan. 2005, 27599/1413; 31 Jan. 2005, 31628/2540.

employee before terminating him. The employer should test the employee's capacity by engaging him in other types of work as well as by warning him on his deficiencies in performance or conduct.

2. Points to Consider in Terminating the Contract Due to the Operational Requirements of the Enterprise, Establishment or Job

688. In terminations due to operational requirements of the enterprise, establishment or the job itself, the employer must have been thrust into a situation where the performance of the job by the employee is no longer needed either because of a sustained reason emanating from outside or inside the organization. In other words, the employer must be in a situation where he is forced to operate the establishment with fewer employees. This downsizing may stem from a downturn in the business cycle or a necessity to reorganize work due to managerial or technological reasons. With a view to determine whether or not the employer's action was arbitrary, the court may investigate the extent to which the alleged cause of the termination is justified. As termination may involve a group of employees, sometimes culminating in collective dismissals affecting certain section(s) of the establishment, the question lies in the criteria to apply in the employer's choosing the employees who are to be terminated. Turkish legal teaching holds that the employer is free to use his discretion in this case. The High Court holds that while the employer is free in taking managerial decisions, an arbitrary managerial decision must be subject to judicial review and should the same results be achieved by managerial decisions other than termination, resolving the issue through termination could not be held to be a valid decision.[270] Notwithstanding this view, however, it is espoused that the employer's discretion in implementing lay-offs may be restricted by collective agreements. In fact many collective agreements carry provisions which foresee the application of criteria such as priority to be given first to voluntary quits and second to those who have reached retirement age, third the application of the 'last in, first out' principle and finally, super-seniority to be granted to union officials and shop stewards who shall be the last to be terminated In the event of dismissals involving a group of employees, the Court of Cassation has tended to emphasize recently the 'social choice' criterion, especially with reference to respecting the principle of equal treatment in view of Article 5 of the Labour Act, but the Court does not seem to apply the said criterion consistently in many of its later decisions.[271]

3. Cases Which Do Not Constitute a Valid Reason

689. In line with ILO Convention 158 (Articles 5 and 6), the following cases, *inter alia*, shall not constitute a valid reason for termination (Article 18(3)):

270. Court of Cassation, 9th Div., 16 Dec. 2004, 27003/27998; 12 Jan. 2005, 12373/522; 1 Feb. 2005, 30981/2829; 18 Sep. 2007, 26494/26906; 25 Feb. 2008, 3735/2001.
271. *See, e.g.*, Court of Cassation, 9 Feb. 2009, 1186/1832.

(a) union membership or participation in union activities outside working hours or, with the consent of the employer, within working hours;
(b) acting or having acted in the capacity of, or seeking office as, a union representative;
(c) the filing of a complaint or participation in proceedings against an employer involving alleged violations of laws or regulations or recourse to competent administrative or judicial authorities;
(d) race, colour, sex, marital status, family responsibilities, pregnancy, confinement, religion, political opinion and similar reasons;
(e) absence from work during maternity leave when female employees must not be engaged in work, as foreseen in Article 74;
(f) temporary absence from work during the waiting period due to illness or accident foreseen in Article 25/(1)-b.

690. Obviously legal consequences associated with the relevant legislation (namely, the Labour Act and the Unions Act) concerning invalid terminations shall be applicable in cases where the contract is terminated in relation to the above-stated reasons. The crucial point here is the reversal of the 'burden of proof', that is, while in principle the burden of proof has been placed on the employer where the plaintiff (employee) claims that the alleged reason was not valid, Article 20(2) provides that the employee shall bear the burden of proof if he claims that his dismissal was in fact caused by a motive different from the one alleged by the employer (i.e., his joining a union or participating in union activities).

691. Moreover, Article 25/(1)-b refers to the employee's absence from work due to illness or accident which may or may not be attributed to his fault. Therefore, here the employer's right to terminate the contract for a valid reason shall take effect following the lapse of the time foreseen in Article 25/(1)-b.

E. The Manner of Terminating the Contract

692. Notice of termination must be given by the employer in written form, showing the reason for termination which must be specified in clear and precise terms, Article 19(1). Here written form should be construed as a condition of validity of the transaction the violation of which would result in an invalid termination.[272]

693. The employee's refusal to accept the written notice of termination must be documented in a signed report prepared on the spot in accordance with the procedure envisaged in Article 109 of the Labour Act.

694. The time when notice must be given is not clear in cases concerning the employee's conduct or capacity. In line with ILO Recommendation 166, it is

272. The Court of Cassation ruled in this direction in several verdicts: 9th Div., 11 Sep. 2003, 14676/14287; 15 Oct. 2003, 16116/17101; 27 Oct. 2003, 18040/18119; 27 Sep. 2004, 5522/19993.

asserted that for termination the employee's behaviour must have been repeated at least once and yet not corrected despite the lapse of a reasonable time period. As for the employee's incapacity, his performance must have remained unchanged within a reasonable time period despite the employer's instructions and written warning. The written warning must also be served in cases concerning the employee's conduct. The payment of notice and severance pay by the employer does not entitle the dismissed employee to claim, solely by making use of fellow employees' testimony, that his termination was not based on a valid reason.[273]

695. The Act is silent on when the termination must be implemented should a valid reason materialize. In line with ILO Recommendation 166 and Article 344 of the Obligations Act of Turkey, however, notice of termination must be given within a reasonable time period following the occurrence of the valid reason.

696. Except for the employer's right to break the employment contract in accordance with Article 25/II of the Labour Act (summary dismissal for serious misconduct or malicious or immoral behaviour of the employee), the employment of an employee working under an open-ended contract shall not be terminated for reasons related to his conduct or performance before he is given an opportunity to defend himself against the allegations made, Article 19(2). As inferred from the beginning phrase and stated in the last sentence, there is no requirement to receive the defence of the employee in summary dismissals under Article 25/II, a point which may be criticized as a violation of the concept of 'due process of law'. It would be feasible therefore, for reasons of due process, to set forth a written defence requirement in summary dismissals as well. In many cases, in practice, with a view to substantiating justification of termination, employers usually get the employee's written defence in terminations under Article 25/II. But the opponents of such a requirement argue also that in summary dismissals there is usually an urgent need to take prompt action, and in any case the employee has the right to contest the termination decision in court where he will naturally have the right to defend himself.

697. In some cases, in order to receive severance pay and other entitlements, it is the employee who asks the employer to terminate his contract, with a commitment that he shall not contest the dismissal, i.e., a sort of constructive discharge. Initially a controversial matter, the Court later ruled that the employee's petition to that effect would be valid, provided that the lawsuit for reinstatement later filed by the worker who has made that commitment and received his notice and severance pay was not acceptable.

F. Procedure of Appeal against Termination

698. With a view to seeking redress, the employee who alleges that no reason was given for the termination of his employment contract or who claims that the reason(s) stated were not valid to justify the termination is entitled to lodge an

273. Court of Cassation, 9th Div., 18 Dec. 2003, 20315/22148.

appeal against that termination with the mediator within one month of receiving the notice of termination in accordance with the provisions of the Labour Courts Act No. 7036. In the event of failure to come to agreement as a result of mediation, a lawsuit may be filed with the labour court within two weeks from the delivery of the mediator's final report. If the parties so agree, the dispute may be referred to private arbitration within the same period of time (Article 20(1)). Due to the refusal of the lawsuit on grounds of having bypassed mediation first, the decision of refusal shall be communicated to the mediator officially. Recourse to the mediator may be made within two weeks from the date of official communication of the finalized decision on refusal.

699. In proving that termination was based on a valid reason, the burden of proof shall rest on the employer. If the worker claims that the termination was based on a different reason, he is under the obligation to prove his argument.

700. The case shall be promptly concluded. If the court's decision is appealed, the regional court of appeal (*istinaf*) shall award its final decision promptly Article 20/4). In deciding on the worker's wage and job security compensation, the court or the arbitrator shall take the current wage level prevailing on the date of litigation.

701. In practice and teaching, however, controversy has arisen as to the date on which the employee's right to appeal his termination will become effective. In terminations involving a period of notice, the said date should be the end of the notice period since the contract is deemed to be in force within the duration of that period; in other words, termination must have actually materialized for the period of statutory limitation to begin. In immediate terminations by advance notice pay, on the other hand, the statutory limitation shall begin on the date when notice to terminate has reached the worker.[274]

702. In an attempt to alleviate the work load of labour courts, Act No. 4857 brought as a new avenue the recourse to arbitration for the settlement of disputes concerning job security. Arbitration of collective rights disputes was already a known method in Turkish practice, but the Court of Cassation has usually upheld the validity of arbitration only in disputes between the parties to collective bargaining involving collective entities and, for that matter, mainly in disputes related to the interpretation of the collective agreement. Inevitably in practice, however, an interpretation suit entailing fulfilment of a certain obligation normally affected the rights of the individual employee as well.

703. In the face of the constitutional principle that judicial power can be exercised only by independent courts (Article 9, Constitution), recognition of the arbitrability of job security disputes in Act No. 4857 led to legal controversy whereby some writers insisted on the unconstitutionality of the provision.[275] Considering the

274. *See* M. Uçum, 'İşe İade Taleplerinde Dava Açma Süresinin Başlangıcına İlişkin Sorunlar', *İşHukuku ve Sosyal Güvenlik Hukuku Dergisi*, pp. 1302–1318.

275. For various criticisms, *see* M. Yücel, 'İşGüvencesi Kapsamında Özel Hakem Şartı', *İşHukuku ve*

tendency of the judicial authority to interpret legislation strictly in literal terms, there was a strong likelihood that the Constitutional Court might strike private arbitration out of the job security system. However, this unconstitutionality debate was misplaced for various reasons. First, legislative regulations which envisage arbitration of disputes even in public service type contracts are possible now under the amended version of Article 135 of the Constitution which says that 'disputes arising from public contracts may be settled through national and international arbitration'. Second, arbitration of rights disputes has been a long-recognized and well-established process envisaged in Turkish procedural law, entailing a binding decision which can normally be appealed to the Court of Cassation only for procedural reasons (i.e., the Act on Civil Procedures, No. 1086, Articles 533–536; and the new Act on Civil Procedures, No. 6100, Articles 407–444). Third, although the arbitration mechanism which may be foreseen in the collective agreement (Article 52(1,2), Act No. 6356) relates to disputes between the parties to the collective labour agreement, arbitral decisions thus awarded also create an impact for the individual employee's fulfilment claims, as noted above. And finally, Act No. 4857 had now, though in a narrowly specified area (namely in termination disputes), imbued collectively bargained private arbitration with a clearly prescribed jurisdiction which included cases concerning the alleged invalidity of termination (i.e., requests for reinstatement or compensation in lieu of reinstatement and wage claims for the time during which the employee is not engaged in work, up to four months) (Articles 20–21). The arbitrator or the arbitration board should, however, decide on such compensation without stating the actual amounts in question.[276]

704. In view of the constitutional principle that the individual's right to have recourse to court proceedings must not be rescinded, it is held that the employee has the option of choosing either to accept arbitration or to have recourse to court.[277] For the system's viability and sustainability, however, the author thinks that the arbitration clause inserted into the collective agreement should, due to the supremacy of the collective agreement over the employment contract, be binding on both the employee and employer as a rule governing the execution and termination of the employment contract.[278] In view of Article 31 of the Unions Act No. 282 or Article 25 of the new Act No. 6356 which prohibits discrimination between members and non-members, except for wage-related matters, this principle should be applicable to all employees, members of the signatory union and non-members alike. Furthermore, the parties may improvise protective measures to provide for the impartiality of the arbitrator. The following provision is a case in point: 'If the parties cannot agree on the identity of the arbitrator or the chairman of the arbitration board, he shall be named and appointed by the court.'

Sosyal Güvenlik Hukuku Dergisi, *Legal*, No. 4, 2004, pp. 1347–1365, and *see* footnote 87 in Çelik, *supra*, p. 214.

276. Court of Cassation, General Council Decision, 22 Mar. 2004, 5846/5621.

277. D. Ulucan, '4773 Sayılı Kanun Çerçevesinde İş Güvencesi', *İş Güvencesi Semineri*, Galatasaray Üniversitesi, İstanbul, 2003, p. 34.

278. Çelik, *supra*, pp. 259–262. For more on arbitration in Turkey, *see* paras 861–866, 872–881 below.

705. These views notwithstanding, the Constitutional Court overruled the validity of collectively negotiated arbitration in termination disputes.[279] However, the decision for nullity does not affect the employer's and employee's agreeing to arbitration in termination disputes. In other words, the Constitutional Court upheld the unconstitutionality of only the collective agreement terms on arbitration in job security disputes. Following the intervention of the Constitutional Court, the last sentence of Article 20/I now reads as follows: 'If the parties so agree, the dispute may also be referred to private arbitration within the same period of time' (i.e., within one month of receiving the notice of termination). But now the controversy relates to when the parties may agree on recourse to arbitration (i.e., during the conclusion or execution of the employment contract, or after termination has materialized?). The rulings of the Court of Cassation have wavered on this matter, but recent verdicts of the Court support the last option. The underlying rationale is the allegedly bounded free will of the worker at the time of the conclusion as well as during the execution of the employment contract because of his/her subordinate position to the employer.[280] Thus with the further restriction of the mandate of arbitration, the case load of labour judges who will necessarily become mired in termination disputes at an ever-increasing rate is likely to be in surmount.

G. *Burden of Proof*

706. In response to the employee's appeal against the notice of termination, the burden of proving that termination was based on a valid reason rests on the employer. However, if the employee claims that the termination was based on a reason different from the one stated by the employer, the burden of proof is then on the employee. The shifting of the burden of proof to the employee in this last incidence is not of much practical significance except when the employee claims that the employer's real motive in termination was the employee's acting as a union-shop steward (Article 18(3 a)), or his participation in union activities (Article 18(3b)). In this case, the employee shall be entitled to a compensation above the amount foreseen in Article 21 of the Labour Act, that is, an amount to be not less than his total annual wages (Article 25 of the Unions Act No. 6356) rather than between four and eight months' wages.

707. When the employer cannot prove his reason, therefore, the employee, in order to receive this higher compensation, must be able to prove that his contract was terminated due to his acting as a shop steward or his union membership or participation in union activities. The Act's treatment of this matter in this manner could certainly be criticized. Besides, a meaningless distinction was created between those who were covered by the job security provisions of the Labour Act and those who were not. In view of Article 31(7) of the now-repealed Unions Act No. 2821, the employer had the burden of proof in lawsuits connected to dismissals due to union

279. Decision of the Constitutional Court, 19 Oct. 2005, 66/72 Official Gazette 24 Nov. 2007, No. 26710.
280. Court of Cassation 9th Div., 26 May 2008, 10997/12660; 20 Jan. 2009, 44630/537.

membership or participation in union activities filed by the employees subject to the Maritime Labour Act No. 854, to Press Labour Act No. 5953, to the previous Obligations Act No. 818 and employees engaged in activities deemed as agricultural as well as employees excluded from the job security provisions (Articles 18 to 21) of the Labour Act. In such cases, general principles of the Labour Courts Act No. 5521 should apply and the compensation to be paid to the aggrieved employee should not be less than his total annual wages. Thus, in so far as the burden of proof was concerned, a groundless differentiation was made between employees accorded general job security by Act No. 4857 and against the interests of those excluded from the protection of its Articles 18–21.[281]

708. Concerning the procedure of trial, Article 20(3) provides that the court must apply fast-hearing procedures and conclude the case within two months. If the decision is appealed, the Court of Cassation must render its definitive verdict within one month. Although Article 20(3) has made reference to a 'definitive verdict', the High Court has occasionally reversed some court decisions for reasons of insufficient evidence or insufficient scrutiny, thereby protracting the trial.[282]

709. However, if the employee also requests other items in addition to his request for reinstatement (such as a wage claim or some other employment-related compensation), the trial will normally take longer than that foreseen in this article especially as such claims are subject to oral hearings. Therefore, trials concerning reinstatement-compensation for invalid terminations and trials for other claims were to be subjected to pertinent legal actions separately.[283] According to Article 316(d) of the new Act on Civil Procedures No. 6100, these trials are to be conducted through 'simple hearing' procedures, meaning that requests for reinstatement and monetary claims may now be adjudicated under the same (unified) trial.

H. Consequences of Invalid Termination

710. If the court or the arbitrator concludes that the termination was unjustified because no valid reason was given or the alleged reason was invalid, the employer must reinstate the employee in work within one month. If, upon the application of the employee, the employer does not reinstate and reengage him in work, compensation to be not less than the employee's four month's wages and not more than his

281. For the complications caused by the said differentiation, *see also* Ünal Narmanlıoğlu, 'İş Güvencesi Kapsamına Giren İşçinin Sendikal Tazminat Talebi', *İşHukuku ve Sosyal Güvenlik Hukuku Dergisi, Legal,* No. 5, 2005, pp. 239–251.

282. Court of Cassation, General Council Decision, 20 Nov. 2004, 9-510/557; 9th Div., 13 May 2004; 650/11630; 1 Nov. 2004, 8628/24546 (with new amendments to the law of procedures which will become effective in October 2011, the Court's verdicts based on fast-hearing processes are likely to change course).

283. Court of Cassation, 9th Div., 11 Sep. 2003, 14994/14267; 24 Sep. 2007, 14002/27728. 'The employee's failure to prove that he was terminated due to his union membership shall not relieve the employer of his obligation to prove his own valid reason'. Court of Cassation, 9th Div., 1 Feb. 20101093/1810. However, the High Court has not changed its position on this matter. *See* Court of Cassation, 9th Div., 21 Mar. 2013, 26152/2004.

eight months' wages shall be paid to him by the employer. In its verdict ruling the termination invalid, the court shall also designate the amount of compensation to be paid in case the employee is not reinstated (Article 21(1,2)). It must be noted that, in designating the amount of compensation, the court or the arbitrator should take into consideration factors like the length of the employee's service, his age, family responsibilities, wage level, the nature of his job as well as the reasons for the termination of his contract and possible causes of the employer's reluctance to reengage him in work.

711. In computing this compensation, the employee's last basic wage is to be considered. The law provides that the employee is entitled only to request reinstatement, and the choice to reinstate or to pay compensation instead has been left to the employer.

712. For reinstatement, the employee must make an application to the employer within ten working days of the date on which the finalized court verdict or arbitrator's decision was communicated to him. If the employee does not apply within the said time period, termination shall be deemed valid, in which case the employer shall be held liable only for the legal consequences of that termination (Article 21(5)). If the employee makes the said application, the employer must reengage him in work for his job at the establishment under the same conditions.[284]

713. The employee shall be paid up to four months' total of his wages and other entitlements for the time he is not at work until the finalization of the court's or arbitrator's verdict. In implementing this provision which aims to provide the employee with income security during the court litigation period, whether or not the employee is reinstated shall have no effect (Article 21(3)). Although not clarified in the High Court's decisions, it is held that, in order to be entitled to remuneration up to four months' wages and other claims, the employees' application within ten days is not a sufficient condition; he must also demonstrate his wish to return to his job, complying with the employer's call for reinstatement.

714. In the event of reinstatement, if advance notice pay or severance pay had already been paid to the reinstated employee at the time of his termination, these amounts shall be deducted from (traded off with) the compensation computed in accordance with Article 21(1) (compensation up to four months' wages). In the event of non-reinstatement, if term of notice has not been respected nor advance notice pay paid, the wages corresponding to the term of notice (in addition to the severance pay if the employee was entitled to that pay and yet not paid) shall be paid to the employee who has not been reinstated (Article 21(4)). If the employer does not reengage the employee in work despite the court's or arbitrator's decision which has rendered the termination invalid, his reluctance to reinstate the employee will be deemed to be a 'termination', in which case the employee's other entitlements accrued between the date of initial termination and employer's refusal to

284. Court of Cassation, 9th Div., 2 Jun. 2004, 1080/13416; 12 Jun. 2007, 8740/18743.

reengage him in work must also be paid to the employee.[285] In its decision rendering the termination invalid, the court also designates the amount of compensation to be paid in lieu of reinstatement (from four up to eight months' wages). This compensation is to be calculated on the basis of the worker's last basic wage.

715. The last subsection of Article 21 provides that provisions of subsections (1), (2) and (3) of this article shall not be altered by any agreement whatsoever, and any agreement provisions to the contrary are to be deemed null and void. Thus the rules embodied in these provisions shall be considered to be absolutely binding.

716. The Court of Cassation has, since the passage of Acts No. 4773 and 4857, reached various decisions generally consistent with the pertinent provisions cited above.[286] As for the level of compensation, however, one should note that the High Court tends to rule at the lower level to be paid to the employee in almost all cases brought before it.

I. Change in Working Conditions and Termination of the Employment Contract

717. Any change by the employer in working conditions based on the employment contract or the rules of work annexed to the contract as well as on other sources and workplace practices may be made only after a written notice is served by him to the employee. Changes that are not in conformity with this procedure and not accepted by the employee in written form within six working days shall not bind the employee. If the employee does not accept the offer for change within this period, the employer may terminate the contract by respecting the term of notice, provided that he indicates in written form that the proposed change was based on a valid reason or there was another valid reason for termination. In this case, the employee may file suit according to the provisions of Articles 17 and 21 (Article 22(1)). 'By mutual agreement the parties may always change working conditions. Change in working conditions may not be made retroactive' (Article 22(2)).

718. In view of Article 117(4) of the new Penal Code No. 5237, a prison term from six months up to three years has been foreseen for persons who, by using force or threats, cause employers or employees to change the prevailing wages or working conditions or to suspend operations. Under the provisions of Article 22, however, the relevance of Article 117 of the new Penal Code is questionable.

---

285. M. Ekonomi, 'Hizmet Akdinin Feshi ve İş Güvencesi', *Çimento İşveren Dergisi*, Ekim, 2003, pp. 1–40. The High Court found inappropriate the designation by the judge of the wages and the said compensation in numerical amounts (Court of Cassation, 20 Nov. 2003, 19548/19644; 24 Jun. 2004, 3740/15625; 8 Jul. 2004, 17868 17365; 6 Jul. 2009, 20151 19581).

286. *See*, *e.g.*, the following decisions of the High Court: Court of Cassation, 9th Div., 8 Jul. 2003, 12442/13123; 16 Sep. 2003, 15784/14563; 6 Nov. 2003, 18733/18729; 29 Jan. 2004, 499/1489; 10 Feb. 2004, 23396/1896; 12 Feb. 2004, 484/2029; 8 Nov. 2004, 12698/25058; 2 Feb. 2005, 31715/2889; 24 Sep. 2007, 14002/27728. *See also* Ekmekçi, *supra*.

719. Under the previous Labour Act No. 1475, the employee was entitled to terminate the employment contract for just cause if the employer made essential alterations in working conditions which he did not accept. Article 24/II of the present Act which regulates the termination of the employment contract by the employee for just cause does not contain a similar provision; instead, Article 22 now aims to regulate the changes made in working conditions by providing some continuity in the employment relationship. This new provision is also linked to the general mechanism of job security. Essential alterations in working conditions may be made only upon the consent of the employee; changes not accepted in written form by the employee within six working days shall not bind him, meaning that employee's silence cannot be taken as implicit acceptance. Also, a general announcement to employees to that effect will not be sufficient; the employer must communicate the written proposal for change to the individual employee. If the employee does not give his written approval, the employer must indicate, again in written form, that the proposed change is based on a valid reason in which case he may terminate the contract by respecting the term of notice and the employee can have recourse to legal action.

720. Controversy arose, however, on the application of Article 22 as to what action should be taken if in the employment contract, the collective agreement or rules of work the employer had reserved his right to make essential alterations in the workplace or the working conditions. While some asserted that such a clause would be binding on the employee due to the purpose of the Act as well as the principle of freedom of contract and fair dealing,[287] the Court of Cassation ruled that the dissenting employee should still have access to the provisions of Article 22, thereby requesting the termination of his employment contract by the employer to be held invalid.[288]

§3. Breaking the Individual Employment Contract for Just Cause (Termination Without Having to Respect a Term of Notice)

I. The Notion

721. 'Breaking' can be defined as 'the act by which the employer or the employee unilaterally and immediately terminates the employment contract for just cause'. In this category, irrespective of whether the contract is open-ended (definite) or fixed-term (definite), either party is entitled to end the contract promptly, for reasons of just cause indicated in the pertinent articles and by not having to respect the terms of notice, or before the expiration of the fixed-term. In breaking, the fact that termination is based on a just cause must be clarified; however, the 'just cause' need not be expressed in a concrete manner. But, the breaking party must

287. G. Alpagut, *Çimento İşveren Dergisi*, September 2004, pp. 61–62.
288. Court of Cassation 9th Div., 26 Jan. 2004, 23105/1204; Court of Cassation, General Council Decision, 11 Nov 2006, 9-613/644; 9th Div., 28 Jan. 2010, 14809/1480.

clarify the reason for the breaking act upon the request of the other party. The breaking party is bound by his reason for breaking the contract once he has clarified it; he may not predicate it on a different just cause later.[289] If both parties have mutually terminated the contract for just cause, the legal consequences must be determined according to which one of the terminations has materialized first.[290] If more than one just cause has been alleged, materialization of only one just cause shall be deemed sufficient for termination.

722. In termination by respecting notice terms or in immediate termination where notice pay has not been paid, either party may terminate the contract if a just cause emerges within the duration of the notice term since the contract is deemed to be in effect within that period.[291]

723. The contract does not automatically end with the emergence of just cause per se; the party wishing to break the employment relationship must notify the other party of his intention to terminate the contract.

724. The employee claiming that the alleged just cause has not in fact materialized may file a lawsuit according to Articles 18–21 in order to avail himself of the provisions on job security (Article 25, last subsection).

II. The Breaking of the Employment Contract by the Employee

725. The employee may terminate the employment contract, whether for a definite or indefinite period, before its expiry or by not observing the notice term, respectively, in the following cases.

A. *For Reasons of Health*

726.

(a) If the performance of the work stipulated in the employment contract endangers the employee's health or life for a reason stemming from the nature of his contract.[292]

(b) If the employer or another employee who is constantly near the employee and with whom he is in direct contact is suffering from an infectious disease or from a disease incompatible with the performance of his duties. In order for the termination of the contract by the employee to be valid, the cited reasons must have been medically approved.

---

289. Court of Cassation, 9th Div., 6 Nov. 1969, 8351/10480; 23 Jun. 1997, 7706/12598.
290. Court of Cassation, 9th Div., 13 Jun. 1977, 6449/9189; 25 Feb. 1988, 206/1674.
291. Court of Cassation, 9th Div., 1 Sep. 2004, 13738/3488; 11 Mar. 2004, 4474/4788.
292. In the opinion of the High Court, the said cause does not have to be a deadly danger. Court of Cassation, 9th Div., 20 Sep. 2004, 4481/19426.

B. For Immoral, Dishonourable or Malicious Conduct or Other Similar Behaviour

727.

(a) If, when the contract was concluded, the employer misled the employee by stating the conditions of work incorrectly or by giving him false information or by making false statements concerning any essential point of the contract;
(b) if the employer is guilty of any speech or action constituting an offence against the honour or reputation of the employee or a member of the employee's family, or if he harasses the employee sexually; (i.e., insulting the employee or his family, swearing, mobbing, sexually harassing; to be invoked by the employee), Such acts shall not necessarily need to be criminal offences under the Turkish Penal Code;
(c) however, Article 105(1) of the new Penal Code No. 25611 which came into force on 1 June 2005 provides that, in the event of sexual harassment and upon the complaint by the aggrieved person, the harasser shall be sentenced to a prison term from three months up to three years or a legal fine. If sexual harassment is committed in the course of the employment relationship, the penalty shall be increased by half of the decided amount, and the prison term shall not be less than one year if due to sexual harassment, the aggrieved was forced to quit her (his) job (Article 105(2)). The place where the act of sexual harassment is committed bears no significance. Depending on where the lawsuit is filed, the labour court and the criminal court shall be competent to look into the case independent of each other. Neither the Labour Act nor the new Penal Code has brought any clear definition of sexual harassment. This void notwithstanding, these new clauses have been welcomed as positive steps towards an important dimension of employment conditions in the workplace; however, the Labour Act has not dealt with the act of mobbing' in any manner, although the acts of mobbing or bullying with related legal consequences do exist in practice;
(d) if the employer assaults or threatens the employee or a member of his family to commit an illegal act, or commits on offence against the employee or a member of his family which is punishable with imprisonment or levels serious and groundless accusations against the employee in matters affecting his honour;
(e) if, in cases where the employee was sexually harassed by another employee or by third persons in the establishment, adequate measures were not taken although the employer was informed of such conduct; (in this case, the sanction foreseen by the Penal Code is a prison term from three months up to two years; if the employer did not take adequate measures and the employee broke the employment contract as a result, the penalty should be a minimum prison term of one year);
(f) if the employer fails to make out a wages account or to pay wages in conformity with the Labour Act and the terms of the contract;[293]

293. Court of Cassation, 9th Div., 14 Jan. 1997, 17400/145; 8 May 2001, 5254/8030; 25 Sep. 2003, 15685/15438. The High Court has passed various other judgments entitling the employee to break his contract for non-payment of his wages or wage-related items, overtime pay, bonuses, etc. Also financial difficulties confronting the employer shall not deprive the employee of the right to break

(g) if, in cases where wages have been fixed at a piece or task rate, the employer assigns the employee fewer pieces or a smaller task than he could accomplish and fails to make good this deficit by paying him according to time, or if he fails to implement the conditions of employment.

C. Force Majeure

728. Force majeure necessitates the suspension of work for more than one week in the establishment where the employee is working (Article 24(3)). Force majeure may result from unexpected events such as fire, accidents and the technical breakdown of machinery as well as from natural disasters such as floods, earthquakes and the like. It may also result from legal developments such as the seizure of the establishment by the government for public good. Reasons such as losses incurred by the employer due to his fault or other causes, cleaning and maintenance of the machinery, seasonal drops in sales or increases in stocks shall not be considered force majeure.[294]

729. The employer is not obliged to pay the employee any wages if the latter has not broken the contract by the end of the first week; he shall pay the employee only his half wages for each day up to one week if the latter is not given work because of force majeure (Article 40). Upon the expiration of the 'one week' period, the employee may remain at the disposal of the employer, pending the arrival of work, or terminate his contract.

730. It should be noted that the Act's provisions on job security are applicable also on 'the termination for just cause' category. Objection to termination for just cause can be made within one month from the date of termination declaration. As pointed out in the reasons for the Act, where the employer breaks the employment contract for just cause, he does not have to communicate the declaration of termination. In this case, statutory limitations start on the date of the official (written) declaration. In line with the established jurisprudence of the Court of Cassation, limitation on the forfeiture of rights due to lapse of time shall begin from the date of oral communication of the termination. The Labour Courts Act provides that in 'just cause' terminations (summary dismissals) mediation shall come to an end if (a) the mediator has been unable to reach the parties, (b) meetings and negotiations

---

the contract; 9th Div., 7 May 1991, 137/8207. Non-payment of social security contributions by the employer shall entitle the employee to terminate the contract and receive severance pay/Court of Cassation, 9th Div., 22 Oct. 1986, 8408/9469; 1 Mar. 2004, 14584/3876; 22 Jan. 2008, 43146/34348. In the event the collective agreement is adjusted by the court due to conditions of economic crisis, the employee's terminating the contract for non-payment of wages on due time shall not entitle him to break the contract; 9th Div., 5 Nov. 1996, 12434/20519. *See also* paras 726–729 below.

294. The Court of Cassation ruled that in the event the work was suspended for one month due to economic crisis and employees were put on unpaid leave, the employee could break the contract for force majeure but was not entitled to notice pay; Court of Cassation 9th Div., 24 Jan. 1996, 24809/685.

have not been held due to the lack of the parties' participation, (c) the parties have reached an agreement as a result of negotiations and (d) where negotiations have resulted in disagreement.

III. The Breaking of the Employment Contract by the Employer

731. The employer may terminate the employment contract for just cause before the expiry of the fixed-term or, in the case of open-ended contracts, by not observing the notice term, in the following cases.

A. *For Reasons of Health*

732. Here there are two categories which must be distinguished. First, according to Article 25/I-a, 'if the employee has contracted a disease or suffered an injury owing to his own deliberate act, loose living or drunkenness and, as a result, is absent for three successive days or for more than five working days in a month', the employer may terminate him immediately for just cause. Second, according to Article 25/I-b, 'if the Health Committee has determined that the suffering is incurable and incompatible with the employee's ability to perform his duties', the employer may again terminate his contract (summary dismissal). In two special cases, though, a waiting period has been foreseen; that is, 'in cases of illness or accident which are not attributable to the employee's fault and which are due to reasons outside those set forth in (a) above, and in cases of pregnancy or confinement, the employer may terminate the employee's contract if recovery from the illness or injury continues for more than six weeks beyond the notice terms set forth in Article 17.

733. In cases of pregnancy or confinement, the period mentioned shall commerce upon the expiry stipulated in Article 74'. (Article 74 provides that a female employee who is pregnant must be allowed a leave of absence for a period of sixteen weeks, consisting of eight weeks immediately before the anticipated date of her confinement and eight weeks immediately following her confinement. This means that the employer may break the employment contract of such an employee only after the lapse of the sixteen-week period plus the notice term (between two and eight weeks) and the six weeks mentioned above.) Last subsection of Article 25/I provides that no wages are to be paid to the employee for the period during which she or he fails to report to work due to the suspension of his (her) contract.

B. *For Immoral, Dishonourable or Malicious Conduct or Other Similar Behaviour*

734. The employer may terminate the contract:

(a) if, when the contract was concluded, the employee misled the employer by falsely claiming to possess qualifications or to satisfy requirements which constitute an essential feature of the contract, or by giving false information or making false statements;[295]

(b) if the employee is guilty of any speech or action constituting an offence against the honour or dignity of the employer or a member of his family, or levels groundless accusations against the employer in matters affecting the latter's honour or dignity;[296]

(c) if the employee sexually harasses another employee of the employer;

(d) if the employee assaults or threatens the employer, a member of his family or a fellow employee, or if he violates the provisions of Article 84 c, that is, entering the establishment while drunk or under the effect of narcotics or to consume alcoholic beverages or to take narcotic substances within its premises;[297]

(e) if the employee commits a dishonest act against the employer such as a breach of trust, theft or disclosure of the employer's trade secrets;[298]

(f) if the employee commits an offence on the premises of the establishment which is punishable with seven days or more imprisonment without probation;[299]

(g) if, without the employer's permission or a good reason, the employee is absent from work for two consecutive days, or twice in one month on the working day following a rest day or on three working days in any month;[300]

(h) if the employee refuses, after being warned, to perform his duties;[301]

(i) if either wilfully or through gross negligence the employee imperils safety or damages machinery, equipment or other articles or materials in his care, whether

---

295. 'False statements given by the security guard on his application form during his recruitment shall entail his dismissal by the employer for just cause', *see* Court of Cassation, 9th Div., 6 Jun. 2000, 4727/7993. On the other hand, the contract of the employee who did not reveal his union membership or her pregnancy during the recruitment process cannot be broken for just cause, in view of Art. 31 of Act No. 2821 and Art. 11 of the International Convention on prohibition of discrimination against women ratified by Act No. 3232. S. Süzek, *DH Hukuku*, Istanbul, 2002, p. 479.

296. Of the many court decisions relating to this subsection, *see*, *e.g.*, among others: Court of Cassation, General Council Decision, 23 Jun. 1982, 1980/9-1229, 1982/719; 8 Apr. 1988, 2513/3945; Court of Cassation, 9th Div., 31 Mar. 1998, 3213/6233; 4 Mar. 1999, 1866/4119; 28 Jun. 2000, 6641/9976; 19 Apr. 2004, 20093/8643.

297. Court of Cassation, 9th Div., 21 Feb. 1994, 13441/2600; 16 Jun. 1998, 8260/10375; 28 Jun. 2000, 6641/9976; 21 Nov. 2000, 11059/17243; 23 Feb. 2004, 13841/3064; 23 Feb. 2004, 13841/3064; 9 Oct. 2006, 18364/2651.

298. Court of Cassation, 9th Div., 24 Sep. 1996, 8900/17744; 17 Oct. 1996, 9798/19634; 2 Apr. 1997, 648/6556; Court of Cassation, General Council Decision, 2 Jul. 1997, 9-446/641; Court of Cassation, 9th Div., 4 Apr. 2000, 2465/4716; Court of Cassation, General Council Decision, 20 Sep. 2000, 9-1100/1155; 15 Feb. 2001, 19076/2751; 16 Jan. 2002, 5510/266.

299. Court of Cassation, 9th Div., 25 Mar. 1987, 2842/3156.

300. Court of Cassation, 9th Div., 14 May 1982, 4239/4843; 28 Jan. 1992, 12148/690; 6 Jun. 2001, 6770/10950; 6 Feb. 2002, 17196/2375; 27 Feb. 2003, 15430/2676; 1 Dec. 2003, 8554/19389; 15 Dec. 2003, 10202/21982. The employee's absenteeism must have been documented in a written report. M. Kılıçoğlu, *İş Kanunu Gerhi*, 2nd edn, pp. 1291–1292. For examples of 'good reason', *see* the decisions of the Court of Cassation 9th Div.: 25 Nov. 1994, 12175/16615; 14 May 1998, 6425/8900; 5 Jul. 1998, 9374/11734; 2 Jun. 2001, 6770/10950; 28 Apr. 2004, 225/10066.

301. Court of Cassation, 9th Div., 21 Jan. 1997, 2517/740; 19 Jan. 1998, 57/149; 20 Nov. 1999, 12411/16519; 20 Apr. 2000, 2112/5991; 29 Jun. 2000, 6859/10069; 22 Apr. 2008, 16142/9973.

these are the employer's property or not, and the damage cannot be offset by his thirty days' pay.[302]

C. Force Majeure

735. Force majeure, preventing the employee from performing his duties for more than one week. The consequences are the same as those alluded to in Article 24/III above, but here the effects of force majeure must have been on the employee per se rather than on the establishment; that is, the employer may break the contract of an employee unable to reach and work at the establishment for more than one week for reasons such as floods, heavy snow and the like.

D. The Employee's Detention or Arrest

736. If, due to the employee's being taken into custody or to his arrest, his absence from work exceeds the notice term indicated in Article 17, the employer may break his employment contract (Article 25/IV). Here, detention or arrest results from an offence committed outside the establishment, as distinct from the case mentioned in Article 25/II-f.

737. Employees who are covered by the job security provisions of Act No. 4857 may have recourse to the labour court and file suit according to Articles 18, 20 and 21 by claiming that the termination was not in conformity with the subsections of Article 25. Thus, the employee asserting that the reason(s) cited by the employer had not in fact materialized and therefore his termination was unjustified may request reinstatement under Act No. 4857. Employees who claimed their termination was unjustified could demand notice pay and severance pay plus other damages under Act No. 1475 (compensation for unfair dismissal). Presently, employees outside the scope of job security legislation shall avail themselves of similar pay as compensation.

738. In the lawsuit filed by the employee encompassed within the protection of job security provisions, the court may rule the termination invalid and reinstate the employee; on the other hand, it may hold the termination unfair but valid in which case the employee may claim his notice pay and severance pay. A lawsuit on reinstatement is to be concluded by applying fast-hearing procedures, whereas the latter case will be subject to oral procedures which normally last longer. Therefore, rather than filing a two-pronged lawsuit (*terditli dava*) in one legal action in such controversial disputes, the necessity to initiate two separate suits has been asserted as being more feasible in the teaching.[303] Apparently on this matter different procedures between the manner of termination for 'just cause' according to Article 25 and

302. Court of Cassation, 9th Div., 9 Apr. 1992, 16257/3937; 10 May 1993, 13356/7960; 27 Jan. 1997, 17797/1212; 15 Sep. 1999, 11383/13234.

303. Ekmekçi, 'Yeni İş Kanununda Yargı, Dava Süreci ve Olası Sorunlar', *Mercek*, Temmuz 2003, p.

for 'valid reasons' according to Articles 18–21 (i.e., statutory limitations, the need take the employee's defence) have led to ambiguities in legal actions.[304] Therefore desirability of establishing uniformity in these two types of terminations has also been voiced in the literature.

739. Under Article 25(4) (last subsection) which enables the employee to invoke job security provisions in the event of an unjustified termination, the relevance of *mora creditoris* explained above has become questionable. Application of the Obligations Act's concept of 'employer's default to accept the labour of the employee' may tempt the employer to neutralize the job security protections granted to the employee. In an effort to avoid the costs associated with job security (reinstatement or compensation), the employer may choose to refuse to accept the labour of the employee, thus invoking merely the provisions of the Obligations Act on employer's default which was the routine view held before the enactment of Act No. 4857.

740. Under the present system, it is held that the employer's conduct should be treated, in accordance with the principle of 'honesty', as a declaration of mind to terminate the employee, provided a reasonably long period of waiting has elapsed, in which case the employee must be entitled to invoke provisions of Article 25/IV for reinstatement or compensation. As for workers not subject to job security provisions of the Act, consequences associated with unjustified termination (i.e., notice and severance pay and, where relevant, compensation for abusive termination) should be applicable.

741. In the event of an employment contract with a definite term or for precisely indicated work, unjustified termination before the expiry of the fixed term or before the work is finished shall entitle the injured party to an amount of compensation equal to the remuneration (wages) for the remainder of the fixed term or for the time to finish the uncompleted work. The right to claim additional indemnity for the unfair breaking of the contract – for example, for the defamatory way by which the contract was broken – is also reserved. No notice pay may be requested. In some cases the Court of Cassation has ruled also for severance pay on behalf of the unjustly terminated employee.[305]

742. In the meantime, however, the employee may have found other employment whereby the relevant provisions of the Obligations Act, Article 408 on the employer's default, may be applicable. In this case, the above-stated compensation will be paid after the deductions foreseen in Article 408 of the Obligations Act are made. The employee will not be able to make any claim if he has found employment after his dismissal at the same or a higher wage rate. If his pay on the new job is higher, the difference must be subtracted from the remuneration which will be met

138; F. Şahlanan thinks, however, that a two-pronged suit may also be initiated. See F. Şahlanan, 'Yeni İş Kanununu Değ erlendirme Konferans Notları', *Türk-İş Dergisi*, Eki, Ankara 2003, p. 86.

304. Court of Cassation, 9th Div., 24 Feb. 2004, 22581/3229; 13 Jun. 2005, 30616/322; 31 Jan. 2005, 31628/2540; 6 Feb. 2006, 39001/2268.

305. Court of Cassation, 9th Div., 18 Mar. 1998, 2611/5145; 13 Apr. 1998, 3198/6469; 19 Sep. 2003, 2296/14832; 21 May 2009, 41429/13673.

by the previous employer; if it is less on the new job, his claim may cover only the difference between the pay in his previous and the present job.[306] It is held that the amount the employee has failed to gain by not doing some other work with no valid reason must also be subject to the same deduction.

E. *Agreements on the Restriction of the Right to Break the Employment Contract for Just Cause*

743. The validity of agreements aiming to restrict the right to terminate the contract for just cause, in particular for the categories envisaged in Article 25/II, is a disputed matter in Turkish legal teaching. It is generally held that the parties may agree to leave certain events outside the scope of the 'just cause' categories, construed as meaning that such conduct is not deemed as justifying immediate breaking of the contract. Altering the conditions is generally conceived of being applicable only in favour of the employee due to the protective nature of labour law. Foreseeing that the employee's absenteeism for three (rather than two) successive days would entitle the employer to break the contract for just cause is a good case in point.[307] However, in the teaching one encounters contrary views asserting that, based on the notions of honesty and good faith, the right to break the contract for just cause cannot be waived by agreements *a priori*, especially in areas where the absolutely binding rules of the law and the protection of personality rights are concerned.[308]

744. Similarly, broadening the scope of 'just cause' categories by agreement is also a disputed matter. In other words, could the parties add new cases of 'just cause terminations' to those set out in Article 24/II and 25/II? Some note that agreements which do not contravene mandatory provisions of law and which are based on good faith should be held valid, whereas others assert that the articulation of 'just cause cases' stem from the mandatory clauses of the Labour Act and Obligations Act; therefore they must not be broadened.[309]

745. Notwithstanding these views, it should be held that certain dimensions of a secondary nature can be added to the categories of 'just cause terminations' cited in Article 25/II especially in the face of the title phrase of that Article which says 'for malicious, immoral or dishonourable malicious conduct or other similar behaviour'. 'Similar behaviour' must be interpreted in a strict manner, though; construed

306. Court of Cassation, 9th Div., 25 May 1970, 717/5293; Court of Cassation, General Council Decision, 1 Feb. 1984, 1981/9-761, 1984/52; 28 Dec. 1989, 7899/11458; 19 Jun. 2007, 11049/19514; 11 Mar. 2008, 36234 4526, ruling that a reasonable reduction must be made from this amount.

307. Court of Cassation, 9th Div., 30 Jan. 1996, 16136/1031; 7 Jul. 1997, 10808/13866; 28 Nov. 2000; 13058/17556.

308. *See* the critique of the High Court's verdict by G. Alpagut in *Kaşılaştırmalı Hukukta İşçinin Feshe Karşı Korunması*, Galatasaray Üniversitesi-İstanbul Barosu 2001 Yılı Toplantısı, pp. 79–117 (Court of Cassation, 9th Div. Ruling 22 May 2001, 6099/8722).

309. S. Süzek, *İşHukuku*, İstanbul, 2002, pp. 523–524; K. Oğuzman, *Türk Borçlar Hukukuna ve Kanununa Göre Hizmet Akdinin Feshi*, İstanbul, 1955, p. 39.

as meaning that 'conduct which is lighter' and for that reason would not entitle the employer to break the contract. In other words such additional categories must not infringe on the existing employee rights.[310] Similarly, the parties may agree on restricting or eliminating some of the 'just cause categories' which do not directly relate to public order and good morals Such an approach would also be consistent with the contemporary notions of 'progressive discipline'.

F. Restriction of the Employer's Right to Break the Contract through Collective Labour Agreements; the Case of Joint Discipline Committees

746. In the absence of job security legislation before the enactment of Act No. 4857, attempts to provide employees with job security by individual employment contracts were encountered only in exceptional cases, but many collective agreements carried provisions which aimed to restrict the employer's right to break the contract for just cause or even to terminate it by his respecting the notice term (where, for example, collective agreements provided that the employer should not lay-off the employee except for reasonable causes like mechanization, automation, rationalization of work and the like). However, in most instances the courts did not uphold the validity of such arrangements on the ground that termination rights had to do with public order and were therefore of a mandatory character. In the presence of the new job security legislation, this void has now been filled.

747. On the other hand, most collective agreements provided for joint discipline committees (sometimes in conjunction with grievance committees) which also dealt with discharge cases. In the working methods of these committees, agreed procedures occasionally foresaw a higher quorum in order to reach a decision on discharge cases which meant that, even where the labour side occupied only the minority of the seats, employee representatives had to join the employer's vote in order to discharge an employee. Discipline rules were sometimes stiffened to break the contract (e.g., absenteeism for three consecutive working days rather than two in a discharge case). And sometimes conduct which would lead to immediate termination according to the Labour Act was deleted altogether. Especially in the 1970s, union representatives had increased their influence on such committees which was acclaimed by labour as effective participative schemes. Although terminations without recourse to, or despite the contrary decision, of a joint committee embodied in the collective agreement were regarded initially as 'unfair breaking of the employment contract',[311] the Court of Cassation ruled in the opposite direction in later years. Its verdicts have in fact wavered on this issue throughout the past decades. In most of its verdicts in the 1980s the Court of Cassation did not uphold the decisions of 'discipline committees', thereby encouraging employers to bypass them altogether and unilaterally dismiss the accused employee for alleged just

---

310. Court of Cassation, 9th Div., 3 Feb. 1984, 343/916; 15 Oct. 1987, 8452/9106; 25 Oct. 1997, 18665/22741; 6 Nov. 2001, 11445/17320.
311. Court of Cassation, General Council Decision, 26 Oct. 1977, 2904/807; and various other decisions in this direction.

cause.[312] These verdicts provided that the mere violation of the discipline committee's judgment by the employer or its avoidance altogether did not constitute an unfair dismissal per se; the employee could go to court and prove that the alleged just cause had not in fact materialized, in which case he would be granted compensation, and not reinstatement.

748. In the mid-1990s, however, the High Court changed its stance again and rendered verdicts ruling that the employee's discharge through the employer's bypassing the discipline committee which was embodied in the collective agreement should be treated as unfair dismissal, as the availability of access to the labour court would not justify ignoring a mechanism addressed by the collective agreement.[313]

749. This change in judicial opinion reflected in a sense the effects of the newly approaching job security milieu in Turkey shaped by the ratification of ILO Convention 158 in 1994.

750. In the presence of job security legislation now, it is more than likely that future court decisions will buttress recourse to discipline and grievance committees and uphold their decisions, even for the employees not covered by the Act's provisions on job security. As for the parties' mutual agreement to restrict the just cause cases cited in Article 25/II, a distinction could be made between those offences which contravene public order and general good morals and which are more serious by their nature – like certain subsections of Article 25/II mentioned above – that would lead to summary dismissal and those which are not so serious in character. The employees outside the scope of job security protection retain the right of recourse to the labour court and request compensation for unfair dismissals.

G. Manner of Termination by Means of Breaking the Contract

751. The party wishing to break the employment contract for malicious, immoral or dishonourable conduct must do so within six working days of knowing the facts on such behaviour, and in any event the right to terminate ceases to be operative one year after the commission of the act, Article 26(1). 'Six days' limitation begins to be operative on the day following the commission of the act, and weekly rest days and holidays are not included.[314]

The one-year statutory limitation shall not be applicable, however, if the employee has also extracted material gain from the act itself (Article 26(1)). This is

312. Court of Cassation, 9th Div., 17 Jan. 1978, 12530/531; 28 Jan. 1981, 15325/1065; 9 Mar. 1984, 2019/2532.

313. Court of Cassation, General Council Decision, 1 Jun. 1994, 9-71/381; 8 Oct. 1997, 9-1998/12367; 31 May 1999, 7665/9472; 22 May 2000, 3958/7162; 13 Jun. 2001, 11791/15490; 15 Mar. 2010, 1913/6803. The Court of Cassation had also ruled that the discharge of an employee without his defence taken – which was foreseen in the collective agreement – constituted an unfair dismissal. Court of Cassation, 9th Div., 7 Oct. 1997, 15909/17344; 17 May 1998, 7405.

314. Court of Cassation, 9th Div., 4 Nov. 1997, 11983/18417.

a new subsection which did not exist in Act No. 1475. Thus acts which involve theft, embezzlement and the like shall not be subject to this statutory limitation.

It is safe to argue that foreseeing mediation, as a precondition for court action in the case of terminations for just cause is misplaced and somewhat ironic. Subsections in Articles 24/ II and 25/II involve offenses which may require urgent action. They generally do not lend themselves to the process of mediation which is likely to distort or obstruct real justice. But however controversial in terms of the due process of law principle, the actual results of the newly introduced mediation procedure indicate that in practice it has clearly lightened the burden of the courts. Of the one-and half-million disputes about 60% have been settled by the agreement of the contesting parties at the mediation stage. Considering the advantages and disadvantages of the mediation process, therefore the healthy and rational avenue for the settlement of this issue seems to lie in the improvement of the labour court and voluntary arbitration systems of Turkey.

With regard to the six working days within which the right to break the contract must be exercised, it should be noted that, if an investigation has been foreseen to disclose the presence of just cause (such as by a discipline committee), the period of six working days shall become operative after the completion of the investigation process.[315]

752. The investigation may cover matters like uncovering the fault or deliberate behaviour involved or the amount of damage caused.[316] In the event of work slowdowns and similar acts of a continuous nature, the 'six-working days' shall become operative upon the ending of such acts.[317] Rather than being a statutory limitation, the 'six working days' is a period after which the right to break the contract is to be forfeited; that period cannot be discontinued or suspended; if exceeded, the dismissal becomes unjustified (unfair) termination.[318] The burden of proof in substantiating that the contract was terminated within the prescribed 'six working days' rests on the employer if he was the terminating party.[319]

753. If the contract is terminated by the employee or the employer for any of the reasons cited in Article 24/II and 25/II within the periods indicated above, the terminating party is entitled also to compensation to cover the material and/or immaterial damages he may have suffered. No compensation may be claimed, however, in cases of breaking the contract for health reasons or for force majeure. The Court of Cassation has also ruled that the employee breaking the contract for just cause may not claim compensation corresponding to the term of notice (notice pay).[320]

---

315. Court of Cassation, 9th Div., 4 Nov. 1998, 13233/15588; 12 Apr. 2000, 1544/5057; 16 Mar. 2004, 13538/5169; 5 May 2005, 26759/15633; 6 Feb. 2008, 1978/13460.
316. Court of Cassation, 9th Div., 9 Nov. 1999, 12749/16914.
317. Court of Cassation, 2 Feb. 2009, 9790/1003; 14 May 2009, 2008252/13471.
318. Court of Cassation, 9th Div., 28 Feb. 2000, 19931/2169.
319. Court of Cassation, 9th Div., 21 Oct. 1993, 4330/1509; 15 Nov. 1994, 11438/15891.
320. Court of Cassation, General Council Decision, 3 May 1975, 1972/9-76, 1974/478; Court of Cassation, 9th Div., 6 Dec. 1977, 10430/16989.

§4. Collective Dismissal

754. When the employer contemplates collective terminations for reasons of an economic, technological, structural or similar nature necessitated by the requirements of the enterprise, the establishment or activity, he must provide the union shop stewards, the relevant regional directorate of labour and the Employment Organization of Turkey with written information to that effect at least thirty days prior to the intended lay-off (Article 29(1)). Terms of notice will take effect upon the lapse of that thirty-day period. This written communication must include the reason for the intended lay-off, the number and groups to be affected as well as the length of time the procedures of termination are likely to take (Article 29(3)).

755. The provisions of Act No. 4857 on collective dismissal are consistent in general with the principles set out in ILO Convention 158 and the relevant EU Directive 98/9/ EC. Article 29(2) provides that a collective dismissal would occur when (a) in establishments employing between 20 and 100 employees, a minimum of 10 employees and (b) in establishments employing between 101 and 300 employees, a minimum of 10% of employees and (c) in establishments employing 301 and more employees, a minimum of 30 employees are to be terminated in accordance with Article 17 on the same date or at different dates within one month.

756. According to Article 29(4), consultations which must be made with union shop stewards after the above-mentioned written notification shall deal with measures to be taken in order to avert or to reduce the terminations as well as the measures to mitigate or minimize their adverse effects on the employees concerned. Consultations must be made within the thirty-day notification period and in any case before notices of termination are served to employees. A document showing that the said consultations have been held shall be drawn up at the end of the meeting (Article 29(5)). The document to be drawn up need not include decisions; the motive is merely sharing of information and consultation.

757. The first draft bill prepared by the nine-member academic committee had foreseen the election of employees' representatives in order to implement the said consultations in establishments where shop stewards appointed by an authorized union did not exit. This was conceived of as a step paving the way for the establishment of a works council or an information-consultation system as envisaged by EU Directives. But due to strong reactions of labour unions, and as the employers also agreed, election of employees' representatives in non-unionized plants was cast off altogether. Under the present system, how the process of consultations will work in non-union plants is not clear. It has suggested the introduction of a works council or workers' representatives system to fill in the said void with a view to implement the said consultations; but due to the absence of political will the project has not been activated as a viable alternative yet.

758. In the event of closing the entire establishment which involves a definite and permanent stoppage of activities, the employer shall notify, at least thirty days prior to the intended closure, only the regional directorate of labour and the Employment Organization of Turkey, and shall post the announcement at the establishment. Terms of notice of termination shall begin upon the lapse of that thirty days' period. Terminations by way of advance notice pay is also possible, again taking effect by that date. If the employer wishes to recruit employees for the same kinds of jobs within the six-months' period following the lay-off date, he shall call back the laid off employees whose qualifications are suitable, giving them priority over other applicants (Article 29(7)). In this case the employer must rehire the applying ex-employees under their working conditions rather than conditions for new employees to be recruited. In this category no information-giving and consultation has been required. Further, 'if in seasonal and campaign work lay-offs are carried out by reason of the nature of such work, provisions on collective dismissals shall not apply' (Article 29(8)).

759. No legal employer liability applicable in the event of non-compliance with the requirement to rehire the laid-off employee has been envisaged. Only for criminal liability a fine of 250 million lira for each terminated employee has been foreseen for the employer or his representative who violates the provisions of Article 29.[321]

760. The employer must not use the provisions on collective dismissals in an attempt to evade or head off the application of Articles 18 to 21 on job security; otherwise the employee may initiate legal action in accordance with these articles (Article 29(9)).[322]

§5. Leaving Employment for Military or Statutory Labour Duty

761. If an employee is recalled to military service to take part in manoeuvres or for any other reason, or if he leaves employment to perform statutory labour service, his employment contract shall be deemed to have ended only after the lapse of two months from the date of his departure. To be entitled to this suspension term, however, he must have been employed for a minimum of one year. Employees who have been employed for more than one year are allowed two additional days for each year of service, provided that the total period of absence must not exceed ninety days. Without prejudice to the provisions of other legislation on this matter, the employee is not entitled to wages within this period which must elapse for his employment contract to be deemed terminated. Even where notice has been given by either party, the legal term of notice for termination shall begin to be operative

321. Also upheld by the Court of Cassation, 9th Div., 26 Nov. 1980, 18844/12214, 26 Jan. 2004, 1321/1175; 1 May 2006, 8138/1228.
322. For a ruling concerning the employer's decision to subcontract work where the High Court did not allow the dismissed employees to invoke Arts 18–21, *see* Court of Cassation, 9th Div., 14 Oct. 2004, 22472/23187.

after the lapse of the suspension period indicated. If the employment contract is a fixed-term one, however, it may expire within the said suspension period (Article 31(1,2,3)).

762. If the employee who leaves his employment to carry out any military or statutory duty applies to his employer within two months of the completion of such duties, the employer must rehire him under the prevailing conditions by giving priority over other applicants when there is a vacancy equal or similar to his previous job. If there is no vacancy, the employer must rehire him to the first job which will become vacant. In the event of non-compliance, the employer shall pay the applying ex-employee compensation equal to three months' wages (Article 31(4)).

§6. Legal Consequences of the Ending of the Employment Contract

I. In General

763. With the ending of the employment contract, the obligations of the parties, and in particular the duty of the employee to work and the duty of the employer to pay him wages, also come to an end. The employee is entitled to claim all his wages accrued but as yet unpaid. 'Upon the expiration of the employment contract, employee's wage claims as well as all the benefits based on the employment contract and law must be paid in full' (Article 32(5)). In the event of the employer's non-compliance with this principle, interest may be changed as of the date on which the default by the employer becomes effective. The employee too must return to the employer all the tools, materials, work clothes and documents provided for him by the employer.

II. Certificate of Work

764. The employer must furnish the employee who is leaving employment with a certificate stating the nature and duration of his employment (Article 28(1)). Providing the employee with a letter of recommendation depends on the will of the employer. If the employer chooses to do so or upon the employee's request, he may draw up a letter of recommendation as well.

765. The employee or his new employer who suffers a loss may claim compensation from the previous employer for the latter's failure to furnish the certificate on due time or for the incorrect information contained in it (Article 28(2)).

766. The employee must leave work in a manner commensurate with the requirements of his contract. He must work until the expiration of a fixed-term contract, or in the case of an open-ended contract, without prejudice to conditions foreseen for seeking new employment, 1 until the end of the term of notice if the contract has not been terminated by means of advance payment of wages for the term of notice. Otherwise, the employee is liable to pay damages for the loss inflicted on his employer. In addition to the employee's liability for ending the contract in this manner, the new employer is also liable jointly with the employee toward the previous employer if the new employer has incited the employee to act in this manner (employee raiding), or if he has hired the employee even though he was aware of the employee's behaviour, or if the new employer has kept the employee in his service even after becoming acquainted with his act contrary to the employment contract (Article 23). The motive here is obviously to deter employers from raiding on other employers' employees and to protect the former employer. The former employer, as a result of joint liability, can claim the payment of damages he has suffered from the employee or the new employer, or from both of them. However, the burden of proof regarding the damage caused is on the former employer.[323]

III. Certificate of Discharge

767. Although not regulated by the Labour Act, a 'certificate of discharge' signed by the employee is generally taken from the employee upon the termination of his employment contract. The employee is requested to state in this signed document that he has received all his claims from the employer, thereby relieving the employer of any other employee claims in the future. Although its opinions have generally wavered on this issue, the Court of Cassation has ruled that, unless items such as notice and severance pay, pay for vacations and overtime work have been clearly stated, the certificate of discharge attests only to relieving the employer of the employee's wage claims. According to various judgments of the Court of Cassation, a blank paper or a printed form called the certificate of discharge signed by the employee during his recruitment on employment is null and void.[324] Through the years, though, the High Court was unable to find a viable solution to this practice which apparently operated to the detriment of the vested rights of employees. According to various rulings of the Court of Cassation, the certificate of discharge is merely a receipt, construed to mean that the terminated employee is still entitled to request other claims accrued but not indicated on the certificate, especially when there is a disproportionate difference between the two.[325] More recent verdicts of the Court tend to validate the certificate of discharge if the claimant has clearly inserted a waiver clause as regards his rights to sue the employer for any other claims. In the presence of such a waiver clause the employee shall not be able to claim that the certificate was merely a simple receipt.[326] In order to be valid, the certificate must have clarified on which claims the employee has relieved the employer. Otherwise, the certificate must be treated simply as a receipt. If, as a result of court litigation, it is found that there are further unpaid claims still remaining, the court must decide on the right amount by subtracting the amount indicated

323. Court of Cassation, 9th Div., 11 Dec. 1998, 20968/1381; 21 Sep. 1999, 8717/14063.
324. Court of Cassation, 9th Div., 25 Feb. 1997, 2119/3817; 8 Dec. 2003, 8998/20326; 25 Apr. 2008, 16918/10275; so is a certificate of discharge with no date on it (9 Mar. 2007, 22037/8814.
325. Court of Cassation, 9th Div., 5 Oct. 1993, 2285/14105; 9 Mar. 2000, 9561/2021; 13 Apr. 2004, 1580/3956.
326. Court of Cassation, General Council Decision, 16 Apr. 1997, 9-86/339; 24 Nov. 1999, 9-968/983.

on the receipt from the total value to which the employee is entitled.[327] A printed blank form to be filled out or a forged document shall not be considered valid.[328] To eliminate the ambiguities and the continuing controversy, regulating this issue by clear-cut provisions in the Labour Act is recommendable. Suffice it to say that, as noted in paragraph No. 487 below, the new Obligations Act which went into force in July 2012 has brought new rules on the certificate of discharge, including 'a one-month period' following the termination of the employment contract within which the employee may provide the employer with the certificate of discharge.

768. The new Obligations Act has set forth rules on the 'certificate of discharge' generally consistent with the past rulings of the Court of Cassation. These rules stipulate that the certificate of discharge aiming to relieve the employer of the employee's claims must be in written form, that a minimum of one month must have elapsed after the termination of the employment contract, the type and amount of the claims must be clearly indicated and the transaction must be executed through a bank. Certificate of discharge and an agreement thereto shall be null and void. Any records which do not signify that worker's claims have been defrayed in real terms shall be treated merely as a receipt (Article 420(2,3), Obligations Act).

769. The clause requiring that a minimum of one month must have elapsed after the termination date of the employment contract is undoubtedly pro-labour, aiming to stave off certain abusive practices of the past; but it is also apt to lead to practical problems. For instance, an employee who has taken legal action against his termination will be reluctant to deliver this signed document and release the employer of possible debts, thus causing hardship and complications in the system. Further, it may tempt the employer to delay the payment of notice and severance pay to the employee to the expiration of the one-month period. Following which he will request the employee to sign the certificate of discharge. Second, designating a numerical sum involving claims on weekly rest days, public and national holiday, annual vacation pay, etc. in the so-called certificate of discharge to be arranged after the lapse of the one-month waiting period is also likely to cause difficulties.[329]

327. Court of Cassation, 9th Div., 24 Apr. 2000, 2242/6176.

328. Court of Cassation, 9th Div., 8 Dec. 2003, 8998/20326; 3 Mar. 2005, 17310/7218.

329. Gülsevil Alpagut, 'Türk Borçlar Kanununun Hizmet Sözleşmesinin Devri', Sona Ermesi, Rekabet Yasağı, Cezai Şart ve İbranameye İlişkin Hükümleri, *Legal İş Hukuku Dergisi*, 2011/31, pp 956–957.

Chapter 9. Severance Pay

§1. The Notion and Developments

770. The Labour Act of 2003, No. 4857, did not foresee any new rules on the employee's severance pay, except for the clause which envisaged the establishment of a 'severance pay fund' in the transitional Article 6, providing that without prejudice to employees' vested rights, Article 14 of the repealed Labour Act No. 1475 will remain in force until the enactment of new legislation on that matter. Due to the meagre state of employment protection in Turkey before the enactment of the new Labour Act in 2003, severance pay, somewhat inflated over the years, was seen as the only means of providing the employee with some degree of income and job security. With the adoption of a stronger job security and the long-awaited unemployment insurance scheme in 1999, the argument for increased severance pay levels seemed to lose clout.

771. As employers had long insisted on the revision of the existing severance pay system as a precondition for the introduction of stronger job security, the committee of academicians, while working on the draft bill for the new Labour Act, prepared also a second draft with a view to establishing and working methods of the proposed severance pay fund. During the legislative process, however, both the employers and labour unions strongly reacted to the proposed version of the so-called fund, albeit for different reasons. The said draft envisaged the reimbursement of the severance pay only in cases of the employee's retirement or death, without prejudice, however, to existing vested rights, coupled with a few additional articulations. Labour unions' objections centred on the alleged curtailment of labour's acquired rights. Employers protested the imposition of added costs as well as the complications involved in the management of the fund. As a result of increased controversy and tension, the proposal on the severance pay fund could not be integrated into the Labour Act, pending the arrival of new amendments through enhanced social dialogue between the parties. Due to the incorporation of new norms on job security into Act No. 4857, as alluded to in the preceding sections, labour came out of the process, for the time being at least, having gained more than the employers, but employers kept insisting on the revision of the severance pay system. Due to lack of agreement, therefore, Article 14 of Act No. 1475 was left as it was until relevant changes could be made in the future. At the moment the present government seems willing to fashion the rules for the establishment of the so-called severance pay fund. The future may witness, therefore, stiff negotiations in order to reach a balanced trade-off between the social partners.

772. Severance pay is the sum of money paid by the employer to an employee who has completed a certain length of service and whose employment contract has been terminated under certain conditions specified in Article 14 of the Labour Act, No. 1475. It was first introduced into Turkish law by the Labour Act of 1936 No. 3008, and has remained in effect since then, with certain amendments made in the Labour Acts of 1967 No. 931 and of 1971 No. 1475 and Act of 1980 No. 2320, Act of 1981 No. 1457, Act of 1982 No. 2762 and Act of 1983 No. 2869. But perhaps the most controversial development of recent years was Act No. 1927 passed in 1975 amending certain sections of Act No. 1475, and significantly Article 14 on severance pay. The 1975 amendment increased the sum of severance pay from fifteen days' pay to thirty days' pay for each complete year of service.

773. While under the previous system it was payable to an employee who had been employed by an employer at least for three years, the 1975 Act lowered the required minimum period to one year and also expanded the scope of the 'contract termination' categories which entitled the employee to severance pay. Since the minimum levels set by labour legislation were automatically exceeded by collectively bargained provisions, the impact of the 1975 amendment on employers had been allegedly profound, touching off heated debates in labour–management circles and arguments that severance pay expenditures placed heavy burdens on enterprises and even led to frequent plant shutdowns. The 1975 amendment (Act No. 1927) set a maximum ceiling on the amount of severance pay, and although the Court of Cassation issued several rulings to the effect that the ceiling should not be exceeded, both unions and employers avoided it either on the grounds that free collective bargaining could not be restrained by labour law provisions which had to be, for the most part, 'relatively binding' or, while abiding by the ceiling, they improvised other forms of pay plans under the pretext of names such as 'extra compensation for contract termination', 'extra leave pay' and the like. Following a suit brought before it, the Constitutional Court repealed the ceiling, though for procedural reasons, on 15 April 1979. Nevertheless, the provisional military government of 12 September 1980 gave the ceiling an absolutely binding effect by slightly changing the wording of Article 14. With the amendments made in 1975 and 1980 to 1983, severance pay took its present shape in Turkey. Meanwhile parallel amendments were made also in the Maritime Labour Act.

774. There was no clear-cut and uniform agreement as to the purpose and nature of 'severance pay' in Turkish labour law. Some writers interpreted it as a kind of payment to reward the employee's commitment to, and loyal performance for the establishment, while others regarded it as a form of redundancy payment which, in the absence of a formal job security system and unemployment insurance, served to provide some degree of employment stability by making it costly for the employer to lay-off workers, as well as securing some income security for the displaced employee. Some treated it as a form of compensation to make good the employee's losses incurred in the course of the employment relationship. Thus, depending on the interpretation adopted, differing views have been instrumental in instigating specific amendments at different times. As a result, severance pay has taken on a sui generis character, bearing the combined overtones of all these different interpretations which prompted the various amendments in the past.

§2. Conditions

775. To be entitled to severance pay, the employment contract must have ended under specified categories of contract termination or on the death of the employee (in which case the payment must be made to the employee's legal heirs), and the employee's length of service must be at least one year. Categories of employees cited in Article 4 of Act No. 4857 under 'exceptions' and working under the Obligations Act shall not be paid severance pay.

I. Specified Categories of Contract Termination or the Death of the Employee

776. Severance pay is to be paid in the event of the termination of the employment contract by the employer for reasons other than those set forth in Article 25/II (i.e., on account of the employee's malicious, immoral or dishonourable conduct or other similar behaviour); but it shall be paid to the employee who terminates his contract for reasons envisaged in Article 24. This means that severance pay shall be paid if the employer terminates the employment contract with a term of notice (Article 17), or without a term of notice for reasons concerning the employee's health (Article 25/I) or force majeure (Article 25/III), or if the employee terminates the contract without term of notice for reasons of health, for immoral or dishonourable conduct or similar behaviour of the employer, or for force majeure (Article 24/I, II, III or IV), but not if the employee himself gives notice of termination according to Article 17. However, negotiated provisions in some collective agreements did stipulate that the employee who ended the employment relationship by respecting a term of notice was entitled to receive severance pay, and many collective agreements contained such provisions which usually required a length of service longer than that stipulated in Article 14. However, this practice was later declared unlawful in the rulings of the High Court.

777. In addition, the employee is entitled to severance pay in the event that he or the employer terminates the employment contract on account of the employee's being called up for regular (compulsory) military service, or if the employee terminates his employment contract for the purpose of qualifying for an old-age pension, disability benefits or a lump-sum payment from legally established social security funds (Article 14(4)). An employee claiming benefits under this section must produce a certificate from the insurance administration to the effect that he is entitled to a pension or lump-sum payment, and he must have submitted a claim to this effect to the insurance administration. And lastly, the severance pay of a deceased employee shall be paid to his legal heirs. As severance pay cannot be conceived of as a wage payment, statutory limitations to apply to severance pay claims should be ten years according to Article 146 of the Obligations Act.

778. The Court of Cassation has ruled that the burden of proof concerning that the employment contract was terminated according to a category that did not entitle the employee to severance pay would rest on the employer.[330]

330. Court of Cassation, 9th Div., 26 Dec. 1996, 17260/24330.

779. No distinction has been drawn in Article 14 between contracts for a definite period (fixed term) and contracts for an indefinite period (open-ended) with respect to severance pay. However, the category of entitlement to severance pay through the termination of the contract by the employer with a term of notice is valid only for contracts for an indefinite period. The employment contract for a definite period expires at the end of the specific period with no severance pay involved. However, the employee working under a contract for a definite period is entitled to severance pay if the employer breaks the contract before the expiration of the specified period for reasons of health (Article 25(1)) or for force majeure (Article 25(3)), or if the employee breaks it according to Article 24(1,2,3)), as well as for the employee's death or the ending of the contract for military duty or in the case of the employee's entitlement to social security benefits (old age pension, disability benefit or lump-sum payment from social security funds). The employee working under a contract for a definite period shall also receive severance pay if the employer terminates his contract before the expiration of the specified period without any just cause – in which case the termination is considered to be an 'unfair dismissal'. On the other hand, the employee whose contract – whether for a definite or an indefinite period – is broken by the employer because of the employee's involvement in an unlawful strike (Article 70(1) of Act No. 6356 (the Act on Unions and the Collective Labour Agreement)) is not entitled to severance pay, while an employee who breaks his contract because of the employer's perpetration of an unlawful lock-out (Article 70(3) Act No. 6356) shall receive severance pay.

780. Furthermore, according to the amendment made by Act No. 2869 in 1983, the female employee who terminates her employment on her own will within one year of her marriage is entitled to receive severance pay.[331] In this case, termination is by respecting the term of notice. If notice term has not been respected, she must pay the employer notice pay but is not deprived of receiving severance pay.

781. In the case of the so-called chain contracts made for definite periods the same legal consequences concerning employment contracts for an indefinite period should prevail, and this includes the payment of severance pay by the employer.

782. The Court of Cassation had ruled that the employee who had worked under chain contracts made for definite periods was to be entitled to severance pay. Under Act No. 4857, a fixed-term contract if renewed should automatically be deemed an open-ended employment contract, and therefore the employee is to be entitled to severance pay when this contract ends under the qualifying conditions mentioned above.

331. Court of Cassation, 9th Div., 6 Jun. 1994, 3797/8597; 22 Nov. 1995, 17712/34485; 11 May 2004, 16699/11271. The High Court also ruled that the woman's divorce followed by remarriages in short intervals was an abusive practice, thus refusing her entitlement to severance pay; Court of Cassation, 9th Div., 14 Jan. 1987, 1986/11078, 1987/11078; 26 Nov. 1987, 10028/10420; 18 Sep. 1989, 6776/6979; 15 Jan. 1990, 7628/118; Court of Cassation, General Council Decision, 14 Feb. 1990, 1990/9-1990.

783. There is no clarity as to whether or not the employee working in the public sector should receive severance pay upon his transfer to the 'public servant' status. Except for a few cases, the High Court has generally not favoured the practice of making the payment and ruled that the person's past service under the employee status should be considered in determining his future seniority as public servant.[332] If the employee has begun working as a public servant shortly after the termination of his employment contract due to the privatization of the public establishment, he should be entitled to notice and severance pay.[333]

II. Length of Service

A. In General

784. To be entitled to severance pay, the employment contract (terminated in accordance with one of the above-mentioned conditions or ended because of the employee's death) must have lasted at least one year. In computing this minimum 'one-year length of service', the periods during which the execution of the employment contract was suspended – with the exception of the time spent by the striking or locked-out worker during a strike or lock-out – should also be taken into account.

B. Computation of the Employee's Length of Service

785. The beginning of the employee's length of service is the date on which the employee has actually started work, not the date on which the employment contract is concluded. However, the time during which an employee has no work to perform pending the arrival of further work, but remains at the employer's disposal, is included in the employee's length of service since such periods are reckoned as part of the statutory hours of work (Article 66/I-c). The whole period corresponding to the duration of the employment contract constitutes employee's length of service. This means that the trial period, if the contract carries a trial clause, as well as all the statutory hours of work regardless of whether or not the employee has actually worked, are to be reckoned as part of the length of service. The determination of the end of the employee's length of service depends on the manner of terminating the employment contract. If the contract is terminated without a term of notice (according to Article 25/I-III and Article 24), the end of the length of service is the date on which the notice to break the contract reaches the other party. If the contract is terminated by making an advance payment corresponding to the term of notice to which the employee is entitled, it should be the last day of the notice period rather

332. Court of Cassation, 9th Div., 13 Feb. 1984, 386/1331; 27 May 1985, 2893/5761; 15 Feb. 2000, 18558/1532; 12 Sep. 2001, 9919/13517.

333. Court of Cassation, 9th Div., 12 Nov. 2001, 18406/17559; 11 Jan. 2005, 5936/453. If the public servant is transferred to 'contract worker' status, he shall receive severance pay as of the date of the transfer. (Court of Cassation., General Council Decision, 12 Nov. 2003, 9-685/690). If he transfers to the 'contract worker' status on his own will, he shall not receive severance pay (Court of Cassation, General Council Decision, 7 Mar. 2007, 9-119/119).

than the day on which notice was given.[334] If termination is implemented by observing a term of notice (Article 17), it is the last day of the notice period. In the case of a deceased employee, it is the date on which the death occurred.

C. *Situations Which Do Not Interrupt the Continuity of the Employee's Length of Service*

786. In determining an employee's length of service the whole period of his employment in one or more establishments belonging to the same employer is counted, whether it has been under the same employment contract since the beginning or under two or more such contracts for different periods (Article 14(2)). If, however, the employee has received severance pay and left the establishment, a new length of service (seniority) starts in the event that he enters the establishment of the same employer. Since, according to Article 14, severance pay is not payable more than once in respect of a given period of service (Article 14(8)), his previous service under the same employer is not taken into account when calculating his new severance pay. Whether or not to compensate the employee for the combined sum of all his periods of service under the same employer has been debated both in legal writings and in court rulings.[335] The question is whether to pay severance pay for each period of service separately, or to compensate for all the periods of service in a combined fashion over the employee's last wage rate and deduct the previous severance payments if any such payments have been made upon the employee's leaving the undertaking in the past. The Court of Cassation has rendered conflicting judgments in both directions on various occasions.[336] Recent rulings have favoured the former opinion, that is, no deduction is to be made and severance pay is to be calculated on the basis of each period of service.[337] If, however, the employee has not been compensated for his previous service periods under the same employer, then the total sum of all periods must be considered in determining the length of service for severance pay. Also, the employee shall be entitled to severance pay if the sum of his periods of service under the same employer exceeds 'one year', even though each separate period is less than the minimum length of service required in order to qualify for severance pay.

787. Another controversial issue concerns the period of service of an employee whose employment contract has been terminated for reasons which do not entitle

---

334. However, the Court of Cassation has issued rulings in the opposite direction. *See* Court of Cassation, 9th Div., 19 Jan. 1976, 1975/34675, 1976/23999; 21 Dec. 1977, 16243/17510; Court of Cassation, General Council Decision, 5 Jun. 1987, 1986/9-666, 1987/457; Court of Cassation, 9th Div., 6 Nov. 1995, 13352/33432; 27 Mar. 2000, 3470/3357.

335. For various opinions on this issue, *see* Çelik, *supra.*

336. Court of Cassation, 9th Div., 17 Jun. 1965, 5125/5414; 18 Jan. 1971, 14088/261; 30 May 1975, 14193/33856 and others.

337. Court of Cassation, 9th Div., 13 Apr. 1976, 8765/11824; Court of Cassation, General Council Decision, 28 Apr. 1976, 974-9/763, 1284; 9th Div., 9 Jun. 1987, 5929/5707; 15 Feb. 1991, 11573/2383; 8 Jul. 1996, 3169/15470; 6 Apr. 2000, 1085/4863; 3 Mar. 2005, 17017/7206; 15 May 2007, 35660/15229.

the employee to severance pay. The question has arisen specifically with regard to the length of service of an employee who has been discharged for just cause according to Article 25/II (for immoral or dishonourable conduct or other similar behaviour) but later reengaged by the same employer. Here the Court of Cassation has again issued conflicting awards with regard to the question of whether or not the employee's previous period of service (which ended in discharge for dishonourable conduct) should be counted in the event of the second termination of his employment contract by the same employer under conditions which now entitle him to severance pay. According to most court decisions both periods of service should be considered by the employer in calculating the employee's severance pay, since Article 14, in referring to the whole period of employment in one or more undertakings of the same employer under two or more contracts for different periods, does not specify as to the manner in which the former contracts were terminated. In several rulings, however, the Court of Cassation held that an employee discharged for a disciplinary cause and then reengaged by the employer should not demand severance pay for the period which ended in discharge for a disciplinary cause unless pardoned explicitly by the employer.[338]

D. Length of Service of Seasonal Employees

788. In the absence of any provision concerning the severance pay of seasonal employees in Article 14 of the Labour Act, the Court of Cassation has, in many of its verdicts on this issue, upheld the view that the length of service for severance pay and the term of notice for such employees must be determined by adding the statutory and actually worked hours each year, and that work which covers merely a certain season cannot entitle an employee to a full year's seniority unless there is a provision to the contrary in the collective agreement.[339] However, this is a contentious point, since the parties to such employment contracts do not usually intend, either explicitly or implicitly, to end the contract. Rather, they aim to continue their employment relationship throughout the following season. So, viewed from a different angle, the contract should in fact be deemed 'suspended' during the interim periods when work is discontinued until the next season. Therefore, the periods during which the execution of the labour contract is suspended, as well as actual working time and other statutory hours of work, should be taken into account in calculating the employee's length of service. Repeated seasonal contracts turn into a contract for an indefinite period and therefore entitle the worker to severance pay.[340] It has been claimed by opponents of this view, however, that the suspension of an employment contract during certain seasons does possess an absolute character and that treating such periods of suspension as part of the employee's length of

338. Court of Cassation, General Council Decision, 15 Jun. 1977, 1976/9-1939, 1977/610; 6 Jun. 1984, 1982/9-724, 657; Court of Cassation, 9th Div., 11 Mar. 2004, 15480/4782. 4 December, 2007, 22866/36816.
339. Court of Cassation, 9th Div., 2 Mar. 1977, 2311/4121; 22 Mar. 1988, 1344/3384.
340. Court of Cassation, 9th Div., 2 Apr. 1984, 1983/9712, 1984/464.

service would not be fair.[341] Suspension applies only to time spent on illness, on strike or leave of absence granted by the employer.

E. Part-time Employees

789. Another point of controversy had arisen in the past with regard to the severance pay of part-time employees. The Court of Cassation judged that, for the employee who worked certain hours on three days of each week, the length of service should be computed by adding the number of hours worked and the employee would be entitled to severance pay if this number exceeded one year.[342] This ruling was criticized on the grounds that since Article 14 merely mentioned 'the number of years of service', without making any reference to as to whether the employee has worked on a full-time or part-time basis, computation of the employee's length of service according to the duration of his employment contract would indeed be more consistent with the purpose of the Labour Act. Furthermore, this would not be an unfair solution, as the amount of severance pay would not be too high because of the relatively low wages earned by part-time employees.

790. It should be noted that on this issue the Court has changed its opinion in its recent rulings. It now considers the total period of the part-time employee's employment regardless of the actual time and days worked.[343] This view should in fact be applicable in other cases concerning the determination of the employee's seniority. In the event of an employee engaged to perform 'on call work', it is held that the same principle should be applicable.[344]

F. Change of Employer or Moving of the Establishment

791. In the event of a change of employer as the result of a transfer or an inheritance or such like, or the moving of the establishment to a different place, the employee's length of service must be determined by adding together his periods of service in the establishment. Both the previous and the new employer have been held liable for compensation for the length of service accrued at the time of the publication of Act No. 1927. But the liability of the previous employer (transferor) is limited by the length of time during which he had the employee under his employment and the wage rate which the employee was receiving at the time of the changeover. If the change of employer took place before the publication of Act No.

341. M. Çenberci, *İş Kanunu Şerhi*, Ankara, 1984, p. 311.
342. Court of Cassation, 9th Div., 24 Oct. 1977, 3902/15481; 16 Mar. 1978, 3256/3791; 21 May 1991, 753/8770.
343. Court of Cassation, 9th Div., 27 Sep. 2000, 8184/12733; 21 May 2001, 6063/8620; Court of Cassation, General Council Decision, 12 Mar. 2003, 21-143/159.
344. Court of Cassation, General Council Decision, 12 Mar. 2003, 21-143/159.

1927, then the compensation corresponding to the whole length of service must be paid by the new employer unless there is a provision to the contrary in the takeover agreement (Article 14(11, 111)).

792. Article 6 of Act No. 4857 on the transfer of the establishment or one of its sections provides that the mere fact of a transfer shall not justify the breaking of the contract and a request for the payment of severance pay; in the transfer of the establishment to a new employer the transferor and transferee shall be jointly liable for the obligations which have arisen before the transfer and which must be defrayed on the date of the transfer; the liability of the transferor is limited, however, to the two-year period following the date of the transfer. The special rule envisaged in Article 14(2, 3) shall however still prevail.

G. Computation of the Length of Service of Employees Working in Public Organizations

793. A significant number of workers are employed by public organizations and public enterprises in Turkey. In figuring out the severance pay of an employee in the public sector, the periods of service spent in different establishments in the public sector must be added together (Article 14(4)). However, this provision is limited only to those categories of severance pay where the employment contract is terminated by the employee in order to receive an old-age, disability or lump-sum payment from the social security funds established by law. Furthermore, when adding together the periods of service in different undertakings belonging to the same public employer, the length of service spent with the status of 'public servant'[345] shall not be counted.[346] But, this exclusion does not cover those persons who, although subject to the Public Servants Pension Fund, are considered as 'employees' rather than public servants. A subsequent amendment to Article 14 entitled the employee to severance pay only upon the termination of the contract with the aim to receive old-age, disability or lump-sum payment from a social security institution. Any period of service spent in a public organization where the employment contract had previously been terminated under a condition which did not entitle the employee to severance pay is not to be counted as part of the length of service for severance pay.

794. 'Public servant' status is one such condition. In addition, the termination of the employment contract by the employer according to Article 25/II and by the employee according to Article 17 are categories which do not entitle the employee to severance pay.

795. Concerning the severance pay of workers employed by subcontractors in the public sector, Act No. 6552, in an effort to guarantee the payment of

---

345. For the 'public servant' and 'employee (or worker)' distinction, *see* below.

346. *See* the verdicts of the Court of Cassation in both directions: Court of Cassation, 9th Div., 1 Feb. 1977, 288/2166; 27 May 1993, 1992/14673, 1993/9121; 28 Apr. 1994, 9587/10202; 29 May 1997, 6823/10306; Court of Cassation General Council December, 11 May 2005, 9-318/327.

subcontractor's worker's severance pay, brought the following supplement to Article 112 of the Labour Act on the severance pay of some workers employed in certain public institutions and organizations:

> Concerning the severance pay of workers employed by subcontractors within the scope of Article 62(1e) of the Public Tenders Act No. 4734, dated 4 January 2002, (a) irrespective of changes in subcontractors, those who have worked without interruption at the same establishments belonging to the same public institutions and organizations the length of time which will serve as a basis for entitlement to severance pay will be the total time spent at establishments of the same public institution or organization; severance pay of those whose employment contracts with the last subcontractor have ended in accordance with Article 14 of the Labour Act with entitlement to severance pay shall be paid by the said public institution or organization; (b) concerning workers employed by the same subcontractor but at different institutions or organizations under the same employment contract, those whose employment contracts have ended according to Article 14 of the Labour Act No. 1475 under conditions with entitlement to severance pay, by taking account of the total time spent at different public institutions and organizations within the scope of Article 62 of Act No. 4734, severance pay shall be deposited to the bank account of the worker by the last public institution or organization. Concerning the severance pay of workers whose employment contracts with the subcontractor have not ended but continued under the subcontractor at an establishment other than those outside the scope of administrations covered by Act No. 4734 and terminated during such work under a condition with entitlement to severance pay, that portion of severance pay corresponding to the time spent in the said public institution or organization shall be deposited, upon the written request of the worker, to his bank account by the last institution or organization; in this case, the worker's wage in the last establishment will be prorated by years taking account of rates of increase in the minimum wage. If the computed severance pay turns out to be lower than the sum he would receive at the wage rate on the date of the termination of his employment contract for the same length of employment, the worker may request the subcontractor to pay the difference. If severance pay has been defrayed over the total time periods worked at different public institutions or organizations, the last one which has paid the severance pay shall redeem from them the portion corresponding to employment in these institutions or organizations However this transaction of redemption shall not apply in the case of public administrations which fall within the scope of central administrations.

796. Although seemingly of minor importance in the big picture, these detailed clauses signal the significance of the various problems inherent in the payment of severance pay in the public sector's subcontracting relationships.

H. The Proposed Severance Pay Fund

797. The employer is barred from having his severance pay obligation insured either by private persons or by insurance companies (Article 14 (15, 16). Apparently the aim of such a prohibition was to guarantee some job security for employees by forcing the employer to meet severance pay expenditures himself in lump-sum form. However, the establishment of a 'severance pay fund' is envisaged in the next subsection of the article, which provides that a 'severance pay fund' could be established by the employer and under the employer's responsibility in a government institution, or in an institution established by legislative enactment, or in a bank or institution where the government owns more than 50% of the shares. However, payments out of this fund could be made only for those cases in which the employee was entitled to severance pay for old-age, retirement, disability, death or a lump-sum payment. In other words, the employer is obliged to pay severance pay himself out of his own funds when the contract is terminated by him with a term of notice (Article 17) or according to Article 25/I and II, or by the employee according to Article 24. Obviously, the aim was again to provide the employee with some of job security. The details concerning the establishment of the 'severance pay fund' were to be regulated by special legislation.

798. While preparing the draft bill for the new Labour Act, the academic committee drew up also the principles governing the so-called severance pay fund in a separate proposal. In the face of new job security rules incorporated first into Act No. 4773 and later into the new Labour Act No. 4857, the committee's intention was to strike a delicate balance between job security, unemployment insurance instituted in 1999 and severance pay – which over the years had reached staggering levels, thereby allegedly putting unbearable costs on employers. As labour unions and employers reacted to the idea of the fund, albeit for different reasons, the 'severance pay fund' proposal was suspended by the Ministry of Labour and Social Security, and was deferred to an unknown date for further deliberations. This was one reason why Article 14 of the repealed Act No. 1475 was left in force (by Article 120 of Act No. 4857). The revision of the severance pay system and the establishment of the so-called severance pay fund are still on the agenda of the government.

§3. The Amount of Severance Pay

799. The amount of severance pay which an employee shall receive by meeting the above-stated criteria is thirty days' pay for each year of service. (Before the amendment by Act No. 1927 in 1975, it was fifteen days' pay for each year of employment.) Any period in excess of each full year is to be compensated on a prorated basis. (Before the 1975 amendment, any period of employment more than six months used to be treated as a whole year, while periods of less than six months were not taken into account.) The basis for severance pay is the employee's last gross wage (before taxes and other deductions), plus other benefits of a continuous nature, either monetary or measurable in monetary terms, paid to the employee by virtue of the employment contract, collective agreement or by law (Article 14(9)).

The same rule applies to the calculation of notice pay envisaged in Article 17 mentioned above. This means that the daily amount of all benefits (wage supplements) like bonuses, premiums, family allowances, heating, clothing and health benefits, etc. must be added to the employee's daily basic wage. In those cases where remuneration is made in terms of piece rates, certain work to be performed or on a percentage basis, the average daily pay is to be computed by dividing the total amount of wage payments during the employee's last year of service by the number of days worked within that year. However, if a wage increase has been granted within the last year of service, the daily pay which will serve as the basis for the employee's severance pay is to be determined by dividing the amount of wages (and other wage supplements), received by the employee between the date of the termination of his contract and the date on which the wage increase was granted, by the number of days worked within that period (Article 14(10)). In the opinion of the High Court, the total sum of actual wages paid in a year must be divided by 365 in order to determine the daily wage earnings.[347] The daily amount thus computed must be multiplied by 30 so as to find the basic amount of severance pay for each year of service. However, sporadic payments and fringe benefits which are not continuous (i.e., pay for work on rest days and holidays, wages for annual leave, pay for overtime work) shall not be included in the calculation of the 'thirty-days' pay' for severance pay.[348] Likewise, certain premiums based on sales volume as well as the employer's share in social security contributions are not included.[349]

800. The Court of Cassation has ruled that because severance pay is a kind of compensation rather than remuneration, claims concerning severance pay cease to be operative after ten years have elapsed, in accordance with Article 146 of the Obligations Act.[350] On the employer's default, the judge rules on the payment by the employer of the highest interest rate charged to bank deposits (Article 14(11)).

801. Act No. 1927 imposed a ceiling on the amount of severance pay by providing that 'the thirty days' pay to be considered for each year of service of the employee in calculating his annual severance pay should not exceed 7.5 times the thirty days' sum of the prevailing daily minimum wage fixed in accordance with the Labour Act'. This meant that the ceiling could rise only when increases were made in the legal minimum wage. However, since Article 14 stated that the thirty-day period serving as the base for each year of service could be raised in favour of the employee by means of individual contracts or collective agreements, the parties usually exceeded this ceiling by way of negotiated provisions which increased the 'thirty-day' dimension as well as by benefiting from the relatively higher wages

347. Court of Cassation, 9th Div., 11 Nov. 1997, 14608/18836; 20 Mar. 2001, 866/4409; 18 May 2004, 3586/12160.
348. Court of Cassation, 9th Div., 16 Dec. 1974, 11158/28952; 27 Apr. 1976, 9532/18600; 17 Feb. 1977, 863/3014; 20 Feb. 1992, 13871/2045; General Council Decision, 3 Mar. 2004, 9-86124; 9th Div., 28 Jun. 2004, 17373/15887.
349. Court of Cassation, 9th Div., 17 Dec. 1992, 5593/13728; 27 Jan. 2000, 18403/950.
350. Court of Cassation, 9th Div., 8 Oct. 1970, 8210/10492; 2 Jul. 1971, 9230/12994; 17 Feb. 2005, 14043/4567. The statutory limitation shall not be applicable to previous entitlements under the same employer; 21 Feb. 1995, 16560/5227.

granted in the privileged sectors of the economy. In several verdicts, however, the Court of Cassation ruled that the ceiling should not be exceeded, thus interpreting Article 14 as an absolutely binding provision which could not be tampered with by the free will of the parties. In the view of the High Court, the 'thirty-day' period could be raised only up to the upper limit of that ceiling.[351] The majority view in legal theory favoured the idea of exceeding the limit, predicating their view mainly on the principle of free collective bargaining.[352]

802. Finally, on 15 April 1979, the Constitutional Court repealed the provision in Article 14 concerning the ceiling on the grounds that its enactment was not consistent with the Constitution and the procedural requirements of the legislative process. The repealing award was to be effective as of one year from the date of its publication in the Official Gazette, but no legislative action was taken after that. Thus, the 'ceiling' issue remained as one of the most disputed and controversial matters in Turkish labour law until finally, the provisional military government passed Act No. 2320 of 17 October 1980 which re-imposed the ceiling as an absolutely mandatory provision of Article 14.

803. It proclaimed that the thirty-day period serving as the basis of severance pay for each year of service by the employee could be increased by individual employment contracts or collective agreements, provided that the annual amount of severance pay did not exceed 7.5 times the thirty days' sum of the prevailing minimum wage (fixed in accordance with the Labour Act). Act No. 2320 also exempted from income tax the total amount of severance pay which employees covered by Act No. 1475 and Act No. 854 (the Maritime Labour Act) receive. However, employees covered by Act No. 212 (the Press Labour Act) are exempted from tax only for that part of the severance pay, not in excess of the first 24 months' pay. Finally, Act No. 2367 of 1982 removed the link between the ceiling and the minimum wage. As it stands now, the thirty days' pay which may be increased by individual employment contracts or collective agreements for each year of service must not exceed the maximum monthly amount of retirement bonus which the highest-ranking public servant is entitled to receive upon his retirement. This figure changes over the course of time as it is adjusted periodically.

804. The amendment to the Income Tax Act No. 2320 exempted severance pay of employees covered by the Labour Act No. 4857 and the Maritime Labour Act No. 854 from income tax. And up to 24 months' pay of employees covered by the Press Labour Act is exempt from income tax.

805. In practice, 'severance pay' seems to have had various adverse effects both on the employer and the employee. The provisions which were drawn up in order to provide some job and income security for the working man quite often led to job

---

351. Court of Cassation, 9th Div., 31 Mar. 1976, 5480/10651; 8 Nov. 1976, 18102/20771; 23 Jan. 1978, 664/817.
352. Ekonomi, *supra*, p. 215; M. Kutal, 'Son Değişiklikler', *Peryön Sempozyumu*, p. 213 and several other writers.

insecurity by tempting employers to lay-off employees before they completed the 'one year of service' requirement for entitlement to severance pay. Moreover, the employee is not entitled to severance pay if he himself terminates the contract by respecting the relevant term of notice. The collectively negotiated arrangements granting severance pay to employees ending the contract on their own will have been found invalid by the Court of Cassation.[353]

806. Furthermore, if one of the aims of severance pay is to reward the employee for his past performance or commitment to his work, then there is no point in depriving the employee who has been hired under a fixed-term employment contract of the right to severance pay. Also, many employees have been tempted to lead the employer into terminating the labour contract 'with term of notice' by slowing down production and/or engaging in certain acts which do not strictly correspond to the 'malicious, immoral and dishonourable behaviour' envisaged in Article 25/II, but which may result in the termination of the contract with severance pay. It is also paradoxical that when an employee who has worked for his employer for many years quits his job is deprived of severance pay, while another employee who is discharged for having had a disease or suffered an injury owing to his own deliberate act, loose living or drunkenness (Article 25/I-a) is granted severance pay. Moreover, it does not seem fair to deprive an employee with long seniority of severance pay if he is absent from work for just a few days (Article 25/II-f). The proposed severance pay fund aims to eliminate such contradictions, as it foresees payment of severance pay mainly in the case of the employee's retirement.

353. Court of Cassation, 9th Div., 2 Apr. 1982, 3021/4158; 22 Jan. 1990, 7863/389; 28 Mar. 1994, 1993/17107, 1994/4716.

Chapter 10. Inventions by Employees: Settlement of Individual Labour Disputes – Labour Courts

§1. Inventions by Employees

807. In Turkey, employee's inventions are protected under the Obligations Act, Article 427. Because the Labour Act does not make any reference to inventions by employees whatsoever, the provisions of the Obligations Act shall apply in situations of inventions by employees. Since an invention is the product of the employee's creative thinking, the law entitles the inventor to put his invention to commercial use. Invention is an activity not normally stipulated in the employment contract. As a rule, both the ownership of and the benefits resulting from, an invention belongs to the inventor even though he may be working under an employment contract. However, there are two exceptions to this general rule. The first exception refers to inventions by employees who have been engaged for the purpose of inventing; the process of inventing is therefore a part of the implementation of the employment contract. The ownership of this type of invention belongs to the employer. The second exception relates to cases whereby the employee invents something not in the course of the implementation of the employment contract but in relation to it indirectly. In this case, the act of inventing has materialized using the materials of the undertaking during working hours, but randomly. The ownership of this type of invention is due to the employer only if it has been explicitly agreed upon in the employment contract. The employer is also entitled to the ownership of such an invention if it has been stipulated in the 'rules of work'.[354]

808. If the invention is of significant economic value the inventing employee is, according to Article 427 of the Obligations Act, entitled to claim some reward in compliance with the relevant legislation on patent rights even though it may have been agreed in the employment contract that the invention would be owned by the employer. Because this right has been guaranteed by law, the employee's entitlement to claim a certain reward is protected even if the employment contract is silent or carries a provision to the contrary.[355]

§2. Settlement of Individual Labour Disputes

809. Labour disputes are grouped into two categories in Turkish law, namely individual labour disputes and collective labour disputes. While the latter may be either a rights dispute or an interest dispute, individual disputes refer, in principle, only to alleged violation of individual rights.

810. Individual labour disputes are generally settled by the labour courts. They can be initiated either by the employee or the employer, and if the employee is a

354. Court of Cassation, 9th Div., 3 May 2021, 2017/427; 2021/685..

355. K. Tunçomağ, *İş Hukuku*, 1979, p. 211. For a new and comprehensive study on employee inventions and innovations, *see* Talat Canbolat, *İşçi Buluşları* (Beta 2007).

union member, the trade union will normally pay his legal expenses and occasionally a union attorney will present his case. Appeals against the final judgments of labour courts may be made to the Court of Cassation which gives a decision on the judgment of the labour court within two months, either upholding or reversing the ruling of the lower court.

811. Verdicts concerning claims which do not include a certain amount may not be appealed to the Court of Cassation. Details of the composition and competence of the labour courts will be given below, but suffice it to say here that Article II of the Labour Courts Act (No. 5521) charges the labour courts with trying suits in connection with individual employment contracts and the Labour Act as well as suits brought by and against trade unions. Likewise, Article 33 of the Trade Unions Act No. 2821 enables unions to act as either plaintiff or defendant in matters arising out of legislation, custom and collective agreements, as well as in legal actions concerning rights under individual contracts. However, criminal courts are involved in cases where criminal offences cited by labour legislation have been committed.

812. Some writers have claimed that individual disputes may also be settled through arbitration if the employer and the employee both agree to make use of it,[356] but the view of the Court of Cassation has been in the opposite direction.[357] However, this is a contentious point and will be dealt with below. Furthermore, the new Labour Act No. 4857 has foreseen the settlement of job security-related disputes by arbitration if the parties have so agreed.

813. Though detailed statistics are not available on the breakdown of cases by individual and collective labour disputes, the majority of cases adjudicated by the labour courts seem to address individual disputes concerning allegations of invalid or irregular termination or unfair/abusive dismissals and claims for compensations and severance pay thereto. Because the employee is reluctant, for fear of reprisal, to sue his employer for individual grievances arising in the course of the individual employment contract, the majority of cases coming before the labour courts seem to have been initiated by employees whose contracts have already been terminated.

§3. Labour Courts

814. Act No. 5521, respecting labour courts and dated 30 January 1950, stated in Article 1: 'wherever it appears appropriate to do so, labour courts must be established to deal with legal disputes between employers and employees as defined in the Labour Act (i.e., excluding those employees engaged in sea and air transportation – except stevedoring and ground services at airports, also excluding agriculture except rural manufacturers, construction and agricultural machinery repair shops;

356. B. Kuru, *Hukuk Yargılama Usulü*, Ankara, p. 733.
357. Court of Cassation, General Council Decision, 10 Nov. 1965, 9-643/405; Court of Cassation, 9th Div., 7 May 1974, 4038/4615.

family home-workers – and excluding public servants), and employers and employers' representatives in connection with employment contracts or claims of any kind under the Labour Act.

815. Labour courts try (a) suits brought by unions in cases covered by Article 4-e of Act No. 5018 (that is, the Unions Act now repealed) and suits brought against unions and (b) suits arising out of disputes between the Workers' (Social) Insurance Organization and the insured persons or their dependents. In places where no labour court has been established, the local court is charged with dealing with such cases by applying the principles and rules laid down in this Act. This provision shall likewise apply where, on account of legal impediment or physical impossibility, the labour court is unable to sit.

816. Article 2 envisaged that the labour court should be composed of one employers' representative and one employees' representative and presided over by a judge appointed for the case. However in 1971 the Constitutional Court repealed, along with several other articles of the Act, the provision concerning the election of employers' and employees' representatives to labour courts on the grounds that the judicial power should be autonomous and independent of any outside influences.[358]

817. Suits could be brought before the court in charge for the locality where the party is domiciled within the meaning of the Civil Code on the date of commencing proceedings, or in the court for the locality where the establishment is situated. Any agreement to the contrary is null and void. At hearings before the labour court, the rules regarding fast-hearing (i.e., the accelerated version of ordinary written method used in court proceedings) were to be followed, but the new Act on Civil Procedures which came into force in October 2011 changed the court's working method to 'simple hearing' (i.e., court proceedings even simpler and faster than the ordinary written form). The court endeavours to reconcile the parties at its first hearing. If conciliation fails, or if one of the parties is absent or is not represented, the proceedings must continue and judgment must be given on the facts at issue. Appeal against the final judgment of the labour court could be made within eight days of the pronouncement thereof. The relevant division of the Court of Cassation must give a decision of approval or reversal of the judgment of the labour court within two months. As a rule the decisions of the Court of Cassation are not subject to review, but if the labour court insists on its judgment then the General Council of the Court of Cassation, which consists of members of other divisions of the High Court, issues a final and binding award on the case, thereby turning down or upholding the court's decision. Since labour courts apply fast-hearing procedures, requesting the correction of this award is not acceptable even for procedural reasons. However, even the awards of the General Council are not binding on similar cases which may arise, although, of course, judges are expected to take the High Courts'

358. *See* the verdict of the Constitutional Court, dated 13 Apr. 1971, 1970/63, 1971/38; Official Gazette, 16 Nov. 1971. Likewise, Arts 3, 4, 6, 12, 13 and 14 of the Act were scrapped by the Constitutional Court on the same date.

decisions into consideration. Further, if the General Council is faced with conflicting awards in similar cases, it may issue a Unification of Jurisprudence Award which then becomes legally binding on similar cases which may arise in the future.

818. The Labour Courts Act of 1950 was an outdated, almost obsolete, law, especially in the face of developments in collective labour relations since 1963. Therefore, was a need to revise it with a view to adapt it to emergent conditions. Also, the Ministry of Justice should endeavour to increase the number and efficiency of labour courts, the functions of which have taken on greater significance in the past forty years or so, particularly after the enactment of Act No. 4857 which has led to an enormous amount of legal actions involving requests for reinstatement. In order to alleviate the heavy caseload of the Court of Cassation, the government is in the process of setting up intermediate-level courts of appeal, as also foreseen in the new Act on Civil Procedures. In an attempt to replace the Labour Courts Act of 1950 and to speed up the settlement of labour disputes, the legislature passed the new Labour Courts Act of October 2017, No. 7036, which was supplemented also by a 'mediation' process as well as various amendments in labour legislation. With a view 'to speed the processes of dispute settlement procedures and improve the efficiency of the labour courts'.

819. Article 2 of the new Act on the establishment of labour courts provides that labour courts shall be set up as units under the chairmanship of a single judge each in the manner of peace courts of first instance in districts designated by the Ministry of Justice upon the opinion of the Council of Judges and Prosecutors. Where the workload requires, more than on division of a labour court may be conceived. In regions where labour courts have not been established, courts of first instance shall be in charge of adjudicating matters which fall into the jurisdiction of labour courts.

820. Mediation as a Precondition for Filing a Lawsuit: Article 3 provides the following main points as a precondition for filing a lawsuit with the labour court:

> 'wage and compensation claims of workers and employers based on law, employment contract or collective labour agreement and job security-based legal actions for re-instalment recourse first to the mediator is a precondition for filing the lawsuit with the labour court. If the mediation results in a failure to agree, the plaintiff must attach the copy of failure to agree to his petition for initiating his lawsuit. If this procedure has not been fulfilled, the court shall send to the plaintiff a warning for the submission within one week of the failure of agreement'. Where the submission of this warning results in a failure of action, the request for filing a lawsuit shall be refused for procedural reasons. If it is found that the suit has been initiated without recourse to mediation, the suit shall provide the necessary information to the respective parties according to which the media communicates with them Also the mediator may carry on any investigations he deems necessary. Based on all the deeds and procedures completed, he shall invite the contesting parties to the first meeting. The mediator may not take into consideration the first meeting, payment of litigation costs shall rest on the parties concerned.

821. The mediator shall conclude the mediation procedure in three weeks from the date he has been placed in charge of the mediation process. In case of need he may extend his term for an additional week at the most. In cases where reaching the mediator was not possible or where the parties have not participated in the process, or where they were unable to negotiate for any reason, the mediator shall end the procedure and communicate this information to the office.

822. In cases where the mediation process comes to an end because one of the parties has not participated in the first meeting without any valid reason, the absentee party shall be mentioned in the final report; regardless of his being found partially or entirely justified in the process, he shall be responsible to pay the total costs. In procedures of court litigation following mediation where both parties have refrained from participating in the first meeting, payment of litigation costs shall rest on the parties concerned. 'In the event mediation results in the mutual agreement of the parties, the fee of the mediator shall be shared on an equal basis unless otherwise has been decided by the parties. 'Allegedly these clauses imply that the legislature is concerned mainly with the actual initiation of mediation where the assumption is to force the employee to be content with less than he was actually entitled to.' In negotiations concerning claims for job-security based compensation (with demands for reinstatement) the fee of the mediator shall be held to be the amount equal to the total sum of the job security compensation to be reimbursed to the employee.

823. In mediation procedures where the main employer-subcontractor relationship is involved with a request of the employee for reinstatement, in order for the mutual agreement between the contesting parties concerned to materialize, both employers (the main employer and the subcontractor) must have participated in the mediation meeting jointly, with their demands consistent with each other on the subject matter of the dispute.

824. The time interval between recourse to the mediation office and the delivery of the final mediator report shall not be considered in the computation of statutory limitations; this interval shall not be operative in the forfeiture of rights due to lapse of time.

825. The journalists employed under the Press Labour Act of 1952, No. 5953, and seamen working under the Maritime Labour Act of 1967, No. 854 shall be considered to be 'employees' within the scope of Article 3/20. Where this article is silent, the general Act Mediation of 7 June 2012, No. 6325 shall be applicable, if compatible.

826. Article 4 of the Labour Courts Act deals with the requirement to call on the Social Security Organization in disputes based on social security and health insurance legislation. Article 6 is concerned with matters of competence of labour courts. The method of adjudication by labour courts shall be 'the simple trial method'.

Where the number of suits increases considerably, the burden of proof and evidential facts shall be evaluated separately for each claim concerned. Relevant clauses of Act No. 6100 (of 2011) shall be applicable for verdicts awarded by the labour courts.

827. The Labour Courts Act provides that the court decisions in the lawsuits and transactions mentioned below are to be final construed meaning they shall not be appealed to higher-level courts for review:

(a) Decisions about objections to declarations of employment termination given in conjunction with Article 20 of the Labour Act No. 4857 (i.e., on job security-based claims).
(b) Decisions in lawsuits concerning the nullification of disciplinary penalties given by the employer in conjunction with the collective labour agreement or work-place ace rules.
(c) Decisions on the Labour Unions and the Collective Labour Agreement Act, 2012, No. 6356.
(d) Decisions concerning the union shop-stewards', non-professional union leader's or the union's request for reinstatement (Article 24 (1,5) of Act No. 6356.
(e) Court decisions on Article 34/4 of Act No. 4857 on the consequences of the employer's failure to pay wages on due date.
(f) Decisions on matters concerning the employee's right to annual leave with pay (Article 51, Act No. 485).
(g) Decisions on the determination of the legality of a strike or lock-out (in which case the intermediate court of appeals shall decide in one month).
(h) Act No. 4688 on Public Servants' Unions and collective Agreement, in lawsuits concerning Article 10(8) and 14(4) dealing with the acquisition of membership.

I. A Critique of the Act on Labour Courts with Reference to Mediation as a Precondition for Legal Action

828. The new Labour Courts Act of 25 October 2017 seems to have brought a drastic change in the well-established conceptualizations of Turkish labour law in terms of the distinction between 'rights disputes' versus 'interest disputes'. While rights disputes refer to employee -employer disagreements on the interpretation and application of existing contracts or legislation, interest disputes emanate from disagreements over new demands for wage increases (new demands on wage-effort bargain, etc.) It is generally held that processes like mediation, conciliation and arbitration are suited rather to solving interest disputes, while court action and private arbitration are methods of solving rights disputes. But under the new system mediation seems to have been shifted to the domain of rights disputes.

829. This is very likely to give rise to various drawbacks, mainly for the worker and, perhaps to a lesser degree, for the employer as well in some cases. The employer may also prefer the real and reliable adjudication of rights disputes, a formal legal procedure in upholding his calculated claims rather than the arbitrary interventions of a mediator whose neutrality he may not be trusting

830. In the final analysis the task of reliable adjudication of rights disputes within reasonable time periods by sufficient number of courts and independent judges seems to be a more preferred avenue.

831. In creating an efficient method of settling rights disputes, another avenue could be encouraging voluntary arbitration (rather than compulsory edition) the basic principles of which are already found in the procedural law of Turkey. It is deplorable, however, that application of voluntary arbitration has not found a widespread usage in Turkish practice.

832. In the clumsy design of the new compulsory mediation in Turkey, the lawmaker has approached the parties as equals. This view is certainly misplaced and mistaken. On the contrary, the pro -labour Turkish labour law treats the employer and worker as unequal whereby the worker is the weaker party that must be protected.

833. In most cases the worker is not in a favourable position to compute the amount of his claims. How much should he claim and how much should he admit as acceptable?

834. In job security-related lawsuits (with requests for reinstatement generally) where the litigation takes a relatively long time, the employee faced with economic difficulties is likely to accept a compensation level lower than his actual worth.

835. Clauses on mediation are confusing indeed, likely to lead to problems in practice. The Act may be subject to a lawsuit before the Constitutional Court on grounds of its unconstitutionality.

836. Answers to many potential questions which may arise in the application of this Act have been treated in a regulation. But leaving the solution of such essential problems to a regulation may lead to a nullification suit on grounds of unconstitutionality.

837. Clauses of the new Labour Courts Act and those on mediation, unlike the interest mediation in collective bargaining, are confusing indeed, likely to lead to problems in practice.

838. These new amendments in legislation requiring compulsory mediation as a precondition even in legal actions filed with a request for reinstatement and/or union compensation are special targets for criticism as they violate freedom of association principles.

839. Act No. 7036 in Article 11 has brought a supplement to Article 20 of Act No. 4857 on the Labour Act has provided that 'if the lawsuit has been filed with the labour court before passing through the mediation stage, the request for court action shall be denied for lack of procedural requirements, whereby the decision of denial shall be communicated promptly to the parties involved. Recourse to mediation may be made within two weeks of communicating the finalized decision on refusal. The time interval within which recourse to mediation must be made before taking legal action for requests on reinstatement as well as the time within which the lawsuit must be filed in the event of disagreement in the mediation process, however, the clauses concerning the time intervals are likely to cause problems in practice. Besides, the idea of considering the mediation process as a precondition for calling on 'arbitration' (where and if the parties have agreed on recourse to arbitration voluntarily) seems to run counter to the notion of voluntary arbitration.

§4. The New Act of Obligations

840. As mentioned above, in an attempt to bring the Obligations Act (law of contracts) of 1926, No. 818, into conformity with contemporary developments, a new Obligations Act, No. 6098 was adopted by the Grand National Assembly on 11 January 2011 (Official Gazette, 4 February 2011, No. 27836). In order to allow for a preparatory adjustment period, however, it was decided that the new law would go into force on 1 July 2012.

841. As the preceding chapters have shown, the Obligations Act forms the basis of many private law sources. Its sections on the employment contract (which it refers to as the 'service contract') bears special significance for labour law, first, for employees who are not protected by labour legislation (i.e., the Labour Act, Maritime Labour Act and the Press Labour Act) and second, on matters where the labour legislation is silent its provisions are directly applicable. This means that the references made to Act No. 818 in the previous editions of this monograph have been revised according to the new Obligations Act in this edition. Because the present labour legislation does not carry provisions on such concepts as the certificate of discharge, covenant of non-competition, the use of the employee's personal data by the employer, the penal condition, protection of the worker's privacy and the transfer of the employment contract, the relevant clauses of the new Obligations Act will be directly applicable.

842. Noteworthy here at first glance is the fact that no coherent relationship has been established between the provisions of labour legislation and the relevant concepts of the new Obligations Act. As a result, almost an entirely different legislative framework seems to have been created on matters like the annual leave with pay, notice terms, the compensation the worker must pay the employer if he leaves employment by ignoring notice terms, fixed-term contracts and the designation by the judge of a compensation for terminations for no just, cause, etc. Differences as such are likely to lead to discriminatory practices between those (workers and employers) covered by labour legislation and those subject to the Obligations Act.

The new Obligations Act is also saddled with ambiguous clauses from which one can hardly draw clear meanings. Article 394 provides, for example, that 'an employment contract which is found to be invalid at a later stage shall have all the consequences of a valid contract until the expiration of the employment relationship'. It is not certain how the invalidity of the contract is to be determined. Similarly, according to the statement of Article 419, the employer can use the worker's personal data only to the extent of his adaptability to the job or as required for the execution of the employment contract. Article 417 which requires the employer to take measures to prevent 'mobbing' behaviour in the establishment has not clarified the meaning of mobbing. Though it is a positive step, 'mobbing' should be defined more clearly; otherwise many labour disputes which may arise due to ambiguities in the concept may prove to be detrimental to workplace discipline and labour peace.[359]

843. Besides, as alluded to above, Article 420 of the new Obligations Act deals with the practice of the employer's obtaining a signed statement from the worker (certificate of discharge), releasing the employer of possible claims by the worker upon his termination. Insofar as the date on which the certificate of discharge may be obtained from the employee. The article provides that a minimum of one month must have elapsed after the termination date of the contract. The clause is undoubtedly pro-labour, aiming to stave off certain abusive practices of the past; but it is also apt to lead to various practical problems. For instance, the worker who has taken legal action against his termination will be reluctant to deliver this signed document, thus causing hardship and complications for the system. In view of such critical points, therefore, the stakeholders likely to be involved in such controversies will probably prod the legislature to make corrections in the text of the new Act.

359. For similar criticisms, *see* Ş. Aktekin, *MESS İşveren Gazetesi*, February 2011, p. 12.

Part II. Collective Labour Relations

Chapter 1. Union Freedom (Freedom of Association)

§1. Concepts and Definitions

I. The Concepts of 'Unions' and 'Employee and Employer Organizations'

844. The word *sendika* has been used by the Constitution and labour laws of Turkey to denote a specific form of employee and employer organization. To avoid confusion for the English reader, the expression 'labour union' will be used throughout this monograph to refer to employees' (workers') organizations, while the expression 'employers' unions' will denote employers' organizations, both of which are governed by the Unions and the Collective Agreement Act No. 6356) and referred to as unions (*sendika*). Act No. 2821 had dropped the term 'occupational organizations of employees and employers' which was frequently used by the repealed Unions Act of 1963, No. 274. However, the term 'employee and employer organizations' is occasionally used to imply unions of both groups in a broad sense. Yet there are also such occupational organizations as the Chambers of Commerce and Industry, the Bar Association and the like. It should be noted, however, that labour unions and employer unions differ from these categories in many respects. Also, the 'association', when used in its broader sense in Turkish law, refers to a certain type of voluntary organizations dealt with by the Associations Act No. 5253 which, along with other entities in this category, also comprises unions as used in their specific connotations throughout this monograph.

845. The right of employees and employers to form and join unions is guaranteed by the Constitution of Turkey. Article 51 of the 1982 Constitution states that, in order to protect and promote their economic and social rights and interests in labour relations, employees and employers are free to establish unions as well as upper-level union organizations without having to obtain any prior permission. By referring to 'upper-level union organizations', the Constitution has aimed to enable the legislature to determine the types of such organizations. In line with this constitutionally guaranteed principle, the Unions Act of 1983, No. 2821, envisaged the establishment of labour unions and employers' unions as well as their confederations, thus implying the abolition of federations and regional councils (*birliks*) which existed under the previous system. The same structure has been retained in the present Act No. 6356.

846. The new Act on Unions and the Collective Labour Agreement No. 6356 begins by giving definitions of certain concepts used in its text. For reasons of clarity and convenience they are cited below:

Article 2

(1) In the implementation of this Act, the meanings/definitions of the terms/concepts below are as follows;
   (a) Ministry: The Ministry of Labour and Social Security;
   (b) Framework agreement: the industry branch-level agreement concluded between labour and employers' unions affiliated with the ESC;
   (c) Competent authority: for the 'establishment level' collective labour agreement, the Provincial Directorate of Labour and Employment Organization (PDLEO) where the establishment is located; for the 'enterprise level' collective labour agreement, the Provincial Directorate of Labour and Employment where the centre of the enterprise is located; and for the 'group collective labour agreement' involving establishments which fall into the jurisdiction of the same Provincial Directorate of Labour and Employment Organization, the PDLEO with which the said establishments are associated; and for the group collective labour agreement which falls into the jurisdiction of more than one PDLEO, the Ministry;
   (ç) Group collective labour agreement: the collective labour agreement between the labour and employers' union covering the establishments and enterprises belonging to more than one employer active in the same industry branch;
   (d) Enterprise collective labour agreement: the collective labour agreement covering more than one establishment belonging to a real or corporate person or to a public institute or organization in the same industry branch;
   (e) Employer's representative: the person who manages the entire enterprise on behalf of the employer;
   (f) Confederation: the organization with corporate status formed by the affiliation of more than five unions active in different industry branches;
   (g) Organizations: unions and confederations;
   (h) Union: organization with corporate status formed by the association of at least seven employees or employers active in an industry branch with a view to protect their rights and promote their common economic and social interests in their working conditions,
   (i) Upper level organization: confederation;
   (j) Administrator: member of the administrative board of the organization and the branch of the organization.

(2) Employer's representative shall be considered to be 'employer' in the implementation of this Act.

(3) The definitions given for the concepts of 'employee', 'employer' and 'establishment' by the Labour Act No. 4857 shall also apply to the implementation of this Act.
(4) Real persons who perform work for wages as an independent professional activity in accordance with transportation, job, agency, publishing, commission or ordinary partnership contract shall be regarded as 'employees' in terms of the second and sixth sections of this Act.

847. Thus, Article 2 of the new Act on Unions and the Collective Labour Agreement has also used the term 'organizations' to denote both 'unions' and 'confederations.' Among the elements of labour and employer organizations, one could cite (a) common objectives of protecting and promoting members' economic and social rights and interests, (b) freedom to establish without prior authorization, (c) the independence of labour and employers' organizations from each other as well as from the state, political parties and religious organizations, from associations, occupational organizations of a public nature, artisan and craft organizations. In view of Article 2(1)g of Act No. 6356, labour and employers' organizations do possess legal corporate personality subject to private law.

II. Relations Between the Right to Organize Labour and Employers' Unions and the Right to Form Associations

848. Drawing the line between unions and associations seems to be a difficult task. According to Article 63 of Act No. 2821 and Article 80 of Act No. 6356, all unions and union confederations are subject to those provisions of the Civil Code and the Associations Act which are not contrary to the Unions Act. Thus, labour and employers' unions are to be treated as private law corporate bodies like all other associations in a general sense. Nonetheless unions differ from associations in various ways. While the right of association has been envisaged in the Second Part of the Constitution under the title 'Individual Rights and Duties' (Article 33), the right to organize unions has been guaranteed in the Third Part under the title 'social and Economic Rights and Duties' (Article 51). But foremost among these differences are the special guarantees granted to unions by the Constitution and the unique competences and functions that have been accorded to them by special legislation. Although unions are private law institutions in a strict sense, they have acquired certain attributes which serve public order and public interest, as they help to establish checks and balances intended to protect the rights and improve the interests of a large number of working people in society.

849. Also, employees' and employers' unions enjoy special privileges as compared to associations in general. While the decision of a competent court is required for the suspension of a union's activities as well as for its abolition and liquidation, the activities of associations may be suspended, even before the competent court takes a decision to that effect, by administrative bodies authorized by law if the unity of the state, national security, public order and general morals warrant such action (Constitution, Article 33).

850. Compared to the now-repealed Act of 1963, No. 274, Act No. 2821 had brought many detailed and wide-ranging clauses pertaining to unions and therefore greatly alleviated the need to apply provisions of the Associations Act to unions. Presently Act No. 6356 seems to have lessened these details. However, as Article 63 of the Act No. 2821 and Article 80 of Act No. 6356 have provided, unions and union confederations shall be subject to those provisions of the Civil Code and Associations Act which are not contrary to union legislation, construed as meaning that in the event there is no applicable provision in the Unions Act, pertinent provisions of the Civil Code and the Associations Act would apply to unions as well. In fact the Associations Act enumerates, along with related penalty provisions, the clauses which shall also apply to unions.

851. With a view to devising more liberal legislation on associations, the Parliament passed Act No. 5253, on 23 November 2004, which replaced Act No. 2908 and lessened the links between associations and Act No. 2821 on unions. Article 35 of the new Associations Act enumerates those provisions which shall apply to unions and confederations on subjects where union legislation is silent. These are Articles 19, 20, 23, 26, 28, 29, 30 and 31. Also, by repealing or amending the contradictory provisions, Act No. 5253 has now been brought into conformity with the Civil Code.

852. Major changes made in the Associations Act concerning unions are the following: in contrast to Act No. 2908, associations may now exchange material aid with labour and employers' unions as well as with other associations having similar objectives and political parties (Article 10(1)). As the new Associations Act had succeeded Act No. 2821 in time, it could be affirmed that unions could accept aid from associations provided the competent organ of the union takes a decision to that effect consistent with the union's objectives. Regarding unions' extending aid to associations, there is no restriction in union legislation, but they can do so only if providing aid as such is consistent with their objectives as indicated in the law and the union constitution. Still the decision must have been adopted by the union's general congress (general assembly), and the union's administrative board must have been authorized accordingly. As regards receiving aid from foreign sources, there is no conflict with the Associations Act.

853. Article 2(f) and Article 25 provide that associations may form common 'platforms' (an informal collaboration with no legal personality) among themselves as well as with foundations, labour unions and similar civic organizations. Limited to subject matters not prohibited by legislation, the platform must also be related to the objectives of the said organizations. Further, participation in the platform must be based on the decision of the union's administrative board taken to that effect.

854. Having completed the legal age of 18 was one of the conditions in order to become a founding member of the union. Since the new Act has not made any reference to age, this condition will no longer be required. And Article 2 of Act No. 5253 provides that the minimum number of founders must still be seven, as was the case under Associations Act No. 2908, so there must be at least seven real persons (or in the case of employers' unions, seven legal bodies represented by employer's representatives) must come together in order to found a union, according to the reference by Article 80 of Act No. 6356. Besides, Act No. 6356 has now explicitly provided that there must be at least seven persons in order to found a union.

855. On the convening of the union's general congress, the administrative board must make an invitation, in line with the Civil Code Article 77, including the date, place and agenda of the meeting, at least fifteen days prior to the meeting of the general congress. If the required quorum is not obtained in the first meeting, a maximum time span of fifteen days has been foreseen for the convening of the second meeting. The minimum time length that should elapse for holding the second meeting was one week under the Associations Act No. 2908. Since Act No. 5253 is silent here, the second meeting may be held now without having to observe the passage of a certain minimum.

856. Article 35 of Act No. 5253 provides that provisions contained in the following articles shall apply also to unions and confederations: (a) the obligation of associations to make annual declarations on their income and expenses and their supervision by the competent authority (Article 19); (b) the power of security forces (Article 20); (c) declaration of the general congress and names of persons elected to the organs of the organization (Article 23); (d) establishments to be formed upon obtaining permits (Article 26); (e) names of associations (Article 28); (f) restrictions on using certain names and signals (Article 29); (g) prohibited associations and activities (Article 30); and (h) official language of communication (Article 31).

857. Article 20 provides that security forces may not enter and search associations, unless they have obtained a court order with a view to protect public order or to prevent the commission of criminal acts. If for reasons of urgency the administrative authority has been forced to issue a decision to that effect, it must submit that decision to the approval of the judge in charge, in twenty-four hours. The judge must pass his judgment in forty-eight hours.

§2. Union Freedoms: Categories and Definitions

I. Individual Positive Union Freedom

A. The Notion

858. Positive union freedom means the freedom of employees and employers to form and join unions and confederations of their own choosing. This right is guaranteed by Article 51 of the Constitution which provides that 'employees and employers can form unions and confederations without having to obtain the prior permission of the government. Their constitutions, administration and operations must not be contrary to the basic principles of the Republic and the rules of democracy'. The principle of union pluralism is also constitutionally guaranteed. Positive union freedom includes also the freedom of the employee or the employer to join the union of his own choice. And naturally, more than one union may be constituted in the same industry branch (sector).

859. Considering these dimensions of union freedom as embodied in the Constitution and the Unions and the Collective Agreement Act, a general definition of employees' and employers' organizations could be as follows: 'being corporate bodies subject mainly to private law, unions are independent organizations of employees and employers, established freely and in accordance with democratic principles and basic features of the Republic in order to protect and promote their members' economic and social rights and interests'. Thus, the major characteristics of employees' and employers' organizations are the pursuance of common goals for their members, their being established freely and voluntarily, the requirement that they must be independent organizations and their formation and operation must be consistent with democratic principles, 'Independence' is construed to mean (a) independence of employees' and employers' organizations from each other, (b) independence from the government and (c) independence from political parties and religious organizations.

B. *Categories Granted the Right to Organize and Join Labour Unions*

860. Contrary to the Unions Act of 1947 which had granted the right to unionize only to manual employees, the Act of 1963, No. 274, by abolishing the distinction between intellectual and manual work in its definition of the employment contract, entitled white-collar as well as blue-collar employees to form and join unions. Article 2 of the Unions Act of 1983, No. 2821, had also provided definitions of 'employees' and 'employers' who could form and join unions.

861. As Article 2(3) of Act No. 6356 states, 'the definitions given for the concepts 'employee', 'employer' and 'establishment' by the Labour Act of 22 May 2003, No. 4857, shall also apply to the implementation of this Act. Thus, any person working under an employment contract is considered to be an 'employee'. Also, any person considered as an employee in accordance with the Labour Act as well as the Maritime Labour Act and Press Labour Act or the Obligations Act (agricultural wage-earners included) is covered by this definition. But Article 2(4) of Act No. 6356 has expanded the concept of 'employee' to cover certain other categories: Real persons who perform work for wages as an independent professional activity in accordance with transportation, job, agency, publishing, commission or ordinary partnership contract, other than employment contract, shall be regarded as 'employees' in terms of the second and sixth sections of this Act, construed as meaning that they will not have access to the provisions of Act No. 6356 on the collective agreement.

862. It should also be noted that the person wishing to become a member of a union must be working in an establishment in the branch of activity in which the union has been established.

C. Employers, Employers' Representatives and the Issue of 'Non-covered Employees'

863. Real persons or corporations or non-corporate public bodies employing employees are considered to be 'employers'. Any person authorized to manage an entire enterprise in the name of the person or corporation or non-corporate public bodies considered as employer' is defined as 'employer's representative'. The employer's representatives are considered 'employers' for the purposes of this Act (Article 2/(1)e and Article 2(2)). Employer's representatives as defined in this article may only join employers' unions.

864. The concept of 'employer's representative', as defined differently in various legal sources, has led to somewhat contradictory practices. The conflict stems mainly from the definitions given by the Labour Act (No. 4857, previously No. 1475) and the Unions Act (No. 2821 and now Act No. 6356). In view of Article 2/(5) of the Labour Act, the term 'employer's representative' means 'any person acting in the establishment (workplace, plant) on behalf of the employer and charged with the direction of the work, the establishment and enterprise'. This is a rather broad definition and covers all persons with delegated management authority right down the line to foremen (first line-supervisors). The Unions Act, on the other hand, provides a narrower definition: 'any person authorized to manage an entire enterprise in the name of the employer is the "employer's representative"'. Here, the main criterion is the authority to manage the entire enterprise (company, corporation, non-corporate public body, etc.), but not a department, nor the authority to supervise certain types of work as in the case of a supervisor. Since the Unions Act of 1963 (No. 274) had mentioned only the phrase 'authority to manage an entire enterprise', it did create this narrow concept of the 'employer's representative'.

865. Thus, under the 1963–1980 system, it was the general manager of a corporation, for instance, who was to be regarded as the employer's representative, for he was empowered to manage the whole enterprise consisting of various establishments (workplaces). The conflict between the definitions gave rise to several problems in Turkish industrial relations. Persons regarded as 'employer's representatives' (that is, only top managers) and therefore treated as 'employers' were thus entitled to join employers' unions only, while all other managerial categories were considered 'employees' and therefore could join labour unions along with the rank-and-file. Because conflicts of interest were apt to arise from the unionization of such managerial personnel, the parties to collective bargaining devised the concept of 'coverage of collective agreements', that is, certain categories of employees with managerial authority who were legally unionizable were to be excluded, by mutual agreement of parties, from the coverage of collective agreements, in which case it was assumed that the employer would provide them with wages and benefits at least equal to, or usually better than, those granted by the collective agreement.

866. Also, the recognition of the right to form and join unions to middle and lower managerial levels allegedly prompted employers to have the so-called yellow unions (company unions) established through such personnel. The legal definition of the 'employer's representative' versus the 'employee' thus became a crucial question in Turkish practice. In the course of time, expansion of the 'non-covered' employee categories through employer pressures has been one of the factors leading to the loss of the union's majority status, thus aggravating the problem of de-unionization. In its original form Act No. 2821 somewhat expanded the scope of the concept so as to cover also the person who was authorized to manage the entire establishment (workplace-plant). Unlike the situation in the previous system, directors of bank branches or captains of ships, for instance, both of which are considered establishments (workplaces) – were to be treated as 'employer's representative'. They were, therefore, entitled to join employers' union which was not possible under the old system. This did not eliminate, however, the problems of 'covered versus non-covered personnel' in collective agreements, for employers still insisted on excluding other managerial personnel from the coverage of collective agreements. Second, it seemed odd to treat as 'employees' other managerial personnel of the 'enterprise' who were positioned higher than the manager of the establishment in the hierarchical echelons of the organization. Evidently, the actual managerial authority of establishment managers could be much more limited than many of such managerial people at the enterprise level who, by definition, were, employees' and therefore could join only labour unions.

867. Probably due to its inability to bring a viable solution, let alone the contradictions it entailed, Act No. 4101, dated 4 April 1995, amended Article 2(6) of Act No. 2821 so as revert the definition of 'employer's representative' back to its earlier form under Act No. 274. Therefore, 'employer's representative' was to be defined again as 'any person authorized to manage an entire enterprise on behalf of the person or corporation or non-corporate public body which is deemed to be the employer'.

868. As the status of the great majority of lower-level managerial personnel in Turkey – i.e., foremen, supervisors – is closer to that of rank-and-file members than to that of management, it would perhaps not be advisable to deprive them of the right to unionize. It might be argued, however, that entitling certain categories of managerial and supervisory personnel to form their own unions (cadre unions) could perhaps prove to be a better solution to the many problems which have arisen in the recent past. Notwithstanding this view, the structure of collective bargaining as envisaged in the Constitution of Turkey did not permit the co-existence of more than one collective agreement at the establishment. The practice of excluding certain employee categories from the coverage of collective agreements by decision of the employer and the union beyond and above their will is certainly contrary to principles of equal treatment and freedom of association. Since the relevant definitions as well as actual practice have not changed, the 'covered versus non-covered personnel' phenomenon remains to be a major flaw besetting the Turkish industrial relations system.

D. Voluntarism

869. As indicated above, the formation of labour and employer's unions is free and voluntary. No person may be forced to form or not to form, to join or not to join, such organizations. This voluntarism is constitutionally guaranteed. Unions and confederations may be constituted without prior authorization. However, one of the motives underlying present legislation was to curb the number of unions without legally undermining trade union freedoms. To realize this objective Acts No. 2821 and 2822 had brought various indirect measures. One such measure was found in Article 5(1) of Act No. 2821 which stated that the founding members of a union must be actively employed within the industry in which the union is to be constituted. The constitutional amendment by Act No. 4709 deleted this provision from the text of Article 51 of the Constitution.

E. Pluralism

870. A natural consequence of the principle that the formation of and membership to labour unions should be free is multi-unionism (or union pluralism). The same rule holds true for employers' unions as well as for confederations. Employees and employers may join the unions of their own choosing, and if they are not satisfied with the performance of their organizations, they may break away and set up new ones. Likewise, more than one confederation of labour and employer's unions may be constituted, and membership to such high-level organizations is also voluntary and free.

871. Since under the previous system employees and employers were free to join more than one union at a time, there were many alleged cases of duplicated membership which occasionally complicated the task of determining the 'majority union'. The Constitution of 1982 (Article 51) and Act No. 2821 prohibited membership of an employee to more than one union at a time. Recently, the Constitutional amendment of 7 May 2010, by Act No. 5982, has repealed this ban on the employee's multiple union membership in the same industry branch of activity, but the restriction in Act No. 6356. still remains in a somewhat relaxed manner.

872. Taking into consideration the expansion of part-time work, Article 17(3) of Act No. 6356 provides the following:

> Joining the union is free. No person shall be forced to join or not join the union. Employees and employers shall not join more than one union in the same industry branch at a time. However employees employed in establishments belonging to different employers in the same industry branch may join more than union. In the event of employees or employers belonging to more than one union in contravention of this rule, the latter memberships shall be invalid.

F. Persons Who Are Not Allowed to Become Members of Unions

873. According to Article 21 of the Unions Act No. 2821 of 1983 in its original form, the following persons were not allowed to constitute or to join any labour or employers' unions: (1) members of the armed forces (excluding 'employees' in undertakings attached to the Ministry of National Defence, the General Command of the Gendarmerie and the Coast Guard Command); (2) inspectors, auditors, directors and any other persons fulfilling similar or higher functions in the governmental establishments, institutions, administrations, agencies, banks and insurance companies (referred to in Article 40/2); (3) persons carrying out religious functions and services; (4) students and (5) teaching staff of private schools subject to Act No. 625 of June 1965.

874. Subsections 3 and 4 of this article were removed by Article 17 of Act No. 3449 on 25 May 1988. Subsections 2 and 5 were repealed by Article 15 of Act No. 4101 on 4 April 1995; the only restriction which remains presently is, therefore, subsection 1 referring to military personnel. Since members of armed forces (professional officers) are considered to be public servants subject to a special act, they represent the only category excluded from the right of unionization at present.

875. The restriction concerning teaching institutions found in Act No. 625 was removed by Act No. 5580 which replaced Act No. 625 (Official Gazette, 14 February 2007, No. 26434). So at present, private school teachers may organize and bargain collectively. More recently, Act No. 6356 has lifted the ban on the right to strike in educational institutions. On the other hand, being under public servant status, unionization of teaching staff of public schools is governed by special legislation on public servants' unions Act No. 4688.

876. Security personnel employed in establishments covered by Act No. 2495 on the Protection and Security of Certain Organizations could not form and join unions. This restriction was repealed by Act No. 5188 of 26 June 2004 which replaced Act No. 2495. However, the ban on their right to strike, as well as the requirement that during a lock-out they must keep working at the locked-out establishment continues.

II. The Freedom Not to Join, to Resign (to Withdraw) or Not to Resign from a Union (Individual Negative Union Freedom)

877. Article 51(3) and (4) of the Constitution and Article 25(1) of the Unions and the Collective Labour Agreement Act No. 6356 both emphasize the freedom of the individual not to join a union or to refrain from resigning, or to resign from the union of which he is a member. Also according to Article 25(1), Act No. 6356, the recruitment of workers shall not be made subject to any condition as to their membership of a labour union, or obliging them to join or refrain from joining a given union or to remain a member of or resign from a given union. Thus 'union-shop' clauses as well as 'yellow-dog contracts' are clearly prohibited. The worker enjoys full freedom to join or not to join, as well as to resign or not to resign from, a union.

III. Collective Union Freedom

878. It is held that the right of employees and employers to form and join unions and higher level union organizations (confederations), as embodied in Article 51 of the Constitution, also involves the concept of 'collective union freedom', as these organizations have the capacity to handle their affairs as autonomous entities. Needless to say, a significant part of collective union freedom is the autonomy of such organizations to engage in free collective bargaining. However, rather than mentioning unions, Articles 53 and 54 of the Constitution, like Article 47 of the 1961 Constitution, have specifically mentioned 'employees' and 'employers' in referring to the right to enter into collective agreements and to strike and lock-out. Before 1980, therefore, some writers pointed to the unconstitutionality of Act No. 275 (on Collective Agreement, Strikes and Lock-Outs) on the grounds that, contrary to the wording of the Constitution, the Act had specifically authorized unions as monopolies to engage in collective bargaining and strike activity'.[360]

879. In reply to this argument, it was claimed that in the light of the basic principle laid down in the Constitution, the legislature had granted the competence to exercise these rights to autonomous employee organizations rather than to employees themselves with a view to empowering them to use such rights more effectively. By using the term 'employees', the Constitution must have implicitly referred to employees organized in labour unions.[361] The same arguments are valid today as far as the Constitution of 1982 is concerned. Thus, Articles 51, 53 and 54 of the Constitution taken together, it is held that both individual and collective union freedoms, construed to mean the freedom to engage in collective and concerted action, have been accorded constitutional guarantees. However, compared to Articles 46 and 47 of the 1961 Constitution, Articles 51 to 54 of the new Constitution carry certain restrictions concerning the full exercise of union freedoms.

880. Certainly, union activities do not comprise solely collective bargaining and strike actions. Collective union freedoms are to be construed as meaning all kinds of activities in which unions engage in accomplishing the goals of 'protecting the rights and furthering the interests of their members', as envisaged in Articles 51 and 53 of the Constitution.

881. Another dimension of collective union freedom is the right of unions to form and join higher level, multi-union organizations. This, too, has been accorded constitutional protection in Article 51. Since Act No. 2821 abolished federations, the

360. M. Kemal Oğuzman, 'Toplu Sözleşme, Grev ve Lokavt Kanunu Tasarılarının Tahlil ve Tenkidi', *Istanbul Üniversitesi Hukuk Fakültesi MecmuasK*, 1962, Vol. XXVII, No. 2, p. 423.
361. Constitutional Court, 19–20 Oct. 1967, 1963/337, 1967/31; Official Gazette, 2 May 1969, 13188, p. 4.

only higher level national union organization is the 'confederation' under the present system. Unions may also affiliate to international union organizations without having to obtain the prior permission of the government. Thus, the right to form or not to form, and to join or not to join confederations and international union organizations has been vested in unions as corporate bodies; but because decisions along these lines are to be taken by the general congress of unions, the final locus of decision-making with regard to this dimension of collective union freedom rests on the will of the rank-and-file members.

§3. Protection of Union Freedoms in Turkish Labour Law

I. Protection of Individual Union Freedom

A. *Guarantees Provided for Union Membership*

882. Due to the direct and mandatory effect of the Constitution (Constitution of Turkey, Article 11), any agreement or action contrary to the positive and negative union freedoms guaranteed by the Constitution is null and void. Special guarantees concerning individual union freedoms have been provided by Article 25 of Act No. 6356 (similar to Article 31 of the previous Act No. 2821 on Unions) Below Article 25 of Act No. 6356 on the protection of individual freedom of association is given first in its original form along with the related criticisms, followed by the statement of the Constitutional Court verdict of 22 October 2014 which overruled it as null and void.

883. In view of Article 25(1), 'the recruitment of employees shall not be made subject to any conditions as to their membership of a labour union, or obliging them to join or refrain from joining a given labour union or to remain a member of or resign from a given labour union. No conditions contrary to this provision may be contained in any labour contract.' Any provision in an employment contract contradicting this rule is null and void. This means that as in the previous systems, union security clauses like 'closed-shop' or 'union-shop' have been effectively prohibited by Turkish law. 'It shall be unlawful for an employer to make discrimination between employees who are members of a labour union and those who are not, or those who are members of other unions with respect to the arrangement of employment conditions or termination of employment' (Article 25(2)). Thus, the Act emphasizes individual union freedoms not only with respect to the recruitment and hiring of employees, but also with respect to other employment practices and the termination of employment contracts between workers who are members of a labour union and those who are not, or those who are members of another labour union, with respect to recruitment, arrangement and distribution of work, promotion, wages, bonuses, premiums, social and fringe benefits, discipline rules or provisions concerning other questions, including termination of employment. It should be noted, however, that the employer taking into consideration objective standards such as the level of training, seniority, etc., as well as subjective criteria like skill and diligence, may apply differential treatment among his employees with respect to their remuneration, premiums and other conditions of employment.

884. The law has also clarified the limits of the above-stated positive and negative union freedoms concerning individual members. After laying down the general rule prohibiting discriminatory practices by employers between members and non-members, it specifies that 'no exceptions shall be made to the provisions of collective agreement with respect to wages, bonuses, premiums and social and fringe benefits' (Article 25(2)). As a rule, therefore, only the members of the 'signatory union' may benefit from the provisions of the collective agreement on wages, bonuses, fringe benefits, etc. However, as will be explained below, employees who are not members of the union which has concluded a collective agreement are entitled to avail themselves of such benefits if they pay a monthly 'solidarity contribution' to the said union.[362]

885. Still further, Article 25(3) reiterates the wording of ILO Convention 87 by stating that 'employees shall not be terminated nor subjected to discriminatory treatment for their membership or non-membership of a union or for their participation in activities of labour organizations nor for their union-related activities outside working hours or during working hours with the employer's permission'. So far, protections of the new Act for individual union freedoms seem to have been provided parallel to the well-entrenched articles of Turkish law since 1963. The problem begins with the articulation of sanctions in the event of violations by the employer concerning the termination of the employee due to his joining the union or to his participation in union-related activities. As Article 25(4) provides, 'except for the case of termination, if the employer acts in contravention of the above-mentioned paragraphs, an amount not to be less than the employee's total annual wages shall be paid to the employee as union compensation', meaning that the so-called union compensation shall be payable only in anti-union discriminatory practices at the employee's recruitment stage (albeit in a vague manner) as well as during the life of the employment contract, i.e., in the application of employment conditions, but not in union-related dismissals. Furthermore, as understood from Article 25(5), the only category that was granted full protection was limited to those covered by the job security provisions of the Labour Act of 2003, No. 4857, i.e., those with a minimum seniority of six months and employed under open-ended employment contracts, in establishments with a minimum of thirty employees and more. As Article 25(5) says, in the termination of the worker's employment contract for any union- related reason, the worker has the right to file suit in accordance with Articles 18,20 and 21 of the Labour Act No. 4857. If it is determined by the court or arbitrator that the employment contract of the worker within the scope of job security provisions was terminated for a union-related reason, the employee shall be entitled to receive union compensation irrespective of his application for reinstatement or his actual reinstatement or non-reinstatement by the employer', a statement which may be indirectly construed as meaning that the reinstatement decision, if any, is likely to be meaningless since upon the employee's application the

362. Nuri Çelik, *İş Hukuku Dersleri*, 26th edn 2013, Beta, İstanbul, p. 440.

employer shall be reluctant to reinstate a worker who has been dismissed by him for a union-related cause, plus the fact that the worker would l be granted union compensation anyhow. Further, 'in case of non-reinstatement (as reinstatement is not mandatory in Act No. 4857), the additional compensation envisaged in Article 21(1) of Act No. 4857 to be between 4 months up to 8 months wages of the worker shall not be payable', in view of Article 25(5).

886. Therefore one could safely argue that since in union-related terminations taking legal action had been foreseen only for employees within the coverage of Articles 18–21 of the Labour Act No. 4857, a sizable portion of workers seemed to have now been denied 'union compensation' (i.e., the sanction associated with the protection of freedom of association). Providing employees with union compensation only for the employer's anti-union conduct during the life of the employment contract (i.e., in the application of employment conditions) and yet denying protection against union-related dismissals to a considerable portion of the workforce who are outside the coverage of job security is ironic, for losing a job is a more devastating outcome for the worker with serious consequences. As mass dismissals following union organizing drives are more common in smaller undertakings, the approach taken here in Article 25 contradicts the legislature's avowed goal of paving the way for greater freedom of association in Turkey.

887. Besides, granting union compensation to the worker discriminated at the recruitment stage and yet denying it for those who are outside the scope of job security during the application and termination of the employment contract is paradoxical, for termination due to a union-related reason is a more serious violation of freedom of association.

888. Yet controversy arose in academic circles (with respect to the interpretation of Article 25 in view of the constitutional principles of equal treatment and freedom of association) from a rather vague statement found in the last sentence of the same clause of Article 25(5) which provides that 'the reluctance of the employee to take legal action according to the above-mentioned provisions of Act No. 4857 shall not preclude him from demanding union compensation'. Relying on this statement one could also argue that workers falling outside the coverage of job security protection may also file suit in accordance with the Labour Courts Act with a view to requesting union compensation in the event of union-related dismissals.[363] Further, according to a detailed analysis of this matter, there are two options inherent in the wording of Article 25; the first is to file a job security-based suit in accordance with the pertinent articles of the Labour Act, an avenue which was available to workers covered by the job security provisions of The Labour Act where the worker has a privileged position in terms of 'burden of proof'. The second option relates to those workers falling outside the scope of job security coverage of the Labour Act as well as those subject to the Obligations Act, the Maritime Labour Act and the Press

363. Nuri Çelik, *İş Hukuku Dersleri*, 26th edn 2013, Beta, İstanbul, p. 439; for a similar interpretation, *see also*, Can Tuncay and Toplu, *İş Hukuku*, İstanbul, Beta.

Labour Act who may all resort to legal action in accordance with the general provisions of the Labour Courts Act. This latter category has an option of either demanding 'abusive dismissal compensation' as termination for a union-related reason qualifies also as an abusive exercise of the right to terminate the employment contract in view of Article 17 of Act No. 4857, or the option of a general legal action according to Article 25(5-last sentence) where the burden proof shall rest on the worker.[364] Suffice it to say that being a far-fetched view, this optimistic interpretation did not seem realistic as it ran counter to the main emphasis of Article 25 which mentions workers who are within the scope of job security thresholds of Act No. 4857 as the main players who may resort to legal action in union-related dismissals. This stance is further bolstered by the statement made in the Parliament during the passage of Act No. 6356 which proclaimed that 'with the amendment made in the first sentence of Article 25(5), employees who are under the scope of job security have now been enabled to receive union compensation'. Here one could argue that what the legislature really meant was certainly not the workers who, although they were covered by the job security threshold, have not for any reason taken legal action in accordance with Articles 18–21 of the Labour Act. This pessimistic, yet more realistic interpretation represented a clear and deplorable regression not only in comparison to the Ministry's earlier draft bill submitted to the Parliament (which, by using the phrase 'irrespective of the scope of job security provisions') enabled all employees to receive 'union compensation' but also in contrast to Article 31 of the now-repealed Act No. 2821 which enabled all workers to receive union compensation for acts of anti-union discrimination, including those covered by the Labour Act as well as those subject to other relevant legislation, i.e., the Obligations Act, the Maritime Labour Act and the Press Labour Act. The final say on this matter would rest on the interpretations of the judiciary. If the more likely pessimistic view prevailed, not only would it deny protection to many workers against employers' anti-union action in terminations, but it would also run counter to the principle of equal treatment enshrined in international norms as well as the Constitution of Turkey. Fortunately, the 22 October 2014 decision of the Constitutional Court has eradicated this pessimistic view by granting union compensation for union-related terminations to all workers regardless of job security coverage.

889. On the burden of proof, Article 25(7) provides that 'in the suit filed against the termination of the employment contract for union-related reasons, the burden of proving that the reason for termination shall rest on the employer; but the employee who claims that his dismissal was not based on the reason given by the employer must prove himself that his dismissal was motivated by a union-related reason. Except for the case of termination, the employee shall have the burden of proving his plea concerning the employer's union-related discriminatory conduct. But where the employee can show a strong likelihood of the employer's union-related discriminatory conduct, the employer shall have to prove the reason underlying his action. Based on the assumption that no employer shall accept that it was he who terminated the employee for a union-related cause, it is very likely that almost all

364. Fevzi Şahlanan, unpublished paper submitted to the Academic Forum held in Antalya, October 2013.

employers will show reasons other than union-related motives. This means that eventually the worker shall be compelled to prove that his dismissal was due to the employer's union-related motive. For real protection, therefore, a clause should be added to the article providing that the employer shall have the burden of proving that termination was not based on a union-related cause.

890. Notwithstanding the controversial interpretations, Article 25 seemed problematic with its poorly written content, and if the pessimistic view prevailed, a considerable number of workers would be denied protection against dismissals for union-related reasons.[365] It also represents a serious regression in comparison to the protections provided by the previous system. In order to eradicate confusion, the sanction of 'union compensation' should be detached from its present connection to the so-called job security coverage.[366] In fact, in its 2014 report, the ILO Committee of Experts expressed its concern over Article 25(5) for the government's unclear reply to this issue which referred to the pending litigation in the Constitutional Court based on a request for the nullification of the said article along with around thirty other articles of Act No. 6356. In this connection, the ILO Committee of Experts requests the government to establish a system for collecting data on anti-union discrimination (in both private and public sectors) and to provide information on the concrete steps taken in this respect. On the other hand, experience has shown that the sanctions of the Penal Code of 2004, No. 5237, foreseeing a prison sentence of six months up to two years for violators of freedom of association have not proven sufficient in practice.

891. These remedies and safeguards notwithstanding, the ILO and labour unions have been quite critical of Turkey for the insufficiency of protections against anti-union activities of employers. With the passage of job security legislation, however, these complaints seem to have attenuated since the year 2002. At the time of writing, there were no court decisions yet on the application of Article 25, but the Constitutional Court had just rendered its verdict on the request for nullity of Article 25 as well as on three additional issues (among some thirty articles claimed to be unconstitutional by the plaintiff).

892. In fact, as a positive development, in response to the lawsuit filed by the RPP (the major opposition party) with a request for the nullification of various articles of Act No. 6356, the Constitutional Court, in its decision on 22 October 2014, found the phrase 'except for the case of termination' in Article 25(4) as well as the reference to 'Article 18' in Article 25(5) unconstitutional – which together denied workers who fall outside job security coverage protection against union-related dismissals (i.e., compensation not to be less than the aggrieved worker's total annual wages). Thus the Court declared that the said references were null and

365. Murat Özveri, Sendikal Haklar:6356 Sayılı Sendikalar, *Toplu İş Sözleşmesi Yasası*, 83–94, İstanbul Birleşik Metal Publishing, 2012.
366. T. Dereli, '6356 Sayılı Sendikalar ve Toplu İş Sözleşmesi Kanunu: Süreçler, Sorunlar ve Öneriler', *Çimento İşveren*, Vol. 28, No. 1, Ocak 2014, pp. 17–19.

invalid. In its decision, the Court heard the social partners' views in addition to considering the reasons raised by the plaintiff as well as the criticisms voiced by academic circles.

893. However, it should be noted that even before the Constitutional Court's decision of 22 October 2014, the Court of Cassation, by relying on the principle of 'equal treatment' as well as on the international norms of freedom of association, had already reversed a lower court's decision which denied the payment of 'union compensation' to a worker for his dismissal due to a union-related cause.[367]

894. On the other hand, in its decision dated 4 April 2007 concerning Tek Gıda İş Union (United Food Workers' Union), the European Court of Human Rights has concluded that the protections foreseen by Turkish legislation on the freedom of association are not effective enough. In this special case the employer was able to get rid of the union altogether by denying reinstatement to union members and paying them all their court-decided union compensations.[368] Proposals have been put forward, consequently to equip employees with stronger protection (similar to that of the union shop steward). In fact, in a project proposing to institute a dual-channel representation in Turkey, a similar protection was defended for members of the works council or employee representatives – which in such a case was apt to eliminate the privileged position of the shop steward over individual union members.[369]

895. To sum up, the guarantees provided by present legislation as well as to add the latest developments in Article 25 of Act No. 6356, the following remarks should be made: The worker's right to call on-court action for a union-related reason is guaranteed regardless of whether or not he is covered by the job security norms of Turkish labour law (i.e., Articles 20–21 of Act No. 4857.) We must note, however, that even here recourse to mediation by the worker first is compulsory before calling on the court for a lawsuit.[370] In the event of termination for a union-related reason, the worker is entitled to file a lawsuit in accordance with Articles 20 and 21 of Act No. 4857, construed as meaning 'after passing through the mediation process first'. Here the mandatory rule still prevails that 'where union compensation has been decided, request for job security compensation also should be denied'. Where the worker has requested the payment of union rather than job security compensation, no reference shall be made to the latter in the mediator's report of agreement, meaning that the report should mention only the amount of union compensation, and this amount must be paid to the worker even if he has not started work.

896. In addition to union compensation foreseen by Act No. 6356, the Penal Code of Turkey No. 5237 of 26 September 2004 brings penal sanctions which shall

367. *See* Court of Cassation 9th Div., 25 Mar. 2014, 13993/10049.
368. Muhittin Astarlı, AİHM, nin Sendika Hakkının Korunmasına Ilişkin Tek Gıda İş Sendikası Kararı ve Türk Hukuku Bakımından Çıkarımlar, Çalışma ve Toplum, 61, 2019, pp. 1237–1258.
369. T. Dereli, P. Soykut, A. Taşbaşı & E. Kaynak, *Institution-Building on Shop-Floor Employees' Representation with Reference to International Norms and Representative Industrial Democracy: A First Attempt to Model Dual-channel Representation in Turkey*, 5 (75) 2613–2637 (2022).
370. Ünal Narmanlıoğlu, 'İşe İade Davalarında Arabuluculuk,' Sicil, no. 38, 2017, p. 2148.

apply to those who, by using force or threats, obstruct the exercise of trade union rights, with the objective of compelling a person to join or not to join a union, to participate or not to participate in union activities or forcing him to leave a post in union administration, ranging from a prison term of six months up to two years. The sanction to apply in the case of obstructing a union's activities shall be a prison term of one year up to three years (Article 118). The prison sentences foreseen by the new Penal Code are distinct from and, in a sense in conflict with, the monetary compensations envisaged by the relevant articles of Act No. 6356.

B. *Labour Union Administrators and their Protection*

1. General Provisions Concerning Labour Union Administrators

897. As the Labour Unions Act sees it, the members of the administrative board of a union and confederation are considered to be union administrators (Article 2(1)).

898. This means that members of the auditing board and discipline board or any other board which the union may set up in order to meet its specific needs are not regarded as administrators for purposes of the Act, although in practice they are also referred to as administrators. In order to assume office in the mandatory organs of a labour union or confederation, the candidates must meet the requirements concerning the founding members, as set forth in Article 6 Upon application by the governor or the ministry after deciding that the elected member does not bear the said qualifications, the court shall terminate his membership in the relevant organ. The court's decision is final (Article 9(3)).

899. There is a legal requirement that the founders and administrators of organizations and their branches must make declarations about the assets belonging to them, their spouses and children under their guardianship in accordance with the Act on Declaration of Assets, dated 19 Aril 1990, No. 3628 and the adjoining regulations (Articled 29(4)).

900. The documents issued by the notary public stating that these declarations have been received shall be submitted to the auditors of the confederation, union, or union branch. Irrespective of whether they are re-elected or not, these persons are bound to deposit another declaration of assets on the expiry of their term of office. Any person who fails to fulfil this obligation shall automatically cease to be the officer one month after the date on which the declaration should be made. If the officials do not meet this obligation, the administration of the organization is to be entrusted to one or three trustees appointed by the labour court until new elections are held to determine new administrators.[371]

371. For more on labour union officials and related matters in the past, *see* the 2011 edition of this monograph paras 511–514).

2. Protection of Labour Union Administrators

901. According to Article 29 of the now-repealed Act, No. 2821, if an employee who would leave the employment of his own free will after being elected as a member or chairman of the managing board of a labour union, union branch or confederation wished to be reinstated in his previous employment upon ceasing to hold office because of his failure to be re-elected, or his reluctance to run for office or his resignation from office. In this case, the employer was obliged to reinstate him within one month from the date on which he requested reinstatement, under the existing working conditions, in his previous post or a post adapted to his previous one, giving him priority over all other candidates. Such a person would retain all his seniority rights as regards wages and the lay-off procedure. The employee concerned was entitled to exercise this right on condition that he had made an application at any time during the three months following the date on which he had ceased to hold office in the labour union.

902. The Court of Cassation ruled, however, that the employer was not obliged to reinstate the applicant if his previous job or a job similar to his previous job did not exist at the workplace'.[372] Besides, the sanctions pertaining to what was referred to as the 'compulsion to conclude a labour contract' were not clear. According to a ruling of the Court of Cassation, the employee concerned could not apply to the court and request his reinstatement if the employer had refused his application for reinstatement. According to the court', if the employee's application was refused he should be entitled only to the benefits which should be payable in case of the termination of his contract (notice pay, severance pay, etc.). Under such circumstances, the employer was held liable only to pay a fine. as mandatory reinstatement was possible only for shop stewards under the previous law.[373]

903. However, there were opposing views on this issue in Turkish legal doctrine.[374]

904. Decisions by the High Court entitling the union official to severance pay in case his request for reinstatement was denied led to controversy in legal teaching. Since the union official had quit his former employment of his own free will, he should not have access to severance payment in view of Article 14 of the Labour Act. In a case related to a similar issue, the High Court ruled that the union official whose function in the union was continuing should not be entitled to severance payment.[375] With a view to bringing clarity to the mandatory reinstatement issue, the draft bills prepared in the recent past have foreseen that the employment contracts

372. Court of Cassation, 9th Div., 22 Sep. 1981, 7270/10691; 10 Oct. 1995, 20805/30830; 24 Nov. 1998, 13637/16333.

373. Court of Cassation, 9th Div., 10 Feb. 1986, 1343/1346. Further, the High Court did not uphold the validity of collectively bargained provisions which mandated the reinstatement of union officials, seeing this practice as an infringement on the employer's management rights (Court of Cassation, 9th Div., 10 May 2000, 2888/6824).

374. Ekonomi, *supra*, p. 109.

375. Court of Cassation, 9th Div., 17 Jun. 2004, 3330/15141.

of union officials leaving employment upon being elected to union managing boards would be deemed suspended during their terms in union posts.

905. A union official could maintain his insurance rights in his former place of employment by continuing to pay his social insurance contributions to the relevant social security organization together with the employer's contributions.

906. It is clear that, by providing some employment security for union officials, the aim of the legislature was to encourage employees to run for union leadership positions in a professional capacity. Yet another motive was the idea of strengthening union democracy by providing the professional leader with some degree of job security in case he was not re-elected, thus weakening his resistance to the democratic process. However, past experience has shown that very few professional leaders, if any, have welcomed the idea of returning to their previous jobs if not re-elected. In some cases, their previous workplaces did not exist any longer by the time their leadership had expired. On the other hand, while professional union leaders had been granted some degree of security and shop stewards an even greater degree of security culminating in reinstatement, the non-professional union officials – those who had not quit their jobs after being elected to union posts – were not accorded any protection, except of course the compensation provided for union members envisaged in Article 31 of Act No. 2821. In order to provide non-professional union officials with full job security, some unions appointed them also as shop stewards, but the Court of Cassation, addressing this issue, ruled that this practice was unlawful, stating that two different functions could not be undertaken by the same person'.[376]

907. The new Act No. 6356 now seems to have brought remedies to fill in the existing voids on this matter. The first remedy is to treat the employee's leaving his job for a professional union administration post as resulting in the 'suspension' rather than the termination of his employment contract. Article 23(1) provides that 'the employment contract of the employee who leaves his job upon becoming the administrator (member of the administrative board) of a labour organization shall be suspended. If he so wishes, he may terminate his employment contract, without any need to observe the notice term of the open-ended contract or the expiration date of the fixed-term contract, on the date of his leaving employment and become entitled to receive severance pay. If the administrator terminates his contract within the duration of his duty as administrator, his severance pay shall be computed on the basis of comparable wages. Thus, in so far as other rights are concerned, this new clause has envisaged safeguards for various alternatives. As the employment contract is deemed to be legally in existence, there is no longer any concern as to how reengagement in work will materialize.

908. In view of Article 23(2), 'the union administrator whose employment contract with the employer has thus been suspended may make an application to the employer within one month upon ceasing to hold office because of the union's loss

376. Court of Cassation, 9th Div., 26 Sep. 1994, 7903/12632.

of corporate status, or his reluctance to rerun for office, or his failure to be re-elected, or he himself resigns from office.' In these cases, within one month of such application, the employer must engage him in work under prevailing conditions in his previous job or in a job adapted to his previous job; otherwise the employment contract shall be deemed to have been terminated by the employer. Thus, by considering problems faced in the past, the new Act has articulated alternative safeguards for professional union leaders' job-related rights. As a further positive point, the new Act has deleted the clause found in the previous legislation which stated that persons convicted of any offence committed in the course of their duties as union administrator should lose the right to reinstatement. Further, Article 23(3) also foresees the payment of severance pay to other union administrators whose duty in the union expires for any reason other than those mentioned. Here perhaps termination of the employment contract by the union administrator while it is in suspension may lead to some legal controversy. Further, given the numerical threshold foreseen by the job security clauses of the Labour Act No. 4857 (i.e., the '30 or more workers' criterion for coverage)), whether or not he can file a lawsuit for reinstatement if he is not given employment may be viewed as another dubious point.

C. *Union Shop Stewards and Their Protection*

1. Appointment of Shop Stewards

909. Article 27 of Act No. 6356 carries provisions on the appointment of union shop stewards (union's workplace representatives, as the Act names them) in terms parallel to the now-repealed Act 2821.

910. The 'employee representatives' who used to be elected from among the employees of the establishment under the now-repealed Labour Act of 1936 had already been replaced by union shop stewards by the Unions Act of 1963 No. 274 and Act No. 2821 had further revised shop stewards' appointment and functions in greater detail. Since the 1963 legislation union shop stewards were the only category granted full job security against dismissals including reinstatement. According to Article 27(1) of Act No. 6356, a labour union whose bargaining authorization in an establishment has been certified shall appoint shop stewards from among its members in the establishment in the following manner, and communicate their identities to the employer within fifteen days: (a) one shop steward, if the number of employees in the establishment does not exceed 50; (b) not more than two, if the number of employees is between 51 and 100; (c) not more than three, if the number of employees is between 101 and 500; (d) not more than four, if the number of employees is between 501 and 1,000; (e) not more than six, if the number of employees is between 1,001 and 2,000; and (f) not more than eight, if the number of employees exceeds 2,000.

911. One of the shop stewards may be designated as the chief shop steward. The tenure of the shop steward shall continue as long as the union carries the certified authorization status for collective bargaining. If the union constitution provides for the designation of union shop stewards by election, the elected members shall be appointed as shop stewards (Article 27(2)).

912. In the event of an 'enterprise collective agreement' it is held that the union which has concluded such an agreement is entitled to appoint shop stewards for each establishment covered by the enterprise-level collective agreement.

913. The conditions required of founding members set out in Article 6 also apply to shop stewards.

2. Functions of Shop Stewards

914. Article 27(3) of the Unions Act delineates the functions of shop stewards in the following manner: Their duties being limited to the establishment, union shop stewards and the chief shop steward shall be in charge of taking notice of employees' requests and handling grievances, promoting and sustaining cooperation and harmony at work and maintaining peaceful relations between employers and employees, protecting the rights and interests of employees and assisting and supervising the application of working conditions set out in labour legislation and the collective agreement. Shop stewards shall perform their functions without hindering their work and work discipline. Establishments shall provide shop stewards with adequate facilities to enable them to fulfil their duties quickly and efficiently (Article 27(4)).

915. Shop stewards have been accorded certain functions by the individual labour law and related regulations. Article 29 of the Labour Act No. 4857 requires consultations with shop stewards in the event of collective dismissals, and the regulation on Annual Leave with Pay has put shop stewards in charge of certain duties in the election of employee representatives to vacation committees. In establishments where there are no shop stewards, employee representatives to sit on vacation committees shall be elected directly by the employees (Article 15). They have also been imputed with several functions by the occupational health and safety legislation.

916. Shop stewards' functions may also be regulated by collective agreements. Most collective agreements contain provisions which equip shop stewards with certain tasks in the initial steps of the grievance procedure, on discipline committees and in the handling of meals and work clothing which are administered as part of the fringe benefit programme. Despite the stipulation of Article 27 that shop stewards must carry out their activities on condition that their own work and work discipline is not hindered, it is generally professed that collective agreements may enable them to fulfil their functions and/or be granted time-off with pay during working hours, as was also the case under most collective agreements before 1980. Unless the collective agreement carries such provisions or the employer gives his consent, however, shop stewards cannot perform their duties within working hours, nor may they be granted time-off with pay.[377]

3. Tenure of Shop Stewards

917. In its earlier version, Article 35 of Act No. 2821 provided that the functions of shop stewards would terminate with the expiration of the collective agreement. Although Act No. 274 which was in effect before 1980 was silent on the issue, the Court of Cassation had also reached a similar conclusion.[378] Once the authorized union concluded the collective agreement it could appoint shop stewards in establishments covered by the agreement. Such appointment would be valid until the expiration date of the collective agreement at most, depending on the provisions of the union's constitution or, if no such provisions existed, according to the discretion of the competent organ of the union. In other words, shop stewards' tenure could be terminated and new stewards could be appointed by the union concerned even before the expiration of the collective agreement. However, the steward's term would automatically end upon the expiration of the agreement.[379] This meant that there would be virtually no union representation at the establishment level once the collective agreement expired. Considering the fact that the normative provisions of an expired agreement were to remain in force until the making of a new collective agreement, there would still be a functional need for shop stewards in protecting the rights and interests of workers and handling their grievances even after the expiration of a collective agreement. Besides, these workers were deprived of job security during a period when they probably needed such security most. Amendment to Article 34 by Act No. 3449 in 1988 provided that the shop stewards' tenure would continue so long as the union possessed bargaining status. Yet this did not resolve the issue altogether.

918. In an attempt to cope with such practical problems and meet the demands of unions that criticized the above-stated practice, Article 9 of Act No. 4101, dated 4 April 1995, amending Article 35, provided that the tenure of shop stewards, who would be appointed by the union upon its obtaining the authorization certificate, would continue as long as the union maintained its certified status. Yet, still further problems may arise in practice. In accordance with Article 7(3) of Act No. 2822 on Collective Agreements, Strikes and Lock-outs, 'the process for bargaining authorization for a fresh collective agreement could be initiated within 120 days before the expiration of the existing collective agreement, provided that the new collective agreement should not enter into force before the expiry of the previous agreement'. In such a case, two unions – one being the newly authorized union, the other the union signatory to the existing agreement – could be in a position to appoint shop stewards. To do away with overlapping functions, it was held that the tenure of shop

377. The Court of Cassation had reached the same conclusion before 1980 when there was no such legal provision on the issue. *See* Court of Cassation, 9th Div., 10 Nov. 1969, 6613/10599.
378. Court of Cassation, 9th Div., 19 Jun. 1979, 8825/9593; 5 May 1981, 5462/6537.
379. Court of Cassation, 9th Div., 24 Nov. 1983, 8061/9656; 25 Feb. 1991, 1990/11603, 1991/2759.

stewards appointed by the signatory union should remain effective until the expiry of the collective agreement. In the event no further authorization was granted to any union, a deadline could be set beyond which the term of the shop stewards should be terminated automatically. These interpretations are likely to prevail under the new system introduced by Act No. 6356.

919. Act No. 2821 was silent on the effects of fluctuations in the number of employees at the establishment on the number of shop stewards to be appointed. In a specific case the Court of Cassation ruled that the employer should not forfeit the shop steward's status unilaterally simply by depending on the reduction in the number of employees since the union signatory to the collective agreement in force had the sole power to appoint shop stewards.[380] The signatory union can, however, reduce the number of shop stewards upon receiving the employer's request based on a reduction in the workforce.[381] In the event of an increase in the workforce, it is held that the signatory union should not increase the number of shop stewards until the finalization of its next collective bargaining certification by the Ministry of Labour and Social Security.

4. Protection of Union Shop Stewards

920. According to the original version of Article 30 of the Unions Act, No. 2821, the employer could not terminate the contract of shop stewards working in his establishment unless he indicated clearly and precisely a just cause for termination. The shop steward or his union might lodge an appeal with the competent labour court within one month of the date the notice of termination was communicated to him. The court should apply fast-hearing procedures and conclude the case within two months. The decision of the court was to be final. The termination had to be annulled if the court ruled that the shop steward was to be reinstated in his job. In this case the employer should pay the shop steward's full wages and all other benefits to which he was entitled, taking effect from the date on which his employment was terminated, even if he had been given no work during his period of office as shop steward. Thus, 'shop stewards' were the only category that had been granted full job security under Turkish Law.

921. As the Court of Cassation had ruled in the pre-1980 period, in order for the shop steward to be reinstated in his job by the labour court, the cause of dismissal did not have to stem solely from his engagement in union activities; that is, he should be reinstated if the termination of his contract was proven to fall into any category of 'unfair dismissal'.[382] However, in the opinion of the High Court, the

380. Court of Cassation, 9th Div., 4 May 1992, 17583/4966; 29 May 1997, 8277/10507.
381. A.R. Okur, *İş Hukuku Dergisi*, April–June 1992, pp. 266–270.
382. The court also stresses in this verdict that the employment contract of the discharged shop steward shall be deemed to be valid even though he may not be actually reengaged in work. *See* Court of Cassation, 9th Div., 20 Dec. 1978, 12263/16174.

mere fact of having been appointed a shop steward should not preclude the termination of his employment contract for the operational requirements of the establishment.[383]

922. The law was mute, though, as to what would happen in those cases where the shop steward was forced by the employer to terminate the labour contract for just cause (according to Article 16 of the Labour Act No. 1475, now Article 24 of Act No. 4857). The Court of Cassation ruled that, if the shop steward had terminated his contract due to the changing of his workplace by the employer without his consent, there should be no reinstatement even though the shop steward might request it. This meant that reinstatement was possible only in those cases where the employment contract was terminated by the employer'.[384] Nevertheless, the Court of Cassation had regarded the employer's action as an abusive practice already in 1997 and 1999 and ruled on the reinstatement of the shop steward. Similar rulings were passed in 2003 and 2004.[385]

923. Some collective agreements provided shop stewards and other non-professional union officials (that is, those union leaders still working for an employer under an employment contract) with additional protection above these legal minimums, such as the ability to resort to voluntary arbitration for reinstatement and/or to demand extra indemnities, but the legal validity of such negotiated arrangements remained unclear. The Court of Cassation did not favour the adjudication of individual disputes by private arbitration.[386]

924. As the new Labour Act No. 4857 which incorporated job security provisions of Act No. 4773 brought protection against dismissals for employees working in establishments with 30 or more employees with a minimum seniority of six months, Article 30 of Act No. 2821 was amended to read as follows:

> the relevant provisions of the Labour Act shall apply to the termination by the employer of the open-ended employment (indefinite-term) contract of the shop steward (meaning Articles 18–21 of Act No. 4857). In the event the shop steward's contract is terminated solely because of his activities as shop steward, the compensation to be paid to him by the employer foreseen in Article 21(1) should not be less than his total annual wages.

925. Here it should be noted that, under the amended system of Act No. 2821, union shop stewards were no longer granted full job security which encompassed

383. Court of Cassation, 9th Div., 21 Oct. 2004, 6558/23719.
384. Court of Cassation, 9th Div., 9 Jul. 1979, 8153/10403; 25 Feb. 1993, 3396/2966.
385. Court of Cassation, 9th Div., 10 Apr. 1997, 1645/7252; 13 Jan. 1999, 19710/57; 20 Nov. 2003, 19327/19592; 26 Feb. 2004, 13385/3403. The shop steward who does not resume work within the legal time limit shall not be entitled to the said compensation (Court of Cassation, 9th Div., 26 Feb. 2004, 13385/3403). The mere fact of being a union steward does not preclude the termination due to operational requirements (Court of Cassation, 9th Div., 21 Oct. 2004, 6558/23719).
386. As the courts were the empowered organs to deal with union-related disputes, the shop steward's right to apply for judicial review was reserved in any case.

almost absolute reinstatement under the previous systems. Further, the protection to be accorded to shop stewards who fell outside the scope of provisions on job security was not clear.

926. Moreover, as a result of the subsection added to Article 21, the burden of proving that the termination was caused for his union-related activities would rest on the shop steward. There was some ongoing controversy, therefore, concerning the job security of union shop stewards which had thus been somewhat weakened in comparison to the previous system.

927. In an attempt to do away with these shortcomings, Act No. 6356 reverted the shop steward's job security to its earlier version which existed before Acts 4773 and 4857. The new approach of the Act on Unions and the Collective Agreement stands out as the strongest and most positive dimensions of the new Act insofar as the protection of union freedoms is concerned. Article 24(1) of Act No. 6356 now provides:

> No employer may terminate the employment contract of the shop steward unless he indicates clearly and precisely a just cause for termination. The shop steward or his union may lodge an appeal with the competent labour court within one month of the date the notice of termination is communicated to him. If appealed, the regional Court of Appeals (istinaf) shall give its final and binding verdict.

928. Termination shall be annulled if the court rules that the shop steward must be reinstated, provided that he makes an application to resume work within six working days; in this case the employer must pay the shop steward's full wages and all other entitlements accrued even if he had been given no work during his period of office as shop steward, taking effect from the date on which his employment was terminated. This provision shall apply in the case of a fresh appointment.

929. In fact, this means actual reinstatement even if the shop steward is given no work. Further, taking account of past practices and court rulings, an additional phrase was added to Article 24 in order to head off covert and abusive employer actions against shop stewards. It says: 'unless he obtains shop steward's written consent, the employer must not change the establishment where he is working, nor may he make essential alterations in his work. Otherwise the change of the establishment or changes in his work shall be deemed null and void' (Article 24(4)). While the system has always had safeguards for full-time union administrators who were no longer attached to the employer, union administrators who kept working for the employer under an employment contract, i.e., the so-called amateur union leaders, had no protection other than the general clauses on protection of freedom of association for workers. The new Act now fills this void by granting non-professional union officials the full job security of the shop steward by providing that 'the protections warranted by Article 24 for shop stewards shall be applicable also for non-professional union administrators who keep working in the establishment' (Article 24(5)).

930. It is safe to argue that Article 24 is likely to bring an end to the ongoing controversy surrounding the job security of the shop steward. By using the concept of 'just cause' rather than 'valid reason' as well as by avoiding the reference to Articles 18–21, the amendment aims to equip shop stewards, regardless of job security coverage of the Labour Act, with the right to reinstatement, as was the case under the previous systems. Further, the amendment provides non-professional union officials with the same job security as that foreseen for shop stewards. Needless to say, however, that much will depend here on the interpretations of the labour judges along lines intended by the new legislation.

II. Protection of Collective Union Freedoms

931. As mentioned above, the right to organize has been guaranteed not only for individuals, but also for unions themselves. In line with the constitutional provision which grants unions the right to form and join multi-union, upper-level organizations, Article 20 of the Labour Unions Act (No. 6356) regulates affiliation of unions to confederations and Article 21 to international bodies. Moreover, Article 26(6) has emphasized the autonomy of labour and employer's unions. Employees and employers must not join organizations of one another. Likewise, such organizations are prohibited from intervening directly or by means of representatives or members or through any other intermediary in the constitution or activities of one another. Employee and employer organizations must not exercise any influence on each other. It is also unlawful to carry on any activity for the purpose of bringing about a state of affairs where a labour union would be financially supported by an employer or employers' organization. The autonomy and activities of the union must also be protected *vis-à-vis* the government, its own members – within the limits set by the requirements of union democracy – third persons and rival unions, especially in the case of inter-union rivalry when authorization disputes concerning the acquisition of bargaining agent status leads to exacerbated strife, accusations and unrest from within the union movement itself. A union which has lost its 'majority status' as a result of unfounded intrusion and meddling by a rival union may request the nullification of the latter's bargaining status and demand indemnities thereto according to Article 49 of the Obligations Act.

932. The freedom of unions to engage in organizing activities and other trade union work through their members at the shop level is also related to the concept of 'collective union freedoms' and yet it is a disputed matter in Turkish industrial relations practice. The only provision on the issue is found in Article 25(3) which states that 'no employee shall be dismissed on account of his participation in the activities of labour unions or confederations outside his hours of work or during hours of work with the employer's permission'. The constitutional provision according to which union work at the workplace would not justify 'not working' (the repealed Article 52/II of the Constitution) indirectly recognized such activities by union members at the shop level, although the said provision was related basically to the functions of shop stewards. It is held that the employer must not interfere with such activities merely by relying on his ownership rights since Article 35 of the Constitution has envisaged the restriction of ownership rights for public good. Such union work may be carried out only during work breaks, without hindering work discipline and productivity, and with due respect to equality amongst the various unions in a milieu where the principle of multiple (rival) unionism prevails.

Chapter 2. Labour Unions and Employers' Unions

§1. Organization and Structure of Labour and Employers' Unions

I. Historical Background: The Principle of 'Industrial Unionism'

933. The Turkish legislature has almost from the beginning adopted the principle of 'unionization by industry branches' or 'industry sectors' – by 'branches of economic activity' as the law has termed it – rather than by 'craft' or 'occupation'. However, neither the 1947 nor the 1963 Trade Unions Act had explicitly prohibited the formation of craft and occupational unions. In fact, a few craft or semi-craft type unions had emerged after 1947, especially in those establishments which consisted mainly of employees belonging to the same craft or occupation, but with the strengthened position of the national-industrial unions and federations after 1960, these craft type unions withered away. The only exception to the absence of craft unionism was the structure of some of the public servant unions which were formed between 1965 and 1970 in accordance with the now-repealed Public Servants Unions Act No. 624. Thus, what was characteristic of almost all the union structures in the developing nations today, as opposed to the unions in early industrialized countries, had materialized in Turkey as well; that is, due to the relative absence of sufficient numbers of skilled workers in the labour force at the inception of Turkey's industrialization, craft unionism did not have much chance to itself on the Turkish labour scene.

934. Furthermore, the Unions Act of 1983 (No. 2821) explicitly prohibited the formation of labour unions on an occupational or craft basis (Article 3(1)). Thus, probably due to the legislature's dominant motive to create a neat and simple union structure, the Act seemed to have brought a ban on the formation of craft unions which in fact had never existed in Turkey.

935. Unlike the previous system under which branches of activity were determined by a regulation of the Ministry of Labour, Act No. 2821 had enumerated 28 industries according to which unions were to be structured. In view of Article 60 of Act No. 2821, these branches of activity were as follows: (1) agriculture, forestry, hunting and fishing; (2) mining; (3) petroleum, chemicals and rubber; (4) food (tobacco, beverages and related industries included); (5) sugar; (6) textile; (7) leather; (8) woodworking; (9) paper; (10) press, publishing and broadcasting; (11) banking and insurance; (12) cement, ceramics and glass; (13) metal-working; (14) shipbuilding; (15) construction; (16) energy; (17) commerce, clerical works, education and fine arts; (18) inland transportation; (19) rail transportation; (20) sea transportation; (21) air transportation; (22) warehouse and storage; (23) communication; (24) health; (25) accommodation and entertainment; (26) national defence; (27) journalism; (28) general services.

936. Article 60 also stated that the allied and related work of a major activity in an establishment would be covered by the major branch of activity. Thus, waiters and cooks employed in the cafeteria of a textile mill, for instance, must join a union active in the branch of activity No. 6 (textiles), while waiters and cooks working in a regular restaurant are to join a union in the branch of activity No. 25 (accommodation and entertainment). Compared to the previous method of determining the industries by regulations of the Ministry of Labour, incorporating them into the Unions Act seemed to be a better solution, since empowering the Ministry to implement unforeseen changes had resulted in complications and alleged cases of politically abusive practices in the past. Several suits aimed at repealing these changes were brought before the Council of State (the highest court in charge of public law cases), and as a result labour and employers' unions were plagued with instabilities and unanticipated harassment resulting from changes in the classification of industries ruled by the Council of State. Now that the branches had been prescribed by the law itself, such instabilities seemed to have ended. However, one could argue that this new approach had made the divisions quite rigid. The need to revise and reorganize the types and number of industries when technological developments and market relocations necessitated change was apparent. Thus, revising the classification of industries by government-issued bylaws (*tüzük*) rather than incorporating them into the law would prove to be a more flexible method. Compared to the Ministry of Labour regulations, bylaws would probably eliminate unforeseen differences of opinion since the latter was automatically subject to the judicial review of the Council of State.

937. While under the previous system there were 34 industries, Act No. 2821 reduced that number to 28. Obviously one of the effective means of creating a clear-cut union structure which seems to have been one of the legislature's major aims is to reduce the number of industries by legal definition.[387] Yet the new industrial divisions, despite the amendments brought by Act No. 2882 dated 28 August 1983, were still the subject of criticism. Examples of unnecessary and irrational divisions were food and sugar, road, rail, sea and air transportation sectors, banking, insurance and clerical-commercial-educational sectors which should in fact be merged for the sake of a neater structure.

938. In an effort to create still a neater and more rational union structure, draft bills aiming to amend Act No. 2821 proposed to reduce the number of 'branches of activity' to 18 from the existing of figure 28. However, these proposed texts did not envisage a strict banding of all the branches. The above-mentioned branches (food and sugar, air, railroad, sea and land transportation, etc.) which are closely related were to be merged, a process which might lead to opposition from existing unions and a great deal of political lobbying and manoeuvring, as evidenced by the various complaints filed with the ILO Committee of Experts in 2005 and afterwards.

387. When Türk-İş attempted to centralize the union structure in the early 1960s, it had devised a reorganization plan based on 16 industries patterned after the West German model. However, this plan never materialized for various reasons. A reorganization scheme involving 32 industries was later adopted by Türk-İş. Likewise, DİSK had adopted an organizational structure based on 16 industries. For these *see* T. Dereli, 'Türk Sendikacılığında Merkezileşme Temayülleri ve Muhtemel Neticeleri', *Sosyal Siyaset Konferansları*, Vol. 17, İstanbul, 1966, pp. 45–92; *see also* the Constitution of DİSK, Art. 66.

939. As envisaged in Article 60, the subgroups of all the work and operations under each branch of activity were to be defined in a bylaw, taking account of international standards and the views of labour and employers' confederations. This bylaw was issued by the Council of Ministers in 1983.[388] Also, according to Article 60, the Ministry of Labour shall publish statistics in January and July of each year, showing the number of employees working in each branch of activity, the number of organized and unorganized workers and the breakdown of organized workers by their unions. Article 62 stipulated that each employer should t notify the Ministry of Labour and the regional directorate of labour within fifteen days of any hiring of employees or termination of employees for any reason. These provisions were aimed at facilitating the determination of unions' bargaining status as well as settling 'authorization disputes' upon request by interested parties.

940. Article 4 of Act No. 2821 dealt with the settlement of disputes concerning the clarification as to which industry a certain establishment should belong. It said that, in the event of a dispute, the branch of activity covering the establishment should be determined by the Ministry of Labour and Social Security, with the decision of the Ministry being published in the Official Gazette. 'The parties concerned may lodge an appeal against the Ministry's decision with the labour court within fifteen days of its publication; the court shall give a ruling on the appeal within two months. Where this ruling is appealed, a final ruling shall be given by the Court of Cassation within two months.' Evidently, this procedure was to be initiated only in those cases where the party concerned raised an objection pertaining to the industry claimed to cover an establishment or enterprise. In view of the Court of Cassation, the objecting party in an authorization dispute must be granted some additional time for application to the Ministry of Labour and for the ensuing court litigation if an authorization dispute[389] involved beforehand the determination of the branch into which the establishment in question fell.[390]

941. It should be noted that the interested party could make an application to the Ministry irrespective of the stage at which the collective bargaining was proceeding. A change of employer would not alter the results of the process of determining the pertinent branch of activity into which the establishment would fall.[391] Further, in any determination to this effect, the main activity performed in the establishment ought to be taken into consideration rather than the tasks or activities auxiliary to the main activity. As the bylaws on the branches of activity provided, tasks and operations which were auxiliary to the main activity should be regarded as an integral part of the main branch of activity.

---

388. *See* the Official Gazette, 16 Jun. 1983, No. 18079, as amended by Act No. 2882, Official Gazette, 6 Dec. 1983, No. 18243.
389. *See* the 'Decisions to Call a Strike and Lock-Out and Implementation' heading.
390. Court of Cassation, 9th Div., 31 Jul. 1985, 8207/7590. The '15 days' period' is a statutory limitation (11 Mar. 1987, 2597/2807). The determination for the subcontractor's establishment must be made independent of the establishment of the principal employer (10 Jul. 2007, 24627/23105).
391. Court of Cassation, 9th Div., 15 Oct. 1996, 18580/19561.

II. The Structure of Labour Unions and Employers' Unions under Acts Nos. 2821 and 6356

A. The Notion

942. Article 51(2) of the 1982 Constitution has ensured the rights of employees and employers to form 'unions' and 'upper-level union' organizations. Since no reference was made to the types of 'upper union structures', the legislature, like in the previous system, was free to regulate the types and number of such structures as it might deem appropriate. In line with this reasoning, Act No. 2821 envisaged the formation of 'confederations' as the only 'upper-level (multi) union' structure, thus removing federations, local unions confined to a certain geographical locality, and regional union councils (*birlik*) which were horizontal structures with political functions that dominated the Turkish labour scene at varying degrees before 1980. In the pre-1980 era federations could be formed through the affiliation of at least two local unions active in the same branch of activity or in related branches of activity. Like industry-based national unions, a federation was accorded legal competence to bargain at the industry-level if it represented the majority of employees in the industry in which it was constituted. Local level bargaining could be implemented only by the affiliated or autonomous local unions. An industry-based national union, on the other hand, had legal competence to bargain both at the industry level and at local levels informally through its branches – which were deprived of a separate corporate status of their own.

943. Thus, as far as the competence to make collective agreements at different levels was concerned, national unions seemed to have been granted a greater degree of flexibility.[392] Perhaps the most salient criterion distinguishing industry-based, national unions from federations was the degree of autonomy accorded to local levels. Whereas local unions affiliated to federations retained their autonomy to a considerable extent, branches of national unions were deprived of corporate status and did not have much say in their own affairs. In 'national' unions almost all power was vested in the head office and union constitutions usually compelled branch offices to transfer all the dues collected locally to the headquarters of the national union. Federations, on the other hand, did not have much authority over their affiliates, nor did the autonomous local affiliates give enough financial support to the federations with which they were affiliated. The 'national' union seemed to be a stronger organization financially, but federations, with their loose structure, had proved to be more democratic in their relations with autonomous local affiliates.

944. Perhaps due to a number of reasons – i.e., the abolition of industry-wide bargaining, the relatively weakened position of federations, the legislature's motive to reduce the number of unions in the country – the Act of 1983, No. 2821, wiped out the federations from the Turkish labour scene altogether, thus retaining only two

392. T. Dereli, '6356 Sayılı Sendikalar ve Toplu İş Sözleşmesi Kanunu: Süreçler, Sorunlar ve Öneriler', *Çimento İşveren*, Vol. 28, No. 1, Ocak 2014, pp. 17–19.

structures, namely 'unions' – which were to be patterned after the 'national industrial union' model of the pre-1980 period, and 'confederations'. Simply by dropping the definition of regional union councils – *birlik* – from the Trade Unions Act, the 1970 amendment (Act No. 1317) had already removed them from the union structure in Turkey.

945. The national industrial union model which was thus adopted rendered the formation of federations unwarranted in any case since the definition and structuring of the union was foreseen as being an entity whose activities would be widespread throughout Turkey at the branch of activity concerned.

B. Labour Unions

946. The legal definition of labour union was given in Article 3/I of Act No. 2821 in the following manner: 'Labour unions shall be constituted on an industrial basis by workers employed in establishments in the same branch of activity with the purpose of their activity being widespread throughout Turkey'. Embodied in this definition is the creation of industrial unions active nationwide, buttressed also by the rule that 'labour unions shall not be constituted on an occupational (craft) or establishment basis (Article 3/III)'. As these provisions imply, the main motive of the 1983 legislation was the creation of a clear-cut 'industrial union' structure, with broad-based, large and 'stronger' units in order to do away with the so-called union inflation which had beset the Turkish industrial relations system in the pre-1980 era. Furthermore, the system did not foresee the formation of labour unions in related branches of activity, which was possible under the previous system.

947. The prohibition placed on forming establishment-based (company) unions, coupled with the provision that unions must be active on an industrial basis nationwide, indirectly precluded the creation of local unions in Turkey. These new structural stipulations have caused resentment and criticism from certain union circles and the ILO on the grounds of their allegedly violating union freedoms, i.e., employees' right to form and join unions of their own choosing freely. The legislature's aim, however, was to eliminate 'company unionism' altogether. A union confined to one establishment only, or even to various establishments in the same branch of activity owned by an employer (company, enterprise), could not be independent and strong enough to defend member interests; it was bound to be weak subject to employer's meddling and pressures, its life being circumscribed by the life of the establishment or company. In fact, these views were used by the government representative's comments in ILO platforms in reply to the criticisms of the Committee of Experts.

948. The stipulation that the 'union's activities must be industry-wide throughout Turkey' was somewhat confusing. It is generally held that unions covering only certain segments of an industry on a local or regional basis may no longer be established. But a newly constituted union is apt to be small, limited to a few workplaces at least during its formative stages, since seven founding employees can give birth to a union legally. Apparently, no force can be applied on a labour union to compel it to be active industry-wide throughout Turkey.

949. Implicit in the wording of Article 3(1) of Act No. 2821 was the idea that the labour union should expand its scope by establishing branches (which under Turkish legal system do not possess separate legal corporate status) so as to cover a considerable portion of the industry. It was also held that it must organize all the specified subgroups within the industry. A union established in the branch of activity 'banking and insurance' for example, should organize not only banking institutions but also insurance establishments. A union branch could nonetheless cover a certain subgroup within the industry in question. Coupled with the avowed goal of reducing the number of unions for the sake of 'stronger unionism', several indirect provisions serving the same goal (i.e., to gain bargaining status, a union should first represent at least 10% of the workers in the respective industry branch as well as more than 50% of the employees in the establishment) have actually led to a neater union structure in Turkey after 1983. Naturally the emerging unions were apt to represent varying degrees of strength and scope in practice. Following 1983, federations and unions reshaped themselves so as to adapt to the new structure, as was envisaged in Transitional Article I of the Act No. 2821. With the effect of these and related provisions, the number of labour unions which totalled around 900 before 1980 dropped to about 100 after 1984. And approximately half of them seemed to have met the minimum 10% representation requirement.

950. Unions could establish local branches on condition that this was specified in their constitutions and pursuant to the decision of the general congress. The union's administrative board might also establish local branches if it was authorized by the general congress to do so.

C. Employers' Unions

951. The structure of employers' unions was also to be designed along lines parallel to labour unions. 'They should be constituted on an industrial basis by employers in the same branch of activity with the purpose of their activity being widespread throughout Turkey'. An exception to this rule was brought in for employers' unions in the public sector. 'For public sector employers' unions, the condition that they must be constituted by public employers in the same branch of activity is not required'. Accordingly, three major public sector employers' unions were set up each covering a multitude of SEEs and public corporations operating in different industries (namely, *Kamu-Sen*, *Kamu-*İş and *Tühis*). This heterogeneous structure has led to a great deal of controversy, mainly because the principle of organization along vertical industrial lines was violated and the distinction between unions and confederations had become somewhat blurred.[393] The underlying reasons mentioned in the reasons' statement of the law in order to justify this new heterogeneous structure as well as opposite views encountered in the literature are as follows.

393. Çelik, *supra*, pp. 465–466.

952. The government cannot find a sufficient number of employers who can act as founding members in each branch of activity in order to organize employers' unions. This was not a defensible cause, for Act No. 2821 at least until the 1995 amendment which had expanded the definition and, thus the number of employers' representatives.

953. Another motive was to create consistency in wages and other employment conditions among the various industries in the public sector.[394] This argument could also be refuted as irrelevant since the government could implement its wages policies even when public sector employers' unions had been organized strictly along homogenous lines. Besides, staff experts in such public employers' unions cannot develop the necessary collective bargaining expertise required to grasp the broad spectrum of various industries together. Although these negotiators handle many of the bargaining issues at initial stages, the last word on wages and wage-related problems was usually uttered by the minister concerned or the Prime Minister himself.[395] Furthermore, SEEs could still join private sector employers' unions and actually there are such affiliations, so there was no need for public and private employers to organize separately.

954. And finally, merging several related industries (i.e., food and sugar) so as to form a single branch of activity could have served the same goal as well as help create a neater labour union structure.

D. Confederations

955. Confederations of labour and employers' unions were defined as top level organizations with corporate status formed by the affiliation of at least five unions operating in different branches of activity (Article 2(7)). Though Act No. 2821 abolished federations' which were a certain type of industry-based national organization, the term 'confederation' was retained to denote top-level union organizations like Türk-Is, DİSK, Hak-Is and TİSK (Employers' Unions Confederation of Turkey).

E. Changes Brought by the New Act No. 6356 in the Relevant Definitions Relating to the Structure of Unions

956. Articles 3, 4 and 5 of the new Act No. 6356 provide the following:

> Organizations (labour unions and employers' unions) shall be established without prior authorization in conformity with the pertinent principles and procedures set out in this Act. Provided that conformity with the relevant principles

394. F. Şahlanan, *Sendikalar Hukuku*, İstanbul, 1995, p. 58.
395. For these criticism, *see* M. Kutal, Türkiye'de Endüstri İlişkilerinin Yasal Çerçevesi, *Türk Denizciler Sendikası Yayını*, No. 6, İstanbul, 1986, pp. 23–24.

and procedures envisaged by this Act prevails, organizations may be established freely. Unions shall carry out their activities in the industry branch in which they are established (Article 3/1). The condition that the employers' union must be established by employers active in the same industry branch shall not be a requirement for public sector employers' unions (Article 3/2.)

'Industry branches are shown in the tabulated list annexed to this Act' (Article 4/1). Works auxiliary to the main activity carried out in an establishment are deemed to fall into the main industry branch wherein the main activity is performed (Article 4/2). Determination of the industry branch to which an establishment belongs shall be made by the Ministry, to be published in the Official Gazette. Within fifteen days of the decision's publication, the interested parties may file suit against the said determination. The court shall decide in two months. If appealed, the Court of Cassation shall render its definitive verdict in two months (Article 5/1). If the process of bargaining authorization for a new collective agreement has already begun, the decision entailing a change in the relevant industry branch shall apply to the next collective agreement term. Requests concerning the determination of the relevant industry branch and legal actions filed thereto shall not qualify as protracting reasons for collective bargaining authorization procedures and for related legal actions (Article 5/2). Change of the industry branch shall not have any effect on the existing collective agreement effective in the establishment (Article 5/3).

The above-cited articles and their subsections thus delineate the pertinent forms and procedures concerning structure Except for a few differences, procedures pertaining to the determination of the establishment's corresponding industry branch and appeal mechanism are similar to the previous system.

957. Although the new Act has deleted the notion envisaged by the previous Act No. 2821 that the union should be industry-based, with its activities widespread throughout Turkey, by providing in Article 3 that unions should carry out their activities in the industry branch where they are established, it has indirectly emphasized the basis of union organization still to be industry based. Unlike the previous legislation, the new Act has deleted the bans which were imposed on the formation of occupational/craft and company unions, a point which, albeit of secondary importance, was occasionally criticized by labour union circles as well as by the ILO, but the requirement that unions shall carry out their activities in the relevant industry branch precludes the formation of craft and company unions anyhow. Further, deletion of the phrase 'to be active nationwide' shall lead to the likelihood of the formation of area-based, local and regional unions, thus perhaps leading to an unanticipated increase in the number of labour unions, an option which the legislature was reluctant to accept in the past.

958. Act No. 6356 has foreseen the reduction of the relevant industry branches from 28 to 20, a process which will involve mergers between the existing industry branches and consequently between various unions active in these branches. In view of the tabulated list annexed to Act No. 6356, the industry branches, determined by considering international norms and after receiving the opinion of labour and employers' organizations, are as follows: (1) hunting, fishing, agriculture and forestry; (2) food; (3) mining and quarries; (4) petroleum, chemicals, rubber, plastics and pharmaceuticals; (5) textiles, confectionery and leather; (6) wood and paper; (7) communications; (8) press, publishing and journalism; (9) banking, finance and insurance; (10) commerce, clerical works, training and fine arts; (11) cement, ceramics and glass; (12) metals; (13) construction; (14) energy; (15) transportation; (16) shipbuilding, sea transportation, storage and warehousing; (17) health and social services; (18) hotel and entertainment; (19) defence and security; (20) general services. It is held that as before, in order to qualify as a competent industrial union organization, the union must aim to be active in the sub branches of the industry branch (e.g., in industry branch (4), in petroleum, chemicals, rubber, plastics and pharmaceuticals).

959. According to the Transitional Article 1 of Act No. 6356, 'within one month from the publication of the regulation referred to in the third subsection of Article 4, unions by way of administrative board decisions shall designate the industry branch in which they will be active'.

§2. Founding of Labour and Employers' Unions and the Acquisition of Corporate Status

I. The Notion

960. While labour unions may be founded by real persons only, employers' unions may be established by real as well as legal (corporate) persons. And self-evidently confederations may be founded only by unions acting jointly as qualifying organizations with a corporate status. Of course, even in the case of legal entities with a corporate status, the actual founders shall always be real persons acting on behalf of the corporate body.

II. Basic Requirements for Founders

961. In view of Article 6(1) of Act No. 6356, real and legal (corporate) persons that possess 'action competence' and who are currently active have the right to found unions. Only a real person currently working under an employment contract (or a few other contract types mentioned, i.e., independent professional work in transportation, agency, publishing, commission or ordinary partnership contract) is entitled to found a labour union. Irrespective of the time limitations specified in Article 53 of the Penal Code No. 5237 of 2004, persons convicted for acts of embezzlement, bribery, theft, fraud, breach of trust, fraudulent bankruptcy, collusive conduct in public tenders and in the performance of obligations, fraudulent acquittal from unjustified enrichment resulting from criminal conduct and smuggling may not qualify to become founders. Article 6 has thus somewhat relaxed the offences which were cited in Act No. 2821 among the obstacles to becoming a founder. The procedures for founding and formation of union organs and their powers have also been simplified.

962. The conditions 'to be a Turkish citizen, to be currently active in the industry branch concerned, to be literate (able to read and write) in Turkish' which were stipulated by the previous legislation have been deleted from the text of the present legislation partly to be consistent with European Union and ILO standards.

963. It must be recalled that the same conditions stipulated in Article 6 also apply to those seeking or holding office in unions' and confederations' administrative and auditing boards.

964. No age requirement has been stipulated for founding members. It was held, however, that the founders should have completed the age of 18 – which was the lawful age according to the former Associations Act. But as the new Associations Act No. 5253 does not make any reference to age, having completed the legal age will no longer be considered as a requirement for the founders of unions. As the Unions Act does not contain any numerical requirement, the general rule set forth by the Association Act (Article 1 and now in clear terms by Article 2/1(g) of the new Act No. 6356) applies to labour and employers' unions as well, according to which at least seven persons must come together in order to found an association. In cases where any founding member of an employers' union is a corporate body, the real person representing it must meet all the above conditions, with the exception of active employment within the branch of activity.

965. Of course for an employers' union, the founders must in the first place qualify as employers' or 'employer's representatives' within the meanings foreseen by the Labour Act No. 4857 of 2003. On other related issues, the Act is silent on 'confederations', except for the definition that the confederation has been defined as 'the organization with corporate status formed by the affiliation of more than five unions active in different industry branches' (Article 2/1 f), but since it is held that the founders of confederations must submit all the documents normally required from the founders of unions to the governor of the province until the first general congress is held, it is to be understood that the confederations too should meet all the criteria envisaged in Article 6.

966. Unions and confederations may be established without prior permission and authorization (Article 51/I of the Constitution, Article 7,8 of Act No. 6356) The founders must draw up the constitution of the union, in written form, and must submit it, along with other required documents mentioned in Article 7, to the Governor of the Province where the registered office of the organization is to be located. In the event of founding a confederation, copies of the decisions taken by the general congress of the respective unions to constitute a confederation must also be added. If any of these persons are not elected officers of the founding unions, they are obliged to submit all the other documents required from the founding members of a union. The union or the confederation shall acquire legal corporate status as soon as the constitution and other required documents have been deposited with the governor. The governor shall immediately forward copies of these documents to the Ministries of Labour and Social Security.

967. For organizations, written statements by the founders attesting to the fact that they possess the required conditions, and for upper-level organizations, general congress motions of relevant organizations shall be attached to the application petition (Article 7(1)). As these provisions indicate, the formation of labour and employers' unions is free and no prior permission of the public authorities is needed, nor is there any requirement for registration as a precondition for gaining corporate status. The organization acquires corporate status upon the delivery of the said documents. Within fifteen days the governor must send the constitution and the list of founders to the Ministry. The Ministry shall announce the name, centre and the constitution of the organization through the official internet site in fifteen days (Article 7(2)). The regional directorate of labour keeps a record of unions and a copy of the record is forwarded to the Ministry of Labour.

968. In the event the constitution or the information contained in the documents are found to be contrary to law or where it is understood that the conditions for founding the organization set out in Act No. 6356 have not been met, the governor shall request the corrections of contraventions or the filling of existing voids within one month. If the said corrections or completions are not provided for within one month, the court, upon the application of the Ministry or the governor concerned and after hearing the testimony of the founders, if deemed necessary, may, with a view to dispel contraventions or fill in the voids, may decide to suspend the operations of the organization within three working days. The court shall grant a time allowance not exceeding sixty days for the correction of contraventions or completion of voids(Article 7(3)).

969. 'When the organization's constitution and related documents are brought into conformity with the law, the court shall lift the suspension order. Where the said conformity has still not been realized upon the expiry of the time allowance granted, the court shall decide to close down the organization' (Article 7(4)). Changes in the organization's constitution shall be announced in accordance with Article 7(2). Announcement shall be applicable to changes in the constitution and other transactions in cases concerning contraventions or voids in procedures (Article 7(5)).

970. According to Article 8, the following must be indicated in the constitution of the union and confederation: (1) the name, headquarters and address of the union or confederation; (2) the objective; (3) the industry branch in which the union will be active; (4) the full names, trade and occupations and the places of residence of the founders, their industry branches, names and addresses of the unions forming the upper-level organization; (5) the conditions and procedures for the acquisition of membership and withdrawal and expulsion from membership of the union or confederation; (6) the formation of the general congress, holding of meetings, functions and powers of the general congress, voting by members and delegates, working methods and principles; quorums for meeting and decision-making; (7)

governing organs other than the general congress; their formation, functions, powers and responsibilities; working methods and principles in holding the meetings, quorums for meeting and decision-making; (8) the formation of union branches, procedures for their mergers or dissolution; representation of union branches and regional branches in the general congress of the union; (9) procedures and principles concerning the fixing of membership dues and salaries of union administrators; (10) procedures and principles concerning the sale of assets; (11) procedures of internal auditing; (12) provisions for the amendment of the union's constitution; (13) liquidation of the assets in the event of dissolving the organization; (14) the full names and addresses and places of residence of the members of the provisional administrative board authorized to represent and administer the organization until the governing organs of the organization are duly formed.

971. Thus, Act No. 6356, like the previous Act No. 2821 has, in a rather detailed manner, enumerated the items which union constitutions must carry. The detailed delineation of these items in legislation has been the subject of criticism by the ILO for allegedly violating the freedom of employees to draw up the constitutions of their organizations freely as they wish. The government has responded to this criticism by arguing that, these points should be regarded simply as guidelines aimed to achieve uniformity in union constitutions rather than as mandatory items concerning content.

§3. Membership

I. The Categories and Basic Principles

972. According to Article 17(1) of Act No. 6356, persons who have completed the age of fifteen and defined ad employees according to this Act may join labour unions. Thus, consistent with the age coverage of the Labour Act, the age limit which was 16 under Act No. 2821 has been lowered to 15. Persons who are considered to be employees within the meaning of Article 2(4) may join labour unions, meaning in addition to those working under an employment contract real persons who perform work for wages as an independent professional activity in accordance with transportation, job, agency, publishing, commission or ordinary partnership contract, are to be regarded as 'employees' in terms of the second and sixth sections of Act No. 6356, construed as meaning that these latter categories' unions shall not be granted competence to conclude collective agreements.[396]

973. Any employer within the meaning of the Labour Unions Act may join employers' unions (Article 17(2)). According to Article 2(3) of Act No. 6356 in reference to the definitions of the Labour Act No. 4857, 'any person or corporation or non-corporate public establishment employing workers is considered to be an employer'. The law has thus enlarged the scope of the concept of 'employer' by

396. For further details found in the definitions given by Act No. 2821 on these categories, *see* the 2011 version of this monograph, p. 281.

including also public organizations which may not have corporate status. Consequently, the increase in the number of employers in the public sector thus facilitated the formation of public-sector employers' unions.

974. In the same manner 'employer's representative', who is defined as any person authorized to manage an entire enterprise in the name of the person or corporation or non-corporate public bodies that are treated as employer, may join employers' union. Thus, the president or general manager of a company may join the employers' union along with the corporate body itself. As explained above, owing to the narrow scope of the definition of employer's representative in the collective labour law of Turkey, all managerial and non-managerial personnel who are deemed to be employers' representatives in view of the Labour Act No. 4857 are treated as 'employees' within the meaning of Act No. 6356 and may therefore join labour unions, a phenomenon which has led to the outgrowth of the practical distinction made between 'covered' versus 'non-covered workers' within the collective bargaining system of Turkey since the 1960s', an ironic situation allegedly contravening freedom of association and the principle of 'equal treatment'.

975. Self-evidently, the above-stated categories may join labour or 'employers' unions provided that they are active in the industry (branch of activity) in which the union has been established. Initially, membership was circumscribed by the constraints set forth in the 1982 Constitution. While guaranteeing union freedoms and voluntarism, Article 51 of the Constitution stipulated that employees and employers should not join more than one union at a time. The Labour Unions Act of 1983, No. 2821, had stressed the same principle with the clarification that membership to more than one union 'in the same branch of activity' was prohibited. In the case of membership to more than one union, the latter would be void. Certainly, the rule envisaged by the Labour Unions Act is more realistic since workers and employers alike may be actively engaged in more than one industry (branch of activity) at the same time. Despite this specific provision, however, the Court of Cassation had ruled that a worker should not join more than union even though he/she might be working in jobs falling into different industries. The High Court had thus given precedence and a strict interpretation to the constitutional phrase.[397] However, the amendment in Article 51 of the Constitution by Act No. 4709 solved this problem by including the phrase 'in the same branch of activity'. Thus, freedom of association of employees who worked, for example, part-time in different branches were also guaranteed under the Constitution. More recently, the said constraint was repealed by the Constitutional amendment of 7 May 2010, Act No. 5982, approved also by a national referendum held on 12 September 2010, But the restriction in Act No. 2821 remained pending new legislation for conformity with the Constitutional amendment. Presently Act No. 6356 has paved the way for the employee's simultaneous memberships to more than one union in the same branch of activity.

976. Employees working in an allied (auxiliary)branch of the establishment may join only the labour union constituted in the branch of activity covering the main

397. Court of Cassation, 9th Div., 10 Jul. 1985, 7738/7474.

establishment (Article 17(4)). For example, employees in the printing press of, say, a bank can join only a union in the banking and insurance branch. This is a direct consequence of the principle of industrial unionism.

II. Acquisition of Membership

977. An important novelty on this subject is the removal of public notary approval which was required by the previous legislation (Act No. 2821) for the worker's acquisition of as well as withdrawal from union membership, a condition that was harshly criticized for many years by international labour circles, namely the ILO and the EU, for its alleged intrusion into freedom of association by making union membership more difficult and costly for the employee.[398] Now the public notary channel has been replaced by an electronic system to be set up in the Ministry of Labour. In view of Article 17(5), 'membership of a labour union shall be acquired by the worker's application to the e-State portal and upon the approval of his membership by the union's competent organ)administrative board) again over the e-State portal.' Unless refused within thirty days, the request for membership shall be deemed to have been approved; the employee whose application is refused without a just cause may take legal action within thirty days; in this case, the court's ruling shall be final and binding as of the date of the union's decision to reject the application for membership. Similarly, 'withdrawal' (resignation) of the employee from his membership shall be by communicating his resignation through the e-State portal. Resignation notice over the e-State portal shall be forwarded to the Ministry and the union simultaneously.' As in the previous system, 'resignation shall become effective one month after notification is made to the union' (Article 19(2 and 3)). Provisions concerning the expulsion of the employee from union membership by the decision of the union's general congress have also been predicated on similar procedures to be made through the e-State portal. 'The expulsion decision of the general congress shall be communicated to the Ministry electronically over the e-state portal and the employee shall be notified accordingly in written form. The expelled member may contest the expulsion decision before the court within thirty days of the notification of expulsion. The court shall render its final verdict within two months. Membership shall subsist until the finalization of the expulsion decision' (Article 19(4)).

978. In its report for the year 2014, the ILO Committee of Experts expressed its concern that procedures over the e-State portal could impact adversely the right to organize of workers for whom this means is not accessible as well as create difficulties for workers in the informal economy. Besides, the information on union membership, which is by definition accessible to all the parties concerned, could pose a serious risk of exposure of labour union members, or workers wishing to become union members, to reprisals and anti-union discrimination, contrary to ILO

398. For information on the reasons which accounted for the introduction of 'public notary approval' requirement in joining the union as well resigning from the union, *see* pp. 294–296 of the 2011 version of this monograph.

Conventions on freedom association. Therefore, leaving the acquisition as well as loss (withdrawal) of membership merely to forms to be signed by workers themselves is advisable; or necessary measures must be taken to ensure that the information on the e-State portal does not become public.

III. Rights and Obligations of Members

A. *Rights*

979. Membership rights, arising from the legal relationship between the union and the member, are based either on law or on the union constitution. According to the Unions Act and generally to the rules governing 'associations' and 'persons' in Turkish law, members' rights can be grouped into three categories.[399]

1. The Right to Participate in the Management and Activities of the Union

980. The right to vote seems to be the most important one in this category (Civil Code, Articles 73 and 69). Every member is entitled to participate in union meetings, especially in the general congress, and to cast his/her vote on the issues under consideration, and this right cannot be obstructed by any member (Trade Unions Act, Article 13(3)). As having all of a union's members participate in meetings may pose difficulties in the bigger organizations, members may exercise their right to participate through their delegates who are elected in accordance with the rules laid down by the law (Unions Act, Article 10(1)) and in the union constitution. On each issue, the member is entitled to just one vote. The rules of union constitutions concerning the election and responsibilities of delegates must be consistent with democratic principles, as envisaged in Article 51 of the Turkish Constitution.[400] The Court of Cassation has also ruled that any union rules subjecting the election of delegates to the will of the union's managing board are null and void.[401] Apart from its regular meetings, the general congress must convene upon the written request of one-fifth of the members (Civil Code, 75(1), Unions Act Article 12(4)). Members are also guaranteed the right to criticize, file complaints and resort to court litigation against the actions or decisions taken by the competent bodies of their unions (Civil Code, Article 83).

2. The Rights Aimed at Protecting the Freedom of Members in Unions

981. Among the rights in this category, one can cite the right of the members to be protected in the event of a change in the union's objectives (Civil Code, Article

399. Çelik, *supra*, p. 476.
400. For more on union democracy in Turkey, *see* Bengü Dereli, *Türkiye'de Sendika Demokrasisi*, İstanbul, 1977.
401. General Council of the Court of Cassation, 18 Jun. 1969, 9-486/632.

67), the right to withdraw (resign) from the union (Unions Act, Article 19(2)) and the right to equal treatment (Unions Act, Article 26(3)).

3. The Right to Benefit from the Services and Activities of the Union

982. This includes the right to benefit from establishments such as union-operated clubs, training programmes, libraries and seminar rooms, as well as the various union activities.

B. Obligations of Membership

1. The Obligation to Abide by the Rules and Regulations of the Organization

983. The member must respect the order established by the constitution and regulations of the union. He must refrain from engaging in actions or uttering statements which may impair the union's common objectives or its development. The member who does not respect the union rules and regulations may be punished by means of penalties envisaged in the union's constitution and union bylaws, normally by the union's discipline board cited among the mandatory organs of the union under the present system. The major sanctions found in most union constitutions range from serving a warning to expulsion from the union.[402]

2. The Obligation to Pay Union Dues

984. Of foremost importance among membership obligations is the duty to pay union dues in return for the right to benefit from the union's activities. A member must pay his union dues regularly, except perhaps if he is sick or has lost his job, cases which may justify non-payment of dues.

985. In view of Article 18/1 of Act No. 6356, the amount of dues to be paid by the members to trade unions and confederations that have not been suspended from activity shall be fixed by the organizations' constitutions. This means that the obligation to pay dues exists only as long as unions and organizations are active. The same principle also applies to the payment of solidarity dues, as set out in Article 39 of Act No. 6356.

986. In a manner similar to the provisions of Act No. 2821, the Unions and the Collective Agreement Act has foreseen the collection of dues through the check-off mechanism. Article 8 of the new Act provides the following:

402. Fevzi Demir, *Sendikalar Hukuku*, İstanbul, 1989, p. 144.

> (1)The amount of membership due shall be determined according to the procedures and principles set out by the constitution of the organization. (2) Upon the written application of the union authorized for collective bargaining to the employer the membership and solidarity dues shall be deducted from the employee's wage and then paid to the union concerned. (3) The employer who does not deduct and pay the above-stated dues or does not remit the deducted dues to the relevant union within one month shall be liable without any need for notification to pay the said dues plus the highest interest rate charged by banks to business transactions. Procedures and principles pertaining to the collection of dues shall be described in a regulation to be published by the Ministry.

987. The obligation of the employer to deduct dues from the employees' wages shall take effect with the union's request from the employer and delivery of the workers' names to him.

988. The application of automatic check-off rights to more than one union in the pre-1983 system was, in fact, one of the causes enabling smaller and weaker unions to survive, thus contributing to the exacerbation of the so-called union inflation problem. By granting this right only to the union certified for collective bargaining (i.e., the authorized union), the rule brought by Act No. 2821 and now reiterated by Act No. 6356, coupled with the effects of other provisions, seems to have played some role in reducing the number of unions after 1983.

IV. Termination of Membership

A. Cessation of Membership

989. Membership ceases to be valid with the loss of membership qualifications mentioned above. In fact, membership ceases to exist when a member loses his 'employee' status.

990. Likewise, any person who loses his status as employer or employer's representative automatically loses membership to and any function he has in an employer's union or confederation, to be effective on the date of losing such status. But, membership of any corporate body in an employer's union continues even where the representative of that body in the union has lost his status as representative. The function of such a representative in the organs of the union or confederation automatically terminates with the loss of that status (Article 19(5)). For example, the general director of a corporation may be the president of the managing board of an employers' union. The membership of the corporation in that employers' union does not expire if that person leaves the corporation, but his job as president of the union's managing board terminates automatically. In this case, the new person who will act on behalf of the corporate body shall be designated. The same rule shall also apply in cases where that person moves to another corporation in the same branch of activity since he was elected to the post of the president in relation to his representing the former corporation.[403]

991. The law has also considered those cases where the membership status would continue or should be suspended. Employees who become members of managing boards, boards of auditors or discipline boards of a labour union retain their membership in the union of which they were members when they assumed such functions. Also, persons entitled to join unions who are members, in the capacity of employers, or employers' or employees' representatives, of the board of management or any similar organ of any establishment or organization by virtue of the law also retain their union membership (Article 19(5)).

992. With the abolition in 1984 of the workers' participation scheme in the management boards of the SEEs, established back in 1964 by Act No. 440, the latter provision seems to be no longer functional in so far as employees are concerned.

993. Likewise, with the unemployment of the employee, his membership in the union is not affected provided that his unemployment does not last longer than one year (Article 19/9).

994. Furthermore, membership relationship of the person drafted for any military duty shall be suspended for the duration of such duty.

995. Membership expires with the death of the person or his being declared legally missing (Civil Code, Article 28(1)); or in the case of corporate entities, with the dissolution or abolition of the organization. Whether or not the loss of a person's legal discretion results in the termination of membership is a contentious point in legal theory. Some have advocated the view that, although membership status does not end, the member may not exercise his membership rights as long as his loss of discretion continues.[404] Membership should terminate if the loss of the person's discretion is of a permanent nature.

996. The worker who leaves employment to receive old-age, retirement or disability benefits or lump-sum payments from social security organization or pension funds established by law or accepts employment in another industry branch, loses his membership and any function in the organs of the union, its branches or the confederation. However, this clause shall not apply to those who continue to work as well as to those who receive old-age, disability or lump-sum payment during their tenure in the administrative, auditing and discipline boards of organizations and branches (Article 19/(6,7)).

997. Also, assignment of the union member to work in the organs of a labour organization or in the union branch shall not terminate union membership (Article 19(8)).

403. Ö. Eyrenci, *Sendikalar Hukuku*, İstanbul, 1984, p. 122.
404. T. Esener, *İş Hukuku*, Ankara, 1978, pp. 352–353.

B. Withdrawal from the Union

998. Article 51 of the 1982 Constitution of Turkey provides that workers and employers are free to resign from the unions of which they were members. It also states that no person shall be forced to maintain or relinquish his membership in a union; Article 19(1 and 2) of Act No. 6356 reiterates these principles.

999. Major dimensions of the employee's resignation from union membership have been covered by Article 19 (1–4) of Act No. 6356. As provided by these subsections:

> (1) The employee and the employer may not be forced to remain in or withdraw from union membership. (2) Every member may withdraw from membership by communicating his resignation through the e-State portal. Resignation notification over the e-State portal shall be forwarded to the Ministry and the union simultaneously. (3) Withdrawal from membership shall become valid one month after notification is made to the union. In the event of the employee's joining another union within the one-month period, the new membership shall become effective upon the expiration of the one-month period.

1000. The said one-month waiting period entails the member's entitlement to all the membership rights as well as his obligation to keep paying the union dues within that one-month waiting period.[405] The said employee shall also be counted in the threshold foreseen for the union's acquisition of majority status.[406] The amendment made to Article 25 of Act No. 2821 by Act No. 3449 in 1988, providing that in the event of the resignee's joining another union the latter membership should commence upon the expiry of the said period, was aimed to solve the various legal problems which had arisen in the past. In fact, the Court of Cassation had ruled in this direction even before the 1988 amendment.[407]

1001. It is generally held that the rationale for requiring the lapse of such a waiting period is to alleviate the problems which may arise from abrupt changes in union's membership as well as from delays in notifications, to provide sufficient time for the implementation of the required procedures and to bring some stability to membership shifts among unions. It has been claimed, however, that the previous three-month waiting period foreseen by Act No. 2821 before the said amendment was too long to justify its purpose and thus hindered the member's freedom of withdrawing from the union. Therefore a period of one month would be sufficient for

405. As a matter of fact, by laying down this principle, the legislature's intention was to forestall the emergence of the various legal and practical problems which had arisen under the previous system.
406. Court of Cassation, 9th Div., 22 Jan. 1998, 149/407.
407. Ruling of the Court of Cassation, 9th Div., 26 Dec. 1984, 12250/12045; 20 Aug. 1985, 9065/7614; Ruling of the General Council of the Court of Cassation, 20 Dec. 1987, 1986/9-404, 1987/112.

providing the Ministry of Labour with the needed time in documenting and verifying the unions' membership figures.[408] Act No. 4101 changed the waiting period to one-month, in line with such views and Act No. 6356 has maintained the same limit.

C. Expulsion of a Member from the Union

1002. According to Article 19(4) of Act No. 6356, the decision n to expel a member from a union or confederation is to be taken by the general congress. Though not stated in the Act, the expulsion motion must be consistent with the law and the constitution of the union. The decision of expulsion must be communicated to the Ministry electronically over the e-State portal and the employee shall be notified accordingly in written form. Within thirty days following the notification of the decision, the member concerned may contest the expulsion sanction before the court. The court must take a final decision within two months. Membership shall subsist until the decision of expulsion is finalized.

§4. AFFILIATION OF THE UNION TO A CONFEDERATION AND INTERNATIONAL ORGANIZATION

I. Affiliation to National and International Upper-Level Organizations

1003. Concerning the membership of unions to national upper-level organizations (confederations), Article 20 of Act No. 6356 provides the following: (1) application for membership to an upper organization shall be based on the decision of the general congress. Affiliation to upper level organization shall be acquired upon the acceptance of the competent organ designated in the constitution of the upper organization. Membership to more than one upper organization at a time is not permitted. Otherwise latter memberships shall be null and void. (2) Withdrawal of membership from upper organization shall be pursuant to the decision of the general congress. Withdrawal shall be valid one month after notification is made to the upper organization. (3) Expulsion from upper organization shall be pursuant to the decision of the upper organization's general congress.

1004. One should note here that the restriction on the affiliation to more than one upper level organization is likely to run counter to the principles of freedom of association which may entail various problems in practice. In fact, labour unions in Turkey have joined such organizations, as there is no obstacle to affiliation with more than one upper level organization at the international level. Act No. 6356 has relaxed the additional restrictions of Act No. 2821 concerning affiliation to international labour and employers' organizations. As a matter of fact, Article 21(1) provides that, 'with a view to helping achieve their objectives as set forth in their

408. For a different view, *see* H.K. Elbir, *İş Hukuku*, Istanbul, 1987, p. 149.

constitutions, the organizations may become founders of labour and employer organizations; they are free to join or withdraw from such organizations as well as to enter into collaborations with and send representatives to them'. In view of Article 21(2), 'by receiving the opinion of the Ministry of Foreign Affairs and the permission of the Ministry of Interior, international labour and employer organizations may set up representative offices and affiliate with upper organizations in Turkey'. And Article 21(3) provides the sanction to apply for violations: 'In the event of contravention of the above subsections, the Ministry of Interior, with a view to annul the affiliation or suspend or close down the representative office, may file suit at the place where the centre of the organization or representative office is located.'

1005. The labour and employers' organizations active in the Turkish Republic of Northern Cyprus are entitled to become members of the confederations founded in Turkey (Article 21(4)). In line with this article, Türk-Sen of Cyprus has become a member of Türk-İş, Confederation of Labour Unions of Turkey.

§5. Participation or Merger of Organizations

1006. A union or confederation (or several unions and confederations) may merge with other unions or confederations; likewise, unions and confederations may amalgamate among themselves. It should be noted that mergers and amalgamations differ from the affiliation of unions to confederations. Whereas in affiliation the organizations concerned retain their independent corporate entity, the merging or amalgamating organizations lose their previous status. As Article 22(1) states, 'when an organization participates in another organization of the same nature, 'all the rights, obligations, powers and interests of the participating organization shall automatically pass on to the organization participated in.

1007. Article 22(2) deals with mergers (amalgamations): 'all the rights, obligations, powers and interests of merging organizations shall automatically pass on to the new corporate body formed as a result of the merger.' Concerning the status of organization's members, Article 22(3) provides that 'members of the participating or merging organizations shall automatically become members of the organization participated in or formed as a result of the merger.

1008. According to a decision of the Court of Cassation, for mergers and amalgamations a decision to that effect must have been taken by the general congress of each organization concerned.[409] Also, it is clear that the merging and participating unions must be active in the same branch of activity (industry). The provisions of Article 20 concerning the procedures and formalities required for affiliation to confederations shall also apply to mergers and participations.

409. Court of Cassation, 9th Div., 1 Jun. 1989, 2737/5098.

§6. Internal Structure of Labour and Employers' Unions

I. Organs: In General

1009. The Unions and the Collective Agreement Act No. 6356 explicitly specifies the mandatory organs of labour and employers' unions (Article 9(1)). There are four mandatory organs which unions must have, as opposed to the three which associations have to establish according to the Civil Code. These are the general congress (general assembly), the administrative board, the auditing board and the discipline board. The Act allows confederations and unions to set up other organs to meet their needs. These are referred to as voluntary organs. However, the powers, functions and responsibilities of the mandatory organs may not be delegated or transferred to these subordinate (voluntary) organs (Article 19(2)).

1010. The provisions of Article 6 concerning the founding members apply also to candidates wishing to assume office in the mandatory organs of a labour union and its branches as well as the confederations. Upon application by the Governor or the Ministry after deciding that he does not possess the said qualifications, the court shall terminate his membership in the relevant organ. The court's decision is final (Article 19(3)).

1011. In view of Article 2(1) No. 6356 only members of the administrative board are treated as union administrators.

1012. In conjunction with general principles of law, labour and employer organizations are to be held liable as a result of the legal transactions of their organs The organs themselves as well as the persons forming the organs are also liable personally for their faulty conduct (Civil Code Article 50).

1013. Act No. 2821 had imposed ceilings on the number of terms for re-election of union administrators. But as subsequent legislation had strengthened union democracy by providing detailed rules and regulations on union elections which rendered these restrictions unnecessary, the so-called ceilings on the maximum number of terms of re-election was deleted from legislation by the 1995 amendment, Act No. 4101.

1014. 'The full names of members elected to organs of organizations and branches other than the general congress, as well as the branches set up and closed, shall be communicated to the Governor and announced in accordance with Article 7(2); 'if those elected to organs other than the general congress are convicted of any offences cited in Article 6, their functions in the relevant organs shall automatically expire (Article 9(5)).

1015. Article 19(6) includes an important restriction which in the past as well as at present has been on the agenda of ILO criticisms. It provides: 'The functions of administrative board and discipline board members of the organization and branches shall automatically expire is they are elected as Parliament members or mayors.'

1016. As one of the common provisions on organs, Article 19(7) provides: 'Unless a higher quorum has been foreseen in the organization's constitution, the quorum for the holding of meetings in the organs other than the general congress is the absolute majority of members and the quorum for decision-making is the absolute majority of those participating in the meeting.'

II. General Congress (General Assembly)

A. The Formation of the General Congress and Elections

1017. As in associations and other corporate bodies, the general congress is the highest decision-making and auditing (control) organ of unions. In line with the rule enshrined in the Constitution (Article 51) which emphasized that the administration and operation of unions should not be contrary to democratic principles, Act No. 6356 brought additional regulations in order to ensure the efficient functioning of democracy in unions.

1018. Article 10 of the Act on the formation of the general congress is as follows: (1) The general congress of the organization shall be composed of members or delegates in view of their constitutions. Members of the administrative, auditing and discipline boards of organizations and branches shall participate in their capacities as such in the general congress meetings. (2) The status of delegates shall continue until the date of the next delegate elections to be held for convening the forthcoming ordinary meeting of the general congress' Act No. 2821 had foreseen numerical limits on the number of members beyond which election of delegates would be mandatory; but Act No. 6356 has removed such limits by leaving the matter merely to the constitutions of organizations. As provided by Article 10(3), 'the principles and procedures concerning the election of delegates shall be designated in the constitution of the organization. However, no provisions obstructing the members' election as delegates may be included in an organization's constitution.' However, the removal of the said numerical limits cited in Act No. 2821 and leaving the matter solely to organizations' constitutions may cause problems in practice, emanating mainly from alleged infringements on union democracy, as the Turkish system has a deep-rooted tradition of relying on legislation rather than voluntarist arrangements. Nevertheless it is held that an employee not working in the branch of activity where the union is active may not be elected to the mandatory organs of the union.[410]

1019. Act No. 2821 of 1983 had subjected union elections to judicial scrutiny and supervision. Regarding union elections at the branch level, however, an amendment in 1988 had removed the supervision of the judiciary over the election procedure at the local branch level due to the reactions by unions for practical reasons, as it was virtually impossible to assign judges to thousands of local elections. However, since the basis of union democracy is rooted at the rank-and-file level, it is

410. Court of Cassation, 9th Div., 10 Apr. 2007, 11004/10227.

generally asserted that it is at the workplace (establishment) level where the election of delegates and branch leaders should be directly supervised by the judge. The said amendment was, therefore, criticized by those vying for more democracy and honesty in union elections.[411]

1020. Elections at the branch level were, then, to be conducted according to the union's constitution. It was possible; however, to initiate an indirect appeal procedure against the election of delegates at the branch level, in line with the general provision which states that all conflicts and disputes concerning the application of Act No. 2821 should be resolved in labour courts.[412]

1021. Act No. 6356 has now brought a direct and clear effect to this matter After providing in Article 16(11) that the election of delegates outside the general congress shall be free, based on equal and secret voting, open counts and classifications in accordance with the organization's constitution, Article 16(2) clearly paves the way for ensuring a fair objection process to elections at this level.[413] In view of subsection 2 of Article 16 now, 'objections to the election of delegates outside the general congress (meaning local elections at the establishment level) which must be made within two days after the announcement of election results shall be settled by a definitive verdict of the court. In the event of cancellation of delegate elections by the court, runoff election must be held in fifteen days.'

B. Meeting of the General Congress

1022. The first general congress of a union or confederation must meet within six months of the date on which it has acquired legal corporate status; the first general congress of the branch must convene within six months from the date on which it has been founded (Article 12(1)). The ordinary general congress must convene every four years at the latest (Article 12(2)). But, the constitution of the union or confederation may provide for more frequent meetings. In practice, almost all the unions and confederations hold their congresses every four years. The administrative board must convene the meetings of the general congress. If the said board does not convene the general congress, it may be removed from office by the judge upon the application of a union member to the labour court. In this case the court appoints one or three curators who must convene the general congress in the shortest time possible and handle the current affairs of the organization until the election of a new administrative board.

1023. The Act has also provided for the holding of the extraordinary congress. The extraordinary congress shall meet when deemed necessary by the administrative board or the board of auditors or at the written request of at least one-fifth of

411. Çelik, *supra*; Ö. Eyrenci, *Sendikalar Hukukunun Güncel Sorunları*, İstanbul, 1987.
412. Ruling of the Court of Cassation, 9th Div., 26 Oct. 1991, 12791/12470.
413. Ünal Narmanlıoğlu, 'Toplu İş İlişkileri Kanun Tasarısının Getirdikleri', *Sicil İş Hukuku Dergisi*, September, 139–155, 2012.

the members or delegates within sixty days with a view to discuss the priority issue stated in the written request (Article 12(4)). It is the administrative board again that must call the convening of the extraordinary congress Where the number of delegates requesting the convening of the extraordinary congress falls below the one-fifth ratio afterwards, the administrative board is not required to call the meeting.[414]

1024. In the event the request to convene the extraordinary congress has been turned down in violation of the law, the delegates have the right to file suit with the labour court, with a view to having the administrative board removed from office, thus requesting the general congress to convene at the nearest time possible and the appointment of one or three curators to handle the affairs of the union until the election of the new administrative board according to Article 12(6) of the Civil Code of 2001, No. 4721.

1025. The absolute majority of the total number of the members or the delegates is required to form a quorum at the general congress meeting. A larger quorum may be provided for in the constitution of the organization. If there is no quorum in the first meeting, the congress is to be postponed for not more than fifteen days. The quorum for this second meeting must not be less than one-third of the total number of members or delegates.

1026. Non-delegates and non-members may not be included in the quorum of the general congress and they do not have the right to vote. The participation of members or delegates in the general congress as well as their right to vote may not be restricted in any manner. In reaching decisions, the absolute majority votes of the members or delegates present at the general congress is required. However, this figure must not in any case be less than one-fourth of the total number of members or delegates On matters concerning changes in the organization's constitution, organization's dissolution, merger, participation or founding an upper organization or international organization, affiliating to or withdrawing from an upper or international organization, the decision quorum shall be the absolute majority of the total number of members or delegates unless a higher quorum has been foreseen by the organization's constitution (Article 13(1,2,3,4)).

1027. The Act has foreseen the supervision by the judiciary of the election of delegates or members to the mandatory organs of unions and confederations. Emphasizing that elections must be held on the basis of free, equal and secret ballot and open returns, it has foreseen detailed procedures on the conduct, date and time of elections in Article 14.

1028. Along with an attached statement involving the agenda, place, date and time of the meeting and details concerning the second meeting if the quorum is not achieved in the first meeting, lists of members or delegates who will participate in

414. Ruling of the General Council of the Court of Cassation, 12 Oct. 1988, 9-304/774.

the general congress will be given to the chairman of the competent election committee at least fifteen days before the general congress meeting where elections are to be held (Article 14(2)).

1029. Objections to the chairman of the election board to be made within the announcement period shall be examined and concluded by a definitive decision within two days at the latest. After receiving the judge's approval, the lists thus finalized shall be forwarded to the relevant organization or branch' (Article 14(4)). The judge who is the chairman of the local electoral board shall appoint an electoral polls committee in charge of elections and the classification of the votes.

1030. Claiming that the general congress meeting and elections were held in a manner contrary to law, to the constitution or that there were irregularities in violation of the law which may have an adverse impact on election results, the ministry as well as the organization's members and delegates may file suit for the cancellation of these transactions or the general congress within one month of the date of the general congress. The trial shall be finalized within two months. In case of an appeal, the Court of Cassation shall award its definitive verdict in fifteen days (Article 15(2)).

1031. In cases where the judge declares the elections null and void due to violation of Article 14 or for procedural deficiencies or unlawful practices having an adverse effect on the outcome of elections, he must arrange for new elections to be held in not less than two and not more than seven days and inform the organization concerned of the date of new elections. Fresh elections shall be held under Article 14 and other provisions of the law on the designated date scheduled only for the holding of elections.

1032. Further, as explained above, in an attempt to offset the absence of the judge at delegate elections at the local (establishment) level, Article 16(1,2) provides the following as an indirect objection measure: Election of delegates outside the general congress shall be free, based on equal, secret balloting, open counts and classification and shall be held in accordance with the organization's constitution. Objections which may be made to the election of delegates outside (other than) the general congress within two days after the announcement of election results shall be settled with a definitive verdict of the court. In the event of the cancellation of the elections of delegates by the court, runoff elections shall be held in fifteen days.'

C. Annulment of the General Congress

1033. Neither the Unions Act, nor the Associations Act had provided any clause for the annulment of the general congress. In practice, the right to request the annulment of the general congress as well as the resolutions of the general congress was predicated on Article 83 of the Civil Code. The union or association member might exercise this right within one month as from the date of the holding of the congress.[415]

1034. In the opinion of the High Court in a case in the year 2004, election of the chairman of the board of directors of a company as the president of the union was in violation of Article 38 of the Labour Unions Act No. 2821 which aimed to ensure the autonomy of labour and employers' unions, thereby required the cancellation of the general congress, limited however only to the election of the union president as there was no other employer or employers' representative elected to the organs of the labour union.[416]

On this matter Act No. 6356, Article 15(2) now provides the following:

> Claiming that the general congress meeting and elections were contrary to law, to the constitution, or that there were irregularities in violation of the law which may have an adverse impact on election results, the Ministry or the organization' members and delegates may file suit for the nullification of these transactions or the general congress within one month of the date of the general congress. The suit shall be finalized within two months in accordance with simple trial procedures. In case of appeal, the Court of Cassation shall render its definitive verdict in fifteen days (Article 15(3)).
>
> 'In the event a decision to cancel the general congress or the election of an organ in the general congress, the court shall appoint one or three curators (trustees) who will convene the general congress in the shortest time possible to hold fresh elections and administer the organization until a new administrative board is elected in accordance with the provisions of Act No. 4721' (Article 15(3)).

D. Powers and Functions of the General Congress

1035. Like in all associations, the general congress is the highest decision-making and control organ in unions. It is also the highest level of the appeal mechanism in unions. Functions and powers of the general congress have been enumerated in Article 11(1). These are: (a) electing the organs, (b) amending the constitution, (c) delegating power to the administrative board to make corrections on matters deemed contrary to law by the authorities concerned and courts, provided that such changes must be submitted to the approval of the first upcoming general congress and shall not have any effect retroactively, (d) reviewing the reports submitted by the administrative and auditing boards and by the certified (independent) auditors, (e) acquitting (absolving) the administrative and auditing boards, (f) approving the budget, (g) determining the salaries, compensation, travel allowances, payments and other benefits to be paid to members of the administrative, auditing and discipline

415. Court of Cassation, 9th Div., 2 Dec. 1996, 20558/22348.
416. Court of Cassation, 9th Div., 9 Jun. 2004, 13365/14374 (*see also* Court of Cassation, 9th Div., 7 Jun. 2001, 8559/9790).

boards, (h) empowering the administrative board to buy and sell immovable property, (i) to establish upper-level organizations, to affiliate with and to withdraw from upper-level organizations, (j) opening, merging or closing branches, empowering the administrative board in such transactions in accordance with the principles foreseen by the organization's constitution, (k) merging with or participating in other organizations, (l) acting as a founder of or affiliating with or withdrawing from international organizations, (m) dissolving the organization, (n) completing other procedures foreseen by law or organization's constitution concerning the general congress and deciding on issues not entrusted to the jurisdiction of other organs.

1036. The powers of the general congress of union branches are limited As Article 11(2) provides, the general congress of the branch shall be competent only in functions mentioned in (a), (d), (e) and (n)) of Article 11(1). In fact, branches do not possess any corporate status and therefore lack the capacity to file suit, as attested to in the various verdicts of the Court of Cassation.[417]

III. Administrative Board

A. *Composition and Functions*

1037. The administrative board of a union and its branches is to be composed of at least three and not more than nine members; the administrative board of the confederation is composed of at least five and not more than 29 members (Article 9(1)).

1038. Act No. 6356 does not carry specific provisions relating to the functions of administrative boards. Referring to the relevant provisions of the previous Act No. 2821, it could be inferred that, the main powers and functions of the administrative board are the following: representing the organization, administering the organization under the powers vested in it by legislation and its constitution; managing the income and expense accounts, preparing the draft budget for the coming term and submitting it to the general congress and carrying out the duties entrusted to it by the general congress.

1039. The constitution of the confederation or union fixes the time and the quorum of the meetings. The quorum may not be fixed at less than the absolute majority of the total number of members The quorum required for decision-making is the absolute majority of the members present in the meeting. In the event of a tie at a meeting, the chairman shall have a casting vote. If the number of the management board members of the union or the confederation is, for whatever reason, less than half of the total even after filling the vacancies with the substitute members, the remaining members of the administrative board or the board of auditors shall call the general congress to meet within one month. In the case such a call is not made, the local labour court at the request of a member shall appoint and instruct three of

417. Court of Cassation, 9th Div., 3 Oct. 1987, 9401/9694; 23 Jan. 1989, 136/313; Ruling of the General Council of the Court of Cassation, 19 Apr. 1989, 9-153/283; 27 Mar. 1990, 595/4071.

the members to convene the general congress within one month. In the event of vacancies on the administrative board of the branches, the branch administrative board must make the necessary arrangements for the election of a new administrative board for that branch.

B. Liability of the Administrative Board

1040. The Unions Act No. 6356 does not carry any clause on the liability of the administrative board. Making reference to the provisions of the Code of Obligations on the relations of the 'association' with its administrative board, it is generally held that in the event of administrative board members' having been elected for a certain period, rules governing 'agency contract' (Code of Obligations, Article 502) and 'representation' (Article 40 and the following) as well as 'employment contract' (Article 393 and the following of the Code of Obligations) shall apply.[418] In conjunction with the agency contract and the employment contract, then, the administrative board must carry out its activities with care and diligence, Article 393 and the following. and be accountable for its affairs to the general congress as well as provide it with pertinent information (Article 508).[419] Also, administrative board members are to be held jointly liable for the damage suffered by the organization as a result of their misconduct and wrongdoing.

1041. If the administrative board is not absolved by the general congress, its members are held liable for the damage and loss inflicted on the union,[420] subject to statutory limitations of ten years, Obligations Act, Article 146. Absolving and acquittal must have been granted in clear and comprehensive terms.

IV. The Board of Auditors

1042. The board of auditors is composed of a minimum of three and maximum nine auditors elected by the general congress (Act No. 6356 Article 9(1)). The branch of a union may have a single auditor. Act No. 6356 has not specified the functions of the auditing board. It may be inferred from Act No. 2821 that the functions of the board of auditors would include seeing to it that the administrative board functions in line with the decisions of the general congress, conducting administrative and financial audits in accordance with the union constitution, and if deemed necessary, requesting the management board to convene the extraordinary general congress and preparing the audit report.

---

418. N. Çelik, *İş Hukuku Dersleri*, 26th edn, 2013, pp. 492–494.

419. However, the Court of Cassation ruled that the relationship between the members of the union's administrative board and the union was not based on an employment contract. Court of Cassation, 9th Div., 8 Feb. 1991, 1288/1454.

420. Fevzi Demir, *supra*, p. 123; Fevzi Şahlanan, *Sendikalar Hukuku*, p. 157; The Court of Cassation has resolved that the approval of its working report by the General Congress does not absolve the administrative board of its liability; Court of Cassation, 4th Div., 10 Oct. 1976, 8348/8885.

V. Discipline Board

1043. The discipline board is composed of at least three and not more than nine members. Again based on the pertinent articles of Act No. 2821 the functions of the discipline board may cover the following: examining the charges pressed against the members of the union or confederation for violation of the rules, regulations, objectives or principles of the organization. The board applies the sanctions set out in the constitution, other than expulsion from membership and communicates information to all the interested parties and the general congress.

§7. Revenues and Expenditures of Unions and Confederations

I. Revenues

1044. According to Article 28(1) of Act No. 6356, the revenues of organizations (labour and employers' unions) are to be composed of (1) members' paid-up dues and solidarity dues; (2) income from activities authorized carried out in accordance with the organization's constitution; (3) donations; and (4) the yield from their assets and earnings derived from the transfer and sale of their assets.

1045. The question of whether or not unions can request extra payment from their members for their services, such as providing legal aid or organizing entertainment and concerts has been a matter of controversy. It has been argued that members pay for such services through membership dues in any case. Others have claimed, however, that as the law has restricted the maximum level of membership dues, unions may demand a fair payment for such services.

1046. Act No. 6356 prohibits unions from receiving aid and donations from certain external sources. According to Article 28(2), it is unlawful for unions and confederations to accept financial aid and donations from the following public organizations or institutions with a public law character. Article 28(2) provides: 'organizations must not receive aid or donations from public institutions and organizations, as well as organizations of tradesmen and craftsmen and from occupational organizations of a public nature.'

1047. With a view to safeguarding the autonomy and independence of organizations, Article 28(3) brings restrictions on labour and employers' organizations from the vantage point of aid, donations and other similar pay-outs. The clause provides:

> Labour organizations must not accept aid and donations from employers and organizations of employers established under this Act or under other legislation; employers' organizations must not accept aid and donations from labour organizations established under this Act or other legislation. Provided that they make notification to the Ministry, organizations may receive aid and donations

from persons, institutions and organizations abroad. However, labour organizations may not receive aid and donations from employer organizations abroad. Receipt of monetary aid and donations must be implemented through bank transactions.

1048. The strict restriction on receiving aid from international sources which required the approval of the government under the previous system of Act No. 2821 has thus been removed.

1049. Article 28(5) foresees the sanction to apply in case of violations. 'In the event of receiving aid and donations in contravention of the above-stated provisions, upon the application of a member or the Ministry the amounts thus received shall be transferred to the Treasury by the decision of the court.'

1050. Organizations must deposit all their revenues in banks. Their constitutions shall designate the amount of petty cash the organization may retain at hand to meet their necessary expenses (Article 28(5)).

1051. Act No. 6356 does not carry any specific clauses on the expenditures of unions and confederations. There is a general provision in Article 28(6) which says that 'organizations are not allowed to spend or donate their revenues for activities other than those indicated in this Act and in their constitutions'.

1052. In an effort to enable organizations to extend aid to devastated areas, Article 28(7) paves the way for a special kind of aid. It provides that, 'based on the decision of the administrative board and in amounts not exceeding 10% of their cash and with a view to establish housing, education and health centres, organizations may directly or through competent authorities extend aid to public institutions and organizations, in kind and cash, to be used by national and international regions hit by national disasters'.

1053. The following subsection has been supplemented to Article 26 of Act No. 6356 by Article 10 of Act No. 6552 (the 'bag law' of 10 September 2014): 'On condition that their constitutions provide for it and their general congress has adopted the relevant resolution, employers' unions may form mutual solidarity and aid funds to be spent for the payment of the employers' share of workers' insurance contributions in an amount not to exceed twenty-five% of their cash.'

1054. Act No. 2821, the legislation preceding the new Act No. 6356, had imposed a mandatory expenditure on labour unions. It provided that 'labour unions and labour confederations shall disburse at least 10% of their revenues in order to improve the occupational and general educational level of their members' (Act No. 2821, Article 44/II as amended by Act 4104 dated 4 April 1995). It is interesting to note that the law had imposed this requirement (which was first introduced by Act No. 274 in 1963) only on labour organizations. Act No. 6356 has repealed this clause, leaving training and education activities merely to unions' own initiative.

§8. Activities of Organizations (Labour and Employers' Unions)

I. Activities

1055. Unlike the previous Act No. 2821 which had enumerated the activities of unions in a detailed fashion, the new Act No. 6356 has chosen to leave this domain to the constitutions of organizations. Article 26 provides that 'in representing their members or heirs of members, labour and employers' unions may freely perform the activities cited in their constitutions'. However, the provision in Article 26(5) requiring that organizations must not deal with activities which fall outside the objectives cited in their constitutions implies that the law's emphasis is still on perceiving unions merely as occupational entities rather than as broad-based civic organizations. Furthermore, a few restrictions which existed under the previous legislation shall prevail under the new system as well. According to Article 26(7), for example, 'organizations must not use the names, emblems, signs or symbols of political parties'. As the stricter restrictions imposed on unions' political functions by the 1982 Constitution and subsequent legislation were removed during the past decades, this limitation here seems to be of minor importance, since it is held that unions may deal with political activities in a general and broad sense Coupled with another restriction in Article 9(6), however, the scope of political activity recognized to unions may still be deemed to be quite narrow. Article 9(6) provides that 'the functions of union and branch administrators (i.e., members of the administrative, auditing and disciplinary boards) shall automatically expire if they are elected as Parliament members or as mayors'. Criticized by the ILO Committee of Experts during the past decades as a contravention of union freedom, this restriction, which did not exist before 1980 is, in fact, based on Article 82 of the 1982 Constitution which mentions union work as one of the categories not compatible with the status of Parliament members. Drawing up a new Constitution for Turkey, a goal which is on the agenda of the current Parliament, may abrogate the said restriction

1056. Article 26(8) has reiterated the pre-existing clause that 'unions must not deal with commercial activities, but, based on the decision of the general congress, they may make investments in industrial and economic ventures in amounts not exceeding 40% of their cash on hand'. As indicated above, Article 44 of Act No. 2821 had imposed on labour unions the requirement to spend a minimum 10% of their revenues for the education and training of their members, but Act No. 6356 has deleted this requirement, leaving it to unions' constitutions. Further, in view of Article 26(9), which is also a replica of the previous legislation, 'organizations must not distribute their income among their members and constituents, except for the said they may extend in accordance with their constitutions to their members during strikes and lock-outs or for training purposes'. Also, Act No. 6356 has broadened the power of unions and confederations to represent their members in legal actions as plaintiff or defendant, even after the termination of their membership status, provided that the ex-member has given his written approval. In an effort to protect the organization's autonomy in respect to freedom of association, Article 28 has banned the receipt of aid or donations from organizations of a public nature as well as from employers' organizations, with the exception of aid from foreign organizations provided that they give advance notice to the Ministry.

1057. In carrying out their activities and services, unions and confederations must ensure equality among their members. As Article 39(1) provides, 'members of the labour union which is the signatory party to the collective agreement shall avail of the benefits provided by the collective agreement.' In view of Article 26(4), 'without prejudice to provisions in the seventh and twelfth sections of this Act, extension to non-members of rights and benefits provided by organizations for their members as a result of their activities shall depend on the written approval of the organization'. Thus non-members may benefit from these rights and services only upon the written consent of the union or confederation No exception is permitted, however, to the provisions of Act No. 6356 on the wages and benefits granted by the collective labour agreement. This means that by paying solidarity dues to the signatory union, non-members may avail themselves of the benefits brought by the collective agreement. The written permission of the union may be required merely in the event where non-members wish to benefit from union services other than the advantages brought about by the collective agreement. The union may also allow non-members to take advantage of the collective agreement even without paying solidarity dues, but no such case has been encountered in practice so far.

II. Union Activities in Actual Practice

1058. With the exception of the 1980–1983 transitional period during which free collective bargaining had been suspended, the most significant, and sometimes the only, activity of unions in Turkey has been collective bargaining since the passage of Act No. 275 in 1963. In fact the role played by collective bargaining has been so prominent that, should the bargaining power of unions be curbed, as was the case during the 1980–1983 period, the Turkish union movement would lose much of its strength. Of secondary significance among trade union activities is the legal aid provided for members. Since spending a minimum of 10% of their income on improving their members general education and culture was imposed as a legal obligation, most labour unions organized periodic seminars and lectures for their members; however the degree to which the unions actually fulfilled this obligation was questionable in most cases.[421] Union publications seem to have increased in numbers in recent years. Also, a few unions have successfully launched health services and recreational facilities for their members.

421. H.F. Erginsoy, *Türk İşçi Hareketi Üzerine Bir Deneme*, İstanbul, 1968, p. 67; M. Kutal ve M. Ekonomi, 'Türk Endüstri İlişkileri Sisteminin Yasal Çerçevesi ve Başlıca Sorunları', *Endüstri İlişkileri Semineri*, pp. 103–104; T. Dereli, *Türk Sendikacılığının Ekonomik ve Sosyal Etkileri, Uluslararası Deneylerin Işığında Türkiye'de Endüsti* İlişkileri, İstanbul, 1977, pp. 173–174; C. Tuncay, 'Sendikaların Faaliyetlerinin Yasal Düzenlemesi Üzerine Düşünceler', *Tühis*, Temmuz, 1981, pp. 9–11.

1059. Another development in recent years has been the increase in unions' strike funds.[422] As mentioned above, the only legislative reference to strike funds and distributing strike benefits is found in Article 39/III which states that 'unions and confederations must mot distribute any of their income or revenues among members, but this provision should not apply to any strike and lock-out benefits paid to their members as provided in their constitutions'. Some unions have been able to support their members on strike by providing strike pay of up to 60% of their basic wage.[423]

1060. With respect to helping members set up cooperatives, an activity on which Article 33/V of Act No. 2821 as well as previous legislation had placed special emphasis, unions, with the exception of a few consumer cooperatives, do not seem to have achieved much.[424]

1061. Likewise, unions' investments in economic and industrial ventures – not to exceed 40% of their cash assets (Article 33/VII), a target which the legislature conceived of as encouraging unions to contribute to the national economy – have not amounted to much so far. However, in recent years in an effort to slow down large-scale privatization and to protect employment in SEEs, unions have shown increasing interest in buying out some plants through joint ventures with other partners. The Karabük Iron and Steel Plant (*Kardemir*) is a case in point.[425,426]

III. Prohibited Activities: Areas in Which Labour and Employers' Unions Must Not Engage

A. *Basic Prohibitions*

1062. Unions and confederations must not carry on any activity prohibited under Article 14 of the Constitution of the Republic of Turkey, nor shall their administration and operation be contrary to the democratic and fundamental principles as set out in the Constitution. Activities prohibited under Article 14 of the Constitution are as follows: (1) to disrupt the indivisible integrity of the state with its country and nation, (2) to jeopardize the existence of the Turkish state and republic, (3) to eradicate fundamental rights and freedoms, (4) to place the administration of the state under the rule of one person or to establish the supremacy of one social class over other social classes and (5) to create discriminations based on language, race,

422. T. Dereli, 'Türkiye'de Sendikacığın Ekonomik ve Sosyal Etkileri', *supra*, pp. 179–181; N. Gerek, *Sendikaların Kooperatifçilik ve Yatırım Faaliyetleri*, Eskişehir, 1983, p. 47.
423. T. Dereli, 'Türkiye'de Sendikacığın Ekonomik ve Sosyal Etkileri', *supra*, pp. 179–181; N. Gerek, *Sendikaların Kooperatifçilik ve Yatırım Faaliyetleri*, Eskişehir, 1983, p. 47
424. N. Ekin, *Endüstri İlişkileri*, İstanbul, 1976, p. 264.
425. *See* H.Y. Ersöz et al., *The Effects of Privatization on Turkish Industrial Relations through Employee Ownership: The Case of Kardemir*, 20(4) The International Journal of Comparative Labour Law and Industrial Relations 605–629 (2004).
426. Y.P. Soykut-Sarıca, *Employee Ownership and Management: The Case of Kardemir Iron and Steel Mill Industry*, 5(33) African Journal of Business Management 12872–12881 (2011).

religion and sect or to establish a state predicated on these concepts and ideas. The democratic and fundamental principles specified in Article 2 of the Constitution proclaim that the Republic of Turkey is a democratic, secular and social state of law, based on social peace, national solidarity and justice, respectful of human rights and committed to Atatürk nationalism.

B. Restrictions on Political Activities

1063. The strict prohibitions placed on unions' political activities by the Constitution of 1982 and Article 37(2) of Act No. 2821 have been repealed through successive amendments. Presently, in addition to Article 26(5) of Act No. 6356 which states that 'organizations shall not deal with activities which fall outside their objectives as espoused in their constitutions, Article 26(7) carries only a mild reference to union-political party relations. It provides that 'organizations shall not use the names, emblems, signs or symbols of political parties'.

C. Prohibitions on Relations Between Workers and Employers' Unions

1064. Labour and employers' unions must be totally independent of each other. Employees, their unions and confederations must not be members of employers' unions or employers' organizations established under any other act; likewise, employers and their organizations must not be members of labour unions and confederations. These organizations must not intervene, either directly or by means of representatives or members or through any other intermediate person, in the constitution, administration or activity of one another. It is also unlawful to put a labour union or confederation under the control of an employer or employers' organization or to encourage or to cause the formation of a labour union or confederation under the influence of an employers' organization (Article 26(6)).

1065. However, bearing the status of 'employee' or 'employer' within the meaning of Act No. 6356 does not preclude a person from joining at the same time an organization set up under Act No. 507 respecting handicrafts and small industries.

D. Other Prohibitions

1066. In view of Article 26(7), 'organizations must not deal with commercial activities. But based on the decision of the general congress, they may make investments in industrial and economic ventures in amounts not exceeding 40 per cent of their cash on hand'.

1067. Article 39(1) of Act No. 2821 had provided that unions and confederations should not nominate any candidate to the organs of public occupational and professional organizations or their higher bodies, nor should they carry on any activity or propaganda for or against any of the candidates. This restriction had been removed by Act No. 4277 of 28 June 1997.

E. Restrictions Imposed by the Associations Act

1068. Article 35 of the associations Act No. 5253 provides that some of the restrictions imposed on associations shall also apply to unions and union confederations. These are as follows: (a) the obligation to make certain declarations and inspection (Article 19), (b) Inspection by security forces (Article 20), (c) declaration of the general assembly and elected officers to competent administrative bodies (Article 23), (d) establishments which can be set up upon permission (Article 26), (e) restrictions on using certain names and emblems (Article 29), (f) prohibited associations and activities (Article 30) and (g) official communication language (Article 31).

1069. It is held in principle that 'where the Unions Act is silent, provisions of the Civil Code and the Associations Act which are not contrary to union legislation shall apply to unions and confederations'. Article 35 of the new Associations Act No. 5253 has enumerated its provisions which shall also apply to unions and confederations. Although such a link has now been established between the two Acts, it is very likely that in unforeseen cases where the Unions Act will still be mute the need to invoke the pertinent clauses of the Associations Act will always be felt also in the future.

§9. Auditing and Inspection of Organizations

1070. In the past, in addition to control and auditing from within, unions were subject to external inspection as well. External inspection was implemented through administrative and financial controls by the Ministry of Labour and the Ministry of Finance at least once in an election term. Unions could also be inspected for general security purposes. Act No. 4277 of 28 June 1997 repealed the inspection of unions by the government and left the auditing issue entirely to the constitutions of unions and confederations themselves. Addressing this issue, Article 47 now reads:

> In implementing the administrative and financial auditing of the unions and confederations from within, the auditing board or the auditors shall examine the revenues and expenditures of the organization as well as the related procedures with a view to ensuring their conformity with the laws, bylaws and the decisions of the general congress. The principles of auditing were designated in a bylaw prepared upon obtaining the written opinions of the labour and employer confederations.

1071. Article 48 of Act No. 2821 had provided that the confederations of which labour and employers' unions were members would inspect the revenues and expenditures as well as all kinds of activities of such affiliated organizations. Although the aim here was to establish democratic control from within the union movement, it was criticized for having equipped the confederations with power over their affiliates which should be autonomous organizations. Auditing by confederations was finally removed by Article 15 of Act No. 4101, dated 4 April 1995.

1072. If deemed necessary and requested by the President, unions and confederations may also be inspected by the State Inspection Board linked to the Presidency in accordance with the Constitution of Turkey, as well as by the Inspection Board of the Prime Minister upon his request. Both types of inspection are of an extraordinary nature, though, and are rarely used in practice. Of more significance, however is the inspection by security forces foreseen in Article 20 of the Associations Act mentioned above.

1073. The Martial Administration Act (No. 1402) brought, in its amended Article 3, sanctions entitling martial law commanders, if martial law was in effect in the region – to enter and search all types of associations, political parties, unions and clubs, as well as private lodgings and persons, without need for any request or written order and to seize the illegal items or criminal evidence. The strict rules envisaged by the Martial Administration Act reflected the precautionary attitudes of the legislature in the turbulent political environment of the 1970s and 1980s riddled with escalating violence of the leftist and separationist movements. The Act's mandate was limited, however, only to the duration of and the area that was s subject to martial administration, which at the time of this writing was no longer in force.

1074. Under the present Associations Act No. 5253, the power of security forces to enter and search unions with a view to protect public order or to prevent the commission of criminal acts has been made conditional upon obtaining a court decision to that effect or pending the approval of the judge in charge where urgent administrative action is warranted by the circumstances.

1075. Compared to previous legislation, Act No. 6356 liberalized and simplified the procedures concerning the auditing of unions and confederations. In view of Article 29(1) 'the auditing of organizations shall be executed by the organization's auditing board in accordance with the law and the provisions of the organization's constitution. Auditing shall ensure inspecting the administration and operations, revenues, expenditures, balance sheets and related procedures so as to verify their conformity with legislation, organization's constitution, bylaws, and the decisions of the general congress.' Act No. 6356 has foreseen a new type of financial inspection: according to Article 29(2), financial auditing of organizations in regard to their revenues and expenditures shall be performed by certified (external) financial consultants competent in accordance with the Independent Accounts, Financial Auditing and Consultancy Act of 1 June 1989, No. 3568 every two years at the latest. This external auditing shall not abrogate the liability of the organization's auditing board. Also, the founders and administrators of organizations must make declarations about the assets belonging to them, their spouses and children under their guardianship in respect of the Act No. 3628, dated 19 April 1990 (Article 29(4)).

§10. Books and Registers to Be Kept by Organizations

1076. Article 30(1) requires the employers' and labour unions to keep the following books and registers:

(a) lists of membership and expirations of membership;
(b) books on decisions of the general congress, administrative, auditing and discipline boards;
(c) registers of incoming and outgoing communications and debits;
(d) registers of dues, 'daily registers' book, inventory book, and the main registers book;
(e) registers and books for revenues.

'All items and materials shall be registered in the book for movable stocks in accordance with the Act on Tax Procedures of 4 January 1961, No. 213' (Article 30(2)). It should be noted that giving the listing of books and registers in a such a detailed manner is not consistent with the general approach of the new Act which purports voluntarism rather than strict adherence to written rules and regulations.[427]

427. Aydın Başbuğ, *Toplu İş İlişkileri ve Hukuk, Şeker İş yayını*, Ankara 2012, p. 154.

Chapter 3. Closing, Suspension and Dissolution

§1. Closing and Suspension

1077. As Article 31(1) provides, 'the organization which engages in activities contravening the principles of the Republic espoused in the Constitution of Turkey shall be closed by court decision upon the request of the Chief Prosecutor of the Republic who is in charge in the jurisdiction of the organization's centre. If the conduct in violation of the said principle has been perpetrated by the organization's administrators individually, the Court's decision shall involve merely the removal of the administrator from office.'

1078. The case may involve suspension of activities and removal from office only temporarily. As Article 31(2) affirms, 'in conjunction with legal actions filed in relation to Article 31(1) above, the court may, upon a request during the trial or directly, decide to suspend the operations of the organization and remove its administrators from office temporarily'. In the cases entailing suspension, 'one or three trustees (curators) shall be appointed in line with Act No. 4721 to ensure the management of the organization and to safeguard its interests as well as to convoke the general congress to be held upon the expiration of the suspension term'.

1079. As explained above, the general congress which is the highest decision-making organ of the union is competent to dissolve the organization as well as to reach decisions resulting in mergers and amalgamations.

§2. Dissolution and Liquidation

1080. As the Unions Act is silent on the subject, the general principles of law and the Associations Act are applicable in the case of an organization's dissolution by itself. The organization shall be dissolved (shall cease to exist) in the event of general inability, or if the formation of its management board in accordance with its constitution becomes impossible, or if the regular (ordinary) general congress cannot be convened for two successive terms.

1081. The general congress may decide to liquidate the organization (Civil Code, Article 78/II). At least two-thirds of the members of the general congress must be present in order to take the decision to liquidate the organization. If the two-thirds quorum is not obtained in the first meeting, however, the members shall be summoned again and the general congress convenes regardless of the number of members present at this second meeting. The decision to liquidate the organization must be taken with at least two-thirds vote of the members who are present.

1082. In some cases the corporate status of an organization may be revoked by court decision. The categories of liquidation in this category are as follows. According to the Civil Code, the organization may be liquidated by a court order if it becomes involved in the pursuance of goals which are contrary to law or general morals. The court decides to abolish the organization if it has not convoked its first general congress within six months of its having acquired legal corporate status, or if its regular general congress has not been convened within the time limit prescribed in its constitution or if its legally compulsory organs have not been elected.

1083. If the organization's activities have been suspended because of the contraventions in its constitution and/or due to required procedures being incomplete or in contravention of law during the founding process, the court grants the union or the confederation a time allowance of not more than sixty days. If the organization has not brought its constitution into conformity with the law or nor completed the required procedures within that time limit, the court decides to close and liquidate the union or the confederation. This decision is final.

1084. The movable and immovable property as well as the assets and liabilities of a dissolved or liquidated organization is to be managed by persons appointed in accordance with the provisions of the Commercial Code.

1085. According to Article 32(1) of Act No. 6356, provided there is a pertinent clause in its constitution, the assets of a union whose corporate status is to expire may be handed over to another organization of a similar nature established under this Act or to an upper organization with which it is affiliated or, if it is not a member of an upper organization, to another upper organization of the same nature. In the case of the upper organization being dissolved, its assets may be transferred to its affiliates. If there is no provision in the organization's constitution, the general congress deciding to dissolve the organization may transfer its assets in line with the above-mentioned principles.

1086. Here, Article 32(2) considers a final alternative in that 'if the constitution does not provide for it or if there is no general congress decision to dissolve the organization or if the transfer of assets is not accepted by the relevant organization, the monies left as a result of dissolution and liquidation shall be transferred to the Unemployment Insurance Fund and commodities in kind shall be handed over to the Employment Organization of Turkey'.

Chapter 4. Basic Facts on Major Labour Confederations

§1. Confederation of Trade Unions of Turkey (Türkiye İşçİ Sendikalari Konfederasyonu – Türk-İş)

1087. Formed in 1952 in Bursa, Türk-İş developed in the ensuing decades as the general confederation of the Turkish labour movement. Since its founding, the confederation has adopted a centrist character and adhered to a policy of supra-party politics, that is, non-alliance with any political party. As the management boards of Türk-İş have always been composed of leaders with differing political opinions and party affiliations, it is likely that this policy was dictated by pragmatic considerations rather than by a genuine desire to stay out of politics.

1088. Despite its avowed adherence to the supra-party principle, Türk-İş lobbied for pro-labour candidates and supported certain political parties in a number of national elections. Its seventh and eighth national conventions, held in 1968 and 1970, respectively, adopted a declaration titled the 'Twenty-four Principles of Türk-İ ş', which demanded social and economic reforms and basic rights for labour. Moreover, a strong Social Democratic faction developed from within Türk-İş during the 1970s. In 1971, the leaders of four Türk-İş-affiliated unions, who were personally associated with the left-of-centre Republican Peoples' Party (RPP), issued a report that stressed the need for a Social Democratic movement within Türk-İş. These people rejected an alliance with the TİP, which had, allegedly, 'pursued an illegal policy'. Instead, they advocated support for the RPP, which had proved its commitment to labour questions, or, alternatively, for the establishment of a Workingmen's Party. As the response of Türk-İş to this call was not positive, the four withdrew their proposals. However, their initiative eventually led to the production by 12 Türk-İş unions of a detailed document titled 'A Social Democratic Order for the Turkish Labour Movement'. This document strongly reasserted the twenty-four principles embodied in the Türk-İş constitution. Henceforth, the Social Democratic movement represented a significant faction within the structure of Türk-İş.

1089. Türk-İş was suspended by the military regime in 1980, but it was allowed to function again a few months later and its secretary-general took office as minister of social security in the military government. This led to the suspension of Türk-İş by the ICFTU to which it had belonged since 1960; however, in 1983, Türk-İş was readmitted to full membership in the ICFTU. In 1988, it joined the European Trade Union Confederation. Türk-İş is also an affiliate of the Trade Union Advisory Committee to the OECD and its national affiliates are members of the appropriate international trade secretariats.

1090. Türk-İş has a loosely confederated structure, with only limited authority over its affiliates. Its official organs are the Management Board, the Executive Committee, the Auditing Board and the Disciplinary Board; however, growing power has been vested in the Presidents' Council – an informal organ composed of the presidents of all the affiliated national unions.

1091. The confederation has been increasingly subject to internal criticism from the Social Democratic Faction, the more radical elements of which are the unions representing petroleum, chemicals and rubber workers; leather workers and cordwainers; glass, cement, ceramics and quarrying workers; civil aviation workers.

1092. Türk-İş organized its first demonstration since 1980 in February 1986. The call was for economic reforms and restoration of trade union freedoms. Since then, it has taken the lead in the revival of trade union activity. Türk-İş has called demonstrations and initiated symbolic protests. In 1987 and, again, in January 1991, its program contained a plank allowing for possible recourse to a general strike. Türk-İş leaders have been interrogated by the general prosecutor and subjected to occasional harassment for these activities. In general, relations between Türk-İş and the government came under increasing strain throughout the late 1980s and during the financial crises of 1994, 1999 and 2001. Although the Confederation's relations with the political establishment have somewhat softened in contrast to earlier decades, it seems to have intensified its opposition to the government's liberal economic policies, especially to the staggering rates of unemployment prevailing despite the officially proclaimed rates of gross national product (GNP) growth.

1093. Although the laws do not grant the confederations any competence to engage in collective bargaining, Türk-İş, in 1989, 1991 and afterwards during the late 1990s up until recently, helped some of its affiliates to coordinate their bargaining in the public sector. This was welcomed as a sign of the confederation's rising prestige and power, albeit informally, in the area of collective bargaining. The coordinated strikes Türk-İş organized in October 1995 proved to be effective in toppling the government.

1094. In 2022, Türk-İş, with 33 affiliates in the 28 industry branches defined by law, represented a total membership of 1,213,000. It has its headquarters in Ankara and Ergün Atalay is the current president and Pevrül Kavlak is the general secretary.

§2. Confederation of Progressive Trade Unions of Turkey (Devrimci İşçi Sendikalari Konfederasyonu – DİSK)

1095. Established in 1967 as a breakaway from the Confederation of Labour Unions of Turkey (Türk-İş), DİSK associated itself with the TİP founded in 1961 and assumed the character of a militant socialist union confederation with a Marxist wing. The term *devrimci* in its title implies progressive or even revolutionary as well as reformist in Turkish. DİSK was active primarily in the private sector, where it conducted many strikes. Before 1980, it was the second largest union confederation in Turkey, with an estimated membership of about 450,000. It was allegedly involved in the escalating political violence of the 1970s and was itself a target of that violence.

1096. Following the 1980 army coup, the activities of DİSK and its affiliates were suspended. In 1981, many DİSK members were brought before a military court and indicted under several articles of the Turkish Penal Code. In addition, a large number of leaders and others with links to DİSK fled the country at that time to avoid prosecution. The trials continued until 1986, when the court passed a sentence of imprisonment on many of those indicted and ordered the dissolution of DİSK and 28 of its 30 affiliated unions. The court's decisions were appealed to the military High Court of Appeals. Meanwhile, defendants were released from prison and DİSK president Baştürk and secretary-general Işıklar both won seats in the parliament in the November 1987 elections.

1097. DİSK was actively supported through the trials by the World Federation of Trade Unions (WFTU), the World Confederation of Labour, the ICFTU and the European Trade Union Confederation (ETUC). These international organizations, particularly the ETUC, opposed the increasing normalization of relations between Turkey and Western Europe so long as trade union rights continued to be infringed and sought to block Turkey's application to become a full member of the European Community. DİSK was officially affiliated with the ETUC in 1985 and had informal ties with the WFTU.

1098. In May 1991, the repeal of the relevant articles of the Turkish Penal Code nullified the offences for which DİSK and many of its leaders had been sentenced.

1099. On 16 July 1991, the military High Court of Appeals finally passed its long-awaited judgment and dropped the pending indictments against DİSK and its leaders. It was generally agreed that, since DİSK was to be reactivated, its assets, heretofore under the supervision of court-appointed trustees, would be given back to its leaders.

1100. After 1984, when collective bargaining was revived in Turkey, many former DİSK members joined Türk-İş affiliated unions. In 1991, as they sought to enlist new members and restructure the organization along the lines envisaged in recent legislation, DİSK leaders confronted novel challenges, including having to cope with the resumption of legal battles and organizational conflicts. Due to heightened international competition in the global economy, however, DİSK's leftist stance and aggressive ideology tended to take on milder overtones, as evidenced by the Confederation's increased collaboration with Türk-İş and the government during the last decade.

1101. Notwithstanding these difficulties, in the spring of 1992 DİSK held its first general congress since 1980 and seemed to be making headway in enlarging its membership base. It represents 17 affiliated national unions organized in 17 industries; general services, food, rubber, chemicals and petroleum, metal-working and textiles represent industries where DİSK seems to be strongly organized, in relative terms. In January 2004, it represented a total membership of 388,318 (13.9% of total membership). The headquarters of DİSK is in İstanbul. It is affiliated with ICFTU,

ETUC and OECD/TUAC. Süleyman Çelebi had to leave the presidency because of his election to the Parliament in the 2011 elections.

1102. Kani Beko is the current president of DİSK. According to its reported official statistics, DİSK represents a total membership of 111,398 workers organized in 19 affiliated national unions.

§3. Confederation of Righteous Trade Unions of Turkey (Türkiye Hak İşçi Sendikalari Konfederasyonu (Hak-İş)

1103. Hak-İş was established in 1976 by the affiliation of seven unions in different industries. The confederation is committed to the goal of 'creating harmony between workers and employers' by adhering to moral values. According to Hak-CF, the main factor leading to class struggle is the unjust wage system. The activities of Hak-İş, like those of other trade union confederations, were suspended by the army coup of September 1980. Following official inspection, the union was allowed to function again six months later. Thereafter, Hak-İş openly opposed the 1983 legislation and organized effective strikes in several industries.

1104. Hak-İş affiliates are organized in seven industries: food, textiles, metalworking, agriculture, general services, health and woodworking. Six of these unions appear to have met the minimum 10% requirement for industry-level representativeness. In order to be able to engage in collective bargaining in other industries as well, Hak-İş has advocated the reduction of the industry representativeness requirement from 10 to 5%. According to official statistics, Hak-İş membership in 2022 stood at 762,439.

1105. Adhering as it does to religious and spiritual values, Hak-İş proved its commitment to serious-minded and responsible unionism. Its research and publishing activities were especially commendable.

1106. The headquarters of Hak-İş is in Ankara. Mahmut Arslan is the current president.

§4. Confederation of Nationalist Trade Unions of Turkey (Türkiye Milliyetçi İşçi Sendikalari Konfederasyonu – MİSK)

1107. Established in 1970, MİSK adopted the ideology of the Nationalist Action Party (MHP), which advocated 'nationalist principles' and was allegedly involved in escalating the war against the extreme partisans of the left. Upon seizing power, the military National Security Council shut down the MHP in 1980, but the party was reorganized in 1983 under a new name, the Nationalist Workingmen's Party (*Milliyetçi Çalışanlar Partisi* – MÇP). Later, the party was renamed MHP again and, as a coalition partner, was instrumental in forming the 57th government in 1999.

1108. As a labour confederation, MİSK initially espoused 'one union in each industry' and 'compulsory union membership', emphasized national consensus and repudiated class struggle. On 12 September 1980, MİSK, too, was suspended by the military government, but it began to function again in 1984. When the number of its affiliated unions fell below five, the Ministry of Labour took steps to dissolve it. In 1991, It was liquidated.

1109. In addition to the above-mentioned confederations, the non-affiliated, independent unions represent a total membership of 37,923.

Chapter 5. Collective Bargaining

§1. The Notion

I. The Right to Bargain Collectively and to Conclude Collective Labour Agreements

1110. Article 53(1) of the Turkish Constitution of 1982 provides that employees and employers have the right to conclude collective labour agreements, with a view to regulate their mutual economic and social standards and determine the conditions of employment. Collective Labour Agreements, Strikes and Lock-outs Act of 1983, No. 2822, governed the rules and procedures for the constitutionally guaranteed right to collective bargaining in a detailed fashion. Although the Constitution and Act No. 2822 as well as Act No. 6356 now have entitled both the employees and employers to enter into collective labour agreements, it is clear that the main party that benefits from the right to collective bargaining are the employees, for it is through the means of concerted action that employees are enabled to improve their working and living conditions. As in other pluralistic systems, Turkish collective labour law stresses that the process of collective bargaining should be free of any outside intervention. In this sense, the 'autonomy of collective bargaining' is construed to mean the freedom of the parties to mutually determine the conditions of employment and their relations without any outside interference. There have been certain periods in Turkey, however, even after the adoption of the free collective bargaining buttressed by the right to strike in 1963, during which the autonomy of collective bargaining was restrained, the aim being, for the most part, to curb the allegedly inflationary effects of collectively bargained wage rates. The expansion after 1982 of the no-strike activities and areas where compulsory arbitration has been the rule, coupled with wage restraint policies, in particular, has always been criticized, nonetheless, as infringements on the principle of the autonomy of collective bargaining.

II. Definition of the Collective Labour Agreement

A. *The Notion*

1111. Article 2(1 h) of Act No. 6356 defines the collective labour agreement as 'a contract concluded between a labour union and an employers' union or an employer not affiliated with the employers' union, with the object of making provision for the conclusion, content and termination of individual employment contracts.' collective agreement shall not be valid unless it is made in written form (Article 35(1)). In view of Article 33(2), 'a collective labour agreement may also contain other stipulations as to the mutual rights and obligations of the parties, application and supervision of the agreement and settlement of disputes'. Taking these legal elements into consideration, then, the following definition could be given: a collective labour agreement is a written contract concluded between a labour union and an employers' union or employer as defined by the law, with the purpose of regulating the conclusion, content and termination of individual employment contracts, as well as other aspects of employee–employer relations, the mutual rights and obligations of the parties and provisions concerning the application and supervision of working conditions and the settlement of disputes.

B. Relations between the Collective Agreement and the General Agreement

1112. The Obligations Act of 1926 adapted from Switzerland had entitled groups of employees to conclude with the employer what was referred to as the 'general agreement', but due to the absence of labour unions until 1947 and the lack of the right to strike until 1963, the practice of making general agreements, as envisaged in the Obligations Act, did not become operative. Collective bargaining, recognized by labour unions and employers and buttressed by the right to strike and lock-out in 1963, proved to be a more viable and effective instrument as compared to the concept of 'general agreement'. Article 3(11) of Act No. 275 of 1963 envisaged that the provisions of a collective agreement should replace those of any general agreement in force in an establishment if the provisions of the latter were at variance with those of the collective agreement, provided that any provisions of the general agreement which were more favourable for the employees would remain in force.

1113. Act No. 2822 of 1983 on Collective Agreements, Strikes and Lock-outs did not abrogate provisions of the Obligations Act on 'general agreements', nor did it establish any link between the collective agreement and the general agreement. In the event of any problem which might arise in practice, it was affirmed that the principle which was envisaged in Act No. 275 should be adhered to, meaning the more specific clauses foreseen in Act No. 2822 should take precedence over the broader principles of the Obligations Act. The new Obligations Act of Turkey, No. 6098 does not make any reference to the 'general agreement'.

§2. CONTENT OF THE COLLECTIVE AGREEMENT

1114. It may be inferred from the foregoing definition that the content of a collective labour agreement consists of two major parts:

(a) the normative part; and
(b) the obligatory part.

I. The Normative Part of the Collective Labour Agreement

1115. The normative part of a collective agreement relates to those clauses concerning the conclusion, content and termination of employment contracts. The clauses which regulate the conclusion of employment contracts may comprise such matters as the form of employment contracts. Employment contracts concluded in a manner contrary to the rules stipulated by the collective agreement must be deemed null and void. However, the specific form may have been required as a condition of proof rather than validity. Where it is not possible to determine the nature of clauses concerning form, they must be construed as meaning a condition of proof rather than validity. Some clauses may prohibit the making of certain employment contracts or require their conclusion under specified conditions. For instance, the collective labour agreement may stipulate that certain categories of employees (like women, children or unskilled workers) shall not be engaged in certain types of work, although such clauses are actually rare in Turkish collective labour agreements. On the other hand, some collective agreement clauses may require the conclusion of employment contracts with certain types of employees (i.e., the requirement to hire disabled persons or ex-convicts above the numbers stipulated by the legislation; when hiring new workers, the requirement to give priority to persons previously employed at the establishment).

1116. Among the clauses which concern the content of employment contracts are those aiming to improve the economic and social well-being of workers, namely wages – the minimum wage fixed for the establishment as well as negotiated wage increases – overtime wages, premiums, bonuses and other fringe benefits, leave pay, working time, etc.

1117. Turkish collective labour agreements seem to provide for various types of wage increases. Some increases are flat-rate, across-the-board type and some foresee percentage increases. Some involve varying rates of increase, using objective criteria such as types of jobs, seniority of the employees, or groups of jobs, as in the case of developing job evaluation systems. It is held that applying differing rates of increase to workers in different job classifications, different skills and different ranks in the organization is not contrary to the principle of equal treatment, since the employer is entitled to differentiate wages and wage increases among employees in different categories according to objective criteria. Discriminating against employees in the same job category, however, would run counter to the principle of equal pay for equal work or for work of equal worth. Applying different rates of increases to employees employed under contracts made for a definite and indefinite period would, of course, violate the said principle.

1118. One important feature of Turkish collective labour agreements has been the growing proportion of many monetary and non-monetary fringe benefits, i.e., heating allowance, bonuses, paid leave, meals or food allowance, holiday pay, marriage, child birth and death allowances, etc.[428]

1119. Some collective labour agreement clauses, on the other hand, appear to be mere repetitions of legal norms, that is, restatement of rules provided for by the Individual Labour Act No. 4857. This was encountered mostly in the agreements negotiated by unions with weaker bargaining power, particularly at the revival of

428. In fact, fringe benefits, both in terms of absolute numbers and proportionally, seem to have outweighed basic wages, a phenomenon frequently criticized by employer groups in recent years.

the free collective bargaining system in the early 1980s. In some cases, the management of certain issues is left to the discretion of the employer, occasionally with minor restrictions. For instance, the employer is accorded the right to change the job of the worker, but only for a temporary period and with no reduction in the employee's wages.

1120. In the wording of Article 2 of Act No. 2822, other aspects of employer––employee relations were also held to fall into the domain of the normative part, a point that was a controversial issue under Act No. 275 which tended to treat such relations under the obligatory particle. The present Act No. 6356 does not mention this element; it is reaffirmed, therefore, that 'other aspects of employer-employee relations' should be included in the normative part.[429]

1121. The participation of union members in various union–management committees, discipline and grievance committees, as well as the implementation of plant-level rules and regulations such as the control of the plant's entrance, the no-smoking rule, conduct of the day-care centres, cafeterias, bathrooms etc., which place certain obligations on the employer are examples in this category.

1122. Those clauses of the collective labour agreement concerning the termination of the individual employment contracts usually deal with the length of terms of notice, the payment of severance pay and restrictions on the employer's right to terminate the labour contract. Some collective labour agreements seem to lengthen the term of notice which the employer has to respect. Some provisions have restricted the number of contract termination categories which do not normally entitle the employee to severance pay and some are aimed at limiting the employer's right to terminate the employment contract for just cause, usually foreseeing the referral of the case to a joint disciplinary committee. However, the legal nature of such clauses has been a matter of controversy in practice.[430]

II. The Obligatory Part of the Collective Agreement

1123. As Article 2(1 h) indicates, the collective agreement 'may also contain clauses as to the mutual rights and obligations of the parties, application and supervision of the agreement and the peaceful settlement of disputes'. Thus, the obligatory part does not seem to be a necessary element for the formation of a collective agreement since the article carries the phrase 'may contain'. Obligatory provisions may be studied under two headings.

429. Nuri Çelik, *İş Hukuku Dersleri*, İstanbul: Beta, 26th edn, 2013, p. 529.

430. For discussions on whether or not recourse to a disciplinary committee envisaged for terminating the employment contract would fall within the scope of normative part, *see* Devrim Ulucan, *Temel Sorunlar Semineri*, Ankara, 1990, pp. 61–76.

A. Mutual Rights and Obligations of the Parties

1124. A significant aspect of mutual rights and obligations is usually implied in those clauses which foresee the execution of mutual duties in good faith. Of foremost importance among these is the 'peace obligation'. Since under the Act No. 275 of 1963 it was possible to resort to strike and/or lock-out action for rights disputes within the duration of a collective agreement, one could speak of the peace obligation only in relative terms in that period.

1125. Under the present system, however, 'peace obligation' is absolute as industrial conflict is permitted only for interest disputes, as borne out by the wording of the Constitution of 1982 and Act No. 2822 and 6356. Besides, the reopening of negotiations is not allowed even on topics which fall outside the scope of the collective agreement within its duration. It is a known fact, however, that the parties are free to include in the collective agreement clauses which foresee the revision of wages and fringe benefits within the life of the agreement; but in the context of the present legislation which forbids industrial action during the term the agreement, no strike or lock-out is allowed for disputes arising from the revision of such clauses.[431]

1126. Among other obligatory clauses of a collective labour agreement, one could cite the functions of union shop stewards regarding their obligation to maintain labour peace, the methods of conducting their functions and the operation of other committees established at the workplace.

B. Clauses Concerning the Application and Supervision of the Agreement and the Settlement of Disputes

1127. Most collective agreements in Turkey carry clauses regarding the application and supervision of the collective agreement. Grievance procedures governing the resolution of disputes which may arise from the interpretation or application of the agreement are examples of obligatory provisions in this category. The grievance mechanism, occasionally linked to clauses on disciplinary procedures, generally culminate at the final step in resort to private arbitration. Some agreements also cite the right to take the dispute to the labour court. The organizations which are party to the collective labour agreement are under an obligation to see to it that their members abide by its provisions. They may exert such informal sanctions on their members as influencing them psychologically, providing information or giving warnings; or they may apply direct legal sanctions which usually take the form of imposing fines or expulsion from membership.

431. Fevzi Şahlanan, *Toplu İş* Sözleşmesi, İstanbul, Banksis Yayınları, No. 70, 1992, p. 23.

III. The Legal Nature of the Collective Agreement

1128. The legal nature of the collective agreement is such that it combines both normative and contractual characteristics, the latter predicated on the law of obligations. This is also implied by Article 80(2) of Act No. 6356 which states that 'in the absence of any relevant provisions on the collective labour agreement in this Act, the provisions of the Civil Code No. 4721, the Code of Obligations No. 6098 and other laws pertaining to employment contracts, which are not contrary to this Act, shall apply'. The normative part of the collective agreement carries provisions bearing the characteristics of objective legal norms which do not exist in other types of contracts. Thus, the collective agreement is a unique contract subject to private law combining both normative and obligatory features.

§3. The Level and Structure of Collective Bargaining and the Collective Agreement

I. The Notion, Historical Development and the Present Framework

1129. According to Act No. 2822, a collective labour agreement could be concluded at the establishment (plant) level or it might cover more than one establishment. Depending on the required circumstances, the collective labour agreement could also be made at the enterprise (company) level. The law had thus repealed the industry-level collective labour agreement which existed under Act No. 275 of 1963. In the pre-1980 system, an establishment could be covered by two concurrent collective agreements, provided that one was concluded at the 'establishment' level and the other at industry level. But the question of the precedence of industry-wide *vis-à-vis* local establishment bargaining proved to be one of the most controversial issues throughout the 1960s and 1970s. Act No. 275 was not clear as to the precedence and content of these two types of agreements. The legality of a strike to be called at an establishment which was already subject to a local bargain but which the union aimed to subject to a new industry-wide agreement remained to be an unsettled issue and the judicial rulings on this issue were often contradictory. In practice, genuine industry-wide bargaining did not materialize in Turkey for various reasons, including inter-union rivalry, the difficulties encountered in gaining 'majority' status at the level of industry, the relatively undeveloped state of employers' unions and the legal problems caused by the overlapping of industry versus local-level agreements. Thus, the nucleus of collective bargaining was pitched at the local establishment level in Turkey. In order to consolidate this pre-existing structure and to do away with the various complications engendered by the dichotomy of industry-wide versus local-level agreements, Act No. 2822 attempted to simplify the bargaining structure, at least from a legalistic viewpoint, by removing the industry-wide agreements from the system altogether.

1130. The Constitution of 1982 did not bring any stipulation as to the level of collective bargaining. It simply stated that no more than one agreement could be made for an establishment at a given time span, meaning that the establishment should not be subject concurrently to more than one agreement for the same period, regardless of the level of bargaining (Article 53(3) the Turkish Constitution of 1982).

1131. The amendment to the Constitution on 7 May 2010 by Act No. 5982 has repealed this ban, possibly with a view to pave the way for a multi-layered bargaining structure in Turkey as revealed by the statement of reasons for the change, but the restriction still remains somewhat indirectly in Act No. 6356 through the wording of Article 34(1) dealing with the coverage and level of the collective labour agreement by saying that 'a collective labour agreement may cover more than one establishment in the same industry branch'.

1132. While devising the system of Act No. 2822, the legislature was certainly free to provide for either the industry-wide or establishment/plant-wide agreements, but there should be no possibility to subject the establishment to more than one agreement for a designated term. The main motive underpinning this now-repealed constitutional stipulation was in fact the elimination of multiple industrial actions and the maintenance of labour peace during the term of an existing agreement. In Act No. 2822, the preferred alternative of the legislature was the adoption of a single form of bargaining level, that of establishment(s) collective labour agreement, a version of which was to be the enterprise (company) collective labour agreement. According to Acts No. 2822 and 6356, however, if collective bargaining authorization for the next term is initiated within the 120 days before the expiration of the existing collective labour agreement according to Article 35(4), a new agreement may be concluded for the following term within the duration of an agreement, but it must not go into effect before the existing agreement expires.

1133. Article 34 of Act No. 6356 regulates the scope and level of collective labour agreements in the following manner: (1) A collective labour agreement may cover one or more than one establishment in the same industry branch (i.e., the latter to be construed also as meaning indirectly a 'group collective labour agreement' if the employers of establishments are affiliated to an employers' union). (2) In cases where there are more than one establishment belonging to a real person or corporate body or to a public institution or organization (i.e., 'enterprise'), the collective labour agreement may be made only at the enterprise level covering all the establishments concerned. (3) Provided the parties so agree, the 'group collective labour agreement' may be concluded between a labour union and employers' union with a view to cover establishments and enterprises belonging to more than one affiliated employer in the same industry branch. (4) Disputes as to whether or not the establishments shall be subject to an enterprise collective labour agreement shall be settled in fifteen days at the latest by the labour court where the centre of the enterprise is located. In the case of an appeal, the Court of Cassation shall settle the dispute with a definitive decision in fifteen days.

1134. As Act No. 6356 has given rise to a new type of agreement called the 'framework agreement', some exploratory remarks to shed light on this new concept seem to be a convenient point in studying the scope and level of bargaining in Turkey.

A. Framework Agreement

1135. As provided by Article 2 of Act No. 6356, the 'framework agreement' is the industry branch level agreement concluded between labour and employers' unions affiliated to the ESC The framework agreement may be made upon the invitation by one of the parties and for a duration of one year minimum and three years maximum, to apply to members of the signatory labour and employers' union; it may carry provisions concerning vocational training, occupational health and safety, social responsibility programs and employment policies. Thus, the conclusion of the framework agreement is based on the voluntary agreement of the parties, thereby not requiring any formal procedures and conditions. Apparently the extent to which a framework agreement shall be considered binding is a dubious matter, nor is certain its precedence over local, establishment and enterprise collective labour agreements. Legislation does not provide anything viable, i.e., arbitration, mediation or recourse to strike action in respect to how the agreement would be reached in the event of a labour dispute. As a matter of fact, legislation has carefully and deliberately avoided using the term 'collective labour agreement' for this category. One could safely argue that the legislature, so far unable to find answers to the aforementioned problems faced in the past to create a multi-layered bargaining structure, chose this option as a testing ground to pave the way for industry-wide bargaining. Whatever intention is involved, however, one might anticipate the likely emergence of certain dysfunctions hampering free collective bargaining by way of the framework agreement, like collusive arrangements between social partners against rival unions with a view to weaken genuine bargaining relationships in a sector. Given the fact that in the development of Turkish industrial relations, legislation rather than voluntarism has played the major role, one cannot make an optimistic estimate for the future success of the so-called framework agreement. Besides, the precondition that the framework agreement may be concluded only by labour and employer's unions affiliated to confederations represented in the ESC is likely to be a target for criticism at the ILO platforms.

II. Establishment(s), Multi-establishment (Enterprise) and Multiemployer (Group) Collective Labour Agreements (Group Bargaining)

1136. Act No. 2822 had provided that a 'collective labour agreement might cover one or more establishments within the same branch of activity'. Thus, an authorized union could make a collective labour agreement covering only one establishment, or it could conclude the collective agreement so as to cover more than one establishment concurrently belonging to different employers, provided it met the bargaining requirements in each of these establishments or enterprises. The latter form, that is, the multi-employer collective labour agreement, generally called the 'group agreement', had in fact become quite fashionable in Turkish practice in the pre-1980 era. Adhering to the notion of industry-wide bargaining and yet realizing the difficulties involved, some had even advocated the adoption of area-based multi-employer agreements as an intermediate stage in the transition from local to industry-wide bargaining.[432] As a matter of fact, regional multi-employer bargains which covered a segment of a certain industry could perform economic and social functions similar to those of genuine industry-wide agreements (i.e., the equalization of labour costs in the labour market, the realization of equal pay for work of equal value, standardization of working conditions throughout the industry and so on). This is particularly true when a union concludes several 'group agreements' so as to cover wider geographical areas. Indeed, successful 'group agreements' were concluded in the late 1970s along these lines in the metal-working and textile industries'.[433] However, a 'group agreement' does not necessarily have to cover only the employers of an industry in a specified area. If market conditions allow or require, broad-based group agreements cutting across wider geographical areas in an industry may also be concluded, especially when union structures and the organization of employers permit this type of multi-employer bargaining. In fact, although legislation had nowhere used the term 'group', this version of broad-based group agreements became quite fashionable in the post-1980 industrial relations of Turkey. Although this trend was prompted basically by employers, labour unions, though initially opposed to it, have tended to acknowledge, albeit reluctantly, some of the advantages associated with group bargaining for themselves as well.

1137. The structure of industry-based national unions envisaged by Act No. 2821 of 1983 seemed to lend itself rather easily to this kind of 'group bargaining'. Thus, the federations which existed mainly for the purpose of industry-wide bargaining were abolished and industry based (national) unions conducive both to local and group bargaining began playing an enhanced role in Turkish industrial relations. The growing importance of employers' unions in the post-1980 era, particularly their predominance in metal-working, food, textile, petroleum, rubber and petrochemicals, also contributed to the widening of bargaining territory.

1138. In Turkey, however, collective bargaining as defined from a strictly legal point of view is focused on the establishment level.[434] Nowhere had Act No. 2822 used the term 'group agreement'. A variation of this rule is the enterprise (undertaking, company) agreement, where the term enterprise denotes an entity comprised of multiple establishments (more than one) in the same industry belonging to an employer, a topic dealt with below in detail. Obviously, now (as well as in the past)

---

432. For a general evaluation of the structure of collective bargaining, *see* the paper in English by N. Süral, 'Evolving Structure of Collective Bargaining in Turkey (1990–2004)', to be published in *Middle Eastern Studies*.
433. Metin Kutal, 'Grup Toplu İşSözleşmeleri Hakkında Bazı Düşünceler', *İktisat ve Maliye*, Vol. XXVI, No. 2, May 1979, pp. 91–97.
434. Erdogan Çubukçu, 'Uygulamada Grup Toplu İşSözleşmesi Adı Verilen Birden Çok İşyerini Kapsayan Toplu İş Sözleşmesinin Toplu İş Hukukumuz Açısından Değ erlendirilmesi', *İHD*, Ekim-Arallık 1991, pp. 581–588.

the 'group collective labour agreement' may cover enterprises as well as independent establishments belonging to different employers in the same industry branch.

1139. The question of 'group agreement' has led to legal controversies in practice. According to the rulings of the Court of Cassation issued in 1986, 'the forms of collective agreements designated by Act No. 2822 are merely establishment and enterprise agreements; for this reason, it is not tolerable for a party to collective bargaining to compel the counter-party to enter into a group-based bargaining relationship; however, this does not preclude the parties from concluding group agreements by mutual agreement'. In the particular case the labour union had not shown willingness to enter into group bargaining.[435] This view, reiterated by the Court of Cassation in another case in 1988 and buttressed even further by its General Council upon the resistance of the lower court[436] was debated extensively in the teaching and practice of labour law.

1140. Critics of the High Court's view predicated their argument on the wording of Article 3(1) of Act No. 2822 which stated that the collective labour agreement might cover 'establishments' as well as a single establishment or enterprise', 'establishments' being construed to mean 'group' as a distinct level of bargaining. Moreover, according to the same critics, the labour union, certified as the bargaining agent for each establishment could force the employers' union to enter into a multi-establishment agreement by calling strikes concurrently after passing through the mediation stage. However, if the labour union did not comply with the employers' union's request for group bargaining, the latter would not be able to force the labour union to enter into group-level bargaining by resorting to lock-out actions because, according to Article 27 of Act No. 2822, the employer was not authorized to order 'lock-out' unless the union had called the strike.[437]

1141. Past legislation as well as some relevant court rulings are repeated here as they are still valid under Act No. 6356. The labour union, rather than forcing employers into a single 'group (multi-employer) bargaining', may choose to act in a number of alternative ways. Even in the event of the union having been granted bargaining certification for various establishments and employers, it may prefer to subgroup them, or choose to bargain with employers on an individual basis. If individual employers refuse to bargain, the labour union has the option to initiate separate disputes; thus, after passing through different mediation processes rather than working with a single mediator for the whole group, it may direct employers to making separate agreements, using the strike weapon if necessary.

1142. Self-evidently, a group collective labour agreement may be concluded by the parties only on a voluntary basis, that is, without one party compelling the other

435. Court of Cassation, 9th Div., 24 Apr. 1986, 3377/4325.
436. Court of Cassation, 9th Div., 18 Apr. 1988, 4524/4293; Ruling of the General Council of the Court of Cassation, 21 Dec. 1988, 9-695/1021.
437. K. Oğuzman, *Türkİş Mevzuatı Açısından Grup Toplu İşSözleşmeleri*, İstanbul, MESS Yayını, 1989, p. 6.

party to enter into a multi-employer bargain. If the labour union, for example, has obtained separate bargaining certificates for different establishments and/or enterprises, the parties may voluntarily agree to wind up making only a single agreement; or in the case of concurrent certifications covering more than one establishment or enterprise paving the way for group (multi-employer) bargaining, the parties may choose to subgroup them under different categories, or they may even convert the whole process into making individual collective labour agreements, entirely differentiated and individualized. Obviously, in such a case, they will be operating with different media And taking multiple strike decisions if necessary. Even in the event of a single comprehensive group agreement, the parties may differentiate certain items depending on the unique conditions of each establishment or enterprise. The only clarification brought by Act No. 6356 relates mainly to the condition that employers in the group collective labour agreement must be represented by an employers' union established in the same industry branch.

III. Enterprise Collective Labour Agreement

A. *The Notion*

1143. Enterprise level bargaining is a concept brought by the 1983 legislation. Act No. 2822 provided that 'in an undertaking belonging to a corporate body, corporation or a public organization or institution which has more than one establishment in the same branch of activity (industry) where the nature of work requires the transfer of employees from one establishment to another, only one collective agreement should be made covering all the establishments of the undertaking'. Such an agreement was to be referred to as the 'enterprise collective labour agreement' within the meaning of the Act.

1144. Due to the difficulties arising from the interpretation of the notion of 'work requiring the transfer of employees from one establishment to another', the wording of the Article was modified by Act No. 3299 in 1986. Thus, in its new form, the concept of the enterprise agreement became broader. Article 3(2) of Act No. 2822 provided that 'in an undertaking belonging to a real person, a corporate body or a public organization or institution which has more than one establishment in the same branch of activity, only one collective agreement shall be made covering all the establishments of the enterprise. Even where establishments belonging to public organizations or institutions have separate corporate status, they too shall be subject to the same, single enterprise agreement.'

1145. As provided by the Act and clarified by the rulings of the Court of Cassation,[438] the incorporation of different establishments and organizations with independent corporate status into the concept of a single 'enterprise' holds true only for

438. Court of Cassation, 9th Div., 17 Oct. 1986, 3383/9306; 7 Dec. 1990, 12748/12914.

public organizations and organizations. In other words, this is an exception which shall not be applicable in the case of corporate entities in the private sector.[439]

1146. It is worth noting that the enterprise agreement may not cover all the establishments belonging to the same employer. This category of collective labour agreement may be concluded to cover only those plants of the enterprise which fall into the same branch of activity (industry). When there is such an entity, the establishments may not be subject to separate bargaining certifications by the Ministry of Labour.

1147. Act No. 3299 passed in 1986 thus broadened the scope of enterprise agreements in various respects. First, in the private sector, the concept of enterprise is no longer limited to entities with a corporate status, that is, private employers as real persons are also subjected to such an agreement if they operate multiple establishments in the same industry. Second, the stipulation that transfer of employees amongst their various establishments (plants) be a requirement of the operations has been deleted from the Act, an amendment which both simplified and broadened the scope of the concept. Third, even those establishments belonging to public organizations and institutions with separate and different corporate status shall constitute an enterprise, provided they are active in the same industry.

1148. A controversial point concerning public organizations and institutions was the status of establishments, associated partnerships and participations which were designated by Executive Order No. 233 as subunits which constitute such public entities. While it is clear that establishments have separate corporate status, the situation of associated partnerships as to whether or not they fall under the concept of an enterprise has been the subject of conflicting judicial rulings. These are defined as corporations more than half of whose capital is owned by a SEE or by a public economic institution. In a ruling of the Court of Cassation passed in 1986, the associated partnership was held to fall within the scope of the enterprise, as the share and managerial influence of the public was considerable.[440] However, in a different verdict issued in 1990, the Court of Cassation ruled that it would not make sense to treat them within the boundaries of an enterprise since they have been subjected to the principles of private law with a General Directorate of their own; besides, no mention has been made of the associated partnership in the pertinent Act No. 3299. Yet in the same ruling of the High Court, viewed from the standpoint of Executive Order No. 233, associated partnerships should not be included in the scope of the enterprise agreement due to their unique nature and legal status.[441]

1149. In the teaching, however, because the majority of capital is furnished by the state, it is held that the 'associated partnership' should be viewed within the meaning of Article 3(3).[442] In other words, associated partnerships of SEEs should

439. Court of Cassation, 9th Div., 9 Feb. 1990, 1719/1242.
440. Court of Cassation, 9th Div., 17 Oct. 1986, 8383/9306.
441. Court of Cassation, 9th Div., 17 Dec. 1990, 12748/12914.
442. Court of Cassation, 9th Div., 17 Dec. 1990, 12748/12914.

be covered by the same enterprise agreement in cases where they are operating in the same industry as other establishments, etc., regardless of the different and independent corporate status which they may possess.[443]

1150. The 'participations' of the SEEs are not to be construed within the meaning of Article 3/II, however, as they are corporations where SEEs or their associated partnerships have a share of between 15% and 50% of the capital.[444]

B. Disputes Concerning Enterprise Collective Labour Agreements

1151. Any disputes arising from ascertaining whether or not the establishments concerned constitute an enterprise within the meaning of the Act shall be decided by the local labour court where the centre of the enterprise is located within fifteen days. In the event of an appeal, the Court of Cassation shall give a final ruling within fifteen days. Following the amendment by Act No. 3299 alluded to above; the number of such disputes has tended to drop.

1152. A serious controversy has arisen, however, with respect to strike and lock-out restrictions in certain industries and sub-branches of industries, set out in articles dealing with strike bans. There seemed to be considerable ambiguity as to how the collective agreement would have been concluded where one or several establishments within the scope of an enterprise were subject to strike and lock-out prohibitions; this means that the dispute, after mediation had failed, should be settled through compulsory arbitration in such establishments while in the rest the employees might enjoy the right to strike As it was stipulated that in an enterprise comprised of establishments in the same industry, only one agreement should materialize.

1153. According to one opinion, if recourse has been made to compulsory arbitration[445] (that is, the YHK) for the settlement of the dispute in the no-strike workplaces, the award of the YHK would be binding for the whole enterprise and the strike and/or lock-out, if called in the remaining establishments, would have to be halted.[446] This view was criticized on the grounds of its denying the constitutionally guaranteed right to strike to employees who should otherwise enjoy it in the settlement of their disputes. Another opinion asserted that the strike and the no-strike plants should be treated separately as independent units. This view was also refuted because it ran counter to the indivisible unity of the 'enterprise agreement' in Turkish law.[447] Besides, there is no concept of 'bargaining unit' in Turkish labour law. It has also been suggested that the dispute should go to the YHK if more

443. Fevzi Şahlanan, *supra*, pp. 37–38.
444. *Ibid.*
445. That is, the Supreme Arbitration Board.
446. S. Reisoğlu, *2822 No lu Toplu İş Sözleşmesi, Grev, ve Lokavt Kanunu Şerhi*, Ankara, 1986, pp. 277–278.
447. M. Ekonomi, 'İşletme Toplu İşSözleşmeleri ve Uygulamada Karşılaşılan Başllıca Sorunlar', *Kamu-İş, Cilt* 1, No. 1, 1987, pp. 20–21.

than half of the employees in the enterprise as a whole are employed in those plants subject to strike bans; otherwise, the dispute should be settled through resort to the strike action.[448] Yet, such a numerical solution was not found acceptable either.[449] Another proposed solution was the exercise of the strike action in those plants where strikes were permissible and then the application of the settlement to the whole enterprise.[450] And yet, since either party is free to make application to the YHK in the event of a dispute in the no-strike sectors, the employer is very likely to make this application to initiate the compulsory arbitration process. Besides, the union may have very few members in those plants where the strike is permissible and therefore, this option may not be a viable one in those cases where the union's strike power is weak.

1154. The Court of Cassation, in its decision upholding a lower court ruling, adopted a solution aimed at combining the settlement reached through the strike action with the binding decision of the YHK for the no-strike workplaces, thus adhering to the principle of 'one collective agreement for the whole enterprise'.[451] Yet, the Court's solution seemed fraught with legal complications and controversy. As in the other ambiguous areas where the judiciary has failed to find a viable solution, a legislative amendment is needed to bring clarity to this issue. One possible remedy could be providing the labour union with the option of choosing one of the two alternatives well in advance, that of preferring either the strike route or the compulsory arbitration option, possibly before the commencement of negotiations.

1155. In an attempt to find a solution to this problem, several draft bills prepared have proposed to amend the law in a manner to allow strike action in those establishments of the enterprise for which no such strike restrictions have been envisaged. The collective agreement concluded pursuant to negotiations or strike and/or lock-out action, shall then apply to all the establishments which constitute the enterprise.

1156. Obviously in the event the ownership of one of the plants (establishments) belonging to the same employer is transferred to another employer, it shall no longer fall into the scope of the enterprise agreement to be concluded with the employer who has sold it off. In a verdict of the Court of Cassation, however, the employer who had taken over one of the plants of a mining company was treated as a contractor performing certain tasks for the principal employer and in so doing, engaging workers on behalf of the latter. Relying on Article 1(5) of the Labour Act No. 1475 – which stated that where a subcontractor operated a certain section of the establishment the principal employer and the subcontractor are to be held jointly liable for the obligations ensuing from the Labour Act or from the employment contracts of the employees employed by the subcontractor working exclusively in the

448. C. Tuncay, *Çimento İşveren Dergisi*, Eylül, 1988, p. 19.
449. N. Çelik, *İş Hukuku Dersleri*, İstanbul, 2004, pp. 521–522.
450. F. Şahlanan, *Toplu İş Sözleşmesi*, İstanbul, Banksis Yayınları, No. 70, 1992, pp. 40–42.
451. Court of Cassation, 9th Div., 13 Jul. 1990, 7963/8221.

establishment concerned – the Court ruled that the plant in question should be subject to the same enterprise agreement covering the company of the principal employer.[452] The Court's treating the buyer employer as a subcontractor subject to the management and control of the seller company was criticized by various writers.[453]

1157. Considering the existing ambiguities on this matter, Article 38 of Act No. 6356 has envisaged, in three alternatives, a novel but perhaps not satisfactory improvisation on the transfer of the establishment within the scope of an enterprise agreement or one of its sections to another employer. Here on this matter, Article 38(1) says: in the transfer of an establishment or a section thereof to another employer, rights and obligations emanating from the collective labour agreement which was in force in the transferred establishment(s) shall continue as employment contracts if the transferee employer has already a collective labour agreement effective in the establishment(s) in the same industry branch. If there is no collective labour agreement effective in the establishment(s) of the transferee employer, rights and obligations arising from the collective labour agreement effective at the transferred establishment shall continue as collective labour agreement terms until a new collective labour agreement is made. As a third alternative Article 38(2) provides: 'In the transfer of an establishment not covered by any collective labour agreement to an employer who is the signatory party to an enterprise collective labour agreement, the transferred establishment shall come under the scope of the enterprise agreement.'

§4. Competence and Authorization for Collective Bargaining

I. The Notion and Controversy

1158. Labour and employers' unions established in compliance with the requirements set out in Act No. 6356 are competent bodies which can conclude collective labour agreements. Confederations are not competent to be a party to the collective labour agreement. A natural outcome of the concept 'freedom of association' is 'union pluralism' or 'rival unionism', concepts which bring up the question of determining which union shall be empowered to bargain on behalf of the workers in a given establishment. This process referred to as 'authorization' for concluding the collective agreement or for collective bargaining has been perhaps the most crucial issue in shaping the character of industrial relations in Turkey since the inception of collective bargaining in Turkey in 1963. There were even times back in the 1970s when, owing to the complications faced in practice, authorization for collective bargaining was determined as a last resort by calling on workers' open declarations' or

452. Court of Cassation, 9th Div., 17 Apr. 1992, 11139/64359.

453. N. Çelik, 'Türk İşHukukunda Asıl İşveren-Alt İşveren İlişkilerinden Doğan Bazı Uygulama Sorunları', *Münir Ekonomi Armağ anı*, Kamu-İş, pp. 163–178; T. Canbolat, *İHD*, Nisan-Haziran 1993, pp. 263–272.

'election by secret ballot' under the supervision of the labour judge or the competent authority.[454] While the 1963 legislation had foreseen only one criterion for the labour union to be authorized, 1983 law, Act No. 2822, mainly for the sake of lowering the high number of labour unions, required the co-existence of two thresholds, the so-called the basic unit of bargaining is an unacceptable condition which hamper free collective bargaining double criteria' whereby, in order for the labour union to be authorized for collective bargaining at any establishment or enterprise, it had first to represent a minimum of 10% of workers working in the industry branch concerned and then second, more than half of the workers in the establishment or enterprise to be covered.

1159. Based on the premise that any numerical thresholds or structural affiliations above and beyond, the so-called double criteria had become the subject of heated debates in national and international fora since the early 1980s. In spite of the ILO's and EU's continued insistence on the abolition of the double criteria, Act No. 6356 turned out to be even more conservative than the approach taken by a few earlier draft bills, a preference reflecting the built-in bias of the parties to shield themselves against the unknowns of what they traditionally called 'union inflation', especially of the government and employers and even some labour unions.

1160. Prior to the passage of Act No. 6356, collective bargaining seemed to have reached a deadlock in some sectors as various unions had lost their authorization status owing largely to their failure to meet the industry branch representativeness threshold. In fact, coupled with the effects of globalization, neo-liberal policies, restrictive measures of the 1983 legislation and increased foreign competition, union density seems to have dropped drastically in Turkey. Although ratios showing membership density vary depending on the type of base figures used, of the roughly 12 million wage and salary earners in private and public sectors combined, only about 10% were unionized by the year 2012, displaying a drop of almost 40% during the last decade.[455] This was a clear justification of how right and fair the ILO was over the years for its insistence on the abolition of the 'double criteria'. Even if the industry branch threshold was fixed at 1%, it was estimated that, out of the 51 unions meeting the 10% threshold at the time of the passage of Act No. 6356, ten would lose their authorization status.

1161. Collective bargaining can materialize only between two competent parties, namely a labour union and an employer, employers or an employers' union established in the industry branch to which the establishments to be covered by the collective agreement belong.

1162. The establishments of the employer in the same industry constituting the enterprise are regarded as an integrated unit and the majority status is to be

454. *See* T. Dereli, 'Toplu Sözleşme Yetkisini Saptama Yolları ve Oylama Yöntemi', *Sosyal Siyaset Konferansları*, Vol. 28, 1976, pp. 28–46.

455. Onur Bakır and Deniz Akdoğan, 'Türkiye'de Sendikalaşma ve Özel Sektörde Sendikal Örgütlenme', Iss, 383, Türk-İş Dergisi, 90 (2009).

calculated on the basis of that integrated whole, regardless of the number of members in each establishment of the enterprise.

1163. In determining the majority status of the union, it is held that all employees, including the sales personnel in the field, those employed on a part-time, on call, temporary or seasonal basis, employees posted to another employer on a temporary basis as well as those who are legally prohibited to join unions are taken into account. Managers who act as employer's representative in collective negotiations are to be included. To be excluded are the employer's representative who manages the whole enterprise and persons in the public servant and contract employee status if there are any. The non-covered employees are also included and counted although in the past the Court of Cassation had held paradoxically that they should not be counted.[456] Inclusion of the employees of the subcontractor was a controversial matter. It was generally asserted that the employees of the subcontractor devoted exclusively to the principal employer's establishment were to be counted if they worked in the same industry as the regular workers of the establishment.[457] However, with the clarification of the principal employer-subcontractor relationship by Act No. 4857, employees of the subcontractor are no longer to be considered.

1164. Originally Articles 41 to 45 of Act No. 6356 addressed the issue of authorization for collective bargaining. Article 41(1) posited the basic rule that 'provided a labour union represents as members a minimum of 3% of employees working in the industry branch where it has been set up, it shall be authorized to conclude the establishment-level collective labour agreement if it also represented more than half of the employees in that establishment, or a minimum of 40% of the employees in the enterprise concerned. So, the industry branch threshold was set at 3%. 'In determining the 3% ratio of the employees working in an industry branch, the statistics published by the Ministry in January and July of each year shall serve as the basis.' In these statistics figures of the Social Security Institution shall be taken into consideration. These statistics shall show the total number of employees and members of labour unions in each industry branch. The said statistics shall be valid for collective labour agreement and related procedures until the publication of new statistics. 'The authorization status of the union which has made an application to receive the authorization certificate or which has already received that certificate shall not be affected by the statistics which are published afterwards (Article 41(5)).[458] The statistics not contested within fifteen days of their publication shall become final and binding. 'An application challenging the accuracy of the statistics may be made to the Labour Court of Ankara within this period. The court shall finalize the objection

456. Court of Cassation, 9th Div., 22 May 1997, 6968/9701; 16 Feb. 2004, 14444/14989; 17 Feb. 2004, 2660/2673. The workers who are currently in the establishment during the process of authorization are also included (15 Sep. 2006, 21611/22886).

457. The Court of Cassation has passed contradictory judgments on this point. Court of Cassation, 9th Div., 26 Nov. 1993, 15308/17400; 7 Dec. 1993, 16138/18206.

458. The system aims to speed up the process. Therefore objection to a union's industry branch jurisdiction just before or during the authorization process is an abusive exercise of a right, i.e., or contrary to law, a violation of the principle of 'bargaining in good faith' in other words. Court of Cassation, 9th Div., 16 Feb. 2022, 1166/1823.

within fifteen days. The Court's decision may be appealed by those concerned as well as by the Ministry. The court of Cassation shall finalize the requested appeal with a binding decision in fifteen days' (Article 41(6)).

1165. In transitional articles annexed to Act No. 6356 the industry branch threshold was foreseen to apply as 1% until the year 2016 and as 2% until the year 2018 to result in 3% at the ultimate stage. But it was already known that even the 1% threshold could hinder free collective bargaining seriously. Further, the application of transitional provisions only to certain unions, i.e., those affiliated to confederations represented in the ESC, is a controversial matter in view of ILO's principles on freedom of association. Had the industry branch representation criterion been definitely eliminated after a specified transitional period, ILO criticisms could be alleviated, at least partially.[459]

1166. Owing to reactions of labour unions and academic circles to the 3% threshold which is likely to hinder collective bargaining rights of workers in many sectors, Act No. 6552 of 10 September 2014 (the so-called bag law) reduced the ratio of representation to 1%. Article 20 of Act No. 6552 now provides that 'the ratio of 3 per cent cited in Article 41(1 and 5) as well as in Article 43(2 and 4) has been changed to 1 per cent'. Yet, considering the new base figures in industry branches due to the larger Social Security coverage as well as to projected mergers among industry branches, the 1 per cent ratio seems destined to cause the loss of collective bargaining authorization status for about 10 of the existing 51 labour unions meeting the threshold. Still further, in view of Article 21 of Act No. 6552 the annex Article 1 to Act No. 6356 foresees that the said ratio shall still be '3 per cent for labour unions not affiliated to the Economic and Social Council', a rule open to serious criticism in national and international circles on grounds of its alleged infringement on the principles of equal treatment and freedom of association.

1167. As Act No. 6552 has set the industry branch ratio presently at 1% level definitely, Article 146(f) has repealed the transitional Article 6(1) of Act No. 6356 which had foreseen varying ratios for certain unions to be effective in different years.

1168. Another novelty in the Article is the reduction of the second criterion for only 'enterprise level bargaining' from 50 plus 1 to 40%. For the enterprise collective labour agreement 40% representation shall be computed by considering the establishments within the scope of the enterprise as an integrated whole, Article 41(2).'If more than one labour union meet the 40% or more majority at the enterprise, the labour union having the highest number of members on the date of its application shall be granted authorization for collective bargaining' (Article 41(3)).

459. Metin Kutal, 'İnsan Haklarına İlişkin Uluslararası Çalışma Sözleşmeleri Işığında Türk Hukukunda Örgütlenme ve Toplu Pazarlık Hakları', *Sicil İş Hukuku Dergisi*, No. 143, March 2013. For estimates on the possible effects of alternative schemes relating to industry branch thresholds, *see* 'Sendikalar ve Yetki Sorunu Raporu-2', *DİSK Araştırma Enstitüsü*, 7 Ekim 2012.

1169. It should be noted that, although industry branch threshold is now 1%, given the size of the basic figures as denominator which will now include workers under social security coverage, rather than workers communicated to the Ministry by employers as in the previous system, plus considering the projected mergers among industry branches, the industry branch threshold may be estimated to be now still roughly the equivalent of a real ratio of 10–15%. Under these circumstances, like the 10% ratio of the previous system, the 1% ratio is likely still to result in the loss of collective bargaining rights for many labour unions.

II. Authorization Process

1170. The process of authorization for collective labour agreement begins with the application of the labour union to the Ministry with a request to have its authorization status verified. 'An employer's union is authorized to conclude the collective labour agreement for the establishment or establishments belonging to its affiliated employers; an employer not affiliated to the employers' union is also authorized to conclude a collective labour agreement for his own establishment(s).' Also, in an attempt to have the authorized labour union identified, the employers' union or a non-union employer may apply to the Ministry. Upon the verification of the labour union's authorization status based on the Ministry's records, the Ministry shall communicate within six working days the said application as well as the number of workers and union members at the establishment or enterprise to the labour unions in the same industry branch as well as to the relevant employers' union or the non-union employer (Article 42 (1,2)). The intention here is to ascertain whether or not an objection to the union's application is likely to come from rival unions or the employer. If it is found that the applying union does not meet the required conditions or that there is no labour union meeting the conditions, the relevant information shall be forwarded only to the union which has made the application (Article 42(3)). This is a point for criticism in the teaching.

1171. Employees for whom notices for social insurance status have not been given to the Social Security Institution on due time shall not be considered in determining the authorized union. This is one of the drawbacks of holding social security figures as the base in the authorization process, meaning that most workers in the informal economy will be denied access to free collective bargaining. A worker working in the informal sector is, by definition an employee who can legally join a labour union, but as most workers in the unregistered sector do not carry a social security number, union attempts to organize them will be in vain in terms of access to freedom of association, a dilemma running counter to the unions' goal of fighting informal employment by organizing unregistered workers. Besides, a worker also needs to have a social security number to join the labour union through the e-State portal.

1172. Following the intervention by the Ministry comes the second stage, i.e., the judicial process involving the unions' or employer's objection to the Ministry's determination.

1173. The labour or the employers' union or the unaffiliated (non-union) employer that has received the communication sent in view of Article 42 may file with the court an objection within six working days and claim that one or both of the parties do not meet the required conditions or that it itself is qualified for authorization (Article 43(1)). In this case, a dispute referred as 'the authorization dispute' is deemed to have begun. The labour union whose membership is less than 1% of the workers in the industry branch cannot make an objection. If the court's decision is appealed, the Court of Cassation shall announce its binding and definitive ruling in fifteen days (Article 43(1,2,3)).

1174. Act No. 2822 was silent on the outcome of a negative reply by the court to the request of the applying union. In the past, this void was filled by court decisions. Now Article 43(4) provides the following:

> The labour union which has been informed by the Ministry that it fails to meet the required conditions in view of Article 42 (2) may file suit with the labour court within six working days. The court shall communicate the initiated suit to labour unions which represent a minimum of 1% of workers employed in the relevant industry branch. The court shall finalize the case within two months. The labour union's objection shall suspend the authorization process until the court's final and definitive decision (Article 43(5)).

1175. The focal point in the authorization process is providing the labour union with an authorization certificate. 'If within the time limit no objection was filed against the Ministry's notification relating to the labour union's authorization, or if an objection was filed and yet turned down, or in the case of an objection by the labour union contesting the initial refusal of the Ministry to grant authorization, upon the approval of the court which rules that the union meets the required qualifications, the labour union shall be given a certificate of authorization by the Ministry within six working days' (Article 44).

1176. Though the law holds that statistics published subsequent to the certification process shall not affect the 1% representativeness status of the union, the Court of Cassation has ruled that, with a view to uncovering the true situation, the authorities are entitled to scrutinize and evaluate all the required data and documents.[460]

1177. The double criteria and specifically the requirement of 10% representation at the branch level had been subject to repeated criticisms by the ILO Committee of Experts on grounds of alleged violation of Convention No. 98. Several draft bills of the recent past had reduced the said ratio to 5%, 1% or even to 0.05%, moves which will likely fail to satisfy the ILO since they still maintain the double

460. Court of Cassation, 9th Div., 24 Sep. 1990, 10132/9595.

criteria.[461] Taking all the controversy over the double criteria and the falling of various major unions below the 1% threshold recently, the abrogation of the industry (branch) level representativeness requirement in an amendment to Act No. 6356 is advisable.

1178. An employers' union has the power to conclude a collective agreement covering all the establishments owned by the employers belonging to that employers' union. And any employer who is not a member of an employers' union is empowered to enter into a collective agreement with a labour union covering the establishment or the enterprise belonging to him. Thus, the competent party is either the employers' union or the employer not affiliated with an employers' union. The employer, if he is a member of an employers' union, is not allowed to enter into an agreement with the labour union independent of the employers' union with which he is affiliated. Likewise it is the employers' union that can act as defendant or plaintiff in the lawsuits concerning the member employer.

1179. Once the Ministry's determination based on membership register at the time of the application by the labour union or the employer has been made, subsequent drops in the union's membership figures do not adversely affect the union's bargaining rights.[462] Negotiations must continue and further steps respected even though changes might occur in membership at later stages. The law has thus had to fixate a certain point in time in order for the system to function smoothly.

1180. Any labour union or employers' union or an unaffiliated employer that receives the information communicated may lodge an appeal with the labour court within six working days after the receipt of such communication. The labour court is the one at the locality of the regional directorate of labour where the establishment is registered. With that appeal, it may contest the authorization of one or both of the parties or assert that it does have the required majority. This appeal must also indicate the reasons involved. If collective bargaining concerns establishments under the jurisdiction of more than one regional directorate of labour, the appeal must be made to the labour court in Ankara. An appeal concerning an enterprise-level agreement must be made to the court at the location where the centre of the enterprise is located. The appeal must first be registered with the relevant regional directorate of labour or the Ministry of Labour and then lodged with the labour court. The Court of Cassation has ruled that in the event of contravention of these legal requirements or after the lapse of the six working days' time limit, the appeal must be turned down by the labour court.[463]

461. Since the statistics affect all the unions interested, the appeal must be directed not only against the Ministry but also against other unions active in the branch (Court of Cassation, 9th Div., 10 Jun. 1999, 9533/10565).

462. Decision of the General Council of the Court of Cassation, 4 Nov. 1992, 9-469/639; 9th Div., 14 Oct. 1999, 15658/15844.

463. Court of Cassation, 9th Div., 10 Nov. 1989, 9545/9685.

1181. Furthermore, according to the last sentence annexed to Article 15(1) by the 1988 amendment with Act No. 3451, labour unions which do not meet the 'minimum representation requirement' in the respective industry branch are not entitled to make an appeal for authorization. This provision intended to stave off unnecessary appeals has been criticized for allegedly violating union freedoms.[464]

1182. On appeals concerning time limits or material error, the court must reach a final decision within six working days without a hearing. The court must hold a hearing on any other appeal and take a decision. If the court's decision after the hearing is appealed, the Court of Cassation must give a final ruling within fifteen days. Appeal to the court suspends the procedures to fix authorization until the final ruling. In cases where an appeal has been made on the accuracy of the statistics concerning the industry branch representation (the Court of Cassation has ruled that the case on the authorization dispute is not to begin until the trial on the accuracy of the statistics has been finalized).[465]

1183. In the event of a determination made by the Ministry of Labour, an appeal concerning an enterprise level collective-agreement must be made to the labour court at the location of the centre of the enterprise Disputes may arise, however, during the authorization process at the establishment level, whereby it may be claimed that the establishment in question is part of an enterprise belonging to the employer who owns other establishments in the same industry. In such cases the local labour court may be required to defer the settlement until the determination as to the nature of the 'enterprise' is finalized.[466] The Court of Cassation has ruled, however, that, due to the mandatory nature of the provisions on enterprise-level agreement, the judge investigating the authorization dispute must first, directly and personally, scrutinize the issue to determine if in the case under review there is the likelihood of an enterprise-level entity.[467]

III. Authorization Certificate

1184. If no appeal has been lodged, the Ministry issues a certificate of authorization to the union concerned after the expiry of the time limit allowed for an appeal, or in the case of an appeal, within six working days of receiving notice of the court's decision if the court has rejected the contestant's appeal. Having access to the certificate of authorization is pivotal to the implementation of the collective bargaining function.

1185. Due to the various complications resulting from inaccurate statistics and false membership notifications by unions, authorization for collective bargaining

464. Mesut Gülmez, *Sendikal Hakların Uluslararası Kuralları ve Türkiye*, Ankara, 1988, p. 442.
465. Court of Cassation, 9th Div., 19 Aug. 1993, 11862/12220; 15 Jun. 1995, 20983/21992.
466. K. Oğuzman, *Hukuki YöndenİşçiİşverenİlişkileriLi*, İstanbul, 1984, p. 41; Çelik, *supra.*
467. Court of Cassation, 9th Div., 23 Mar. 1990, 2093/1797; Eahlanan agrees with the opinion of the Court of Cassation. *See* F. Şahlanan, *supra*, p. 74.

has always been a much-debated issue in Turkish practice. Confronted with various criticisms, the authorities searched in the late 1970s for alternative ways as the last resort, such as election by secret ballots or open declarations of mind by the employees as the last resort.[468] However, due to their alleged incompatibility with the existing system – which is based on unions' representation through registered memberships, these proposals and even *de facto* practices could not be incorporated into legislation. Nevertheless, the controversy still prevails. Election by secret ballot (the so-called referendum in Turkish) is at present advocated as a preferred alternative by DİSK.

§5. Nullity of the Collective Agreement

1186. Where a collective agreement has been concluded without a certificate of authorization, the nullity of the collective labour agreement, if alleged by one or both of the parties that the required condition have not been met, the Ministry of Labour or any interested party may lodge an appeal with the labour court within forty-five days of its determining that no valid authorization certificate exists, claiming that the agreement should be declared null and void. The competent court is the one at the locality of the regional directorate of labour where the establishment is registered. If the collective agreement covers establishments under the jurisdiction of more than one regional directorate, the appeal must then be made to the labour court in Ankara. The court may also suspend the application of the collective labour agreement until the finalization of court proceedings (Article 44). To safeguard the interests of workers, nullity does not take effect retroactively. But, in all these cases, the judge, upon request or at his own discretion, may suspend the execution of the collective agreement until a decision to that effect is taken.

§6. Invitation to Collective Negotiations and the Process of Negotiations

I. Invitation to Bargaining

1187. Following the finalization of the union's bargaining status for an establishment or establishments or for an enterprise, the negotiation process must begin. The labour union or an employers' union or an employer not affiliated to an employers' union that receives the Ministry's communication determining the unions' authorization, or the certificate of authorization, must issue an invitation to meet for collective negotiations to the other party within fifteen days of receipt of the communication or the certificate. The date of invitation shall be communicated to the

468. T. Dereli, 'Toplu Sözleşme Yetkisini Saptama Yolları ve Oylama Yöntemi', *Sosyal Siyaset KonferanslarK*, Vol. 18, İstanbul, 1977, pp. 75–76; M. Kutal, 'Toplu Sözleşme Yetkisinin Saptanmasında İşçilerin Oyuna BaşvurulmasıL Sistemi', *İktisat ve Maliye Dergisi*, February 1976, pp. 481–482.

competent authority by the inviting party (Article 46(1)). If invitation is not made within this period, the authorization certificate (of the labour union) shall become invalid (Article 46(2)).

1188. Within six working days from the date the invitation is delivered to the other party, the date, place and time of negotiations must be fixed between the parties and the competent authority shall be so informed. In the absence of such agreement, the competent authority shall, upon the request of either party, immediately fix the date, place and time of the first meeting and notify the parties accordingly (Article 47(1)). If the labour union does not attend the first meeting within thirty days of the invitation date or fails to start negotiations within the same time period, its (labour union's) authorization status shall become void. The inviting party is under the obligation to enclose all proposals and demands it wants to put forward in the collective negotiations. In other words, the piecemeal approach in negotiations is not possible. 'However, due to the logic of bargaining, during the negotiations the parties are free to make changes in their respective proposals and counter proposals' (Article 46(3)).

II. Negotiations

1189. As was the case under Act No. 2822, 'the duration of negotiations shall be 60 days from the date of the first meeting' according to Act No. 6356, Article 47(3). Due to the logic of bargaining, the new Act, like the old one, did not foresee any specific rules on the conduct of negotiations. In practice, the parties follow the general bargaining tactics developed in the industrial relations systems of democratic countries. A statistical survey made on unions' bargaining behaviour in Turkey has revealed that of the four main criteria employed by labour unions on wage negotiations i.e., cost of living increases, comparable wages, ability to pay (profits) and productivity, the criterion 'comparable wages' tops the list.[469]

1190. The process begins with the parties' presenting their authorization documents to each other. The first meeting deals with deciding on policy issues, methodical and procedural aspects of negotiations, the dates on which successive meetings should be held, etc. Then negotiations on proposals and counterproposals pick up; controversial items perceived as being too difficult to settle are generally postponed to subsequent meetings. Items on which agreement is reached are recorded and co-signed at the end of each meeting. One problem which had plagued the previous system was the extremely prolonged nature of negotiations, but with the imposition of new time limits the violation of which entails the forfeiture of bargaining rights as well as the requirement that the negotiations stage may last only up to sixty days, unreasonable delays in the bargaining process seem to have been headed off under

469. Y.P. Soykut Sarıca, *Wage Determination under Collective Bargaining: Inflation, Productivity and Profitability Relationships – An Empirical Study on Relations Between Inflation, Productivity and Profitability* (VDM 2008).

the present system. The fact that Act Nos 2822 and 6356 have both enabled the parties to initiate the authorization and bargaining process 120 days before the expiration of the existing agreement has also been instrumental in speeding up the bargaining process.

1191. Looking back at the parties' behaviour at most bargaining tables of the 1970s as well as the predominantly neo-liberal times of the 1980s, one can safely argue that collective bargaining was heavily of the 'distributive' type rather than 'integrative'. Although with the weakening of union power during the last two decades, the highly strike-prone years may seem to be a phenomenon of the past, even issues. Even where an integrative approach was expected to prevail (i.e., formation of joint committees, grievance mechanisms, etc.), the attitudes were basically still conflictual rather than cooperative. The fragmentation and rivalry among unions have had a paralysing effect on social dialogue in collective bargains, influenced also by economic factors (e.g., the excessively high rates of inflation during the 1970s), as well as cultural (e.g., the distorted and stereotyped perceptions of the social partners for each other). The absence of formal participative schemes (e.g., co-determination, works councils) may be another factor accounting for the predominantly distributive character of collective negotiations in Turkey.

1192. Certainly after the formal sixty-day negotiations stage is exhausted, negotiations may continue through the mediation and strike-lock-out-stages, until the date on which a final settlement is reached on all disputed items and this is usually the case in most tough bargaining cases. The fact of the matter is that, with the introduction of the above-mentioned provisions, the interminable length of negotiations which lingered on long after the termination of the existing collective agreement has now been considerably shortened.[470]

1193. As provided by a ruling of the Court of Cassation, the moving of the establishment to a different location during collective negotiations should not preclude the conclusion of the collective agreement, provided there was no change in the nature of the establishment for which authorization was obtained.[471]

1194. Negotiations have also an impact on the definition of the concept, employer's representative', that is, in addition to 'employer's representative' as defined in Article 2 (1 e) of Act No. 6356, any person acting as a party to a collective agreement or representing the employer during collective bargaining shall be deemed to be an employer' (for the purposes of this Act) (Article 39(7)).

470. For the changing nature of negotiation tactics over the years, *see* N. Süral, 'The Evolving Structure of Collective Bargaining', *supra*.
471. Court of Cassation, 9th Div., 13 Jul. 1987, 7421/7183.

Chapter 6. Main Features of Collective Labour Agreements

§1. The Nature and Characteristics of the Collective Labour Agreement

I. The Form and Change in the Collective Labour Agreement

1195. Upon reaching an agreement on all the items during negotiations or at the mediation or the strike–lock-out stage, the collective agreement is concluded in written form. Written form is a condition of validity.

1196. The collective labour agreement may be made for a minimum period of one year and a maximum period of three years. The duration of the collective labour agreement may not be extended or shortened by the parties after it has been signed, nor may it be terminated before the expiration of the agreed upon term. In activities which last less than one year, the duration of the collective labour agreement may be shorter than one year. If the work is not completed, such an agreement shall be in force till the end of the one-year period' (Article 35(2,3)). 'Application for a fresh collective bargaining authorization may be made within the 120 days prior to the expiry of the existing agreement' (Article 35(4)).

1197. Though the Act is silent as to whether or not changes can be made during the life of the collective agreement, it is generally held that the parties are free to modify it by mutual agreement.[472] Modification of the collective labour agreement must also be made in written form. By written form is meant 'ordinary written form'. Three copies of the collective agreement must be delivered to the competent authority and one copy must be posted at the establishment. Non-observance of these requirements does not affect the validity of the collective agreement.[473]

1198. Article 37 deals with the change in the status of the parties as it relates to the validity of the collective labour agreement. 'The loss of legal corporate status of the union signatory to the collective labour agreement or suspension of the union's activities as well as the loss of the union's bargaining authorization status and the change of the employer or the industry branch to which the establishment covered belongs shall not cause the termination of the collective labour agreement' (Article 37(1)).

II. The Binding Effect of the Collective Agreement on the Employer Affiliated with an Employers' Union

1199. Unlike the pre-1983 legislation, Act No. 2822 and 6356 have strengthened the position of the employers' union *vis-à-vis* the member employers. Article

472. K. Oğuzman, *Hukuki Yönden İşçi-İşveren İlişkileri*, İstanbul, 1984, p. 95.

473. M. Ekonomi, 'Toplu İş Sözleşmesinin Niteliğ i, Hükümleri, Uygulama Alanı ve Sona Ermesi', *Yargıtay Kararlarının Değ erlendirilmesi Semineri*, Aralık, 1984, Ankara, pp. 63–64.

37(2) provides that any employer who was affiliated with employers' union on the date of invitation to collective negotiations shall remain bound by the invitation made to the union even after the expiration of the employer's membership to the employers' union (Article 37(2)). 'Any employer who was a member of an employers' union party to the collective agreement at the date of its conclusion remains bound by its provisions even though he may have subsequently severed his relations with the employers' union' (Article 37(3)). It is clear that severing relations with the employers' union involves cases such as the employer's expulsion as well as his resignation from the employers' union. If during negotiations the employer enters into an independent relationship and signs a collective agreement with the labour union on his own initiative, the employers' union may file a suit with a view to nullify that agreement. Another sanction may be the employer's expulsion from the employer's union.

III. Relations between the Collective Agreement and the Individual Employment Contracts

A. *The Direct and Automatic Effect of the Collective Labour Agreement on the Individual Employment Contract*

1200. The precedence of collective agreements over individual employment contracts is emphasized in Article 6(1) of Act No. 2822 and now in Article 36(1) of Act No. 6356 has been embodied in the following statement:' unless otherwise stated in the collective labour agreement, the provisions of individual employment contracts may not be contrary to those of the collective labour agreement. The provisions of an individual employment contract which are at variance with those of the collective agreement shall be replaced by the provisions of the latter'. This means that, with the autonomy granted to them by the Constitution, the parties to collective bargaining are empowered to set forth normative rules which, like statutory law, exert a direct and mandatory impact on individual employment contracts.[474]

1201. Thus, the normative clauses of a collective agreement do have an automatic and direct impact on those provisions of employment contracts (of employees covered by the collective labour agreement) which are contrary to or less beneficial than those provided by the collective labour agreement. The clauses in the individual employment contract which are contrary to the collective agreement are, therefore, null and void. However, in order to protect the employee, the individual employment contract per se is not considered to be null and void. Only the less favourable provisions shall automatically be supplanted by the normative provisions of the collective labour agreement.[475] However, the parties may have agreed

474. Court of Cassation, 9th Div., 9 Apr. 1968, 157/4628; General Council Decision, 21 Feb. 1975, 9-1040/227; 20 Apr. 1987, 3816/3991.
475. Court of Cassation, 9th Div., 4 Apr. 2001, 5641/5576.

to the contrary in the collective labour agreement, but this is not a practice encountered in most Turkish collective labour agreements. The direct and mandatory effect involved here applies to the following cases:

- individual employment contracts which existed at the time of the conclusion of the collective labour agreement may have been changed later so as to contain provisions contrary to the collective agreement;
- new employment contracts may have been made involving provisions contrary to the collective labour agreement;
- existing employment contracts may contain clauses contravening a newly-made collective labour agreement; and
- abusive and malicious terms intended to evade the mandatory effects of the normative provisions of the collective labour agreement may have been inserted into the individual employment contract (in which case such clauses are to be deemed void and therefore must be automatically supplanted by the pertinent provisions of the collective agreement).

Also, the provisions of a collective labour agreement must apply in all cases not covered by the individual employment contract.

B. The Validity of the Clauses of the Individual Employment Contract Which Are More Favourable for the Employee

1202. Article 36(1) also foresees that the terms of an employment contract which are more favourable for the employee must apply in cases where the collective labour agreement is at variance with such terms. Thus, the legislative and collectively bargained provisions constitute minimum standards which may be exceeded by individual employment contracts in accordance with the principle of freedom of contract. Clearly, in view of Article 36(1), the employer is not obliged to provide individual employees with benefits above and beyond those set out in the collective agreement. The purpose of this clause is to enable the employer and the individual employee to determine employment conditions freely above and beyond the collectively bargained provisions. The employee in question here is the one who is qualified to benefit from the collective agreement (member, or the non-member who pays a solidarity due to the union). Thus, differential remuneration to reward the higher performance and merit of certain employees is possible. It is therefore affirmed that differential treatment within reasonable limits is an exception to the rule of equal treatment of employees under the collective bargaining system. As a measure to strengthen 'union security' further, under the collective bargaining system between 1963 and 1983 (Act No. 275), however, the union was empowered to compel the employer to agree to the contrary. Over the years, however, the supremacy of the collective labour agreement over the individual contract seems to be waning, as evidenced, for example, by the avoidance by the Constitutional Court of collective agreement-based arbitration in job security disputes or the refusal to recognize the validity of some collectively bargained flexibilization arrangements (e.g., the balancing act in the compressed workweek), cases where individual rights seem to take precedence over union security.

1203. The validity of individual employment contract provisions which are more favourable for the employee takes effect irrespective of whether the contract was concluded before or after the collective labour agreement. Although theoretically the employer is free to provide certain employees with working conditions more favourable than those of the collective labour agreement, these 'more favourable working conditions' usually refer in practice to wages rather than to clauses related to working time, organization of work and other working conditions. In fact it is not appropriate or even easy to discriminate among workers in terms of working conditions other than wages and wage-related items.

C. *The Consequences of an Expired Collective Agreement*

1204. Article 36(2) provides that the terms of an expired collective agreement concerning employment contracts shall continue to be binding until a fresh collective agreement enters into force. To benefit from this possibility, the worker does not have to pay any union dues whatsoever. This rule aims to protect the working conditions of employees during the time interval between the expiration date of the existing collective agreement and the making of a new collective agreement which is usually concluded with a certain delay due to prolonged negotiations. Despite the possibility provided by Act No. 2822 and 6356 enabling the parties to start negotiations even before the expiration of the existing agreement, the signing of the new collective labour agreement usually materializes several months later.

1205. It should be noted that only the employment contracts which existed under the expired collective agreement should continue to be binding, that is, the individual employment contracts for new employees may be freely concluded in the time interval concerned. Second, the obligatory part of the collective agreement, i.e., rights and obligations of the union and the employer, cease to exist with the expiration of the collective labour agreement. In other words, it is only the normative part of the expired collective agreement that shall remain in force as employment contracts until a fresh agreement is concluded. The normative part of a collective agreement comprises those provisions related to the making, content and termination of the individual contracts. It should also be noted that only those provisions concerning the content (e.g., wages, working time) and termination (e.g., severance pay) of individual contracts shall remain effective, since the employer and a new employee to be hired would be free in concluding a new individual employment contract in any manner they deem fit.

1206. The following points must also be considered in applying the above-stated rule. If the newly signed contract is made retroactive so as to take effect before the date on which it was signed, the normative provisions of the expired collective agreement should continue to be binding until the date on which the new agreement becomes effective rather than the date on which it was signed. Second, upon the termination of the collective agreement the employee and the employer are both free to modify the individual employment contract, provided that they agree to do so. Third, the rule that the normative provisions of an expired collective agreement continue to be effective until the making of a fresh agreement should not be construed to have an absolute meaning; that is, it shall be applicable only in the case of those rights not limited by a certain date or a specified length of time.[476] And fourth, the worker who severs his membership with the union on the date of the expiration of the collective labour agreement may not have access to agreement terms in the form of a continuing individual contract.[477]

D. Relations between the Expired and the New (Renewed) Collective Labour Agreement

1207. The accepted view is that each new collective agreement is an independent and separate entity. The working arrangements adopted for a specified length of time are thus replaced by a new order set out in the new collective labour agreement taking account of changed conditions. The provisions of the new collective labour agreement must therefore be put into effect irrespective of whether they are more or less favourable for the employee than those which existed under the expired agreement. The expired agreement is no longer valid upon the coming into force of the fresh collective labour agreement. The Court of Cassation ruled that the plaintiff could not request the payment of items not provided in the present agreement, nor the difference between the higher sum foreseen in the expired agreement and the amount that was reduced in the present agreement.[478] Thus established rights may be altered or removed altogether by the newly made collective agreements and the concept of 'vested (acquired) rights' does not apply automatically.

1208. However, any rule in the new agreement stating that the previous practice would persist is to be deemed valid, provided the previous practice is identifiable.[479]

1209. The 1982 Constitution of Turkey as well as Act No. 2822 banned the conclusion of multiple collective agreements at an establishment or enterprise in a given period of time. The constitutional amendment of 2010 has abrogated this restriction from the wording of Article 53 of the Constitution altogether and the restriction no longer exists in Act No. 6356. No clause in Act No. 6356 now says that 'not more than one collective agreement may be concluded or executed for the same period in the establishment'. The dichotomy of industry-wide and local (establishment level) collective bargaining with all the resultant problems which had arisen in the pre-1980 era led the legislature in 1983 to try to eliminate the problem of overlapping agreements. New amendments to Act No. 6356 could envisage

476. Court of Cassation, 9th Div., 2 Mar. 2010, 48194/432.
477. Court of Cassation, 9th Div., 1 Oct. 2007, 1866/28586).
478. Court of Cassation, 9th Div., 27 Mar. 1985, 2859/3284; 31 Mar. 1989, 1524/2965.
479. Court of Cassation, 9th Div., 7 Feb. 1975, 80861/28426.

industry-wide as well as establishment-level bargaining, thus paving the way for a multi-layered bargaining structure. The lifting of the ban has raised the possibility of regulating sectoral employment conditions of a general nature by concluding industry-wide agreements while at the same time enabling the parties to make local agreements geared to workplace conditions.[480] But new legislation in this direction should be formulated very carefully by taking the lessons learned in the past into due consideration.

§2. The Territory of the Collective Agreement

I. In Terms of the Level of Bargaining

1210. Since this aspect of territorial scope has already been explained in detail under the structure of collective bargaining above, attention will be focused here on the territory of the collective agreement only in terms of persons and the place to be covered.

II. In Terms of Persons

A. *Members of the Signatory Union*

1211. In view of Article 39(1) of Act No. 6356, the members of a labour union that is a party to a collective agreement shall benefit from that agreement. The non-members may take advantage of the collective agreement only by paying solidarity dues to the signatory union.

1212. Since Article 33(1) of Act No. 6356 in defining the collective labour agreement, has referred only to the 'employment contract', it is clear that those working under several other types of contract and yet entitled to form and join unions (publishing, transportation, job, agency and partnership contracts according to Article 2(4) do not have the right to avail themselves of the collective bargaining process.

1213. As a rule, collective agreement provisions which relate to wages, bonuses, premiums and other monetary benefits as well as those items measurable in monetary terms are applicable only to members of the labour union and to non-members who pay solidarity dues to the union.

1214. In extending the benefits of their activities to their members, organizations must ensure equality and respect the restrictions placed on discriminatory practices

480. For critical views on the existing system, *see* D. Ulucan, *Özerkliğ iin Hukuki ve Uygulamaya İlişkin Güncel Sorunları*, İstanbul, p. 180; F. Sağlam, *Anayasa Hukuku Açısından İşçi Haklaının Güncel Sorunları*, İstanbul, p. 43.

They must abide by the principles of gender equality in performing their functions' (Article 26(3)).

1215. Article 25(2) of Act No. 6356 provides that the employer must not make any discrimination between members and non-members with regard to employment conditions, with the exception that the provisions of the collective agreement respecting wages, bonuses, premiums and social and fringe benefits are reserved. Taken in conjunction with that statement, it follows that working conditions set out in a collective agreement other than wages, bonuses, premiums and other benefits must be applicable to all employees regardless of their membership status. Thus, it is basically those specially articulated benefits measurable in monetary terms that must apply to members of the signatory union. And, those terms of the collective labour agreement other than the items referred to in Article 25(2) are applicable to all employees in the establishment, although this is a controversial matter in practice.[481]

1216. On the issue of the categories and conditions according to which employees may have access to the benefits of the collective labour agreement, Act No. 6356 has reiterated almost the same provisions which existed under Act No. 2822. First, as mentioned above, the general rule is that members of the labour union which is the signatory party to the collective labour agreement shall avail of the benefits provided by the collective labour agreement. Second, the distinction made between the conclusion (signing) date and the date on which the parties have agreed to make the collective labour agreement's provision effective, the rule that was prevalent in the previous system, has been maintained. As Article 39(2) provides, 'those who were members of the labour union on the date of the collective labour agreement's ratification (signing) shall benefit from it as of the date on which it has been put into effect; those who have joined the labour union after the conclusion of the collective labour agreement terms, as of the date on which their membership has been notified to the employer'. Article 39(4) addresses the position of non-members: in order to have access to the benefits of the collective labour agreement, those who were not members of the signatory union, or those who were recruited later and yet had not joined the labour union, as well as those who were members of the union on the date of the conclusion of the collective labour agreement but who had later resigned or were expelled from the union shall benefit from the collective labour agreement's terms, provided that they pay the signatory union 'solidarity dues'.

1217. For this, the approval of the labour union shall not be required. Benefiting from the collective labour agreement by paying solidarity dues becomes valid as of the date on which a request to that effect is made. According to the original version of this clause, requests made before the date of the signing of the collective labour agreement would become effective as of the date of the conclusion of the collective labour agreement, Article 39(4). However in its verdict dated 30 December 2020,

481. Öner Eyrenci, *Toplu İş Sözleşmesinin İşyerinde Çalışan Bütün İşçilere Uygulanacak Hükümleri*, Kamu-İş, Nisan, 1988, p. 13.

the Constitutional Court declared subsection 4 of Article 39 null, thus entitling non-members to benefit from the collective agreement even for the period preceding the signing (ratification) of the collective labour agreement before the conclusion of the collective labour agreement, a confusing decision indeed where only one member of the High Court voted against it on grounds of difficulties involved in collecting solidarity dues for the past periods.

1218. The amount of the solidarity due which was to be two-third of the regular membership due under Act No. 2822 may now be designated freely in the union's constitution, provided that it must not exceed the regular membership due (Article 39(5)). Thus, the ceiling on the amount of 'solidarity due', a concept conceived as a regulatory balance between union freedom and union security way back in the labour relations legislation of 1963 of Turkey, has now been removed.

1219. So far these arrangements are replicas of similar clauses found in Act No. 2822.[482] But there was a void which in the past had given to legal problems in court decisions. The void was related to union members whose employment contracts had expired between the date of the conclusion of the collective labour agreement and the date on which it was held to have become effective. To fill this void, Article 39(3) provides that such workers shall benefit from the collective labour agreement until the expiration of their individual employment contracts. As a positive step, it is hoped that this new clause will bring an end to the ongoing controversy on this matter.

1220. There are certain categories in Turkish law and practice who are denied the right to take advantage of collective labour agreement terms. A group of employees in this category is the so-called non-covered personnel who, according to a verdict of the Court of Cassation, may not benefit from the collective labour agreement even though they may be willing pay the union solidarity dues. Another category defined by the law is the 'employer's representative' within the meaning of this Act, as well as those managers who have participated in collective negotiations as representatives of the employer (Article 39(7)). Also, 'with the exception of those employees who must keep working during the strike in view of Article 65 for the safety of the establishment, machinery, installations, plants and animals, the workers who have not participated in the strike may not take advantage of the collective labour agreement terms concluded pursuant to the strike unless there is an agreement to the contrary (Article 39(8)).

B. Applying the Collective Labour Agreement to Non-Members with the Written Consent of the Union

1221. Act No. 6356 states in Article 26(4) that, without prejudice to the provisions in the seventh and twelfth sections of the Act, the rights and benefits conferred on their members by labour or employers' unions and confederations may be

482. For the pre-2012 system, *see* the 2011 edition of this monograph.

extended to non-members if the organization concerned consents thereto in writing. This means that, with the written consent of the signatory union, non-members may benefit from the services provided by the union as well as from the terms of the collective labour agreement itself. But there is no known practice along this direction. It is not realistic to expect unions, which are opposed even to the practice of non-members' taking advantage of a collective agreement by paying solidarity dues, to grant such a permission which runs counter to the conception of union security.

C. Extension of the Collective Agreement

1222. With slight differences from Act No. 2822, Act No. 6356 in Article 40 addresses the process of the extension of the collective labour agreement by the government to other establishments in an industry branch.

1223. Upon the request of the labour or employers' unions or an employer and pursuant to obtaining the opinion of the YHK, the Council of Ministers may extend a collective labour agreement, either in whole or in part and after making the changes it may deem necessary, concluded by the labour union with the highest membership established in the industry branch which will be subject to extension, to other establishments not covered by a collective labour agreement in that industry branch. The YHK shall give its advisory opinion in fifteen days (Article 40(1)).

1224. 'Provisions of the collective labour agreement dealing with the rights and obligations of the parties as well as the clause on recourse to private arbitration may not be extended' (Article 40(5)).

1225. Unlike the previous Act No. 2822, the new Act does not require that the union whose collective labour agreement is to be extended must first meet the industry-level representation threshold. Such a numerical threshold has now been removed. Extension, which as a process aims to standardize working conditions in an industry branch and eliminate unfair competition among employers, has been for the most part designed along lines parallel to Act No. 2822. Despite its avowed goals and good intentions, however, the past experience of thirty years has shown that the process of extension was unable to perform its intended functions. The second novelty brought by Act No. 6356 is the reduction of the time period to obtain the opinion of the YHK to 15 from 30 days. The third novelty is found in Article 40(7) which provides that 'for the establishment or enterprise to which a collective labour agreement has been extended, application for a fresh collective bargaining authorization may always be made and with the conclusion of a new collective labour agreement, the implementation of the extension process in that establishment or enterprise shall come to an end'.

1226. According to Article 40(2), 'the reasons for extension shall be indicated in the decision for extension. The decision for extension shall be published in the Official Gazette which shall also clarify the date on which it shall be effective; however, the date of its taking effect may not precede the date of its publication in the official Gazette.' The decision for extension shall lose its effect with the expiration of the extended collective labour agreement. When it deems it necessary and by indicating the reasons, the Council of Ministers may abrogate the decision for extension (Article 40(3,4)).

1227. Other important dimensions of Article 40 are the following: 'Decision for extension may not be taken for establishments where an application for collective bargaining authorization has not yet been finalized or, within the duration of the union's bargaining status where a collective bargaining authorization certificate has been granted. For the establishment or enterprise to which a collective labour agreement has been extended, application for a collective labour agreement authorization may always be made and with the conclusion of a fresh collective labour agreement, the implementation of the extended agreement in the establishment or enterprise concerned shall be discontinued (Article 40(6,7)).

1228. The criterion used for the extendibility of a collective labour agreement, i.e., that it must have been made by the labour union with the highest number of members in the industry branch concerned, may be perceived as one of the factors likely to inhibit a viable 'extension' process. Irrespective of a union's membership size, the collective labour agreement by any union with even a lower membership might qualify as being a more ideal document conducive to apply to the characteristics of the industry branch concerned. The extension process which has been applied only a few times in Turkey was envisaged initially also as a substitute for industry-level bargaining which, due to the aforementioned reasons of Turkey, could not materialize in the real sense. The possibility of opting out of the extension coverage upon the conclusion of a fresh establishment level collective labour agreement is an indication of the legislature's preference for local over industry-wide collective bargaining. Procedures concerning the power of the government to decide on the validity of collective labour agreement terms to be extended as well as the possibility of opting out in the event of a new authorization for an establishment or enterprise level bargaining are factors which may also make the application of extension more complicated and difficult. For the 'extendable' collective labour agreement, legislation could lay down certain criteria for a more rational 'collective labour agreement' model.

D. *Providing Unqualified Workers with Benefits Brought by the Collective Agreement*

1229. In principle, employees who qualify to benefit from the collective agreement are those who are either members of the signatory union or those who accept to pay the solidarity dues to the union. Employees who do not meet these two criteria cannot take advantage of the collective agreement provisions on wages, benefits, etc., unless the signatory union has granted its written consent to that effect. If the employer knowingly provides such employees with the same benefits at or higher amounts than those engendered by the collective labour agreement, the union may demand from him the reimbursement of solidarity dues which should otherwise be paid by the employees concerned. In the event such dues are not paid, the union may file a lawsuit against the employer for damages.[483] In other words, the principle of freedom of contract shall not apply in such a case. In practice, many collective agreements carry clauses aimed at obstructing such behaviour and some collectively bargained provisions stipulate that the amounts thus granted to unqualified workers should be given as extra benefits to all union members in the establishment. However, the Court of Cassation ruled that the employer should not be held responsible if the amounts thus deployed were less than what the collective labour agreement had provided for.[484] Notwithstanding such views, it is also espoused by the Court that the employer is free to apply differential treatment to employees of different skills and performance, particularly in regard to promotion policies which entail increases in wages, premiums and bonuses each of which may be the same or about the same as those brought by the collective agreement, or even higher.[485]

E. The Problem of 'Covered Versus Non-Covered' Employees

1230. As alluded to above in the relevant paragraphs, a widespread practice in Turkish industrial relations has been, by agreement of the parties, to exclude some personnel – union members as well as potentially unionizable persons – from the coverage of the collective agreement. These are generally managerial personnel, department heads, supervisors, secretaries and occasionally all the office personnel. The extremely narrow definition of the 'employer's representative' in Article 2(1 e) of Act No. 6356 (beginning way back in the 1963 legislation) has been one of the reasons prompting employers to pressure labour unions into accepting the concept of 'non-covered employees' in collective agreements. The fact that only the person who manages the whole enterprise on behalf of the employer – and those who have participated in collective negotiations in the capacity to represent the employer – are regarded as the employer's representative has meant that all the managerial staff are treated as employees, thus having the right to join unions and enjoy the benefits of the collective bargaining system Top management has been desirous of keeping such managerial and high-level/high-skill employees (supervisors, technicians, professionals) on its side by rewarding them with alluring benefits relieved of restrictive union policies. As labour unions have naturally resented this management policy, the issue of excluding some of the legally unionizable employees from the coverage of the collective agreement has become a controversial topic in negotiations. In successive bargaining rounds throughout the years, labour unions have been thrust into surrendering an increasing number of positions to management, in

483. K. Oğuzman, *supra*, pp. 77–78. In the opinion of the High Court, however, the union may not request the reimbursement of solidarity dues if the employer has granted collectively bargained benefits to unqualified employees only partially (Court of Cassation, 9th Div., 4 Mar. 2003, 16415/2828).

484. Court of Cassation, 9th Div., 3 Jun. 1981, 1930/13733; 12 Sep. 1991, 12106/11981.

485. Court of Cassation, 9th Div., 11 Nov. 1974, 6292/24782; 20 May 1985, 2546/5437.

return for certain concessions obtained from the employer at the last minute. Because a threshold has been reached in recent years beyond which the labour unions' majority status is seriously threatened, unions are now striving to win back at least some of the so-called non-covered personnel into their ranks.

1231. The practice of pushing otherwise unionizable employees outside the scope of the collective agreement – somewhat arbitrarily and without receiving the consent of the employees concerned in most cases – has been criticized in the light of Article 53 of the 1982 Constitution and Article 26 of Act No. 6356 (in the past Article 31 of Act No. 2821).

1232. Article 53 of the Constitution has recognized the right of all employees to enter into collective labour agreements and Article 26 of Act No. 6356 (i.e., Article 31 of the Unions Act No. 2821) mandate that labour unions and employers' unions must ensure strict equality among their members.

1233. Leaving some employees outside the scope of the collective labour agreement seem to violate these constitutional and legislative principles. What is more, non-covered employees cannot benefit from the collective agreement even if they are willing to pay solidarity dues to the signatory union since naturally they have been left entirely outside the collective bargaining system. Act No. 2822 was silent on this issue, so is Act No. 6356 and the Court of Cassation, in several of its verdicts, has upheld the autonomy of the social partners to shove some employees outside the area of collective bargaining.[486] Writers who support the High Court's viewpoint claim that the parties may freely determine who are to be covered by the agreement (462), meaning that those excluded from the coverage cannot benefit from the collective agreement even though they may retain their union membership. In actual practice, of course, the employers have in most cases rewarded such personnel with benefits higher than those provided by the collective agreement. As a result, there have been no serious complaints leading to judicial awards of any significance. Recently, however, there are alleged cases where non-covered employees are paid under collectively bargained levels. In a more recent verdict, the Court of Cassation ruled that even where the collective agreement provided that non-covered employees should not receive lesser benefits than union members, the signatory union, should not demand payment of solidarity dues by them.[487]

1234. In the face of increasing union unrest due to employers' attempts to increase the number of non-covered employees, the future may witness new efforts to clarify the covered versus non-covered personnel dilemma. One solution may be

486. Court of Cassation, 9th Div., 6 May 1974, 2460/8465; 12 Jan. 1976, 31395/1000; 16 Feb. 1976, 1704/5689.

487. Court of Cassation, 9th Div., 20 May 1985, 2547/5436; General Council Decision, 25 Apr. 1986, 9-835/449; Court of Cassation, 9th Div., 23 May 1995, 4219/17027. In another verdict, the High Court found differential treatment of non-covered personnel in wages by the employer contrary to Art. 31/III of Act No. 28221 and Art. 2 of the Civil Code (fair dealing) as well as to the principle of equality embedded in Art. 10 of the Constitution (Court of Cassation, 9th Div., 24 Oct. 1995, 12072/32880).

to expand the scope of the definition of the concept 'employer's representative' so as to move such supervisory and technical-professional personnel into the structure of management. Apparently, the step taken by the original version of Act No. 2822 so as to treat the manager of the establishment also as the employer's representative did not solve the problem either, so the 1995 amendment by Act No. 4101 reverted back to the even narrower definition of the 1963 legislation. What is needed seems to be a more drastic change, like that brought by the Taft Hartley Act where even the foreman is not defined as an employee. Given the nature of the established industrial relations milieu in Turkey, though, deciding where to draw the line is not an easy task. At present a more acceptable solution could be to predicate this practice on the written consent of the worker who is to be excluded from the coverage of the collective labour agreement.

1235. Another solution may involve recognizing such managerial-technical personnel to form their own unions, as is the case in some European countries. But the premise of organizing unions along industrial lines and the still prevalent principle of 'only one collective agreement at a time in a given establishment or enterprise', coupled with the motive to keep the number of unions down, makes this an unlikely alternative to materialize in the foreseeable future.

III. In Terms of Place

A. Establishment(s) and Enterprise

1236. As alluded to above, a collective agreement may cover an establishment or establishments in the same industry branch, or an enterprise in the event of a multiple of establishments belonging to the same employer in the same industry branch. Therefore, the concept of establishment bears significance for the scope of the collective labour agreement in terms of place. While Act No. 2821 reiterated the definition of the establishment given by the Labour Act No. 1475, Act No. 2822 did not supply any specific definition in this sphere. In this connection, the establishment (plant) is where the work is performed and all the related premises and annexes attached to the workplace due to the nature and operation of the work are also considered to be part of the same establishment. The new Labour Act No. 4857 has somewhat expanded the concept of the establishment in Article 2(2,3). The requirement that the premises, annexes and the establishment should be related to each other involves the concept of unity both in terms of management and of technical goal. Since collective bargaining is conducted in relation to establishments within the same industry branch, determining the industry branch into which an establishment falls bears significance. The tabulated list given by the Act No. 6356 enumerates the 20 industry branches; and the classification of all the works and operations under each branch of activity are stated in a regulation. Article 2(2) also foresees that works auxiliary to the main activity of the establishment are deemed to fall into the industry branch wherein the main activity is carried out. This determination is also important in clarifying the competence and authorization (certification) of the labour (and employers') union concerned. The decision as to which branch of activity covers an establishment is to be made by the Ministry of Labour against which the parties concerned may lodge an appeal with the labour court and with the Court of Cassation if an appeal is made.

1237. An issue related to the scope of collective agreement in terms of place is the moving of an establishment to a different location. The Court of Cassation has brought clarity to what would happen to the status of the collective agreement as well as to the bargaining status of the union concerned in the event of the transfer of the establishment to a different location. According to the opinion of the High Court, because the collective agreement is concluded on behalf of the employees of a given establishment, moving the establishment to a different location must not affect adversely the conclusion of a collective agreement by the union which has been certified as the authorized agent for that establishment.[488] If an agreement was already in force at the workplace which was later moved, it shall continue to be effective in the new location where the same establishment is operating presently.

B. *Subcontracting*

1238. Controversy prevailed in Turkish labour law as to whether or not the principal employer should be held responsible in so far as the application of the collective agreement to the employees of the subcontractor was concerned. Acts Nos. 2822 and 6356 are both silent on this matter. With a view to evading the high cost of collectively bargained wage increases, employers and recently especially public employers, were tempted to contract out work to outsiders with increasing frequency in recent years.

1239. In the past unions, claiming that such employer action was aimed at weakening union freedoms and free collective bargaining, have tried to fight back by trying to incorporate anti-subcontracting clauses into collective agreements, but only with limited success. However, the Court of Cassation ruled that the employees of the subcontractor could benefit from the collective agreement concluded with the principal employer in the same manner as the employees of the latter if they became members of the signatory union[489] or otherwise paid solidarity dues. This verdict, approved by the general Council of the High Court was based on Article 1 of the Labour Act No. 1475 which provided that where a subcontractor operated a certain section of the establishment the principal employer and the subcontractor were to be held jointly liable for the obligations ensuing from the Labour Act or from the employment contracts of the employees employed by the subcontractor working exclusively in the undertaking or its subordinate facility.[490] This High Court ruling was harshly criticized by various writers on several grounds. First, it was argued that the clause involving joint liability of the principal employer and the subcontractor

488. Court of Cassation, 9th Div., 13 Jul. 1987, 7421/7183.
489. *See* headings 'Part-Time and Full-Time Contracts'.
490. Ruling of the General Council of the Court of Cassation, 4 Nov. 1987, 9-156/815.

was not linked in any way to obligations arising from the collective bargaining process; rather it aimed at protecting particularly the wage-related rights of the subcontractor's employees. Second, problems were likely to arise when the principal employer was forced to perform duties stemming from the collective agreement for employees of the subcontractor with whom he had no direct employment relationship. Here the employment contract was between the subcontractor and the workers engaged by him. And third, complications would follow when the establishment or its subordinate facility was leased to a third person who, after taking it over, registered it with the appropriate Regional Directorate of Labour as a separate establishment. This breakaway unit might fall into the scope of a different industry branch In a case like this, there was the likelihood of a different union in a different industry (or perhaps in the same industry) to initiate the bargaining process for this separate entity which had now to be treated as an independent establishment. Apparently, the above-stated verdict of the Court of Cassation was hardly applicable to cases like this.[491]

1240. The 1987 General Council verdict of the Court of Cassation notwithstanding, the 9th Division of the High Court, taking the above criticisms into consideration, rendered a decision in the opposite direction in 1996. Addressing a similar problem, the High Court ruled that the principal employer could be held jointly liable for the subcontractor's obligations arising from a collective agreement only if the latter was himself party to a collective agreement covering his own employees. Since there was no relationship between the subcontractor's employee (the claimant) and the collective agreement in force at the establishment, the employee's request to benefit from the collective agreement covering the principal employer's employees could not be justified and should therefore be denied.[492] In a similar case in 1996, the Court of Cassation reiterated the same opinion by ruling that the subcontractor's employee should not be allowed to have access to the provisions of the collective agreement in force at a public establishment simply by relying on ILO Convention 94 of 1949, which had been ratified by Turkey. Although the Convention, in aiming to protect the wages of the contractor's employees, referred also to collective agreement wage rates prevailing at the establishment, subsequent national legislation was not conducive to setting wages of the subcontractor's employees at collectively bargained levels involving the principal (public) employer's employees.[493]

1241. In tackling the question of subcontracting, however, attention must be paid to different forms in practice. There is, first, the practice of the employer to enter into business deals with an outside contractor (i.e., construction of a new building, marketing of the firm's products). The employer's freedom of concluding such contracts which are limited in time and scope must not be questioned, of

491. Çelik, *supra*, p. 629.
492. Court of Cassation, 9th Div., 11 Mar. 1996, 2554/4851.
493. Court of Cassation, 21st Div., 18 Oct. 1996, 2261/5790. For rulings reaching a similar conclusion, *see* Court of Cassation, 9th Div., 29 Apr. 1997, 3762/7742; General Council Decision, 14 Nov. 2001, 9-711/820; 9th Div., 25 Mar. 2004, 16528/5827.

course. A second category is the contracting out of certain activities which do not belong to the domain of the firm's essential operations (e.g., cafeteria services, the provision of meals, cleaning, transportation of employees to and from work). Such auxiliary services which were previously performed by the firm's own employees are now contracted out to a third person who brings his own employees to perform such services. Though this category of contracting out which has become quite common in recent years is apt to lead to membership loss for unions, there seems to be agreement on its acceptability for the sake of increased labour flexibility. And Article 2 of the Labour Act shall not apply as long as employees of the contractor are not employed exclusively at the workplace concerned and keep supplying their services to undertakings belonging to different employers. In the third category, however, part of the firm's main operations are contracted out, often with a view to escaping the union power and lowering labour costs, to a third person – sometimes referred to as the sub-employer in Turkish practice – whose employees are assigned exclusively to the operations of the principal employer. It is this category of subcontracting where the 'joint liability' foreseen in the Labour Act as well as the earlier verdicts of the High Court seemed to make sense to some writers. The above-stated criticisms directed against the extension of a collective agreement to the employees of a different employer still retained their validity from a strictly legalistic viewpoint. But attempts to get away with a certified bargaining agent should not be tolerated. In an attempt to safeguard union and collective bargaining freedoms, the Court of Cassation had improvised a somewhat meagre solution by relying on Article 1 of the Labour Act No. 1475. Good faith (*bona fide*) dealing as embedded in Article 2 of Turkish Civil Code is a principle that should not be overlooked in this case as in other similar cases. Besides, the rule which provided that at a specified establishment (or enterprise) only one collective agreement was applicable also precluded the conclusion of additional collective agreements covering employees of the subcontractor(s), be they in the same industry, by the same union, or by different unions. The employer who, under the disguise of more labour flexibility, had subcontracted part of his essential operations to outsiders had actually engaged in behaviour qualifying as the abusive exercise of a right or simulation (*muvazaa*).

1242. New definitions and articulations brought by Act No. 4857 to the concept of principal employer–subcontractor relationship seem to have ended the ongoing controversy at least partially. In view of Article 2(7, 8)of the Labour Act No. 4857, safeguards against covert abuses and simulated acts on this matter have now been put into force. Where an abuse or simulated act is proven to exist, the subcontractor's employees shall be treated as employees of the principal employer from the very beginning. The subcontractor must, under the present system, register his domain of activity as an independent establishment where he may be the party to a collective agreement for his own employees and the principal employer shall be jointly liable with him for the obligations ensuing from that collective agreement as well as from his employees' employment contracts and labour legislation.[494]

494. For examples of recent court rulings along these dimensions, *see* Court of Cassation, 9th Div., 22 Apr. 2004, 20352/9110; 22 Apr. 2004, 6280/9180; 21 Feb. 2005, 32618/5690.

1243. Similarly, as a result of increasing unrest and legal actions taken in the public sector, forthcoming legislation (e.g., a new *torba kanunu*) is likely hold that, where a latent simulated act is proven to exist and the subcontractor's workers are performing the main work of the establishment, they shall be assigned to the permanent positions of the main employer, to be treated accordingly from the very beginning.

§3. THE DURATION AND ENDING OF THE COLLECTIVE LABOUR AGREEMENT

I. Main Features

1244. Due to the problems encountered in practice, Act No. 2822 had repealed the clauses of Act No. 275 concerning the conclusion of collective agreements made for an indefinite period. Also under the present system, a collective labour agreement may be made only for a definite period. In fact, as mentioned above, Article 35(2) of Act No. 6356 provides that a collective agreement may be concluded for a specified period of not less than one year and not more than three years. However, an exception to that general rule has been provided in Article 35(3) stating that where a collective agreement is to apply to work that is due to last less than one year, the agreement may be concluded for less than one year. However, such an agreement shall be applicable for one year at least if the work in question is not yet completed by the end of that one-year period.

1245. Furthermore, Act No. 6356, like Act No. 2822 stipulates that the duration of a collective agreement may not be changed by agreement of the parties. According to Article 35(2), following the conclusion of a collective labour agreement the parties are not allowed to extend or shorten its duration or terminate it before the expiry date. Concepts 'to extend and to shorten' also involve the connotation 'to renew'. Thus, renewal of a collective agreement which was possible under Act No. 275 of 1963 is no longer permitted. Certainly, in the present system, as was the case under Act No. 2822, 'the procedures for the certification of the authorized union may begin within the 120 days before the expiration of a collective agreement' may be used by all the unions concerned, i.e., the present signatory union as well as any contesting rival union involved. It is thus clear, also in the light of this provision, that the renewal of a collective agreement by the parties concerned is not permissible.

1246. Faced with increasing pressures for more flexibility due to global competitive trends and economic recessions under inflationary conditions, the existing rules concerning the fixed duration and inflexibility of the collective labour agreement have become the subject of criticism in recent years. It has been proposed in various writings that 'due to unforeseen hardships or changed conditions', the parties should be allowed to shorten or lengthen, by mutual agreement, the duration of a collective agreement in force. Of course, even under the present system there is no obstacle precluding the parties from agreeing to incorporate changes into the existing collective agreement, but this can be done only upon mutual agreement and by signing a written document, usually referred to as a 'protocol' in practice.

1247. On the matter of changing monetary items of a collective agreement by way of the parties' mutual agreement, the accepted opinion holds that due to unforeseen hardships reductions may be made in wage-related clauses provided they have not yet materialized in terms of the respective dates specified in the collective agreement.[495] In other words, the change is not possible once the employee's claims to a wage increase have become accrued.[496] The change may be put into legal form, in accordance with the Obligations Act, by a written contract signed by the employees concerned who thus relieve the employer of his obligation to pay the collectively bargained rate.

1248. The parties deemed to be legally competent to modify the collective agreement are the signatory labour union and the employer or the employers' union. The management board of the union may however delegate this power to certain board members or third persons.

II. The Controversy over the Readjustment of the Collective Agreement by Judicial Process

1249. Yet a different issue to be addressed in this connection is whether or not, in the event of the employer's alleged inability to perform his obligations due to extraordinary economic crisis conditions, the judge is empowered to readjust the collective agreement terms or cancel them altogether.

1250. This has become a matter of controversy in conjunction with the General Council rulings of the Court of Cassation which, using the criteria of 'unforeseen hardship' due to the emergence of a just cause and as required by the principle of fair dealing, as envisaged in Article 480(2) of the new Obligations Act No. 6098 relieved the public employer of the obligation to make the second-year's wage payments indexed to inflation on due time. The government refused to make these payments to employees and came up with a protracted pay plan. The employees filed suits for fulfilment, labour courts favoured their requests, but the Court of Cassation

495. Court of Cassation, 9th Div., 20 Jan. 2004, 18300/426.

496. Court of Cassation, 9th Div., 4 Dec. 1996, 20258/2240; 2 Jun. 1997, 7304/10562. However, the High Court had also reached contrary conclusions on this matter (9th Div., 22 Apr. 1996, 906/9229; 8 Jul. 1996, 5525/15513); 21 Dec. 2006, 38526/4481. *See* the Court of Cassation, General Council Decision, 17 Apr. 2013, 2012/9-1893. This General Council Decision represents an interesting case whereby the Court of Cassation reversed the lower court's insistence on the employer's right to lower wages for reasons of economic difficulty, rather than renegotiating the terms of the collective labour agreement with the union. The case also involves other dimensions regarding the workers' wage and severance pay entitlements.

reversed these court decisions. When the courts insisted, the General Council of the Court of Cassation issued its binding awards for each case.[497]

1251. In fact, Article 480(2) of the Obligations Act No. 6098 (Article 365(2) of the previous Obligations Act) provides that if reasons unanticipated or unforeseen by the parties preclude the fulfilment of an obligation or makes it extremely difficult, the judge, using his discretion, may readjust the agreed amount or revoke the contract. Also, Article 435 of the Obligations Act No. 6098 (Article 344 of the previous Obligations Act) entitles the party, for whom the continuation of the employment relationship has taken on an unbearable nature due to extraordinary circumstances, to terminate the employment contract for just cause.

1252. It has also been argued that a solution could be improvised in view of the 'good faith and honesty' principle envisaged in Article 2 of the Civil Code. If, in the wake of changing circumstances after the formation of the contract, demanding the fulfilment of the obligation in accordance with the contract runs counter to the principle of honesty, the claimant may request its readjustment to new conditions or its cancellation. In order to improvise in this manner, however, the change disrupting the equilibrium between the parties' mutual obligations must have been caused by extraordinary circumstances which could not be foreseen during the conclusion of the contract.

1253. The Court of Cassation, while admitting to the principle of 'adherence to the contract' (*pacta sunt servanda*), reversed the labour court's verdict and ruled that in the event of extraordinary economic circumstances which disturb considerably the balance between the parties' mutual obligations, strict adherence to the collective agreement could not be requested in view of the principles of honesty and justice; since the basis for the legal transaction had collapsed, the judge could ratify the readjustment of the payment of wage increases according to a protracted plan of payment.

1254. Opponents of the High Court's stance have argued that the 'unforeseen hardship' criterion of the general law of contracts could not applicable to the domain of collective labour relations. Article 53 of the Constitution and Act No. 2822 and Act No. 6356 have empowered the parties to create objectively binding legal norms. Evading such objective legal norms by judicial decisions or even by legislation contravenes the autonomy of social partners in collective bargaining.[498]

1255. Furthermore, the concept of inability to pay due to impossibility of fulfilment is not held to be an acceptable excuse in monetary debts. The claimant had the right to call upon the enforcement mechanism.[499] Therefore, employees were

497. Rulings of the General Council of the Court of Cassation, 3 May 1995, 9/267/442; 3 May 1995, 9-392/494; also in the same direction, 9th Div., 13 Mar. 1996, 4479/5354; 9th Div., 14 Mar. 1996, 4479/5354; General Council Decision, 26 Feb. 1997, 9-679/119.

498. Çelik, *supra*, p. 876.

499. K. Oğuzman and T. Öz, *Borçlar Hukuku*, Istanbul, 1994, pp. 315–316.

entitled to initiate a suit for fulfilment in accordance with Article 61 of Act No. 2822 and demand the payment of the second-year's wage increase along with the accrued interest charged for business transactions.

1256. Thus the repeated use of the concept 'collapse of the basis for legal transaction' (frustration) by the Court of Cassation became a matter of concern. The academicians, labour unions and workers, worrying that its misuse could entail the demise of the collective bargaining system in the future, voiced their criticism against the opinions addressed by the High Court in 1995 and 1996.[500]

III. Retroactivity in Collective Agreements

A. *In General*

1257. Before 1980, although Act No. 275 was silent on the subject of retroactivity, the date on which the collective agreement would become effective was always made retroactive to the expiry date of the previous agreement. This was largely due to the prolonged nature of collective negotiations. It was reaffirmed that applying a new collective labour agreement retroactively did not contravene the general principles of law, provided it did not undermine the acquired rights of employees. The generally accepted rule was, and still is, that the new agreement becomes effective as of the date of its ratification unless retroactivity has been agreed to and clearly stated in the collective labour agreement. In fact, it was upheld by the High Court that, unless otherwise provided for in the new collective agreement, it should take effect from the date on which it was signed and therefore an employee who had retired before the signing of the collective agreement was not entitled to its new provisions on severance pay.[501] In the post-1980 era, the Court of Cassation has also upheld, albeit indirectly, the practices on retroactivity.[502]

1258. In order for a collective agreement clause to be made retroactive, the obligations which it entails must be of a nature which can actually be fulfilled. Obviously normative clauses such as those pertaining to the content of employment contracts – i.e., wage increases, bonuses, premiums and fringe benefits are of this nature. On the other hand, normative provisions concerning the making of employment contracts – i.e., those provisions which envisage a certain form for the employment contract or which require or prohibit the conclusion of certain contracts – may not be made retroactive. Likewise, provisions concerning the termination of employment contracts may not be subject to retroactivity.[503] It should be noted that provisions which envisage reducing the weekly working time or increasing the terms of notice or annual vacations may be made retroactive through clauses put

500. *See* the debates on the issue in Yargıay'ın 1995 *Kararlarının Değerlendirilmesi Semineri, İşHukuku ve Sosyal Güvenlik Hukuku Milli Komitesi*, İstanbul, 25 Oct. 1996.
501. Court of Cassation, General Council, 12 Feb. 1975, 1974/9-505, 1975/194.
502. Court of Cassation, General Council, 1989, 10-250/361.
503. Court of Cassation, 9th Div., 26 Nov. 1979, 13980/14235.

into the collective agreement to that effect.[504] However, increases in fringe benefits provided in kind and consumed by workers in the past may not be subject to retroactivity.[505] On the other hand, although the obligatory part of the collective agreement may also be subject to retroactivity, those clauses on the application and supervision of the agreement – i.e., union security clauses, grievance procedures, discipline committees – cannot be made retroactive.

B. *Employees Entitled to Benefit from the Provisions of a Collective Agreement Made Retroactive*

1259. As a rule, members of the labour union party to the collective agreement take advantage of its provisions and non-members may avail themselves of the agreement if they pay a monthly solidarity contribution to the labour union concerned. Regarding retroactivity, Article 39(2) provides that employees who were members of the signatory labour union at the date of the conclusion (ratification) of the collective agreement benefit from its provisions as of the date on which the agreement has taken effect (commencement of the agreement); employees who become members after the date of the conclusion (ratification) of the agreement benefit from the agreement as of the date the labour union communicates their membership to the employer.

1260. Article 39(2) also provides that employees who were not members of the signatory union on the date of the conclusion of the agreement or those who were subsequently employed but had not joined the union or those who were expelled or had resigned from the union after the date of ratification would avail themselves of the agreement if they paid a monthly solidarity contribution to the labour union concerned. The consent of the union is not required in any case. Employees who thus pay solidarity contributions to the signatory union would start benefiting from the date on which such a request was made. However, solidarity contributions shall not be paid to labour unions barred from carrying on any activity.

1261. It follows from the wording of Article 39, then, that employees working in the establishment who were members of the signatory union on the date on which the agreement was signed shall take advantage of the agreement provisions retroactively even though they were not members of the union in that past period – and without having to pay any dues for the past period. Those of them who have started work in the establishment between the date on which the agreement came into effect retroactively and the date on which it was signed shall of course benefit from the agreement as of the date of their beginning work. However, those who were not members of the signatory union on the date of the conclusion of the collective agreement are not entitled to benefit from the agreement retroactively in any manner. They may avail themselves of the collective agreement terms only by paying solidarity contributions proactively. This rule has been criticized on grounds of its

504. Çelik, *supra*, pp. 580–586.
505. Esener, *supra*, p. 516.

adverse effects on negative union freedoms – that no one may be forced to join a union in any way, as embodied in Article 51(4) of the Constitution. Nevertheless, it is clear that, by providing for the payment of solidarity contributions, Article 39 aims to maintain a delicate balance between the principles of union freedom and union security. Likewise, those whose membership is severed for any reason whatsoever after the conclusion of the collective agreement must pay the signatory union solidarity contributions in order to avail themselves of the collective agreement.

C. *Workers Whose Employment Contracts Have Expired Before the Conclusion of the New Collective Agreement*

1262. The contentious point is the situation of those who have left the establishment before the signing but after the taking effect (commencement) of the new collective agreement. Under the previous system, the Court of Cassation was of the opinion that, in the absence of any collective agreement clause to the contrary, there was no reason to deprive such persons of retroactively derived benefits (corresponding of course to the length of time they were employed in the establishment after the taking effect of the new collective agreement).[506] More recently, however, the Court has ruled in several of its verdicts that, in the face of the wording of Article 9 of Act No. 2822 entitling only those who were members of the signatory union at the time of the conclusion of the agreement to benefit from its provisions retroactively, employees who have left the establishment before the signing of the agreement should not be permitted to do so.[507] This view was criticized in the literature. It was asserted that such employees should benefit from the provisions of the new agreement made retroactive if the agreement itself has explicitly entitled them to do so.[508] One could go even one step further and claim that, by making the collective agreement retroactive, the parties had the implicit aim of covering all the employees eligible to benefit from its provisions unless they had left certain categories out. Now Article 39(3) has filled this void by stating that workers whose employment contracts have expired between the date of the conclusion of the collective labour agreement and the date on which it was held to have become effective would benefit from the collective labour agreement terms until the expiration of their individual employment contracts.

IV. The Ending of the Collective Labour Agreement

1263. Under the present system in Turkey, a collective labour agreement ends only upon the expiration of the duration agreed to by the parties (i.e., on the date

506. Court of Cassation, 9th. Div., 19 Oct. 1970, 8665/10804.

507. Court of Cassation, 9th Div., 10 Oct. 1987, 9764/9997; 10 Mar. 1988, 691/2792; 7 Feb. 1991, 10159/1364; 2 Apr. 1991, 13766/1802; 11 May 1993, 13024/8004; 13 May 1993, 13910/8316.

508. N. Çelik, Yargıtay'In 1992 Yılı Kararlarları Semineri, *İşHukuku ve Sosyal Güvenlik Hukuku Milli Komitesi*, İstanbul, 1992, pp. 115–116.

foreseen in the agreement itself). As mentioned above, the duration of the collective labour agreement may not be extended or shortened nor may it be ended before its agreed-upon duration.

1264. In order to speed up the collective bargaining process, Article 35(4) entitles the parties to initiate authorization procedures for the upcoming agreement within 120 days before the expiration of the existing collective agreement, provided that the fresh agreement must not enter into force before the expiry of the existing one.

§4. Nullification and Invalidity of the Collective Agreement

1265. Like all legal procedures, the collective labour agreement too must be consistent with the general principles of law in order to be valid. However, Act No. 6356, like Act. No. 2822 carries only a single provision concerning the nullification of a collective agreement and this relates solely to the agreement concluded without obtaining a valid authorization certificate. Article 45(1) of the Act provides that in cases where a collective agreement has been concluded without a certificate of authorization, any interested party or the Ministry of Labour and Social Security may lodge an appeal, within forty-five days of the Ministry's access to the information, that either one or both of the parties was unauthorized and that the agreement should therefore be declared null and void. Appeals to declare the agreement null and void must be lodged with the labour court in the locality of the regional directorate of labour where the establishment is registered. If the agreement covers establishments under the jurisdiction of more than one regional directorate of labour, the appeal must be lodged with the labour court in Ankara. The judge, upon request and if he deems it necessary, may suspend the commencement of the collective agreement until a decision is taken.

1266. In addition to this specific case, if either of the parties is found incompetent, the collective agreement may always be declared null and void, as competence is regarded as a precondition for authorization. A significant case in point here is the union's violation of the specific industry branch requirement mandated by the law. Likewise, a strike or lock-out called by an incompetent labour or employer organization is considered 'unlawful'. Furthermore, a collective agreement which has not been set down in writing is null and void. Avoidance may also be brought if the agreement violates general principles of law, is against public order and general good morals or contravenes individual rights and dignity (Obligations Act, Article 27(1)). Likewise, any interested party may request nullification if the conclusion of the collective labour agreement was fraught with gross mistake, fraud or under threat (Obligations Act, Articles 30–37). In contrast to the prevailing principle of the Obligations Act, the nullity of the collective agreement takes effect only proactively, due to the protective nature of labour law.

1267. Furthermore, in view of Article 5, collective agreements must not contain any stipulations contrary to the indivisible integrity of the state with its territory and the nation, to national sovereignty and the Republic, to public order, national security, public morals and public health or to any mandatory provision of law or regulations, nor shall they include any stipulations encouraging, supporting or protecting acts that are criminal offences under the law (Article 33(5)).

1268. Also, the validity of the collective agreement is not affected in the event of certain developments. A collective labour agreement does not cease to have effect in cases where the signatory union has been dissolved, barred from activity or has lost its authorized (majority) status or because there has been a change of employer in the establishment(s) to which the agreement applies. Self-evidently this provision aims to maintain stability and security of the workplace, a motive which exists in the area of individual employment relationship as well. The change of employer does not affect employment contracts of employees; nor shall the collective agreement which determines the nature of individual employment contracts be affected in any manner, construed as meaning that the collective agreement does not cease to exist in such cases as the death of the employer or the emergence of a new corporation due to the merger of the company (employer) with another company or the transfer of the ownership of the undertaking to a new employer. It is held that the rule must apply also in the case of the change of the employer during the process of authorization, meaning that the certificate of authorization obtained before the change of the employer is binding on the new employer and hence the labour union is not compelled to issue another invitation for bargaining with the new employer. In so far as the cases alluded to above are concerned, the law has not made any distinction as to the normative or obligatory provisions of the collective agreement. Therefore, where the union side no longer exists, it is of course only the normative part of the collective agreement that shall continue to be effective. With the exception of the dissolution of the labour union therefore, both the normative and obligatory part of the collective agreement shall continue to be operative in the above-stated cases.

Chapter 7. Settlement of Collective Labour Disputes

§1. MEDIATION

I. The Notion

1269. Mediation is a step to which recourse must be made for the peaceful settlement of collective interest disputes before taking any strike and/or lock-out action or before resorting to compulsory arbitration where strikes and lock-outs are not permissible. The mediation in this category is certainly quite different from mediation mentioned in the new Labour Courts Act. Unlike the pre-1980 system when strikes and lock-outs should be preceded by the three-member conciliation boards, Act No. 2822 of 1983 and Act No. 6356 of 2012, taking into consideration the shortcomings of the conciliation system, established a one-person mediation process for the settlement of interest disputes (as right to strike for rights disputes was banned). The conciliation boards under the abolished system were to draw up an official non-binding decision which had to be submitted for the approval of the parties. Under the present system, the mediator is not empowered to issue a decision whatsoever. His task is to exert every effort possible in order to bring the parties to agreement and to offer suggestions to that effect. His main function is to help the parties find solutions in the settlement of the disputed items and, though not mandatory, to offer recommendations which he can incorporate into his final report in the event of a failure to reach agreement.

1270. Considering its avowed goals and flexible features, timing, etc., the present system of mediation was inspired by the US system. The parties are free to accept or reject the proposals of the mediator, a principle consistent with the autonomy of the social partners which is the underlying rationale of free collective bargaining. It should be borne in mind, however, that under the present system, the parties must first pass through the mediation stage in order to initiate the subsequent stages of industrial conflict, which was also the rule under the previous conciliation system. In other words, unlike the US system, Turkey has fostered compulsory mediation; though of secondary nature, there was also a category called 'voluntary mediation' under Act No. 2822. There is no formal 'fact-finding' mechanism; but requiring the mediator to espouse his assessment of the facts and recommendations which he may deem helpful for the settlement of the dispute has somewhat imbued the mediator's function with a flavour resembling that of the now-abolished conciliation boards.

1271. In addition to normal (routine) mediation, a second major category of mediation is to be called upon in cases where the government suspends a strike or lock-out. In this case, the process is called 'extraordinary mediation'.

II. Initiation of the Mediation Process

1272. In the presence of a collective interest dispute, the mediation process must be initiated. Conditions under which a collective labour dispute is deemed to have arisen are, according to Article 49(1), as follows:

> If either of the parties fails to appear at the place, date and time fixed for negotiations, or refrains from starting negotiations, or fails to attend the meetings after their commencement, or if the parties indicate their failure to reach agreement within the time limit for negotiations (60 days), or if that time expires without an agreement, one of the parties shall communicate the dispute to the competent authority in six working days. Otherwise, the labour union shall lose its authorization status.

1273. The phrase 'either of the parties' mentioned in Article 49(1) is construed to mean the 'party invited to negotiations' since the bargaining status of the inviting party shall be forfeited automatically if it fails to make an appearance within thirty days of the date on which it has made the invitation.

1274. Invalidating the labour union's collective bargaining authorization in the event of the last four cases mentioned in Article 49 is a new phenomenon brought about by Act No. 6356. Here the target of the said sanction is merely the labour union and workers since for the employer side the process of authorization is meaningless in the strict sense. As such the sanction is lopsided and prone to abusive practices. Following the receipt of the report in conjunction with the failure to reach agreement in accordance with Article 49(1), the next step is naturally the initiation of the mediation process, as was also the case under the previous system. Act No. 6356 has skipped what was called 'voluntary mediation' under Act No. 2822 which, with the request of either party, could be the mediation to be called on upon the lapse of the first thirty days from the beginning of negotiations. Though not frequently used, voluntary mediation was able to serve certain functions within its constraints, generally in cases where negotiations could not start due to the absence of the party invited. So, under the present new system, the process qualifies merely as 'compulsory mediation', a step which must be taken, naturally with no binding outcome, before an industrial action (strike and lock-out, or recourse to compulsory arbitration) can legally begin.

1275. The procedures pertaining to compulsory mediation have been addressed by Article 50 which provides: 'Upon receiving the report indicating the disagreement, the competent authority shall, with the participation of at least one of the parties, appoint a mediator from the official list of the Ministry, or if no party attends, it shall do so directly. Where the parties have agreed on a mediator from the official list (by name), this mediator will be put in charge of acting as the mediator in the dispute' (Article 50(1)). Because it favours voluntarism, the last sentence of Article 50(1) is certainly positive, but empowering the competent authority to appoint the mediator if no party attends the meeting is open to criticism. Furthermore, Article

60(7) has foreseen a stronger form of intervention by the government in conjunction with the strike action. It provides that 'in the settlement of a dispute for which a lawful strike has been decided, the Minister of Labour and Social Security may act as a mediator himself or may appoint another person as a mediator'. Considering that, especially in public sector disputes, the state is the employer by definition, the intervention by the Minister in the dispute as mediator may be serious target for criticism, as it has been cited in the 2014 report of the ILO Committee of Experts.

1276. Contrary to Act No. 2822 whereby the appointment of the mediator in the compulsory category of mediation was to be made by the labour court, this power has now and correctly been vested in the competent authority (Ministry of Labour) Missing in this process is the appointment of a neutral on whom the parties may have voluntarily agreed outside the official list, an option often raised as a desirable route by the advocates of more 'voluntarism'.

1277. With a view to helping the parties to reach agreement, the mediator shall make every effort and offer his suggestions for a settlement to the interested parties (Article 50(2)). The mediator's duty lasts fifteen days, but it can be extended for an additional six working days if the parties so agree (Article 50(3)). If the mediator can help the parties agree on the disputed items, the collective labour agreement is to be drawn up in line with the provisions of Article 48 on the signing and ratification of the collective labour agreement.

1278. 'If on the expiry of the mediator's term agreement has not been reached (on all items in dispute), the mediator shall draw up a report within three days and submit it to the competent authority together with an attached statement including his recommendations for the settlement of the dispute. The competent authority shall deliver the mediator's report to the parties within three days at the latest' (Article 50(5)). Delivery of this report is a critical point in paving the way for taking a lawful strike and lock-out decision or having recourse to the YHK where strikes and lock-outs have been prohibited by law.

1279. The mediator's term of duty starts on the date the communication for his appointment reaches him. An official mediation organization attached to the Ministry of Labour and Social Security has been set up to take the necessary steps and measures for providing official mediation services. The principles and procedures governing the establishment and operation of the official mediation organization and the preparation of the list of persons who may be called upon as official mediators have been provided for by a bylaw issued under Article 65 of Act No. 2822.

1280. The mediator must make every effort to bring about a settlement between the parties and make proposals to the interested parties. The parties and all interested persons are under the obligation to provide the mediator with the information requested by him (Article 50(6)). The fee of the mediator is fixed by the competent authority by considering the scope and nature of the dispute between the lower and upper limits set out in the relevant regulation, and shared by the parties, to be paid in equal amounts.

1281. The strike or lock-out action or resort to compulsory arbitration where strike or lock-out bans exist can be initiated only after exhausting the mediation stage. Any strike decision taken prior to the expiration of the mediation stage is deemed to be illegal.

1282. The mandate of the mediator is limited to the disputed items, but obviously flexibility of making changes in all collectively negotiated items in order to reach a final agreement prevails. The procedure may vary in each case depending on the nature of the dispute and the unique methods used by the mediator. Although the original determination of the dispute and the final agreement or disagreement is to be made in written form, the meetings are to be conducted orally, with an interim report drawn up for each meeting. The mediator may also hold separate meetings with each party and hear the opinions of third parties.

1283. The parties may certainly reach an agreement even before the intervention of the mediator in the dispute. In this case, the competent authority must be notified immediately.

A. *The Mediator's Qualifications*

1284. Despite the detailed rules governing the appointment and functions of the mediator, Act No. 2822 has not made any reference to 'neutrality' as a condition. The bylaws issued in conjunction with Article 59(2) of Act No. 2822, however, foresees some qualities which may be construed as 'neutrality'. The qualifications which the mediator must meet according to Article 26 of the bylaws are as follows: (1) to be citizens of Turkey, (2) to be in full possession of their civic rights, (3) not to have been barred from public service, (4) not to have been found guilty of certain types of felony or convicted of specified categories of criminal acts, (5) not to be engaged in the organs of political parties, of employers' and labour unions and confederations or public organizations, (6) to have graduated from a four-year institution of higher learning, with training in law, social policy, industrial relations or economics and a work experience in labour–management relations for a minimum period of five years, or must have had higher education in a different field but with work experience in labour relations in public institutions for a minimum period of ten years.

B. *The Legal Nature of Mediation*

1285. The recommendations and proposals of the mediator incorporated into his report in the event of disagreement are by no means regarded as a binding decision. In arbitration, on the other hand, the arbitrator's award is binding on the parties. Mediation is a public service function which falls into the domain of public law. Mediators who abuse their functions with malicious intent to the parties or, with the same intent, fail to transmit their reports to the competent authority within the prescribed time limit are liable to a major fine. The official mediators assigned to duty are considered public servants for any offences committed by or against them during their term of duty.

III. Other Forms of Mediation

1286. One should note here that the concept of mediation in collective interest disputes is technically and legally an entirely different form of the mediation explained in the new Labour Courts Act.

1287. Apart from official mediation, the Turkish industrial relations has also witnessed mediation efforts by private persons such as ministers, governors or mayors, or martial law commanders in areas where martial law was in effect and where official mediation had failed.

1288. Where a lawful strike or lock-out has been suspended by the order of Council of Ministers for sixteen days due to public health or national security reasons, mediator designated by the Minister of Labour and Social Security from the official list or the minister himself in line with Article 60(7) shall make every effort for the settlement of the dispute during the suspension period (Article 63(2)). This special category of mediation has been referred to as 'extraordinary mediation' in practice. When the impasse still persists at the expiration of the suspension term or if the parties have not agreed to refer the dispute to private arbitration, upon the request of one of the parties within six working days the dispute shall be settled by the YHK. Otherwise, the labour union's authorization status shall be void, another case where only the labour union's collective bargaining rights seem to have been impaired in a lopsided fashion.

IV. Problems of Mediation

1289. The present system of mediation was instituted by Act No. 2822 with a view to replace the conciliation boards of the pre-1980 era which were criticized for their alleged inefficiency in settling collective interest disputes. The experience of the last decade has shown, however, that the system of mediation is not as effective as was intended at its inception. Lamentations by labour unions, and Türk-İş in particular, have frequently reflected the dissatisfaction with mediation, culminating in even their preference for the removal altogether of any mechanism for the peaceful settlement of labour disputes. Proposals to revert back to the previous three-member conciliation boards have also been made in legal literature, asserting that the decisions of conciliation boards, though not binding, were more effective than mediation in bringing some pressure on the parties in dispute.

1290. Among the factors accounting for the relative failure of mediation in settling interest disputes, the following may be cited: (a) the staggering rate of inflation during the 1970s and 1980s which caused a rapid erosion in real wages, thereby leading to extremely high wage demands by unions in collective negotiations, encountered by stiff resistance by employers who had to keep costs down in the increasingly competitive domestic and international markets; (b) the absence of a full-fledged job security system pressing labour unions to negotiate for extremely high levels of notice pay and severance pay as well as enhanced forms of job security measures aimed to curb lay-offs; (c) the ever-increasing demands for more fringe benefits which tend to lengthen the negotiations process; (d) the denial of sufficient powers to mediators who, as a result, lack any authority to exert pressure or exercise sanctions on the parties; (e) the relatively short term of duty of mediators (fifteen days) and their exclusion from any mediating efforts during the strike stage; (f) the high work load of most mediators most of whom are not full-time professionals in labour disputes; (g) the reluctance of the Official Mediation Organization to publicize the findings of mediators with a view to bringing pressure on the disputing parties.

1291. Such adverse views notwithstanding, there is no question about the fact that some degree of success prevails in the mediation process. According to the official statistics of the Ministry of Labour and Social Security, approximately one-third of labour disputes had resulted in agreement at the mediation stage. However, in terms of the workplaces and the number of employees involved in labour disputes the percentage of those resulting in agreement at the mediation stage is approximately 20%.[509] Still, however, this ratio underestimates the actual contribution of mediators, because, even in unsettled cases, many of the disputed items are resolved by mediators although final settlements in all issues have not yet been effected. Thus one may argue that mediation serves various protracted and disguised functions in helping the parties reduce their differences in the longer run.

1292. A problem which causes delays in the mediation process is the failure of the competent authority as well as the mediators to complete the procedures within the prescribed time limits. Such unintended delays do not make the process invalid, but involve disciplinary sanctions for the officials concerned. In a case where the competent authority missed to implement the voluntary mediation process that was requested, the Court of Cassation did not consider the competent authority's negligence to be a violation of law and gave its approval to the direct initiation of the compulsory mediation process.[510]

1293. Act No. 2822 was silent on whether or not a single mediator would be in charge in multi-employer (group) bargaining disputes. In various group bargaining disputes different mediators have been assigned the task of mediating for each

509. T.C. Çalışma ve Sosyal Güvenlik Bakanlığı, *Çalışma Hayatıı İstatistikleri*, Vol. 62, Ankara, Kasım, 1995, p. 37.

510. Court of Cassation, 9th Div., 30 Apr. 1992, 4808/4881.

employer's enterprise or establishment.[511] The Court of Cassation has approved the validity of that practice.[512] Yet, in some others, a single mediator was chosen to deal with the dispute concerning multi-employer units. Since multi-employer bargaining results in a single 'pattern collective agreement' for all employers concerned, the predominant view seemed to foster the practice of assigning a single mediator to handle the dispute pertaining to such group bargains,(4) which eventually became the accepted practice now under Act No. 6356.[513]

1294. In the presence of various malfunctions besetting the mediation process under the existing system, various proposals may be put forward for improvement. In a draft bill for labour law reform, the Ministry of Labour has suggested repealing the Official Mediation Organization and replacing the existing compulsory system with voluntary mediation, to be conducted by private mediators agreed upon by the parties themselves. Another proposal may foresee a longer term of duty for mediators, to be carried out during the strike action as well. To enhance the effectiveness of the system further, the powers of the mediators may be increased by empowering them, if and when the difference between the parties' final offers have become minimal, to submit the final position of the parties to secret balloting by members of the organizations concerned. Furthermore, the effectiveness of mediation may be enhanced if the Official Mediation Organization uses its power to publicize the findings of mediators, in at least important disputes, as envisaged in Article 59(6) of Act No. 2822. Also, the parties may agree to resort to private arbitration at any stage of a rights or interest dispute. In practice, the parties have agreed to the mediator's acting as a private arbitrator in a few collective interest disputes. The further encouragement of this technique may help develop a viable 'med-arb' system for the peaceful settlement of labour disputes before the strike and lock-out actions take place.

1295. Notwithstanding the problems besetting the mediation system and the various suggestions for its improvement cited above, several draft bills have maintained mediation with minor modifications. The major changes foreseen in these drafts included the participation of the mediator in collective negotiations and the elimination of the category called 'voluntary mediation', a process which had not proven to be effective in practice and therefore repealed under the new Act No. 6356.

511. *See* Court of Cassation, the above ruling.

512. *See* Court of Cassation, the above ruling.

513. K. Oğuzman, *Grup Toplu İşSöleşmelerii Hakkında Yargıtayın Görüşlerinin Değerlendirilmesi*, MESS Yayını, İstanbul, 1989, p. 6; F. Şahlanan, *supra*, pp. 30–31.

Chapter 8. Industrial Conflict; Strikes and Lock-Outs and Their Exceptions

§1. The Right to Strike and Employer's Recourse to Lock-Out: The Notion and Constitutional Basis

1296. The Turkish Constitution of 1982 provides in Article 54 that 'employees have the right to strike in the event of a labour dispute arising during negotiations for the conclusion of a collective labour agreement. The exercise, scope and exceptions of this right as well as employers' resort to lock-out shall be governed by special legislation.' Thus, unlike the 1961 Constitution which had guaranteed only the right to strike, the present Constitution also mentioned employer's resort to lock-out, thereby carefully avoiding using the concept 'right' for the lock-out. Act No. 275 of 1963, however, treating a strike and lock-out as reciprocal rights, had regulated the right to lock-out in a manner parallel to the right to strike. The rationale underlying the wording of the 1982 Constitution as such is construed to mean that under the present system, offensive lock-outs are not seen as a social right, implying that only defensive lock-outs are permissible. As Article 26(2) and Article 27(3) of Act No. 2822 as well as Article 59(2) of Act No. 6356 have now provided, the decision to call a lock-out can be taken only following the labour union's decision to call a strike. This and the constitutional view notwithstanding, the pertinent provisions of Act No. 2822 and Act No. 6356 of 2012 seem to have regulated the right to strike and lock-out almost in parallel terms. Article 60(6) 27(3) of Act No. 2822 involves a special case where the scope of a lock-out may turn out to be broader than the scope of the strike; that is, in group (multi-employer) bargaining where the decision to call a strike covers only certain establishments, the decision to order the lock-out may be taken to cover other establishments as well within the scope of the dispute in question. This dimension of the legislation was recently struck out by the ruling of the Constitutional Court on 25 October 2014 as it had been the subject of criticism in the labour law teaching.[514]

§2. Main Features of the Right to Strike and Lock-Out

I. Definition of Lawful Strikes and Lock-Outs

A. *The Strike*

1297. Act No. 6356 provides the following definition for lawful and unlawful strikes: 'Strike means any concerted cessation by employees of their work with the purpose of halting the activities of an establishment or of paralyzing activities to a considerable extent, or any abandonment by employees of their work in accordance with a decision taken to that effect by an organization' (Article 58(1)).

514. F. Sağlam, *Anayasa Hukuku Açısından İşçi Haklarının Güncel Sorunları*, İstanbul, p. 34; F. Demir, *Sendikalar, supra*, p. 214.

1298. 'Lawful strike means any strike called by employees for the purpose of safeguarding or improving their economic and social position and working conditions in the event of a dispute during negotiations to conclude a collective labour agreement' (Article 58(2)).

1299. This means that only right to strike for interest disputes is guaranteed and permissible.

1300. Unlawful strike means any strike called without fulfilling the conditions required for a lawful strike.

1301. The following elements can be derived from the above legal definition to clarify what is meant by a 'lawful strike'. First, the strike must have an occupational objective related to an interest dispute in order to qualify as 'lawful', as implied in the expression 'safeguarding or improving employees' economic and social position and working conditions in the event of a dispute during negotiations'. Thus, unlike the pre-1980 system, strikes are permissible only in the event of interest disputes.[515] In the opinion of some writers, however, the Constitution has not banned strikes for rights disputes; it has merely bestowed legal guarantee on the right to strike for interest disputes.[516]

1302. Act No. 2822 had banned strikes called for other purposes, general strikes and political strikes as well as other forms of mass resistance. Among the forms of unlawful concerted action, Article 25 of Act No. 2822 had not mentioned sympathy strikes, boycotts and mass demonstrations and 'calling in sick' moves; however, the phrase 'any other acts of resistance' implied that all such forms were prohibited as well. In fact the Court of Cassation has ruled in its several verdicts that such concerted acts by employees should qualify as unlawful strikes,[517] as a result of which the employer could dismiss striking employees for just cause without any obligation to respect terms of notice and to pay severance payment.

1303. The second element of a 'lawful strike' is the condition that the strike decision must have been taken by a labour union which is the party to collective negotiations. Although Article 58(1) refers to 'any concerted cessation by the employees of their work', the employee side of the negotiations, according to the general structure of Act No. 2822 and 6356 and particularly in view of Article 59(2), must always be a labour union. Thus, the strike decision must have been taken by the labour union in order to be valid. In enforcing that decision, the union must aim either to halt the operations of the workplace entirely or to paralyse them to a considerable extent.

---

515. K. Oğuzman, *Hukuki Yönden İşçiİşveren İlişkileri, supra*, pp. 120–121.
516. F. Sağlam, *Anayasa Hukuku Açısından İş Hukukunun Güncel Sorunları, supra*, pp. 36–37.
517. Court of Cassation, 9th Div., 12 Nov. 1991, 12613/14228; 7 Oct. 1993, 3638/14256; 15 Sep. 1999, 10941/13721; 22 Nov. 2002, 20349/593.

1304. The third element involves 'concerted cessation of work by the employees'. This entails that employees must leave the establishment (workplace) after stopping work. Certainly, their commitment to the workplace and to their work is assumed to continue; that is, they have the intention of going back to their work after the strike is over. Although the Act uses the phrase 'concerted cessation of work', it must be noted that no specified ratio of workers is required in order for the strike to be enforced. 'Concerted action' is construed to mean 'cessation of work by more than one employee'. In fact, even though only a few employees may have participated in the strike at its inception, it may turn out to be an effective work stoppage if fellow workers join at later stages. The decision to go on strike and the implementation of the strike in an effective manner are separate issues.

1305. Fourth, the strike must be called and implemented in accordance with a series of requirements stipulated by Act No. 6356. As alluded to above, a strike is permissible only in the event of a collective interest dispute and all the formal requirements including the process of mediation must have been exhausted before the strike can lawfully begin. Anti-union practices by employers once the legally certified union has fulfilled all the lawful requirements do not invalidate the legality of the strike.[518]

B. Lock-Out

1306. As provided by Article 59(1), 'lock-out means any action taken by an employer or his representative, either on his own initiative or in accordance with a decision taken by an employers' organization, to refuse employment to employees so as to completely halt the activities of a given establishment'.

1307. 'Lawful lock-out' means any lock-out ordered in compliance with this Act where there is a dispute in the course of negotiations for a collective labour agreement and a decision to call a strike has already been taken by the labour union.

1308. 'Unlawful lock-out' means any lock-out ordered without fulfilling all the conditions for a lawful lock-out. Given the above definition, the elements of a lawful lock-out can be stated as follows. First, the lock-out must be aimed at an occupational goal and only lock-outs for interest disputes are permissible. Though not specified in the pertinent article clearly, the lock-out must pursue the objective of changing conditions of work, of imposing new conditions or of maintaining the conditions already prevailing. Conditions required for a lawful strike are valid also for a lawful lock-out. And only defensive lock-outs are permissible. As in a lawful strike, a lawful lock-out entails the exclusion of workers from the establishment only temporarily, that is, up until the conclusion of the collective labour agreement

518. The Court of Cassation has ruled that the dismissal of some employees by the employer before the labour union's decision to go on strike does not invalidate the lawfulness of the strike decision taken in accordance with legal requirements. Court of Cassation, 9th Div., 11 Feb. 1993, 1008/1958.

between the parties in dispute, as evidenced by the principle that, similar to the strike, the employment contracts of strikers as well as those who have been locked-out are deemed suspended rather than terminated within the duration of the strike or lock-out (Articles 67(1) and 68(1)).

1309. Second, the denial of work to employees must be based on a lock-out decision taken by the employer or his representative or, if the employer is affiliated with an employers' union, by the employers' union concerned.

1310. Third, in a lock-out the number of workers whom the employer refuses to engage in work must be large enough to halt the operations of the establishment completely, as opposed to the definition of the strike where it suffices to halt the operations merely 'to a considerable extent'. The refusal to engage the workers in work must be temporary in a lock-out, as evidenced by the suspension of employment contracts for the duration of the lock-out. As such, the lock-out is distinct from collective dismissals where the employer lays off employees due to certain objective economic causes rather than any motivation prompted by collective bargaining. However, the Court of Cassation upholds the view that if the shutdown of the workplace is instigated by the employer in an attempt to derive better concessions in collective bargaining rather than by objective factors pertaining to the operations of his undertaking, then such a shutdown should be regarded as an unlawful lock-out.[519]

1311. Certainly, this becomes more apparent in cases where the lock-out has been ordered subsequent to a strike decision or strike action by the union. The Court of Cassation went even further by ruling that the employer could close down his establishment after the certification of the union's majority status but only for objective economic reasons.[520] But the Court also found the shutdown of the establishment based on the employer's claims of unbearable costs caused by excessive wage demands as unjustified and legally unacceptable.[521] In another verdict, the Court of Cassation has deemed the collective dismissal of workers by the employer as an 'unlawful lockout', proclaiming that the employer's motive was unjustified as it was aimed at obstructing the labour union's strike action.[522]

1312. Fourth, as stated above, a significant element characterizing the lawful lock-out is the complete halting of operations in the establishment. The far-reaching consequences this may cause for the employer may actually serve as a deterrent preventing him from calling a lock-out arbitrarily.

---

519. Court of Cassation, 9th Div., 8 Jul. 1977, 8399/10608. For an evaluation of this verdict, *see* D. Ulucan, İHU, 1978/11, TSGLK, 17, No. 5.

520. Court of Cassation, 9th Div., 25 Dec. 1978, 15661/16194; 15 Jan. 1979, 119/670.

521. Court of Cassation, 9th Div., 15 Jun. 1990, 6798/7405.

522. Court of Cassation, 9th Div., 7 Jun. 1991, 9017/9888. However, lay-off of workers due to economic factors whereby some production is still carried out in the establishment should not be treated as an unlawful lock-out. Court of Cassation, 9th Div., 1 Mar. 1991, 2643/3142.

1313. And, last but not least, all the requirements stipulated by Act No. 6356 must have been met. Failure to abide by any of these rules and procedures causes the lock-out to be denoted as 'unlawful'.

1314. The pre-existing bans on calling political strikes, the general strike, sympathy strikes and similar concerted actions of resistance like work slow-downs and sit-ins, all imposed by Turkey's 1982 Constitution and long-criticized by the ILO were removed by the 12 September 2010 constitutional referendum. But although Act No. 6356 does not make any reference to such forms of industrial action, the definition given in Article 58 limits lawful strikes only to interest disputes which arise in the course of negotiations for a new collective labour agreement.

II. The Decisions to Call a Strike and Lock-Out and Implementation

A. *The Decision to Strike or Lock-Out*

1315. Article 60(1) provides that:

> the decision to call a strike may be taken within 60 days from the date on which the communication mentioned in Article 50(5) (mediator's report) has been delivered (to the parties) and may be put into force within that term on the date which must be communicated to the counter-party within six working days beforehand. The failure to take the decision to strike within that term and communicate it within the indicated time shall invalidate the authorization to make the collective labour agreement.

1316. Although here too the main features of Act No. 2822 have been preserved, Act No. 6356 foresees a few new dimensions on the initiation of industrial conflict. The initial six working days cool-off period after the delivery of the mediator's report during which no action could be taken under Act No. 2822 has now be deleted.

1317. 'The employers' union or the employer unaffiliated with the employers' union make take a lock-out decision within sixty days from the date on which the labour union's decision to strike has been communicated to the employers' union or the employer concerned and may be put into force within that term on a date to be notified to the other party within six working days beforehand' (Article 60(2)).

1318. Failure to respect these time limits makes the strike unlawful. Besides, the authorization certificate of the union becomes void if a decision to call a strike is not taken within that prescribed time limit or, where strikes are prohibited, application is not made to the YHK for resolving the dispute.

1319. And the lock-out may be declared only upon receiving the labour union's decision to strike. However, in relation to group collective labour agreements, even though the decision to call a strike covers only some of the establishments involved in the dispute, the decision to order a lock-out may be taken to cover also other establishments within the scope of the dispute (Article 60(6)). As noted above, this clause in Article 60(6) of Act No. 6356 has been declared null by the decision of the Constitutional Court on 22 October 2014.

1320. This latter case, now null and void, which naturally deviated from the notion of defensive lock-outs, applied to 'group' (multi-employer) bargains. In enterprise-level (multi-plant) bargaining where an enterprise with multiple establishments (plants) in the same industry exists, the strike and lock-out decisions have to be taken naturally for all the establishments concerned, since the enterprise with multiple establishments belonging to the same employer in the same industry branch represents an integrated whole.[523]

B. Notification and Announcement of Strike and Lock-Out Decisions

1321. The decision to strike and lock-out shall be immediately announced at the establishment or establishments by the party that has taken the decision (Article 60(3)). Also a decision to call a strike or order a lock-out must be submitted to a notary public to be communicated to the other party within six working days of the date of the decision and one copy of the decision must be submitted to the competent authority. The decision to call a strike or order a lock-out shall come into effect on the date notified to the other party six working days beforehand through the public notary (Article 60(5)). The date of actual enforcement shall be immediately announced by the deciding party at the establishment or establishments (Article 60(3)). The failure of the competent authority to communicate the strike decision to the other party (employer) within six working days does not affect the legitimacy of the strike.[524]

C. Strike Ballot

1322. Act No. 2822, like its predecessor Act No. 275, had foreseen the taking of a strike ballot if a certain number of employees request that such a vote be conducted. Under Act No. 6356 it is Article 61 that regulates the strike ballot with some changes. Aiming to stave off the possible adverse effects of the strike on non-strikers as well as on the employer and other stakeholders, Turkish legislation, beginning with the 1963 Act, has approached the issue of strike vote from a rather negative viewpoint rather than leaving it to the voluntary decision of the labour union and its members. Furthermore, Act No. 6356 has taken a more anti-labour approach to the strike ballot by making a 'no-strike vote' easier than the previous system. In view of Article 61, 'a strike vote must be complied with if one-fourth employees employed in the establishment on the date the strike decision was announced request the competent authority in writing that a strike vote must be

523. *See* Court of Cassation, the above ruling.
524. Court of Cassation, 9th Div., 18 Feb. 1987, 2978/2139.

taken within six working days following the announcement of the strike. The strike ballot must be administered (by secret voting and open counts) by the competent authority within six working days following the written request. If, of the employees who were working in the establishment on the date of the announcement of the strike the majority who take part in balloting vote against the strike, the strike decision shall not be implemented (Article 61(3)).

1323. The one-fourth ratio must be determined in terms of the number of employees on the payroll on the date the strike decision is announced in the establishment. The total number of employees, whether union members or not, must be taken into account in determining the specified one-fourth ratio. The only persons to be excluded are those treated as employer's representatives within the meaning of Act No. 2821 and, of course, public servants (if there are any). This means that even those employees who have been excluded from the coverage of the collective agreement by the mutual consent of the parties shall be counted and may participate in the voting.[525]

1324. In this case if agreement cannot be reached until the expiry of the sixty-day period, or if the labour union does not apply to the supreme Arbitration Board within six working days from the finalization of the 'no-strike' outcome, the labour union's authorization status shall become invalid (Article 51(1)). Another item which is clearly slanted against the labour union which in this case will have to start the whole process from the very beginning. While under Act No. 2822 the strike could not be enforced if the simple majority of employees working at the establishment had voted against the strike, the new Act has referred merely to the 'no-strike' vote of the majority of the actual participants in the strike ballot, thus making it easier to halt a lawful strike. This procedure may pave the way for increased employer pressures on certain worker groups, i.e., managerial employees and workers excluded from collective bargaining coverage (non-covered workers) in order to force them to participate in the ballot in an attempt to extract a 'no-strike' resolution. Furthermore, invalidating the certificate of authorization is another point vulnerable to criticism.[526]

1325. The Act is silent on the effect of the strike vote on the lock-out. It is held that the nullity of the union's bargaining certificate in the event of the failure to reach agreement or to refer the dispute to compulsory arbitration must entail the automatic cancellation of any lock-out decision since the union deprived of bargaining rights need not be forced by any means into agreeing with the employer.[527]

1326. In the event of a dispute pertaining to an enterprise agreement, the request for a strike ballot must be made to the authority where each establishment of the

525. Court of Cassation, 9th Div., 13 Oct. 1975, 28864/46610. On modalities of strike ballot, *see* A. Çifter, Grev Oylaması, *Kenan Tunçomağ'a Armağan*, İstanbul, 1997, pp. 76–100.

526. Murat Özveri, Sendikal Haklar: 6356 Sayılı Sendikalar ve Toplu İş Sözleşmesi Yasası, pp. 159–160.

527. K. Oğuzman, *Hukuki Yönden İşçiiİşveren İlişkilerii, supra*, p. 203; M. Kutal, *Toplu İş Sözleşmesine İlişkin Temel Sorunlar Semineri*, Ankara, 1990, p. 114.

enterprise is located. Ascertaining the appropriate number of employees requesting that the ballot must be taken as well as finalizing the results of the strike ballot following the gathering of the ballots shall be administered by the competent authority to which the centre of the enterprise is attached (Article 61(4)). In group collective bargaining, the request for the strike ballot shall be made to the relevant competent authorities to which establishments and/or enterprises in the group are attached. Ascertaining whether or not the number of employees requesting the strike ballot has reached the required ratio as well as the results of the ballots shall be determined for each establishment separately (Article 61(5)).

1327. Provisions on the strike ballot have been the target of heated criticisms by labour union and pro-labour circles. The critics argued that the strike vote, as it stands, was designed to undermine the union's strike power by letting all the employees of an establishment participate in a voting procedure which may ultimately bar the union from going on strike. Advocates of the voting procedure argue, on the other hand, that by involving all the employees in the strike ballot, the legislation aimed to safeguard the interests of non-members as well as members of a union because everyone will likely be affected adversely by the consequences of a work stoppage. On the employers' side, however, there have been occasions where temporary employees have been hired in order to avert the strike decision of a union by forcing such employees to request and participate in a strike vote.

1328. Some union constitutions include a strike ballot procedure as a measure of union democracy, thereby letting only union members participate in the ballot on the employer's final offer or on the report of the mediator, but the incorporation of this procedure into law is unlikely because of possible reactions from certain unions.

D. Implementation of the Strike and Lock-Out

1329. With a view to filling the void which existed in the pre-1980 system, Act No. 2822 and now 6356 have brought new rules as regards the time limits within which the strike or lock-out would be implemented. A strike or lock-out decision taken in accordance with Article 60 of Act 6356 and submitted to the public notary must be executed within sixty days following its communication to the other party. Within that sixty-day period, the decision to call a strike or order a lock-out shall become enforceable on the date notified to the other party six working days beforehand through a notary public.

1330. There is thus first a maximum period of sixty days within which the strike or lock-out action must actually be put into effect. Second, the employer must be informed of the actual date the strike action will be enforced six working days before which a notarized statement to that effect must have been received by him. The motive underlying these time slices was to do away with the uncertainties which existed under the previous system and to forestall unexpected (surprise) strikes which might harm the establishment and production processes.

1331. If a strike ballot was taken, the sixty-day period starts on the date the results of the ballot are finalized. In temporary bans on strikes and lock-outs, upon the repeal of the ban and in the event of the suspension (postponement) of industrial action by the government, if the government withdraws the postponement decree or the High Court of Administration cancels the postponement, the strike or lock-out is to be executed in accordance with the regular procedures envisaged in Article 60.

1332. A decision to call a strike or order a lock-out which is not submitted to the notary public within the prescribed time for notification to the other party or to the competent authority shall not come into effect. The right to a strike or lock-out which is not initiated on the announced date shall lose its effect. If a decision to call a strike is not put into effect within the prescribed time limit (sixty days), or if there is no order for a lock-out or the decision to order a lock-out is not put into effect within the allotted time, the certificate of authorization shall become invalid. As Article 60(4) provides, 'the right to strike or lock-out shall be forfeited if it is not implemented on the date notified. The authorization certificate shall become void if the strike decision is not put into force within due time as well as in the event of lock-out where there is no lock-out decision or the lock-out has not been put into operation within due time.' The strike or lock-out executed in violation of the prescribed time limits is deemed unlawful. In this case sanctions concerning unlawful strikes or lock-outs shall be applicable.

§3. Consequences of Strikes and Lock-Outs

I. The Requirement to Leave the Establishment

1333. Employees who go on strike are required to leave the establishment once a strike becomes effective. As provided by Article 64(1), 'employees are free to participate or not to participate in the strike. Employees participating in the strike or who are subjected to a lock-out must leave the establishment. Working at the establishment shall not be denied in any way to employees refusing to participate in the strike as well as to those who have initially participated but later refused participating in the strike.' Thus, the freedom to work of the employees who do not participate or who have refused to participate in the strike may not be restricted in any way.[528] 'The employer is at liberty to engage or not to engage in work any employees who are not participating or who have refused to participate in the strike', as the right to refrain going on striking is guaranteed. But, due to the duty of equal treatment, the employer must either engage all of the non-striking employees in work or none of them. Further, a striking employee may later decide to quit the strike and

528. This principle is closely related to the freedom to work of the employer as well as of the employee. Without prejudice to the lawful exercise of the right to strike, the new Penal Code No. 5237 has brought sanctions to apply in the event of the violation of the principle of the freedom to work by the employer or the employee. In view of Art. 117, the person who violates the freedom to work is to be sentenced to a prison term from six months up to two years or to a legal fine. And anyone who obstructs work or causes work to stop shall be sentenced to a prison term from six months up three years, which may be further increased under certain conditions (Art. 119).

work in the establishment. But the employee who has not taken part in the strike, thus keeping on working in the establishment on the date the strike had begun, is not allowed to participate in the strike at a later stage.[529] The law is silent as to whether only members of the union which has initiated the dispute may take part in the strike. In practice, non-members and members (of even other unions) are entitled to participate in the strike action.

1334. If a collective agreement is concluded at the end of the strike action, the agreement, with the exception of those who cannot take part in the strike by virtue of Articles 65, shall not apply to non-striking employees, unless provision to the contrary has been made in the collective agreement (Article 39(8)). In practice, collective agreements usually contain such a permitting clause.

1335. Article 39(8) does not affect the rights of employees who have been excluded from the strike by virtue of Article 39, or non-striking employees in establishments to which the collective agreement has later been extended.

1336. Because, by definition of the law, a lock-out results in the complete halting of operations in the establishment, all employees, whether or not they are members of the union exposed to a lock-out decision, must leave the workplace within the duration of the lock-out.

1337. Employees who are participating in the strike or who are locked out are prohibited from obstructing the entrance or exit of the establishment (Article 64(2)).

1338. Any clauses in collective labour agreements and employment contracts waiving or restricting the right to strike or foreseeing the abdication from or restriction of the right to strike or lock-out are null and void (Article 64(1)). 'The worker's employment contract shall not be terminated for his participation in taking the decision to strike, for encouraging the taking of this decision, for taking advantage of participating in the strike or inciting others to participate in the strike. Within the duration of the strike and lock-out employees shall keep receiving social security benefits in view of the provisions of the Social Insurances and General Health Insurance Act, No. 5510' (Article 66(2,3)).

II. Employees Excluded from Taking Part in a Strike or Lock-Out

1339. As provided by Article 65, 'on condition that their activities are unrelated to the production or sale of goods, a sufficient number of employees are required to work and the employer must employ them during a lawful strike or lock-out'. The object is to ensure the continuity of work in processes which have to be maintained for technical reasons, or to ensure the safety of the establishment and prevent damage to machinery, installations, equipment, raw materials and finished and semi-finished products, or to ensure the protection of animals and plants.

529. Court of Cassation, 9th Div., 23 Sep. 1993, 1714/13599; 27 Jun. 2006, 1570/4778.

1340. Act No. 6356, like its predecessor Act No. 2822, has also spelled out the method of identifying the employees to be excluded from participating in the strike or lock-out. The types and numbers of such employees, including substitutes, must be announced in writing within the establishment by the employer or his representative during the six working days following the commencement of collective negotiations. A copy of this announcement must be sent to the labour union that is the party to collective bargaining. If no appeal against this notice is lodged by the labour union with the local labour court within six working days, the notice becomes final. If an appeal has been lodged, the labour court must take a final decision within six working days (Article 65(2)).

1341. If such employees have not been determined for any reason during the legal time limit, either party may request the competent authority (regional directorate of labour)to determine their types and numbers even after the lapse of the time limit. The competent authority must resolve the issue and notify the parties accordingly in the shortest time possible. Where necessary, the competent authority may take a decision at its own initiative. Either party may lodge an appeal with the local labour court and contest the decision of the competent authority. The court shall render its definitive verdict within six working days' (Article 65(3)). In disputes concerning an enterprise agreement, the competent labour court shall be the one where the headquarters of the enterprise is located and the regional directorate of labour according to the region where each of the establishments is located.

III. The Identification of Employees Who Must Not Participate in the Strike or Lock-Out

1342. Employees excluded from participating in the strike or lock-out are generally such categories as guards, maintenance workers, electricians, firemen and certain repairmen. Also, as employment contracts are suspended during a strike or lock-out, the employer is required to pay on the normal pay day the wages due to the employees on strike or lock-out earned by them prior to the commencement of the strike or lock-out. The employees responsible for making the payment are also required to work. If this requirement is breached, the employer may, after obtaining written permission from the competent authority, recruit new employees in place of the employees who do not work. Furthermore, one or perhaps a few workers may be excluded from the strike or lock-out in order to deal with the wage payments and wage-related procedures of employees who are not participating in the strike.

1343. Act No. 6356 has also provided for the actual naming of the employees to be excluded from the strike or lock-out. The competent authority, within three working days after the receipt of the decision to call a strike or order a lock-out, decide which employees are to continue working in the establishment during a strike or lock-out and notify the employer and the workers concerned in writing. However, if the chairman and members of the management board of the labour union or its branch are employed in the establishment, they may by no means be required to continue working during a strike or lock-out (Article 65(4)).

1344. If employees excluded from the strike or lock-out refrain from working, the employer, after obtaining the written permission of the competent authority may recruit new workers to replace them.

1345. In addition to the employees excluded from taking part in the strike or lock-out according to the criteria explained above, private security personnel employed in certain establishments in accordance with special legislation (Act No. 5188) shall not participate in a strike and they have to continue working during a lock-out.

1346. In an effort to impair the effectiveness of a strike, the employer may attempt to enlarge the scope of the list of employees to be excluded from striking. This point has been raised as a likely adverse effect of the above provisions.

1347. However, actual practice does not seem to have yielded any effect as such. First, there is the requirement that the functions of these employees must be unrelated to the production or sale of goods and services. Besides, a long list means paying wages for employees whose work is not making any contribution to the production and sale functions of the establishment. And finally the labour union is empowered to lodge an appeal with the labour court if it does not agree with the type and number of such employees.

IV. The Effect of Lawful Strikes and Lock-Outs on Individual Employment Contracts

1348. As was the case under Act No. 275 and Act No. 2822, Act No. 6356 has reiterated the notion that employees' employment contracts are not to be terminated during a lawful strike or lock-out; they shall simply be suspended. Act No. 6356 proclaims that 'the employment contracts of employees participating in a lawful strike and of those not participating or who have given up participating in such a strike and yet who were unable to work because of the strike, as well of those affected by a lawful lock-out shall be suspended for the duration of the strike and lock-out' (Article 67(1)). Thus, the rights and obligations under the employment contract of any employee who takes part in a lawful strike or wishes to work in the establishment during the strike but is not called upon to do so by the employer, shall be suspended until the end of the strike.[530]

1349. Also, where an employee is affected by a lawful lock-out, his rights and obligations under the employment contract shall be suspended until the end of the lock-out.

1350. Adjacent to the suspension of the employment contract is the non-payment of wages and other benefits to the employee during a strike or lock-out.

530. On the effects of the strike on individual employment contracts, *see* A. Çifter, *Türk Hukukunda Grevin Hizmet Aktine Etkisi*, Kocaeli, 2001.

Nor shall this period be taken into account in the calculation of the employee's severance pay. Collective agreements and employment contracts must not carry any clause contrary to these rules (Article 67(3)).

1351. Since other time periods during which the employee's employment contract is suspended (according to the Labour Act and Maritime Labour Act) are taken into account in the calculation of his severance pay, the above provision is an exception to this general rule. The employer must, however, pay on the normal pay day all the wages and other benefits of the employees whose employment contracts have been suspended due to the strike or lock-out, accrued before the date on which the strike or lock-out actually began. The personnel in charge of making these payments shall work to perform that duty. Otherwise Article 65(5) shall be applicable (Article 67(2)).

1352. However, as mentioned above, employees continue to benefit from the relevant provisions of the Social Security Act during the period of a strike or lock-out But the wages and other benefits as well as the said deductions of employees who have been excluded from a strike or lock-out must be paid regularly since there employment contracts are operative during the strike our lock-out.

1353. The striking employee as well as the employee subject to a lock-out is not paid the weekly rest day remuneration because, due to the strike, the requirement to have worked during workdays before the rest day, as laid down in Article 46(1) of the Labour Act, has not been met. The same rule applies to employees who are on strike during national holidays since the employee's refraining from work is due to the strike and not because of the fact that it is a holiday. Likewise, since the requirement 'to have worked at least one year' has not been fulfilled (Article 53(1), the Labour Act), the time spent on strike or lock-out is not counted in determining the employee's entitlement to annual leave with pay. A non-striking employee may use his annual leave with pay during the strike. The employee on strike, on the other hand, may avail himself of annual leave with pay after the strike is over. The employee who took his annual leave before the beginning of the strike or lock-out may use his leave during the strike or lock-out,[531] but he may also discontinue his leave and participate in the strike.[532]

1354. Act No. 2822 was silent on the ending of the employment contracts during a strike or lock-out, so is Act No. 6356. Obviously, there is no question about the termination of the employment contract by the mutual consent of the parties or about breaking it for just cause in accordance with Articles 24 and 25 of the Labour Act.[533] An employment contract made for a definite period also ends with the expiration of the specified period during the strike or lock-out. But whether or not the employment contract could be terminated by observing the notice terms and without showing any cause in accordance with Article 13 of the Labour Act No. 1475

531. K. Oğuzman, *Hukuki Yönden İşçi-İşveren İlişkileri, supra*, p. 222.
532. Çelik, *supra*, pp. 671–672.
533. In other words, 'for just cause terminations'.

(now Article 17 under Act No. 4857) was a contentious point. The majority favoured the view that notice to terminate the contract could be given within the duration of the strike or lock-out, but the terms of notice could begin only after the ending of the strike or lock-out.[534] In fact, the Court of Cassation upheld lower court decisions that notice periods should not become operative as long as the execution of employment contracts was subject to suspension.[535] Under the present system of job security, terminating the employee with notice during a strike shall in no way be considered justifiable. For employees not covered by the job security provisions of Act No. 4857, on the other hand, termination in accordance with Article 17 shall be considered an abusive dismissal.

1355. An employee whose rights and obligations under his employment contract are suspended in consequence of a lawful strike or lock-out is not permitted to accept any other employment. If he does, the employer may terminate his employment contract for just cause without notice or compensation However, provided that they do not exceed the remaining time slice of the weekly working time, employees working part-time may be employed at the establishment of another employer (Article 68(3)). Thus, essentially and as a basic rule, the striking or locked out employee may neither accept employment in another establishment nor is he allowed to work in self-employed occupations. Likewise, during a lawful strike or lock-out the employer must not take on any employee in a permanent or temporary capacity or hire any other person as a replacement for a striking or locked-out employee whose rights and obligations under his employment contract have been suspended accordingly (Article 68(1)). Thus strike-breaking is explicitly forbidden in Turkish law.[536] The employer has the right to recruit new employees only in substitution for the ones excluded from participating in a strike or lock-out by definition of Article 65 if their employment contracts have ended during the strike or lock-out (i.e., if they have died or left employment on their own or who have been terminated by the employer for just cause). Violation of this restriction by the employer shall be inspected by the competent authority upon the written request of the labour union (Article 68(1)).

1356. Alleged violation of the 'no strike-breaking' rule by the employers is to be inspected by the regional directorate of labour upon the written application of the strike pickets harnessed by the union concerned. Any employer violating the prohibition to hire strike replacements is liable to a major fine. Persons urging the employer to act in this direction are also held liable.

1357. Employees who are not participating or have refused to participate in a strike may be employed under Article 68(2) only in their own functions and not in substitution for the employees who have taken part in the strike (Article 68(2)).

---

534. K. Oğuzman, *Hukuki Yönden İşçi-İşveren İlişkileri, supra*, p. 213; T. Esener, *supra*, pp. 629–630.
535. Court of Cassation, 9th Div., 8 Jul. 1977, 8389/10606; 24 Apr. 1978, 5535/6756.
536. For the special socio-economic reasons underlying the legislature's motives in explicitly prohibiting strike-breaking in Turkey, *see* T. Dereli, Aydınlar, *Sendika Hareketi ve Endüstriyel İlişiler Sistemi*, İştanbul, 1975, pp. 339–342.

However, this rule applies only to employees who have originally been hired for certain identifiable jobs, meaning those who are routinely assigned to different tasks are not subject to this restriction.[537]

V. Employees' Housing Rights

1358. The employer must not in any circumstances require an employee who has taken part in a lawful strike or been affected by a lawful lock-out to vacate the housing which he has placed at the employee's disposal. The employer may demand from the employees residing in such housing the payment of such expenses as repair costs, water, gas, lighting and heating expenditures as well as the current rent payments incurred within the duration of the strike and lock-out (Article 69(1,2)). During a lawful strike and lock-out the employer is not allowed to restrict gas, water, lighting and heating services for such housing. But the employee may not request the continuation of such services if they have been cut off as direct consequence of the lawful strike and lock-out (Article 69(3)).

VI. Movement of Products Out of the Struck Establishment

1359. As emphasized in Article 54 of the 1982 Constitution as well as in Article 64(1) of Act No. 6356, the freedom to work in the establishment of those employees who are not participating or have refused to participate in the strike must not be restricted in any way by the employees on strike.

1360. A problem related to the right to strike as well as the freedom to work during the strike is the movement of goods and equipment in and out of the struck establishment. The issue was a controversial one and Act No. 2822, with an amendment in 1988 by Act No. 3451, brought the following provision: 'The sale of the goods produced by the employees working and the movement of the necessary materials, equipment and supplies into the establishment shall not be obstructed.' The provisions of Article 68 (prohibition on recruitment of strike replacements or on employees' accepting other employment) shall also apply to the performance of such work. Subsequent to this amendment, the Court of Cassation, changed the position it had adopted in its 1988 verdict[538] and ruled in the following direction:

> The movement of the goods out of the establishment is possible if they have been produced before as well as during the strike by employees who were not participating or who refused to participate in the strike. But the movement of goods produced previously by the striking employees out of the establishment is not permissible. Where necessary, the quantity and proportion of the goods

537. The Court of Cassation had upheld a lower court decision in this direction: 9th Div., 20 Apr. 1967, 2837/3467.
538. Court of Cassation, 9th Div., 5 Oct. 1988, 10143/9127.

produced by the non-striking and striking employees before the commencement of the strike must be determined by expert opinion; and then the movement of only the goods produced by the non-striking employees out of the establishment may be permitted. If this is not feasible, the proportion of striking and non-striking employees must be ascertained and acted upon accordingly.[539]

1361. The Court's apparently pro-union 1992 verdict was criticized on the grounds that let alone determining the said proportion was practically unfeasible, non-striking employees not engaged in actual production but assigned specifically to the handling, transfer and movement of the goods produced should be permitted to move all kinds of finished stocks out of the establishment, provided that such employees could by no means be required to perform the functions of the employees on strike.[540] Besides, it was been asserted that the contrary conclusion was apt to violate the principle of the freedom of non-striking employees to work, (in particular of those employed in warehouse units or engaged in the transport-loading-unloading and sale functions in the establishment).[541]

1362. Before the amendment, the article read as follows: 'The movement of the goods produced by the employees working or any kind of stock out of the establishment, or the sale of such goods, or the movement of the necessary materials, equipment and supplies into the establishment shall also apply to the performance of such work.'

1363. Finally, in 1994 the Court of Cassation changed its stance on this issue again and, parallel to the opinions raised in the literature, ruled that 'the goods previously produced by striking workers may be moved out of the establishment provided that the conditions of Article 43 are as well respected (i.e., non-striking employees must not be engaged in the operations which were performed by the those who are now on strike) in the moving, carrying and loading of such goods. Evidently the effect of the strike is proactive; ascribing retroactive effects to any strike action does not seem feasible'.[542]

1364. It is clear that in its 1992 verdict, the Court of Cassation (albeit confusingly) aimed to further the effectiveness of the strike weapon by limiting the movement of the finished goods out of the establishment. While the opposing views seem to carry some weight, allowing without any distinction the goods produced before and during the strike to be moved out is likely to undermine the effectiveness of the

539. Court of Cassation, 9th Div., 7 Sep. 1992, 9830/9273.
540. N. Çelik, 1992 Yılı Kararları Semineri, *İşHukuku ve Sosyal Güvenlik Hukuku Türk Milli Komitesi*, 1993, p. 122; Çelik, *supra*, p. 520.
541. M. Ekonomi, 'Grevin Uygulanması Sırasında Stokların İşyeri Dışına Çıkarılması, *İHD*, TemmuzEylül 1993, pp. 325–339.
542. Court of Cassation, 9th Div., 26 Dec. 1994, 18347/18558. *See* the paper by M. Ekonomi, 'Yargıtay'ın İşHukukuna İlişkin Kararlarının Değerlendirilmesi 1994', *İşHukuku ve Sosyal Güvenlik Hukuku Türk Milli Komitesi*, İstanbul, 1996, pp. 99–100; Court of Cassation, 9th Div., 4 Feb. 1999, 995/1481.

strike considerably, Besides, the supervisory mechanism to enforce the requirements of the then Article 43 within the establishment is extremely difficult during the strike. There was need for further legislation, therefore, to clarify the meaning of the 1988 amendment.

1365. To deal with this matter, the new Act No. 6356 brought the clear-cut solution envisaged in Article 64: Employees who are participating in the strike or who have been locked-out are prohibited from obstructing the entrance or exit of the establishment. The sale of the items produced before the strike had begun and their movement out of the establishment must not be obstructed. The sale and movement of products produced by non-strikers out of the establishment as well as the movement of necessary items, tools and equipment into the establishment shall not be obstructed by strikers in any manner. For the execution of these acts, provisions of Article 68 shall apply (Article 64 (2, 3 and 4)).

VII. Subcontractor's Employees

1366. Still another problem arising from the principle of freedom to work in the establishment during a strike concerned the employees of the subcontractor. It is generally held that the employees of the subcontractor should enjoy this freedom as well. Since Act No. 6356 has not brought any specific clauses on this matter, court decisions rendered before 2012 are still valid. However, in a case where the principal employer handed over the work in his establishment who was at a collective labour dispute stage to a subcontractor who was one of his previous (retired) employees, the Court of Cassation ratified the lower court decision,[543] ruling that the employer's action was not justified since his main motive was to render the strike ineffective. In the opinion of the 8th labour court in Ankara, the agreement between the main employer and the subcontractor was a simulated one aimed to thwart the upcoming strike. Besides, the subcontracted work involved the main operations of the establishment rather than work of an auxiliary nature.[544] The court invoking Article 2 of the Turkish Civil Code (the principle of fair dealing) concluded that in this case the subcontractor was not an entity independent from the main employer and therefore the statement by the subcontractor (the plaintiff) that his employees were unjustly barred from entering the establishment was not a valid argument. Thus, the action as well as the request for an injunction had to be denied. Article 2 of the new Labour Act No. 4857 brought clarity to the principal employer-subcontractor relationship and the High Court's verdict in the special case mentioned is consistent with the present legislation which forbids simulated acts by the principal employer and subcontractor.[545] Due to the presence of simulation, the right to work of the subcontractor's employees at the struck establishment could hardly be defended.

543. Court of Cassation, 9th Div., 12 Apr. 1991, 7302/7518.

544. *See* Court of Cassation, the above ruling.

545. *See* above 'Part-Time and Full-Time Contracts'.

1367. The High Court also ruled that during a lawful strike the struck employer should not carry on production on the premises of a different employer.[546]

VIII. Strike Pickets

1368. A labour union that has called a lawful strike is entitled, with the object of ensuring that its decision to strike is respected by members, to place strike pickets of not more than four of its members at each exit and entrance of the establishment. The provisions envisaged by Act No. 6356 on strike and lock-out pickets are similar to those foreseen by Act No. 2822. In view of Article 73(1) of the new Act, 'in order to ensure respect for the lawful strike and to monitor members' adherence to the strike decision, the labour union which has called a strike at an establishment may place strike pickets of not more than four of its members at each entrance and exit of the establishment, provided that there shall be no resort to force, violence and threat.' 'The strike pickets shall not obstruct the entrance into and exit from the establishment, nor may they stop people going in or coming out, even for checking purposes' (Article 73(2)). They must not resort to force, violence or threat, their sole aim being to ensure that the members of the union respect the decision to go on strike. The freedom to work is guaranteed in every case.

1369. Article 48(4) of Act No. 2822 provided that the labour union or the employees should not provide any means of shelter such as sheds, huts or tents in and around the establishment for the strike pickets or for employees on strike. An amendment to Article 48 by Act No. 3451 foresaw that a regulation would be issued by the Ministry of Labour to determine the ways and means of meeting the necessary needs of strike pickets. A regulation along these lines was published in the Official Gazette on 11 September 1988. This regulation had foreseen the provision of protective personal devices like umbrella, raincoat and similar means by the striking labour union for strike pickets while the employer was in charge of supplying humanitarian measures like lavatory and toilet arrangements as well as urgent medical intervention in the case of serious illness of strike pickets during their work: the union was responsible to provide food and drinking water for strike pickets, but if non-striking workers were served meals by the establishment, the employer had to offer the same meal to strike pickets as well during their duty to oversee the strike. Based on the assumption the regulation of 1988 was a supplement to the now-repealed Act No. 2822 and without bringing any new arrangements, Act No. 6255 of 2014 has abrogated this regulation altogether, thus entrusting the said functions only to the striking union which has been seen as another sign signalling the anti-union stance of the legislature.

1370. Although Act No. 6356 has struck out some of the details of Act No. 2822 related to the implementation of the strike, its Article 74 on the powers of the administrative authority, heavier than their counterparts in Act No. 2822, is open to criticism, as it is likely to impair the effectiveness of the strike. Article 74(1) provides:

546. Court of Cassation, 9th Div., 15 Jul. 1993, 1992/8607, 1993/10241.

'To cope with probable disruptions, the highest civil authority of the locality shall take the necessary measures to ensure the continuity of services necessary for the daily life of the public and operations of the establishment.' Though Article 74(2) includes some reservations on the use of the powers of administrative authority by saying that 'the measures taken by the highest civil authority relating to the maintenance of public order during the implementation of the strike and lock-out shall not be prejudicial to the execution of a lawful strike or lock-out', the said article is still vulnerable to subjective interpretations.

1371. Parallel to strike pickets, 'the employers' union which has ordered a lawful lock-out is also entitled, with the object of ensuring that its members respect a lock-out decision, to send pickets to the establishments affected by the lock-out. These pickets must not use force and threat' (Article 73(3)).

§4. The Ending of the Strike and Lock-Out

I. Suspension (Postponement) of the Strike or Lock-Out

1372. The power of the government to postpone a strike or lock-out up to sixty days has been a practice under Act No. 2822 in Turkey severely criticized by the ILO since the 1980s. Based on the Constitution of 1982, the same restriction still exists under the new Act No. 6356, as the constitutional reform of September 2010 did not repeal the said constitutional principle. In view of Article 60(7) of Act No. 6356, any lawful strike or lock-out called, ordered or implemented may be suspended by a decree of the Council of Ministers for up to sixty days if it is likely to be prejudicial to public health or national security. After a suspension order has come into effect, the mediator appointed according to Article 60(7) shall make every effort to the settlement of the dispute during the postponement period. During that time the parties may also agree to refer the dispute to private arbitration. If, on the expiration of the sixty-day time limit, the parties have still not been able to reach a settlement, nor agreed to call on private arbitration, upon the request of either party within six working days the dispute shall be settled by the YHK. Otherwise, the labour union's authorization status shall become void (Article 63(1, 2 and 3)).

1373. Obviously, if interpreted in broad terms assessing the degree to which a strike may jeopardize general health or national security may be highly subjective in many controversial disputes. Act No. 2822 provided the parties with an appeal mechanism to contest the executive order with a request for an injunction as well as a decision on the merits of the case.[547] Article 62 has not made any reference to such a judicial review. This void notwithstanding, recourse to legal action is always available since, as a basic principle of public law, legal action is always accessible against the acts of the Administration.

547. For more details on this matter, *see* the 2011 edition of this monograph pp. 367–368.

1374. The suspension of strikes for public health or national security reasons has been practised in Turkey quite frequently, often accompanied by alleged violations of the real intent of the law. In fact, according to interpretations of the ILO's supervisory organs, an area where the strike legally exists, the dispute ultimately culminates in a definitive strike ban leading to compulsory arbitration which, according to the ILO is not acceptable in view of the principles of Conventions 87 and 98. Although the said restriction was one of the requests for nullification in the Republican Party's petition to the Constitutional Court, in its 22 October 2014 ruling the Court denied that request because recourse to compulsory arbitration was a Constitutionally mandated clause in Article 54 of the 1982 Constitution.

1375. The government, claiming that the practice is constitutionally mandated, has responded to these criticisms by emphasizing the availability of appeal to the High Court of Administration or the possibility of the parties' reaching agreement or referring the dispute to private arbitration. The limited number of suspension orders has also been one of the defence points. In fact, a great majority of labour disputes falling within the scope of the then Article 33 of Act No. 2822 were settled either by the parties' agreeing between themselves or by referring the dispute to voluntary arbitration during the postponement period.

1376. It should be noted that during the 1963–1980 era the ILO was not critical of the said suspension transaction applicable for similar reasons because, upon the lapse of the then ninety days' time limit, the parties were free to resume industrial action. The mechanism brought by Act No. 6356 also carries another drawback, i.e., the invalidation of the labour union's authorization status if recourse to compulsory arbitration is not made by either party in the event of an ongoing disagreement on the expiration of the sixty-day suspension term. Thus, another dimension has been added to the list of cases entailing the avoidance of the labour union's bargaining status. Considering the numerous cases of the past, it is likely that the government's power to suspend strikes will remain on the agenda of the ILO supervisory organs, even more so now under the additional pitfalls caused by the new Act. As a deplorable point it must be recalled that, in nine different cases, Act No. 6356 has cited situations where the labour union's certificate of authorization is to be automatically invalidated if certain initiatives are not taken in due time. Paradoxically the employer's capacity to be the signatory party to collective negotiations is not affected in any manner.

II. Abusive Exercise of the Right to Strike and Lock-Out

1377. The right to strike or lock-out must not be exercised contrary to the principle of good faith or in such a manner as to cause harm to society or to destroy national wealth (Article 54(2) of the 1982 Constitution and Article 72(1) of Act No. 6356). Any strike called or lock-out ordered contrary to this rule shall be suspended by the competent court upon the request of either party or the Minister of Labour and Social Security. Here there is uncertainty as to what the outcome of negotiations would be.

1378. The concept of 'good faith and fair dealing' emphasized here is the principle embedded in the Turkish Civil Code which means that any act must have been carried out in a manner consistent with its underlying motives and purposes. Evidently, determining the presence of 'good faith' is a difficult matter, particularly in an area where industrial conflict is involved. On the other hand, ascertaining the extent of damage to society or national wealth is likely to pose even more controversy.

1379. Apparently, the judge will use his discretionary powers in a broad manner and apply both concepts in combination. Besides, the Act has not clarified the outcome of the suspension order in this case. By analogy to similar provisions, it could be inferred that suspension of the work stoppage would entail the cancellation of the authorization certificate of the party concerned.[548] So far, with the exception of the steel strike in 1989, the court has not wielded its power to intervene in a lawful strike activity in accordance with Article 47.

1380. The Court authorized and in charge: 'Disputes arising from the application of this Act shall be handled by courts in charge of dealing with and competent in labour cases. However, the court where the competent authority is located shall be competent in disputes which arise from the application of the seventh and eleventh sections (Article 79).

1381. Application of other legislation: 'In cases where this Act is silent, Act No. 4721 and provisions of the Associations Act of 4 January 2004, No. 5253, that are not contrary to this Act shall apply' (Article 80(1)).

1382. 'On collective labour agreements; in cases where this Act does not carry provisions, Act No. 4721 and the Obligations Act of Turkey, 11 January 2011, No. 6098, as well as provisions of other legislation dealing with employment contracts which are not contrary to this Act shall apply' (Article 80(2)).

1383. Article 64 of the new Act, after reiterating the norms of freedom of workers to strike or not to strike, has foreseen a new dimension for the liability of the labour union in conjunction to damages caused by the strike. 'The labour union shall be liable for the payment of damages inflicted on the establishment caused by its faulty conduct. If the strike has been called without the decision of the labour union, the workers or union officials responsible for the faulty conduct shall be liable as individuals for the payment of damages' (Article 64(5)). Despite the protection foreseen for the labour union as a corporate body here, the sanction still seems to be heavily tilted against the right to strike, which, by definition here, is a lawful action. By its very nature, every strike may result in some degree of damage to the employer's premises. Further, the phrase 'faulty behaviour' used in the article covers much wider ramifications than what would be implied had, rather than 'faulty conduct', the phrase 'by the deliberate and intentional conduct … ' been used.

548. Murat A. Demircioğlu, 'Yasal Greve Yargısal Müdahale', *Kamu-İş, Münir Ekonomi Armağ anı*, pp. 331–347.

1384. Act No. 6356 also carries sanctions for the abusive exercise of the right to lock-out. Article 72(2), similar to Article 47(2) of Act No. 2822 provides: 'If it is determined by the final judgment of a court that a lawful lock-out has been ordered with the object of permanently closing the establishment, the lock-out must cease as soon as the court's judgment is communicated to the employer or the employer's union.'

1385. As for the employees, the consequences associated with unlawful lock-outs in view of Article 70(3) shall apply, meaning that 'employees shall be entitled to terminate their employment contracts for a just cause with all the accrued rights to which they are entitled, including severance pay if they have fulfilled the requirements for such pay. The employer must also compensate any damages suffered by the employee during the lock-out without any obligation on the employee's part to do the corresponding work' (Article 72(2)).

III. Normal Ending of the Strike and Lock-Out

1386. A strike or lock-out normally ceases to be operative under three conditions. These are the following:

- The strike or lock-out normally ends either with a compromise agreement between the parties or with the labour union's or the employer's union's succumbing to the demands of the opposite party. However, a formal decision is required for the strike or lock-out to be deemed ended legally.' The decision to end a lawful strike or lock-out must, on being taken by the party by which the strike or lock-out was initiated, be notified in writing to the other party and to the competent authority by the end of the next working day. The competent authority shall announce the ending of the strike or lock-out. With the announcement made, the lawful strike and lock-out shall come to an end (Article 75(1,2)).
- A decision to end a strike does not affect or terminate a lock-out and a decision to end a lock-out does not affect or terminate a strike (Article 75(3)).
- The second condition ending a strike or lock-out is associated with the changed status of the labour or employer's organization concerned'. The strike or lock-out shall end *ipso facto* where the labour union that initiated the strike is closed, abolished or dissolved for any reason and the authorization certificate shall become void. The lock-out shall end *ipso facto* where the employers' union is closed or dissolved for any reason (Article 75(4,5)).
- The third condition under which the strike comes to an end is the loss of members by the union to the extent that the strike becomes ineffective to a considerable extent. If it is established that three-fourths of the members at the establishment have severed their membership relation with the union that initiated the strike, any of the interested parties may request the competent court to

end the strike.[549] The decision to end the strike must be announced as provided in Article 75(2). Upon the ending of industrial action, the obligations of the parties (i.e., the employee's duty to work and the employer's duty to pay wages) become operative again.

§5. Unlawful Strikes and Lock-Outs

I. Unlawful Strikes

1387. Any strike that does not meet the conditions pertaining to 'purpose' and the requirements stipulated by the law is an unlawful strike. A strike whose purpose falls outside the object of 'safeguarding or improving the employees' economic and social position and working conditions' is an unlawful strike. Also, any work stoppage called without fulfilling all the conditions for a lawful strike is an unlawful strike. Amendments to the Constitution of 1982 by Act No. 5982 of 7 July 2010 have repealed the ban on political, general and sympathy strikes and work slowdowns, but the said prohibitions still remain, albeit indirectly, through the definition of the strike and lock-out in conjunction with the strictly worded 'purpose' element involved industrial conflict, as mentioned above.

Also, in order for a strike to be considered lawful, all the conditions required by the law (legislation) must have been met. The absence of any one of the above-stated legal conditions as well as 'purpose' would therefore cause a work stoppage to be treated as an 'unlawful' strike.

II. Legal Consequences of Unlawful Strikes and Lock-Outs

1388. Article 70(1) of Act No. 6356 provides the following: 'In the event of an unlawful strike, the employer may (without any liability as to notice or compensation (i.e., notice pay and severance pay), terminate the employment contract of any employee who has supported the decision to call that strike or has participated in it or urged others to take part in it or to sustain it'. Termination of the employment contract is deemed to be in conformity with Article 25/II of the Labour Act No. 1475 (just cause dismissals).[550]

1389. In conjunction with a dispute related to this issue, the Court of Cassation ruled that the labour union that had caused an unlawful strike by erring in the fulfilment of procedural requirements for a lawful strike should compensate for the damages suffered by the dismissed employee.[551]

549. Court of Cassation, 9th Div., 2 No. 1998, 15964/15467; 26 Nov. 2002, 25600/22861. This provision involves the loss of the union's members for any reason whatsoever (15 Sep. 2009, 33838/27396).
550. Court of Cassation, 9th Div., 30 Dec. 1988, 13102/13021; 23 Mar. 1992, 2893/3270.
551. Court of Cassation, 9th Div., 5 Nov. 1985, 7135/1065.

1390. Nevertheless, various problems adjacent to this issue are encountered in practice. First, for the termination of the employee's employment contract, his participation in the unlawful strike is not a sufficient condition; the employee must also be defaulting and be aware of or should be in a position to know the unlawful nature of the strike.[552] It has been established that, due to the complicated loopholes accounting for the unlawful strike which the employee can hardly grasp, the burden of proof concerning the alleged default by the employee rests on the employer.[553]

1391. The Act is silent on the time period within which the employee's employment contract could be terminated for his having participated in an unlawful strike. Since, however, the determination suit as to whether or not a strike is unlawful must be concluded within one month, the employment contract may be terminated within six working days following the rendering of the court's decision to that effect. The issue becomes more complicated in those cases where the strike comes to an end before the conclusion of the court litigation or no determination action has been filed with the court. Establishing a parallel between this category of breaking the employment contract and termination for just cause categories envisaged in Article 25/II of the Labour Act,[554] some writers have argued that the right of the employer to break the employment contract because of the employee's involvement in an unlawful strike must cease to be operative six working days after the employer became aware of any such act by the employee and in any event, after one year had elapsed since the commission of the act. Still some other writers and the Court of Cassation have concluded that a justifiable reason for breaking the employee's employment contract would persist for so long as his participation in the unlawful strike continues and, therefore, the prescribed 'six-working-days' and 'one year' periods should become operative not on the day of the employer's becoming aware of the employee's act but following the date on which the strike ended.[555]

1392. Still according to another view opposed to drawing a parallel with Article 25/II of Act No. 4857, it is affirmed that the categories mentioned in Article 25/II of the Labour Act relate solely to those cases where the employment contract may be broken due to the immoral, dishonourable or malicious conduct of the individual employee and not to conduct involving any concerted work stoppage. Besides, neither the Obligations Act nor the Press Labour Act carries provisions on the forfeiture of the termination right due to lapse of time. Therefore, by applying the relevant criteria 'of the Obligations Act, the adoption of a reasonable statutory limitation period geared to good faith and general principles of law and determined in accordance with the requirements of each case has been proposed as a more acceptable solution in this case'.

---

552. K. Oğuzman, Hukuki Yönden *İşçi-İşveren İlişkilerii, supra*, p. 260; Court of Cassation, 9th Div., 20 Nov. 1990, 11449/12316.
553. Court of Cassation, 9th Div., 11 May 1981, 3715/6757.
554. *See*, the heading 'Functions of Shop-Stewards'.
555. Oğuzman, *supra*, pp. 268–269; Court of Cassation, 9th Div., 25 Feb. 1982, 581/2089.

1393. Article 74 of Act No. 6356 on the nature of the determination suit has brought a degree of clarity to solve some practical problems concerning the termination of employment contracts of employees involved in unlawful strikes. Article 71(1) provides that 'either party to a dispute may at any time request the competent labour court to determine whether or not a strike called or executed is unlawful. The court must render its definitive decision within one month. The court's decision shall be is binding on the parties and members of the labour and employers' union and serves as absolute evidence in criminal proceedings' Also, the judge may as an interlocutory precaution suspend the enforcement of the strike or lock-out that has been subject of a lawsuit (Article 71(2)).

1394. In the event of an unlawful lock-out the employees may terminate their employment contracts for just cause. The employer must compensate all the amounts which the employees are entitled to receive under their employment contracts for the duration of the lock-out and any damages they have suffered, without any obligation on the employee's part to perform the corresponding work (Article 76(3)).

III. Payment of Damages Caused in Conjunction with an Unlawful Strike

1395. Any damages sustained by the employer as a result an unlawful strike must be compensated by the labour union which decided to call it or, if it took place otherwise than by the decision of a labour union, by the employees who took part in it (Article 70(2)). In the former case it is asserted that members of the managing board of the labour union involved in an unlawful strike also have personal liability along with the liability of the union. The Court of Cassation has ruled, however, that members of the union's management board must not be held personally liable for the damage caused as a result of an unlawful strike.[556]

IV. Unlawful Lock-outs

1396. The concept of 'unlawful lock-out' is defined along the same lines as those of the unlawful strike, that is, any lock-out that is not motivated by the occupational 'purpose' and is not ordered or conducted in accordance with the conditions set out in the legislation (that is, to be ordered for a dispute in the course of negotiations for a collective agreement subsequent to a decision to call a strike taken by the labour union).

V. Legal Consequences of Unlawful Lock-outs

1397. In the event of an unlawful lock-out, employees are entitled, without any liability as to term of notice or compensation, to terminate their employment

556. Court of Cassation, 10th Div., 11 May 1976, 2146/3437.

contracts with the employer who has ordered it. The employer must pay all the sums which the employee has been entitled to receive under his employment contract and to compensate any damage the latter has sustained, without any obligation on the employee's part to perform the corresponding work (Article 70(3)).

§6. Operations and Areas Where Strikes and Lock-Outs Are Prohibited: Compulsory Arbitration

I. The Notion

1398. According to the Turkish as well as Act No. 6356, the right to strike and lock-out is the rule as the ultimate step in labour disputes, while compulsory (official) arbitration is the exception to be called on in those essential operations or areas where industrial conflict has been forbidden. The parties may agree to resort to voluntary (private) arbitration at any stage of a collective interest or rights dispute, but in interest disputes compulsory (official) arbitration must be invoked after failing at the mediation stage, at the request of either party in those operations and establishments considered essential and critical to the functioning of the economy and therefore excluded from the right to strike and lock-out. The Turkish Constitution of 1982 left the regulation of strike and lock-out restrictions to special legislation (Article 54(4)) and provided for the YHK to deal with the ultimate settlement of disputes in such operations and establishments where strike and lock-out prohibitions exist.

1399. Activities and establishments where strikes and lock-outs are prohibited by Act No. 6356 (Permanent restrictions): in this vein where the ultimate process to settle the labour dispute has to be compulsory arbitration, Act No. 6356 has deleted a few restrictions which existed under Act No. 2822. But, using the ILO criteria, some of the remaining bans still cannot be deemed to fall into 'essential services' in the strict sense of the term, defined by the ILO Committee of Experts as 'those services where the interruption of which would endanger the life, personal safety or health of the whole or part of the population.' According to the Committee, these may be the hospital sector, electricity services, water supply services, the telephone service and air traffic control. In borderline cases, it has suggested one solution might be 'not to impose a total prohibition of strikes, but rather to provide for the maintaining by a defined and limited category of staff of a negotiated minimum service when a total and prolonged stoppage might result in serious consequences for the public'.

1400. Strike and lock-out bans which Act No. 6356 has repealed relate to the following activities and establishments: production of lignite used for thermal power plants, exploration of natural gas and petroleum, notary services, training and education institutions, day nurseries and old-age retirement homes. A positive development has been the abrogation of some strike and lock-out bans in the health sector, i.e., establishments for the production of vaccines, clinics, sanatoriums, dispensaries and pharmacies, thus limiting the bans in the health sector only to hospitals.

1401. Although the legislature had imposed a new ban on strikes in air transportation on 31 May 2012, at a critical time when negotiations were in progress for civil aviation workers, the new Act excluded airways from the scope of strike bans. Despite the elimination of certain prohibitions of Act No. 2822, therefore, Act No. 6356 still includes a fairly wide array of activities and establishments where strike and lock-out action is permanently prohibited. These are the following: 'life and property saving activities; funeral and mortuary services and cemeteries; city water, electricity and natural gas; production, refinery and distribution of petroleum; petrochemical works starting from naphtha or natural gas, banking; establishments run directly by the Ministry of National Defence, General Command of Gendarmeries and the Coast Guard; fire-fighting and mass urban transportation provided by public organizations; and hospitals' (Article 62(1)). Further, shortly after the enactment of Act No. 6356, a clause annexed to Act No. 6362 on capital markets of 6 December 2012, brought a ban on the right to strike in capital markets and financial services. Using the ILO criteria, this and most of the categories cited among the restrictions include activities whose disruption is not likely to cause serious harm to the daily life of the public, either because of their nature or because of the availability of a multitude of alternatives, e.g., banks, urban transportation and petroleum. Thus given the international norms of freedom of association, Act No. 6356 still seems vulnerable to criticisms by international and national circles. More recently, through its 22 October 2014 ruling, the Constitutional Court has repealed existing strike and lock-out bans in 'mass urban transportation by public organizations' and in banking. Repealing the ban in the banking sector is important as in Turkey about 198,000 workers are employed by banks.

II. Temporary Restrictions

1402. In temporary restrictions enumerated in Article 62, strike and lock-out activity may resume taking effect once the conditions necessitating the restriction disappear. Cases of temporary restrictions were more varied under Act No. 2822, but the new Act has struck out some of them. The remaining categories in Act No. 6356 are the following:

1403. 'Where the life of the community is considerably affected by natural disasters, the Council of Ministers may suspend strikes and lock-outs in such establishments as it deems necessary and for such time as the situation requires. Within sixty days after the lifting of the ban, implementation of strike and lock-out may resume by giving notification to the other party six working days beforehand' (Article 62(2)).

1404. The second temporary restriction concerns industrial action during the journey of transport vehicles. 'It is not permissible to implement a strike or lock-out in any means of land, sea or air transport while the vehicle is still engaged in its journey before reaching its final destination within Turkish territory' (Article 62(3)).

1405. Another category involving the restriction of industrial action is the suspension of the strike or lock-out by the order of the Council of Ministers for reasons of general health or national security. Since recourse to the YHK on the expiry of the suspension term is compulsory, this category may be viewed also as a unique version of strike/lock-out restrictions.

III. Recourse to Compulsory (Official) Arbitration

1406. Act No. 2822 had abolished the provincial arbitration boards which existed under the pre-1983 system as the first step of the compulsory arbitration mechanism. Now since Act No. 2822 of 1983 the YHK, which is a Constitutionally based institution, is the competent body (along with, of course, voluntary arbitration where the parties agree on it).

1407. Article 51 addresses, in summary form, the cases where recourse to the YHK is compulsory:

> If a strike vote has been taken, within six working days from the finalization of a no-strike result, the labour union may have access to the Supreme Arbitration Board; in disputes where legal strike and lock-out bans exist, in six working days from the communication of the mediator's report to the parties; and where the dispute still persists at the expiration of the suspension term, in six working days the parties may apply the Supreme Arbitration Board. Otherwise, the labour union shall lose its authorization status (Article 51(1)).
>
> So, in addition to its advisory functions, the Supreme Arbitration Board's mandate centres on three major situations.
>
> In temporary restrictions, if the prohibition is lifted within the six-month period, the strike or lock-out may be put into effect in accordance with the routine procedure. If the ban is not lifted, however, the dispute is bound to be settled by the Supreme Arbitration Board which makes the number of major categories for the Board's mandate 'five' actually. The six-month period starts with the receipt of the mediator's report.
>
> 'Decisions of the Supreme Arbitration Board are binding and shall take effect as a collective labour agreement' (Article 51(2)).

IV. The Composition of the YHK

1408. The YHK which is based on a tripartite structure dates back to the earlier stages of the Turkish industrial relations system. Including the Chairman, the YHK consists of eight members who convene under the chairmanship of the most senior head of the departments of the Court of Cassation in charge of dealing with disputes relating to Act No. 6356. Substitute members are to be elected to substitute for the elected members if they are absent. A member to be selected by the Council of Ministers, from among persons having knowledge and experience in economics, business administration, social policy or labour law, with no ties with labour or employers' organizations and no function in the organs of political parties; a professor of labour law or social security law to be selected by the Higher Education Board; the Director of Labour of the Ministry of Labour and Social Security. In addition to government-appointed members, the Board has two members representing employees elected by the labour confederations with the highest number of members among the labour confederations and two members on behalf of employers, one elected by the employers' confederation with the highest number of members and the other representing public sector employers to be appointed by the government. The only novelty is the exception of a rather positive rearrangement concerning the election of members to represent employees and employers. According to Article 54(1c):

> if the labour confederation to which the labour union involved in the current dispute is affiliated differs from the confederation having the highest number of members, one member from that different confederation shall participate in the Board's meeting in lieu of the second employee member; similarly, where the employers' confederation with which the employers' union involved in the current dispute is affiliated differs from the employers' confederation with the highest number of members, one member to be elected by the confederation with which the employers' union in dispute is affiliated shall participate in the board's meeting in lieu of the second employers' representative.

1409. The members who are designated by election serve for a term of two years, but they may be re-elected. Conditions to be met by the employee and employer members are those stipulated in Article 6 (Article 54(2)).

1410. With the participation of the Chairman and a minimum five of its members, the YHK must convene within six working days of receiving an application. Its decisions are binding as a valid collective agreement. Decision quorum in the YHK is the majority of the participants in the meeting. If the votes are equal, the Chairman has a casting vote. Also, the parties may voluntarily choose to refer the dispute to the YHK to act in the capacity of a private arbitrator.

1411. The YHK must also give its advisory opinion in the suspension of strikes and lock-outs as well as the extension of the collective labour agreement by the government. Labour unions have often been critical of the decisions of the Board which, owing to its composition, were perceived as being heavily slanted against labour's interests. In workers' opinion, in contrast to two workers' and two employer's representatives, the inclusion in the Board of four members elected by public entities results in an employer-dominated structure in the mixed economy of Turkey where the state plays also an important employer role. In ILO platforms, the government has responded to this criticism by the counter-argument that the board where the chairman represents the independent judiciary, the state, with the remaining three members, plays the third party role of overseeing the functioning of the industrial relations system in harmony. Furthermore, despite its alleged unbalanced structure in interest and rights disputes, the stakeholders seem to make more use of the Board's arbitration capacity rather than those of third party neutrals as private arbitrators.

1412. Each case is to be examined by the Board on the basis of the documents in the file. The Board may obtain any information which it lacks from the parties concerned. It may also hear any persons whose opinions it wishes to obtain or may request them to present their views in writing; with a view to inform the Board, the parties to the dispute may also request to be hears or to submit their information or documents (Article 56(2)). Premised on the principle of the autonomy of social partners, the Board's competence is limited only to the disputed items; it is not empowered to intervene and decide on any issues already agreed upon by the parties, nor is it allowed to issue any judicial decisions such as whether or not an establishment is subject to strike prohibitions – a matter which is strictly in the domain of the labour courts.

1413. The awards of the YHK in interest disputes are final and have the same force and binding effect as a collective labour agreement. Its awards in interest disputes may not be appealed to any authority. Article 56(4)deals with the establishment and composition of the Board's secretariat. Further details are provided in a special regulation titled 'Regulation on Recourse to the Arbitrator and Mediator' (Article 57(1)).

Chapter 9. Collective Rights Disputes, Labour Courts and Arbitration

§1. Settlement of Collective Rights Disputes

I. Recourse to the Labour Court

1414. Unlike the system of Act No. 275 which permitted strikes and lock-outs for rights disputes, Act No. 2822 of 1983 as well as Act No. 6356 of 2012, in a manner consistent with the wording of the 1982 Constitution (Article 54(1)), envisaged resort to labour courts or private arbitration as the sole avenue for the settlement of collective rights disputes. In this respect two types of court litigation have been foreseen, those involving interpretation and those fulfilment.

A. *Interpretation Suit*

1415. The interpretation (or determination) suit may be filed by the party to the collective labour dispute (labour union or the employer); the individual employee is permitted to file only a suit for fulfilment. Where there is a dispute arising from the interpretation of a collective agreement in force, either party may lodge a suit with the competent labour court and request an interpretation. As Article 53(1) says, 'a lawsuit may be filed with the court by the parties to a collective labour agreement which is in force.' The court shall award its decision within two months at the latest. In case of appeal, the Court of Cassation shall render its definitive verdict within two months. The right to initiate an interpretation suit is recognized only to the signatory labour or employers' union party the collective agreement in force.[557]

1416. Over the years the judiciary has brought clarifications of various dimensions of legal actions in the settlement of rights disputes. For example, if the defendant in an interpretation lawsuit is an employer affiliated with an employers' union, judicial action should be directed against the employers' union rather than the individual employer concerned.[558]

1417. Also, as emphasized by the Court of Cassation, initiation of an interpretation (determination) action is not possible in cases where the plaintiff concerned is already in a position to file a fulfilment suit.[559] However, situations are encountered in practice where the lawsuit for fulfilment is by its nature one that necessitates the scrutiny of the merits of the dispute, thus requiring interpretation of the case in combination with an action for fulfilment.[560]

557. Court of Cassation, 9th Div., 17 Oct. 1996, 18804/19613.
558. Court of Cassation, 9th Div., 16 Sep. 1988, 8917/8241.
559. Court of Cassation, 9th Div., 8 Feb. 1984, 597/1105; 12 Feb. 1988, 1346/1004; 15 Dec. 1994, 18324/18002.
560. Court of Cassation, General Council, 23 Oct. 1987, 9-612/770.

B. Suit for Fulfilment

1418. The only remedy foreseen for non-fulfilment of an obligation arising from the collective agreement is payment of interest. As provided by Article 53(2), in legal actions for fulfilment, the party held liable to fulfil is to be adjudged to pay, beginning from the date of default, the highest interest rate charged by the banks for credits used in business transactions (subvention interest). Furthermore, the party that fails to fulfil all or part of his obligations may be sentenced to instantaneous fulfilment. The highest interest rate for bank loans is to be charged only for claims arising from the application of the collective labour agreement.[561]

§2. Private (Voluntary) Arbitration in Collective Interest and Rights Disputes

I. The Notion and Pertinent Procedures

1419. Similar to the situation under Act 274 of 1963, Act No. 2822 of 1983 also provided that the parties could agree to resort to private (voluntary) arbitration at any stage of a collective rights or interest dispute. And while the dispute was at the mediation stage, the parties could also agree to the mediator's taking on the role of a private arbitrator.

1420. In the case of collective rights disputes, however, it is held there is no need for the parties' mutual agreement if the collective agreement already carries a clause for recourse to private arbitration at the request of either one of the parties. With the exception of the collective agreement term referring the settlement of a job security dispute to arbitration which was struck down by the Constitutional Court in 2004, in Turkey generally, such collectively bargained clauses have been regarded as valid, in which case the dispute must be resolved by the arbitrator(s).

1421. For a rights dispute to be settled through voluntary arbitration, the Court of Cassation has generally upheld the view that the dispute should pertain to the alleged violation of rights of a collective of workers rather than the grievance of an individual employee; however, actual practices seem to have developed in both directions. Although a strict distinction is usually made between individual and collective rights disputes, the borderline tends to become blurred when it is a labour union that initiates the grievances of a few employees, or occasionally even of a single employee. This is especially evident if problems pertaining to union freedoms are involved, i.e., when a union initiates disputes concerning the allegedly unfair dismissals of shop stewards or of employees because of their union membership or union-related activities. As in essence such disputes relate to collective representation cases, they should also be treated as collective rights disputes even when only a single employee is involved and legal opinion has tended to develop in this

561. Court of Cassation, 9th Div., 20 Apr. 1989, 3391/3764.

direction.[562] However, it should also be noted in this connection that settlement of disputes concerning union freedoms are held to fall into the domain of labour courts rather than the competence of private arbitrators. As the new Labour Act No. 4857 has empowered private arbitrators to decide on litigations concerning job security, the mandate of arbitration in disputes of terminated individual employees involving reinstatement/compensation claims has now been accorded legal recognition with the exception of collective labour agreement-based arbitration.

1422. Although Turkish law entitles the parties in rights disputes to call on either the labour court or private arbitration, a considerable number of collective agreements seem to carry full-fledged grievance procedures (usually linked to joint discipline committees) involving several steps which eventually culminate in voluntary arbitration. But even when a collective agreement-based arbitration process has been envisaged, it is held that the individual employee still retains his constitutional right to file suit for his grievance with the labour court. The Court of Cassation has ruled in several cases that collectively bargained arbitration clauses are not binding on the individual employee.[563] This has led to confusion in cases where a number of workers subject to an arbitration case also sought legal action at the labour court, in which case they had to be deleted from the arbitrator's award, thus entailing at times contradiction between the decisions of the arbitrator and the labour court. Also, in its verdict in 1987, the Court of Cassation re-emphasized that private arbitration could be invoked only for collective rights disputes; a private arbitration clause envisaged in the collective agreement would be binding only on the labour and employers' union party to that agreement, not on the individual employee.[564]

1423. Hence there seemed to be a need in Turkey for the development of a system where labour courts and private arbitration could coexist. The expansion of private arbitrators' competence so as to empower them with discharge cases under the present Act No. 4857 could pave the way for the promotion of a well-coordinated, two-pronged system in the settlement of rights disputes in general, individual or collective.

1424. Obviously, if voluntary arbitration is intended to contribute to the just and speedy adjudication of rights disputes, the Court of Cassation's above-stated awards have hindered the development of a viable private arbitration system in Turkey which should now be revaluated in the light of emerging needs.

1425. In the opinion of the Court of Cassation, the arbitration process should include, according to Article 520 of the previous Act on Civil Procedures, three

562. *See, e.g.*, Esener, *supra*, pp. 572–580.
563. Court of Cassation, General Council, 10 Nov. 1965, 643/D/9, 495; Court of Cassation, 9th Div., 1 Jun. 1970, 4846/5796.
564. Court of Cassation, 9th Div., 14 Sep. 1964, 4983/5929; 7 Sep. 1987, 8058/7373.

arbitrators, unless otherwise provided in the arbitration agreement. Therefore the ruling rendered by a single arbitrator selected by the court entailed the reversal of the award.[565]

1426. The parties to a collective rights or interest dispute may agree to choose the YHK as a private arbitrator at any stage in the dispute. The YHK would then act in the capacity of a voluntary arbitration board.

1427. It should be noted in this connection that about one-third of the labour disputes referred to the YHK in the 1990s were cases where the parties had requested the Board to act in the capacity of a voluntary arbitrator,[566] which could be construed to mean a heightened confidence in the perceived neutrality of the Board. A great majority of such requests came from the public sector, however.

II. The Legal Nature of Arbitration Awards in the Pre-existing and the Present Systems

1428. In interest disputes the award of the YHK or the private arbitrator has the same force and effect as a collective agreement. If the parties have resorted to private arbitration in conjunction with a rights dispute, the arbitrator's award is then governed by general legal rules where principles pertaining to arbitration as set forth in the Act on Civil Procedures must apply. In this category arbitration decisions were binding on the parties as a judicial award and registered by the labour court in the past under Act No. 1086 of 1927. Because similar notions prevail presently under the new Act on Civil Procedures, they are reiterated here as still valid generalizations in the following manner: while the labour court's decisions might be appealed to the Court of Cassation which could reverse them for reasons of substance (merit) as well, arbitrator's awards, if appealed, were to be reviewed by the High Court only for procedural reasons. The Court of Cassation might turn down an arbitration award issued in relation to a rights dispute only if (a) the award has not been rendered within the time limit set out for the arbitration process which is six months unless otherwise decided by the parties; (b) the award concerns an issue not requested by the parties; (c) the arbitrator has exceeded his jurisdiction and authority; and (d) the award has not dealt with each argument and counter-argument brought up by the parties (Article 533, Act of Civil Procedures, No. 1086, July 1927). For those awards reversed by the Court of Cassation for reasons in the last three categories, a new private arbitrator (or arbitration committee) must be selected.

1429. The award not rendered within the arbitration period and thus overruled by the Court of Cassation is null and void. In this case, the dispute must be

565. Court of Cassation, 9th Div., 7 Sep. 1989, 647/6450.
566. T.C. 'Çalışma ve Sosyal Güvenlik Bakanlığ ı, Çalışma Hayatı İstatistikleri', Ankara, *Yayın* No. 59, May 1995, p. 65.

adjudicated by the competent court.[567] Although grievance arbitration awards having a binding effect which can be overruled by the Court of Cassation essentially for procedural reasons mentioned above, it was held that arbitrators should judge each case with equity and according to principles of good faith – a rule set out in the Civil Code of Turkey – and ought not to infringe upon the absolutely binding principles of law as well as public order and general good morals.[568]

1430. Regarding recourse to private arbitration, Article 52(1) of Act No. 6356 provides the following: 'The parties may agree to apply to the private arbitrator at any stage of interest or rights disputes.' The collective labour agreement may include a clause envisioning the revision of certain items by the mutual consent of the parties during the life of the agreement:

> The collective labour agreement may carry clauses which envisage recourse to private arbitration at the request of either one of the parties. In this case, unless there is a clause to the contrary in the collective labour agreement, provisions of the Civil Procedures Act of January 2011, No. 6100, relating to private arbitration shall be applicable. Private arbitrator's awards in collective rights disputes shall be subject to general provisions. If the parties to a collective interest dispute make a written agreement to apply to private arbitration, the provisions concerning mediation, strike and lock-out as well as official arbitration shall not be applicable. Private arbitrator's awards in collective interest disputes shall become effective as a collective labour agreement. The parties may agree to designate the Supreme Arbitration Board as a private arbitrator at any stage of the dispute (Article 52(2,3,4)).

1431. In an attempt to settle disagreements on the revision of disputed items, an arbitration clause may have been set out in the collective agreement or the parties may conclude an arbitration agreement after the emergence of the dispute. However, this should not be construed to mean that the competence of the private arbitrator foreseen in the collective labour agreement could be expanded so as to address disputes which fall outside the scope of his mandate.[569]

1432. The arbitration agreement must be made in written form for interest disputes; otherwise it becomes null and void.

1433. Where an arbitration agreement has been concluded for a rights dispute, neither party may have recourse to the labour court. If, despite the arbitration agreement, however, the employer or the labour union has filed suit with the court, the judge may proceed trying the case unless the defendant, within the time limit allowed for a plea against the merits of the case, contests the litigation, claiming that the dispute should be settled by arbitration rather than by the court.

567. Esener, *supra*, p. 582.
568. For a general evaluation of arbitration in Turkish law, *see* K. Tunçomağ, *Toplu İşUyuşmazlıklarının Çözümünde Uzlaştırma ve Tahkim*, İstanbul, 1973.
569. Court of Cassation, 9th Div., 26 Jun. 1986, 4891/6559.

1434. The arbitrator(s) must be third party neutrals. The arbitrator may have been designated in the arbitration agreement by name (*in persona*). Arbitration agreement becomes void if the designated arbitrator refuses to act as arbitrator, resigns or dies. The parties may appoint a third person to designate the arbitrator. The arbitration agreement becomes void if this person refrains from designating the arbitrator or dies. The arbitration agreement may foresee that the arbitrator is to be co-opted by the agreement of the parties. If the parties are unable to agree on the identity of the arbitrator, the arbitration agreement becomes void. But in rights disputes (grievance arbitration), the arbitrator must be appointed by the competent court if the parties fail in choosing the arbitrator. The question of arbitrability is to be resolved by the competent court if a dispute to that effect arises between the parties.

1435. On top of this background, the new Act on Civil Procedures, No. 6100, dated 12 January 2011 and entered into force on 1 October 2011, has brought detailed provisions on arbitration in its Articles 407 to 444. While it does not change the concept and legal consequences of arbitration to any considerable extent, the new Act has established closer links between the arbitration process and the court system. The new Act is applicable where the place of arbitration is in Turkey and in those areas not subject to the International Arbitration Act of 21 June 2001. The new Act brings definitions on such matters arbitrability (Article 408); the competent court; and, where permitted, the court's contributions to the arbitration process; the nature and written form of the arbitration agreement (Articles 410, 411); objection to the choice of arbitration as a method of resolving the dispute(Article 413); rejection of the arbitrator(s) by the party(ies) concerned (Article 417, 418); failure to reach a decision in arbitration and selection of new arbitrator(s) (Article 420, 421); right to equal and fair hearing in arbitration (Article 423); conclusion of the arbitral process and the request for clarification or correction of the arbitral award; and restitution of the arbitration trial (Articles 435–437). If during the court proceedings in a dispute, the parties agree to have recourse to arbitration, the trial file must be sent to the arbitrator or the arbitration board involved (Article 412). Upon the request of the party concerned, the arbitrator or the arbitration board may take precautionary measures and collect evidential facts on the issue (Article 414). The parties may freely determine the number of arbitrators which must be an odd figure. If the parties have not fixed this number, three arbitrators shall be in charge (Article 416). The arbitration board shall reach its decisions by majority vote; if empowered by the board, the board chairman is also competent to issue the arbitration decision himself (Article 433). The arbitration judgement must be passed within one year, but if the parties so agree the duration of the arbitration process may be extended; in the absence of such an agreement, it may also be extended by the court upon the request of one of the parties (Article 427). In the event of a single arbitrator where the parties cannot agree on naming her (him), the arbitrator shall be designated by the court upon the request of one of the parties. Where more than one arbitrator is in charge, at least one of them must be a lawyer with a minimum of five years' experience in his field of expertise. Arbitration decisions may be challenged only by filing a lawsuit for nullity with the court located at the place of arbitration. In this case the court must finalize the case promptly (Article 439). Arbitration decisions may be nullified

(a) if the party to the arbitration agreement is found to be incompetent or if the arbitration agreement is invalid, (b) if the procedures envisaged in the arbitration agreement or in the section regarding the election of the arbitrator(s) have not been complied with, (c) if the decision was not rendered within due time, (d) if the arbitrator(s) are found to be incompetent in contravention of law, (e) if the arbitrator(s) has ruled on a matter outside the scope of the arbitration agreement, or has not ruled on all the matters covered by the request, or if it has exceeded its powers, (f) if the process has not been conducted in conformity with the procedures set out in the arbitration agreement, or in the absence of such procedures, according to the rules in this section whereby such failure has adversely affected the merits of the case; (g) if the principle of equal treatment and fair hearing has not been respected, (h) if the subject matter is not arbitrable in view of Turkish law and (i) if the arbitration award is found to violate public order.

1436. While under the pre-existing system the arbitration process was perceived as being on a par with the ordinary court ruling which could be appealed to the Court of Cassation basically for procedural reasons, under the new system arbitration is somewhat subordinated to the ruling of the court for nullity which may then be challenged before the Court of Cassation with a request for reversal. However reasons for nullity and reversal are similar to those of the pre-existing system.

1437. In Article 78, Act No. 6356 cites various administrative fines as penal sanctions for the violators of various articles of the Act on Unions and the Collective Labour Agreement.

§3. A Summary Evaluation of the New Act on Unions and the Collective Labour Agreement No. 6356

1438. Following prolonged deliberations over the above-mentioned draft proposals and sustained efforts of social dialogue during the past decade, the legislature finally enacted the new industrial relations law of Turkey, the Act on Unions and the Collective Agreement of 7 November 2012, No. 65356. Aimed at bringing the labour relations law of Turkey into conformity with international norms on freedom of association and free collective bargaining as well as finding solutions to problems encountered in Turkish practice, the new Act carries several positive dimensions, i.e., simplifying some of the procedures; abolishing the condition for public notary approval in the worker's acquisition of and withdrawal from union membership; re-strengthening the job security of union shop stewards; clarifying the rights and security of union administrators. But it also seems seriously flawed in certain dimensions, i.e., the vague loophole in the protection of workers against acts of anti-union discrimination, thus attenuating existing protections for a considerable portion of the workforce (as a positive step, however, the Constitutional Court has eradicated this flaw through its October 2014 ruling, as noted above); maintaining the double criteria required for the labour union's authorization for collective bargaining, that is, while seemingly reducing the first (industry sector level) criterion to 1 from the 10% level and yet, given the aforementioned constraints, making the union's ability to achieve the authorization status much more difficult; re-emphasizing strike bans in some sectors not deemed to fall into 'essential services' in the strict sense of the word; postponement of strikes and lock-outs by the government due to alleged reasons of general health or national security where the process must result in compulsory arbitration; and adding to existing legislation several new cases which will entail the avoidance and nullification of the labour union's authorization status.

1439. Since at present there seems to be consensus on drawing up an entirely new Constitution for Turkey, it would perhaps be more logical to finalize the text of the new Constitution first and then to proceed to giving the industrial relations legislation its definitive form. However, due to the likelihood that the constitutional change process may take considerable time, the legislature must take immediate action by taking the package of industrial relations reform to its present agenda. Concerning the scope and tone of an ideal labour relations law, the author favours, among other things, the following points to be considered in particular: the new legislation, while expanding the freedom of association, should avoid disrupting drastically the deeply ingrained institutions and the general fabric of Turkish industrial relations. Keeping the definition and structure of the 'industry-wide national union' must be given due consideration. Legislation must ease the way to the worker's acquisition and loss of membership, based on a simple application and withdrawal form; and repeal the industry-level representativeness as the first condition for bargaining authorization, although there seems to be an in-built bias of the stakeholders to sustain it; simple majority representation must suffice for local level collective bargaining; strike restrictions must be limited only to 'essential services' in the strict sense of the word, with compulsory arbitration being the ultimate stage in the settlement of such disputes; suspension of strikes and lock-outs by the government for reasons of national security or general health must be regulated as an open-ended process like in the pre-1980 period, meaning that suspension should by no means result in recourse to compulsory arbitration; and, based on the lessons learned in the pre-1980 period, industry-level collective bargaining should be contrived alongside 'group (multi-employer) bargaining' after careful deliberations.

1440. It is unfortunate that, though debated extensively between the social partners just prior to the 100th ILO Conference in June 2011, agreement was not possible on the draft of December 2010. The latest draft did not seem to elicit much optimism either. Meanwhile, work on amending Act No. 4688 on public servants' collective bargaining rights was also in progress. Social dialogue efforts to bring Turkey's industrial relations legislation into conformity with the ILO freedom of association norms had preoccupied the country's legislative agenda for at least twenty years; yet, as the evaluations in the above paragraphs have shown, no satisfactory solution could be achieved even by the enactment of the new Act on Unions and the Collective Agreement in November 2012. Settlement of the aforementioned matters of grave concern both for the ILO and the national social partners is also a precondition for the opening of negotiations over the chapter on Social Policy and Employment in Turkey–EU relations. The painstaking debates in many conference Committee meetings were so frustrating that even the basic ILO tradition of settling the differences through dialogue was shunned in the remarks of the ILO's group spokespersons who could now even imply that if agreement was not possible by dialogue on such critical matters based on conflict of interests, the government, by exercising its political will, should pass the pertinent legislation once and for all. Yet Turkey, a country which has a fairly developed industrial relations system, has accumulated sufficient experience on social dialogue, as evidenced by the appearance of several more mature draft texts in the recent past. Despite the presence of some ongoing problems (e.g., the unsettled issue of personnel reform in the public sector entailing denial of collective bargaining with the right to strike to a large segment of public servants and for workers both in the public and private sectors, the double criteria for collective bargaining certification, strike restrictions in certain sectors not deemed to fall into 'essential services' in the strict sense, etc.), there seems to be sufficient ground for optimism in reaching compromised solutions in the foreseeable future.

1441. At a stage where the government's avowed goal was to launch reforms in an attempt to bring the Turkish industrial system in conformity with international norms of freedom of association, the outcome has been somewhat disappointing, particularly in the face of the seventh paragraph annexed to Article 90 of the Constitution of Turkey which gives precedence to international norms in the application of core fundamental rights.[570] Various dimensions of Act No. 6356 are clearly tilted against works and labour unions. As a matter of fact, a lawsuit was filed with the Constitutional Court on 4 January 2013, shortly after the passage of Act No. 6356 on January 2013, by the RPP (the major opposition party, requesting an injunction and nullification of the Act's more than thirty paragraphs on grounds of their unconstitutionality. As indicated above, the Court rendered its decision on a few articles of Act No. 6356 on 22 October 2014.

1442. In fact, the final draft of the government before the passage of Act No. 6356 was a relatively balanced text reached as a result of continued social dialogue among the stakeholders. Therefore the text of the Act shows the extent to which last minute interventions during the parliamentary process can distort the finer regulatory balances achieved during the earlier phases of social dialogue. Despite the introduction of various positive elements, therefore, the new Act on Unions and the Collective Agreement is likely to continue being challenged in national and international fora, as the ILO Committee of Experts' report for the year 2014 has already demonstrated. Irrespective of whether or not the Constitutional Court declares it unconstitutional, the law-maker must indeed amend the Act to ensure its conformity with international standards of freedom of association.

---

570. For debates on this matter, *see* Mesut Gülmez, İş Hukuku Öğretisi ve Anayasa Madde 90 Sorunu, Ali Güzel'e Armağan, 3030-309, Beta, No. 2319, İstanbul 2011.

Chapter 10. Public Servants' Right to Organize and to Bargain Collectively

§1. The Employee–Public Servant Distinction in the Public Sector

1443. Before addressing the issue of public servants' unions, clarification first of the problems stemming from the deep-rooted ramifications of employee–public servant distinction in the public sector seems to be a convenient starting point. In Turkey, the public sector embraces, in addition to workers employed in SEEs and municipal entities, groups of public servants and other public functionaries working under administrative law in the central and local governmental entities. They are found in the units of the central government and other public corporate bodies as well as in SEEs and their associated partnerships. These groups are placed in positions established by legislation whereby their remuneration and social security rights are governed by the Public Servants' Retirement Fund. But, in addition to public servants and quasi-public servant groups such as the 'contract employees', there are also wage-earners working under employment contracts who are just employees subject to the same labour legislation as that which applies to private sector employees (the Labour Act, the Maritime Labour Act, the Press Labour Act and the Obligations Act). Public servant-employee distinction in the public sector is important since employment conditions and rules which apply to each group are considerably different. As for their general working conditions, public servants are subject to Public Servants' Act No. 657 which, in its Article 27, prohibits the right to strike and quasi-strike actions by public servants. Besides, although new legislation has recognized public servants and 'contract employees' to form and join unions, until the constitutional amendment in 2010, these unions could only engage in collective negotiations with the public employer, construed as meaning that, in the final analysis, they could not conclude binding collective agreements.

1444. The public sector personnel regime was saddled with obfuscations even before the enactment of the Public Servants Act No. 657 in 1965, particularly with respect to the status of technical personnel. With the broader meaning attached to the concept of 'public servant' by Act No. 657, this and similar categories were considered public servants by the Court of Cassation and the Council of State, thereby disregarding the possibility to establish a German-style *Angestellte* category in the public sector.

1445. Due to the reactions of labour unions and namely of Türk-İş, Act No. 1317 amending certain sections of Act No. 274 on Unions in 1970 brought new definitions which treated public servants who were doing manual work as 'employees', but new complications were created by an amendment to Act No. 657 by Act No. 1327. Later Executive Decrees Nos. 7 and 12, issued in 1973 and 1974 as well as Act No. 1897 of 1975 amending certain sections of Act No. 657, all failed to bring a viable solution to the public servant–employee dilemma in the public sector.

1446. Nor did the relevant definitions introduced by the Constitution of 1982 bring clarity to the existing complications. Similar to the wording of the Constitution of 1961, Article 128 of the 1982 Constitution provides that 'the continued and essential services of the state, SEEs and other public corporate bodies to be executed according to the general principles of public administration shall be performed by public servants and other public functionaries'. The types and nature of tasks to be performed by public servants and other public functionaries would be designated by special legislation.

1447. As for the SEEs and their associated partnerships, one should note that, in addition to public servants and employees, an additional category called 'contract employees' was created. With a view to rationalize employment practices in SEEs many of which were slated for privatization, the government issued Executive Decrees No. 233 and 308 in the mid-1980s and afterwards, thereby creating considerable controversy in labour circles due to the denial of union and collective bargaining rights to the so-called contract employees. In an effort to find solutions to various contested issues, the Court of Cassation passed certain judgments which served as ad hoc improvisations. The Constitutional court repealed several provisions of Executive Decrees Nos. 233 and 308.[571] To fill the void caused by the decision of the Constitutional Court, Executive Decree No. 399 was put into effect in 1990. Still upon a lawsuit filed on grounds of unconstitutionality, the Constitutional Court invalidated many provisions of Decree No. 399 following which new amendments were made by Act No. 3771.[572] It should be noted, however, that according to Act No. 3771, contract employees were to be deemed public functionaries, and as such they should not enjoy the right to join labour unions nor to strike and conclude binding collective agreements, construed as meaning that they could join only public servants' unions,[573] as alluded to below. More recently Act No. 6111 of 25 February 2011, which in fact is a general piece of legislation covering many diverse topics, has explicitly emphasized in Article 119 annexing Article 13/A to Decree 399, allowed contract employees to form and join unions (of naturally, public servants), but no right to strike (Article 14). Thus contract personnel are treated as public servants from the viewpoint of Act No. 4688. Similarly, the category cited as 4/C in the Public Servants Act No. 657 are not considered as 'employees'.[574] Contract personnel who are employed in accordance with 4/B of Act No. 657 should be

571. Constitutional Court, 22 Dec. 1988, 1988/5, 1988/55, Official Gazette, 25 Jul. 1989, No. 20232.

572. Constitutional Court, 4 Apr. 1991, 1990/12, 1991/7, Official Gazette, 13 Aug. 1991, No. 20959.

573. For more on the personnel regime prevailing in state economic enterprises, *see* the following: M. Kutal, 'KİT Personel Rejiminin Hukuki Esasları ve Sorunları', paper presented at a symposium organized by TÜHİS on 18–22 Jun. 1999 in Ankara; M. Kutal, 'KCT Personel Rejiminin Esasları ve Sorunları', *Prof. Dr. Nuri Çelik'e Armağan*, Vol.: II, İstanbul, 2001, pp. 1239–1254; *Türkiye'de Kamu Personel Rejiminin Yeniden Yapılandırılması Sempozyumu*, joint publication by Başbakanllık Devlet Personel Başkanlığ ı and TÜHİS, Ankara, 2003. Also, Court of Cassation, 9th Div., 25 Jul. 2008, 22173/22066; 19 Feb. 2009, 37321/3014.

574. Court of Cassation, 22nd Div., 2 May 2011, 12330712876.

treated as working under an employment contract.[575] But the High Court has issued conflicting judgements on this matter, holding that contract personnel are not to be considered 'employees'.[576]

§2. Developments and the Constitutional Amendment of 1995 Paving the Way for Public Servants Unions

1448. Until recently public servants and certain public functionaries performing the continued and essential services of the state in accordance with the general principles of public administration were not covered by any trade union and collective bargaining legislation. However, with a view to granting public servants the right to unionize and negotiate collectively, the ratification of ILO Conventions No. 151 and 87 in 1993 as well as an amendment in 1995 to Article 53 of the Turkish Constitution of 1982 made the enactment of new legislation in this area an urgent matter.

1449. Unlike the 1961 Constitution, the Constitution of 1982 was silent, until the 1995 amendment, on the right of public servants to organize and join unions. The 1961 Constitution, in its initial version, had recognized the right of public servants to form unions, though not the right to engage in collective bargaining or to strike. In fact, in order to guarantee an all-inclusive right to organize, Article 46 of the 1961 Constitution used the term 'working people' rather than 'workers' with a view to extending the right to organize to public servants as well. However, in response to their widespread involvement in militant political action, public servants' unions set up in accordance with the Public Personnel Unions' Act of 1965 (Act No. 624) were outlawed in 1971 and the term 'working people' in Article 46 of the 1961 Constitution was changed to 'workers' by Act No. 1488 which amended certain sections of the 1961 Constitution. This constitutional amendment in Article 119 clearly prohibited public servants from joining unions. This, at least in part, accounted for the aggravation of the problem known as the 'public servant–employee distinction' in the public sector.

1450. Since then several efforts to resolve this dilemma in the public sector by governmental decrees and even by legislation (like the amendment to Article 2 of Act No. 274 by Act No. 1317 in 1971 as well as subsequent attempts at personnel reform) all failed. Persons who, by the nature of the work they performed, should be treated either as blue-collar or white-collar employees in the public sector (which meant a sizable number of public employees in central government and municipalities as well as in-SEEs) were thereby placed into the 'public servant' category merely on the grounds that, being subject to public law, they were not employed under an employment contract. Though the public servant-employee distinction which thus became a chronic problem in the public sector appeared to be a legal-technical matter, it was indeed, in the final analysis, the result of a power struggle. Since public servants were denied the right to organize and bargain collectively, the

575. Court of Cassation, General Council Decision, 27 Jan. 2010, 9-580//1.
576. *See, e.g.*, 22nd Div. 14 May 2012, 17180/9798.

government found an effective way of excluding many of its employees from the coverage of collective labour relations. Consequently, a great majority of public personnel who would have preferred to be under public servant status several decades ago aspired, during the 1970s and 1980s, to be defined as 'employees' in the public sector because of the trade union and collective bargaining rights enjoyed by the latter.

1451. Various public servants' groups were organized into associations in 1971, the year when their right to organize in unions was rescinded, but organizing in associations did not prove to be an effective means of tackling their problems. Civil service regulations involve the revision of public servants' salary scales by indexation of the so-called multiplier and indicator in the budget, but this did not seem to be effective in keeping up the purchasing power of public servants, for it depended largely on the lopsided and arbitrary decisions of the government, nor were there efficient avenues of appeal of which public servants could avail themselves in the event of disciplinary actions by public employers, with the exception of appeals to administrative courts.

1452. As indicated above, the Constitution of 1982 neither prohibited nor guaranteed the right of public servants to organize unions. Relying on this, arguments were put forward that public servants could form and join unions. Yet in the face of the prevailing legal environment, this seemed to be quite difficult, if not impossible altogether. Furthermore, the Associations Act (No. 2908) restricted the right of the majority of public servants to form associations (Article 4) and forbade certain categories from joining associations (Article 16).

1453. These facts notwithstanding, various unions were established by public servant groups (mainly by teachers and municipal public personnel) in the late 1980s and particularly after the ratification by Turkey of the ILO Conventions Nos 87 and 151 in 1993. These unions based their *raison d'être* on Article 90 of the Constitution which provided that international agreements, once ratified by the Parliament, would automatically take on the force of national law and no appeal could be filed against them even with the Constitutional Court on grounds of their unconstitutionality. But in the absence of enabling legislation, judicial verdicts generally did not favour the legality of these unions although many of them seemed quite active and even had formed a confederation of their own. Some municipal unions even concluded collective agreements with municipalities, but the enforceability of these agreements were often questioned by judicial and administrative authorities. Several draft bills were prepared after 1992 by the Ministry of Labour with a view to devising the structure and functions of public servants' unions, but actual legislation could not be enacted due to the political instability of the country in those years.

1454. Finally, amendments made in the Constitution of Turkey by Act No. 4121, dated 23 July 1995, recognized public servants' rights to form and join their unions and to engage in collective negotiations with the Administration. Subsection II of Article 53 of the Constitution read as follows:

> Unions and upper-level union organizations that will be permitted by special legislation to be established by public servants who fall within the scope of Article 128 of the Constitution but who will not be subject to the first and second subsections of this Article and to Article 54 may make application to judicial authorities on behalf of their members and engage in collective negotiations with the Administration in line with their objectives. If agreement is reached as a result of negotiations, a document of agreement shall be drawn up and signed by the parties. This document of agreement shall be placed before the Council of Ministers in order for proper administrative and legislative arrangements to be made. If such a document of agreement has not been signed, the points of agreement and disagreement signed by the parties shall be submitted to the Council of Ministers for consideration. Special legislation shall be enacted with a view to governing the procedures concerning the application of this subsection.

1455. More recently, however, amendments to the 1982 Constitution by Act No. 5982 on 7 May 2010 and then approved in a national referendum held on 12 September 2010 recognized the right of public servants and other public functionaries to make collective agreements, thus deleting the concept of non-binding 'collective negotiations' from the text of the Constitution. In the event of a dispute in reaching agreement, the parties may have recourse to the Public Servants Arbitration Board. Decisions of the Board are final and carry the force of a collective agreement (paragraphs 3 and 4). Still, the Constitution does not guarantee the right to strike for public servants. In the presence of the new constitutional principle; however, overhauling Act No. 4688 with a view to passing legislation on public servants' right to organize and bargain collectively (rather than negotiate) had become an item on the agenda of Parliament. An amendment to Public Servants Act No. 657) by Act No. 4275 of 16 June 1997 had already paved the way for new legislation on public servants' 'right to organize'.[577] Article 22 of Act No. 657 reads: 'Public servants may form and join unions and upper-level union organizations in accordance with the principles embedded in the Constitution and pertinent legislation'.

1456. As noted above, personnel in the public sector have had an unclear status in Turkey. Public employees enjoy the same rights of organizing, bargaining and striking as do private sector employees. Public servants, on the other hand, historically have had job security but no right to organize and bargain. As embodied in Article 128 of the Constitution, public servants and other public functionaries are persons performing what are considered to be essential and continued services of the state and other public bodies in accordance with the principles of general administration' and their salaries are fixed by legislation (the budget act). One problem, however, was that some of the public employees who do not fit into the above definition at all have been classified as public servants and thereby denied collective

577. Official Gazette, 17 Jun. 1997.

bargaining rights. Individuals may be performing the same functions in different parts of the government, but with distinctively different rights. The situation was also compounded by legislation. Turkey had adopted ILO Conventions No. 87 and 151 which together included the rights of public servants to organize and bargain with a view to determining the conditions of their employment. The constitutional enactment in 1995 provided the public servants with a right to organize and negotiate, but the outcome of negotiations would not be binding on the government.

1457. Growth in public servants' unions could provide new dynamism for the labour movement, a voice for the personnel involved and even a useful vehicle for public employers at all levels of government to deal with employee concerns. Subsequent legislation did not grant the right to strike to public servants. Obviously unclear and highly informal bargaining arrangements as implied in the constitutional amendments of the past were not going to be satisfactory in the long run for either party. At this point, one could safely argue that some changes were on the way in order to place the system more in conformity with the ratified ILO Conventions.

§3. The Content of the Present Public Servants' Unions Act

1458. Following extensive debates, public servants' unions were granted legal recognition by Act No. 4688 of 25 June 2001 in line with the principles embodied in Article 53 of the Constitution. Taking some of the views expressed by the ILO, the legislature made a few amendments to Act No. 4688 by Act No. 5198 of 24 June 2004 and Act No. 6289 of 4 April 2012. Below is a summary of the basic provisions of Act No. 4688 as amended.

1459. Article 1 of Act No. 4688 as amended by Act No. 6289 in 2012 provides the following: 'The purpose of this Act is to define the principles and procedures concerning the establishment, organs, powers and activities of unions and confederations to be set up by public servants and other public functionaries with a view to protect and promote their common economic, social and occupational rights and interests, to determine the rights and responsibilities of their administrators and to lay down the methods and procedures for concluding the collective agreement.'

1460. It should be noted at this point that neither Act. No. 4688 nor Act No. 6111 amending Executive Order No. 399 on contract personnel on 13 February 2011 has recognized the right to strike to 'public servants' and 'other public functionaries.' Besides, the Public Servants Act No. 657 maintains the ban on public servants' right to strike.

1461. Article 2 of Act No. 4688 provides that it shall apply to public servants (and other public functionaries) who fall outside the scope and definition of 'employees' – meaning 'contract employees' are covered by the Act as well in administrations with general, annexed and special budgets, provincial administrations and municipalities, SEEs, banks and organizations and their affiliated institutions established by special legislation.

1462. The following terms and concepts used in the Act denote the following: (a) public servants:[578] those working outside the status of 'employee' in the positions of the above-mentioned public institutions and organizations; (b) public employer: the public institution or organization with a corporate or non-corporate status where public servants work; (c) public employer representatives: those persons and their assistants authorized to represent and administer the whole public institution or organization; (d) establishment: place where public service is performed; (e) institution: the entities whose functions, powers and responsibilities have been defined by their respective legislation, covering the multitude of establishments representing an integrated whole for the nature and execution of the public service; (f) unions: organizations with corporate status formed by public servants in order to protect and promote their common economic, social and occupational rights and interests; (g) confederation: the upper-level organization with corporate status established by at least five unions operating in different service branches; (h) collective agreement; the contract signed by the parties resulting from negotiations with a view to determine the financial and social rights of public servants in compliance with the principles set forth in this Act; (i) negotiations record: in the absence of reaching agreement, the record involving the items of agreement as well as non-agreement; (j) union shop steward: the public servant elected by the union with the largest membership at the establishment; (k) establishment union representative: the public servant elected as union representative by a union other than the one with the largest membership.

1463. Principles concerning foundation are as follows: based on the principle of 'service branch', public servants' unions shall be established according to service branches by public servants working in the public establishments in a service branch. They must aim to be active nationwide and founding a union on the basis of occupation or a single establishment is not permissible. More than one union may be established in a service branch (Article 4). Article 5 enumerates the eleven service branches: (1) office, banking and insurance services; (2) training, education and scientific services; (3) health and social services; (4) local administration services; (5) press, publication and communication services; (6) culture and art services; (7) *bayındırlık*, construction and rural services; (8) transportation services; (9) agriculture and forestry services; (10) energy, industry and mining services; (11) religion and foundation services.

1464. Unions and confederations shall be established freely and without the prior permission of authorities. To become a founder, working as a public servant is sufficient. (Article 6). Procedures concerning a 'foundation' are similar to those envisaged for labour unions. Article 7 enumerates the matters to be contained in the constitutions of unions and confederations. For administrative procedures, the Ministry of Labour and Social Security is competent; and for legal actions, competent labour courts shall be in charge.

578. The term 'public servant' used here in its broader connotation includes 'other public functionaries' as well.

1465. Compulsory organs of unions, union branches and confederations are the general congress (assembly), administrative board, auditing (supervisory board) and discipline board. They may establish other organs as well; the organs other than the general congress may delegate functions, powers and responsibilities to these other organs, provided this is specified in their constitutions (Article 8).

1466. Article 9 provides for the election of delegates should the number of members exceed certain levels. The general congress of the union and confederation must be held within six months following the acquisition of corporate status. Provided that it must not exceed four years, Ordinary general congress shall be held at intervals indicated in the union's or confederation's constitution (Article 10). Elections in the general congress shall be conducted under judicial scrutiny, based on free and equal voting, secret balloting, open counts and classification (Article 11).

1467. As for membership, Article 14 provides that the public servant may freely join the union established in the service branch where he is working. Membership to the union shall be acquired upon the application of the public servant to the union with three signed application forms and upon the acceptance of his membership by the union's competent organ. Unless the application for membership is refused by the union within a maximum of thirty days, request for membership shall be considered accepted. If refused without a valid reason, the public servant has the right to appeal to the labour court within thirty days. The union shall submit one copy of the membership certificate to the public servant; one copy shall be by the union; one copy shall be given to the employer to serve as a basis for membership dues. Joining more than one union simultaneously is not permitted. In case of membership(s) to more than one union, subsequent membership shall be invalid (Article 14(5)).

1468. Article 15, dealing with restrictions on membership – and therefore criticized by the ILO as well as by the public servants' unions for its broad scope – cites the following categories as persons who must not join unions: (a) public servants employed by the General Secretariat of the Grand National Assembly, General Secretariat for the Office of the President and General Secretariat for the National Security Council; (b) chairmen and members of higher judicial organs, judges, and prosecutors; (c) chairmen, undersecretaries, directors and their assistants of organizations covered by this Act as well as legal consultants, top directors of regions, mayors and vice-mayors; (d) chairman and members of the Higher Education Board, rectors of universities, deans of faculties, principals of institutes and their assistants; (e) directors of civil administration; (f) members of the armed forces; (g) the National Intelligence Organization; (h) central supervisory staff of the establishments and institutions included in the scope of this Act; (i) security (police) personnel and other public servants employed as security staff; (j) public servants employed in law enforcement establishments.

1469. Regarding these restrictions, the ILO supervisory organs have raised their opposition, especially to the inclusion of civilian personnel employed by the armed forces and the Ministry of National Defence in the categories among the categories denied the right to organize as well as to the rather broad scope of prohibitions on membership. As a matter of fact, following a lawsuit, the Constitutional Court has struck out the ban on the right to organize of civilian personnel employed by armed forces. However, the list of bans on membership is still too long.[579] According to ILO Committee of Experts, restrictions should be limited only to 'positions of trust'.

1470. With respect to termination of membership, Article 16 provides that any member may withdraw from membership freely by indicating it in a resignation statement in three copies. A copy must be given to the member immediately. The public employer shall send a copy of the resignation form to the union in fifteen days. Resignation shall be effective one month after the date of the member's application to the public employer. If the resignee joins another union within this period, the new membership shall be acquired upon the expiration of this thirty-day period. Decision to expel the member from the union is to be taken by the general congress.

1471. The decision of expulsion shall be communicated to the expelled member's employer in written form. Following expulsion, the expelled member may appeal to the competent court within fifteen days. The Court makes its final judgment within two months and membership shall be effective until the decision for expulsion becomes final. The functions of those whose 'public servant' status has expired for reasons cited in Article 16(4) shall be terminated in unions, union branches and union organs (except in confederations). But the duties in the organs of unions and confederations of the public servants who have retired shall continue until the expiry of their terms (Article 16(5)).

1472. Affiliation to confederations and international organizations is regulated in Article 17. A union can join only one confederation. In case of membership to more than one confederation, subsequent memberships shall be invalid. Unions or confederations may freely join or resign from membership of any international organization consistent with their objectives. They are free to invite Turkey members and representatives of international organizations which are consistent with their objectives, and may freely send their members and representatives to meetings abroad.

1473. Article 18 provides for the guarantees provided to union members and union administrators. Public servants shall not be subject to discriminatory practices nor shall they be removed from office due to their participation in the activities of unions or confederations outside working hours or within working hours with the permission of the employer. The public employer must not make discrimination among public servants with respect to their union membership (Article 18(3)). Being a member or non-member shall in no case be a ground for unequal treatment. An important void in the Act is the absence of the sanction to apply in the event of

579. *See* the ruling of the Constitutional Court, dated 10 Apr. 2013, 21/57.

the contravention of the principle of non-discrimination. Here the sanctions foreseen by the Penal Code of Turkey, No. 5237, as well as by Act No. 6356, may be held to be applicable by analogy.[580]

1474. The public employer must not change the workplace of the union shop steward and union establishment representative, provincial union representative, as well as union or branch administrator, without indicating the reason for the change clearly and precisely. Commensurate with the provisions in the union constitution or upon their written request, those elected to the boards of unions or confederations shall be considered to be on leave without salary in their establishments till the end of their duties. Those who have not made such a request may continue to carry on their duties. Members of the administrative board who have not taken the said leave of absence shall be allowed 'one day leave' each week. Upon ceasing to hold office for any reason, the public employer is obliged to reinstate those persons deemed to be on leave without pay in their previous positions or in other appropriate positions if they make an application within one month. Otherwise, in the absence of the said application, they will be considered to have resigned from their positions (Article 18(4)). The members of the administrative boards of union branches, other than those considered to be on leave without salary, shall continue their duties in the relevant public establishments. In view of Article 18(5), branches of unions shall be constituted with a minimum of 400 members.

1475. Although Act No. 4688 does not make any reference, it must be held that, like in the case of all public functionaries, duties in the organs of unions and confederations of those public servants who become candidates in local and general elections shall be suspended for the period of their candidacy, to be terminated if they are elected.

1476. But the terms of union officials who are considered to be on leave without salary shall be evaluated in their retirement entitlements provided that they accept to pay retirement deductions to the Pension Fund of the Republic of Turkey by their unions. In case of temporary removal from office, retirement by decision of the administration, removal from office or appointment, etc., if the public servant makes an appeal and contests such decisions in court, his duty in the union shall continue until the court's decision becomes final. The institutions from which management board members of unions, confederations and union branches take unpaid leave of absence shall continue paying health care expenses of such persons and of members of their families whom they are responsible for looking after.

1477. Despite the above-mentioned guarantees which Act No. 4688 had foreseen, the ILO has expressed dissatisfaction with the insufficiency of protections provided for union members and officials. Taking the ILO's criticisms into account, the amendment by Act No. 5198 has brought a few clarifications to Article 18.

580. Can Tuncay and Burcu Savaş, *Toplu İş Hukuku*, İstanbul: Beta, 2013, p. 440.

1478. In a manner similar to Articles 32 and 33 of Act No. 2821 on unions, Article 19 enumerates the activities with which public servants' unions and confederations may deal. As amended by Act No. 6289 in 2012, Article 19 has incorporated the representation of the public servants' union in the conclusion and application of the collective agreement. Adhering to the principle of gender equality, Article 19 has emphasized for public servants' unions such functions as making proposals to relevant legislative and administrative bodies in the legislation process for the improvement of their members' welfare, training and research activities, making and publishing productivity studies and representation of members and their heirs before administrative and judicial bodies, establishing training, health and recreation centres, libraries and mutual said funds and participating in collective negotiations with the Administration, helping members to establish cooperatives to which (without making donations) they may extend credits not to exceed 10% of their cash assets as well as engaging in relief operations in regions hit by natural disasters, not to exceed 10% of their cash assets.

1479. The administration and operation of public servants' unions must not be contrary to the nature of the Republic of Turkey espoused in the Constitution as well as to principles of democracy (Article 20(1)). As regards prohibitions, restrictions are placed on receiving pecuniary aid from public authorities and political parties; nor may unions extend such aid to political parties and public authorities (except for cases which involve natural disasters) (Article 20(2)). Public servants' unions and confederations must not be organized within the structure of political parties, and they must not use titles, emblems, signs and symbols of political parties. Furthermore, they shall not deal with commercial activities (Article 20(4)).

1480. By referring to establishment-level union shop-stewards, Article 23 governs such issues as their selection, numbers and functions. The union which represents the highest number of public servants in the respective establishments is authorized to choose and appoint the union representatives from the establishment for one term of the general congress. Their number will vary between one and five, depending on the number of public servants (between 200 and more than 2, 000) working in the establishment. One of them is appointed as the chief steward. They shall perform their functions at the establishment for a period of four hours weekly during which they shall be deemed to be on leave. Their functions are: hearing members' problems with the employer or the workplace, forwarding these problems to the relevant authorities and ensuring communication between the union and the employer. The employer shall provide, to the extent possible, the means and facilities for union shop stewards to enable them to carry out their functions. The public employer shall not change the workplace of the union shop steward unless he indicates a clear and precise reason for the change (Article 18(2)). Although the Act has not clarified the sanction to apply in the event of the violation of this principle, it is clear that the shop steward can have access to the administrative court to seek redress of his grievance.

1481. In an attempt to ensure similar functions and coordination, the Act has foreseen designation of 'establishment union representatives' by unions in workplaces other than those which have enrolled 'the highest number of members.

1482. The Public Servants' Unions Act foresees the establishment of joint administrative boards at the institutional level. These joint administrative boards are to be formed to voice opinions on the working conditions of public servants and to see to it that laws on public servants are implemented without discrimination. They are composed of equal numbers of public employer representatives and representatives appointed by the union which represents the largest number of members in its composition (Article 22). They shall convene twice each year.

1483. The supervisory mechanism of the ILO has questioned the place and role of administrative boards in collective negotiations. Apparently, the Supreme Administrative Board which existed under the original text of Act No. 4688 did not play any significant role. In response to criticisms that collective negotiations have been limited by the Act solely to monetary issues, the government claimed that non-monetary issues – working conditions, personnel matters, discipline, etc. – were dealt with by institutional administrative boards. According to the ILO's observations, social partners had suggested that the Supreme Administrative Board be abolished since it had no real function.[581]

1484. Among the revenues of public servants' unions, membership dues rank as the most important item. Other sources of revenues are income earned from the activities of unions, donations and aid and income from the unions' real estate assets. Public servants' unions hall not accept aid and donations without the permission of the government from foreign sources other than the international organizations with which they or the Republic of Turkey are affiliated (Article 24(2)). However, this clause is in conflict with Article 1(1) of the Associations Act, No. 5253. Unions and confederations must deposit their cash income in banks. The maximum amount of cash they may keep at hand for their expenses shall be indicated in their constitutions (Article 24(3).

1485. Concerning expenditures, unions and confederations must not spend their revenues outside their objectives indicated in their constitutions and for purposes circumscribed by law. As in the previous Labour Unions Act No. 2821, they must disburse a minimum of 10% of their income for the improvement of their members' occupational skills and training (Article 26(1,2)). Except for mutual aid funds, unions, their branches and confederations shall not extend loans to their members and administrators, to other persons and institutions, nor shall they distribute their income among members whatsoever.

1486. In an effort to encourage the development of financially strong unions, Article 25, as amended, has foreseen the automatic check-off mechanism in a manner easier than that envisaged in Act No. 2822. Based on the requests by members

581. The amendment to Act No. 4688 has in fact abolished that board.

in their membership applications and the amount designated in the union's constitution. Dues shall be deducted by the public employer from members' salaries and deposited in a bank account of the union within five days; a copy of the payments list must be sent to the relevant union. The amount of the monthly due, to be indicated in the union's constitution, must not be less than four-thousandths or more than one-thirtieth of the net total amount of payments accruing from the monthly salary of the public servant who is in the first-level of the 15th grade of the public servants' salary scale, the minimum salary plus any kind of cost of living increments and indemnities. The union constitutions shall not contain any provisions for deduction of any amounts from members' salaries other than union membership dues. Within the last week of each month, the public employer shall announce the list of members and the dues deducted at a visible site in the establishment and communicate it publicly at the institutional level.

1487. Administrative and financial supervision of the branches, unions and confederations shall be carried out by the supervisory boards or auditors of unions as well as by certified independent accountants authorized to conduct audits in accordance with Act. No. 3568 of 1 June 1989. The audit reports shall be submitted to the approval of the union's general congress.

1488. With slight variations, cases of the termination of the corporate status of a public servants' union and confederation in Act No. 4688 are similar to those envisaged for labour and employers' unions covered by Act No. 6356. In Article 36 mergers, amalgamation and participation of organizations have been regulated along lines parallel to Article 22 of Act No. 6356. The organization may always be dissolved by the decision of the general congress (Article 12). The voids in Act No. 4688 shall be filled by the relevant provisions of the Civil Code and Act No. 6356. Closing of the organization by judicial ruling (in the event of the contravention of constitutional principles, by the labour court upon the request of the Chief Prosecutor of the Republic), the suspension of the union's activities as well as the appointment of trustees to handle the affairs of the union or confederation during suspension and the transfer of assets in the event of dissolution and liquidation, Article 40 shall be executed along lines similar to those in Act No. 6356.

§4. The Collective Agreement

1489. In its previous form before the constitutional amendment of 2010, the parties could reach a document of agreement (or non-agreement) as a result of negotiations, but this agreement document was by no means binding on the parties. This negotiation function was consistent with the wording of Article 53 of the Constitution and presumably with the content of ILO Convention No. 151. However, this approach did not suffice to head off debates in the ILO and union circles as well as in the academia.

1490. Following the constitutional amendment in Article 53, by the amendment on 11 April 2012 by Act No. 6289, Act No. 4688 now recognizes (albeit limited within the constraints of a unique compulsory arbitration mechanism) the right of public servants' unions to conclude binding collective agreements with the administration.

1491. Article 28 provides that collective negotiations shall concern salary coefficients and indices, remuneration, any increments and allowances, the collective agreement bonus, medical treatment and funeral expenses, food and clothing benefits and other incentives of a financial nature. The parties to the collective agreement are the Public Employer Board on behalf of public employers and, on the public servants side, the Public Servants' Unions Board, i.e., authorized unions of public servants established in each service branch as well as the confederations with which these unions are affiliated. The Public Employer Board is composed of the following public officials under the chairmanship of a Minister to whom the State Personnel Directorate is attached: representatives of the Ministry of Labour and Social Security, Ministry of Development, Ministry of Finance, Ministry of Interior Affairs and if deemed appropriate, other ministries as well as the Under-secretary of the Treasury and the State Personnel Directorate.

1492. Under the Chairmanship of a representative designated by the Confederation with the largest membership, the Public Servants' Unions Board is composed of 15 members: a representative designated by each union with the largest membership in respective service branches, representatives from confederations ranking as first, second and third in terms of the total number of members of the affiliated unions. The confederations shall inform the State Personnel Directorate of the names of the chairman and the relevant representatives within fifteen days before the beginning of negotiations.

1493. As the above-mentioned structure shows, the motive is to create a centralized negotiation strategy which eventually disregards the specific features of different service branches to a considerable extent. The ILO seems to disapprove this heterogeneous structure which, nevertheless, lends itself easily to a unique form of coalition bargaining.

1494. The top-level Advisory Public Personnel Board is to be set up with a view to promote social dialogue between 'public servants' unions and confederations' and public administrations on general matters which fall outside the scope of the collective agreement, to review and evaluate public personnel legislation and implementations, to conduct joint studies to improve the structure and functions of public administration, to ensure public servants' participation in administration and to search for solutions to problems encountered in public administration. It shall convene in March and November of each year. Under the Chairmanship of the Minister to which the State Personnel Directorate is attached, it shall be composed of presidents of the three confederations with the largest membership and presidents of public servants' unions with the largest membership in each service branch, plus the State Personnel Director. Depending on its agenda, other authorities may also be invited to its meetings (Article 21).

1495. Authorization of public servants' unions and confederations for collective negotiations has been regulated in Article 30 as amended by Act No. 5198. With a view to determine the pertinent figures and with the participation of two representatives from the respective institution and a representative from each union active in the concerned service branch, a meeting shall be held within five days following 15 May by the public institution concerned. In this meeting the total number of public servants from whom dues have been deducted, together the total number of union members in respective unions shall be designated in a record which will then be combined with similar records sent by local administrative units. The combined record will be communicated to the Ministry of Labour and Social Security until the end of May (Article 30(4,5)). Upon receiving the said records and lists, the Ministry shall verify the total number of public servants and unions' members in respective service branches as well as the total number of confederation members. The results shall be published in the Official Gazette within the month of July each year (Article 30(6)).

1496. Within five working days from the publication of results in the Official Gazette, the public servants' unions and confederation nay contest the accuracy of the figures before the Labour Court of Ankara. The Court shall conclude the case within fifteen days. In view of the Labour Courts Act No. 5521, the challenging party may appeal the Court's decision to the Court of Cassation within eight days.

1497. Negotiations for the collective agreement shall be carried out between the Public Employer Board representing the public administration and the Public Servants' Unions Board representing public servants (Article 29(1)). Negotiations shall be held in years whose last figure represents an odd number. Proposals concerning public servants in general terms shall be prepared by the Confederations' representatives of the Public Servants' Unions Board, together with proposals for each service branch by the representatives of the unions concerned and shall be submitted to the Directorate of the State Personnel Department, to be delivered to the Public Employer Board at least one week before the beginning of negotiations on the first day of the month of August. Negotiations are to be conducted in an integrated fashion by considering the general proposals relating to public servants as well as proposals for each service branch (Article 31(2 and 4)). Collective negotiations must be concluded on the last day of the month of August including the decision of the Public Servants' Arbitration Board. If agreement is reached as a result of negotiations a single agreement shall be reached involving the financial and social rights of public servants in general as well as those concerning each service branch. The part of the collective agreement on public servants in general shall be signed by the chairman of the Public Employer Board and the chairman of the Public Servants' Unions Board, together with the relevant union representative on the sections concerning the respective service branches (Article 29(4)). The signed collective agreement shall be published in the Official Gazette to be valid for two financial years following its conclusion (Article 28(3)). With the exception of the 'collective agreement bonus', no discrimination is permissible in the application of collective agreement terms with respect to members and non-members (Article 28(3)). Monthly pay increases based on the multiplier in the computation of salary increase as well as old age, disability and death benefits subject to the Social Insurance and General Health Insurance have been specified in Article 28 of the Act.

1498. Envisaged by the 2010 constitutional amendment and then incorporated into Act No. 4688 by Act No. 6289, dated 11 April 2012, the Public Servants Arbitration Board is competent to render its binding arbitration award in the event of the parties' failure to reach agreement in negotiations. Within three days from the signing of the record involving the items of agreement and non-agreement in negotiations, or in the case of the parties' failure to sign this record of agreement and non-agreement, the record ascertaining the emerging dispute, the Board shall convene upon the initiative of those authorized to sign the relevant sections of the collective agreement, with its mandate limited to these sections (Article 33). No application is permissible, however for those items which have been approved and signed, nor for any matter which does not fall within the scope of the collective agreement.

1499. The Public Servants' Arbitration Board shall be composed of 15 members elected in the following manner: (1) to act as chairman, a member to be elected by the Council of Ministers (government) from among the chairmen (or acting chairmen) of the Court of Cassation, the Council of Stare (the Supreme Administrative Court), or the Government Accounting Authority (*Sayıştay*); (2) a member to be designated by the chairman of the Public Employer Board from among representatives of the Ministry of Development, Ministry of Finance, Under-secretary of the Treasury, or the State Personnel Department; (3) two members to be designated by the confederations with the largest membership; (4) a member to be designated by the confederations ranking as the second and third in terms of the membership of affiliated unions; (5) a member to be elected by the Council of Ministers from the relevant departments of universities bearing the minimum status of 'associate professor'; (6) three such professors to be elected by the confederation with the largest membership; (7) two such professors to be elected by the confederations ranking as the second and third in terms of the membership of affiliated unions; (8) and one such professor to be elected by the Council of Ministers from among the seven such professors nominated. The chairman and other members of the Public Employer Board shall be designated and their names communicated to the Chairmanship of the State Personnel Department, together with the names of those elected by the confederations, two weeks before the beginning of negotiations. A substitute member shall be appointed for the chairman and each member of the Board. Thus the Public Servants' Arbitration Board is composed of 11 members whereby the composition is clearly slanted against the number of public servants' representatives. The Board shall be convened with the participation of at least eight members. The Board shall render its decision within five days from the date of the application to it. It shall reach its decision by the simple majority vote of those participating members. The Board's members cannot abstain from voting; in the event of equal votes, the decision of the party on behalf of which the chairman has voted shall prevail. The Board's decision shall be communicated to the parties in written form within three days and published in the Official Gazette (Article 34(3,4,5,6,7)).

1500. With a view to determining the so-called social balance payment and upon the proposal of the municipal council, or following the decision of the provincial council in a province, by the governor, an agreement may be concluded between the president of the union with the largest membership in a certain local administration unit and the mayor or the governor of a province within three months following the conclusion of the above-mentioned collective agreement process This agreement shall by no means qualify as a collective agreement and no recourse may be made to the Public Servants' Arbitration Board in relation to it. This agreement is limited by the duration of the collective agreement and its term shall not exceed the date of local elections. Payments in respect of this agreement shall by no means be deemed as vested rights. Agreement is not possible above certain ceilings indicated in Article 32.

1501. As indicated in the above paragraphs, the ILO is critical of Act No. 4688 on various grounds. The Committee of Experts requests, quite rightly, the narrowing the exceptions to membership only to 'positions of trust' in the bureaucratic echelons.

1502. It is also true that the present legislation has not created a viable collective bargaining system supported by the right to strike at least for those public servants not engaged in the administration of the state and that limitation is likely to remain unchanged given the constraints of Article 53(4) of the Constitution which, by referring to compulsory arbitration, denies to public servants the right to strike enjoyed by employees of both the public and private sectors. Coupled by the ban on the right to strike, the composition of the Public Servants Arbitration Board is clearly and heavily pro-employer. As the foregoing paragraphs show, the public servants' collective agreement system does not represent a real collective bargaining relationship; rather it is unique quasi-coalition bargaining pattern resulting in a single and integrated agreement (and, at times, perhaps no agreement at all), with supplements involving provisions relating to specific service branches. Geared to the requirements of a rigid civil service system and budgetary constraints, this sort of bargaining may be found to be a contravention of the representation of adversary interests between the direct employer and union, a fact which is essential for the creation of a genuine bargaining relationship.

1503. Public servants' right to bargain collectively and to strike is an issue of concern for the ILO also in view of subsection 6 of Convention No. 98, that is, to bargain collectively and to strike should also be granted to those categories of public functionaries who are not exercising authority in the name of the state, a criticism raised against Turkey in the Conference Committee since the late 1980s. Some changes must be implemented, therefore, in order to place the system more in conformity with the ratified ILO Conventions.

1504. Employees who are classified as public servants but who should be listed as public employees because of the nature of their work should have their status changed. Thus the size of the public servants' group – which numbers around 1.5 million at present – may be drastically reduced to an estimated number of about half a million. There is thus a need for a comprehensive personnel reform in the public sector. The proposed personnel reforms of the recent past did not turn out to be satisfactory, since they all foresaw converting public servants not engaged in the administration of the state into contract employees, who, by definition, would naturally be covered by Act No. 6488 and who therefore were denied the right to strike. So were the public personnel in the 4/C category of the Public Servants' Act No. 657 who are not deemed to be 'workers'.

1505. Insofar as sheer numbers are concerned, public servants' unionism seems to have made a fairly impressive progress in a relatively short time. By the year 2013, there were many public servants' unions at the 'service branches' level, affiliated to 10 confederations which altogether represented as members a total of 1,468,021 public servants out of a total 2,134,638 public servants (or a membership density of 68.77%, a ratio much higher than that of workers) by the year 2013.

1506. By the year 2021, there were many public servants' unions at the 'service branches' level, affiliated to 13 confederations which altogether represented as members a total of 1,718,984 public servants out of a total 2,658,555 public servants (or a membership density of 64.66%, a ratio much higher than that of workers) by the year 2021.

1507. The major confederations with the highest membership density are Türkiye Kamu-Sen (the Confederation of Public Servants' Unions of Turkey), KESK (the Confederation Public Servants Retirees of Turkey), Memur-Sen (Confederation of Public Servants' Unions), BASK (Confederation of Independent Public Servants Unions) and Hürriyetçi KamuSen (Public Servants for Freedom), in that order.

1508. New legislation (Act No. 7429, dated 22 December 2022) has brought a restriction on public servants' freedom of association. It provides that, to be entitled to the 'collective agreement bonus', the public servant must be a member of the union organization representing a minimum of 2% of public servants. On grounds of its alleged unconstitutionality and violation of the ILO's norms on union freedoms, this minimum 2% representativity requirement has elicited strong reactions from unions which are below this threshold. Being also contrary to the principle of 'equal treatment', the restriction seems to favour Memur-Sen and Kamu-Sen, the two organizations which are sympathetic to the AKP government.

Chapter 11. Some Current Practices and Problems of Industrial Relations in Turkey

§1. Participative Practices in Turkish Industrial Relations

1509. Employees influence management decision-making in Turkey through several channels and in varying degrees. These may be grouped into three categories: the law, shop-level practices implemented by the initiative of the employer and collective bargaining both in the private and public sectors.[582]

I. Participation through Certain Labour Law Provisions

1510. Employees participate in various joint boards and committees in Turkey through several legislated arrangements Among these may be cited the participation of employees' representatives in the 'annual vacation committee' as well as various other committees foreseen in the pertinent articles of Act No. 4857. The occupational health and safety committees to be set up in certain establishments constitute an important form of participation in a legally defined area. Workers' representatives also sit on some of the high-level tripartite boards and general assemblies, such as the minimum wage board, the YHK and the General Assembly of the Social Insurance Organization.

1511. Another tripartite body with consultative functions is the Labour Council. The Labour Council, composed of representatives of the ministries concerned, universities as well as employees' and employers' organizations, is convened upon the request of the Ministry of Labour. It is an advisory ad hoc body whose task is to discuss items on new legislative proposals and other matters of interest to workers and employers and as such it performs functions foreseen in ILO Convention No. 144 ratified by Turkey. More recently in Article 114 of Act No. 4857 the formation of the Tripartite Consultation Board has been envisaged with a view to promote work on the adoption of legislation in conjunction with ILO Convention 144 as well as with the relevant European Union directives. The Tripartite Consultation Board was established in line with Article 114 and has already initiated efforts along the lines set out in its respective Regulations.

1512. With a view to initiating the long-awaited top-level conservative mechanism, a declaration issued by the Prime Minister in 1994 and revised in 1995 and again in 1997 established the ESC. Presently its legal basis is the Act No. 4641, dated 11 April 2001, on the Formation, Functions and Working Methods of the ESC. It is composed of representatives of labour unions (in addition to Türk-İş, other confederations of labour and public servants' unions are also represented) and employers' (both private and public), government and other interest groups (i.e., chambers

582. For a comprehensive account of these schemes, *see* T. Dereli, *Employee Involvement in Turkey* (Kluwer Law International 2004).

of commerce, industry and agriculture) to deal with general questions of concern to the national economy as well as to workers and employers in particular. The ESC is a new experiment and its effectiveness has yet to be tested. It is important to note in this connection that the ESC has not convened so far even in important occasions which seem to necessitate its active involvement. Also, certain criticisms have been levied against the composition of the ESC which is very large, encompassing various interest groups and in which the government seems to be overrepresented.

1513. Established by Act No. 440 (dated March 1964) and put into effect by a bylaw in 1966, a limited form of workers' participation in the management boards of SEEs and their establishments was started by the government with a view to experimenting with new models and extending the outcome to the private sector if the results proved fruitful. After fourteen years of experience with this limited form of participation in the public sector, the government of Ecevit in 1978 attempted to enlarge the scope of participation and prepared several draft bills to that effect. In line with the wording of the social contract which was signed by the government and Türk-CF in July 1978, a draft decree, aimed to create an employees' participation scheme (as well as proposed legislation for enhanced job security) which was more comprehensive and broader in scope than the existing model, was prepared, but as a result of the change of power from the Ecevit to the Demirel cabinet in 1979 the above-mentioned proposals did not materialize. After the military intervention of 12 September 1980, the Parliament went even further in 1984 by abolishing the limited form of workers' participation in the management boards of the SEEs. But expanding the scope and effectiveness of participation first in the SEEs and then introducing similar schemes into the private sector became an ongoing idea frequently voiced in union and pro-labour circles. Forthcoming work on EU-style 'works councils' or Information-Consultation systems envisaged by the pertinent EU directives is likely to revive interest in the Ecevit government's proposals of 1978.

1514. As a step to initiate preparations for the establishment of an European type 'works council' a conference was held on 1 March 2005 under the guidance of Ministry of Labour, but there has been no follow-up work on this matter since then.

II. Contemporary Participative Schemes Practised at the Shop Level

1515. In recent years some of the modem enterprises in Turkey have addressed the use of employee suggestion systems as well as sophisticated labour–management cooperative efforts such as shop-level quality circles, team-building and team work, job redesign and job enrichment. Of particular interest in this category are the experiments made within the skills and imagination of leaders of the Koç and SabancL companies and their unions. The outcome of quality circle experiments in the SabancL group are reported to be quite fruitful while the Koç group's sophisticated human resource management practices have been hailed as alluring efforts. The unions-including even the DCSK-affiliated Lastik-CF organized in BrisSa have been quite cooperative. Yet no union has so far been able to penetrate the ToyotaSa (the Toyota-Sabancı joint venture) which also conducts quality circle programmes with a view to improving quality and productivity. Ironically, the introduction of similar practices in the glass industry was not possible due to the resentment of Kristal-İş the union which was influenced by the ideology of The General Confederation of Labour in France (French: Confédération Générale du Travail, CGT) on this issue. Turk Pirelli, on the other hand, seems to have made significant contributions to quality through such efforts which in turn have helped to increase its share in world markets.

III. Participation through Collective Bargaining

1516. In the absence of a broad-based statutory participation system in Turkey, collective bargaining serves as perhaps the most effective method, albeit only in certain areas, whereby labour is able to influence management decisions in both the private and public sectors. In fact, as Professor Blanpain had pointed out', influence on management decision-making through collective bargaining by which workers' wages and conditions of employment are regulated by agreement between their representatives and employers can, of course, be extremely important, depending on the subject matter and the level of bargaining, as well as the binding effect of the collective agreements.[583]

1517. In Turkey, the scope of participation through collective bargaining has been limited, however, to certain personnel and social matters and high-level financial and economic decisions which are regarded as management prerogatives have generally been excluded from the union's impact. Most Turkish collective agreements endeavour to limit the right of management to hire, transfer and even promote employees without consulting the signatory union. Labour unions have also been successful, to some extent, in influencing the size of the workforce through collectively bargained provisions and, in some cases, have restricted the right of the employer to subcontract work out although the rulings of the judiciary have wavered on this issue. Indeed, providing workers with job security had been one of the major goals of labour unions during the past decades.

1518. Most Turkish collective agreements provided for 'joint discipline committees' which, among other functions, aimed to restrict the employer's right to terminate or break the worker's employment contract. During the 1960s these committees were almost without exception headed by the employer or his representative. When votes were even, it was usually the chairman's (employer's) vote which determined the outcome. However, the 1970s witnessed an increasing influence of employee representatives on discipline committees, especially in cases concerning discharge and lay-offs. Although the opinions of the judicial organs wavered

583. R. Blanpain, *The Influence of Labour on Management Decision-Making: A General Introduction*, 8 Bulletin of Comparative Labour Relations 11 (1977).

and were generally not favourable towards unions' attempts to provide their members with employment security,[584] in many of the more modern undertakings where managers exercised sophisticated personnel policies the decisions of such joint committees were respected.

1519. Later, albeit belatedly, the Court of Cassation seemed to be upholding the legal validity of such joint committees by ruling that the employer's ignoring the committee's decisions should be construed to mean 'unfair dismissal' for which increased compensation rates could be applicable, though not 'reinstatement'. These verdicts of the late 1990s seemed to reflect the already-felt impact of the ratified ILO Convention No. 158 despite the absence of enabling legislation – which could materialize only after the year 2001.[585]

1520. Another form of 'collective bargaining-based participation' relates to the role played by shop stewards in the grievance procedure. Most collective agreements provide for a full-fledged grievance and arbitration process-despite the legal possibility of filing suit with the labour courts. Thus, union-appointed shop stewards function as the first step on the joint grievance committees which in some collective agreements are structured in conjunction with discipline committees and by which most rights disputes are resolved before having to be referred to higher or outside levels of dispute settlement mechanisms.

§2. Privatization and Industrial Relations

1521. By the mid-1970s Turkey's SEEs were becoming increasingly unprofitable in spite of – or partly because of – the various subsidies they received. Their inefficiency was attributed to politically motivated employment policies, poor management, arbitrary government meddling and restrictions on the pricing of their products. It had become customary to give SEE jobs to party supporters after elections. In addition to overstaffing, this practice was responsible for a high turnover among qualified managers who were frustrated by political appointees with little or no knowledge of management. Besides, because of social considerations, SEEs were not free to raise their prices in line with costs in the inflationary environment of the 1970s and 1980s. Their losses were therefore routinely met through government finance. This, in turn, was a major cause of the increase in budget deficits and the accelerating the rate of inflation.

1522. Privatization has been a perennial item on the economic agenda of successive Turkish governments since the early 1980s. Preparations for the contemplated sale of state assets have already led to far-reaching changes in industrial

584. For these developments and related judicial rulings, *see* paras 435–437 above. For an evaluation of 'participative schemes' from a limited sample of Turkish collective agreements, *see* M. Kutal, *İktisat ve Maliye*, Vol. XXVI, Nos 6–7, 1979, pp. 209–307. *See* paras 495–498 above.

585. Court of Cassation, 9th Div., 31 Mar. 1992, 326/3836; 24 Sep. 1992, 3164/120374; General Council of the Court of Cassation, 1 Jun. 1994, 9-71/381.

relations and employment practices in the SEEs, such as the introduction of the 'contract employee' status, tougher bargaining policies with unions and the contraction of employment. Yet the scale of actual privatization and, consequently, its direct impact on industrial relations have so far been limited on account of governments' cautious approach to this controversial issue. Whenever shares in state enterprises were put up for sale, there were rumblings of discontent from the labour unions and, in some cases, considerable controversy. As a result, with the exception of privatization of a few enterprises in block, the process has been confined largely to the sale of minority shares of the state, with relatively long intervals between offerings.

1523. Labour unions in Turkey generally view privatization as a move to weaken and ultimately to destroy the labour movement. They had already witnessed a decline in their membership as a result of preparations for privatization. Labour union statements therefore reflect strong rejection of the privatization program. Frequent criticisms focus on (1) the creation of the contract employees' category in the SEEs; (2) erosion of employees' job and income security; and (3) the creation of a non-union environment. Unions are also concerned that many employees will be made redundant both before and after privatization. In cases of redundancies, they ask who would pay their accumulated benefits, such as severance pay. In addition, they believe that privatization will lead to tougher bargaining since they will have to negotiate with private sector employers competing in world markets.

1524. Union reactions also centre on the policy choices the government is making. A recurrent criticism is that the government, rather than selling off or rehabilitating inefficient SEEs, is in the process of handing over profitable enterprises to the private sector, particularly to foreign multinational corporations that are alien to national interests. Unions claim that monopoly SEEs that might be bought by foreign corporations will not strive to sell their products to domestic consumers at reasonable price levels. They will seek high profits, raising prices and fuelling inflationary pressures.

1525. Unions also see the SEEs as a symbol of Turkey's economic and political independence. To counter allegations of economic inefficiency of the SEEs, some unions emphasize their social contributions, while blaming their inefficiency on political interference, high turnover among managerial staff, mismanagement and overstaffing. They argue that, with their price-regulating and stabilizing functions, the SEEs help to correct imbalances in the distribution of national income. Furthermore, the SEEs have always made significant contributions to workers' and managers' education, thus helping the private sector as well by providing it with trained human resources. Employment created by the SEEs makes an invaluable contribution to social stability. The SEEs have also pioneered many social welfare programs since the 1930s. However, the unions deplore the abolition of the employees' participation scheme in SEEs' management since the enactment of privatization legislation in 1984.

1526. Labour unions also argue that it is unrealistic to expect employees to buy shares in the companies that employ them. Their income is barely sufficient for their families' survival and they cannot afford to put money aside from their earnings to buy shares. If they can, they will have to sell them before long. However, when the government decided to close down the allegedly unprofitable steel mill in Karabük, claiming that its technology was too old to be renovated, union reactions led to the buying out of the enterprise by the workers. The enterprise was sold to workers at a symbolic price; a joint stock company was set up, giving workers and other stakeholders shares. The new company, Kardemir, has been operating with reasonable efficiency under the union's control so far.[586] On the other hand, the attempted buying of Et ve Balık Kurumu, the big state conglomerate processing meat and fish products, by the Hak-CF Confederation, elicited strong reactions from many diverse groups in 1995 which were instrumental in thwarting the Union's bidding.

1527. Lastly some unions criticize privatization as a politically motivated phenomenon rather than an economic one. These unions consider privatization to be in contradiction with citizens' constitutional right to live in a 'social, just and legal' state. At present, labour unions seem to favour restructuring of the SEEs through delegation of increased autonomy to professional managers.

1528. If and when large-scale privatization goes ahead as planned, bargaining units ('establishment' and 'enterprise', using the Turkish labour law terms) will remain essentially unchanged in cases where the whole enterprise is sold. The union will simply move with its members from a public sector unit to a private sector unit, since the same unions function and organize workers in both sectors. If an enterprise collective agreement is in force, it will continue to apply until its date of expiry, in accordance with Article 8 of Act No. 2822 which stipulates that a change of employer does not affect the validity of the collective agreement in force.

1529. If the enterprise is broken up and sold piecemeal on a plant-by-plant (establishment) basis, however, the bargaining structure and union-management relationship may be disrupted. Where separate plants are sold in this way, the privatized plants will form separate bargaining entities with independent legal status, over which different unions may claim bargaining rights. In such cases, the disruption of the bargaining relationship is likely to cause uncertainty and increased inter-union rivalry.[587] Certainly in the event of the transfer of an establishment within the scope of an 'enterprise' or a section thereof, Article 28 of Act No. 6356 shall be applicable.

1530. Attempts to privatize large SEEs in which the state owns the majority or all of the shares have provoked strong criticism from unions and the public. Yet, in the face of chronic financial difficulties and pressures from international institutions, privatization seems to be inevitable. Some SEEs will be sold to private sector owners, while a few others are destined for permanent closure. The government is

586. H.Y. Ersöz, S. Özdemir, A. Yavuz, T. Akgeyik, H. Şenocak, *supra*, pp. 612–613.
587. T. Dereli & I.U. Zeytinoğlu, *Public Sector Industrial Relations on the Eve of Mass Privatization in Turkey*, 132(5–6) International Labour Review 701 (1993).

determined to accelerate privatization, making it the linchpin of its plans for restructuring the economy and reducing the budget deficit and inflation-which also means keeping public sector wages down. The real challenge has come as the AKP government has had to tackle the big public corporations such as SEKA (the paper and pulp industries of Turkey), SÜMERBANK, ETİBANK, TÜRK TELEKOM (telecommunications company), ERDEMİR (steel production group) and Türk Şeker (sugar factories). The AKP government seems to have utilized privatization as a means of financing budgetary deficits, selling off almost everything belonging to the public, even land that is under state ownership. When the SEEs are fully privatized, there will be substantial changes not only in their labour relations, but also in the general context of the administration of the national economy.

1531. The new Act No. 6552 has brought a job security clause for workers affected by privatization. Article 66 provides that workers whose employment contracts are terminated due to privatization and who do not have the right to move into other public institutions or organizations, shall, without having to renew their employment contracts, continue their employment until they become entitled to receive old age or disability pension.

1532. Statements by government representatives suggest that seats on the management boards of SEEs earmarked for privatization might be allocated to union representatives. This could help to ease internal conflicts that are bound to arise because of privatization. It may also help union leaders to understand the inherent problems plaguing the SEEs and employers to understand the views and concerns of their workforce. Ultimately this may pave the way for a smoother transition to new labour relations in privatized SEEs. However, the role of 'political contingency', that is, unions' tendency to effect the final negotiated settlements with pertinent ministers who also were trying to extract political benefits for themselves, will cease to be a factor in collective negotiations in Turkey.[588]

588. T. Dereli, *Problems of the Turkish Industrial Relations System*, in *New Dimensions in Industrial Relations in a Changing World, Proceedings of the First International Industrial Relations Congress*, 12–13 Nov. 1992, Istanbul, p. 42.

Concluding Remarks

1533. As the preceding chapters have shown, a considerable number of reforms envisioned in the earlier editions of this monograph have become a reality by the year 2014 despite a multitude of deficiencies still existing in the new Act on Unions and the Collective Labour Agreement. First and foremost, the notion of 'flexicurity', that is, a delicate balance between the long-awaited job security for employees and a reasonable degree of flexibility which employers have been vying for, has now become a reality. Further, though certain items still remain unresolved, various ameliorations have been successfully incorporated into union and collective bargaining legislation. With a view to bringing the Turkish system into conformity with the ILO and European standards, some additional amendments should be in the pipeline to further improve the effectiveness of labour law and industrial relations in Turkey. Presently the frequently talked about plans in political quarters to draw up an entirely new Constitution for the nation is eliciting optimism for the creation of a stronger basis of freedom of association.

1534. Perhaps the most deplorable trend for Turkey's labour unions and their friends is the declining rate of union density. While union density was 9.5% in 1995, it has dropped to 5.8 in 2002. The picture is worse in the private sector where in 2007 it has fallen to 3.4. The ratio of the workforce covered by collective labour agreements in 2020 was 7.8%, which is less discouraging, however. For public servants' unionism, union density was 57.00% in 2009, much better than the average numerical values, for reasons unique to the civil servants' working environment.

1535. One should note, however, that while the legislative framework is essential, the actual implementation phase is even more important and, in most cases, more difficult to promote unless the actors of the system can develop and sustain an effective social dialogue between themselves. Since a country's industrial relations system and, in particular, its collective relations dimension, is closely intertwined with national culture, traditions and customs, the practice of imitating foreign models is likely doomed to failure, as experience has shown in many cases. Although Turkey's projected accession to the European Union prompts the acceleration of the process of adaptation to EU norms, one should recall that taking strides in haste might entail unanticipated dysfunctions in practice. Fortunately, however, international labour standards are formulated in such flexible and broad terms that they lend themselves rather easily to adaptation to national custom and tradition.

1536. And it is needless to say that no industrial relations system is free of malfunctions. Besides, the industrial relations system of Turkey has had its share of worldwide developments affecting labour adversely everywhere. Compared to the situation even a decade ago, our problems are entirely different at this stage of globalization. Of special significance is the lingering rate of high unemployment and inflation despite satisfactory rates of GNP growth in the economy. This so-called jobless growth seems to be the greatest challenge confronting labour. In fact, the adoption of elaborate rules on freedom of association and the right to collective bargaining look meaningless and far-fetched if the economy fails to achieve a satisfactory employment level with decent jobs.

1537. On the other hand, the idea of upgrading the Turkish system into full conformity with EU norms just for the sake of Turkey's accession to the EU – which still seems to be a far-flung goal – is certainly misplaced. The ultimate goal should be the promotion of a labour law and industrial relations system based on core ILO standards and yet best suited to the interests of Turkey's working people, employers and employees alike.

Selected Bibliography

Self-evidently the following bibliography is not exhaustive. Further, it does not include journal articles some of which have been referenced in the relevant paragraphs of this monograph.

Books

Aktay, A., Nizamettin; Arıcı, Kadir; Kaplan, E. Tuncay, *İş Hukuku*, 2nd edn, Ankara, 2007.

Alpagut, Gülsevil, *Belirli Süreli Hizmet Sözleşmesi*, Tühis, Ankara, 1998.

Altan, Ö Zühtü, *Sosyal Politika*, Eskişehir, 2004.

Başbuğ, Aydın, *Toplu İş İlişkileri ve Hukuk, Şeker-İş yayını*, Ankara, 2012.

Biçerli, M. Kemal, 3rd edn, *Çalışma Ekonomisi*, İstanbul, Beta, 2005.

Canbolat, T., *Türk İş Hukukunda Asıl İşveren-Alt İşveren İlişkileri*, Kazanci Hukuk Yayinları, Istanbul 1992.

Centel, Tankut, Demircioğlu, Murat, *İş Hukuku*, İstanbul, 2006.

Caldwell, Lynton, *Turkish Administration and the Politics of Expediency*. Hopper & Levin eds, 1967.

Çelik, Nuri, *İş Hukuku Dersleri* (26th edn), Beta, İstanbul, 2013.

Çelik, Nuri, Nurşen Caniklioğlu & Talat Canbolat, *İş Hukuku Dersleri* (27th edn), Beta, İstanbul, 2014.

Demir, Fevzi, *Sendikalar Hukuku* (4th edn), İzmir, 1999.

Demir, Fevzi, *İş Hukuku ve Uygulaması*, İzmir, 2013.

Demircioğlu, Murat, *Labour Law in Turkey*. İstanbul Chamber of Commerce Publication, İstanbul, 2010.

Dereli, T., Y. Pınar Soykut Sarıca & Aslı ŞenTaşbaşı (eds). *Labour and Employment Relations in a Globalized World*, Springer, 2014.

Dereli, T., Y. Pınar Soykut-Sarıca & A. Şen-Taşbaşı (eds). R. Blanpain (editor in-chief), *Emerging Patterns of Work and Turkish Labour Market Challenges*, Wolters Kluwer, 2014.

Dereli, Toker, *The Development of Turkish Trade Unionism*, Istanbul, 1968.

Dereli, Toker, Aydınlar, *Sendika Hareketi ve Endüstriyel İlişkiler Sistemi*, İstanbul, 1975.

Dereli, Bengü, *Türkiye'de Sendika-içi Demokrasi*, İstanbul, 1977.

Dereli, Toker, 'Turkey', in *International Handbook of Industrial Relations*, edited by A. Blum, Greenwood, Westport, 1982.

Dereli, Toker, 'Turkey', in *European Labour Unions*, edited by J. Campbell, Greenwood Press, Westport, 1992.

Selected Bibliography

Ekin, Nusret, *Endüstrilişkileri*, İstanbul, 1976.
Ekonomi, Münir, *İş Hukuku I* (3rd edn), İstanbul, 1984.
Elbir, Halit K., *İş Hukuku*, İstanbul, 1987.
Esener, Turhan, *İş Hukuku* (3rd edn), Ankara, 1978.
Eyrenci, Öner, *Sendikalar Hukuku*, İstanbul, 1984.
Gülmez, Mesut, *Sendikal Hakların Milletlerarası Kuralları ve Türkiye*, Todaie, Ankara, 1988.
Gülmez, Mesut, *Avrupa Birliğ i ve Sosyal Politika*, Ankara, 2008.
Güzel, Ali, Ali Riza Okur, *Sosyal Güvenlik Hukuku*, İstanbul, 2004.
Işikli, Alpaslan, *Sendikacılık ve Siyaset*, İstanbul, 1979.
I ̇nce, Ergun, *Çalışma Hukuku*, İstanbul, 1998.
Kerr, Clark, et al., *Industrialism and Industrial Man*, Harvard University Press, Cambridge, 1960.
Kerwin, R.W. (New York 1954), 'Türkiye'de Devletçilik', Çev. N. Coşar, N. Coşar (Ed.), Türkiye'de Devletçilik içinde, İstanbul: Bağlam Yayınları, pp. 97–114, 1995.
Kiliçoğlu, Mustafa, *Sendikalar Hukuku ve Toplu İş Uyuşmazlıkları*, Ankara, 1999.
Koray, Meryem, *Endüstri İlişkileri*, İstanbul, 1992.
Kutal, Gülten, *Türkiye'de İşçi Sendikacılığı*, İstanbul, 1977.
Kutal, Metin, *Teorik Esasları ve Tatbikatı Bakımından Asgari Ücret*, İstanbul, 1969.
Mollamahmutoğ lu, Hamdi, *İş Hukuku* (2nd edn), Ankara, 2005.
Narmanlioğlu, Ünal, *İş Hukuku I*, İzmir, 1998.
Newstrom, J.W., *Organizational Behaviour*, McGraw Hill/Irwin, 2011.
Oğuzman, M. Kemal, 'Turkey; Law of Contracts', in *International Encyclopaedia of Laws*, edited by Roger Blanpain, Kluwer Law International, The Hague, 1996.
Rosen, M. Sumner. 'Turkey', in *Labour in Developing Economies*, edited by Walter Galenson, University of California Press, Berkeley, 1962.
Şahlanan, Fevzi, *Sendikalar Hukuku*, İstanbul, 1995.
Şahlanan, Fevzi, *Toplu İş Sözleşmesi*, İstanbul, 1992. Talas, Cahit, *Toplumsal Politikaya Giriş*, Ankara, 1981.
Soyer, Polat, *Genel İş Koşulları*, İstanbul, 1987.
Soykut-Sarıca, Yesim Pınar, *Wage Determination under Collective Bargaining: Inflation, Productivity and Profitability Relationships – An Empirical Study on Relations Between Inflation, Productivity and Profitability*, VDM, Berlin, 2008.
Sümer, Haluk H., *İş Hukuku*, 15th edn, Konya, 2010.
Sümer, Haluk H., *İş Hukuku Uygulamaları*, 4th edn, Konya, 2010.
Süral, Nurhan, *İş Hukukunda Barişçi Çözüm Yolları*, Ankara, 1982.
Süzek, Sarper, *İş Hukuku*, Beta, İstanbul, 2014.
Tuna, Orhan, Metin Kutal, *Grev Hakkı*, İstanbul, 1968.
Tuncay, A. Can, *Toplu İş Hukuku*, ALFA, İstanbul, 1999.
Tuncay, Can A. and F. Burcu Savaş, Toplu İş Hukuku, Beta, İstanbul, 2013.
Tunçomağ, Kenan, *Topluİş Uyuşmazlıklarının Çözümünde Uzlaş*tırma *ve Tahkim*, I ̇stanbul, 1972.
Türkiye Toprak, Seramik, Çimento ve Cam Sanayii İşverenleri Sendikası, İş Hukuku ve Sosyal Güvenlik Hukuku Akademik Forumu, İstanbul: Legal Hukuk Kitapları No. 285, 2014.

Türkiye Sendikacilik Ansiklopedisi (ed. O. Baydar) (Joint publication of the Ministry of Cultural Affairs and Social History Foundation of Turkey), 3 vols., İstanbul, 1996.

Uçkan, Banu, Deniz Kağ nıcioğ lu, *Endüstri İlişkileri*, Eskişehir, 2004.

Ulucan, Devrim, *Toplu İş Sözleşmesi Özerkliğ i ve Hukuki Niteliği*, İstanbul, 1981.

Ülgener, Sabri, İktisadi İnhitat Tarihimizin Ahlak ve Zihniyet Meseleleri, İstanbul Üniversitesi İktisat Fakültesi, 1951.

Yanardağ, Merdan, *İçtihad Kapısı İslam Dünyasının Süren Ortaçağı*, Kırmızı Kedi yayınevi, 2022.

Yenisey, Kübra Doğan, *Social Security Law in Turkey*, Kluwer Law International, 2013.

Zaim, Sabahaddin, *Çalışma Ekonomisi*, 10th edn, İstanbul 1997.

Journals

Bradburn, Norman M., 'An Achievement, and Father Dominance in Turkey', *Journal of Abnormal and Social Psychology*, vol. 67, no. 5 (November 1963): 464–465.

Çalışma ve Toplum Birleşik Metal-İş, İstanbul.

Çimento İşveren Dergisi, Ankara. *Sicil İş Hukuku Dergisi*, İstanbul.

Fındıkoğlu Z.F., The Social Stratification Related with the Turkish Social Changes' *İstanbul Üniversitesi İktisat Fakültesi Mecmuası,* vol. 20, nos 1–4 (2011): 374–388.

İşveren Dergisi, TİSK, Ankara.

Kamu-İş Hukuku ve İktisat Dergisi, Ankara.

İstanbul Üniversitesi Hukuk Fakültesi Dergisi (*Journal of the Law Faculty of İstanbul University* which includes research articles on labour law).

İktisat ve Maliye Dergisi (Sosyal Hukuk ve UygulamasL, a series of articles by Metin Kutal on labour law and industrial relations), İstanbul. Legal, *İş Hukuku ve Sosyal Güvenlik Hukuku Dergisi*, İstanbul. Mercek Dergisi, Mess, İstanbul.

Proceedings of the Turkish Industrial Relations Association (annual volumes for years 1990 to 2004).

Sosyal Siyaset Konferansları, İstanbul (annual publication of the Faculty of Economics, Department of Labour Economics and Industrial Relations, 56 vols.).

Tühis Dergisi, Ankara.

Türk-İş Dergisi, Ankara.

Concerning various proposals for reform in labour legislation and particularly in Acts No. 2821 and 2822 as well as evaluation of recent legislation, Act No. 6356), see the following articles or chapters:

Centel T., 'The Right to Strike: Turkey', in *The Right to Strike: Studies in Employment and Social Policy*, edited by Brnd Waas, vol. 45, series editors Neal, Alan C. Manfred Weiss, Birgitta Nystrom, Kluwer Law International 2014, 537–548.

Dereli, T., et al. Institution-Building on Shop-floor Employees' Representation with Reference to International Norms and Representative Industrial Democracy: A First Attempt to Model Dual-Channel Representation in Turkey, 2022, 5 (75), 2613–2637.

Dereli, T., '6356 Sayılı Yeni Sendikalar ve Toplu İş Sözleşmesi Knunu: Genel Bir Değerlandirme', *Çalışma ve Toplum Dergisi*, 2013/1, pp. 41–43.

Selected Bibliography

Dereli, T., '6356 Sayılı Sendikalar ve Toplu İş Sözleşmesi Kanunu: Süreçler, Sorunlar ve Öneriler', *Çimento İşveren Dergisi*, Cilt 28, Sayı 1, Ocak 2014, pp. 10–33.

Dereli, T., 'ILO Perspektifiyle Turkiye'de Sendika Özgürlukleri ve Yeni Yasa Taslaklarının Degerlendirilmesi', *Sicil İş Hukuku Dergisi*, Yil 2, No. 6, Haziran 2007, pp. 87–106.

Dereli,T., 'Yeni Anayasa Değ isiklikleri ve Uluslararasi Sendika Özgülüğ ü Normalari', *Mercek Dergisi*, No. 59 Temmuz 2010, pp. 24–31.

Dereli, T.,'Toplu Is Hukuku Mevzuatina Yonelik Degisikliklerin Degerlwndirilmesi', *Mercek Dergisi*, Ocak 2011, pp. 28–41.

Dereli, T., 'The Benefits of Freedom of Association for Turkey, and Selected Cases', paper presented to the ILO Conference at the ILO International Training Centre in Turin, Italy, held on 22–23 June 2010.

Dereli, T., 'TBMMM nin 24, Yasama Doneminde Endustriyel Iliskiler ve Calisma Hayatinda Beklentiler', *Mercek Dergisi*, Vol. 6, No. 63 Temmuz 2011, pp. 11–19.

Kutal, M., 'Toplu Pazarlik Sistemi Açısından Anayasada 5982 Yasa ile Yapilan Son Degisklikler', *Mercek Dergis*, Vol. 15, No. 59, Temmuz 2010, pp. 23–25.

Norman B. Bradburn, 'Interpersonal Relations within Formal Organizations in Turkey', *The Journal of Social Issues*, vol. XIX, no. 1 (January 1963): 61–67.

Presthus, R.V., 'Weberian v. Welfare Bureaucracy in Traditional Society'. *Administrative Science Quarterly*, vol. 6 (1961): 1–24.

Soykut-Sarıca, Y.P. (2011). 'Employee Ownership and Management: The Case of Kardemir Iron and Steel Mill Industry'. *African Journal of Business Management*, vol. 5, no. 33 (2011): 12872–12881.

Tuncay, C., 'Sendikalara Iliskin Son Kanun Tasarısının Getirdilkleri', *Sicil Is HukukuDergisi*, Vol. 7, No. 21, March 2011, pp. 153–164.

Table of Cases

Table of Legislation

Uçum, Mehmet, İşe İade Taleplerinde Dava Açma Süresinin Başlangıcına İlişkin Sorunlar, *İş Hukuku ve Sosyal Güvenlik Hukuku Dergisi*, 2008, 701

Table of Statutes[589,590]

589. Except where the legislation specifies the date on which it shall become effective, any adopted legislation enters into force upon its publication in the Official Gazette. The following list of statutes has been arranged in chronological order, starting from the latest dating back to the earliest.
590. Since the 2017 referendum which has changed the constitutional system of Turkey to a 'presidential' form of government, presidential decrees and orders have gained momentum over legislative acts. The list below includes only 'legislation (acts) enacted by the Grand National Assembly.

Table of Statutes,

Index

The numbers here refer to paragraph numbers.

Index

Index

www.ingramcontent.com/pod-product-compliance
Lightning Source LLC
Chambersburg PA
CBHW071408230926
51846CB00001B/35
9789403534060